RETHINKING HISTORIES OF INDONESIA
EXPERIENCING, RESISTING AND
RENEGOTIATING COLONIALITY

RETHINKING HISTORIES OF INDONESIA

EXPERIENCING, RESISTING AND RENEGOTIATING COLONIALITY

EDITED BY SADIAH BOONSTRA,
BRONWYN ANNE BEECH JONES, KATHARINE MCGREGOR,
KEN M.P. SETIAWAN AND ABDUL WAHID

ANU PRESS

ASIAN STUDIES SERIES MONOGRAPH 20

ANU PRESS

Published by ANU Press
The Australian National University
Canberra ACT 2600, Australia
Email: anupress@anu.edu.au

Available to download for free at press.anu.edu.au

ISBN (print): 9781760466978
ISBN (online): 9781760466985

WorldCat (print): 1526063920
WorldCat (online): 1526064278

DOI: 10.22459/RHI.2025

This title is published under a Creative Commons Attribution-NonCommercial-NoDerivatives 4.0 International (CC BY-NC-ND 4.0) licence.

The full licence terms are available at
creativecommons.org/licenses/by-nc-nd/4.0/legalcode

Cover design and layout by ANU Press. Cover image: *Struggles in the Exotic* (2022). Image courtesy of Zico Albaiquni and Ames Yavuz Gallery.

This book is published under the aegis of the Asian Studies editorial board of ANU Press.

This edition © 2025 ANU Press

WARNING: Readers are advised that this publication describes experiences of a highly sensitive nature, including racism and graphic images of violence, war, death and dying.

Contents

List of illustrations	vii
Abbreviations	xi
Glossary of terms	xiii
Acknowledgements	xv
Contributors	xvii

Part 1. Colonial categories across and beyond the colony

1. Rethinking histories of Indonesia: A decolonial approach — 3
   Sadiah Boonstra, Bronwyn Anne Beech Jones, Katharine McGregor, Ken M.P. Setiawan and Abdul Wahid

2. 'Oedjan belasting, the raining of taxes': Coloniality and the Dutch economic exploitation of the Chinese — 45
   Abdul Wahid

3. Locating colonial Indonesia in colonial Ceylon: Geography, language and belonging — 71
   Ronit Ricci

4. 'So I say my name': Towards a decolonial ethics for reading girls' worlds in letters — 91
   Bronwyn Anne Beech Jones

5. Dealing with modernities: East Java's plantation society in colonial times and the revolution — 121
   Grace T. Leksana

6. Rethinking histories of military atrocity, ethnic violence and photography, from the Aceh War to the Indonesian national revolution — 145
   Susie Protschky

7. Francisca Fanggidaej: A decolonial perspective on colonial elites and the Indonesian revolution — 179
   Katharine McGregor

8. Giving voice to the voiceless: 'Sin Po' and the Chinese massacres during the revolutionary period 205
Ravando and F.X. Harsono

Part 2. Colonial legacies: The persistence of and attempts to dismantle coloniality

9. Beyond the point of no return: The re-emergence of Indonesian debates about concepts of the return of cultural objects 241
Sadiah Boonstra

10. How to liberate the colonised archives? Describing the Djogdja Documenten after their return 273
Michael Karabinos and Rika Theo

11. The rise and fall of Glodok 295
Abidin Kusno

12. Decolonising a colonial fort? The case of Fort Rotterdam, Makassar 321
Ajeng Ayu Arainikasih

13. After recognition: Decolonial re-affect outside/within the museum 347
Brigitta Isabella

14. Confronting coloniality through the courts? Reconsidering the Rawagede case 375
Ken M.P. Setiawan

15. Seeking the Morning Star: Young Papuans and the ongoing struggle against Indonesian colonialism 403
I Ngurah Suryawan

Index 431

List of illustrations

Figures

Figure 1.1 Meme with the hashtag #KamiBersamaBonnieTriyana ('We are with Bonnie Triyana'), 26 January 2022 — 15

Figure 1.2 Untitled meme, 4 February 2022 — 16

Figure 2.1 Newspaper coverage of an anti-tax demonstration in Batavia on 8 September 1924 — 46

Figure 4.1 Word map in *Soenting Melajoe*, 1921 — 100

Figure 5.1 Bridge on the South Semeru Road from Malang to Bondowoso, 1939 — 122

Figure 6.1 Aftermath of the KNIL massacre at Kuta Sukun, Sigli (Aceh), 6 August 1897 — 153

Figure 6.2 Aftermath of the KNIL massacre at Batu Iliq, Samalanga (Aceh), 3 February 1901 — 153

Figure 6.3 Aftermath of the KNIL massacre at Kuta Rih (1), Alas (Aceh), 14 June 1904 — 154

Figure 6.4 Aftermath of the KNIL massacre at Kuta Rih (2), Alas (Aceh), 14 June 1904 — 154

Figure 6.5 Aftermath of the KNIL massacre at the puri Pemecutan, Badung (south Bali), 20 September 1906 — 155

Figure 6.6 C.B. Nieuwenhuis's photograph of the massacre at Kuta Sukun from the '*Oostwaarts!*' ('Eastwards!') exhibition — 158

Figure 6.7 'Mountain gun in position on the Glé Risa Poenggoeng', Samalanga (Aceh), 1901 — 160

Figure 6.8 'Marechaussee brigade from Samagani at Pasar Sibreuë', Aceh, c. 1897–1901 — 163

Figure 6.9 Stafhell & Kleingrothe, 'Execution on a Deli plantation', Sumatra, c. 1880–1901   166

Figure 6.10 'Water transport to the Glé Nang Roë', Samalanga (Aceh), 29 January 1901   168

Figure 6.11 'Coolies and military police assemble before the attack on Kuta Sukun', Sigli (Aceh), August 1897   169

Figure 6.12 'Convict labourers assist soldiers with a river crossing', Samalanga (Aceh), February 1901   169

Figure 6.13 'The draught horse convoy on the plain before the *puri* Denpasar', Badung (south Bali), September 1906   170

Figure 8.1 Photograph of the exhumation of Chinese remains in Karangbendo, Ponggok and Blitar, taken in 1951 by Harsono's father, Oh Hok Tjoe   206

Figure 8.2 An announcement in *Sin Po* made by CHTH Nganjuk on 26 August 1951 regarding the reburial of Chinese victims in Manyung Village   226

Figure 8.3 A Chinese mass grave in Manyung, Nganjuk   226

Figure 8.4 Inscribed tombstones from the Chinese mass grave in Bojong Village, Wonosobo   227

Figure 8.5 A notice in *Sin Po* announcing the reburial of the bodies of the Chinese massacred in Maja   228

Figure 8.6 The mass grave of Chinese massacre victims in Maja   229

Figure 8.7 The Yogyakarta Chinese mass grave in the Pingit area, Bumijo   230

Figure 8.8 The vandalised Chinese mass grave in Grogolan Village, Pekalongan   231

Figure 9.1 Pencilled notes by Ali Sastroamidjojo   257

Figure 9.2 Corrections made by Soesilo to the final Draft Cultural Agreement   260

Figure 11.1 *Sinar Glodok* advertisement at Jakarta Fair   307

Figure 11.2 Graphic slogan in *Sinar Glodok*   308

Figure 11.3 Reporting politics in *Sinar Glodok*   312

Figure 12.1 Fort Rotterdam, Makassar   329

Figure 12.2 La Galigo Museum's permanent exhibition in Building M, 2019   339

Figure 13.1 Replica of Gajah Dompak sword, 2017   364

Figure 13.2 One of the postcards from 'My Message to Tana Toba'   367

Figure 13.3 Performance piece 'Tribute to Boru Lopian', Museum HKA, Antwerp   369

Figure 15.1 Victor Yeimo (centre) and, on the left, the late West Papuan independence activist Filep Karma (1959–2022), at Karma's release from Abepura Prison coinciding with the seventh anniversary of the formation of the KNPB, 19 November 2015   408

Figure 15.2 KNPB demonstration in support of Papua joining the international Pacific Forum, 7 September 2015   415

Figure 15.3 KNPB street demonstration in Abepura, Jayapura   420

Figure 15.4 Women of the KNPB protest on Trikora ('People's Triple Command') Day, Lingkaran Abepura, Jayapura, 19 December 2016   424

Figure 15.5 KNPB demonstration to protest Trikora Day in Jayapura, 19 December 2016   426

Maps and table

Table 2.1 Chinese population of the Netherlands East Indies, 1860–1930   54

Map 5.1 Agricultural enterprises in East Java (Surabaya, Kediri, Pasuruan, Probolinggo and Besuki), adapted from original drawings by Mr H. P^h. T^h. Witkamp, 1892   124

Map 8.1 Map of the First Dutch Military Aggression in Java, July–August 1947   215

Map 9.1 Federal Indonesia, 1948–1949   249

Abbreviations

ANRI	Arsip Nasional Republik Indonesia (National Archives of the Republic of Indonesia)
BFO	Bijeenkomst voor Federaal Overleg (Federal Consultative Assembly)
CHTH	Chung Hua Tsung Hui (Federation of Chinese Organisations in Indonesia)
KNIL	Koninklijk Nederlandsch-Indisch Leger (Royal Netherlands East Indies Army)
MP	Member of Parliament
NA	Nationaal Archief (National Archives of the Netherlands)
NEFIS	Netherlands East Indies Forces Intelligence Service
NIOD	NIOD Institute for War, Holocaust and Genocide Studies
Pesindo	Pemuda Sosialis Indonesia (Socialist Youth of Indonesia)
PKI	Partai Komunis Indonesia (Communist Party of Indonesia)
RTC	Dutch–Indonesian Round Table Conference (Konferensi Meja Bundar)
THHK	Tiong Hoa Hwee Koan
UN	United Nations
UNESCO	United Nations Educational, Scientific and Cultural Organization
UNTEA	United Nations Temporary Executive Authority
VOC	Vereenigde Oost-Indische Compagnie (Dutch East India Company)

Glossary of terms

Belanda Hitam	'Black Dutchmen', a term used to refer to soldiers in the colonial army of African background whose ancestors were brought to the East Indies as enslaved persons from the Gold Coast (modern-day Ghana), as well as Moluccans whom the Dutch awarded European status.
Bersiap	'Be ready', referring to a period of violence in the early phase of the revolution during which republican supporters attacked Indo-Europeans and other minorities, between September 1945 and November 1946.
Bumiputera	'Son of the earth', a politically charged term used as a form of racial classification to refer to 'natives' or local inhabitants. The term has sometimes been used to imply that some Indonesians are more 'Indonesian' than others.
coloniality	Refers to the structures of power, ideas and practices underpinning colonisation, which persist to the present.
decoloniality	To detach from structures of coloniality and to (re)establish old and new ways of thinking, languages, ways of life and being in the world that coloniality rejects.
Inlanders	A colonial term used to refer to 'native' Indonesians.
Kampong	(also *kampung*) A village or hamlet
Madiun Affair	(*Peristiwa Madiun*) When in August 1948 factions in the Indonesian military seized control over the city of Madiun in East Java, which the republican government declared was an illegal uprising.
martial races	A myth used by the Dutch during the colonial era to characterise certain ethnic groups, particularly Moluccans, as supposedly having superior martial skills and a ferocious manner.

New Order	(*Orde Baru*) A term adopted by President Suharto to describe his regime (1966–98), contrasting with President Sukarno's Old Order (*Orde Lama*).
Pangreh Praja	The branch of the civil service staffed by locals in the colonial era.
Peranakan	Chinese who were born in the Netherlands East Indies.
Pribumi	'Native of the soil', a term used to refer to local Indonesians; sometimes also used to exclude those considered to be of migrant descent.
puputan	Dynastic ending in Bali
Renville Agreement	A ceasefire agreement in January 1948 that confirmed Dutch territorial gains in return for a plebiscite in Dutch-occupied parts of Java, Madura and Sumatra as to whether they would join the republic or become separate states.
Thirtieth of September Movement	(also G30S, *Gerakan Tiga Puluh September*) The formal name of the movement that launched the 30 September 1965 coup, led by Colonels Untung and Latief, in which six generals and one general's aide were kidnapped and killed.
Vreemde Oosterlingen	'Foreign Orientals', a term coined by the Dutch to classify Chinese, Arab and Indian communities during the colonial period.

Acknowledgements

In the past decade there has been increased attention on Indonesia's colonial history, both in the country itself and in the Netherlands, Indonesia's former colonial power, from scholars, activists and artists. These engagements reflect the overall state of ambiguity regarding colonial history in both countries. In Indonesia, a challenge is how to write new histories of the period of Dutch colonial rule, including how to address firmly nationalist views of history, especially when dealing with violence, and how to include different historical subjects in writing, including women and Chinese Indonesians. Similarly, in the Netherlands, there has been criticism of that country's focus on the 1945–49 period, thereby overlooking the longer history of colonialism and how to deal with some of its darkest aspects, such as economic exploitation and violence. It is evident that the process of addressing histories of colonialism remains highly contested in both countries and requires sustained critical attention.

This volume is the first to comprehensively attend to these contestations and seeks to foreground Indonesian voices and perspectives. The project arose out of discussions with leading historians Eveline Buchheim, Bambang Purwanto and Remco Raben, who suggested that we critically examine processes of and sensitivities around writing colonial history. They also provided generous feedback on an early concept note for this volume.

The contributions to this volume are based on a series of workshops that were held in July 2021 and January 2022. These workshops were made possible through the support of the Indonesia Democracy Hallmark Research Initiative (IDeHaRI) at the University of Melbourne. We wish to acknowledge Bronwyn Beech Jones, who provided invaluable assistance in preparing and organising the workshops. We also thank the external discussants who shared their valuable insights and feedback on draft chapters at the January 2022 workshops: Eveline Buchheim, Vannessa Hearman, Wayne Modest, Bambang Purwanto and Alicia Schrikker.

Most of all, we are grateful to our contributors, who worked closely with us to develop their chapters during these workshops and beyond. It is important to mention that we started this project during the Covid-19 pandemic, when many of our contributors were facing extraordinary challenges. We thank them for generously offering their time and energy to this project.

Last, we thank those who supported us with the finalisation of the manuscript. We are grateful for the financial support provided by the Faculty of Arts at the University of Melbourne and for Ratna Erika Suwarno's research assistance. We thank Jan Borrie for editing support. Finally, we would like to express our sincere appreciation to James Fox and ANU Press, as well as two anonymous reviewers, for their support in publishing this volume.

Contributors

Sadiah Boonstra is a historian and curator based in Jakarta, where she is CEO and founder of CultureLab Consultancy Indonesia, a postdoctoral researcher at Vrije Universiteit Amsterdam and Honorary Senior Fellow at the University of Melbourne. Sadiah was previously collections and curatorial specialist at the Indonesian Heritage Agency, Asia scholar at the University of Melbourne, curator of public programs at Asia TOPA Melbourne, senior manager of programs at National Gallery Singapore, a postdoctoral fellow at Royal Holloway University London and the British Museum, and a fellow at the Alliance for Historical Dialogue and Accountability, Institute for the Study of Human Rights at Columbia University, New York.

Bronwyn Anne Beech Jones teaches gender and Southeast Asian history at the University of Melbourne, where she completed her PhD in 2024 supported by the Hansen Scholarship in History. Her doctoral research examined women's and girls' self-fashioning in early twentieth-century Sumatra through three women's newspapers. Bronwyn's primary research interests are everyday life, gender, education, resistance and literary practices in colonial Indonesia. She is a member of the steering committee for the University of Melbourne's History, Memory and Decolonial Futures Research Collective.

Katharine McGregor is Professor of Southeast Asian History in the School of Historical and Philosophical Studies at the University of Melbourne. Kate has researched many topics related to Indonesian history and struggles with memory and violence from the colonial period through to the present. Her most recent book is *Systemic Silencing: Activism, Memory, and Sexual Violence in Indonesia* (Critical Human Rights Series, University of Wisconsin Press, 2023). Kate is also a research lead for the University of Melbourne's History, Memory and Decolonial Futures Research Collective.

Ken M.P. Setiawan is Senior Lecturer in Indonesian Studies at the Asia Institute, University of Melbourne, and an associate at the Centre for Indonesian Law, Islam and Society at the Melbourne Law School. Ken was born in Indonesia and grew up primarily in the Netherlands, where she studied Indonesian language followed by a Master of Arts in Southeast Asian Studies and a PhD in law at Leiden University. Ken's main research interests are the politics of human rights in Indonesia. Her most recent book, co-authored with Dirk Tomsa, is *Politics in Contemporary Indonesia: Institutional Change, Policy Challenges and Democratic Decline* (Routledge, 2022).

Abdul Wahid is a lecturer in the Department of History, Universitas Gadjah Mada, Indonesia. From 2017 to 2021, he was also a KITLV postdoctoral researcher. His research interests include the following themes: the political and economic history of colonial and postcolonial Indonesia, the social dimensions of violence in modern Indonesia (the revolutionary period of 1945–50 and 1965–66) and sociopolitical issues of minorities, particularly the Chinese in colonial and postcolonial Indonesia.

Ajeng Ayu Arainikasih is pursuing a PhD at Leiden University in the Netherlands. Her research focuses on decolonisation and museums in postcolonial Indonesia. Ajeng is a lecturer at the University of Indonesia and is the founder and Lady Boss of Museum Ceria, an independent museum consultancy based in Jakarta. Her major and recent academic publications are, written collaboratively with Adrian Perkasa, 'Looking Back from the Periphery: Situating Indonesian Provincial Museums as Cultural Archives in the Late-Colonial to Post-Colonial Era' (*Wacana* 24, no. 3 [2023]) and 'A Story of Entanglement between Indonesian National Heroes, Museums, and Decolonization' (*ICOFOM Study Series* 52, no. 1 [2024]).

F.X. Harsono is a prominent Indonesian artist whose work explores the role of artists in society and claims for recognition and justice. Harsono's work focuses on self-identity, working directly with the Chinese Indonesian community of his ancestry to document their stories in a variety of media, including film. Harsono was awarded the 2014 Prince Claus Award honouring his 'crucial role in Indonesia's contemporary art scene for forty years' and, in 2015, the Joseph Balestier Award for the Freedom of Art. His work has been shown in more than 100 exhibitions around the world.

Brigitta Isabella is a researcher, curator and editor, who navigates her encounters with people, objects and discourses through various knowledge-production platforms that operate at the intersection of art history, critical theories and cultural activism. She has been affiliated with a self-organised research group based in Yogyakarta, the Kunci Study Forum, since 2011 and is a member of the editorial collective of the peer-reviewed journal *Southeast of Now: Directions in Contemporary and Modern Art*. She teaches in the Visual Arts Department, Indonesia Institute of the Arts Yogyakarta.

Michael Karabinos is a lecturer in Archival Studies in the Media Studies Department at the University of Amsterdam. From 2023 to 2024, he was a member of the Dutch Council for Culture's committee on colonial archives. Previously he was a Deviant Practice Research Fellow at the Van Abbemuseum in Eindhoven, Netherlands, researching within the museum's archive and curating exhibitions using its material. In 2021 he joined the Collecting Otherwise working group at the Nieuwe Instituut's National Collection of Dutch Architecture and Urban Planning in Rotterdam, Netherlands.

Abidin Kusno is professor in the Faculty of Environmental and Urban Change at York University, Toronto, and former director of the York Centre for Asian Research. His publications include *Visual Cultures of the Ethnic Chinese in Indonesia* (Rowman & Littlefield, 2016) and *Jakarta: The City of a Thousand Dimensions* (NUS Press, 2023).

Grace T. Leksana is assistant professor in Indonesian history in the Cultural History section of Utrecht University, Netherlands. She is the author of *Memory Culture of the Anti-Leftist Violence in Indonesia: Embedded Remembering* (Amsterdam University Press, 2023). Since 2007 she has been working on the issue of state violence in Indonesia, particularly the anti-leftist violence in 1965. Her interests cover memory studies, oral history, histories of the Left, (de)colonisation and knowledge production.

Susie Protschky is Professor of Global Political History at Vrije Universiteit Amsterdam. Her current book project is a history of colonial war photography in Indonesia titled *Seeing Like a Soldier: Photography and Colonial War Photography in Dutch Indonesia*. Her previous book, *Photographic Subjects: Monarchy and Visual Culture in Colonial Indonesia* (Manchester University Press, 2019), won the Asian Studies Association of

Australia and the Royal Studies Journal book prizes. She is also the author of *Images of the Tropics: Environment and Visual Culture in Colonial Indonesia* (KITLV Press/Brill, 2011).

Ravando is the inaugural John Legge Postdoctoral Research Fellow at Monash University, Melbourne. He received his PhD from the University of Melbourne in 2023. Before this, he taught history at Universitas Gadjah Mada, Indonesia. His doctoral thesis examined the Chinese Indonesian newspaper *Sin Po* (1910–65) as a lens to explore political movements and transnational connections of Chinese Indonesian society in the Dutch East Indies. Ravando's monographs include *Perang Melawan Influenza: Pandemi Flu Spanyol di Indonesia Masa Kolonial, 1918–1919* (*The War Against Influenza: The Spanish Flu Pandemic in Colonial Indonesia, 1918–19*) (Penerbit Buku Kompas, 2020) and *Merawat Kehidupan: 100 Tahun Rumah Sakit Husada (Jang Seng Ie)* (*Nurturing Life: A Centennial of Husada/Jang Seng Ie Hospital*) (Penerbit Buku Kompas, 2025).

Ronit Ricci is the Sternberg-Tamir Chair in Comparative Cultures and a professor in the departments of Asian Studies and Comparative Religion at the Hebrew University of Jerusalem. She is also affiliated with The Australian National University. Her main academic interests are Javanese and Malay manuscript cultures, translation studies and Indonesian literature. She is the author of *Islam Translated: Literature, Conversion, and the Arabic Cosmopolis of South and Southeast Asia* (University of Chicago Press, 2011) and *Banishment and Belonging: Exile and Diaspora in Sarandib, Lanka and Ceylon* (Cambridge University Press, 2019). She edited *Exile in Colonial Asia: Kings, Convicts, Commemoration* (University of Hawai'i Press, 2016) and *Storied Island: New Explorations in Javanese Literature* (Brill, 2023).

I Ngurah Suryawan lectures in the Anthropology Department at the University of Papua in Manowkari, West Papua Province. His PhD thesis, 'Siasat Elit Mencuri Kuasa: Dinamika Pemekaran Daerah di Papua Barat [Elite Strategies for Stealing Power: The Dynamics of Regional Expansion in West Papua]', was completed at Universitas Gadjah Mada in 2015. His postdoctoral research focuses on the 'Cultural Ecology and Dynamics of Natural Resources in Marine Communities Merauke, Papua' (ANU-ELDP London, 2016–17) and 'The Making of Local Elites in West Papua 1961–1998' (KITLV Netherlands, 2017–18). He is currently working on comparative studies on indigenous peoples and natural resources exploitation in West Papua and Bali.

Rika Theo is an archivist, librarian and researcher working on the silences in the Indonesian displaced archives. She received an OnsArchief archival fellowship in 2022 to research problematic custody and hidden narratives of the Indonesian Left archives in the Netherlands. Previously a journalist in Jakarta, she won a scholarship to study in the Netherlands, obtaining her MA in international political economy, an MA in archival studies and a PhD in international development. She is a librarian at the University of Amsterdam and an archivist at the International Institute of Social History. She is also involved with the activist group Watch65.

Part 1.
Colonial categories across and beyond the colony

1
Rethinking histories of Indonesia: A decolonial approach

Sadiah Boonstra, Bronwyn Anne Beech Jones,
Katharine McGregor, Ken M.P. Setiawan
and Abdul Wahid

> I beg of you do not think of colonialism in the classic form which we of Indonesia, and our brothers in different parts of Asia and Africa, knew. Colonialism has also its modern dress, in the form of economic control, intellectual control, actual physical control by a small but alien community within a nation. It is a skilful and determined enemy, and it appears in many guises.[1]

In his opening address at the famous 1955 Bandung Conference, Indonesian president Sukarno laid out the many challenges the people of Asia and Africa confronted in the post–World War II period. Ten years after the declaration of Indonesian independence, Sukarno signalled the continuing struggle to realise full independence across multiple spheres of life. The Bandung Conference and its emphasis on the enduring nature of colonialism are a theme about which many intellectuals, including decolonial thinkers, from across Asia, Africa and, later, South America continued to theorise for decades to come.

---

1   Sukarno, '"Let a New Asia and Africa be Born": Extract from the "Opening Address Given by Sukarno", 18 April 1955', in *Indonesian Political Thinking: 1945–1965*, eds Herb Feith and Lance Castles (Ithaca: Cornell University Press, 1970), 458.

In the late 1980s, the sociologist Aníbal Quijano coined a term for the systemic nature of colonialism: the 'coloniality of power' or 'coloniality' for short.[2] Coloniality opened a path into further interrogating the incomplete process of decolonisation. Quijano proposed an analysis that, as María Lugones puts it, 'provides us with a historical understanding of the inseparability of racialisation and capitalist exploitation as constitutive of the capitalist system of power'.[3] This global capitalist, colonial, modern system of power or 'coloniality of power' that Quijano describes began in the Americas in the sixteenth century and spread to other parts of the world, including Southeast Asia, where it continues to exist.

Importantly, Quijano makes a distinction between 'colonialism' and 'coloniality'. In Quijano's conceptualisation, colonialism refers to Western imperial/colonial expansion that 'laid the foundation for modern/colonial globalisation' and an economic system we today call capitalism.[4] Coloniality, by contrast, refers to the structures of power and control underpinning colonisation that persist to the present. Coloniality can thus be understood as referring to the epistemic, *enduring* legacies of imperialism, which continue to impact current cultural, social, economic and political systems, including knowledge and its production.[5] The concept of coloniality also helps sharpen our understanding of decolonisation. In many cases, the local elites who gained control of the government failed to fully overthrow (or overcome) 'coloniality' and continued to replicate what the colonisers did, but in the name of national sovereignty.

The construction of coloniality and the workings of the 'colonial matrix of power'[6] in the Indonesian context run as a red thread through the contributions to this volume. To critically consider coloniality, contributors draw inspiration from the related concept and praxis of decoloniality as outlined by Catherine Walsh and Walter Mignolo.[7] Considering that

---

2   Aníbal Quijano, 'Coloniality and Modernity/Rationality', *Cultural Studies* 21, nos 2–3 (2007): 168–78, doi.org/10.1080/09502380601164353, at 171.
3   María Lugones, 'Toward a Decolonial Feminism', *Hypatia* 25, no. 4 (2010): 742–59, doi.org/10.1111/j.1527-2001.2010.01137.x, at 745.
4   Alvina Hoffmann, 'Interview—Walter Mignolo/Part 2: Key Concepts', *E-International Relations*, [Bristol], 21 January 2017, www.e-ir.info/2017/01/21/interview-walter-mignolopart-2-key-concepts/.
5   Quijano, 'Coloniality and Modernity/Rationality'; Lugones, 'Toward a Decolonial Feminism'; Walter D. Mignolo and Catherine E. Walsh, *On Decoloniality: Concepts, Analytics, Praxis* (Durham: Duke University Press, 2018), doi.org/10.1215/9780822371779.
6   Walter Mignolo and Arturo Escobar, eds, *Globalization and the Decolonial Option* (New York: Routledge, 2010), doi.org/10.4324/9781315868448, 3.
7   Mignolo and Walsh, *On Decoloniality*.

political decolonisation—meaning the formal end of colonial rule—did not entail an end to coloniality, this approach aims to comprehend how Western modes of thought and knowledge systems have been universalised to highlight the plurality of such systems and undo 'the hierarchical structures of race, gender, heteropatriarchy, and class that continue to control life, knowledge, spirituality, and thought'.[8] At the same time, decoloniality means detaching from structures of coloniality and (re-)establishing old and new ways of thinking, languages, ways of life and being in the world that coloniality rejects. This volume is animated by theories of coloniality and decoloniality because of the critical attention they bring to understandings of colonial history. Decoloniality and decolonial thinking seek to highlight the plurality of systems of knowledge and thought and the simultaneous existence of multiple frameworks of knowledge, and of thinking beyond the framework of coloniality.

The central premise of *Rethinking Histories of Indonesia: Experiencing, Resisting and Renegotiating Coloniality* is that it is time for a critical evaluation of histories of Indonesia extending back to the formal period of colonisation right through to the present using the scholarly lens of coloniality and decoloniality to capture the enduring legacies of and processes that reproduce coloniality. The book therefore aims to lay bare the workings of coloniality and to take the first steps towards undoing it. We have paid careful attention to representing a range of perspectives in this volume. Our chapters have been written by scholars from across the world working in the fields of history, area studies, archive studies, legal studies, artistic practice, literary history, urban history, visual history, sociology, museum studies and anthropology. Of our 16 contributors, nine are Indonesian and 10 are women. We have adopted a collaborative research process of sharing our work, thinking and resources.

Across the book, we consider how colonial categories and related propaganda functioned across a range of fields and sites to justify and reinforce colonial ideology and projects ranging from tax law and the technologies associated with plantations to the operations of colonial ideology within the Dutch military and other parts of the colonial bureaucracy, and an elite Eastern Indonesian family. The chapters dealing with colonial categories and ideologies engage critically with Dutch colonial sources or provide new analyses of Malay and Indonesian-language sources including newspapers,

---

8   ibid., 17.

interviews and memoirs that offer alternative windows on to colonial history and local perspectives leading up to and including the Indonesian revolution of 1945–49. Taking up the theme of the ongoing resonance of colonial history in the present, later chapters ask to what extent colonial categories were dismantled or repurposed, and whether there was a shift away from colonial thinking after 1945, in both Indonesia and the Netherlands, as former coloniser, and how we might explain such (dis)continuities. These chapters consider how colonial influences and structures of thought continued to inform fields of cultural production, heritage preservation, urban space and law as well as how Indonesian nationalism reproduces colonial assumptions.

The innovation of this book lies in the fact that it is the first volume to critically analyse the connections, resonances and influences of coloniality across periods of Indonesian history that traditionally have been studied in isolation. For several reasons, explained below, despite the prominence of Indonesians in anticolonial and anti-imperial movements, postcolonial approaches have never really thrived there. We ask why and begin to offer an alternative conceptualisation of Indonesian history through the lens of coloniality.

Anticolonial thinking and the limited influence of postcolonial history in Indonesia

Vijay Prashad offers an excellent summation of 'the Bandung spirit' as 'a refusal of both economic subordination and cultural suppression'.[9] While Bandung represented the culmination of sentiments expressed across the centuries by peoples subjected to colonialism, it was not the first nor the only expression of such views. Such resistance dates to at least the Haitian revolution (1791–1804) that successfully challenged slavery and established an independent republic.[10] Despite their absence at Bandung, women across Asia and Africa also launched fierce challenges of both colonialism

---

9 Vijay Prashad, *The Darker Nations: A People's History of the Third World* (New York: New Press, 2007), 46.
10 Michel Rolph Trouillot, *Silencing the Past: Power and the Production of History* (Boston: Beacon Press, 1995).

and patriarchal oppression.¹¹ Nor was Bandung the last expression of the Bandung spirit. The conference gave rise to a range of different Asian–African organisations such as the Afro-Asian People's Solidarity Organisation, the Afro-Asian Journalists' Association and the Afro-Asian Writers Association, all of which tried to challenge the global hegemony of the West.¹² In the 1950s and 1960s, Indonesians were at the centre of these global movements to address 'social, racial, political and economic justice among the formerly colonised nations'.¹³

Anticolonial thinkers and leaders from the 1940s to the 1960s, such as Sukarno, Mahatma Gandhi, Kwame Nkrumah and Frantz Fanon, were key sources of inspiration for postcolonial studies. The field can be very broadly characterised by efforts to adopt 'a particular vantage point from which to apprehend the world'—one that is critical of colonial ideology and systems and of modernity, decolonisation, neo-colonialism, nationalism and teleological thinking.¹⁴ Palestinian literary scholar Edward Said foundationally identified how colonial discourses characterised the 'West' in opposition to an always deficient non-Western 'Other', showing how the links between knowledge, culture and power reproduced colonialism.¹⁵

---

11   See, for example, Elisabeth Armstrong, 'Before Bandung: The Anti-Imperialist Women's Movement in Asia and the Women's International Democratic Federation', *Signs* 41, no. 2 (2016): 305–31, doi.org/10.1086/682921; Paul Bijl, 'Legal Self-Fashioning in Colonial Indonesia: Human Rights in the Letters of Kartini', *Indonesia* 103 (2017): 51–71, doi.org//10.1353/ind.2017.0002; Katharine McGregor, 'Indonesian Women, the Women's International Democratic Federation and the Struggle for "Women's Rights", 1946–1965', *Indonesia and the Malay World* 40, no. 117 (2012): 193–208, doi.org/10.1080/13639811.2012.683680; Katharine McGregor, 'The Cold War, Indonesian Women and the Global Anti-Imperialist Movement, 1946–65', in *De-Centering Cold War History: Local and Global Change*, eds Jadwiga E. Pieper Mooney and Fabio Lanza (London: Routledge, 2013), 31–51; Rosalind Parr, 'Solving World Problems: The Indian Women's Movement, Global Governance, and "the Crisis of Empire", 1933–46', *Journal of Global History* 16, no. 1 (2021): 122–40, doi.org/10.1017/S1740022820000169.
12   Katharine McGregor and Vannessa Hearman, 'Challenging the Lifeline of Imperialism: Reassessing Afro-Asian Solidarity and Related Activism in the Decade 1955–1965', in *Bandung, Global History, and International Law: Critical Pasts and Pending Futures*, eds Luis Eslava, Michael Fakhri and Vasuki Nesiah (Cambridge: Cambridge University Press, 2017), 161–76, doi.org/10.1017/9781316414880.012; Carolien Stolte and Su Lin Lewis, eds, *The Lives of Cold War Afro-Asianism* (Amsterdam: Amsterdam University Press, 2022).
13   Taomo Zhou, 'Global Reporting from the Third World: The Afro-Asian Journalists' Association, 1963–1974', *Critical Asian Studies* 51, no. 2 (2019): 166–97, doi.org/10.1080/14672715.2018.1561200, at 167.
14   Rochona Majumdar, 'Postcolonial History', in *Debating New Approaches to History*, eds Marek Tamm and Peter Burke (London: Bloomsbury Academic, 2018), 49–74, doi.org/10.5040/9781474281959.0007, at 70.
15   Edward Said, *Orientalism* (London: Penguin, 1978); and Edward Said, *Culture and Imperialism* (New York: Knopf, 1993).

Early postcolonial studies were also propelled by 'subaltern studies' that arose from Indian intellectuals who sought to draw attention to the subaltern—the marginalised and forgotten subjects of history.[16] Writing histories of subaltern subjects involved finding new ways of reading colonial texts and using alternative sources such as oral history.[17] Following Dipesh Chakrabarty, postcolonial history also challenges the idea that Europe is and always has been the centre of world history and the related global inequity that arose from the Eurocentric idea that 'large sections of the world's populations are relegated to the imaginary "waiting room" of history where they are told that they are "not yet" ready for rights that are in principle considered universal'.[18]

Despite the prominent involvement of Indonesians in decolonisation movements, postcolonial history has not been highly influential in Indonesia for several reasons. As identified by Sukarno, the intersection of decolonisation and the Cold War led to the emergence of new forms of coloniality. These influenced how Indonesia was positioned in the global order from its declaration of independence. Here it is crucial to consider what Sabelo Ndlovu-Gatsheni refers to as 'Cold War coloniality'— a process that led countries of the Global South to become 'entrapped in a global ideological warfare' preventing 'authentic political and economic formulations and creations'.[19] This ideological warfare saw competition between universalist and expansionist ideologies emanating from the Soviet Union and the United States.[20] These ideologies drove Western powers to work with the Indonesian army to both remove Sukarno and destroy the political left because of the perceived threats they posed to

---

16   Rochona Majumdar, '*Subaltern Studies* as a History of Social Movements in India', *South Asia: Journal of South Asian Studies* 38, no. 1 (2015): 50–68, doi.org/10.1080/00856401.2014.987338.

17   See, for example, Ann Stoler, *Along the Archival Grain: Epistemic Anxieties and Colonial Common Sense* (Princeton: Princeton University Press, 2010); Ann Stoler and Karen Strassler, 'Castings for the Colonial: Memory Work in "New Order" Java', *Comparative Studies in Society and History* 42, no. 1 (2000): 4–48, www.jstor.org/stable/pdf/2696632.pdf; G. Roger Knight, 'Colonial Knowledge and Subaltern Voices: The Case of an Official Enquiry in Mid-Nineteenth-Century Java', in *Sources and Methods in Histories of Colonialism*, eds Kirsty Reid and Fiona Paisley (London: Routledge, 2017), 85–99, doi.org/10.4324/9781315271958-6.

18   Majumdar, 'Postcolonial History', 54. For the full argument see Dipesh Chakrabarty, *Provincializing Europe: Postcolonial Thought and Historical Difference* (Princeton: Princeton University Press, 2007), doi.org/10.1515/9781400828654.

19   Sabelo J. Ndlovu-Gatsheni, 'When Did the Masks of Coloniality Begin to Fall? Decolonial Reflections on the Bandung Spirit of Decolonisation', *Bandung: Journal of the Global South* 6, no. 2 (2019): 210–32, doi.org/10.1163/21983534-00602004, at 214; see also Sabelo J. Ndlovu-Gatsheni, *Decolonization, Development and Knowledge in Africa: Turning Over a New Leaf* (London: Routledge, 2020), doi.org/10.4324/9781003030423, 46.

20   Odd Arne Westad, *The Global Cold War* (Cambridge: Cambridge University Press, 2007).

Western capitalism.[21] The destruction of the political left and the strength of anticommunism in Indonesia had important ramifications for the slow and limited take-up of postcolonialism in Indonesia. This is not to suggest that the political left was completely aligned with postcolonialism; indeed, postcolonialism also includes major critiques of the teleological dimensions of Marxism, but at the very least the political left shared with postcolonial thought important critiques of structures of power in Indonesian society.

Several Indonesian scholars have to date reflected on why postcolonial approaches are not common in Indonesia. Hilmar Farid, for example, offers some reasons for this.[22] First, he connects the neglect of postcolonial perspectives, which are highly alert to ongoing inequalities in structures of power, to the absence for many years in Indonesian scholarship of Marxist or class perspectives. This in turn is a product of the destruction in 1965–68 of the political left and the longstanding taboos around taking up issues related to class due to intense anticommunism.[23] Second, at the time postcolonial studies was escalating in the 1980s and 1990s in Indonesia, due to the direction of the New Order government (1966–98), attention focused instead on modernisation, development and authoritarianism.[24]

Bambang Purwanto notes that there were efforts from as early as the 1950s to write Indonesia-centric versions of history, yet because history was utilised politically for nation-building purposes, there was a tendency to produce 'ultra nationalist history that leaned more towards rhetoric', such as the claim by Mohammad Yamin that the roots of the Indonesian flag extended back 6,000 years.[25] Writing shortly after the fall of the Suharto regime in 1998, Purwanto highlighted the need for more critical approaches to Indonesian history writing and a move away from a focus on elite political actors to the exclusion of everyday people, which stands in direct contrast to subaltern

---

21 Katharine McGregor, Jess Melvin, and Annie Pohlman, 'New Interpretations of the Causes, Dynamics and Legacies of the Indonesian Genocide', in *The Indonesian Genocide of 1965: Causes, Dynamics and Legacies*, eds Katharine McGregor, Jess Melvin, and Annie Pohlman (London: Palgrave Macmillan, 2018), 1–26, doi.org/10.1007/978-3-319-71455-4_1; Bradley R. Simpson, *Economists with Guns: Authoritarian Development and U.S.–Indonesian Relations, 1960–1968* (Stanford: Stanford University Press, 2008), doi.org/10.1515/9780804779524.
22 Hilmar Farid, 'Postcolonial Perspectives from Southeast Asia', Presentation to Postcolonial Perspectives from the Global South, Goethe-Institut, Jakarta, 24–25 January 2019, www.youtube.com/watch?v=1M53NvufNb4.
23 ibid., 50:55–52:11 mins.
24 ibid., 51:24–52:11 mins.
25 Bambang Purwanto, 'Historisisme Baru dan Kesadaran Dekonstruktif Kajian Kritis terhadap Historiografi Indonesiasentris [A New Historicism and Awareness of Critical Deconstructive Studies for Indonesia-Centric Historiography]', *Humanoria* XIII, no. 10 (2001): 32–33.

studies. During the New Order period, there were systematic efforts to use history for the purposes of reinforcing militarist and anticommunist values.[26] In the post-Suharto era there have been intense debates about the direction of Indonesian history and many efforts to escape what Mestika Zed refers to as the 'tyranny of national history' or highly politicised versions of history.[27] This has encompassed new attention particularly to local histories and, to a more limited extent, marginalised historical subjects;[28] but on the most sensitive periods of Indonesian history, including the events of 1965 and the revolution, there is continuing pressure from institutions such as the military to not deviate from certain interpretations of these events.[29]

As explained above, key anticolonial thinkers across Asia and Africa inspired postcolonial thinking, yet postcolonialism also includes critiques of independent states for reproducing assumptions about modernity in nationalist projects. This might include history writing and ongoing potential processes of 'othering' groups of people in efforts to define who is included or excluded from a nation. In *The Wretched of the Earth*, Fanon argues that national consciousness 'will in any case only be an empty shell, a crude and fragile travesty of what it might have been'.[30] Due to the compromises nationalists make, he argued, they also replicated colonial-era thinking and structures of power.[31] Building on these insights, this volume reconsiders 'colonial' history and interrogates the legacies, as well as the reproduction, of colonial structures of power and colonial ways of thinking.

---

26   Katharine McGregor, *History in Uniform: Military Ideology and the Construction of Indonesia's Past* (Singapore: NUS Press, 2007).
27   Mestika Zed, 'Menggugat Tirani Sejarah Nasional [Contesting the Tyranny of National History]', Paper presented to Seventh National History Conference, Jakarta, 28–31 October 2001.
28   The multi-volume 2012 history *Indonesia Dalam Arus Sejarah*, for example, included attention to historical subjects such as *ulama* (Islamic scholars), farmers, fishing communities and students and topics such as the history of gender discourse and education. See Taufik Abdullah, 'Kata Pengantar [Introduction]', in *Indonesia dalam Arus Sejarah* [*Indonesia in the Flow of History*], eds Taufik Abdullah and A.B. Lapian (Jakarta: Ichtiar Baru van Hoeve, 2012).
29   Take, for example, the reactions of sections of the military, police and religious organisations to efforts to open discussions about the 1965 violence around the fiftieth anniversary of these events, which challenged the official New Order narrative that the killings were justified. See Katharine McGregor, 'Historical Justice and the Case of the 1965 Killings', in *Routledge Handbook of Contemporary Indonesia*, ed. Robert W. Hefner (London: Routledge, 2018), 129–39, doi.org/10.4324/9781315628837-10.
30   Frantz Fanon, *The Wretched of the Earth*, trans. Constance Farrington (New York: Grove Press, 1963), 148.
31   Gyan Prakash, *After Colonialism: Imperial Histories and Postcolonial Displacements* (Princeton: Princeton University Press, 1995), doi.org/10.1515/9781400821440.

Recent debates about colonial history and cultural repatriation

In the past decade several controversies about colonial history and how the process of decolonisation is understood and narrated have erupted in the Netherlands, the former colonial power of Indonesia. By contrast there has been less discussion of representations of colonial history in Indonesia so far, but there are signs that this is changing. Recently there have been more vociferous demands, for example, for the return of cultural objects still held in the Netherlands. These debates help highlight the continuing resonance of colonial history and its meanings in the present as well as the persistence of coloniality.

In February 2022, for example, the national museum of the Netherlands, the Rijksmuseum, opened the much talked about exhibition '*Revolusi!* Indonesia Independent'. The exhibition focused on the tumultuous period 1945–49, which followed the Netherlands' refusal to recognise Indonesia's declaration of independence and the attempt to recolonise the Indonesian archipelago by force. The curatorial team comprised two curators from the Rijksmuseum, Harm Stevens and Marion Anker, and two Indonesian curators, historian Bonnie Triyana and art historian Amir Sidharta. The content and title of the exhibition and the constitution of the curatorial team indicate that the Rijksmuseum was striving to foreground Indonesian rather than Dutch voices and experiences of the revolution. The Rijksmuseum curators seemed to understand the need to decolonise not only the institution they represented, its collections and its exhibition practices, but also Dutch history at large and, first and foremost, the colonial past.

Despite these important moves to accommodate a more Indonesia-centric interpretation of the 'revolution', when the Indonesian curator Triyana announced in a newspaper piece that the Rijksmuseum would not 'use "bersiap" as a common term to refer to violence during the revolution'[32] in the exhibition, this created public controversy, indicating ongoing

---

32   Bonnie Triyana, 'Schrap de term Bersiap want die is Racistisch [Delete the Term *Bersiap* Because it is Racist]', *NRC*, [Amsterdam], 10 January 2022, www.nrc.nl/nieuws/2022/01/10/schrap-term-bersiap-voor-periodisering-want-die-is-racistisch-a4077367. The debate only escalated once this article in the leading liberal national newspaper the *NRC* was picked up by more populist Dutch press outlets such as *De Telegraaf*, which used alarmist language to frame the issue. See, for example, 'Rijksmuseum: Toch Aandacht voor Term Bersiap [Rijksmuseum: Still Attention for the Term *Bersiap*]', *De Telegraaf*, [Amsterdam], 14 January 2022, www.telegraaf.nl/nieuws/1757408305/rijksmuseum-toch-aandacht-voor-term-bersiap.

sensitivities about how the colonial past is recalled in the Netherlands. The term '*bersiap*' ('be ready') is a slogan from prewar boy scouting used by Indonesian youths to warn each other about the enemy or to take action.[33] For many Indo-Europeans, however, the term reminds them of the terrible violence directed against them by young Indonesian revolutionaries in September to December 1945.[34] There were more than 40,000 victims of the violence in this period, of whom 5,723 (or 12.5 per cent) were Indo-Europeans.[35] So, the attacks during this period were not exclusively on Indo-Europeans, although that image persisted in the Netherlands for a long time.[36] Triyana's piece attempted to historicise and contextualise *bersiap*, arguing that the term cannot be used as a shorthand for all the violence that occurred in this period during which, for example, a social revolution was also under way. He also argued that *bersiap* has racist undertones because the way it is popularly understood is divorced from the historical context of Dutch colonialism and the collapse of the Japanese Empire and because the perpetrators are presented as 'primitive, uncivilised Indonesians'.[37]

---

33 For a discussion of this term and its use in the Netherlands, see William H. Frederick, 'Shadows of an Unseen Hand: Some Patterns of Violence in the Indonesian Revolution, 1945–1949', in *Roots of Violence in Indonesia: Contemporary Violence in Historical Perspective*, eds Freek Colombijn and J. Thomas Lindblad (Leiden: Brill, 2002), 143–72, doi.org/10.1163/9789004489561_009, at 145.
34 This memory has become 'institutionalised' by means of both memoirs and historical studies written mostly by survivors and their families, such as Herman Bussemaker, *Bersiap! Opstand in het Paradijs: de Bersiap-periode op Java en Sumatra 1945–1946* [*Bersiap! Revolt in Paradise: The Bersiap Period on Java and Sumatra 1945–46*] (Zuthpen: Walburg Pers, 2005). Such memories are also reinforced in the annual commemoration on 15 August at the Indies Monument in The Hague. See Nationale Herdenking 15 Augustus 1945 [15 August 1945 Commemoration Foundation], *Commemorations in the Netherlands* (The Hague: Nationale Herdenking 15 Augustus 1945, 2024), 15augustus1945.nl/en/other-commemorations/). There is also a plan to build a *Bersiap* monument in The Hague, which is likely to be sponsored and supported by the Indo-European community in the Netherlands. See The Indo Project, 'Bersiap, Decolonization Research and Postcolonial Uproar: A Summary', *The Indo Project*, 26 February (Boston: The Indo Project, 2022), theindoproject.org/bersiap-decolonization-postcolonial-uproar/.
35 Henk Schulte Nordholt, 'Waarom het Woord "Bersiap" Zoveel Woede Oproept [Why the Word "Bersiap" Invokes So Much Anger]', *Trouw*, [Amsterdam], 18 January 2022, www.trouw.nl/opinie/waarom-het-woord-bersiap-zoveel-woede-oproept-b8013df3/; Esther Captain and Onno Sinke, *Het Geluid van Geweld Bersiap en de Dynamiek van Geweld Tijdens de Eerste Fase van de Indonesische Revolutie, 1945–1946* [*Resonance of Violence: Bersiap and the Dynamics of Violence in the First Phase of the Indonesian Revolution, 1945–1946*] (Amsterdam: Amsterdam University Press, 2022), 188.
36 Nordholt, 'Why the Word *Bersiap* Invokes So Much Anger'.
37 Further to these observations, leading Indonesian historian Bambang Purwanto notes that 'the whole framework of historiography about "bersiap" arose from the surrounding context of Dutch efforts to rebuild their colonial power' and the word continues to be used to 'erase all the wrongful actions of the Dutch in Indonesia'. Bambang Purwanto, 'Bersiap, Kutukan Kemerderkaan Indonesia yang Menghantui Belanda [*Bersiap*, the Curse of Indonesian Independence that Haunts the Netherlands]', *Media Indonesia*, 23 August 2022. mediaindonesia.com/opini/516800/bersiap-kutukan-kemerdekaan-indonesia-yang-menghantui-belanda.

The general understanding of *bersiap* also simplifies the basis on which people were targeted in the violence: rather than race alone, people were often targeted based on perceived loyalty to the Dutch.

Select representatives of the Indo-European community furiously protested Triyana's article. They felt they were being dismissed as racists and that Triyana obscured the suffering they experienced.[38] The Dutch Indies Federation (Federatie Indische Nederlanders), a small media-savvy organisation established in 2017 by third-generation Dutch East Indies people that purports to protect and promote historical legacies and knowledge related to this community, reported Triyana to the police, alleging 'group insult' of the Indo-European community and that the museum's decision was 'war propaganda coming from Indonesia'.[39] Shortly thereafter, the Rijksmuseum reneged on its position, announcing that it would retain the term in the exhibition.[40] In response, the Committee of Dutch Debts of Honour (Komite Utang Kehormatan Belanda), a group advocating for redress for colonial violence, lodged a complaint against the Rijksmuseum for 'group insult against Indonesians'.[41]

The *bersiap* controversy raged for several weeks among activists and sections of the East Indies community, indicating that the colonial past is very much part of the present. What these debates exposed is that colonially constructed discourses, categories and hierarchies of race continue to be deeply embedded in the social fabric of Dutch society today. The value some

---

38   Esther Wills, 'Rijksmuseum Schrapt Bersiap [Rijksmuseum Deletes *Bersiap*]', *Indies Tijdschrift*, [*Indies Magazine*], 13 January 2022; Lizzy van Leeuwen, 'Het Rijksmuseum als Speelbal van Woke [The Rijksmuseum as Plaything of Woke]', *De Telegraaf*, [Amsterdam], 14 January 2022; Theodor Holman, 'Zo Verhul je de genocide [This Is How You Disguise Genocide]', *Het Parool*, [Amsterdam], 12 January 2022. On the violence against this community, see William H. Frederick, 'The Killing of Dutch and Eurasians in Indonesia's National Revolution (1945–1949): A "Brief Genocide" Reconsidered', in *Colonial Counterinsurgency and Mass Violence: The Dutch Empire in Indonesia*, eds Bart Luttikhuis and A. Dirk Moses (London: Routledge, 2014), 133–54, doi.org/10.4324/9781315767345-7.
39   Federatie Indische Nederlanders [Federation of Dutch East Indies] (FIN), 'Aangifte tegen Bersiap-ontkenner Triyana [Complaint Filed Against *Bersiap* Denier Triyana]' (FIN, 11 January 2022), www.federatie-indo.nl/2022/01/11/22-01-11/; and 'Woede over Niet Gebruiken van Term "Bersiap" op Indonesië-expositie [Anger Over Not Using the Term "Bersiap" at Indonesia Exhibition]', *NOS Nieuws* [*Dutch Broadcasting Foundation News*], 12 January 2022, nos.nl/artikel/2412770-woede-over-niet-gebruiken-van-term-bersiap-op-indonesie-expositie. Group insult—insulting a group of people or a population group—is a crime under Dutch criminal law.
40   Bart Funnekotter, 'Bersiap Blijft, en het Rijksmuseum is niet Woke [Bersiap Stays and the Rijksmuseum is Not Woke]', *NRC*, [Amsterdam], 14 January 2022, www.nrc.nl/nieuws/2022/01/14/bersiap-blijft-en-het-rijksmuseum-is-niet-woke-a4079433.
41   'Aangifte tegen Rijksmuseum om gebruik Term "Bersiap" [Complaint Against Rijksmuseum for Use of Term "Bersiap"]', *Noordhollands Dagblad*, [Alkmaar, Netherlands], 22 January 2022, www.noordhollandsdagblad.nl/cnt/dmf20220121_77416427.

members of the Indo-European community placed on their experiences privileged them over the experiences of ethnic Chinese, Moluccans, communists and others who were similarly targeted. In Chapter 8, Ravando and F.X. Harsono produce important new insights into the scale and patterns of violence against Chinese Indonesians on the island of Java. For Indo-Europeans, recognition of their historical suffering in the former colony is an important source of legitimation and identity.[42] This sits alongside historical and ongoing experiences of discrimination and assimilation in the Netherlands.[43] This contestation was underpinned by issues of power and control: Who gets to write the past? Whose stories and experiences prevail and whose do not?

Whereas in the Netherlands the *bersiap* issue was very controversial, in Indonesia, only a few media outlets covered the debate.[44] Much of this involved explaining the term *bersiap* itself, which barely has a place in Indonesian historiography. This reporting also included chronologies of the *bersiap* discussion in the Netherlands and the reporting of Triyana to the police. The latter resulted in much confusion on social media because netizens were under the false impression that Triyana had been arrested and held by the police. This was framed in social media discussions in colonial and nationalist terms. Memes (see Figures 1.1 and 1.2) depicted Triyana and the *bersiap* controversy as a case of coloniser–colonised power relations, including Triyana as Indonesian national hero Diponegoro in Raden Saleh's 1857 painting *The Arrest of Pangeran Diponegoro* and sitting on the floor before a colonial court (*landraad*) in a diorama. Figure 1.1 also features the hashtags #Talkingabouthistoryisnotacrime and #Savecuratorialindependence. More serious objections were voiced by prominent historian Anhar Gonggong,

---

42   This includes being identified as victims of suffering during the Japanese occupation; *bersiap* was also recognised legally through compensation payments paid by the Dutch Government for wartime victims. See Elly Touwen-Bousma, *Op Zoek Naar Grenzen: Toepassing en Uitvoering van de Wetten voor Oorlogslachtoffers* [*Looking for Boundaries: Application and Implementation of the Laws for War Victims*] (Amsterdam: Boom, 2010).

43   Esther Captain, 'Harmless Identities: Representations of Racial Consciousness among Three Generations Indo-Europeans', in *Dutch Racism*, eds Philomena Essed and Isabel Hoving (Leiden: Brill, 2014), 53–69, doi.org/10.1163/9789401210096_004.

44   See Eveline Buchheim, Satrio Ody Dwicahyo, Fridus Steijlen, and Stephanie Welvaart, eds, *Sporen vol betekenis/Meniti Arti: In gesprek met 'Getuigen & Tijdgenoten' over de Indonesische onafhankelijkheidsoorlog/ Bertukar Makna bersama 'Saksi & Rekan Sezaman' tentang Perang Kemerdekaan Indonesia* [*Traces Full of Meaning: In Conversation With 'Witnesses and Contemporaries' about the Indonesian Independence War*] (Amsterdam: Amsterdam University Press, 2022), especially pp. 178–95.

who, in response to Triyana's reporting, urged the Indonesian Government to withdraw its support of the '*Revolusi!*' exhibition and deny requests to loan objects.⁴⁵

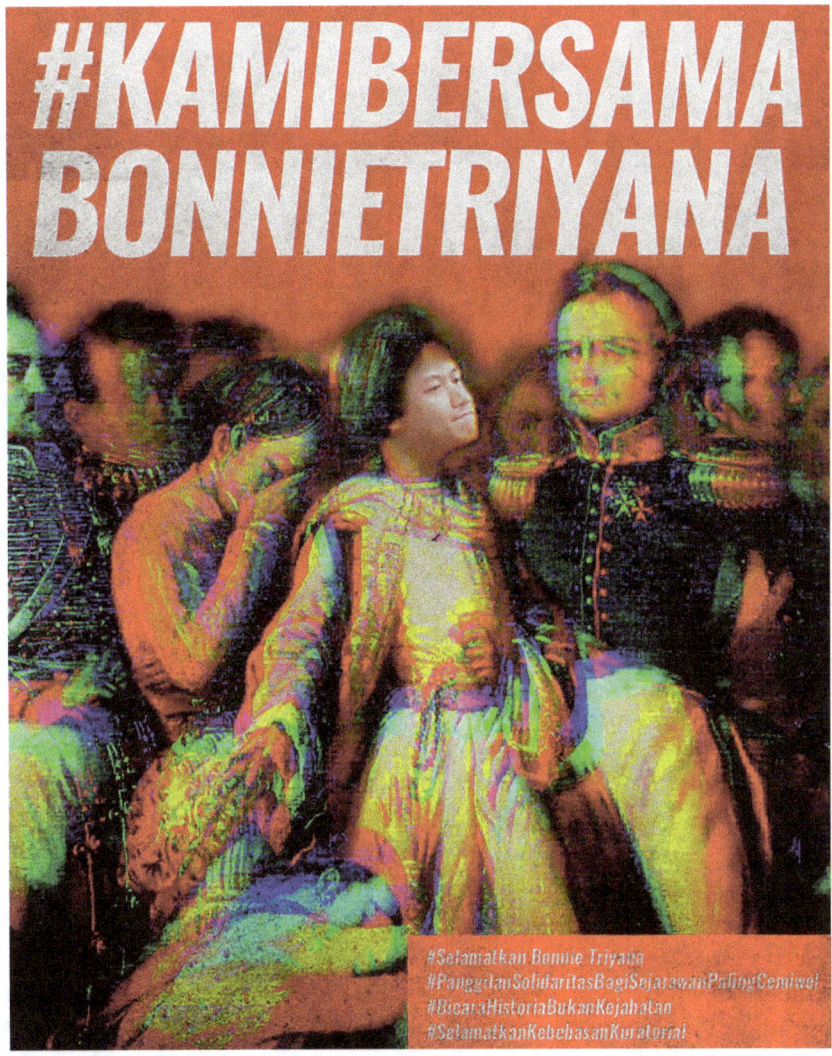

Figure 1.1 Meme with the hashtag #KamiBersamaBonnieTriyana ('We are with Bonnie Triyana'), 26 January 2022
Photo: Courtesy of Alit Ambara.

---

45   'Anhar Gonggong Desak RI Cabut Partisipasi Pameran Rijksmuseum Belanda [Anhar Gonggong Urges Republic of Indonesia to Withdraw Participation in Dutch Rijksmuseum Exhibition]', *CNN Indonesia*, 27 January 2022, www.cnnindonesia.com/nasional/20220127152144-20-752067/anhar-gonggong-desak-ri-cabut-partisipasi-pameran-rijksmuseum-belanda/.

Figure 1.2 Untitled meme, 4 February 2022
Photo: Courtesy of Alit Ambara.

In Indonesia debates related to the ownership and repatriation of cultural objects held in museum collections in the Netherlands have become noticeably more pronounced. In 2019 the Dutch Government returned about 1,500 objects from the Museum Nusantara in Delft and, in 2020, Diponegoro's *keris* (ritual dagger).[46] In October 2022, I Gusti Agung Wesaka Puja, the chair of the Indonesian Government's repatriation team, announced a further list of priority objects requested for return at a seminar organised by the Association of Indonesian Museums (Asosiasi Museum

---

46 Callistasia Wijaya, 'Indonesia–Belanda: Ratusan Ribu Benda Bersejarah Indonesia Dimiliki Belanda akan Segera Dikembalikan [Indonesia–the Netherlands: Hundreds of Thousands of Indonesian Historical Objects in Dutch Hands Will Be Quickly Returned to Indonesia]?', *BBC News Indonesia*, 13 March 2020, www.bbc.com/indonesia/indonesia-51749544. See also Jos van Beurden, 'Returns by the Netherlands to Indonesia in the 2010s and the 1970s', in *Returning Southeast Asia's Past: Objects, Museum, and Restitution*, eds Louise Tythacott and Panggah Ardiyansyah (Singapore: NUS Press, 2021), 187–209, doi.org/10.2307/j.ctv1r4xctd.13.

Indonesia), which was submitted by Director-General of Culture Hilmar Farid to the Dutch Government in July that year.[47] This list included the Pita Maha collection, the reins of Diponegoro's horse, a Balinese *keris* from the early twentieth-century Puputan Klungkung, the Hindu-Buddhist Singasari statues, the Lombok royal treasure (*pusaka*) taken in 1894, regalia from the Luwu Kingdom in South Sulawesi, a Qur'an belonging to Acehnese resistance leader Teuku Umar held at the Dutch National Museum of Ethnology and the Eugène Dubois fossils in the collection of the Naturalis Biodiversity Center in Leiden. The Eugène Dubois collection, comprising 40,000 fossils excavated by Dutch naturalist Eugène Dubois in the late nineteenth century—notably including the skull, molar and thigh bone of *Pithecanthropus erectus*, famously known as 'Java Man'—stirred the most commotion.[48] In 2023, 472 items—including 355 objects from the Lombok collection looted in 1894, four statues from the thirteenth-century Singasari temple, a *keris* from Klungkung and 132 pieces identified as the Pita Maha collection—were returned to Indonesia. Dubois' fossil collection is still under review by the Dutch repatriation committee.

There were differing responses to the public debate. Director of the National Museum of World Cultures (Nationaal Museum van Wereldculturen) Marieke van Bommel stated that the museum would cooperate in the requests for return, whereas the Naturalis Biodiversity Center responded with the utmost reluctance, claiming that the research and museum infrastructure in Indonesia is insufficient to properly care for the fossils.[49] The latter response echoed broader contested distinctions between cultural historical objects produced as arts and handicrafts and fossils, with claims that 'it would not have been found if the Dutchman, Dubois, had not searched for it'[50] and that the fossils were 'not seized or involuntarily handed over'.[51] In response,

---

47 Fenneke Sysling, 'Er is een Lijstje met de Eerste 8 Koloniale Collecties die Indonesië terugeist van Nederland [There is a List with the First 8 Colonial Collections Claimed by Indonesia from the Netherlands]!', @fsysling, *Twitter* [X], 17 October 2022.
48 Merijn van Nuland, 'Indonesië eist Java-mens en Andere Topstukken terug van Nederland [Indonesia Demands Java Man and Other Top Pieces Back from the Netherlands]', *Trouw*, [Amsterdam], 18 October 2022, www.trouw.nl/binnenland/indonesie-eist-java-mens-en-andere-topstukken-terug-van-nederland-be6860e9/.
49 ibid.
50 As quoted in ibid. For more on this, see Caroline Drieënhuizen and Fenneke Sysling, 'Java Man and the Politics of Natural History: An Object Biography', *Bijdragen tot de Taal-, Land- en Volkenkunde [Journal of the Humanities and Social Sciences of Southeast Asia]* 177, nos 2–3 (2021): 290–311, doi.org/10.1163/22134379-bja10012, at 293.
51 Louis Zweers, 'Veel is al in bezit van Indonesië [Much is Already Owned by Indonesia]', *Nederlands Dagblad*, [Amersfoort], 8 November 2022.

the secretary of the Indonesian Government's repatriation committee, Bonnie Triyana, underlined the inherent double standards at the heart of these cases in an interview with the Dutch newspaper *Trouw*, stating:

> Someone can say 'this object belongs in the Netherlands because a Dutchman went to Indonesia, dug in the ground and after a good while searching found a skull'. But that is like if someone travels to another country, finds oil there and says, 'it is mine, I may use it and sell it'. The fact that you excavated it on someone else's land does not mean that the object directly belongs to your country.[52]

These recent discourses form part of a much longer history of demands for repatriation. Two chapters in this volume take us back to early discussions at the 1949 Round Table Conference related to cultural decolonisation more broadly (Chapter 9) and regarding ownership and ongoing colonial categorisations within the partially repatriated archive known as the Djogdja Documenten (Chapter 10).

Colonial categories across and beyond the colony

Throughout this volume, we examine colonial categories and propaganda from multiple angles. We use the concept of colonial categories to signal groupings applied to and used by Indonesians throughout and beyond the formal period of Dutch colonisation, with references also to the British Empire. This includes legal classifications imposed by the Dutch colonial state and their wider effects, as well as less formal categories such as references to the *Belanda Hitam* ('Black Dutchmen') and 'martial races'. We also seek to capture alternative conceptualisations of identity used by locals, such as the concepts of *bangsa* ('race' or 'people') or 'Malay'. 'Race' is a social construct, but this does not diminish its effects. As Patrick Wolfe has argued in relation to colonialism, 'different racial regimes encode and reproduce the unequal relationships into which Europeans coerced the populations concerned'.[53] The racial regime used by the Dutch in the colony of the Netherlands East Indies rested on the 1854 law that crudely classified people for legal purposes as 'European', 'Foreign Oriental' or

---

52 As quoted in van Nuland, 'Indonesia Demands Java Man'.
53 Patrick Wolfe, 'Settler Colonialism and the Elimination of the Native', *Journal of Genocide Research* 8, no. 4 (2006): 387–409, doi.org/10.1080/14623520601056240, at 387.

'Native'. The category 'Native' or 'Inlanders' referred to most locals and was applied across many spheres of colonial society, particularly in medicine and science.[54] Esther Captain argues that the term implied 'these people were part of the indigenous flora and fauna of the archipelago instead of being human beings'.[55] The category 'Foreign Oriental' worked to racialise those of Chinese and Arab descent as 'foreign' and therefore separate from other Indonesians. The related differential treatment of such people produced a range of harmful assumptions with long-lasting and often violent impacts.

There has been sustained attention on Chinese Indonesians due to their unique and important position throughout history.[56] In a survey of the research, Mary Somers Heidhues has identified several key themes. Of most importance for this volume is the pioneering research that took a postcolonial approach rather than state-oriented studies focusing on issues such as citizenship, political representation, violence against Chinese Indonesians, Chinese organisations, religious practices, diverse identities and connections to China.[57] One trend Heidhues misses is the increased number of Chinese Indonesian scholars and public intellectuals contributing to academic discourse about their own society and history. This is especially evident since the fall of the New Order in 1998 when many Chinese Indonesian intellectuals and scholars participated in the new 'democratic atmosphere' of academic freedom by producing or publishing work in Bahasa Indonesia about various aspects of their 'own history'. These works reveal insider and 'popular' perspectives of the ill-fated position of this community throughout Indonesian history. A prime example of this work is that of Beni G. Setiono.[58] In an encyclopedic book, Setiono critically analyses the recurrence of anti-Chinese violence from the eighteenth century to the present, while also analysing the contributions of Chinese Indonesians to the shaping of modern Indonesia.

---

54 See Hans Pols, 'Psychological Knowledge in a Colonial Context: Theories on the Nature of the "Native Mind" in the Former Dutch East Indies', *History of Psychology* 10, no. 2 (May 2007): 111–31, doi.org/10.1037/1093-4510.10.2.111; Fenneke Sysling, *Racial Science and Human Diversity in Colonial Indonesia* (Singapore: NUS Press, 2016), doi.org/10.2307/j.ctv9hj794.
55 Captain, 'Harmless Identities', 55.
56 We choose to use the term Chinese Indonesians when referring to modern periods of Indonesian history because we consider this the most inclusive term, which includes recognition of the fact that Indonesians of Chinese descent are foremost also Indonesian.
57 Mary Somers Heidhues, 'Studying the Chinese in Indonesia: A Long Half-Century', *Sojourn: Journal of Social Issues in Southeast Asia* 32, no. 3 (2017): 601–33, doi.org/10.1355/sj32-3c.
58 Beni G. Setiono, *Tionghoa Indonesia dalam Pusaran Politik* [*Chinese Indonesians in the Political Maelstrom*] (Jakarta: Transmedia, 2008).

The Dutch colonial category 'European' ostensibly included people of European background, but recent scholarship has highlighted the more complex dimensions of this category. Bart Luttikhuis has argued that being European was measured not so much by 'whiteness' as by a multitude of factors, of which class and language competency were also important.[59] Through her careful study of elite culture, Susie Protschky has shown that people classified into other groups could achieve 'European' status if they demonstrated appropriate mimicry of European traditions.[60] Although ethnicity alone did not determine whether someone was 'European', all three legal categories reinforced social hierarchies and led to further exploitation.

Across scholarship on colonial categories, a key point of debate has been to what extent race, gender or class determined social hierarchy.[61] Gender and class are key axes around which hierarchies of power operated in colonial society. Research into gender has been at the forefront of efforts to interrogate colonial categories. From the 1990s, new histories were written about relationships between women of different classes in colonial society, such as Indonesian domestic workers and Dutch women, and the changing position of Indo-European women.[62] These studies, however, tended to focus on Dutch-produced discourses about Indonesian people.

More recently scholars have examined how Indonesians negotiated and resisted the multiple structures of power of the colonial regime by using sources that better capture Indonesian perspectives on class and race. Using the so-called wild publications (*batjaan liar*) of the 1920s written in low Malay, Hilmar Farid and Razif highlight critiques launched by radical nationalists

---

59 Bart Luttikhuis, 'Beyond Race: Constructions of "Europeanness" in Late-Colonial Legal Practice in the Dutch East Indies', *European Review of History* 20, no. 4 (2013): 539–58, doi.org/10.1080/13507486.2013.764845.
60 Susie Protschky, 'Teacups, Cameras and Family Life: Picturing Domesticity in Elite European and Javanese Family Photographs from the Netherlands Indies, ca. 1900–42', *History of Photography* 36, no. 1 (2012): 44–65, doi.org/10.1080/03087298.2012.636503.
61 Susie Protschky, 'Race, Class, and Gender: Debates Over the Character of Social Hierarchies in the Netherlands Indies, Circa 1600–1942', *Bijdragen tot de Taal-, Land- en Volkenkunde [Journal of the Humanities and Social Sciences of Southeast Asia]* 167, no. 4 (2011): 543–56, doi.org/10.1163/22134379-90003584.
62 Julia Clancy-Smith and Frances Gouda, eds, *Domesticating the Empire: Race, Gender and Family Life in French and Dutch Colonialism* (Charlottesville: University of Virginia Press, 1998); Ann Stoler, *Carnal Knowledge and Imperial Power: Race and the Intimate in Colonial Rule* (Berkeley: University of California Press, 2002); Frances Gouda, *Dutch Culture Overseas: Colonial Practice in the Netherlands Indies, 1900–1942* (Amsterdam: Amsterdam University Press, 1996); Elsbeth Locher-Scholten, 'So Close and Yet So Far: The Ambivalence of Dutch Colonial Rhetoric on Javanese Servants in Indonesia, 1900–1942', in *Domesticating the Empire: Race, Gender and Family Life in French and Dutch Colonialism*, eds Julia Clancy-Smith and Frances Gouda (Charlottesville: University of Virginia Press, 1998), 130–53.

of racialised classifications.⁶³ Using colonial decrees and accompanying newspaper reportage, Arnout van der Meer identifies Indonesian resistance to the Dutch practice of mobilising colonial feudality.⁶⁴ From the perspective of the history of medicine, Hans Pols has analysed how trained Indonesian (including Chinese Indonesian) physicians both challenged racism and countered social-Darwinist conceptions of 'the Javanese' and 'Malays'.⁶⁵ Ayu Saraswati has articulated the various meanings attached to 'whiteness' in Indonesia's history.⁶⁶ Research on Chinese Indonesians, as noted, has been at the forefront of interrogating the effects of colonial categories.

In researching colonial categories and thinking about how they operated, scholars face several constraints, the first relating to sources. Chapters in this volume dealing with the colonial period use images produced by Dutch colonial agents, state colonial records as well as sources produced by Indonesians and other communities who were the subjects of colonial power. Yet, in trying to analyse how colonial categories worked, we are, as Susie Protschky reminds us, equally constrained by the primary sources we consult and 'the analytical perspectives that these materials enable (and disable), and the meanings attributed to terms of reference'.⁶⁷ Throughout this volume, we draw critical attention to colonial naming practices, such as use of the term *bersiap*, and how these were both replicated and challenged within and beyond the colonial era.

We use a diverse range of visual and written sources from the colonial period that cover not only Dutch, but also Indonesian perspectives. In so doing, we reconsider how these colonial categories and related propaganda operated across a range of fields. These include colonial photographic visualisations of daily life and of colonial warfare designed to reinforce structures of power and thinking related to particular ethnic groups, a taxation system that penalised Chinese Indonesians, an army that built its identity on ideas about 'martial races', the exploitative plantation system that was centred on making land and peasants 'productive' and 'modern' and the reproduction of colonial power within the families of colonial civil servants who were

---

63 Hilmar Farid and Razif, '*Batjaan Liar* in the Dutch East Indies: A Colonial Antipode', *Postcolonial Studies* 11, no. 3 (2008): 277–92, doi.org/10.1080/13688790802226694.
64 Arnout van der Meer, *Performing Power: Cultural Hegemony, Identity, and Resistance in Colonial Indonesia* (Ithaca: Cornell University Press, 2020), www.jstor.org/stable/10.7591/j.ctv1hbf2dd.
65 Hans Pols, *Nurturing Indonesia: Medicine and Decolonisation in the Dutch East Indies* (Cambridge: Cambridge University Press, 2018), doi.org/10.1017/9781108341035, especially pp. 71–92, 93–115.
66 L. Ayu Saraswati, *Seeing Beauty, Sensing Race in Transnational Indonesia* (Honolulu: University of Hawai`i Press, 2013), doi.org/10.21313/hawaii/9780824836641.001.0001.
67 Protschky, 'Race, Class and Gender', 550.

at once included and excluded from the category 'European'. We focus on how Indonesians experienced, negotiated and resisted these colonial categorisations.

Consistent with the emphasis the concept of decoloniality places on local belief systems, we also examine alternative sources of identity and senses of self that operated within and beyond the boundaries of the colony. As Thongchai Winichakul has so aptly demonstrated, colonial boundaries and colonial maps imposed on people a form of imagined geographical connection.[68] But this did not supersede other forms of community based on language and traditions such as the broader community of Malays spread across Sumatra, British Malaya and Dutch/British Ceylon (now Sri Lanka). Using Malay-language newspapers produced by Sumatran women and the Ceylon-based Malay diaspora, we ask how these two communities of people conceptualised, alternatively, the world, the boundaries of their communities, gender, class and ethnicity (see Chapters 3 and 4).

Although the Indonesian revolution is often romanticised as a radical break from the colonial era, the concept of coloniality encourages us to consider how contests related to colonial categories and longstanding justifications of diverse forms of colonial violence spilled over into this struggle.[69] Here, we consider what colonial war photography reveals about a range of modes of colonial violence and how the category 'martial races' worked within the colonial army (see Chapter 6). We pay careful attention also to how and why one community, Chinese Indonesians, became caught between the republican forces and the Dutch and how members of this community narrated their experiences during and shortly after the revolution (see Chapter 8). Again, centring Indonesian voices, we examine how a member of another more marginalised community, an Eastern Indonesian woman revolutionary, reflects on the extent to which the revolution entailed a dismantling of colonial structures of power (see Chapter 7).

---

68   Thongchai Winichakul, *Siam Mapped: A History of the Geo-Body of a Nation* (Honolulu: University of Hawai`i Press, 1997), doi.org/10.1515/9780824841294.
69   This is a theme that artists, writers and filmmakers have also explored from as early as the 1940s. See, for example, the work of painters such as Agus and Otto Djaya, S. Sudjojono, Basuki Abdullah, Henk Ngantung, Hendra Gunawan, Affandi and Trubus Soedarsono; writers Pramoedya Ananta Toer and Chairil Anwar; composer Ismail Marzuki; and filmmaker Usmar Ismail.

Colonial legacies: The persistence of and attempts to dismantle coloniality

Both former colonising powers and former colonised nations commonly present decolonisation in national histories as a rupture with the past, whether a withdrawal from colonial territory and influence or a moment when indigenous rulers reclaimed power and created a new nation.[70] In the context of Indonesia and the Netherlands, this emphasis on political discontinuity marked by significant dates is illustrated by continuing debates about the recognition of the Indonesian declaration of independence on 17 August 1945. For a long time, the Dutch insisted that Indonesia became an independent state after the 'transfer of sovereignty' on 27 December 1949. Then Minister of Foreign Affairs Ben Bot made only a minor concession on this debate in 2005 when he stated that 'the Dutch Cabinet and people liberally accept that Indonesian independence, politically and morally, commenced in fact in 1945'.[71] Nonetheless, the statement did not legally recognise the declaration of independence, nor did it refer to the longer period of colonialism.

Over time, the Dutch Government started to pay attention to the violence committed between 1945 and 1949; however, this violence was generally conceived of as exceptional and was not broadly recognised as a key dimension of colonial structures. Dutch Government policy since 1969 had held that, overall, the armed forces behaved correctly in Indonesia and there had been only a limited number of isolated 'excesses'.[72] Activism relating to demands for compensation for colonial violence escalated from about 2011, with demands for redress for executions committed by Dutch forces during the revolution, which led to apologies and compensation.[73] Nonetheless, the

---

70   Els Bogaerts and Remco Raben, 'Beyond Empire and Nation', in *Beyond Empire and Nation: The Decolonisation of African and Asian Societies 1930s–1960s*, eds Els Bogaerts and Remco Raben (Leiden: KITLV Press, 2012), 7–19, doi.org/10.1163/9789004260443, at 13.
71   Lizzy van Leeuwen, 'Postcolonial Neglect in Holland', *Inside Indonesia* 103 (January–March 2011), www.insideindonesia.org/postcolonial-neglect-in-holland.
72   Vincent J.H. Houben, 'A Torn Soul: The Dutch Public Discussion on the Colonial Past in 1995', *Indonesia* 63 (April 1997): 47–66, doi.org/10.2307/3351510.
73   On two prominent cases and related activism, see Stef Scagliola, 'Cleo's "Unfinished Business": Coming to Terms with Dutch War Crimes in Indonesia's War of Independence', *Journal of Genocide Research* 14, nos 3–4 (2012): 419–39, doi.org/10.1080/14623528.2012.719374; Katharine McGregor, 'From National Sacrifice to Compensation Claims: Changing Indonesian Representations of the Westerling Massacres in South Sulawesi, 1946–47', in *Colonial Counterinsurgency and Mass Violence: The Dutch Empire in Indonesia*, eds Bart Luttikhuis and Dirk A. Moses (London: Routledge, 2014), 282–307, doi.org/10.4324/9781315767345-14; Rémy Limpach, *De Brandende Kampongs van Generaal Spoor* [*The Burning Kampongs of General Spoor*] (Amsterdam: Boom, 2016).

narrative of excessive violence continued to be reproduced, as illustrated by the apology of the Dutch King Willem-Alexander during his 2020 official visit to Indonesia in which he stated: 'I express regret and apologise for *excessive* violence on the part of the Dutch in those years.'[74]

This stood in contrast to the emerging findings of scholars, commencing with Rémy Limpach's research, which concluded that violence was more systematic.[75] It was in this context that researchers affiliated with the NIOD Institute for War, Holocaust and Genocide Studies at the Royal Netherlands Institute of Southeast Asian and Caribbean Studies and the Netherlands Institute of Military History began a research program called 'Independence, Decolonisation, Violence and War in Indonesia, 1945–1950'. The four-year project (2017–21) received funding from the Dutch Government and investigated violence committed by all sides during the period 1945–49.[76] Following the delayed presentation of the research results in 2023 in a parliamentary debate, the Dutch State recognised the proclamation on 17 August 1945 as a historical fact, but maintained that the statement was made without legal consequences.[77]

The conclusions of this project, presented just one week after the opening of the '*Revolusi!*' exhibition at the Rijksmuseum, were that the violence committed by Dutch troops during 1945–49 was indisputably structural and not incidental—a finding that reinforced Limpach's conclusions and challenged the previously held consensus that Dutch uses of extreme violence were rare 'excesses'.[78] The research team used the term *bersiap*,

---

74 [Emphasis added.] 'Dutch King Apologises for "Excessive Violence" in Colonial Indonesia', *Reuters*, 10 March 2020, www.reuters.com/article/us-indonesia-netherlands-idUSKBN20X15L.
75 Limpach, *The Burning Kampongs of General Spoor*.
76 The results of the research project are available for public access at: www.aup.nl/en/series/onafhankelijkheid-dekolonisatie-geweld-en-oorlog-in-indonesie-1945-1950.
77 Yvette Tanamal, 'Dutch PM Recognises 1945 as Indonesia's Independence', *Jakarta Post*, 16 June 2023. The transcript of the parliamentary debate can be found online at: www.tweedekamer.nl/downloads/document?id=2023D33139. For the reaction to this, see NOS Nieuws, 'Nederland erkent 17 augustus 1945 als onafhankelijkheidsdag Indonesië [The Netherlands Recognises 17 August 1945 as Indonesia's Independence Day]', *NOS Nieuws* [*Dutch Broadcasting Foundation News*], 14 June 2023, nos.nl/artikel/2478878-nederland-erkent-17-augustus-1945-als-onafhankelijkheidsdag-indonesie.
78 For a summary of the project's findings, see the volume Kon. Inst. v. Taal-, Land- en Volkenkunde [Royal Netherlands Institute of Southeast Asian and Caribbean Studies] (KITLV), Nederlands Instituut voor Militaire Historie [Netherlands Institute for Military History] (NIMH), and NIOD Inst. v. Oorlogs-, Holocaust- en Genocidestudies [NIOD Netherlands Institute for War, Holocaust and Genocide Studies], *Beyond the Pale: Dutch Extreme Violence in the Indonesian War of Independence, 1945–1949* (Amsterdam: Amsterdam University Press, 2022), doi.org/10.1515/9789048557172. The prior consensus was based on government-sponsored research and the 1969 report known in the Netherlands as the *Excessennota* or '*Memorandum of Excesses*'.

but broadened understandings of this to include violence experienced not only by the Indo-Dutch community but also by marginalised communities within the Indonesian archipelago.[79]

Reactions in the Netherlands to the project were pronounced, with some veterans, for example, condemning what in their view was an unfair assessment of the behaviour of all veterans. Chairman of Veterans Platform, Hans van Griensven, stated that 'while only a small percentage of the 200,000 men sent there misbehaved, now everyone is labelled a war criminal'.[80] In an attempt to mediate this, then Dutch prime minister Mark Rutte apologised to 'all the Indonesian people' and to 'all the Dutch people' affected by the systemic violence committed during the 1945–49 period.[81] Yet, his apology generated mixed reactions in the Netherlands, including some who felt it was insufficient and more extreme nationalist views such as those of Geert Wilders from the far-right Party for Freedom. Via Twitter (now X), Wilders not only questioned the apology, but also requested a similar apology from the Indonesian side for 'their violence and for bersiap'; he also claimed the Dutch veterans were heroes.[82]

In Indonesia, by contrast, responses to the apology varied from lukewarm to complete silence from the Indonesian Government. Writer and prominent intellectual Goenawan Mohamad, who grew up during the 1940s, wrote:

> I prefer to see Rutte's apology not as a conscientious policy, but rather a political act or, if you will, a proxy. It is a *mea culpa* without pathos. After all, his government had no part in the ugly chapter of the Dutch colonial history.[83]

---

79 Captain and Sinke, *Resonance of Violence*.
80 Tonny van der Mee and Raymond Boere, '"Geschiedvervalsing" of "geen nieuws"? Kenners sterk verdeeld over onderzoek naar dekolonisatie Indonesië ["Fake History" or "No News"? Experts Strongly Divided About Research into the Decolonisation of Indonesia]', *Het Parool*, [Amsterdam], 17 February 2022, www.parool.nl/nederland/geschiedvervalsing-of-geen-nieuws-kenners-sterk-verdeeld-over-onderzoek-naar-dekolonisatie-indonesie-b4ade2e3/.
81 Rijksoverheid, '1e Reactie van Minister-President Mark Rutte na de Presentatie van het Onderzoeksprogramma "Onafhankelijkheid, Dekolonisatie, Geweld en Oorlog in Indonesië, 1945–1950" [First Reaction of Prime Minister Mark Rutte after the Presentation of the Research Program "Independence, Decolonisation, Violence and War in Indonesia, 1945–1950"], Speech, 17 February 2022, Government of the Netherlands, www.rijksoverheid.nl/documenten/toespraken/2022/02/17/eerste-reactie-van-minister-president-mark-rutte-onderzoeksprogramma-onafhankelijkheid-dekolonisatie-geweld-en-oorlog-in-indonesie-1945-1950.
82 Geert Wilders, 'Waar zijn de Excuses [Where Are the Apologies]', @geertwilderspvv, *Twitter* [X], 18 February 2022.
83 Goenawan Mohamad, 'Maaf [Sorry]', *TEMPO*, [Jakarta], 19 February 2022.

In arguing that the contemporary Dutch Government has no connection to the actions of governments of the past, Goenawan Mohamad implied a neat, but in our view problematic, separation of colonial history from the present. He importantly acknowledged, however, the structural nature of colonialism and colonial violence by claiming:

> Colonialism is an evil institution, built on arrogance and greed, based on an 'ideology' that was used to justify treating Indonesians (and many other peoples elsewhere) as less than human, as subhuman slaves. And that is something I can never forgive.[84]

The research project itself was criticised for overlooking the larger context of colonialism, the research process and the role Indonesians were given. Historian Hilmar Farid, who wrote the epilogue to the Dutch research report, noted that the most fundamental issue underlying the systemic violence of the 1945–49 period remained unaddressed: the fact that both 'physical and symbolic violence' were part and parcel of the method of colonial rule for gaining and maintaining power.[85] In his view, the colonial wars of the nineteenth century in all parts of the archipelago, the 'penal sanctions on plantations' and all kinds of violence and other acts of wrongdoing 'created a social landscape that became fertile ground for outbreaks of extreme violence in the subsequent periods'.[86] He therefore reiterated the need to take a longer view of colonial history to understand the 1945–49 period. Further to this, he critiqued the Dutch-centric approach taken to the research, by which he meant a strong reliance on Dutch archives and the neglect of recent Indonesian historical debates and research such as those featured on the online platforms *Historia* and *Tirto*.[87] In addition to criticisms of the small number of Indonesian researchers appointed to the team (including one of the authors of this chapter) and the fact they were not given leading

---

84 ibid.
85 Hilmar Farid, 'Dealing with the Legacies of a Violent Past', in *Beyond the Pale: Dutch Extreme Violence in the Indonesian War of Independence, 1945–1949*, by Kon. Inst. v. Taal-, Land- en Volkenkunde (KITLV), Nederlands Instituut voor Militaire Historie (NIMH), and NIOD Inst. v. Oorlogs-, Holocaust- en Genocidestudies (Amsterdam: Amsterdam University Press, 2022), 473–86, at 481.
86 ibid., 481.
87 ibid., 477. This includes discussion of topics such as the revolution and children and the complex position of Chinese Indonesians in the revolution. See Hendri Johari, 'Tionghoa Prianganan Pusaran Revolusi [Chinese Prianganans in the Maelstrom of the Revolution]', *Historia*, [Jakarta], 13 February 2021, historia.id/militer/articles/tionghoa-priangan-dalam-pusaran-revolusi-vVWNk/page/1; and Hendri Johari, 'Kisah Petumpur Cilik dalam Revolusi Indonesia [The Story of An Everyman Fighter in the Indonesian Revolution]', *Historia*, [Jakarta], 20 November 2020, historia.id/militer/articles/kisah-petempur-cilik-dalam-revolusi-indonesia-6kkk1.

roles, there was a misguided suspicion that because the project was funded by the Dutch Government the researchers would not thoroughly interrogate Dutch violence against Indonesians.[88]

The project, however, prompted some Indonesian academics to reflect on the boundaries of Indonesian history. As historian Sri Margana asks, will a Dutch state-sponsored project finding evidence of Dutch structural violence challenge Indonesian researchers to uncover and acknowledge Indonesian violence towards minorities during the 1945–49 period?[89] To date, this has been a highly sensitive issue due to sacralisation of the Indonesian revolution and the tendency towards nationalist framings of history that focus on a binary understanding of conflict between colonisers and the colonised. Margana's comments point to ongoing challenges in terms of acceptance of more complex narratives of Indonesian history that necessarily challenge simplistic nationalist historiography.

Indonesian commentators also raised the fact that the continued emphasis on the 1945–49 period is problematic because it conceals longer histories of colonialism, meaning that little attention is paid to the power structures that underpinned the violence. As we posit in this volume, (de)colonisation cannot be neatly organised or demarcated by applying certain dates or time frames. Rather, we conceptualise decoloniality more broadly as a process that involves not just ousting colonial power, but also dismantling the long legacies and modes of thinking that permeate almost all aspects of society.[90] As such, decolonisation is a multifaceted and complex process, often contradictory and of limited success, especially when new local elites replicate colonial practices in the name of nationalism.[91] Colonial structures often remained intact, with inequalities further entrenched, rather than eliminated. In addition, as time went by, some former colonised nations became colonisers themselves.

In the chapters of this book that consider the post-1949 period, we examine and evaluate the challenges of decolonisation today. These include contributions in the field of archives and heritage, including negotiations

---

88 Jeffry Pondaag and Francisca Pattipilohy, 'Questions about the Dutch Research Project "Decolonisation, Violence and War in Indonesia, 1945–1950"', [Open letter], *Histori Bersama*, 27 November 2017, historibersama.com/questions-about-the-dutch-research-project/.
89 Sri Margana, 'Konsekuensi dari Kesimpulan Tim Peneliti Belanda [Consequences of the Conclusions of the Dutch Research Team]', *Historia*, [Jakarta], 18 February 2022, historia.id/militer/articles/konsekuensi-dari-kesimpulan-tim-peneliti-belanda-vxg3J/page/3.
90 Mignolo and Walsh, *On Decoloniality*; Quijano, 'Coloniality and Modernity/Rationality'.
91 Hoffmann, 'Interview'.

about access and control. In these chapters, we also interrogate the persistence and legacies of colonial categories such as the spatial organisation of Glodok in Jakarta (Chapter 11). Authors reflect on the extent to which museums in both the Netherlands and Indonesia have 'progressed' in terms of decolonisation and how this is pursued. As insightfully identified by Brigitta Isabella (Chapter 13), attempts to decolonise institutions, such as through issuing apologies or staging exhibitions with 'alternative' framings, can be regarded as a manifestation of a 'colonial anxiety that requires the atonement of guilt through the politics of recognition'. Isabella and other authors problematise the extent to which 'recognition' can be sought in museums and courts and more equitable and just ways of relating created. The chapters in Part 2 of this book also discuss how legal proceedings and activism attempt to address both colonial injustices of the past and ongoing colonialism in Indonesia today.

Chapter outlines

The book is divided into two parts. Part 1, 'Colonial Categories Across and Beyond the Colony', focuses on how Indonesians experienced, negotiated and resisted colonial categorisations from the nineteenth century to the period of the revolution. Part 2 investigates the lasting impacts of colonialism in both Dutch and Indonesian societies up to today, starting from the understanding that decolonisation is a continuing process. Chapter 2 examines how the Dutch State created and reinforced colonial categories and markers of difference across the colony. In Chapter 2, '"*Oedjan Belasting*, the Raining of Taxes": Coloniality and the Dutch Economic Exploitation of the Chinese', Abdul Wahid examines how colonial categories and economic exploitation worked hand in hand in the colony. The colonial state used taxation from 1917 to 1942 to squeeze all Indonesians, but especially Chinese Indonesians, due to fears about their rising economic strength. Wahid documents the evolution of and rationale behind the tax system and the deliberate targeting of this group and how Chinese Indonesians navigated and indeed protested these impositions.

Chapters 3 and 4 shift our focus from the colonial state and its agents to consider alternative political and cultural communities and their projection of bases of identity. Ronit Ricci in Chapter 3, 'Locating Colonial Indonesia in Colonial Ceylon: Geography, Language and Belonging', moves beyond the formal boundaries of the colony of the Netherlands East Indies to the Malay colonial diaspora in Ceylon, a community at once connected to, but also separated from, Indonesia. Ricci connects British and Dutch colonialism. Through a close reading of the Malay newspaper *Wajah Selong*, published in Ceylon from 1895 to 1898, Ricci asks how ties with the archipelago and other Malay communities were maintained and how the paper promoted an alternative category of person, the Malay, in this part of the British Empire.

In Chapter 4, '"So I Say My Name": Towards a Decolonial Ethics for Reading Girls' Worlds in Letters', Bronwyn Anne Beech Jones provides an analysis of how West Sumatran and Tapanuli elite girls conceptualised the world, their selves and a sense of solidarity. Using letters they published in the newspaper *Soenting Melajoe* ('*Malay Headdress*') (1912–21) and a translated short story from the agricultural periodical *Minangkabau* (1918), the chapter considers how, through writing, girls imagined and lay claim to an alternative modern future in which there was greater equality between men and women. She argues that in some ways these ambiguous world views challenged dominant modes of colonial subjectification but, in others, writers also reproduced inequalities, particularly across the classes.

Chapters 5 and 6 focus more closely on class and the reproduction of colonial hierarchy and difference from the late colonial period through to the revolution. Chapter 5, 'Dealing with Modernities: East Java's Plantation Society in Colonial Times and the Revolution', by Grace T. Leksana traces the propaganda around the introduction of plantations and related infrastructure such as roads into East Java in the 1930s and local reactions to this process. Using colonial reports, newspaper coverage and oral history interviews, she reflects on the clashes between colonial concepts of modernity and attempts by plantation owners to transform 'unproductive land' into wealth-producing plantations. She charts the reactions of labourers and other community members to new concepts of ownership and increased surveillance as well as violence directed at labourers.

Chapter 6, 'Rethinking Histories of Military Atrocity, Ethnic Violence and Photography, From the Aceh War to the Indonesian National Revolution', by Susie Protschky focuses on the photographic records of embedded war photographers. Protschky argues that these sources reveal multiple forms of 'approved' colonial violence, including unfree labour and rule by racialised difference in the colonial Royal Netherlands East Indies Army (Koninklijk

Nederlandsch-Indisch Leger). She also reflects on racialised discourses about the so-called martial races of Eastern Indonesia and their utility in subjugating ethnic 'Others' for the Dutch colonial state.

Chapters 7 and 8 consider how class and race-based hierarchies operated from the late colonial period through to the Indonesian revolution, during which Indonesians experienced racialised violence. Chapter 7, 'Francisca Fanggidaej: A Decolonial Perspective on Colonial Elites and the Indonesian Revolution', by Katharine McGregor unpacks Fanggidaej's observations about growing up in an elite family from an Eastern Indonesian island from the late colonial era through to the revolution. Using Fanggidaej's 2006 memoir and other ego documents, McGregor analyses how, as a revolutionary and a member of an ethnic group labelled 'Moluccans' (often stereotyped as being loyal to the Dutch), Fanggidaej critiqued the elitism and reproduction of colonial hierarchies. How did she conceptualise the revolution and related ongoing forms of coloniality in diplomatic negotiations and agreements?

In Chapter 8, 'Giving Voice to the Voiceless: "Sin Po" and the Chinese Massacres during the Revolutionary Period', Ravando and F.X. Harsono use reporting in *Sin Po*, a newspaper run by members of the Chinese Indonesian community, and mass graves to focus on one legacy of the 'othering' of ethnic Chinese. This chapter presents an alternative narration of the Indonesian revolution from the view of a group of people for whom this was a largely terrifying experience. They were caught in the middle between Dutch and republican forces and mistrusted and/or abandoned by both.

The contributions in Part 2 of this volume, 'Colonial Legacies: the Persistence of and Attempts to Dismantle Coloniality', examine the enduring legacies of colonialism up to the present in Dutch and Indonesian society, and start from the premise that decolonisation is an ongoing process. Contributors consider what 'decolonisation' means in the context of Indonesian history, culture and politics, tracing how decolonisation proceeded after Indonesia proclaimed independence. Key questions include the extent to which colonial categories were dismantled or repurposed, especially across the spheres of culture and heritage, and how they continue to impact the law and even the organisation of urban space. In so doing, the authors reflect on the critical question of whether coloniality has really ended.

Chapters 9 and 10 focus on the restitution of colonial objects and archives and consider how coloniality continues to inform thinking about, and practices of, restitution. Commonly, discussions about restitution foreground the perspectives of former colonisers. In Chapter 9, entitled 'Beyond the Point of No Return: The Re-Emergence of Indonesian Debates About and Concepts of the Return of Cultural Objects', Sadiah Boonstra shifts the gaze by considering Indonesian perspectives on debates about the return of cultural objects by examining Indonesian discussions underlying the Draft Cultural Agreement that was formulated during the Dutch–Indonesian Round Table Conference negotiations in 1949. By reconstructing Indonesian discourses of object restitution, Boonstra analyses how Indonesia prioritised the return of cultural objects and their role in the country's cultural future as imagined in 1949, as well as how this continues to be the basis of contemporary discussions about the restitution of colonial objects.

In Chapter 10, 'How to Liberate the Colonised Archives? Describing the Djogdja Documenten after Their Return', Michael Karabinos and Rika Theo consider repatriation of archival collections. They focus on the Djogdja Documenten, records seized during the Second Dutch Military Aggression in Yogyakarta (1948)—a collection that contains records created by Indonesian republican institutions and leaders. Karabinos and Theo examine how coloniality informed the theft of the archives and their classification. They consider how, in the 1970s and 1980s, following the repatriation of the archives to Indonesia, these colonial frameworks persisted, thereby reproducing Dutch perspectives on the Indonesian revolution. They also raise the issue of archives and collections that have still not been returned to Indonesia, including the objects placed on display in the '*Revolusi!*' exhibition mentioned above.

Chapter 11 considers colonial legacies, particularly in relation to colonial categories, stretching from the colonial period to the early years of independence and post-1998 Indonesia. In 'The Rise and Fall of Glodok', Abidin Kusno examines urban space and spatial politics during the colonial period and how this affected the identity formation of Chinese Indonesians over time. Kusno focuses on Glodok, Jakarta's Chinatown, as the centre of Chinese trading. He then examines how spatiality influenced both colonial and postcolonial ordering of space, as well as the production of Chinese Indonesian identity. Kusno asks how, in the aftermath of anti-Chinese violence in 1998, the identity of Chinese Indonesian traders was influenced by their relationship to Glodok and the extent to which a 'new' Chinese Indonesian identity developed.

Chapters 12 and 13 consider coloniality within museums in Indonesia, the Netherlands and Belgium and efforts to undo these colonial structures. In 'Decolonising a Colonial Fort? The Case of Fort Rotterdam, Makassar', Ajeng Ayu Arainikasih traces the legacies of space in the colonial Fort Rotterdam, in Makassar. After independence, Fort Rotterdam was turned into a museum and tourist destination. Arainikasih examines the extent to which this fort was decolonised as a postcolonial museum, considering what and whose histories are being depicted and, by extension, who and what were excluded. Arainikasih's chapter highlights how deeply entangled are colonialism, nationalism and decolonisation in the spaces of museums.

In Chapter 13, 'After Recognition: Decolonial Re-Affect Outside/Within the Museum', Brigitta Isabella picks up questions of representation and positionality within museums in the former colonising nations of the Netherlands and Belgium. She examines the efforts of these museums to decolonise their collections by inviting researchers and artists from former colonies to reinterpret the collections, drawing on local knowledge and literature. Isabella argues that these interventions enable audiences to critically engage with the injustices preserved by museums and to articulate self-recognition—an active subjectivity breaking out of a binary of giver–receiver. As such, these endeavours may contribute to knowledge production that forges new, and equal, relationships, yet they also raise deeper questions about the politics of recognition and the affective labour of researchers and artists.

The final two chapters turn their focus to the legacies and persistence of colonial violence. In Chapter 14, 'Confronting Coloniality Through the Courts? Reconsidering the Rawagede Case', Ken M.P. Setiawan turns the lens on how Dutch courts have addressed cases of colonial violence. Focusing on the 1947 Rawagede massacre, which was heard in the Civil Court in 2011, and using Dutch and Indonesian media sources, Setiawan argues that the case in fact reproduces dominant historical narratives, in both the Netherlands and Indonesia. Moreover, the court case reflects persistent inequalities between the former coloniser and the colonised.

In Chapter 15, 'Seeking the Morning Star: Young Papuans and the Ongoing Struggle Against Indonesian Colonialism', I Ngurah Suryawan investigates contemporary colonialism in Indonesia and forms of resistance by Papuan activists. He traces the beginnings of the Papuan youth movement during the last few decades of the Dutch colonial era and identifies connections in more recent forms of organising. Focusing on the intellectual legacies of the Papuan youth leader Victor Yeimo, Suryawan pays attention to the historical roots of Papuan nationalism, contemporary experiences of colonialism—including those related to violence, arrest, education and settlers—as well as how colonialism might be resisted.

Together, the chapters in Part 2 attend to the various spheres where coloniality endures: culture and heritage, spatial organisation, law and politics. The many areas where the legacies of colonialism persist and take on new forms underline the need for decolonisation to be seen from a broader perspective that is more profound than political disengagement between coloniser and colony alone. Instead, decoloniality requires, first, an awareness and acknowledgement of coloniality and its workings within and across structures of life and knowledge. It is through this process of recognition that the workings of coloniality can be understood and, once a deep understanding is reached, work can begin on undoing its enduring structures.

References

Primary sources

CNN Indonesia. 2022. 'Anhar Gonggong Desak RI Cabut Partisipasi Pameran Rijksmuseum Belanda [Anhar Gonggong Urges Republic of Indonesia to Withdraw Participation in Dutch Rijksmuseum Exhibition].' *CNN Indonesia*, 27 January. www.cnnindonesia.com/nasional/20220127152144-20-752067/anhar-gonggong-desak-ri-cabut-partisipasi-pameran-rijksmuseum-belanda/.

Federatie Indische Nederlanders [Federation of Dutch East Indies] (FIN). 2022. 'Aangifte tegen Bersiap-ontkenner Triyana [Complaint Filed Against *Bersiap* Denier Triyana].' 11 January. FIN. www.federatie-indo.nl/2022/01/11/22-01-11/.

Funnekotter, Bart. 2022. 'Bersiap Blijft, en het Rijksmuseum is niet Woke [*Bersiap* Stays and the Rijksmuseum is Not Woke].' *NRC*, [Amsterdam], 14 January. www.nrc.nl/nieuws/2022/01/14/bersiap-blijft-en-het-rijksmuseum-is-niet-woke-a4079333.

Holman, Theodor. 2022. 'Zo Verhul je de genocide [This is How You Disguise Genocide].' *Het Parool*, [Amsterdam], 12 January.

Johari, Hendri. 2020. 'Kisah Petumpur Cilik dalam Revolusi Indonesia [The Story of An Everyman Fighter in the Indonesian Revolution].' *Historia*, [Jakarta], 20 November. historia.id/militer/articles/kisah-petempur-cilik-dalam-revolusi-indonesia-6kkk1.

Johari, Hendri. 2021. 'Tionghoa Prianganan Pusaran Revolusi [Chinese Prianganans in the Maelstrom of the Revolution].' *Historia*, [Jakarta], 13 February. historia.id/militer/articles/tionghoa-priangan-dalam-pusaran-revolusi-vVWNk/page/1.

Muryanto, Bambang. 2015. 'RI Offered Return of Historical Objects from Delft Museum.' *Jakarta Post*, 19 October. www.thejakartapost.com/news/2015/10/19/ri-offered-return-historical-objects-delft-museum.html.

Nederlandse Omroep Stichting [Dutch Broadcasting Foundation] (NOS). 2022. 'Woede over Niet Gebruiken van Term "Bersiap" op Indonesië-expositie [Anger Over Not Using the Term "Bersiap" at Indonesia Exhibition].' *NOS Nieuws [Dutch Broadcasting Foundation News]*, 12 January. nos.nl/artikel/2412770-woede-over-niet-gebruiken-van-term-bersiap-op-indonesie-expositie.

Noordhollands Dagblad. 2022. 'Aangifte tegen Rijksmuseum om gebruik term "bersiap" [Complaint Against Rijksmuseum for Use of Term "Bersiap"].' *Noordhollands Dagblad*, [Alkmaar, Netherlands], 22 January. www.noord hollandsdagblad.nl/cnt/dmf20220121_77416427.

Reuters. 2020. 'Dutch King Apologises for "Excessive Violence" in Colonial Indonesia.' *Reuters*, 10 March. www.reuters.com/article/us-indonesia-netherlands-idUSKBN20X15L.

Rutte, Mark. 2022. '1e Reactie van Minister-President Mark Rutte na de Presentatie van het Onderzoeksprogramma "Onafhankelijkheid, Dekolonisatie, Geweld en Oorlog in Indonesië, 1945–1950" [First Reaction of Prime Minister Mark Rutte after the Presentation of the Research Program "Independence, Decolonisation, Violence and War in Indonesia, 1945–50"].' Speech, 17 February. Government of the Netherlands. www.rijksoverheid.nl/documenten/toespraken/2022/02/17/eerste-reactie-van-minister-president-mark-rutte-onderzoeksprogramma-onaf hankelijkheid-dekolonisatie-geweld-en-oorlog-in-indonesie-1945-1950.

Sukarno. 1970. '"Let a New Asia and Africa be Born": Extract from the "Opening Address Given by Sukarno", 18 April 1955.' In *Indonesian Political Thinking: 1945–1965*, edited by Herb Feith and Lance Castles, 458. Ithaca: Cornell University Press.

Triyana, Bonnie. 2022. 'Schrap de term "Bersiap" want die is Racistisch [Delete the Term "Bersiap" Because it is Racist].' *NRC*, [Amsterdam], 10 January 2022. www.nrc.nl/nieuws/2022/01/10/schrap-term-bersiap-voor-periodisering-want-die-is-racistisch-a4077367.

van Leeuwen, Lizzy. 2022. 'Het Rijksmuseum als Speelbal van Woke [The Rijksmuseum as Plaything of Woke].' *Telegraaf*, [Amsterdam], 14 January.

Secondary sources

Abdullah, Taufik. 2012. 'Kata Pengantar [Introduction].' In *Indonesia dalam Arus Sejarah [Indonesia in the Flow of History]*, edited by Taufik Abdullah and A.B. Lapian. Jakarta: Ichtiar Baru van Hoeve.

Armstrong, Elisabeth. 2016. 'Before Bandung: The Anti-Imperialist Women's Movement in Asia and the Women's International Democratic Federation.' *Signs* 41, no. 2: 305–31. doi.org/10.1086/682921.

Bijl, Paul. 2017. 'Legal Self-Fashioning in Colonial Indonesia: Human Rights in the Letters of Kartini.' *Indonesia* 103: 51–71. doi.org/10.1353/ind.2017.0002.

Bogaerts, Els, and Remco Raben. 2012. 'Beyond Empire and Nation.' In *Beyond Empire and Nation: The Decolonisation of African and Asian Societies 1930s–1960s*, edited by Els Bogaerts and Remco Raben, 7–19. Leiden: KITLV Press. doi.org/10.1163/9789004260443.

Buchheim, Eveline, Satrio Ody Dwicahyo, Fridus Steijlen, and Stephanie Welvaart. 2022. *Sporen vol betekenis/Meniti Arti: In gesprek met 'Getuigen & Tijdgenoten' over de Indonesische onafhankelijkheidsoorlog/Bertukar Makna bersama 'Saksi & Rekan Sezaman' tentang Perang Kemerdekaan Indonesia [Traces Full of Meaning: In Conversation With 'Witnesses and Contemporaries' about the Indonesian Independence War]*. Amsterdam: Amsterdam University Press.

Bussemaker, Herman. 2005. *Bersiap! Opstand in het Paradijs: de Bersiap-periode op Java en Sumatra 1945–1946 [Bersiap! Revolt in Paradise: The Bersiap Period on Java and Sumatra 1945–1946]*. Zuthpen: Walburg Pers.

Captain, Esther. 2014. 'Harmless Identities: Representations of Racial Consciousness among Three Generations Indo-Europeans.' In *Dutch Racism*, edited by Philomena Essed and Isabel Hoving, 53–69. Leiden: Brill. doi.org/10.1163/9789401210096_004.

Captain, Esther, and Onno Sinke. 2022. *Het Geluid van Geweld Bersiap en de Dynamiek van Geweld Tijdens de eerste Fase van de Indonesische Revolutie, 1945–1946* [Resonance of Violence: Bersiap and the Dynamics of Violence in the First Phase of the Indonesian Revolution, 1945–1946]. Amsterdam: Amsterdam University Press.

Chakrabarty, Dipesh. 2007. *Provincializing Europe: Postcolonial Thought and Historical Difference*. Princeton: Princeton University Press. doi.org/10.1515/9781400828654.

Clancy-Smith, Julia, and Frances Gouda, eds. 1998. *Domesticating the Empire: Race, Gender and Family Life in French and Dutch Colonialism*. Charlottesville: University of Virginia Press.

Drieënhuizen, Caroline, and Fenneke Sysling. 2021. 'Java Man and the Politics of Natural History: An Object Biography.' *Bijdragen tot de Taal-, Land- en Volkenkunde [Journal of the Humanities and Social Sciences of Southeast Asia]* 177, nos 2–3: 290–311. doi.org/10.1163/22134379-bja10012.

Fanon, Frantz. 1963. *The Wretched of the Earth*. Translated by Constance Farrington. New York: Grove Press.

Farid, Hilmar. 2019. 'Postcolonial Perspectives from Southeast Asia.' Presentation to Postcolonial Perspectives from the Global South, Goethe-Institut, Jakarta, 24–25 January. www.youtube.com/watch?v=1M53NvufNb4.

Farid, Hilmar. 2022. 'Dealing with the Legacies of a Violent Past.' In *Beyond the Pale: Dutch Extreme Violence in the Indonesian War of Independence, 1945–1949*, by Kon. Inst. v. Taal-, Land- en Volkenkunde (KITLV), Nederlands Instituut voor Militaire Historie (NIMH), and NIOD Inst. v. Oorlogs-, Holocaust- en Genocidestudies, 473–86. Amsterdam: Amsterdam University Press.

Farid, Hilmar, and Razif. 2008. '*Batjaan Liar* in the Dutch East Indies: A Colonial Antipode.' *Postcolonial Studies* 11, no. 3: 277–92. doi.org/10.1080/13688790802226694.

Frederick, William H. 2002. 'Shadows of an Unseen Hand: Some Patterns of Violence in the Indonesian Revolution, 1945–1949.' In *Roots of Violence in Indonesia: Contemporary Violence in Historical Perspective*, edited by Freek Colombijn and J. Thomas Lindblad, 143–72. Leiden: Brill. doi.org/10.1163/9789004489561_009.

Frederick, William H. 2014. 'The Killing of Dutch and Eurasians in Indonesia's National Revolution (1945–1949): A "Brief Genocide" Reconsidered.' In *Colonial Counterinsurgency and Mass Violence: The Dutch Empire in Indonesia*, edited by Bart Luttikhuis and A. Dirk Moses, 133–54. London: Routledge. doi.org/10.4324/9781315767345-7.

Gouda, Frances. 1996. *Dutch Culture Overseas: Colonial Practice in the Netherlands Indies, 1900–1942*. Amsterdam: Amsterdam University Press.

Hoffmann, Alvina. 2017. 'Interview—Walter Mignolo/Part 2: Key Concepts.' *E-International Relations*, [Bristol, UK], 21 January. www.e-ir.info/2017/01/21/interview-walter-mignolopart-2-key-concepts/.

Houben, Vincent J.H. 1997. 'A Torn Soul: The Dutch Public Discussion on the Colonial Past in 1995.' *Indonesia* 63 (April): 47–66. doi.org/10.2307/3351510.

Knight, G. Roger. 2017. 'Colonial Knowledge and Subaltern Voices: The Case of an Official Enquiry in Mid-Nineteenth Century Java.' In *Sources and Methods in Histories of Colonialism*, edited by Kirsty Reid and Fiona Paisley, 85–99. London: Routledge. doi.org/10.4324/9781315271958-6.

Kon. Inst. v. Taal-, Land- en Volkenkunde [Royal Netherlands Institute of Southeast Asian and Caribbean Studies] (KITLV), Nederlands Instituut voor Militaire Historie [Netherlands Institute for Military History] (NIMH), and NIOD Inst. v. Oorlogs-, Holocaust- en Genocidestudies [NIOD Netherlands Institute for War, Holocaust and Genocide Studies]. 2022. *Beyond the Pale: Dutch Extreme Violence in the Indonesian War of Independence, 1945–1949*. Amsterdam: Amsterdam University Press. doi.org/10.1515/9789048557172.

Limpach, Rémy. 2016. *De Brandende Kampongs van Generaal Spoor* [*The Burning Kampongs of General Spoor*]. Amsterdam: Boom.

Locher-Scholten, Elsbeth. 1998. 'So Close and Yet So Far: The Ambivalence of Dutch Colonial Rhetoric on Javanese Servants in Indonesia, 1900–1942.' In *Domesticating the Empire: Race, Gender and Family Life in French and Dutch Colonialism*, edited by Julia Clancy-Smith and Frances Gouda, 130–53. Charlottesville: University of Virginia Press.

Lugones, María. 2010. 'Toward a Decolonial Feminism.' *Hypatia* 25, no. 4: 742–59. doi.org/10.1111/j.1527-2001.2010.01137.x.

Luttikhuis, Bart. 2013. 'Beyond Race: Constructions of Europeanness in Late Colonial Legal Practice in the Dutch East Indies.' *European Review of History* 20, no. 4: 539–58. doi.org/10.1080/13507486.2013.764845.

Majumdar, Rochona. 2015. '*Subaltern Studies* as a History of Social Movements in India.' *South Asia: Journal of South Asian Studies* 38, no. 1: 50–68. doi.org/10.1080/00856401.2014.987338.

Majumdar, Rochona. 2018. 'Postcolonial History.' In *Debating New Approaches to History*, edited by Marek Tamm and Peter Burke, 49–74. London: Bloomsbury Academic. doi.org/10.5040/9781474281959.0007.

Margana, Sri. 2022. 'Konsekuensi dari Kesimpulan Tim Peneliti Belanda [Consequences of the Conclusions of the Dutch Research Team].' *Historia*, [Jakarta], 18 February. www.historia.id/militer/articles/konsekuensi-dari-kesimpulan-tim-peneliti-belanda-vxg3J/page/3.

McGregor, Katharine. 2007. *History in Uniform: Military Ideology and the Construction of Indonesia's Past*. Singapore: NUS Press.

McGregor, Katharine. 2012. 'Indonesian Women, the Women's International Democratic Federation and the Struggle for Women's Rights, 1946–1965.' *Indonesia and the Malay World* 40, no. 117: 193–208. doi.org/10.1080/13639 811.2012.683680.

McGregor, Katharine. 2013. 'The Cold War, Indonesian Women and the Global Anti-Imperialist Movement, 1946–65.' In *De-Centering Cold War History: Local and Global Change*, edited by Jadwiga E. Pieper Mooney and Fabio Lanza, 31–51. London: Routledge.

McGregor, Katharine. 2014. 'From National Sacrifice to Compensation Claims: Changing Indonesian Representations of the Captain Westerling Massacres in South Sulawesi (1946–47).' In *Colonial Counterinsurgency and Mass Violence: The Dutch Empire in Indonesia*, edited by Bart Luttikhuis and Dirk A. Moses, 282–307. London: Routledge. doi.org/10.4324/9781315767345-14.

McGregor, Katharine. 2018. 'Historical Justice and the Case of the 1965 Killings.' In *Routledge Handbook of Contemporary Indonesia*, edited by Robert W. Hefner, 129–39. London: Routledge. doi.org/10.4324/9781315628837-10.

McGregor, Katharine, and Vannessa Hearman. 2017. 'Challenging the Lifeline of Imperialism: Reassessing Afro-Asian Solidarity and Related Activism in the Decade 1955–1965.' In *Bandung, Global History, and International Law: Critical Pasts and Pending Futures*, edited by Luis Eslava, Michael Fakhri, and Vasuki Nesiah, 161–76. Cambridge: Cambridge University Press. doi.org/10.1017/9781316414880.012.

McGregor, Katharine, Jess Melvin, and Annie Pohlman. 2018. 'New Interpretations of the Causes, Dynamics and Legacies of the Indonesian Genocide.' In *The Indonesian Genocide of 1965: Causes, Dynamics and Legacies*, edited by Katharine McGregor, Jess Melvin, and Annie Pohlman, 1–26. London: Palgrave Macmillan. doi.org/10.1007/978-3-319-71455-4_1.

Mignolo, Walter D., and Arturo Escobar, eds. 2010. *Globalization and the Decolonial Option*. New York: Routledge. doi.org/10.4324/9781315868448.

Mignolo, Walter D., and Catherine E. Walsh. 2018. *On Decoloniality: Concepts, Analytics, Praxis*. Durham: Duke University Press. doi.org/10.1215/978082237 1779.

Mohamad, Goenawan. 2022. 'Maaf [Sorry].' *TEMPO*, [Jakarta], 19 February.

Nationale herdenking 15 augustus 1945 [15 August 1945 Commemoration Foundation]. 2024. *Commemorations in the Netherlands*. The Hague: Nationale herdenking 15 augustus 1945. 15augustus1945.nl/en/other-commemorations/.

Ndlovu-Gatsheni, Sabelo J. 2019. 'When Did the Masks of Coloniality Begin to Fall? Decolonial Reflections on the Bandung Spirit of Decolonisation.' *Bandung: Journal of the Global South* 6, no. 2: 210–32. doi.org/10.1163/21983534-00602004.

Ndlovu-Gatsheni, Sabelo J. 2020. *Decolonization, Development and Knowledge in Africa: Turning Over a New Leaf*. London: Routledge. doi.org/10.4324/9781003030423.

Nederlandse Omroep Stichting [Dutch Broadcasting Foundation] (NOS). 2023. 'Nederland erkent 17 augustus 1945 als onafhankelijkheidsdag Indonesië [The Netherlands Recognises 17 August 1945 as Indonesia's Independence Day].' *NOS Nieuws [Dutch Broadcasting Foundation News]*, 14 June. nos.nl/artikel/2478878-nederland-erkent-17-augustus-1945-als-onafhankelijkheidsdag-indonesie.

Parr, Rosalind. 2021. 'Solving World Problems: The Indian Women's Movement, Global Governance, and "the Crisis of Empire", 1933–46.' *Journal of Global History* 16, no. 1: 122–40. doi.org/10.1017/S1740022820000169.

Pols, Hans. 2007. 'Psychological Knowledge in a Colonial Context: Theories on the Nature of the "Native Mind" in the Former Dutch East Indies.' *History of Psychology* 10, no. 2: 111–31. doi.org/10.1037/1093-4510.10.2.111.

Pols, Hans. 2018. *Nurturing Indonesia: Medicine and Decolonisation in the Dutch East Indies*. Cambridge: Cambridge University Press. doi.org/10.1017/9781108341035.

Pondaag, Jeffry, and Francisca Pattipilohy. 2017. 'Questions about the Dutch Research Project "Decolonisation, Violence and War in Indonesia, 1945–1950".' [Open letter], *Histori Bersama*, 27 November. historibersama.com/questions-about-the-dutch-research-project/.

Prakash, Gyan. 1995. *After Colonialism: Imperial Histories and Postcolonial Displacements*. Princeton: Princeton University Press. doi.org/10.1515/9781400821440.

Prashad, Vijay. 2007. *The Darker Nations: A People's History of the Third World*. New York: New Press.

Protschky, Susie. 2011. 'Race, Class, and Gender: Debates Over the Character of Social Hierarchies in the Netherlands Indies, Circa 1600–1942.' *Bijdragen tot de Taal-, Land- en Volkenkunde* [*Journal of the Humanities and Social Sciences of Southeast Asia*] 167, no. 4: 543–56. doi.org/10.1163/22134379-90003584.

Protschky, Susie. 2012. 'Tea Cups, Cameras and Family Life: Picturing Domesticity in Elite European and Javanese Family Photographs from the Netherlands Indies, ca. 1900–42.' *History of Photography* 36, no. 1 (February): 44–65. doi.org/10.1080/03087298.2012.636503.

Purwanto, Bambang. 2001. 'Historisisme Baru dan Kesadaran Dekonstruktif Kajian Kritis terhadap Historiografi Indonesiasentris [A New Historicism and Awareness of Critical Deconstructive Studies for Indonesia-Centric Historiography].' *Humanoria* XIII, no. 1: 32–33.

Purwanto, Bambang. 2022. 'Bersiap, Kutukan Kemerderkaan Indonesia yang Menghantui Belanda [Bersiap, the Curse of Indonesian Independence that Haunts the Netherlands].' *Media Indonesia*, 23 August. mediaindonesia.com/opini/516800/bersiap-kutukan-kemerdekaan-indonesia-yang-menghantui-belanda.

Quijano, Aníbal. 2007. 'Coloniality and Modernity/Rationality.' *Cultural Studies* 21, nos 2–3: 168–78. doi.org/10.1080/09502380601164353.

Rele, Anne ter. 2022. 'Indonesische Roofkunstcommissie Vindt dat Deze Stukken bij het Indonesische Verhaal Horen [Indonesian Stolen Art Committee Believes That These Objects Belong to the Indonesian Story].' *Trouw*, [Amsterdam], 18 October. www.trouw.nl/buitenland/indonesische-roofkunstcommissie-vindt-dat-deze-stukken-bij-het-indonesische-verhaal-horen~b61d3841/.

Said, Edward. 1978. *Orientalism*. London: Penguin.

Said, Edward. 1993. *Culture and Imperialism*. New York: Knopf.

Saraswati, L. Ayu. 2013. *Seeing Beauty, Sensing Race in Transnational Indonesia*. Honolulu: University of Hawai`i Press. doi.org/10.21313/hawaii/9780824836641.001.0001.

Scagliola, Stef. 2012. 'Cleo's "Unfinished Business": Coming to Terms with Dutch War Crimes in Indonesia's War of Independence.' *Journal of Genocide Research* 14, nos 3–4: 419–39. doi.org/10.1080/14623528.2012.719374.

Schulte Nordholt, Henk. 2022. 'Waarom het Woord "Bersiap" Zoveel Woede Oproept [Why the Word "Bersiap" Invokes So Much Anger].' *Trouw*, [Amsterdam], 18 January. www.trouw.nl/opinie/waarom-het-woord-bersiap-zoveel-woede-oproept~b8013df3/.

Setiono, Beni G. 2008. *Tionghoa Indonesia dalam Pusaran Politik* [*Chinese Indonesians in the Political Maelstrom*]. Jakarta: Transmedia.

Simpson, Bradley R. 2008. *Economists with Guns: Authoritarian Development and U.S.–Indonesian Relations, 1960–1968*. Stanford: Stanford University Press. doi.org/10.1515/9780804779524.

Somers Heidhues, Mary. 2017. 'Studying the Chinese in Indonesia: A Long Half-Century.' *Sojourn: Journal of Social Issues in Southeast Asia* 32, no. 3: 601–33. doi.org/10.1355/sj32-3c.

Stoler, Ann. 2002. *Carnal Knowledge and Imperial Power: Race and the Intimate in Colonial Rule*. Berkeley: University of California Press.

Stoler, Ann. 2010. *Along the Archival Grain: Epistemic Anxieties and Colonial Common Sense*. Princeton: Princeton University Press.

Stoler, Ann, and Karen Strassler. 2000. 'Castings for the Colonial: Memory Work in "New Order" Java.' *Comparative Studies in Society and History* 42, no. 1: 4–48. www.jstor.org/stable/pdf/2696632.pdf.

Stolte, Carolien, and Su Lin Lewis, eds. 2022. *The Lives of Cold War Afro-Asianism*. Amsterdam: Amsterdam University Press.

Sysling, Fenneke. 2016. *Racial Science and Human Diversity in Colonial Indonesia*. Singapore: NUS Press. doi.org/10.2307/j.ctv9hj794.

Sysling, Fenneke. 2022. 'Er is een Lijstje met de Eerste 8 Koloniale Collecties die Indonesië Terugeist van Nederland [There is a List with the First Eight Colonial Collections Claimed by Indonesia from the Netherlands]!' @fsysling, *Twitter* [X], 17 October.

Tanamal, Yvette. 2023. 'Dutch PM Recognises 1945 as Indonesia's Independence.' *Jakarta Post*, 16 June.

Telegraaf. 2022. 'Rijksmuseum: Toch Aandacht voor Term Bersiap [Rijksmuseum: Still Attention for the Term *Bersiap*].' *Telegraaf*, [Amsterdam], 14 January. www.telegraaf.nl/nieuws/1757408305/rijksmuseum-toch-aandacht-voor-term-bersiap.

The Indo Project. 2022. 'Bersiap, Decolonization Research and Postcolonial Uproar: A Summary.' *The Indo Project Blog*, 26 February. Boston: The Indo Project. theindoproject.org/bersiap-decolonization-postcolonial-uproar/.

Touwen-Bousma, Elly. 2010. *Op Zoek Naar Grenzen: Toepassing en Uitvoering van de Wetten voor Oorlogslachtoffers* [*Looking for Boundaries: Application and Implementation of the Laws for War Victims*]. Amsterdam: Boom.

Trouillot, Michel Rolph. 1995. *Silencing the Past: Power and the Production of History*. Boston: Beacon Press.

van Beurden, Jos. 2021. 'Returns by the Netherlands to Indonesia in the 2010s and the 1970s.' In *Returning Southeast Asia's Past: Objects, Museum, and Restitution*, edited by Louise Tythacott and Panggah Ardiyansyah, 187–209. Singapore: NUS Press. doi.org/10.2307/j.ctv1r4xctd.13.

van der Mee, Tonny, and Raymond Boere. 2022. '"Geschiedvervalsing" of "geen nieuws"? Kenners sterk verdeeld over onderzoek naar dekolonisatie Indonesië ["Fake History" or "No News"? Experts Strongly Divided About Research into the Decolonisation of Indonesia].' *Het Parool*, [Amsterdam], 17 February. www.parool.nl/nederland/geschiedvervalsing-of-geen-nieuws-kenners-sterk-verdeeld-over-onderzoek-naar-dekolonisatie-indonesie-b4ade2e3/.

van der Meer, Arnout. 2020. *Performing Power: Cultural Hegemony, Identity, and Resistance in Colonial Indonesia*. Ithaca: Cornell University Press. www.jstor.org/stable/10.7591/j.ctv1hbf2dd.

van Leeuwen, Lizzy. 2011. 'Postcolonial Neglect in Holland.' *Inside Indonesia* 103 (January–March). www.insideindonesia.org/postcolonial-neglect-in-holland.

van Nuland, Merijn. 2022. 'Indonesië eist Java-mens en andere topstukken terug van Nederland [Indonesia Demands Java Man and Other Top Pieces Back from the Netherlands].' *Trouw*, [Amsterdam], 18 October. www.trouw.nl/binnenland/indonesie-eist-java-mens-en-andere-topstukken-terug-van-nederland~be6860e9/.

Westad, Odd Arne. 2007. *The Global Cold War*. Cambridge: Cambridge University Press.

Wijaya, Callistasia. 2020. 'Indonesia–Belanda: Ratusan Ribu Benda Bersejarah Indonesia Dimiliki Belanda akan Segera Dikembalikan [Indonesia–the Netherlands: Hundreds and Thousands of Indonesian Historical Objects in Dutch Hands Will Be Quickly Returned to Indonesia]?' *BBC News Indonesia*, 13 March. www.bbc.com/indonesia/indonesia-51749544.

Wilders, Geert. 2022. 'Waar zijn de Excuses [Where Are the Apologies].' @geertwilderspvv, *Twitter* [X], 18 February.

Wills, Esther. 2022. 'Rijksmuseum Schrapt Bersiap [Rijksmuseum Deletes *Bersiap*].' *Indies Tijdschrift* [*Indies Magazine*], 13 January. www.indiestijdschrift.nl/3104/0/publications/nieuws-2022/rijksmuseum-schrapt-bersiap [page discontinued].

Winichakul, Thongchai. 1997. *Siam Mapped: A History of the Geo-Body of a Nation*. Honolulu: University of Hawai`i Press. doi.org/10.1515/9780824841294.

Wolfe, Patrick. 2006. 'Settler Colonialism and the Elimination of the Native.' *Journal of Genocide Research* 8, no. 4: 387–409. doi.org/10.1080/14623520601056240.

Zed, Mestika. 2001. 'Menggugat Tirani Sejarah Nasional [Contesting the Tyranny of National History].' Paper presented to Seventh National History Conference, Jakarta, 28–31 October.

Zhou, Taomo. 2019. 'Global Reporting from the Third World: The Afro-Asian Journalists' Association, 1963–1974.' *Critical Asian Studies* 51, no. 2: 166–97. doi.org/10.1080/14672715.2018.1561200.

Zweers, Louis. 2022. 'Veel is al in bezit van Indonesië [Much is Already Owned by Indonesia].' *Nederlands Dagblad*, [Amersfoort, Netherlands], 8 November.

2

'*Oedjan belasting*, the raining of taxes': Coloniality and the Dutch economic exploitation of the Chinese[1]

Abdul Wahid

Introduction

On Monday morning, 8 September 1924, an unusual scene unfolded in the area between Sirene-Park and the Sociëteit de Harmonie, one of most iconic colonial buildings in the heart of Batavia, the capital of the Netherlands East Indies. Thousands of people from different ethnic backgrounds, but mostly non-Europeans, flocked around the main street surrounding the office building of the Gemeente-Secretarie (Municipal Secretary), wearing European-style clothes, some with bicycles and banners decorated with writing. As can be seen in Figure 2.1, this was a mass demonstration of predominantly Chinese people who claimed to be representatives of '*pendoedoek dari gemeente Batavia*' ('the residents of the municipality of Batavia'). Accompanied by the music played by Tiong Hoa Im Gak Hwe, a Chinese music group affiliated with Tiong Hoa Hwee Koan (THHK),[2] the prominent Chinese

---
1 The phrase *Oedjan Belasting* ('The Raining of Taxes') is the title of an article in *Sin Po: Wekelijksche Editie* [Weekly edition], 21 February 1925.
2 On the THHK and its role in promoting Chinese schools in the East Indies, see Didi Kwartanada, 'The Tiong Hoa Hwee Koan School: A Transborder Project of Modernity in Batavia, c. 1900s', in *Chinese Indonesians Reassessed: History, Religion and Belonging*, eds Siew-Min Sai and Chang-Yau Hoon (London: Routledge, 2013), 27–44.

organisation which promoted and supported Chinese nationalism in the Indies, the Chinese protesters expressed their grievances against government tax policies, particularly those issued by the Batavia municipal government.³

Figure 2.1 Newspaper coverage of an anti-tax demonstration in Batavia on 8 September 1924
Source: *Sin Po* [Weekly edition], 13 September 1924.

---

3   'Een Massa-Demonstratie [A Mass Demonstration]', *Algemeen Handelsblad voor Nederlandsch-Indie* [*General Trade Magazine for the Dutch East Indies*], 11 September 1924.

The demonstration ended about 4 o'clock in the afternoon without any significant incidents and a committee representing the protesters handed a signed petition to the *Burgemeester* ('Mayor') of Batavia. *Sin Po*, the prominent Chinese Malay-language newspaper, reported several days later that the petition included two demands: 1) the Batavia Mayor should abolish the municipal tax service, and 2) the taxes levied by the central and municipal governments should be merged into a single levy.[4] The petition was seemingly a consequence of the *Decentralisatie Wet* ('Decentralisation Law'), a policy introduced by the Netherlands East Indies Government from 1903. The law delegated some of the central government's authority to local governments, including municipal governments in the big cities across the colony. This included a fiscal aspect that gave the municipal government authority to levy new taxes to finance its programs. Therefore, municipal taxes were introduced on top of the central government's taxes, creating an additional tax burden for residents of municipalities, especially the Chinese, most of whom settled in urban areas due to the enhanced opportunities for trade.

This street demonstration was notable because of the assertiveness of the crowd and the clear evidence it provided of everyday efforts to resist colonial exploitation. *Sin Po* vividly explains:

> Those participating in the demonstration were mainly not white people, but Indigenous, Chinese and Arabs. Streets were fully occupied by participants and spectators. No riot happened. This is the second time Batavia residents showed their unhappiness with the work of Municipal government.[5]

In the 1920s, this kind of politically motivated mass gathering aimed at criticising the colonial government had become increasingly normal in urban areas of Java but also elsewhere, as the colonial government introduced a series of 'democratic experiments' from the early twentieth century allowing

---

4   'Demonstrasi Oeroesan Belasting [Demonstration on Tax Matters]', *Sin Po: Wekelijksche Editie* [Weekly edition], 13 September 1924. For analysis of *Sin Po* during and after the Indonesian revolution, see Ravando and Harsono's Chapter 8 in this volume.
5   'Demonstration on Tax Matters', *Sin Po*: 'Jang toeroet ambil bagian teroetama ada pendoedoek jang boekan berkoelit poeti, jalah bangsa Boemipoetra, Tionghoa dan Arab. Djarang orang Tionghoa dan Arab berkompoel. Djalanan sampe penoe dengan orang jang ikoet dan jang menonton. Tidak ada keriboetan apa-apa. Ini ada boeat kadoea kalinja, jang pendoedoek Batavia oendjoek ia orang poenja koerang senang hati pada mintrad poenja tjara berkerdja [The participants are non-White populations, namely Natives, Chinese, and Arabs. The Chinese and Arab are seldom to make such a gathering. Street was fully occupied by participants and observers. There was no chaos. This is the second time Batavia populations show their antipathy toward the way the Gemeente worked].'

the development of 'civil society'. This included permission for people to produce printed media and engage in associations, political parties and politics, especially in urban areas.[6] Yet, a mass demonstration to protest the colonial government's tax policies involving such 'apolitical groups' as the Chinese and Arabs was quite extraordinary, especially for Batavia, the colonial administration's capital, because, consistent with the logic of coloniality and the inseparable link between 'racialisation and capital exploitation',[7] the colonial government had tried to carefully control these groups and place them in key economic roles in the colony. The protest and its diverse participants suggest the heavy tax burden was becoming a shared and pressing political issue among 'citizens of the Netherlands East Indies', particularly non-Europeans. Unlike previous anti-tax protests that took the old-fashioned form of armed rebellions,[8] this time, the residents of Batavia organised modern, non-violent protest through a demonstration and a petition to exercise 'their right' to question the government's tax policies. In fact, the 8 September 1924 demonstration was the last 'anti-tax' demonstration, as the colonial government introduced a repressive approach, forbidding political gatherings of any kind after the outbreak of leftist-inspired rebellions in February 1926 and January 1927, allowing political aspirations to be channelled only through the parliament.[9]

These popular grievances arose because of the increasingly burdensome taxes the Dutch introduced due to the deteriorating position of the public finances of the Netherlands East Indies, especially in the 1920s. The official statistics show that, in that period, the government was suffering the biggest fiscal

---

6   This was evident from the formation of the Volksraad and the Gemeenteraad ('Municipal Council'). See Freek Colombijn, 'The Colonial Municipal Council in Padang (Sumatra) as Political Arena', *Journal of Southeast Asian Studies* 26, no. 2 (1995): 263–88, doi.org/10.1017/S0022463400007104; Remco Raben, 'Decolonization and the Democratic Moment in Southeast Asia', Paper presented to Eclipse of Empire: Colonial Resistance, Metropolitan Decline and Imperial Crises in the 19th and 20th Centuries Conference, Universitat Pompeu Fabra, Barcelona, 2–3 June 2010; Abdul Wahid, 'City and "Colonial Governance" in Late Colonial Indonesia: Towards an Agenda for Historical Research', *Paramita: Historical Studies Journal* 28, no. 1 (2018): 25–37. Indonesian historians view this period as representative of the birth of 'the nationalist movement of Indonesia'. See, for example, Sartono Kartodirdjo, *Pengantar Sejarah Indonesia Baru: Sejarah Pergerakan Nasional* [*Introduction to New Indonesian History: History of the National Movement*] (Yogyakarta: Penerbit Ombak, 2014).
7   María Lugones, 'Toward a Decolonial Feminism', *Hypatia* 25, no. 4 (2010): 742–59, doi.org/10.1111/j.1527-2001.2010.01137.x, at 745.
8   Sartono Kartodirdjo, *Protest Movement in Rural Java: A Study of Agrarian Unrest in the Nineteenth and Early Twentieth Centuries* (Singapore: Oxford University Press, 1973).
9   Merle C. Ricklefs, *A History of Modern Indonesia Since c. 1200*, 3rd edn (London: Bloomsbury Academic, 2008), doi.org/10.5040/9781350394582; Abdul Wahid, 'From Revenue Farming to State Monopoly: The Political Economy of Taxation in Colonial Indonesia, 1816–1942' *Bulletin of Indonesian Economic Studies* 50, no. 2 (2014): 294–95, doi.org/10.1080/00074918.2014.896245, 283.

deficit since the start of the century, amounting to a total f336.6 million.[10] Among others, one reason for the debt was colonial repression and the extravagant military expenditure since the last decade of the nineteenth century to finance campaigns in Aceh and Lombok, and the lavish 'welfare projects of the Ethical Policy', which was an attempt to assuage colonial guilt.[11] According to some economic historians, the Netherlands East Indies ran continuous deficits from the abolition of the 'Cultivation System' in the 1870s and was in surplus only during the enforcement of this system from the 1830s to the 1860s.[12]

In response to the deficit, the colonial government increased revenues from taxes. This was evident statistically from the share of total revenues provided by taxes, which steadily grew in the last four decades of the colonial period. Economic historian Anne Booth has calculated that, by 1939, the share of tax revenue in total revenue was 67 per cent, while the real total yearly average of government tax revenue in the period 1930–39 was f262 million.[13] The considerable growth of the importance of tax as a source of government revenue came at a cost to indigenous, but also Chinese taxpayers who carried the largest burden of taxes on their shoulders. On this issue, prominent colonial servant W. Huender warned the government that the burden of taxation for indigenous people in the colony, at least in Java, meant they had reached 'their utmost limit' and further increases would jeopardise their general welfare.[14]

The tax burden on indigenous people was confirmed by Huender and Ranneft's 1926 investigation.[15] Yet, what is less recognised is that Chinese people, especially after 1920, faced a particularly extreme situation due to the multiple ways in which they were exploited as a colonially produced minority group. Early evidence to support this argument is the fact that the largest proportion of government tax revenue was accrued from personal and corporate income taxes, which in the period 1936–40 accounted for

---

10   f = guilders.
11   W.M.F. Mansvelt and Pieter Creutzberg, eds, *Changing Economy in Indonesia. Volume 7: Balance of Payments, 1823–1939* (The Hague: Martinus Nijhoff, 1987), Tables 2–4; Anne Booth, *The Indonesian Economy in the Nineteenth and Twentieth Centuries: A History of Missed Opportunities* (London: Palgrave Macmillan, 1998), doi.org/10.1057/9780333994962.
12   Jan L. van Zanden and Daan Marks, *An Economic History of Indonesia, 1800–2010* (London: Routledge, 2012), 50.
13   Booth, *The Indonesian Economy in the Nineteenth and Twentieth Centuries*, 146.
14   ibid., 147.
15   J.W. Meijer Ranneft and W. Huender, *Onderzoek naar den Belastingdruk op de Inlandsche Bevolking* [*Investigation into the Tax Burden on the Native Population*] (Weltevreden: Landsdrukkerij, 1926).

30 per cent of total tax revenues, in comparison with land tax (*landrente*), which accounted for only 7.7 per cent.[16] Income taxes (personal and corporate) were only levied on Chinese and European people who were categorised as upper-income groups in the colony, while land tax was levied only on the indigenous population, the lowest income group. In addition to being categorised as an upper-income group, the Chinese, according to a racialised logic, were subjected to various 'new taxes' such as the war-profit tax, corporate tax, property tax and many others that were introduced in the first two decades of the twentieth century.[17] Under such conditions, the Chinese experienced what *Sin Po* described as '*Belasting Bersoesoen-sooesoen*'[18] ('multilayered taxes'), which forced them on to the streets of Batavia on 8 September 1924 to express their grievances.

This chapter seeks to analyse why and to what extent the Chinese were heavily taxed by the Dutch colonial government (and its successors). To answer the question, I investigate how and why the war profit and income taxes were levied. Combining information from colonial archives, official publications and Chinese newspapers, this chapter argues that the exploitation of the Chinese in the colonial taxation system was integrally connected with the Dutch construction of the sociopolitical and legal position of the Chinese as *Vreemde Oosterlingen* ('Foreigners or Foreign Orientals'). Through this category, Dutch colonialists positioned the Chinese as a 'middleman minority' sitting between the Europeans at the top and indigenous people at the bottom of the social pyramid of colonial society. As such, the Dutch colonial rulers allowed the Chinese to expand their economic influence but carefully monitored their political influence on the local population, which, from a fiscal perspective, was a strategic way to render them 'manageable subjects' who presumably would not protest various forms of taxation.[19] The link between racialised categories and economic exploitation accentuates the 'coloniality of power' introduced in

---

16   Wahid, 'From Revenue Farming to State Monopoly', 51.
17   ibid., 43–48.
18   'Belasting Bersoesoen-soesoen [Multilayered Tax]', *Sin Po: Wekelijksche Editie* [Weekly edition], 15 May 1926.
19   Various scholars have theorised the Chinese position in colonial Indonesia and elsewhere as a 'trading minority', 'middleman minority', 'entrepreneurial minority' and 'essential outsiders'. See Wim F. Wertheim, *East–West Parallels: Sociological Approaches to Modern Asia* (The Hague: W. van Hoeve, 1964); Edna Bonacich, 'A Theory of Middleman Minorities', *American Sociological Review* 38, no. 5 (1973): 583–94, doi.org/10.2307/2094409; Christine Dobbin, *Asian Entrepreneurial Minorities: Conjoint Communities in the Making of the World Economy, 1570–1940* (London: Curzon, 1996); Daniel Chirot and Anthony Reid, eds, *Essential Outsiders: Chinese and Jews in the Modern Transformation of Southeast Asia and Central Europe* (Seattle: University of Washington Press, 1997).

Chapter 1 of this volume. By focusing on the position of the Chinese as the subjects of taxation, this study contributes to the new histories of taxation in colonial Indonesia, which in the past few decades have focused heavily on opium revenue farming,[20] land tax,[21] taxation's contribution to economic development and public finance,[22] its connection with colonial state formation and governance[23] and its sociopolitical impacts.[24] In discussing the position of the Chinese as the subjects of colonial tax exploitation, this study takes as an insight Louis Althusser's theory that the 'tax system reflects the underlying ideology of the state, just like other parts of the state apparatus do'.[25] Following this line, this study views the Dutch colonial tax system as a container of colonial ideology, reflective of the way the colonial state operated. Furthermore, it shows how one group was forced to fund

---

20 James Rush, *Opium to Java: Revenue Farming and Chinese Enterprise in Colonial Indonesia, 1860–1910* (Ithaca: Cornell University Press, 1990); Claudine Salmon, 'A Critical View of the Opium Farmers as Reflected in a Syair by Boen Sing Ho (Semarang 1889)', *Indonesia* [SI] (1991): 25–51, doi.org/10.2307/3351253; Fritz W. Diehl, 'Revenue Farming and Colonial Finances in the Netherlands East Indies, 1816–1925', in *The Rise and Fall of Revenue Farming: Business Elites and the Emergence of the Modern State in Southeast Asia*, eds John Butcher and Howard Dick (London: Palgrave Macmillan, 1993), 196–232, doi.org/10.1007/978-1-349-22877-5_12.
21 W.R. Hugenholtz, 'The Landrent Question and its Solution, 1850–1920', in *The Late Colonial State in Indonesia: Political and Economic Foundation of the Netherlands Indies, 1880–1942*, ed. Robert Cribb (Leiden: KITLV Press, 1994), 139–72; Anne Booth, 'Land Taxation in Asia: An Overview of the 19th and 20th Centuries', *Oxford Development Studies* 42, no. 1 (2014): 1–18, doi.org/10.1080/13600818.2014.880413.
22 Booth, *The Indonesian Economy in the Nineteenth and Twentieth Centuries*; Anne Booth, *Economic Change in Modern Indonesia: Colonial and Post-Colonial Comparison* (Cambridge: Cambridge University Press, 2016), doi.org/10.1017/CBO9781316271438; Ewout Frankema and Anne Booth, eds, *Fiscal Capacity and the Colonial State in Asia and Africa, c. 1850–1960* (Cambridge: Cambridge University Press, 2020), doi.org/10.1017/9781108665001.
23 Wahid, 'From Revenue Farming to State Monopoly'; Maarten Manse, 'From Headhunting to Head Taxes: Violence, Taxation and Colonial Governance on Seram, c. 1860–1920', *Bijdragen tot de Taal-, Land- en Volkenkunde [Journal of the Humanities and Social Sciences of Southeast Asia]* 177, no. 4 (2021): 524–58, doi.org/10.1163/22134379-bja10023; Maarten Manse, 'Promise, Pretence, and Pragmatism: Governance and Taxation in Colonial Indonesia, 1870–1940' (PhD diss., Leiden University, Netherlands, 2021).
24 Onghokham, 'Pulung Affair: Pemberontakan Pajak di Desa Patik, Beberapa Aspek Politik di Madiun Pada Abad ke-19 [Pulung Affair: Tax Rebellion in Patik Village, Some Political Aspects in Madiun in the Nineteenth Century]', *Majalah Ilmu-ilmu Sastra [Indonesian Literary Sciences Magazine]* 7, no. 1 (1977): 1–25; Onghokham, 'Pajak dalam Perspektif Sejarah [Tax in Historical Perspective]', *Prisma* 14, no. 4 (1985): 74–85; The Siauw Giap, 'Socio-Economic Role of the Chinese in Indonesia, 1820–1940', in *Economic Growth in Indonesia, 1820–1940*, eds Angus Maddison and Gé Prince (Dordrecht: Foris Publications, 1989), 159–202; Sartono Kartodirdjo, *Laporan-laporan tentang Gerakan Protes di Jawa pada Abad XX [Reports on the Protest Movement in Java in the Twentieth Century]* (Jakarta: National Archives of the Republic of Indonesia, 1981); Kenneth A. Young, *Islamic Peasants and the State: The 1908 Anti-Tax Rebellion in West Sumatra*, Yale Center for International and Area Studies Monograph No. 40 (New Haven: Yale University Press, 1994).
25 Louis Althusser, 'Ideology and Ideological State Apparatuses (Notes Toward an Investigation)', in *The Anthropology of the State: A Reader*, eds Aradhana Sharma and Akhil Gupta (Malden: Blackwell Publishing, 2006), 86–111, at 90.

the colonial project. My analysis adopts a decolonial lens by linking this racial logic to colonial exploitation and charting sources of resistance to this exploitation.

The socioeconomic and legal positions of the Chinese

Chinese from different parts of China had migrated to and settled in Java and other parts of the archipelago long before the coming of Europeans. Their presence was a product of centuries-old relations between mainland China and the archipelago, and most of them came from the southeast in an area that is today between the provinces of Guangdong and Fujian.[26] When the Dutch finally took control of most of the archipelago and established Batavia as their trading and administrative headquarters, they realised the economic importance of Chinese migrants, especially in international and local trade.[27] After the Dutch established a monopoly on international trade through the Dutch East India Company (Vereenigde Oost-Indische Compagnie, VOC), they exploited the Chinese to support their ambition to build Batavia as the centre for administration, but also to expand their political and economic influence in the archipelago. Under the VOC's tutelage, the Chinese were incentivised to become or assigned roles as intermediary traders, contractors for public works, sugar planters, owners of or workers in sugar mills, arrack distilleries and sawmills, artisans, and many other occupations.[28] These growing opportunities attracted more Chinese migrants to Batavia, which in the long run overwhelmed Batavia's carrying capacity and created various social problems that led to the horrible massacres by the Dutch of thousands of Chinese in 1740.[29] For analysis of this event and the creation of colonial categories, including spatially, see Abidin Kusno's analysis in Chapter 11 of this volume.

---

26   Ong Eng Die, *Chineezen in Nederlandsch-Indië: Sociografie van een Indonesische Bevolkingsgroep* [*The Chinese in the Netherlands Indies: Sociography of an Indonesian Population Group*] (Assen: Van Gorchum & Co., 1943), 29.
27   On the early Dutch venture in Batavia and elsewhere in the archipelago through the VOC, see Femme S. Gaastra, *The Dutch East India Company: Expansion and Decline* (Zutphen: Waalburg Press, 2003).
28   The Siauw Giap, 'Socio-Economic role of the Chinese in Indonesia', 159.
29   Leonard Blussé, *Strange Company: Chinese Settlers, Mestizo Women, and the Dutch in VOC Batavia*, KITLV Verhandelingen Series No. 122 (Leiden: KITLV/Foris Publications, 1986).

2. 'OEDJAN BELASTING, THE RAINING OF TAXES'

Despite the 1740 massacre, which indicates the mixed feelings of the Dutch about the Chinese, the important position of the Chinese in the local economy remained. The Dutch used the Chinese extensively as intermediaries in the sale of imported goods such as opium, liquor and cotton, but also for the sale of locally produced commodities like coffee, tobacco, indigo, sugar and so on. But, from a fiscal perspective, the most important role that the Dutch granted to the Chinese was in the system of farming out monopolies, particularly the licences to collect taxes from the population, which is known in the Dutch literature as *pachtstelsel* ('tax farming'). According to Howard Dick, this kind of tax collection system was an early stage of state formation.[30] The VOC adopted the system as a solution to the lack of human resources and the limited political infrastructure in the first decades of their settlement in Batavia. After the VOC's collapse, however, and throughout the nineteenth century, the Dutch retained and even institutionalised the system on a larger scale as part of the colonial state administration. By the end of the nineteenth century, the system was almost exclusively controlled by the Chinese elite, allowing them to expand and strengthen their economic influence, at least in Java.[31]

The Chinese population in the Netherlands East Indies grew significantly from the mid-nineteenth century, due largely to the influx of new immigrants from China who were attracted to seek their fortune amid the burgeoning economic opportunities or join relatives who had already settled and made a living in the archipelago. By 1802, the total Chinese population in Java and Madura was 23,311 people. Fifty years later, it had increased more than five times to 123,871 people and, in the next 50 years, it almost doubled, to 227,265 people.[32] The first statistical information about the Chinese population in the entire colony is for the year 1860, when the total Chinese population was reported as 221,438 people, 149,424 of whom were living in Java and Madura and the remainder of whom were living in other islands—known in colonial publications as the 'Outer Islands'. Table 2.1 provides a complete picture of the growth of the Chinese population and its geographical distribution in the period 1880–1930.

---

30   Howard Dick, 'A Fresh Approach to Southeast Asian History', in *The Rise and Fall of Revenue Farming: Business Elites and the Emergence of the Modern State in Southeast Asia*, eds John Butcher and Howard Dick (London: Palgrave Macmillan, 1993), 3–18, doi.org/10.1007/978-1-349-22877-5_1, at 5–6.
31   Rush, *Opium to Java*; Diehl, 'Revenue Farming and Colonial Finances in the Netherlands East Indies'.
32   Peter Boomgaard and A.J. Gooszen, *Changing Economy in Indonesia. Volume 11: Population Trends, 1795–1942* (Amsterdam: Royal Tropical Institute, 1991), Table 6b.1, 127.

Table 2.1 Chinese population of the Netherlands East Indies, 1860–1930

Year	Java & Madura	Outer Islands	Netherlands East Indies
1880	206,931	136,862	343,793
1890	242,111	218,978	461,089
1900	277,265	260,051	537,316
1905	295,193	268,256	563,449
1920	383,614	425,423	809,039
1930	582,431	650,783	1,233,214

Source: Departement van Economische Zaken [Department of Economic Affairs] (1931).

One notable insight from Table 2.1 is that the number of Chinese living in the Outer Islands grew faster than that in Java and Madura from 1890. By 1920 and 1930, the number of Chinese living in the Outer Islands exceeded that in Java and Madura. This is because, after 1860, the Outer Islands emerged as new destinations for Chinese immigrants who wanted to make a living as *koeli* ('workers') due to the expansion of tobacco plantations in East Sumatra, tin mining in Bangka and Belitung, coalmining in western Sumatra, oil factories in many parts of Sumatra, goldmining in western Borneo and many other opportunities. According to an official report, 223,507 Chinese contract workers moved to these regions in the period 1912–31. Meanwhile, 231,706 Chinese non-contract or free workers came to Java and Madura in the period 1900–31—far below the number moving to the Outer Islands (639,396 people). This means that in the last three decades of the colonial period, the geographical concentration of the Chinese settlements shifted from Java–Madura to the Outer Islands, especially Sumatra. This geographical shift meant that, in Java and Madura, most Chinese were born in the Netherlands East Indies (and were known as *Peranakan*), while most of those in the Outer Islands had been born in China (and were known as *Singkeh*).[33]

Table 2.1 also shows that the total Chinese population in 1930 was 1,233,214, which accounted for only 2 per cent of the total East Indies population, which comprised 59,138,067 indigenous people (97.4 per cent),

---

33   Ong Eng Die, *The Chinese in the Netherlands Indies*, 39–40. Yet, most Chinese contract and free workers came from the same areas as their predecessors—namely, Guangdong and Fujian. The Chinese population comprised the following ethnic (or dialect) groups: Hokkien (47 per cent), Hakka or Keh (16.9 per cent), Kwongfoe (11.44 per cent) and Tio Ciu or Hoklo (7.38 per cent). See Departement van Economische Zaken [Department of Economic Affairs], *Volkstelling 1930 [Census 1930]*. Volume VII (Batavia: Landsdrukkerij, 1931), Table 21, 104.

240,417 Europeans (0.4 per cent) and 115,535 other 'Foreign Asians' (0.2 per cent). According to Ong Eng Die, the Chinese in the East Indies made up only 0.3 per cent of the global Chinese population of 450 million, but represented 12 per cent of the almost 11 million overseas Chinese living outside the mainland, particularly in the Pacific region.[34] According to the *Koloniaal Verslag* ('*Colonial Report*') for 1907–08, the Chinese occupational structure in Java and Madura in 1905 was as follows: 33,959 were employed in commerce, 10,902 in manufacturing and mining, 7,970 in agriculture and fishing, 1,083 in transport, 835 in services, with 23,693 in other industries. The occupational structure of Chinese living in the Outer Islands was quite different, with agriculture and fishing as the biggest sectors, employing 94,358 people, followed by manufacturing and mining (25,096), commerce (21,263), transport (1,711), services (935) and other (37,774).[35] The Chinese were the ones who engaged in trade and therefore it was mostly those in Java and Madura who were targeted with the harshest tax policies, although all Chinese were subject to a greater number of taxes than other residents in the colony.

In the early decades of the twentieth century, the Chinese strengthened their economic control over the trade in retail exports and imports in Java, Madura and elsewhere in the colony. By 1930, the proportion of Chinese control of large-scale trade was already 35.4 per cent, far exceeding European control, which stood at just 13.4 per cent, and indigenous control, which was only 5.4 per cent. In terms of retail trade, the Chinese had almost full control through medium and small-scale trading companies, shops and '*klontong*' (traditional small shops), which were scattered throughout the cities and towns of Java.[36] In addition to their control over the trading sector, at the beginning of the twentieth century, the Chinese managed to expand their economic influence in other sectors. According to The Siauw Giap, this expansion was supported by the increased availability of capital among the Chinese elite after the abolition of a monopoly-lease system. This allowed them to reinvest their capital in various modern economic sectors to compete with Europeans in the capital and technology-intensive sugar industry but also in other sectors, including transportation, banking, services and other large and medium-sized industries.[37]

---

34   Ong Eng Die, *The Chinese in the Netherlands Indies*, 13.
35   M.R. Fernando and David Bulbeck, eds, *Chinese Economic Activity in Netherlands India: Selected Translations from the Dutch* (Singapore: ISEAS, 1992), doi.org/10.1355/9789814379410, 87–89.
36   Ong Eng Die, *The Chinese in the Netherlands Indies*, 104.
37   The Siauw Giap, 'Socio-Economic Role of the Chinese in Indonesia', 177.

Responding to increased Chinese economic influence, the colonial government introduced several policies to control them. First, in 1885, the Dutch decided to make the Chinese subject to European commercial law to simplify their dealings with the growing number of their enterprises. Chinese businesspeople were permitted to form legally recognised modern enterprises or companies, which previously had only been possible for Europeans or those with Europeans' legal status. For the Chinese, this was quite a radical policy as they were initially equated with 'native' people (together with Arabs, Indians and other Asians)—in terms of their legal and administrative positions—under the racially based *Regerings-reglement* ('Constitutional Regulation') of 1854.[38] The policy to make Chinese the subjects of European commercial law, according to Cribb and Kahin, brought about a gradual institutionalisation of the group known as Foreign Orientals as a third racial classification, after Europeans and Inlanders, as legally defined in the revised constitution of 1925 (Art. 163).[39]

A more progressive policy concerning the legal position of the Chinese was taken by the Dutch in 1892 with the enactment of the Citizenship Law, which designated the Chinese as 'foreigners' and not 'citizens', but they were still considered Dutch subjects if they domiciled in the Netherlands East Indies. Almost a decade later, the Dutch amended the 1892 bill with a more 'aggressive' law known as the *Netherlands Citizenship Act* (s. 296) of 10 February 1910. Based on the principle of *jus soli* ('right of soil'), the new law stipulated that all Chinese, as well as members of other ethnic groups who were born in the East Indies of parents who settled and lived there, were Dutch subjects even if they were not Dutch citizens.[40] Many scholars view the law as a Dutch response to rising Chinese nationalism in the Indies and the formation of the Republic of China with its 'aggressive' citizenship

---

38 In comparison, Japanese in the East Indies had, by 1889, been granted full European-equivalent status—something the Chinese wanted but never achieved and that made them envious. Cees Fasseur, 'Cornerstone and Stumbling Block: Racial Classification and the Late Colonial State in Indonesia', in *The Late Colonial State in Indonesia: Political and Economic Foundation of the Netherlands Indies, 1880–1942*, ed. Robert Cribb (Leiden: KITLV Press, 1994), 31–56, at 37.
39 However, this racial classification was not entirely fixed. About this matter, Cribb and Kahin explain: 'Movement between [racial] categories was possible by means of *gelijkstelling* ['alike-making'], under which a person of native or foreign oriental status could gain full legal European status if he could demonstrate that he was culturally assimilated to the European community or had special legal need for European status.' See Robert Cribb and Audrey Kahin, *Historical Dictionary of Indonesia* (Lanham: Scarecrow Press, 2004), 363.
40 Donald E. Willmott, *The National Status of the Chinese in Indonesia* (Ithaca: Cornell University Press, 1956), Ch. 2.

policy that claimed all Chinese abroad as Chinese citizens.[41] From an economic perspective, the *Citizenship Act* of 1910 clearly shows the real intention of the Dutch was to fend off the citizenship claims of the Republic of China over the Chinese, particularly those born in the Indies. The Dutch did not want to lose the Chinese, with their significant economic power, as 'taxable subjects', as will be shown in the following section.

The tax burden on the Chinese and their responses

In the last decade of the nineteenth century, the Dutch colonial administrators launched a series of tax reforms with the intention of establishing a modern, unified and just tax system and administrative state in the East Indies. One of the most important tax reforms, and highly related to the political and economic position of the Chinese, was the abolition of the *pachtstelsel* system. The system had been in operation since the early nineteenth century, with the licences almost entirely in the hands of the Chinese elite, covering many taxes and monopolies, and had become a significant source of revenue for both the colonial government and the Chinese *pachters* ('licence-holders'). Reform was implemented through three different measures: first, the complete abolition of toll bridges and taxes on markets, forest exploitation and the sale of palm sugar; second, conversion into state-collected taxes, including taxes on the slaughter of cattle and pigs, the trade of edible birds' nests, the sale of liquor, tobacco and fish, Chinese gambling, and a poll tax; and third, conversion into state monopolies of the taxes on the sale of opium, pawnshops and the production and sale of salt.[42]

These reforms brought about a significant change in the role and position of Chinese under the colonial tax administration, from partial government partners in tax collection to pure taxpayers. Because of their economic position, as mentioned above, in their capacity as taxpayers, the Chinese naturally became the most important group after the Europeans and those equated with them. Under the new system, by the mid-1910s, the Chinese were liable to 'old taxes'—such as the head tax, excise and stamp duties and

---

41   For example, Leo Suryadinata, *Peranakan Chinese Politics in Java, 1917–1942* (Singapore: NUS Press, 1981); and Patricia Tjiook-Liem, De Rechtspositie der Chinezen in Nederlands-Indië 1848–1942 [*The Legal Position of the Chinese in the Netherlands Indies, 1848–1942*] (Leiden: Leiden University Press, 2009).
42   Wahid, 'From Revenue Farming to State Monopoly', 180.

taxes on exports and imports, the slaughter of cattle and pigs, lotteries, dogs and Chinese gambling licences—but also liable to pay the newly introduced taxes, such as property, business and income taxes.[43] The Chinese also had to pay other taxes that were levied by the Netherlands East Indies Government in relation to certain conditions or policies—for example, taxes on war profits (*oorlogswinstbelasting*) and luxury goods (*luxe-belasting*) were introduced in the wake of World War I and new taxes were levied by the municipalities as part of the decentralisation policy.[44]

Interestingly, under the reformed tax system, the Chinese found themselves in a dual and hence exploited position. In the case of some taxes, they were considered liable because of their legal status as '*gelijkgesteld met de inlanders*' ('equated with indigenous people'), but for others, such as property and income taxes, they were perceived as being equal to Europeans.[45] In other words, the Chinese were liable to a wide range of taxes levied on either Europeans or indigenous people, which is how they came to bear a heavier tax burden than both. It was why they deemed the Indies' taxation system unjust and excessively severe towards them. As a result, in the early twentieth century, taxation in the East Indies was a major source of Chinese grievance, which they articulated openly towards the government through any forms of expression possible at that time. According to Lea E. Williams, Chinese resentment towards government taxation was primarily caused by the fact that they paid high taxes but received only 'small reward' and no 'decent compensation, for example in the form of such important public services as education, health care, etc'.[46]

---

43 J. Paulus, ed., *Encyclopaedie van Nederlandsch-Indie. Volume 1* (Leiden: E.J. Brill, 1917), 224; J. Visser, *Overzicht van het Belastingwezen van Nederlandsch-Indië: Voor Onderwijs en Praktijk* [*Overview of the Netherlands Indies' Tax System: For Education and Practice*] (Batavia: Van Dorp & Co., 1924), 43–44.
44 Wahid, 'From Revenue Farming to State Monopoly', 172.
45 Visser, *Overview of the Netherlands Indies' Tax System*, 142–43.
46 Lea E. Williams, *Overseas Chinese Nationalism: The Genesis of Pan-Chinese Nationalism in Indonesia* (Glencoe: The Free Press, 1960), 27. In contrast to what the Chinese population felt about their tax burden, the Dutch colonial administrator thought the Chinese paid 'extremely little' in taxes compared with European and indigenous people. Surely, such a contention offended the feelings of Chinese people and raised their grievances about other issues. Aside from tax issues, Williams further explains that the Chinese in the early decades of the twentieth century were offended by the tax-farming system (*passenstelsel*) and zoning system (*wijkenstelsel*) that restricted their freedom and the placing of Chinese under the jurisdiction of the courts for natives (*politierol*).

Few statistical data are available for the period 1910–30 about the amount of tax the Chinese paid and the proportion of public revenue it comprised or the tax burden placed on the Chinese population. The existing quantitative data about the tax burden are related mostly to the indigenous population, as exemplified by the extensive survey of the diminishing welfare of indigenous people in 1904–14 and a further survey on the tax burden on the indigenous population in the early 1920s.[47] Yet, we can ascertain the extent of the burden from the Chinese newspapers published before and after the introduction of the new taxes, including evidence from the first half of the 1920s when the colonial government introduced the war-profit tax and property tax. The following paragraphs will discuss these taxes and how the Chinese population reacted to them.

The Netherlands East Indies Government officially introduced the war-profit tax in 1917 through a decree, *Staatsblad 1917 No. 592*.[48] The tax was part of a package of crisis regulations designed to address government losses incurred in the last two years of World War I, when exports of colonial products and the import trade were seriously disrupted by a shortage of shipping capacity due to German submarine warfare.[49] The tax was levied progressively, reaching, at its highest, a rate of 30 per cent of the short-term profits of individuals (and corporations) made during the first two to three years of the war. During this time, the colonial economy benefited from the enormous increase in world market prices, combined with the Netherlands'

---

47   The surveys were launched under the framework of the 'Ethical Policy', as the colonial government considered overtaxation was contributing to the diminishing welfare of indigenous people. See C.J. Hasselman, *Algemeen Overzicht van de Uitkomsten van het Welvaart-Onderzoek Gehouden op Java en Madoera in 1904–1905: Opgemaakt Ingevolge Opdracht van Zijne Excellentie den Minister van Koloniën* [*General Overview of the Results of the Welfare Research in Java and Madura 1904–1905: Drawn Up by Order of His Excellency the Minister of Colonies*], Koloniaal Verslag [Colonial Report] 1907–1908 ('s-Gravenhage: Martinus Nijhoff, 1914); Meijer Ranneft and Huender, *Investigation into the Tax Burden on the Native Population*; and Frans Hüsken, 'Declining Welfare in Java: Government and Private Inquiries, 1903–1914', in *The Late Colonial State in Indonesia: Political and Economic Foundation of the Netherlands Indies, 1880–1942*, ed. Robert Cribb (Leiden: KITLV Press, 1994), 213–27.

48   Arsip Nasional Republik Indonesia [National Archives of the Republic of Indonesia] [hereinafter ANRI], *Arsip Algemene Secretarie serie Grote Bundel Besluit* [*General Secretariat Archive Large Bundle Decree Series*], 1891–1942, Nomor Inventaris 3683, No. Arsip Bt. 1941-07-31/30, Inkomstenbelasting, Bedrijfs – en Patentbelasting [Income Tax, Corporate and Patent Tax].

49   van Zanden and Marks, *An Economic History of Indonesia*, 97. Despite the Netherlands East Indies not being involved directly in World War I and taking a neutral stance, the war in Europe affected 'the domestic political situation, the relationship between motherland and the colony, and the economic performance of the Netherlands Indies'. See Kees van Dijk, *The Netherlands Indies and the Great War, 1914–1918* (Leiden: KITLV Press, 2007), doi.org/10.26530/oapen_389234, at vii.

neutral position in the war, which allowed it to continue doing business normally, bringing high profits and high demand, such as the lucrative exports of commodities like oil, sugar and rubber.[50]

This means individual businesspeople or enterprises engaged in export–import trade received most of the benefits and profits from this wartime condition; hence, they were the targets of the war-profit tax. It can be assumed that the Chinese businesspeople were the main payers of this levy for two reasons: first, they played a significant role in the export–import sector in the East Indies; and second, many Dutch individuals and enterprises were exempt from the tax because their registered offices were in the Netherlands, so they paid tax there. Indeed, the archives show many Chinese businesspeople in the East Indies were liable for this tax. With its high rate of 30 per cent implemented progressively, the war-profit tax turned out to be a major blow for Chinese businesspeople. Many failed to pay their tax assessments on time and faced penalties, from amercements and confiscation of assets to imprisonment.[51]

The archive of the Department of Finance provides detailed examples of the effects of these taxes. In one case, Soen Bie Seng, the owner of a trading company in Batavia, had to pay war-profit tax of $f7,560$ in 1918 and $f36,780$ in 1919. Soen Bie Seng paid the bill in two instalments: $f10,000$ in October and $f1,591$ in November 1919. This was less than half the bill, leaving another $f25,189$ to be paid. Soen Bie Seng was unable to pay the remainder by the deadline and, as a result, his company was sealed, his assets were taken over and he was sent to jail.[52] Another case was that of N.V. Sin Hong Ho from Semarang, which operated as an exporter of agricultural products like sugar, peanuts and coffee. This family company was registered to three owners: Lai Wong Poh, Thong Tek Li Sip and Eng Jo Sip. After a thorough examination, it was revealed that the company had to pay a total tax bill of $f525,306.65$ as an accumulated tax debt from 1914 to 1918. The company set out to pay this enormous sum at the end of 1919 but failed. As a result, the company's legal permit to operate was

---

50   A report reveals that, from 1917 until 1923, the colonial government collected total revenue as high as $f193$ million from this tax. It was abolished in 1923, when the world economy had recovered its normal conditions. J.L. Vleming and J. van Gelderen, *Theorie en Praktijk van de Indische Belastingen, Lezingen Gehouden te Weltevreden in de Openbare Vergadering van 4 April 1923* [*Theory and Practice of the Indies Taxation, Lectures Delivered in Weltevreden in the Public Meeting on 4 April 1923*] (Weltevreden: Indonesisch Drukkerij, 1923), 13.
51   ANRI, *Arsip Financiën* [*Financial Archives*], No. Inventaris 392, 'Catatan global pajak laba perang 1919 [Global Notes of War Profits 1919]'.
52   ANRI, *Arsip Financiën* [*Financial Archives*], No. Inventaris 413, 'Pajak Laba Perang [War Profit Tax]'.

annulled, its assets were frozen and the owners were sent to jail.⁵³ Revealing the serious consequences of the tax problem, a study shows that some Chinese individuals tried to manipulate the auditing process of their profits or, in extreme cases, to flee Java or the East Indies for good. This is what Oei Tiong Ham, one of the richest Chinese in the East Indies, did in 1918, fleeing to Singapore.⁵⁴

From the examples above, it is clear the war-profit tax was not only excessive for many Chinese businesspeople, but also harshly implemented—to the extent that the tax weakened the performance of Chinese enterprises, sometimes threatening their survival. It is no wonder Chinese businesspeople were unhappy with the tax, and critics popped up in the newspapers and in the Volksraad ('People's Council') through their representatives. The *Sin Po* weekly edition of 27 October 1923, for example, criticised the timing and the way the tax was collected. Although *Sin Po* accepted the government's reason for levying the war-profit tax, they insisted it was introduced at the wrong time, when trade, the market and economic conditions were beginning to decline. *Sin Po* also criticised the government's method of levying and collecting the tax, stating it was done too late, because the profits incurred by businesses had already been spent. Many Chinese had spent their wartime profits and then lost their capital due to the worsening economic conditions in the last year of World War I. For them, the tax rate was excessive, the assessment system was imperfect and the timing was unreasonable. As a result, *Sin Po* concludes:

> [T]raders, especially those who don't understand and are afraid to have an issue with the government, become so frightened and worried, while that kind of fear and concern have already killed their spirit and contentedness to engage in trade. Because of all this, a lot of capital disappeared.⁵⁵

---

53   ANRI, *Arsip Financiën* [*Financial Archives*], No. Inventaris 414, 'Pemeriksaan Buku Perusahaan-perusahaan [Inspection of Companies' Books]'. This bundle contains more than 100 companies that had an issue with the war-profit tax. Most were Chinese companies or individuals, but there were also a few Dutch and other Europeans who struggled with this tax.
54   Jamie Mackie, 'Towkays and Tycoons: The Chinese in Indonesian Economic Life in the 1920s and 1980s', *Indonesia* [SI] (July 1991): 83–96, doi.org/10.2307/3351256, at 87.
55   '[O]rang-orang dagang, teroetama jang koerang mengarti dan takoet beroeroesan dengan Pamarentah, djadi sanget katakoetan dan berkoatir, samentara ini perasaan takoet dan koeatir soeda boenoeh sebagian marika poenja napsoe dan kagoembirahan dalem perdagangan. Banjak kapitaal jang djadi mandek lantaran ini.' 'Belasting-belasting [Taxes]', *Sin Po: Wekelijksche Editie* [Weekly edition], 23 October 1923.

While the dust around the war-profit tax was still far from settled, the Chinese were shocked by the government's plan to introduce a new unified income tax and tax on luxury goods for those living in Batavia and its surrounds.

As discussed in the opening of this chapter, the Chinese were unhappy with the government's plan and organised a demonstration to object. *Sin Po*, as the most influential Chinese newspaper, also contributed to this movement by voicing the grievances of the Chinese in Batavia and providing harsh criticism of the government. In the edition of 23 October 1923, *Sin Po* suspected the real reason the government was introducing new taxes was because of its own 'lavish expenditure and its incompetent financial management'.[56] In other editions, *Sin Po* openly characterised the government tax policies as constituting a situation in which it was '*oedjan belasting*' ('raining taxes'),[57] they were '*bajar belasting doea kali*' ('paying tax twice')[58] and paying '*belasting bersoesoen-soesoen*' ('multilayered taxes').[59] All this evidence reflects the prevalent feeling among the Chinese population that the Netherlands East Indies Government's tax policies were unjust and excessive towards the Chinese. These criticisms highlight the link between racial categories and economic exploitation in the capitalist colonial system.

Yet, after 1926, these kinds of criticisms disappeared from newspapers, as the colonial government imposed stricter press surveillance. The Chinese 'fight' against the government's tax policies did not stop but continued through formal institutions like the Siang Hwee ('Chamber of Commerce') and by Chinese representatives in the Volksraad. Minutes of the Volksraad meetings, especially those concerning the East Indies' annual budget, show how Chinese representatives like Hok Hoe Kan, Khouw Kim An and Loa Sek Hie tried their best to voice the interests of their constituents on the burden of taxation and other related issues. In cooperation with Indonesian senators, they raised the tax issue as part of the *anti-Nederlands-onderdaanschap* ('anti-Dutch nationality') campaign, and later as part of a petition to the Dutch Government to give the East Indies government greater autonomy.[60]

---

56 'Pemandangan Oemoem tentang Malaise [General View on Malaise (Crises)]', *Sin Po: Wekelijksche Editie* [Weekly edition], 23 October 1923.
57 'The Raining of Taxes', *Sin Po*.
58 'Bajar Belasting Doea Kali [Paying Tax Twice]', *Sin Po: Wekelijksche Editie* [Weekly edition], 7 March 1925.
59 'Multilayered Tax', *Sin Po*.
60 Suryadinata, *Peranakan Chinese Politics in Java*, 34; Mona Lohanda, *The Kapitan Cina of Batavia, 1837–1942: A History of Chinese Establishment in Colonial Society* (Jakarta: Djambatan, 1996), 150.

Despite their advocacy, there were no substantial changes to the government's tax policies until the end of the Dutch colonial period. The Chinese had almost no option but to obey as 'Dutch subjects' and pay all the taxes. Their grievances were met with the 'iron hand' of the colonial government, which used its legal and administrative instruments to constrain the bargaining position of the Chinese, while exploiting their indispensable economic resources. This situation confirms the premise of the classic theory of a middleman minority, which assumes that the Chinese in colonial Java and elsewhere were trapped between the colonisers and the colonised; they had to serve the interests of the superior Dutch colonisers with very limited power to launch expressions of dissent and link the indigenous producers with local or regional markets, on the one hand, and sometimes with the colonial administration on the other. Until the end of the colonial period, the Chinese position remained unchanged; most were confined to the middleman-trading minority, although an increasing number of Western-educated members of the younger generation began to occupy the newly emerging professions in urban areas.[61] In the longer run, this 'legal pluralism' upheld racial ideology, with grievous consequences, because it fed into indigenous resentment of the Chinese, which often led to violence.

From a fiscal point of view, the position of the Chinese as primary taxpayers in the colony remained constant as they continued to be one of the main targets of government taxation. Despite the political turmoil and regime change that took place in the 1940s, relatively little changed regarding political and administrative functions. The Japanese military regime (1942–45) and the competing authorities in the revolutionary period (1945–49)—both the Dutch and the Indonesian Republic—manipulated both the economic wealth of Chinese people and their political weakness for their own benefit. In such a difficult situation, whatever political stand the Chinese took to defend themselves brought unfavourable consequences, particularly a series of violent attacks.[62] Yet, a separate study is needed of the Chinese fiscal position during this transitional period of modern Indonesia.

---

61   Wertheim, *East–West Parallels*, 42–82; Wahid, 'From Revenue Farming to State Monopoly', 179–80.
62   See Mary Somer Heidhuis, 'Anti-Chinese Violence in Java during the Indonesian Revolution, 1945–49', in *Colonial Counterinsurgency and Mass Violence: The Dutch Empire in Indonesia*, eds Bart Luttikhuis and A. Dirk Moses (London: Routledge, 2014), 155–76, doi.org/10.4324/9781315767345-8.

Conclusion

This chapter has shown how, in the last three decades of the colonial period, through the Netherlands East Indies' taxation system, the Dutch exploited the Chinese population along with indigenous people. Driven by desperate financial shortages due to the high military expenditures on the Aceh and Lombok conquests, the ambitious infrastructure projects of the Ethical Policy and shifting global economic conditions before, during and after World War I, the Netherlands East Indies Government in the first decade of the twentieth century sought alternative sources of revenue. It introduced tax reform and new taxes as solutions to the financial problems. While the tax-reform programs were presented as rational, efficient and fair, the introduction of new taxes was in fact driven by the desire for more revenue to drive Dutch economic development. The introduction of the war-profit tax is a good example. Introduced during World War I, it was designed to progressively tax profits realised by individuals and companies during the war years thanks to rocketing prices for oil, sugar, rubber and so on due to high global demand. The tax was levied over a short period on a very pragmatic basis; it therefore reflects the dual 'face' of the colonial state—namely, its innovative but also greedy nature in finding new sources of revenue.

From this new taxation, the colonial government collected a significant sum of revenue, but mostly at the cost of the Chinese population. Sociopolitically constructed as 'foreigners' and economically as intermediaries between indigenous peasants and Europeans, the Chinese became the primary taxpayers in the colony. Their economic power was targeted through various taxes, both old and new, introduced by the central or local governments. By 1920, the Chinese found themselves overtaxed, with their tax burden increasing all the time. Despite their difficult minority status, the Chinese resisted and began to express their grievances, by protesting via newspapers, street demonstrations or petitions in formal institutions like the Chamber of Commerce and the Volksraad. All these efforts were fruitless, however, as the colonial government continued with its tax program, ignoring the outcry of Chinese and indigenous taxpayers.

This chapter shows how the coloniality of power worked in the colonial political structure, within which the Chinese were placed as 'foreigners', and how this constrained and weakened their bargaining position, making them 'constantly exploited'. The institutionalisation of this sociopolitical structure, keeping the Chinese weak politically while exploiting them economically, became one of the most problematic but long-lasting legacies in postcolonial Indonesia and thus an enduring feature of coloniality.

References

Primary sources

Algemeen handelsblad voor Nederlandsch-Indië. 1924. 'Een Massa-Demonstratie [A Mass Demonstration].' *Algemeen handelsblad voor Nederlandsch-Indië [General Trade Magazine for the Dutch East Indies]*, 11 September.

Arsip Nasional Republik Indonesia [National Archives of the Republic of Indonesia] (ANRI). n.d. *Arsip Financiën [Financial Archives]*, No. Inventaris 413, 'Pajak Laba Perang [War Profit Tax].' Jakarta: National Archives of the Republic of Indonesia.

ANRI. n.d. *Arsip Financiën [Financial Archives]*, No. Inventaris 414, 'Pemeriksaan Buku Perusahaan-perusahaan [Inspection of Companies' Books].' Jakarta: National Archives of the Republic of Indonesia.

ANRI. 1891–1942. *Arsip Algemene Secretarie serie Grote Bundel Besluit [General Secretariat Archive Large Bundle Decree Series]*, 1891–1942, Nomor Inventaris 3683, No. Arsip Bt. 1941-07-31/30. Inkomstenbelasting, Bedrijfs – en Patentbelasting [Income Tax, Corporate and Patent Tax]. Jakarta: National Archives of the Republic of Indonesia.

ANRI. 1919. *Arsip Financiën [Financial Archives]*, No. Inventaris 392, 'Catatan Global Pajak Laba Perang 1919 [Global Notes of War Profits 1919].' Jakarta: National Archives of the Republic of Indonesia.

Departement van Economische Zaken [Department of Economic Affairs]. 1931. *Volkstelling 1930 [Census 1930]. Volume VII.* Batavia: Landsdrukkerij.

Encyclopaedie van Nederlandsch-Indië [Encyclopedia of the Netherlands Indies]. 1905. Parts 1–4. 's-Gravenhage/Leiden: Nijhoff/Brill.

Hasselman, C.J. 1914. *Algemeen Overzicht van de Uitkomsten van het Welvaart-Onderzoek, Gehouden op Java en Madoera in 1904-1905: Opgemaakt Ingevolge Opdracht van Zijne Excellentie den Minister van Koloniën [General Overview of the Results of the Welfare Research in Java and Madura 1904–1905: Drawn Up by Order of His Excellency the Minister of Colonies]*. Koloniaal Verslag [Colonial Report] 1907–1908. 's-Gravenhage: Nijhoff.

Meijer Ranneft, J.W., and W. Huender. 1926. *Onderzoek naar den Belastingdruk op de Inlandsche Bevolking [Investigation into the Tax Burden on the Native Population]*. Weltevreden, Java: Landsdrukkerij.

Sin Po. 1923. 'Belasting-belasting [Taxes].' *Sin Po: Wekelijksche Editie* [Weekly edition], 23 October.

Sin Po. 1923. 'Pemandangan Oemoem tentang Malaise [General View on Malaise (Crises)].' *Sin Po: Wekelijksche Editie* [Weekly edition], 23 October.

Sin Po. 1924. 'Demonstrasi Oeroesan Belasting [Demonstration on Tax Matters].' *Sin Po: Wekelijksche Editie* [Weekly edition], 13 September.

Sin Po. 1925. 'Oedjan Belasting [The Raining of Taxes].' *Sin Po: Wekelijksche Editie* [Weekly edition], 21 February.

Sin Po. 1925. 'Bajar Belasting Doea Kali [Paying Tax Twice].' *Sin Po: Wekelijksche Editie* [Weekly edition], 7 March.

Sin Po. 1926. 'Belasting Bersoesoen-soesoen [Multilayered Tax].' *Sin Po: Wekelijksche Editie* [Weekly edition], 15 May.

Secondary sources

Althusser, Louis. 2006. 'Ideology and Ideological State Apparatuses (Notes Towards an Investigation).' In *The Anthropology of the State: A Reader*, edited by Aradhana Sharma and Akhil Gupta, 86–111. Malden: Blackwell Publishing.

Blussé, Leonard. 1986. *Strange Company: Chinese Settlers, Mestizo Women, and the Dutch in VOC Batavia*. KITLV Verhandelingen Series No. 122. Leiden: KITLV/Foris Publications.

Bonacich, Edna. 1973. 'A Theory of Middleman Minorities.' *American Sociological Review* 38, no. 5: 583–94. doi.org/10.2307/2094409.

Boomgaard, P., and A.J. Gooszen. 1991. *Changing Economy in Indonesia. Volume 11: Population Trends, 1795–1942*. Amsterdam: Royal Tropical Institute.

Booth, Anne. 1980. 'The Burden of Taxation in Colonial Indonesia in the Twentieth Century.' *Journal of Southeast Asian Studies* 11, no. 1: 91–109. doi.org/10.1017/S0022463400019007.

Booth, Anne. 1998. *The Indonesian Economy in the Nineteenth and Twentieth Centuries: A History of Missed Opportunities*. London: Palgrave Macmillan. doi.org/10.1057/9780333994962.

Booth, Anne. 2014. 'Land Taxation in Asia: An Overview of the 19th and 20th Centuries.' *Oxford Development Studies* 42, no. 1: 1–18. doi.org/10.1080/136 00818.2014.880413.

Booth, Anne. 2016. *Economic Change in Modern Indonesia: Colonial and Post-Colonial Comparison.* Cambridge: Cambridge University Press. doi.org/10.1017/ CBO9781316271438.

Butcher, John, and Howard Dick, eds. 1993. *The Rise and Fall of Revenue Farming: Business Elites and the Emergence of the Modern State in Southeast Asia.* London: Palgrave Macmillan. doi.org/10.1007/978-1-349-22877-5.

Chirot, Daniel, and Anthony Reid, eds. 1997. *Essential Outsiders: Chinese and Jews in the Modern Transformation of Southeast Asia and Central Europe.* Seattle: University of Washington Press.

Colombijn, Freek. 1995. 'The Colonial Municipal Council in Padang (Sumatra) as Political Arena.' *Journal of Southeast Asian Studies* 26, no. 2: 263–88. doi.org/ 10.1017/S0022463400007104.

Cribb, Robert, and Audrey Kahin. 2004. *Historical Dictionary of Indonesia.* Lanham: Scarecrow Press.

Dick, Howard. 1993. 'A Fresh Approach to Southeast Asian History.' In *The Rise and Fall of Revenue Farming: Business Elites and the Emergence of the Modern State in Southeast Asia*, edited by John Butcher and Howard Dick, 3–18. London: Palgrave Macmillan. doi.org/10.1007/978-1-349-22877-5_1.

Dick, Howard. 1993. 'Oei Tiong Ham.' In *The Rise and Fall of Revenue Farming: Business Elites and the Emergence of the Modern State in Southeast Asia*, edited by John Butcher and Howard Dick, 272–80. London: Palgrave Macmillan. doi.org/ 10.1007/978-1-349-22877-5_18.

Diehl, Fritz W. 1993. 'Revenue Farming and Colonial Finances in the Netherlands East Indies, 1816–1925.' In *The Rise and Fall of Revenue Farming: Business Elites and the Emergence of the Modern State in Southeast Asia*, edited by John Butcher and Howard Dick, 196–232. London: Palgrave Macmillan. doi.org/ 10.1007/978-1-349-22877-5_12.

Dobbin, Christine. 1996. *Asian Entrepreneurial Minorities: Conjoint Communities in the Making of the World Economy, 1570–1940.* London: Curzon.

Fasseur, Cees. 1994. 'Cornerstone and Stumbling Block: Racial Classification and the Late Colonial State in Indonesia.' In *The Late Colonial State in Indonesia: Political and Economic Foundation of the Netherlands Indies, 1880–1942*, edited by Robert Cribb, 31–56. Leiden: KITLV Press.

Fernando, M.R., and David Bulbeck, eds. 1992. *Chinese Economic Activity in Netherlands India: Selected Translations from the Dutch.* Singapore: ISEAS. doi.org/10.1355/9789814379410.

Frankema, Ewout, and Anne Booth, eds. 2020. *Fiscal Capacity and the Colonial State in Asia and Africa, c. 1850–1960.* Cambridge: Cambridge University Press. doi.org/10.1017/9781108665001.

Gaastra, Femme S. 2003. *The Dutch East India Company: Expansion and Decline.* Zutphen: Waalburg Press.

Heidhuis, Mary Somer. 2014. 'Anti-Chinese Violence in Java during the Indonesian Revolution, 1945–49.' In *Colonial Counterinsurgency and Mass Violence: The Dutch Empire in Indonesia*, edited by Bart Luttikhuis and A. Dirk Moses, 155–76. London: Routledge. doi.org/10.4324/9781315767345-8.

Hugenholtz, W.R. 1994. 'The Landrent Question and its Solution, 1850–1920.' In *The Late Colonial State in Indonesia: Political and Economic Foundation of the Netherlands Indies, 1880–1942*, edited by Robert Cribb, 139–72. Leiden: KITLV Press.

Hüsken, Frans. 1994. 'Declining Welfare in Java: Government and Private Inquiries, 1903–1914.' In *The Late Colonial State in Indonesia: Political and Economic Foundation of the Netherlands Indies, 1880–1942*, edited by Robert Cribb, 213–27. Leiden: KITLV Press.

Kartodirdjo, Sartono. 1973. *Protest Movement in Rural Java: A Study of Agrarian Unrest in the Nineteenth and Early Twentieth Centuries.* Singapore: Oxford University Press.

Kartodirdjo, Sartono. 1981. *Laporan-laporan tentang Gerakan Protes di Jawa pada Abad-XX [Reports on the Protest Movement in Java in the Twentieth Century].* Jakarta: National Archives of the Republic of Indonesia.

Kartodirdjo, Sartono. 2014. *Pengantar Sejarah Indonesia Baru: Sejarah Pergerakan Nasional [Introduction to New Indonesian History: History of the National Movement].* Yogyakarta: Penerbit Ombak.

Kwartanada, Didi. 2013. 'The Tiong Hoa Hwee Koan School: A Transborder Project of Modernity in Batavia, c. 1900s.' In *Chinese Indonesians Reassessed: History, Religion and Belonging*, edited by Siew-Min Sai and Chang-Yau Hoon, 27–44. London: Routledge.

Lohanda, Mona. 1996. *The Kapitan Cina of Batavia, 1837–1942: A History of Chinese Establishment in Colonial Society.* Jakarta: Djambatan.

Lugones, María. 2010. 'Toward a Decolonial Feminism.' *Hypatia* 25, no. 4: 742–59. doi.org/10.1111/j.1527-2001.2010.01137.x.

Mackie, Jamie. 1991. 'Towkays and Tycoons: The Chinese in Indonesian Economic Life in the 1920s and 1980s.' *Indonesia* [SI] (July): 83–96. doi.org/10.2307/3351256.

Manse, Maarten. 2021. 'From Headhunting to Head Taxes: Violence, Taxation and Colonial Governance on Seram, c. 1860–1920.' *Bijdragen tot de Taal-, Land- en Volkenkunde* [*Journal of the Humanities and Social Sciences of Southeast Asia*] 177, no. 4: 524–58. doi.org/10.1163/22134379-bja10023.

Manse, Maarten. 2021. 'Promise, Pretence and Pragmatism: Governance and Taxation in Colonial Indonesia, 1870–1940.' PhD diss., Leiden University, Netherlands.

Mansvelt, W.M.F., and Pieter Creutzberg, eds. 1987. *Changing Economy in Indonesia. Volume 7: Balance of Payments, 1823–1939*. The Hague: Martinus Nijhoff.

Ong Eng Die. 1943. *Chineezen in Nederlands-Indië: Sociografie van Een Indonesische Bevolkingsgroep* [*The Chinese in the Netherlands Indies: Sociography of an Indonesian Population Group*]. Assen: Van Gorchum & Co.

Onghokham. 1977. 'Pulung Affair: Pemberontakan Pajak di Desa Patik, Beberapa Aspek Politik di Madiun Pada Abad ke-19 [Pulung Affair: Tax Rebellion in Patik Village, Several Political Aspects in Madiun in the Nineteenth Century].' *Majalah Ilmu-ilmu Sastra Indonesia* [*Indonesian Literary Sciences Magazine*] 7, no. 1: 1–25.

Onghokham. 1985. 'Pajak Dalam Perspektif Sejarah [Tax in Historical Perspective].' *Prisma* 14, no. 4 (April): 74–85.

Paulus, J., ed. 1917. *Encyclopaedie van Nederlandsch-Indie. Volume 1*. Leiden: E.J. Brill.

Raben, Remco. 2010. 'Decolonization and the Democratic Moment in Southeast Asia.' Paper presented to Eclipse of Empires: Colonial Resistance, Metropolitan Decline and Imperial Crises in the 19th and 20th Centuries Conference, Universitat Pompeu Fabra, Barcelona, 2–3 June.

Ricklefs, Merle C. 2008. *A History of Modern Indonesia Since c. 1200*. 3rd edn. London: Bloomsbury Academic. doi.org/10.5040/9781350394582.

Rush, James. 1990. *Opium to Java: Revenue Farming and Chinese Enterprise in Colonial Indonesia 1860–1910*. Ithaca: Cornell University Press.

Salmon, Claudine. 1991. 'A Critical View of the Opium Farmers as Reflected in a Syair by Boen Sing Ho (Semarang 1889).' *Indonesia* [SI]: 25–52. doi.org/10.2307/3351253.

Shiraishi, Takashi. 1990. *An Age in Motion: Popular Radicalism in Java, 1912–1926*. Ithaca: Cornell University Press. doi.org/10.7591/9781501737848.

Suryadinata, Leo. 1981. *Peranakan Chinese Politics in Java, 1917–1942*. Singapore: NUS Press.

The Siauw Giap. 1989. 'Socio-Economic Role of the Chinese in Indonesia, 1820–1940.' In *Economic Growth in Indonesia, 1820–1940*, edited by Angus Maddison and Gé Prince, 159–202. Dordrecht: Foris Publications.

Tjiook-Liem, Patricia. 2009. *De Rechtspositie der Chinezen in Nederlands-Indië 1848–1942* [*The Legal Position of the Chinese in the Netherlands Indies, 1848–1942*]. Leiden: Leiden University Press.

van Dijk, Kees. 2007. *The Netherlands Indies and the Great War, 1914–1918*. Leiden: KITLV Press. doi.org/10.26530/oapen_389234.

van Zanden, Jan L., and Daan Marks. 2012. *An Economic History of Indonesia, 1800–2010*. London: Routledge.

Visser, J. 1924. *Overzicht van het Belastingwezen van Nederlandsch-Indië: Voor Onderwijs en Praktijk* [*Overview of the Netherlands Indies' Tax System: For Education and Practice*]. Batavia: Van Dorp & Co.

Vleming, J.L., and J. van Gelderen. 1923. *Theorie en Praktijk van de Indische Belastingen: lezingen gehouden te Weltevreden in de openbare vergadering van 4 April 1923* [*Theory and Practice of the Indies Taxation, Lectures Delivered in Weltevreden in the Public Meeting on 4 April 1923*]. Weltevreden: Indonesisch Drukkerij.

Wahid, Abdul. 2014. 'From Revenue Farming to State Monopoly: The Political Economy of Taxation in Colonial Indonesia, 1816–1942.' *Bulletin of Indonesian Economic Studies* 50, no. 2: 194-95. doi.org/10.1080/00074918.2014.896245.

Wahid, Abdul. 2018. 'City and "Colonial Governance" in Late Colonial Indonesia: Towards an Agenda for Historical Research.' *Paramita: Historical Studies Journal* 28, no. 1: 25–37.

Wertheim, Wim F. 1964. *East–West Parallels: Sociological Approaches to Modern Asia*. The Hague: W. van Hoeve.

Williams, Lea E. 1960. *Overseas Chinese Nationalism: The Genesis of Pan-Chinese Nationalism in Indonesia, 1900–1916*. Glencoe: The Free Press.

Willmott, Donald E. 1956. *The National Status of the Chinese in Indonesia*. Ithaca: Cornell University Press.

Young, Ken. 1994. *Islamic Peasants and the State: The 1908 Anti-Tax Rebellion in West Sumatra*. Yale Center for International and Area Studies Monograph No. 40. New Haven: Yale University Press.

3

Locating colonial Indonesia in colonial Ceylon: Geography, language and belonging

Ronit Ricci

What constituted colonial Indonesia? Where did its borders lie? When thinking about it, should we prioritise territory, descent, longings? And, further, how do the naming practices used over time—that is, 'Javanese', 'Indonesian', 'Malay'—shape our view of the past and obscure certain connections and affiliations? This chapter addresses these questions by focusing on a colonial Indonesian diaspora living in Ceylon (now Sri Lanka) in the late nineteenth century. Can a decolonial approach change the way we conceive of history?

When I set out to find traces of attachment to 'colonial Indonesia' within the diasporic community in Ceylon—known today as Sri Lanka Malays—I envisioned myself going through the pages of the yet-unstudied late-nineteenth-century newspaper *Wajah Selong*, published in Colombo in Malay and written in *jawi* (modified Arabic) script, noting all instances in which places and events in the Dutch East Indies were mentioned, drawing conclusions on attachments from afar. Such attachments, I reasoned, would point to an extension or expansion of the boundaries of what we usually conceive of as the colony, to encompass not only the multiple islands of the Indonesian archipelago, but also an additional small island known as the 'Gem of the Indian Ocean' or, more casually, Ceylon.

Ultimately, after reading all extant issues of the newspaper (published from 1895 to 1898), I had to concede that I would need to change course as the available evidence did not conform to my hypothesis. As a result, I would like to dedicate this chapter to some possible reasons 'Indonesia'—its sites and contemporary events—did not occupy the major role I had foreseen for it within the newspaper's pages. Furthermore, although geography and space as they found shape in the newspaper apparently are not the best lens to employ for better understanding a colonial diaspora like the Sri Lanka Malays, I wish to explore the ways in which *Wajah Selong* does offer alternative inroads that show us that the Malays' homelands in the Indonesian–Malay region and their historical, religious and cultural attachments to those lands played an important role in creating and maintaining their colonial-diasporic identity. Before addressing these questions, I begin with some background.

Introduction: A community rooted in colonial exile

Beginning in the late seventeenth and throughout the eighteenth centuries, the Dutch, who held control over parts of present-day Indonesia and Sri Lanka, sent people from across the archipelago to Ceylon as soldiers, convicts, servants and political exiles. Although coming from diverse backgrounds, the 'Indonesians' who arrived in Ceylon over time, and their descendants, gradually coalesced into a community who spoke and wrote in the Malay language—long the lingua franca of travel, trade, diplomacy and Islamisation across what we now term the Indonesian–Malay world.

The category of political exiles to Ceylon included many who belonged to the ruling elite in their homelands. For example, the Javanese King Amangkurat III, ruler of Mataram, was exiled in 1708 after a bitter struggle over the throne with his uncle, the future Pakubuwana I; the twenty-sixth Sultan of Gowa in South Sulawesi, Fakhruddin, was exiled in 1767 on charges of conspiring with the British to oppose the trading monopoly of the Dutch East India Company (Vereenigde Oostindische Compagnie, VOC) in eastern Indonesia; also exiled during the eighteenth century were, among others, the Prince of Bantam, the Crown Prince of Tidore and the King of Kupang. Even earlier, in 1684, the Dutch exiled Sheikh Yusuf of Makassar,

3. LOCATING COLONIAL INDONESIA IN COLONIAL CEYLON

a leader, religious scholar and 'saint' from Sulawesi.[1] These banishments must be seen within the larger framework of Dutch colonial policies for the removal of individuals who were perceived as a threat to the rulers' authority and punishing those who rose against Dutch rule by shipping them off to faraway places, often never to return. Such policies were applied often within the borders of present-day Indonesia: thus, for example, Pakubuwana VI, Susuhunan of Surakarta, was banished to Ambon in 1830, Tuanku Imam Bonjol of West Sumatra was sent in 1837 to Cianjur and later Ambon and Manado, while, most famously, Pangeran Diponegoro was exiled to Manado and later Makassar following his defeat in the Java War (1825–30). Therefore, whether sent to Dutch territories that would much later be declared as belonging to Indonesia or to those that would not, exile was a common plight and forms a historical phenomenon that transcends political geography when we now revisit histories of colonialism.[2]

In addition to political exiles whose numbers were not high but whose banishment was politically and symbolically significant, many of those sent to Ceylon were soldiers serving in colonial armies. When the British took over the island from the Dutch in 1796, they continued to employ soldiers from the Indonesian archipelago (and their descendants) who were already in Ceylon and to recruit new ones from Java, Madura and the Malay Peninsula.

In the early nineteenth century, Frederick North, Governor of Ceylon, established a special regiment for Malay men within the British colonial army on the island. Like other groups within colonised populations—for example, the Gurkhas and the Sikhs in British India (see also Protschky's Chapter 6 in this volume)—the Malays were viewed, since serving the Portuguese

---

1   On the history of exile to colonial Ceylon during the Dutch period and the development of a colonial Malay diaspora in Ceylon, with an emphasis on diasporic Malay literary culture, see Ronit Ricci, *Banishment and Belonging: Exile and Diaspora in Sarandib, Lanka and Ceylon* (Cambridge: Cambridge University Press, 2019), doi.org/10.1017/9781108648189. On the Sultan of Gowa and his family's life in Ceylon, see Suryadi, 'Sepucuk Surat dari Seorang Bangsawan Gowa di Tanah Pembuangan (Ceylon) [A Letter from a Gowa Noblewoman in the Land of Exile (Ceylon)]', *Wacana: Jurnal Ilmu Pengetahuan Budaya* [*Wacana: Journal of the Humanities of Indonesia*] 10, no. 2 (2008): 214–45, doi.org/10.17510/wjhi.v10i2.194.

2   Even further afield than Ceylon lay another site of exile, the Cape in South Africa (*Nagari Kap*), which was under VOC rule from 1652 to 1795. On forced migration from the Dutch territories in the archipelago to the Cape, see Kerry Ward, *Networks of Empire: Forced Migration in the Dutch East India Company* (Cambridge: Cambridge University Press, 2009), doi.org/10.1017/CBO9780511551628. On the Cape Malays and their religious and literary culture, see Saarah Jappie, 'JAWI DARI JAUH: "Malays" in South Africa through Text', *Indonesia and the Malay World* 40, no. 117 (2012): 143–59, doi.org/10.1080/13639811.2012.683675. A comparative study of the Sri Lankan Malays and Cape Malays is very much warranted but has not been carried out to date.

in Ceylon in the sixteenth and seventeenth centuries, as a 'martial race', admired and often feared for their bravery, determination and brutality.[3] The Malay Regiment was active for several decades until its disbandment in 1873. During these years, it formed a central pillar of community life, with 75 per cent of men and boys serving in it for varying periods, their families living in nearby barracks and religious and literary works in the Malay language written, copied and taught within the regiment's sphere. This last tendency is evidenced in extant nineteenth-century Malay manuscripts in Sri Lanka, many of which attest to ownership by members or retirees of the regiment.[4] While the regiment's loyalty in service and battle was to the British Empire, such manuscripts show a strong, ongoing bond to the literary, linguistic and Islamic traditions of the Indonesian archipelago.

Also important to note is the question of nomenclature. Clearly, there was no Indonesia to speak of in the late nineteenth century and even the borders of the colony had not reached their final limits. Therefore, speaking of an 'Indonesian diaspora' in Ceylon is an anachronism. At the same time, as noted, the 'Malay' community's origins were diverse and encompassed many parts of the archipelago and the Malay Peninsula, so imagining a map that includes their many places of origin conjures a space that is more like Indonesia than any other single state. In his *Syair Faid al-Abad* (*Bounty of the Ages*), a work written in the poetic *syair* metre at the turn of the twentieth century and recounting the community's past in Ceylon, author Baba Ounus Saldin depicted the warriors sent by the British to fight the Kandy Wars thus:[5]

> *Dikirimnya orang ke tanah sabrang dari Betawi Bugis Semarang*
> *Banten Ternate Petani Palembang Tuban Padang Pariaman Kelantan Pulau Penang*[6]

---

3   Anonymous, *Jubilee Book of the Malay Cricket Club* (Colombo: Ceylon Malay Cricket Club, 1924), 158.
4   On the establishment of the Malay Regiment and its subsequent history and demise, see B.A. Hussainmiya, *Orang Regimen: The Malays of the Ceylon Rifle Regiment* (Bangi: Universiti Kebangsaan Malaysia Press, 1990), doi.org/10.1017/s0022463400003003.
5   The Kandy Wars were a series of wars fought against the last sovereign king in Ceylon, Sri Vikrama Rajasinha, in the early nineteenth century, ending several centuries of European engagement with the highland kingdom of Kandy. On these wars and the Malays' complex roles within them, serving on both sides, see Ricci, *Banishment and Belonging*, 181–217.
6   Baba Ounus Saldin, *Syair Faid al-Abad* [*Bounty of the Ages*] (Colombo: Alamat Langkapuri Press, 1905). For a study of some historical and literary aspects of the *Syair*, see Ronit Ricci, 'Along the Frontiers of Religion, Language and War: Baba Ounus Saldin's Syair Faid al-Abad', in *The Routledge Companion to World Literature and World History*, ed. May Hawas (London: Routledge, 2018), 82–92, doi.org/10.4324/9781315686271-7.

> They sent people off to foreign lands from Batavia, south Sulawesi, Semarang
>
> Banten, Ternate, Patani, Palembang Tuban, Padang, Pariaman, Kelantan, Penang Island.

It is beyond our scope here to consider the gradual process through which this diversity of origins came under the umbrella term 'Malay'. Suffice to note that some seventeenth and eighteenth-century Dutch records refer to people from the archipelago as 'Easterners' (*Oosterlingen*)—another blanket term—while others mention the category 'Javanese' and yet others contain a broader range of appellations, including 'Balinese', 'Makassarese', 'Madurese', 'Ambonese' and 'Buginese'. In the late nineteenth century and into the twentieth, at the very least, the twin affiliations *Melayu* ('Malay') and *Jawa* (or *Ja*, 'Javanese') were still employed in Ceylon, and their use depended, in part, on the language in which one was speaking and describing the community.[7]

The point I wish to emphasise here is that naming is rarely neutral but rather is the result and expression of certain circumstances, agendas and struggles. The naming of 'Chinese Indonesians' is perhaps the most debated and contentious example in modern Indonesian historiography but there are others, including *Belanda Hitam* ('Black Dutchmen') (see McGregor's Chapter 7 in this volume), 'Foreign Orientals', '*priyayi*' (elite Javanese), among others, and the use of 'Malay' in colonial Ceylon is no doubt another case in point. Within a discussion of history and its revisiting, questions about the naming of groups and categories of people must be acknowledged and explored: Who holds the power to name? How, when and why do names change? How do names employed in a colonial context continue to inform the decolonial present?

'Wajah Selong': A brief introduction

The biweekly newspaper *Wajah Selong* was published in Colombo from 1895 to 1898 by Baba Ounus Saldin, leader of the Malay community, religious scholar, author and publisher.[8] To the best of my knowledge, only

---
7   For an expanded discussion, see Ronit Ricci, 'Jawa, Melayu, Malay or Otherwise? The Shifting Nomenclature of the Sri Lankan Malays', *Indonesia and the Malay World* 44, no. 130 (2016): 68–80, doi.org/10.1080/13639811.2016.1219491.
8   For autobiographical writing by Saldin, see Baba Ounus Saldin, *Kitab Segala Peringatan* [*A Book of Memories*], MS 137 (Kuala Lumpur: Dewan Bahasa dan Pustaka Library, n.d.).

a single, incomplete set of copies survives, housed at the National Archives of Sri Lanka.[9] A forerunner of this newspaper, one of the world's earliest in Malay and titled *Alamat Langkapuri*, was published in the same city and by the same man in 1869–70 and 1877–78. Despite this, and despite both being written in Malay using the *jawi* script, a clear shift is evident between the two newspapers: the *Alamat Langkapuri* was more locally focused, with most of its items pertaining to the Malay community in Ceylon and events and developments in that colony, while *Wajah Selong* took a more international perspective and was also disseminated across a much larger region, with agents hired in several cities in Java, Sumatra, Singapore, the Malay Peninsula and Siam (Thailand). *Wajah Selong* thus focused less specifically on Ceylon's Malays, but was also more connected to a wider Indonesian–Malay world and its dissemination had the potential to foster networks of shared knowledge and perspective, creating what Benedict Anderson dubbed 'imagined communities'.[10] Thinking in terms of a colonial diaspora and its identity, and its links to a 'home country', *Wajah Selong* therefore offered both less and more than its predecessor. More broadly, the modern newspaper was a new item on the older list of means by which the Malays maintained ties to the archipelago and Southeast Asia via trade, exile and return, the *hajj* and military deployment.

Wajah Selong's distribution pattern was, as mentioned, different from that of *Alamat Langkapuri*. Saldin did not explicitly reflect on his motives for this change in his memoir or in his other available writings, but a recurring theme in *Alamat Langkapuri* was his plea to subscribers to pay their dues; indeed, he had to shut the operation because of financial difficulties. The need for a more stable financial basis for his press may have encouraged him to cast his net more widely. The newspaper was also used to advance additional business interests of its publisher and editor, including the printing and sale of books in Malay, Tamil and Arabic, and advertising various goods for export or import such as silk sarongs from Java and precious stones and

---

9   The set was catalogued under the wrong title and therefore, despite many visits to the archives, I was unaware of its availability until 2017. This could be viewed as a negligible anecdote but points to a significant issue: materials written in the *jawi*/Arabic script could not be read or recognised by any of the National Archives' staff, so have been doomed to further marginalisation and loss within the institution charged with the preservation of Sri Lanka's documented history, mirroring the marginality of the Malays within the national narrative and contemporary political life. The fact that *Wajah Selong* was published only for a brief period and that not all issues survived make reading the entire source possible but also limit the scope of analysis and the ability to draw definitive conclusions. Nonetheless, it provides insights and information that would be difficult to access elsewhere.
10   Benedict Anderson, *Imagined Communities: Reflections on the Origin and Spread of Nationalism* (London: Verso, 1991).

wooden furniture from Ceylon. *Wajah Selong* employed agents (*wakil*) in Singapore (responsible also for Java, Sumatra and cities to the east), Penang, Malacca, Sungai Ujung and Siam, and these sites are mentioned often by name in the newspaper's issues.

For example, in the issue published on 27 September 1896, we read:

> *Segala wakil kepada surat* Wajah Selong
>
> *Bahwa wakil kepada surat ini tuan Ahmad bin haji Hasim nambar 91 Beach Road Singapura. Dan tuan haji 'Abd al-Qadir bin haji Muhammad Salih Qadi nambar 54 Acin Street Pulau Pinang. Dan tuan haji Muhammad Saraj nambar 43 Sultan Road Singapura, adapun tuan ini wakil kami pada pihaq Tanah Jawa dan Sumatra dan nagari2 yang di sebelah timur.*
>
> All agents of the *Wajah Selong* newspaper
>
> Agents for this newspaper are Mr Ahmad, son of *hajji* Hasim, 91 Beach Road, Singapore; and Mr *hajji* 'Abd al-Qadir, son of *hajji* Muhammad Salih Qadi, 54 Acin Street, Penang Island; and Mr *hajji* Muhammad Saraj, 43 Sultan Road, Singapore, who is also our agent in the regions of Java, Sumatra and the lands to the east.

A list of prices also appears in quite a few issues as subscription costs varied depending on place.[11]

Wajah Selong had a distinctly international character. It regularly cited various newspapers in Europe, Asia (especially colonial India) and the United States. It reported news from across the world, with examples including an earthquake in Japan, drought in America, war in Kashmir and events unfolding in Zanzibar, Russia, Armenia and Argentina, among many others. Some topics, like the ongoing conflict between Greece and Türkiye, received frequent and detailed coverage. More generally, news from the Ottoman Empire, which was a Muslim-ruled entity in a world in which most of the powerful were Christian, was given disproportionate attention.

This could be a good place to pause and mention the choice of *Wajah Selong* as the major source on which to base this chapter. Part of furthering a decolonial approach is searching for, exploring and taking seriously non-European sources from the colonial period. For too long, studies of colonial

---

11 For example, in the 15 March 1896 issue, subscription prices were listed for one year, six months or three months, with those for Ceylon approximately 10 per cent lower than for places overseas.

history have relied solely or at least primarily on documents produced by colonial administrators, scholars, soldiers and others who, by virtue of their positionality within the order of things, left us a representation of the past that possesses many blind spots. As scholarship over the past several decades has shown, archives and documentation are never neutral and must be approached with a good measure of healthy scepticism. One way to amend the legacy of heavy reliance on sources inherited from the colonising side, and to see a more nuanced historical picture, is to bring other voices and perspectives into view. The point is not to swing full scale in the other direction and present the colonised perspective as somehow 'truly authentic', but to engage with the different ways of knowing, seeing and acting by members of different social classes, ethnic groups, genders and nationalities during the colonial period and acknowledge the vast multiplicity of experiences and views.[12] *Wajah Selong* as well as other newspapers published within non-European communities in the colonial period (see also Beech Jones's Chapter 4 on West Sumatran women's newspaper writing in this volume) are examples of historical sources that can reveal much about thought worlds, beliefs, values and actions that remain hidden from view within the coloniser's archive.

Locating Indonesia?

So, where did the Dutch East Indies fit in this picture of global reporting? Did the Malays' ancestral lands receive special, perhaps more frequent, mention than other sites? Reading through the newspaper's issues, one finds that places in the Indies, as well as in today's Malaysia, were certainly mentioned, although the term Hindia-Belanda ('Dutch East Indies') is absent. There are readers' letters from Perak and Malacca, a report on 'a tiger in Malaya' (*harimau di Tanah Melayu*), news of a large wedding gathering in Penang and statistics about pilgrims going on the *hajj* from Tanah Jawa and

---

12 For studies on forced migration and exile under colonialism that highlight local, vernacular sources, see Clare Anderson, 'A Global History of Exile in Asia, c. 1700–1900', in *Exile in Colonial Asia: Kings, Convicts, Commemoration*, ed. Ronit Ricci (Honolulu: University of Hawai`i Press, 2016), 20–47, doi.org/10.21313/hawaii/9780824853747.003.0002; Yang, '"Near China beyond the Seas Far Far Distant from Juggernath"'; Timo Kaartinen, 'Exile, Colonial Space, and Deterritorialized People in Eastern Indonesian History', in *Exile in Colonial Asia: Kings, Convicts, Commemoration*, ed. Ronit Ricci (Honolulu: University of Hawai`i Press, 2016), 139–64, doi.org/10.21313/hawaii/9780824853747.003.0007.

Tanah Melayu.[13] These instances by no means overshadow events reported from elsewhere. For example, we might expect that in a Malay newspaper appearing in the 1890s developments in the Aceh War (*Perang Nagari Aceh*) would be followed closely, but they were not, and even when a brief report on that war appeared, the same page included a report on the war in Sudan. And this is not only a quantitative issue about coverage of the archipelago versus other lands; my impression is that, for the most part, the reporting from the former is not more interesting, intimate, detailed or enthusiastic than reporting from the latter. The newspaper tells of many dramatic and emotional events and what it labels *ajaib* ('wonderous', 'strange', 'unusual') occurrences from elsewhere. If the number and content of reports from the archipelago are not a good means for assessing a sense of Malay-ness and a connection to a colony that would come to be called Indonesia by members of its diaspora, what are some alternatives?

In the following pages, I will address three themes that I would like to suggest offer a possible lens on Malay identity and belonging: Islam, a juxtaposition of self and 'other', and Malay language and culture.

Historical records attest not only to ethnic and linguistic diversity among people from the archipelago who arrived in Ceylon during the colonial period, but also to a population that was non-monolithic in religious terms and included Christians and Balinese Hindus in addition to Muslims. Nonetheless, and certainly by the time *Alamat Langkapuri* and *Wajah Selong* were published, the Malays in Ceylon were largely affiliated with Islam. Malay mosques were erected and managed across the island in towns where Malays lived and served—for example, Wekande and Slave Island in Colombo, Badulla and Kandy; Friday sermons were offered in Malay and a range of Islamic texts, written predominantly in Arabic and Malay, were copied (and later also printed) throughout the nineteenth century. The centrality of Islam to *Wajah Selong* can be seen in the use of the *jawi* script, which was taught to children in Ceylon as part of an Islamic education through which they were familiarised with Arabic letters so they could read the Qur'an. Whereas in the Dutch and, to a lesser degree, British territories in Southeast Asia during this period the use of Romanised Malay was growing and, according to Adam, had a decisive impact on the character

---

13   Even in the few examples presented in this chapter one may notice the consistent use of *tanah* ('land') added to placenames, especially Melayu and Java (that is, Tanah Melayu, Tanah Jawa). This phenomenon occurs throughout the newspaper's pages and can be contrasted with the consistent use of *pulau* ('island') whenever Ceylon is mentioned. This is intriguing, especially considering that Java is also an island.

of collective identity that would emerge in Indonesia (that is, less Islam-centric than Malaysia),[14] the use of Romanised Malay in Ceylon was not at all widespread at this time. Thus, the ongoing use of *jawi* attested to the Malays' strong Muslim affiliation. A clear religious and political identity was also expressed in the newspaper's opening sections, as exemplified in the 14 March 1897 issue:

> *Bismillah hamdan musalliyan*
>
> *Kemudian daripada segala pujian2 maka memulailah kami membuat surat dengan beberapa shukur bagi tuhan malik al-shatar yang dighaibkan daripada tiap2 salah dosa kami. Lagi telah disampurnakan dengan lengkap saum Ramadhan pada bulan yang mulia, lagi bertambahnya beribu2 tasbih dan shukur bagi tuhan itu karena dikaruniakan bersuka2an kepada hari raya 'Id al-Fitr. Dan lagi apalah kiranya mudah2an Allah subhan wa ta'ala menjauhi daripada tiap2 balanya daripada segala kupar yang bermusuh serta beroleh kemenangan ke atas khalifat sayyid al-mursalin maulana al-sultan al-Ghazi 'Abd al-Hamid Khan dan sekalian raja2 Islam.*
>
> In the name of God praise be upon Him and prayers upon the Prophet
>
> Then, of all praises, we begin this writing by offering many thanks to God, king Who causes all our sins to vanish. Furthermore, the Ramadhan fast has been completed during the blessed month thus we add thousands of *tasbih* [use of the formula *Subhan Allah*, extolling God's perfection] and thanks to God, who has blessed us with various pleasures on Eid al-Fitr. And further we hope that Allah, may He be praised and exalted, shall distance each and every soldier from all hostile infidels and attain victory for the *khalifa* [successor] of Sayyid al-Mursalin [Master of the Messengers, the Prophet], the *maulana* [learned scholar of religion], the Sultan al-Ghazi Abdul Hamid Khan and all Muslim rulers.[15]

In addition to centring Islam and religious thought and practices, the newspaper reported frequently on events in other parts of the wider Islamic world such as Türkiye, especially Istanbul, and on the Ottoman Sultan Abdul Hamid II, as well as on Muslims in various parts of India. News was

---

14 Ahmat Adam, *Sejarah dan Bibliografi Akhbar dan Majalah Melayu Abad Kesembilan Belas* [*The History and a Bibliography of Malay Newspapers and Magazines in the Nineteenth Century*] (Bangi: Universiti Kebangsaan Malaysia, 1992), 91–92.
15 Abdul Hamid II (r. 1876–1909) was the last sultan to exert effective rule over the Ottoman Empire.

sprinkled occasionally with *hadith* (words of the Prophet) or Qur'anic quotes. An intriguing dimension of *Wajah Selong*'s emphasis on Islam appears in a recurrent interest in converts, reported time and again under the rubric '*Islam Baru*' ('New Muslims').

The new converts depicted included, above all, Westerners, as in news that came from London and Liverpool, including a story about a Jewish woman who took her two daughters to a Muslim man, who cared for children, asking that he teach and convert them. The man consulted with a sheikh, who believed he should go ahead and do so. There were also reports from neighbouring countries, especially India, including from Calcutta and Lahore, with one report (cited from the *Punjab Observer*) telling of two white people who expressed a wish to become Muslims, were told to recite the profession of faith (*do'a kalimah*) and were given new names. A case in Colombo of a white convert, who stood by the road to convince people of other faiths of Islam's truth and succeeded in persuading a young Sinhalese man, was also discussed.[16]

These instances point to a strong commitment to Islam—a faith and way of life that were inextricably tied to the Malays' roots in the archipelago. Another aspect of this commitment to Islam and the identity it fostered can be seen in the second theme, that of the relationship between, and often juxtaposition of, self and other. We have already noted the expression of allegiance and support to the Turkish Sultan and other 'Muslim rulers' (*raja Islam*) appearing in an 1897 issue. The emphasis on Western converts is likely, in part, related to tensions between coloniser and colonised and Christians ruling over Muslim subjects, including in Muslim-majority societies, as was the case in parts of the Dutch East Indies and British India. However, there was an additional group from whom the newspaper seems to have made a clear effort to distinguish its readership. In late nineteenth-century Ceylon, most of the population was Sinhalese (written as *Cinggala* in Malay) and Buddhist. Part of maintaining a diasporic Malay identity was an ethnic and religious differentiation from this majority.

The differentiation was achieved in part by the well-worn method of demonisation. For example, the 7 November 1897 issue contained a report attributing extreme cruelty to a Sinhalese individual under the title '*Perbunuhan*' ('A Killing'). It told of a Sinhalese man in Galle, who

---

16 These events were reported, respectively, in the issues dated 14 March 1897, 28 March 1897 and 26 September 1897.

'worshipped idols' (*memuji berhala*)—a typical way of referring to a Buddhist by employing iconoclastic terminology. The man's wife, it was said, fell for an idolatrous guru (*jadi semuka dengan seorang guru berhala*) and, when the man returned home, his four-year-old child relayed to him all that had happened, with the result that hatred filled the home. One day when the man was away, the woman killed the child, cooked him as a *rendang* (meat dish) and served it to the man. Unfortunately, the relevant page is torn and the middle of the story missing, but the final part tells of the man finding his son's head and reporting his wife and the guru to the authorities.[17] Other reports depicted Sinhalese as killers and drunks. In an interesting case, *Wajah Selong*, citing the *Independent*, reproduced news of a Malay woman, who was tried in court for selling arak in Kampung Kertel, a Malay neighbourhood in Colombo, and was fined and warned by the magistrate that she would be jailed should the offence be repeated. *Wajah Selong* then commented:

> *Tetapi tiadalah kami percaya akan dia seperempuan Melayu, barangkali perempuan Cinggala yang boleh bertutur Bahasa Melayu, bahwa jika ia anaq cucu Islam tiada boleh ia berani membuat perbuatan yang demikian.*[18]

> However, we do not believe that she is a Malay woman, likely she is a Sinhalese woman who speaks Malay. Were she indeed a Muslim, she would not dare behave in this way.

In this instance, when a Malay woman was apparently guilty of an 'un-Islamic' offence, the editor responded defensively, preferring to believe that such behaviour was not possible and, without proof, blaming the actions on a Sinhalese in an attempt to preserve a positive self-image, all the more so for the community's (and especially its women's) presentation in the media. A juxtaposition between Muslim and non-Muslim others with clear endorsement of the former is also evident in reports from India that engage with Muslim–Hindu encounters. Further research is needed to assess whether this type of 'us' and 'them' approach was related to a hardening of boundaries between different groups under colonial categorisation schemes. We do know that there existed common views on the 'typical' Malay and 'typical' Sinhalese in Ceylon that marked them as different—for example, in addition to being considered daring and fearsome warriors, the Malays were believed to be good servants, gardeners and cooks, whereas the Sinhalese

---

17   7 November 1897.
18   6 June 1897.

were often depicted as lazy or, as Robert Percival put it, 'indolent in the extreme'.[19] Such colonial images may have contributed to the shaping or sharpening of the Malays' self-perception.

Finally, I wish to highlight, as a third theme to consider when trying to assess an often-elusive diasporic identity, mention in *Wajah Selong* of the Malay language and the Malays as a collective. More broadly, the ongoing use of the Malay language in colonial Ceylon presented the firmest evidence of historical and cultural bonds to the lands to the southeast. The language was used for speaking and for various forms of writing, including *hikayat* (a genre of prose writing that included tales of romance and adventure, history and pre-Islamic literature), *syair* (poetry), religious compendiums, letters, diaries, documents and of course the newspapers. On 15 August 1897, a letter to *Wajah Selong*'s editor described misbehaviour and ignorance among the youth and called on the preachers (*katib*) to explain what was permitted and forbidden (*halal dan haram*) in the mosques every Friday, and to do so while speaking in Malay.[20] A report cited from a Malay newspaper from Perak emphasised the importance of not forgetting 'the language of one's mother and father' (*bahasa ibu dan bapak*) and of studying it.[21] Books and the printing of invitations and other documents in Malay were advertised regularly. Certain local Malay sites were mentioned often, including Kampung Pangeran, Kampung Jawa and Jawatte—all of which had names that inscribed Java, and Javanese-ness, on to the developing urban landscape of Colombo.[22] These examples also hint at the ongoing presence of other, non-Malay identities and memories—in particular, Javanese ones, which continued to exist alongside and combined with the broad Malay affiliation.

---

19 Robert Percival, *An Account of the Island of Ceylon Containing its History, Geography, Natural History, with the Manner and Customs of its Various Inhabitants: To Which is Added, the Journal of an Embassy to the Court of Kandy* (London: C. & R. Baldwin, 1803), 120 (on the Malays), and 190 (on the Sinhalese).
20 Most Muslims living in Ceylon were Tamils and there were various ties between them and the Malays, so Tamil was likely the alternative language to be employed for the sermons.
21 The newspaper was the *Perak Pioneer and Native States Advertiser*, the first English-language newspaper in Perak (founded in 1894). It is noteworthy that of the many newspapers cited in *Wajah Selong*, very minimal mention is made of those from the Malay world.
22 Kampung Pangeran (Prince Village) was named for one of the exiled princes, likely Pangeran Arya Mangkunagara, the older brother of Pakubuwana II of Kartasura, who was exiled in 1728. Kampung Jawa (Java Village) was home to descendants of Javanese exiles, soldiers and servants; Jawatte (Java Gardens) is an area in western Colombo where the Jawatte Mosque and cemetery are currently located.

Rethinking histories of Indonesia: A view from Sri Lanka

This chapter addressed the question of how we might revisit the history of colonialism in the Indonesian case by thinking beyond geography—that is, beyond the area that eventually, after many wars, decades of exploitation and forced European expansion, coalesced into the future nation-state of Indonesia. This state, like many other newly independent states across Asia, Africa and the Middle East in the post–World War II era, had borders that were determined by the limits of colonial rule. Somewhat ironically, and sometimes tragically, such states inherited and often continued perpetrating not only social, legal and economic structures of coloniality, as discussed throughout this volume, but also, at an even more basic level, acquired the colonial-era spatial contours and imaginaries of their newly declared homelands. However, if we do not limit ourselves to the physical boundaries of the Dutch East Indies turned Indonesia, what other possibilities emerge for assessing the colonial period, its events, communities and emotional and cultural landscapes? The example explored here, the Malay community in colonial Ceylon, should be understood, in part, as a component of such a broadly defined colonial Indonesia. In part, this is because identities are always complex and multidimensional and all Malays possessed a past reaching back to the archipelago, family memories of exiled kings and courageous warriors, and a mother tongue from elsewhere—all of which constitute dimensions of the community's self-understanding.

Returning to the theme of banishment, which is central to Malay history and identity in Ceylon, as it was the reason people from the Indonesian archipelago arrived on the island in the first place, would it be going too far to claim that the Dutch, too, understood Ceylon as part of the East Indies? Batavia was the beating heart of the Dutch empire, and second to it in importance was Colombo. Clearly, in the nineteenth century, the grand 'unit of analysis' for large parts of Asia was empire and not the nation-state, and the two colonies were distinct yet also strongly linked within a single empire, with the ability to exile a disobedient prince alternately to Ambon, Makassar or Jaffna signalling an imagined map in which such places were on a par. However, fast-forwarding to the postcolonial age, despite the fact that the plight of the Malays' ancestors was inextricably linked to colonial forced migration (whether as exiles, slaves or soldiers), their story has been entirely absent from the Indonesian national narrative, and even the sons of royalty banished to Ceylon have been banished once more, this time from textbooks, historical research and popular culture.[23] It could be that the attachment, however diffuse, felt by many Malays to the archipelago as a distant 'homeland' was not mutual and that independent, postcolonial Indonesia did not feel attached to them in return.

A major issue that lurks in the shadows of my discussion and that I view as key to the debate about revisiting histories of colonialism is the presence of two colonial powers, the Dutch and the British, in the region we now term the 'Indonesian–Malay world'.

Exploring Indonesia's past from today's vantage point, it is tempting to limit the discussions to the former Dutch East Indies and especially to its contours in the late colonial period leading up to independence. Nonetheless, for several centuries (the English and Dutch East India companies were founded just two years apart, in 1600 and 1602, respectively), these empires of trade and conquest competed with and fought one another, signed treaties and exchanged territories, all while contributing to the geographical and social shaping of their shifting colonies and the states that would later emerge from them. The historiographical British–Dutch divide obscures many connections, one of which is the Malay diasporic community's ties to the Indonesian–Malay region, but there must be many more.

Thus, can we even speak of 'colonial Indonesia' without 'colonial Malaya'? From the perspective of *Wajah Selong*'s weekly issues in the final years of the nineteenth century, what did one see?

In terms of empire, Ceylon in the days of *Wajah Selong* 'belonged' to the British yet possessed a significant Dutch past (which ended exactly a century earlier, in 1796) that, for the Malays, had determined their very presence in Ceylon. As Alicia Shrikker has shown in her study of the transition from Dutch to British rule, the processes of change were complex and gradual and Dutch legacies often continued to shape British policies and approaches.[24] In the early nineteenth century, Java experienced a regime change (one that was short-lived, yet significant) of the British Interregnum (1811–16) during which the new rulers imposed many changes yet continued, among other Dutch policies, the exiling of local rulers who did

---

23 Sheikh Yusuf of Makassar is somewhat of an exception, perhaps, but even articles and books dedicated to his life briefly gloss over the decade he spent in Ceylon. See, for example, the study by Abu Hamid, *Syekh Yusuf Makassar. Seorang Ulama, Sufi, dan Pejuang* [*Syekh Yusuf Makassar: A Scholar, Sufi, and Warrior*] (Jakarta: Yayasan Obor Indonesia, 1994), 108–11.
24 Alicia Schrikker, *Dutch and British Colonial Intervention in Sri Lanka, 1780–1815: Expansion and Reform* (Leiden: Brill, 2007), doi.org/10.1163/ej.9789004156029.i-272.

not gain their favour.²⁵ These episodes are but two examples of recurring transitions and negotiations in the region. Back in Ceylon, publishing a newspaper in Malay created a natural link with Malay-speaking societies in Southeast Asia and, concurrently, a barrier with neighbouring India just across the Palk Strait, which although under the same British rule had no readership for *Wajah Selong*.²⁶ Some prominent Malay families in Ceylon knew their places of origin (for example, Java, Sumenep, Makassar) and in that respect their connection was to 'Indonesia'. But if we consider the diversity of their origins and their late-nineteenth-century allegiance to a British colony like the Straits Settlements and, above all, the linguistic and cultural commonalities across the vast region that now encompasses Indonesia, Malaysia, Singapore, Brunei and Timor-Leste (as well as southern Thailand and the southern Philippines), we might imagine that the Malays in Ceylon were no more an 'Indonesian diaspora' than a 'Malaysian' one. But that, too, is not what we aim to ask: were they (in retrospect!) more Indonesian or Malaysian? Focusing on this hypothetical question would be a complete cop-out to the forces of nationalism and the selective national narratives this volume seeks to interrogate and challenge. The point is not to present a final answer to a complex historical question but to broaden the horizon, to see new connections and new possibilities as we glance back and wonder where to locate, within the scope of a decolonial viewpoint, this small, geographically marginal yet remarkably resilient community.

The present state of affairs is beyond the scope of this chapter, yet it is worth noting in closing, and in a return to the question of nomenclature, that the category 'Malay', as I hope I have shown, narrowed the scope of the diverse identities of the people from the archipelago who arrived in Ceylon, yet it was also a unifying force through which to remain connected to a distant history and a faraway land throughout the colonial period, under Dutch and British rule, and beyond. After the mid-twentieth century, with decolonisation, the names 'Indonesia' and 'Malaysia' presented challenges of their own—the first lacking echoes with Malay-ness, Java, Ternate and all other historical points of departure to Ceylon and the second closely linked to the community's name but very loosely related otherwise, as few

---

25   On the exile to Penang and later Ambon of Hamengkubuwana II of Yogyakarta by the British, see Sri Margana, 'Caught between Empires: Babad Mangkudiningratan and the Exile of Sultan Hamengkubuwana II of Yogyakarta, 1813–1826', in *Exile in Colonial Asia: Kings, Convicts, Commemoration*, ed. Ronit Ricci (Honolulu: University of Hawai`i Press, 2016), 117–38, doi.org/10.1515/9780824853754-008.

26   Ahmat Adam, in his extensive study of nineteenth-century Malay newspapers, concluded that the Malay press under the two empires, Dutch and British, exhibited many similarities and attested and contributed to a shared Malay identity. Adam, *The History and a Bibliography of Malay Newspapers*, 92.

Malays trace their lineage to sites in contemporary Malaysia. A study of the postcolonial legacies of the Malays' complex history, of their senses of attachment, loyalty, belonging and identification, would shed further light on our understanding of colonial and postcolonial Indonesia and how these entities, real and imagined, continue to be negotiated and renegotiated over space and time.

References

Primary sources

Alamat Langkapuri. 1869–70; 1877–78. Colombo: National Archives of Sri Lanka.

Saldin, Baba Ounus. n.d. *Kitab Segala Peringatan* [*A Book of Memories*]. MS 137. Kuala Lumpur: Dewan Bahasa dan Pustaka Library.

Wajah Selong. 1895–98. Colombo: National Archives of Sri Lanka.

Secondary sources

Abu Hamid. 1994. *Syekh Yusuf Makassar. Seorang Ulama, Sufi, dan Pejuang* [*Syekh Yusuf Makassar: A Scholar, Sufi, and Warrior*]. Jakarta: Yayasan Obor Indonesia.

Adam, Ahmat. 1992. *Sejarah dan Bibliografi Akhbar dan Majalah Melayu Abad Kesembilan Belas* [*The History and a Bibliography of Malay Newspapers and Magazines in the Nineteenth Century*]. Bangi: Universiti Kebangsaan Malaysia.

Anderson, Benedict. 1991. *Imagined Communities: Reflections on the Origin and Spread of Nationalism*. London: Verso.

Anderson, Clare. 2016. 'A Global History of Exile in Asia, c. 1700–1900.' In *Exile in Colonial Asia: Kings, Convicts, Commemoration*, edited by Ronit Ricci, 20–47. Honolulu: University of Hawai`i Press. doi.org/10.21313/hawaii/9780824853747.003.0002.

Anonymous. 1924. *Jubilee Book of the Malay Cricket Club*. Colombo: Ceylon Malay Cricket Club.

Hussainmiya, B.A. 1990. *Orang Regimen: The Malays of the Ceylon Rifle Regiment*. Bangi: Universiti Kebangsaan Malaysia Press. doi.org/10.1017/s0022463400003003.

Jappie, Saarah. 2012. 'JAWI DARI JAUH: "Malays" in South Africa through Text.' *Indonesia and the Malay World* 40, no. 117: 143–59. doi.org/10.1080/136398 11.2012.683675.

Kaartinen, Timo. 2016. 'Exile, Colonial Space, and Deterritorialized People in Eastern Indonesian History.' In *Exile in Colonial Asia: Kings, Convicts, Commemoration*, edited by Ronit Ricci, 139–64. Honolulu: University of Hawai`i Press. doi.org/10.21313/hawaii/9780824853747.003.0007.

Margana, Sri. 2016. 'Caught between Empires: Babad Mangkudiningratan and the Exile of Sultan Hamengkubuwana II of Yogyakarta, 1813–1826.' In *Exile in Colonial Asia: Kings, Convicts, Commemoration*, edited by Ronit Ricci, 117–38. Honolulu: University of Hawai`i Press. doi.org/10.1515/9780824853754-008.

Percival, Robert. 1803. *An Account of the Island of Ceylon Containing its History, Geography, Natural History, with the Manner and Customs of its Various Inhabitants: To Which is Added, the Journal of an Embassy to the Court of Kandy*. London: C. & R. Baldwin.

Ricci, Ronit. 2016. 'Jawa, Melayu, Malay or Otherwise? The Shifting Nomenclature of the Sri Lankan Malays.' *Indonesia and the Malay World* 44, no. 130: 68–80. doi.org/10.1080/13639811.2016.1219491.

Ricci, Ronit. 2018. 'Along the Frontiers of Religion, Language and War: Baba Ounus Saldin's Syair Faid al-Abad.' In *The Routledge Companion to World Literature and World History*, edited by May Hawas, 82–92. London: Routledge. doi.org/10.1017/9781108648189.

Ricci, Ronit. 2019. *Banishment and Belonging: Exile and Diaspora in Sarandib, Lanka and Ceylon*. Cambridge: Cambridge University Press. doi.org/10.1080/21567689.2021.1928932.

Saldin, Baba Ounus. 1905. *Syair Faid al-Abad* [*Bounty of the Ages*]. Colombo: Alamat Langkapuri Press.

Schrikker, Alicia. 2007. *Dutch and British Colonial Intervention in Sri Lanka, 1780–1815: Expansion and Reform*. Leiden: Brill. doi.org/10.1163/ej.9789004 156029.i-272.

Schrikker, Alicia. 2011. 'Caught between Empires: VOC Families in Sri Lanka after the British Takeover, 1806–1808.' *Annales de démographie historique* [*Annals of Historical Demography*] 122, no. 2: 127–47. doi.org/10.3917/adh.122.0127.

Suryadi. 2008. 'Sepucuk Surat dari Seorang Bangsawan Gowa di Tanah Pembuangan (Ceylon) [A Letter from a Gowa Noblewoman in the Land of Exile (Ceylon)].' *Wacana: Jurnal Ilmu Pengetahuan Budaya* [*Wacana: Journal of the Humanities of Indonesia*] 10, no. 2: 214–45. doi.org/10.17510/wjhi.v10i2.194.

Ward, Kerry. 2009. *Networks of Empire: Forced Migration in the Dutch East India Company*. Cambridge: Cambridge University Press. doi.org/10.1017/CBO9780 511551628.

Wilkinson, R.J. 1959 [1901]. *A Malay–English Dictionary*. 2 vols. London: Macmillan & Co.

Yang, Anand A. 2016. '"Near China beyond the Seas Far Far Distant from Juggernath": The Mid-Nineteenth-Century Exile of Bhai Maharaj Singh in Singapore.' In *Exile in Colonial Asia: Kings, Convicts, Commemoration*, edited by Ronit Ricci, 71–93. Honolulu: University of Hawai`i Press. doi.org/10.1515/ 9780824853754-006.

4

'So I say my name': Towards a decolonial ethics for reading girls' worlds in letters

Bronwyn Anne Beech Jones[1]

Introduction

> I greet you with my hand my friend
> So I say my name.
> —Sitti Salamah[2]

This call for recognition and friendship was penned by Sitti Salamah from Panyabungan, a northwestern area of the island of Sumatra. Published in the women's newspaper *Soenting Melajoe* ('*Malay Headdress*') in 1919, Sitti Salamah's poem provides insight into the sentiments of an elite, educated girl in colonial Indonesian society. This chapter contributes to efforts to rethink the limits of a historical understanding of women writers by using the letters

---

1 Thank you to Wayne Modest, the editors and the contributors for their valuable feedback on earlier versions of this chapter, which I dedicate to Fathul Fatimah, who started to learn to read while this chapter was being written.
2 Sitti Salamah B. Dolok, 'Ratap Tangis ni Sitti Salamah Boroe Dolok [The Cry of Sitti Salamah Boroe Dolok]', *Soenting Melajoe* [*Malay Headdress*], 30 May 1919: 2, in *Soenting Melajoe*, 6, no. 1 (1917) – 10, no. 4 (1921), Microfilm, 33168008944734 (Melbourne: Monash University, 1917–21).

of teenagers to whom I refer as girls.³ Drawing on writings produced by girls in two West Sumatran Malay-language newspapers between 1912 and 1921, I trace an approach to understand their senses of the world, including race, modernity, locality and injustice. Girls' perspectives elucidate how conceptions of self and solidarity and dreams of opportunities to participate in a global modernity reinscribed and refused colonial grammars of gender, class and racial differences.

Using thematic case studies, I examine writers' senses of geography, origins, friendship, homeland and hopes. Individual perspectives on self and collective identities have been glossed over in research that has predominantly used *Soenting Melajoe* to probe Minangkabau women leaders and gender politics.⁴ Distinct in their public textual form, letters to newspapers and periodicals were tools girls and women used to fashion senses of self, forge friendships and form political languages. It is possible to track a small number of writers over multiple years in *Soenting Melajoe* and document advocacy, especially for girls' schools.⁵ Conversely, by piecing together senses of the world, this chapter examines who is made visible and whose labour and experiences remain invisible in this archive.

The first section outlines an approach to reading girls' self-making and world-making practices to make visible networks of knowledge. I then present a genealogy of a visualisation—word maps—to contextualise 11-year-old Retna Tenoen's letter to *Soenting Melajoe* about her multiple

---

3   See, for example, Eunike G. Setiadarma, 'Hoedjin: Eksplorasi Metode Penulisan Sejarah Perempuan [Hoedjin: A Methodological Exploration for Writing Women's History]', *Jurnal Sejarah* [*History Journal*] 4, no. 1 (2021): 1–13, msi.or.id/journal/index.php/js/article/download/49/47/112; Anna Mariana, 'Memikirkan Ulang Historiografi Sejarah Perempuan [Rethinking the Historiography of Women's History]', *Jurnal Sejarah* [*History Journal*] 4 (2021): i–iv; Ruang Perempuan dan Tulisan, ed., *Yang Terlupakan dan Dilupakan: Membaca Kembali Sepuluh Penulis Perempuan Indonesia* [*Those Accidentally Forgotten and Those Forgotten: Rereading Ten Indonesian Women Writers*] (Jakarta: Marjin Kiri, 2021); and the group Ruang Perempuan dan Tulisan.

4   Notably, Jeffrey Hadler, *Muslims and Matriarchs: Cultural Resilience in Indonesia through Jihad and Colonialism* (Ithaca: Cornell University Press, 2008); Wannofri Samry and Rahilah Omar, 'Gagasan dan Aktiviti Wartawan Wanita Minangkabau pada Masa Kolonial Belanda [Concepts and Activities of Minangkabau Women Journalists in the Dutch Colonial Period]', *Jebat: Malaysian Journal of History, Politics & Strategy* 39, no. 2 (2012): 24–47; Silfia Hanani, 'Women's Newspapers as Minangkabau Feminist Movement Against Marginalization in Indonesia', *Global Journal Al-Thaqafah* 8, no. 2 (2018): 75–83, at 77; Saskia Wieringa, 'Matrilineality and Women's Interests: The Minangkabau of Western Sumatra', in *Subversive Women: Women's Movements in Africa, Asia, Latin America and the Caribbean*, ed. Saskia Wieringa (London: Zed Books, 1995), 241–68, at 249–50.

5   Bronwyn Anne Beech Jones, 'Textual Worlds: Rethinking Self, Community and Activism in Colonial-Era Sumatran Women's Newspapers' (PhD diss., University of Melbourne, 2023).

sources of geographic knowledge.⁶ The second case examines how girls from Natal and Tapanuli crafted a cohort based on sharing their aspirations in letters in 1918–19. The final case reconstructs the agency of a female translator, who, as far as I know, did not write about herself. Using her translation of Leo Tolstoy's short story 'The Empty Drum', published in the periodical *Minangkabau* in 1918, I argue that Fatimah Rasad scripted a global sense of inevitable justice into an anticolonial vernacular for Pariaman, a trading port north of Padang. Their writing reveals girls' complex subjectivities—aspiring to be modern, claiming an 'authentic' collective identity and expressing self-determination. This chapter extends the volume's aim to understand how coloniality interlaces local experiences with capitalist circuits of power. It reveals multiple ambiguities and subtexts within girls' world views, whispering alternatives that belie the dominant modes of subjectification.

Letters and girls' world-making

The girl writers examined in this chapter were overwhelmingly of the middle to upper classes and enmeshed in colonial political and economic systems through familial employment that enabled formal education. They were among the few Indonesians permitted to attend Dutch-language schools (*Hollandsch-Iinlandsche Scholen, HIS*)⁷ for seven years of primary education. The transformative experience of education for elite girls in colonial-era Indonesia is well documented. Cora Vreede-de Stuers and Susan Blackburn chronicled how associations and new ideas about girlhood and womanhood in the early twentieth century reflected and spurred debates about the interplay between Western-style education, religion and tradition, including in women's newspapers.⁸ Although cohering with a colonial agenda of uplift, girls' schooling had radical unintended consequences, as Blackburn described, 'giving rise to uncertainties, contradictions and conflicts, as well

---

6   Names in this chapter have been reproduced in accordance with how writers referred to themselves in these publications.
7   Dutch-language schools for natives.
8   Cora Vreede-de Stuers, *The Indonesian Woman: Struggles and Achievements* (The Hague: Mouton, 1960), 64; Susan Blackburn, *Women and the State in Modern Indonesia* (Cambridge: Cambridge University Press, 2004), doi.org/10.1017/CBO9780511492198, 56.

as emancipatory implications'.⁹ Communities forged in the classroom and the pages of newspapers presented new possibilities and aspirations, thus literacy was 'a key that opened the door to authority'.¹⁰

In the early 1910s, there was also colonial concern about a limited take-up of government girls' schools, especially on Java.¹¹ A 1913 *Bataviaasch Nieuwsblad* ('*Batavia Newspaper*') article reported officials' attempts to naturalise low female attendance in 'native culture' by claiming that Islam and the prevalence of early marriage discouraged parents from educating girls. *Bataviaasch Nieuwsblad* significantly targeted a contradiction, notwithstanding substantial and diverse gender barriers, between a lack of interest and letters in *Soenting Melajoe* on the imperative of education written by Muslim girls and women of the matrilineal Minangkabau ethnic group.¹² Blackburn contended that, by 1914, government reluctance to guarantee financial support and consider local models constrained girls' schooling more than lack of community interest.¹³ Furthering this, Suwignyo has argued that restricted educational systems ensured the reproduction of social stratification based on race and class.¹⁴

The burgeoning West Sumatran press reflected comparatively high literacy rates, including among elite girls.¹⁵ Literacy nonetheless remained confined; by 1930, only 6.44 per cent of Indonesians were literate in Latin script, subsequent to the Ethical Policy's increased investment in People's Schools (*Volksschool*), some speciality girls schools and flourishing nongovernment schools.¹⁶ Across West Sumatra in 1911, there were 111 People's Schools offering three years of

---

9   Blackburn, *Women and the State in Modern Indonesia*, 38.
10 H.M.J. Maier, *We Are Playing Relatives: A Survey of Malay Writing* (Singapore: ISEAS, 2004), doi.org/10.1163/9789004454606, 152.
11 C. Lekkerkerker, *Meisjesonderwijs, Coeducatie en Meisjesscholen voor de Inlandsche Bevolking in Nederlandsch-Indië, 1914* [*Girls' Education, Co-Education and Girls' Schools for the Native Population of the Netherlands Indies, 1914*] (Padangpanjang, Sumatra: Pusat Dokumentasi dan Informasi Minangkabau [Minangkabau Documentation and Information Centre], 1914), 637, 884.
12 'Gouvernements Onderwijs voor Inlandsche Meisjes [Government Education for Native Girls]', *Bataviaasch Nieuwsblad* [*Batavia Newspaper*], 16 June 1913: 5, resolver.kb.nl/resolve?urn=ddd:011036306:mpeg21:p005.
13 Blackburn, *Women and the State in Modern Indonesia*, 39.
14 Agus Suwignyo, 'The Making of Politically Conscious Indonesian Teachers in Public Schools, 1930–42', *Southeast Asian Studies* 3 (2014): 119–49, at 122.
15 Hadler, *Muslims and Matriarchs*, 144; Ahmat Adam, *Sejarah Awal Pers dan Kebangkitan Kesadaran Keindonesiaan* [*The Vernacular Press and the Emergence of Modern Indonesian Consciousness*] (Jakarta: Hasta Mitra, 1995), 317–18; Ahmat Adam, *Suara Minangkabau, Sejarah dan Bibliografi Akhbar dan Majalah di Sumatera Barat* [*Minangkabau Voices: A History and Bibliography of Newspapers and Magazines in West Sumatra*] (Kuala Lumpur: University of Malaysia Press, 2012).
16 Maier, *We Are Playing Relatives*, 145.

primary schooling financed by local communities, expanding to 358 by 1915 and 548 by 1925, when 40 per cent of students were girls.[17] The first newspaper on which I focus, *Soenting Melajoe*, was published in Padang between 1912 and 1921, edited by women and supported by politician Mahjoedin, known by his title Datoe' Soetan Maharadja.[18] The weekly's editors positioned it as a forum for girls and women to learn, challenge Minangkabau male authority, centre women's status in matrilineal customary law and suggest that God-given maternal strength was pairable with Western modes of education.[19] Conversely, the monthly *Minangkabau* was printed in 1918 in Pariaman[20] and promoted self-sufficiency and published contributions from male agricultural officials. Fatimah Rasad edited *Minangkabau* and translated two short stories. Neither publication was overtly anticolonial but both were inherently subversive by advocating cultural sovereignty and self-help and seeking to form and strengthen communities. Their reading publics portray Stoler and Cooper's idea of contested divisions between coloniser and colonised, with 'ambiguous lines that divided engagement from appropriation, deflection from denial, and desire from discipline', particularly regarding knowledge-making.[21]

Reading girls' letters for world-making requires locating how they wrote about themselves in relation to others directly and indirectly, spatially and temporally. World-making denotes the symbolic ways in which people comprehend the world across multiple radiating scales: individual, neighbourhood, community, national, regional, global.[22] I consider three modes of world-making—geographic connections, cohorts and imagined worlds—that were underwritten by notions of community service. Drawing attention to multiple levels of identity, world-making necessitates remaining attuned to shifting borders of inclusion and exclusion. Paul Bijl theorised that, through letter-writing, women's advocate Raden Adjeng Kartini crafted

---

17   Taufik Abdullah, *Schools and Politics: The Kaum Muda Movement in West Sumatra (1927–1933)* (Jakarta: Equinox Publishing, 2009 [1971]), 19, 70.
18   Initially Zoebediah Ratna Djoewita and Siti Roehana (Ruhana Kuddus), until 1918, when Ratna Djoewita stepped down. Amna Karim (from Bengkulu) became a co-editor in 1917, joined by Sitti Djatiah and Sitti Noermah.
19   Hadler, *Muslims and Matriarchs*, 145; Beech Jones, 'Textual Worlds'.
20   See Mestika Zed, *Saudagar Pariaman: Menerjang Ombak Membangun Maskapai* [*Pariaman Trader: Riding the Waves, Building a Fleet*] (Depok: LP3ES, 2017).
21   Ann Laura Stoler and Frederick Cooper, 'Between Metropole and Colony: Rethinking a Research Agenda', in *Tensions of Empire: Colonial Cultures in a Bourgeois World*, eds Frederick Cooper and Ann Laura Stoler (Berkeley: University of California Press, 1997), 1–56, doi.org/10.1525/9780520918085-003, at 6.
22   Nathalie Karagiannis, 'Multiple Solidarities: Autonomy and Resistance', in *Varieties of World-Making: Beyond Globalization*, eds Nathalie Karagiannis and Peter Wagner (Liverpool: Liverpool Scholarship Online, 2007), 154–72, doi.org/10.5949/UPO9781846314346.009.

'selves' entitled to European rights and law.²³ The writers examined here did not pursue direct claims to European recognition but rather horizontal bonds with educated girls. While focusing on girls, I acknowledge expressions of gender-based solidarity (*bangsa perempoean*) encompassing students, graduates of teacher training colleges, older women and future women that were for some ethnically confined and for others more open.²⁴ While most younger writers were students or school graduates, older women like the co-editor Siti Roehana (Ruhana Kuddus) were taught to read informally in the family. To examine the writing of girls aged between 11 and their late teens, I follow Saraswati and Beta's framework of decolonial knowledge-production that ties girlhood to youthfulness, rather than strictly defined age cohorts.²⁵ Writers coalesced around their mutual membership of a modern, progressive cohort.

To engage with girls' agency in crafting selves and worlds requires multiple modes of slow, reflective reading. These modes respond to Saraswati and Beta's call for a 'knowing responsibly' framework for Indonesian girlhood studies. They foreground how patriarchal projections of victimhood on to contemporary Indonesian girls are sustained by intersecting colonial race and gender hierarchies.²⁶ This chapter focuses on girls who partially refused such subjectification, emphasising how girls engaged in and crafted modernity. To form a feminist ethics of reading, after Saraswati and Beta, I find instructive María Puig de la Bellacasa's conceptualisation of care as a research method acknowledging interdependency—growing analysis around meaning, rather than dissecting it.²⁷ This method of care co-locates with Mignolo and Walsh, whose decolonial approach involves grasping how Western knowledge systems have been universalised to undo hierarchical structures.²⁸ As Indonesian feminist philosopher Gadis

---

23 Paul Bijl, 'Legal Self-Fashioning in Colonial Indonesia: Human Rights in the Letters of Kartini', *Indonesia* 103 (2017): 51–71, doi.org/10.1353/ind.2017.0002, at 51–54.
24 Bronwyn Anne Beech Jones, 'Narrating Intimate Violence in Public Texts: Women's Writings in the Sumatran Newspaper *Soenting Melajoe*', in *Gender, Violence and Power in Indonesia: Across Time and Space*, eds Katharine McGregor, Ana Dragojlovic, and Hannah Loney (London: Routledge, 2020), 1–38, doi.org/10.4324/9781003022992, at 21.
25 Marissa Saraswati and Annisa R. Beta, 'Knowing Responsibly: Decolonizing Knowledge Production of Indonesian Girlhood', *Feminist Media Studies* 21, no. 5 (2021): 758–74, doi.org/10.1080/14680777.2020.1763418, at 761.
26 ibid., 769.
27 María Puig de la Bellacasa, *Matters of Care: Speculative Ethics in More than Human Worlds* (Minneapolis: University of Minnesota Press, 2017), www.jstor.org/stable/10.5749/j.ctt1mmfspt, 70–75.
28 Walter D. Mignolo and Catherine E. Walsh, *On Decoloniality: Concepts, Analytics, Praxis* (Durham: Duke University Press, 2018), doi.org/10.1215/9780822371779, 17.

Arivia has emphasised, a critically reflexive, decolonial approach positions a researcher/reader as a learner of knowledge, rather than a 'discoverer'.[29] A decolonial ethics of care for reading early twentieth-century Indonesian print culture cultivates analysis by reconstructing textual and social worlds while acknowledging a writer's agency and voice.

At the micro, textual level, this approach involves careful, slow reading to understand individual opinions without assuming that a writer's position or terms remain stable. Showcasing individual concerns by selecting and translating quotes attempts to avoid what Gayatri Spivak referred to as the generic 'international translator-ese' through which non-Western women's writing is presented as sources on distant cultures.[30] At a meso, intertextual level, this necessitates tracking relationships within and across newspapers, including, where possible, reader reception. Reading thematically can illuminate silences, indirection and world-making practices that replicated, were influenced by and resisted colonial structures of power.[31] Third, at a more macro-level, applying a decolonial ethics to reading selves and worlds situates perspectives within wider cultural, political and economic shifts and changes across multiple geographic scales. Cutting across these scales are structures that shape perception, expression and visibility, which underscore the importance of intersectional awareness especially in elite textual spaces.

Bridging: Mapping felt connections

Retna Tenoen's January 1921 letter to *Soenting Melajoe* discussed forms of connection she felt with other parts of Asia. Retna was born on 25 January 1909 and her story in *Soenting Melajoe* was threaded with references to Crown Princess Juliana of the Netherlands and the weaving school Retna's parents founded in Pulau Air, Padang. Retna's father, press entrepreneur and Padang City councillor Majoedin (referred to by his honorifics Datoe' Soetan Maharadja), was a cultural nationalist, who carved out spaces to strengthen Minangkabau matrilineal *adat* ('customary law') as the foundation

---

29   Gadis Arivia, 'Menumbuhkan Analisis Dekolonialisasi di Indonesia: Studi Pemikiran Toety Heraty, Kartini, dan Siti Roehana, Sebuah Refleksi Kritis Filosofis dan Feminis [A Philosophical and Feminist Analysis of Decoloniality in Indonesia: A Critical Study of Toeti Heraty, Kartini, and Siti Roehana]', *Jurnal Perempuan* [*Women's Journal*] 27, no. 2 (2022): 93–102, at 94.
30   Gayatri Chakravorty Spivak, 'The Politics of Translation', in *Outside in the Teaching Machine*, 2nd edn (New York: Routledge Classics, 2009), 200–25, at 204.
31   Linda Tuhiwai Smith, *Decolonizing Methodologies: Research and Indigenous Peoples*, 2nd edn (London: Zed Books, 2012), 45.

of a modern community. Minangkabau girls were frequently cast as objects of interventions in newspapers and the weaving school he founded, where Retna's mother, Siti Amrin, taught.[32] At a night market to mark the tenth birthday of the school and the princess in 1919, Retna made a speech in Dutch and presented a Malay-language poem about the weaving school, celebrating the 'loyal and steadfastly charitable' Netherlands.[33] This event presented a hybrid conception of modernity that emphasised culturally salient girls' skills, such as weaving, lace-making and word craft. Retna also featured prominently in the night market craft showcase and won an award alongside five other young competitors aged between seven and 11 years, who were held up by Datoe' Soetan Maharadja as exemplars of a generation skilled at both Palembang-style embroidery and French knots.[34] Before 1921, Retna's letters reflected a common emphasis in the newspaper on being polite and virtuous.[35] To understand how she layered geographic knowledge in a 1921 letter in *Soenting Melajoe* requires first contextualising the word maps that featured in the same edition. These visualisations were developed in *Soenting Melajoe*'s sibling, the daily *Oetoesan Melajoe* ('*Malay Messenger*') (1911–26).[36] Word maps accompanied articles on World War I and origin stories of the Minangkabau ethnic group, bridging readers with faraway places.

These visualisations arranged words in different fonts to represent locations and distances, crafting a cosmopolitan outlook. In 1915, *Oetoesan Melajoe* published a visualisation of World War I battles. Paired with coverage of troop movements (telegraphed from *Sumatera Bode*'s Batavia office), the map encouraged readers to imagine key locations such as Gallipoli and Galata. Word maps cohere with recent studies of contemporaneous data visualisations as pedagogic tools in newspapers, albeit in more technologically crude ways, indicating vernacular publications' limited budgets.[37] Initial word maps evolved to visualise Minangkabau history. For instance, a 1916 map depicted regions of India in relation to the Himalayas, China, Melaka and Siak in Riau. It accompanied Datoe' Soetan Maharadja's

---

32   Beech Jones, 'Textual Worlds'; Abdullah, *Schools and Politics*, 14–15.
33   'Merayakan Hari Lahir Prinses Juliana [Celebrating Princess Juliana's Birthday]', *Soenting Melajoe* [*Malay Headdress*], 2 May 1919: 2–3; Retna Tenoen, 'Ilmoe Pengetahoean [Knowledge]', *Soenting Melajoe* [*Malay Headdress*], 21 January 1921: 2, Microfilm, 33168008944734 (Melbourne: Monash University).
34   'Tentoonstelling Padang 1919 [1919 Padang Exhibition]', *Soenting Melajoe* [*Malay Headdress*], 30 May 1919: 3.
35   For example, Ratna [sic] Tenoen, 'Nasihat kepada Perempoean Gadis Gedang dan Ketjil [Advice to Girls Young and Old]', *Soenting Melajoe* [*Malay Headdress*], 10 October 1919: 3.
36   Adam, *The Vernacular Press*, 317.
37   Murray Dick, *The Infographic: A History of Data Graphics in News and Communications* (Cambridge: MIT Press, 2020), doi.org/10.7551/mitpress/11379.001.0001, 19.

account of historical Minangkabau connections through trade, religion and matriliny. Women weavers featured prominently in his culturally nationalist vision. Explaining the superiority of Keling fabric for sarongs compared with European fabric, he mused that 'perhaps later Minangkabau women skilled at making sarong for our own consumption will have a product to trade'.[38] To scale up production, he looked to the Pulau Air weaving school in Padang, its sister school in Pariaman and classes offered by Keoetamaan Isteri in Padangpanjang. Word maps thus positioned girls within global networks, bridging a Minangkabau past and future.

Word maps published in *Soenting Melajoe* from November 1920 to January 1921 accompanied accounts of Minangkabau origins. These maps emanated from the centre of the Minangkabau *alam* ('realm', 'world'): Mount Marapi in the highlands. Articles recounted the well-known Minangkabau *tambo* ('origin story')[39] about Iskandar the Great's youngest son, Maharadja Diradja, his wife and a philosopher settled near Mount Marapi, where his wife gave birth to a daughter.[40] New generations expanded out, forming Luhak nan Tigo. Word maps also show later settlements like Bonjol, Kumpulan, Lubuk Sikaping and Air Bangis. Merging with patterns of mobility, these visualisations depict Jambi, Aceh, Bandung, Pontianak and Makassar, where, especially from the late nineteenth century, Minangkabau families migrated, including to take up civil service positions. Word maps thus incorporated girls and women spread across the archipelago into a community, visualising what Hadler termed a 'textual and metaphorical *alam*'.[41] Eleven-year-old Retna Tenoen engaged with these accounts to negotiate her own place in the world.

In January 1921, Retna wrote of her sense of belonging, which was geographically broader than her father's accounts of connections. Her January 1921 article explained that '*Indië*' (Hindia) was derived from the River Indus, south of the Himalaya Mountains, which were visually depicted by their prominent position on the accompanying map (Figure 4.1).[42] She continued:

---

38 7 December 1916; reprinted in 'Bombai', *Soenting Melajoe* [*Malay Headdress*], 8 December 1916: 1, Microfilm, 33168008944775 (Melbourne: Monash University].
39 See Evelyn Blackwood, 'Representing Women: The Politics of Minangkabau *Adat* Writings', *The Journal of Asian Studies* 60, no. 1 (2001): 125–49, doi.org/10.2307/2659507.
40 Datoe' Soetan Maharadja in July 1920 presented another common interpretation: that this movement was during Noah's Flood. See Tsuyoshi Kato, *Matriliny and Migration: Evolving Minangkabau Traditions in Indonesia* (Ithaca: Cornell University Press, 1982), 19, 34–35.
41 ibid., 30–31; Hadler, *Muslims and Matriarchs*, 154.
42 Tenoen, 'Knowledge'.

The Hindu people are a very ancient people who have been civilised for thousands of years, according to a Dutch book. The Hindu people then became our ancestors, the people of the Minangkabau World, who until the present are still called Hindus, which means we are one lineage (*kaoem*), one large family (*familie*) of the same clan.[43]

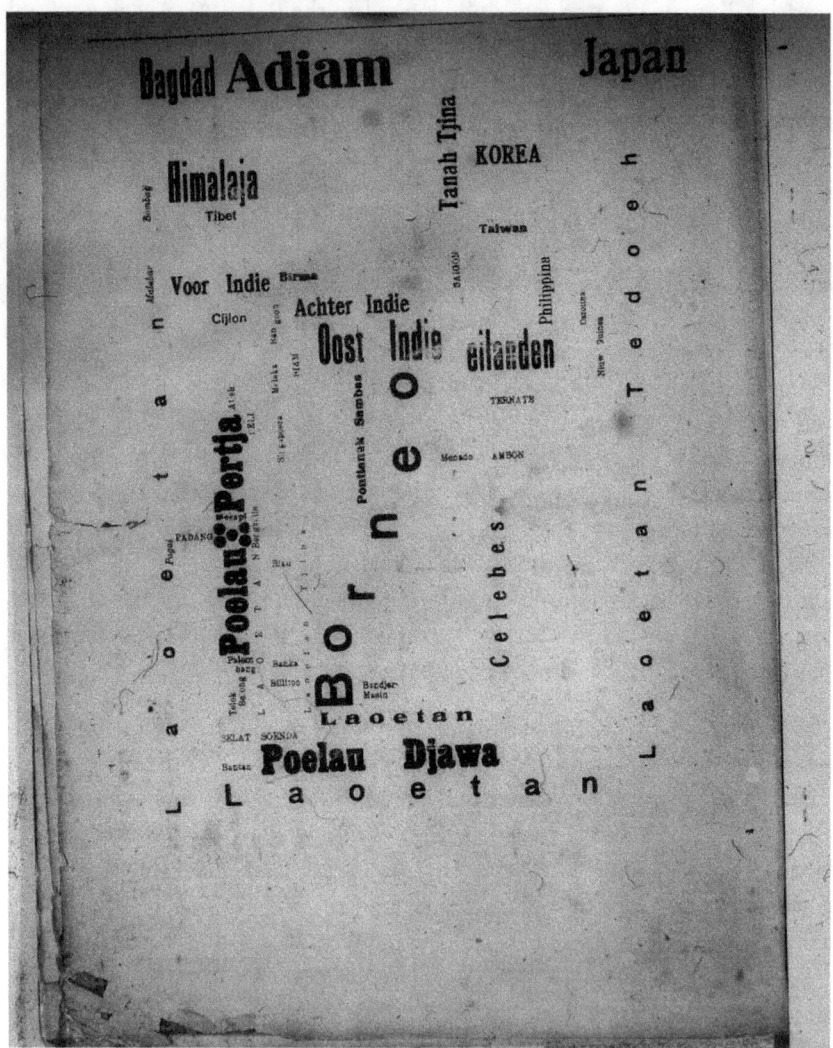

Figure 4.1 Word map in *Soenting Melajoe*, 1921
Source: *Soenting Melajoe*, 14 January 1921.

---

43 ibid., 2.

Similar to scholarship on Malay-ness that has highlighted the influence of colonial hierarchical categories, Retna knitted together origin stories with sources she deemed authoritative.[44] The 'Dutch book' referenced was a P.G. Geysbeek Witsen encyclopedia published in 1861.[45] Six months earlier, Datoe' Soetan Maharadja had used aspects of the encyclopedia entry on India to explain that the Minangkabau were, in his view, descended from the *Kshatriya* ('warrior') caste.[46] While echoing her father's focus on shared lineage, Retna framed her understanding around a quote from the encyclopedia reproduced in *Soenting Melajoe* in Dutch in June 1920: 'Before the Hindus were under the yoke of foreign rulers, they stood on a higher stage of civilization, and their country was the cradle of all arts and sciences.'[47] This account reflects Dutch perceptions of a revered ancient Hindu past set in contrast to a colonised present. Retna reproduced her father's emphasis on common lineage but added the dimension of being a 'family', thus imbuing a sense of her herself and her Minang peers reading the paper as intimately connected across time and space.[48]

Retna's multilayered sense of the world also drew bonds of economic and racial solidarity. She explained that she knew that people from Saigon, Rangoon and Siam (Thailand) had traded with her Minangkabau ancestors 'a very long time ago', had recently supplied the rice she ate and 'helped us in the East Indies when we were struck with the dangers of famine'.[49] News coverage about rice importation embedded certain places with an image of generosity. Despite the Netherlands' wartime neutrality, the importation of rice from Burma was prohibited in 1914 and from French Indochina in 1915. Combined with successive low domestic harvests, this led to progressively higher prices, eventually causing a nearly Indies-wide rice shortage in 1918–19.[50] Retna's focus on cooperation contrasted with discontent expressed in 1918, including in *Soenting Melajoe*, by women working at markets. Her privileged and still-in-formation view abstracted

---

44 Anthony Milner, *The Invention of Politics in Colonial Malaya: Contesting Nationalism and the Expansion of the Public Sphere* (Cambridge: Cambridge University Press, 2002), 51.
45 P.G. Witsen Geysbeek, *Algemeen Noodwendig Woordenboek der Zamenleving* [*General Essential Dictionary of Society*]. Volume 6 (Gouda: Witsen G.B. van Goor en D. Noothoven van Goor, n.d.).
46 Datoe' Soetan Maharadja, 'Asal Oesel Nikik Mojang [The Origin of the Ancestors]', *Soenting Melajoe* [*Malay Headdress*], 23 June 1920: 1. For more on economic and cultural flows, see, for example, André Wink, *Al-Hind: The Making of the Indo-Islamic World. Volume 2* (Leiden: Brill, 2002), 289.
47 Witsen Geysbeek, *General Essential Dictionary of Society*, 290.
48 For uses of *famili*, see Hadler, *Muslims and Matriarchs*, 86.
49 Tenoen, 'Knowledge'.
50 Kees van Dijk, *The Netherlands Indies and the Great War, 1914–1918* (Leiden: KITLV Press, 2007), doi.org/10.26530/OAPEN_389234, 369.

trade to cooperation and friendship, removed from the material realities of food price increases and crop failures. This view of the world led Retna to also suggest that, as a member of the Minangkabau ethnic group and Malay race, she shared racial similarities with people in Siam. Retna's account contained a greater flexibility compared with her father's explanation of a modern world divided into five racial categories.[51] She wrote that 'for people from China and Japan a desirable colour is that which is like their skin, and for people from Siam a desirable colour is that which is like their skin'.[52] L. Ayu Saraswati argued that classification projects in *Soenting Melajoe* demonstrate racial awareness and hierarchies that were resisted in the formation of a non-racial Indonesian-ness.[53] By contrast, Retna's letter looked out to parts of Asia beyond the colonial borders that became the nation of Indonesia to form a decentred sense of beauty and desirability.

Retna's predominant focus on being Minangkabau and Malay generated the historical and contemporary connections she shared with others, particularly girls who similarly learned at a *HIS*. Towards the end of her letter, she posed a series of questions about her identity as a Dutch-educated Minang girl:

> Would it not be good if girls of my people sometimes wore clothes like Siamese girls? Chinese women's clothes are often copied and have become models, and European women's clothes have become exemplars ... What would it be like if we wore the clothes of Siamese girls, we who already understand Dutch; what would happen if we wore clothes like the Siamese?[54]

Retna questioned whether clothes reconstructed a self, strongly contrasting with a 1919 writer who condemned women who wore European-style dresses without head coverings as 'not deeply rooted in their ethnic group and ... not truly of Minangkabau blood'.[55] Her points of reference are reminiscent of earlier writers who looked to Siam with admiration for modernisation and wariness that forms of female work, such as being royal

---

51 Bronwyn Anne Beech Jones, 'Crafting Community', *Inside Indonesia* [SI], no. 144 (April–June 2021), www.insideindonesia.org/crafting-community.
52 Tenoen, 'Knowledge'.
53 L. Ayu Saraswati, *Seeing Beauty, Sensing Race in Transnational Indonesia* (Honolulu: University of Hawai`i Press, 2013), doi.org/10.21313/hawaii/9780824836641.001.0001, 64.
54 Tenoen, 'Knowledge'.
55 Sitti Noersjamsoe, 'De Aanhouder Wint [Persevere]', *Soenting Melajoe* [*Malay Headdress*], 21 March 1919: 2–3; Bronwyn Anne Beech Jones, '"The Age of Women Adept at Writing": Female Voices from the Dutch East Indies in the Early Twentieth Century', *Agora* 56, no. 1 (2021): 69–75.

guards, were narrowing due to Western influence.⁵⁶ Nonetheless, Retna's questions specifically pertained to a subset—'we who already understand Dutch'—underlining an assumed classist requirement to fully embody this modernity. Retna carved out space to consider her evolving sense of self through school, her father and the newspaper. This case nuances Anderson's identification that colonial mapping introduced new, dominant ideas about space by demonstrating multilayering.⁵⁷ In *Soenting Melajoe*, colonial knowledge-making practices such as the categorising and universal intent of encyclopedias and spatial organising were co-located with local understandings of the past and imagined interpersonal connections.

Meeting: Serving local communities

Soenting Melajoe is an archive containing subcommunities of friendships. The newspaper has predominantly been analysed as a product of ethnically Minangkabau women, mirroring its subtitle as a women's newspaper for 'Women of the Minangkabau Alam'. However, attention to the locations of writers reveals how, alongside large cohorts throughout the west coast of Sumatra, contributors were spread in regional centres and towns on Sumatra and trading ports on other islands.⁵⁸ This section explores a coalition of girls who self-identified as being Mandailing, Tapanuli and Batak who have not been the subject of previous analyses.⁵⁹ It adds to a method of reading world-making attention to how homelands were imagined within *Soenting Melajoe* and underwritten by notions of service.

From 1917 *Soenting Melajoe* reported on a weaving school for girls, Panagoe Hagabean in Padangsidempuan, and how girls and women from this area attended weaving schools in Padang. Salamah attended a *HIS* in Padangsidempuan before her father, Maharadja Djamboer djagong Nasoetion Brotan, supported her to undertake craft schoolteacher training in Padang and then return to teach in Panyabungan, Natal.⁶⁰ Salamah and

---

56 Noerela Anwar, 'Gerakkan Perempoean Bangsa Asing [Foreign Nations' Women's Movements]', *Soenting Melajoe* [*Malay Headdress*], 3 August 1912: 1.
57 Benedict Anderson, *Imagined Communities: Reflections on the Origin and Spread of Nationalism*, 2nd edn (London: Verso, 2006), 174.
58 See Beech Jones, 'Narrating Intimate Violence in Public Texts', 21.
59 Adding to the timeline of North Sumatran women's writing in Sartika Sari, *Gagasan Kesetaraan Gender dalam Puisi yang Terbit di Surat Kabar di Sumatera Bagian Utara 1919–1941* [*Ideas of Gender Equality in Poetry Published in North Sumatran Newspapers, 1919–1941*] (Yogyakarta: CV Arti Bumi Intaran, 2018).
60 'Kepandaian oentoek Perempoean [Skills for Women]', *Soenting Melajoe* [*Malay Headdress*], 2 February 1917: 1; Hadler, *Muslims and Matriarchs*, 150–51.

this nongovernment school were nodes in an expanding network of schools in central Sumatra, including Angkola-Batak and Malay-language primary schools and Dutch-language schools for elite girls and boys.[61] Two years later, Salamah dedicated two poems in *Soenting Melajoe* to Siti Hafasah (known as Boeroe Enggan) that encouraged devotion to developing Panyabungan through formal education and learning weaving in Padang. She switched between Malay and Mandailing (underlined).[62] These extracts illustrate how place, community and cause were structured as dialogue.

> Oranges, limes, and pomegranates
> The train from Pariaman arrives
> The cries of Sitti Salamah
> [I] hope she is praised by the people of Panyabungan.
>
> Brought by train from Pariaman
> To Padang
> To the government I entreat
> For the cries of women to be answered …
>
> Listen to the [calls for] progress
> Men and women to advance together
> My cries are no different
> Only that my homeland is no different
> Only a matter for my homeland P. Panyabungan …
>
> But actually nonetheless,
> I do not agree with holding hands
> As is the way of Europeans
> I only wish to advance together …
>
> Even though the old seem like children
> That is what I really wish for
> To the government of Batak lands.
> I hope what I wish for comes true
>
> The ship arrives from Hindustan
> And docks at Pulau Batu
> Oh, Hafasah Boeroe Enggan!
> Greetings of welcome for you.

---

61   Susan Rodgers, 'Sutan Pangurabaan Rewrites Sumatran Language Landscapes: The Political Possibilities of Commercial Print in the Late Colonial Indies', *Bijdragen tot de Taal-, Land- en Volkenkunde* [*Journal of the Humanities and Social Sciences of Southeast Asia*] 168, no. 1 (2012): 26–54, doi.org/10.1163/22134379-90003568, at 32–33.

62   Thank you to Abuy Ravana Siregar and Arpin Siregar for assistance translating Bahasa Mandailing.

Docking briefly at P. Batoe,⁶³
The sailor sings so sweetly,
I greet you with my hand <u>my friend</u>
<u>So I say</u> my <u>name</u> …

Oh B. Enggan, my peer,
<u>Batak *adat*</u>
<u>Is said to be the guide</u>
<u>If we are of different nations</u>
<u>We are family</u>
<u>Loving each other even though it's hard</u>

Oh my <u>sister</u>! If you like confusion in your chest
<u>Since we met</u>
<u>Even though we are far my sister</u>
<u>Here is our meeting place</u>

Oh! B. Enggan (<u>my sister-in-law</u>)
With this I say
Perhaps my sister has not met me
But with SM we meet.⁶⁴

Writing predominantly in Malay connected writers to a larger community of women and girl readers and coded for participating in modernity. As Tom Hoogervorst and Henk Schulte Nordholt have argued in the case of the contemporaneous Javanese middle class, notions of progress, innovation and agency encompassed by modernity were embodied and enacted. Reading and writing in Malay, they suggest, became 'the source of self-identification for the upwardly mobile middle classes, setting them apart from the rural and working-class communities'.⁶⁵ In Malay, Salamah endorsed progress and education and echoed a common critique of women's calls for personal liberty and public handholding in rival publication *Soeara Perempoean* ('*Women's Voice*').⁶⁶ She also reached out to forge friendship

---

63   A small group of islands near Nias.
64   Salamah, 'The Cry of Sitti Salamah Boroe Dolok'.
65   See Tom Hoogervorst and Henk Schulte Nordholt, 'Urban Middle Classes in Colonial Java (1900–1942): Images and Language', *Bijdragen Tot de Taal-, Land- en Volkenkunde* [*Journal of the Humanities and Social Sciences of Southeast Asia*] 173, no. 4 (2017): 442–74, doi.org/10.1163/22134379-17304002, at 453; see also Su Lin Lewis, *Cities in Motion: Urban Life and Cosmopolitanism in Southeast Asia, 1920–1940* (Cambridge: Cambridge University Press, 2016), doi.org/10.1017/CBO9781316257937.
66   For more on *Soeara Perempoean* editor Saadah Alim, see Aura Asmaradana, 'Di Bawah Bayang-bayang Adat: Sebuah Pembacaan atas Hidup, Pemikiran, dan Karya Saadah Alim [Under the Shadow of *Adat*: A Reading of the Life, Thought, and Works of Saadah Alim]', in *Yang Terlupakan dan Dilupakan: Membaca Kembali Sepuluh Penulis Perempuan Indonesia* [*Those Accidentally Forgotten and Those Forgotten: Rereading Ten Indonesian Women Writers*], ed. Ruang Perempuan dan Tulisan (Jakarta: Marjin Kiri, 2021), 150–60.

across distance in the newspaper: 'Perhaps my sister has not met me/ But with SM we meet.' However, the words Salamah chose to express in Mandailing—'people', 'you', 'friend', 'sister', 'family', 'meeting place'— suggest attempts to emphasise thick ties of intimacy and local connection among a subcommunity of readers. This poem to a peer from Panyabungan coheres with Rodgers' observation that the elite sons and daughters in the southern Sipirok region 'were generally proudly multilingual' from the 1880s.[67] Salamah also expressed criticism of her elders for being 'like children', presumably referring to their lack of formal education, to this more intimate Mandailing readership. At the same time, this subcommunity of writers in *Soenting Melajoe* commonly conveyed everyday expressions of Islamic faith—a common world-making effort in the publication, which sought commonality with Minangkabau girls in West Sumatra as well as other Muslim readers.[68] Poems presented vignettes of Ramadan and Eid al-Fitr, and many writers bookended articles with Arabic expressions.

Alongside common language use, Mount Sibualbuali featured as a motif of a Tapanuli homeland, including in titles and embedded in verses. H.W. Siparloengoen signed as the 'Fairy of Sipirok' and wrote in a combination of English (underlined) and Malay. She had moved from Sipirok in 1913 with her family and studied at the American Methodist School in Medan, dreaming of a familiar landscape:

> <u>When the nigt</u> [sic] has come
> From Sirumalun, in Deli
> <u>In my eyes</u> I spot Si Bualbuali,
> <u>Very, very far away</u>, like a stove pot.[69]

Writing about home was a creative endeavour, a testimony and an appeal. H.W. Siparloengoen emphasised that her family was from Hasibun, 100 kilometres north of Sipirok, reflecting multilayered spatial identities and networks.[70] She wrote in a playful combination of English, Malay and Mandailing. For instance, she signed off one May 1918 letter by expressing,

---

67 Rodgers, 'Sutan Pangurabaan Rewrites Sumatran Language Landscapes', 32.
68 Daniel Perret, 'Ethnicity and Colonization in Northeast Sumatra: Bataks and Malays', in *From Distant Tales: Archaeology and Ethnohistory in the Highlands of Sumatra*, eds Dominik Bonatz, John Miksic, J. David Neidel, and Mai Lin Tjoa-Bonatz (Newcastle upon Tyne: Cambridge Scholars Publishing, 2009), 143–68, at 158.
69 K.M. alias Fairy Sipirok, 'Siroemaloen From [From Siroemaloen]', *Soenting Melajoe* [*Malay Headdress*], 18 July 1918: 3.
70 H.W. Siparloengoen, 'Eme Dibaboan From [From a Weeded Rice Field]', *Soenting Melajoe* [*Malay Headdress*], 26 July 1918: 1.

in English: 'I hope my dear sisters, let me hear about Green Field of Sipirok by return of the post.'[71] Other writers named friends living away from their hometown, celebrating students, teachers and assistant teachers in Sibolga, Balige and Medan to document how 'the people of Tapanuli have a role'.[72] Led by middle to upper-class educated Tapanuli youth and reliant on trickle-down benefits, these aspirations for modernity were premised on the universal adoption of newness as a collective aspiration.[73]

Expressions of love for homelands were politically inflected through appeals to service. Siti Hafasah explicitly posed a mission for girls to inspire one another to strive for opportunities in Sipirok, 'so that those in our hometowns, our brothers and sisters, can pick those delicious fruits'— presumably, the familiar ingredients of formal education, employment, consumer goods and physical and social mobility.[74] The next year, she urged compatriots to 'wake up from your sleep' to develop their homeland, which she believed to be 'behind' in consensus-making, intelligence, agriculture and patriotism.[75] Aligning a lack of adequate schooling and agricultural infrastructure with political mechanisms and sentiments shows an ascendent emphasis on organising, which nevertheless commonly appealed to Batak *adat* as a guide, as in Salamah's poem. At the same time, some writers also lamented barriers to enacting this modernity. For instance, Nai Angat Soer Tapanoeli lamented the risks and precarity experienced by young people who left Tapanuli for jobs in Deli, on the east coast of Sumatra, where, according to the apparently popular refrains sung by children, 'I thought I wanted to go to Deli but I don't have enough money for the journey', and where 'the young unemployed are discarded'.[76] Nevertheless, more detailed accounts of personal experiences of disappointment and labour, especially in

---

71   Fairy Sipirok, 'From Sirumalun'.
72   Limbajoeng and Noersitti, 'Kiriman dari Sipirok: Kedatangan jang Pertama [Letter from Sipirok: The First Entry]', *Soenting Melajoe [Malay Headdress]*, 12 April 1918: 2.
73   Jean Gelman Taylor, 'The Sewing-Machine in Colonial-Era Photographs: A Record from Dutch Indonesia', *Modern Asian Studies* 46, no. 1 (2012): 71–95, doi.org/10.1017/s0026749x11000576, at 87.
74   K. Madjenoen, 'Sipirok', *Soenting Melajoe [Malay Headdress]*, 11 January 1918: 2; similar sentiment also expressed in Sitti H., 'Tanah Airkoe Sipirok [My Homeland, Sipirok]', *Soenting Melajoe [Malay Headdress]*, 8 February 1918: 2; Hoogervorst and Schulte Nordholt, 'Urban Middle Classes in Colonial Java', 469.
75   Siti Hafasah Boroe Enggan, 'Bangsakoe Tapanoeli [My Tapanuli People]', *Soenting Melajoe [Malay Headdress]*, 30 May 1919: 2.
76   Nai Angat Soer Tapanoeli, 'Sian Sihadaoan [From Afar]', *Soenting Melajoe [Malay Headdress]*, 9 May 1919: 2.

the plantation economy, were undiscussed in *Soenting Melajoe*, reinforcing its utility in narrating discourses within modernity and coloniality rather than resistance.

This cohort nuances Perret's identification that different communities (*bangsa*) competed against one another to achieve 'progress'.[77] Writers articulated the feeling of falling behind, which does invoke competition to achieve Eurocentric modernity, but this reaction also saw the cultivation of subnational political discourse. Girls adopted a primary language of service that was tied to local communities but also extended beyond ethnic difference to common gender, especially to appeal to Minangkabau peers. Appeals were advanced to established community organisations and educated girl reading publics, rather than linked to perceived differences between women in Minang matrilineal and Mandailing and Batak groups' patrilineal *adat*. This analysis supports Grace T. Leksana's (Chapter 5 in this volume) questioning of the extent to which understandings of coloniality provide space for Indonesian agency to adopt and adapt to modernity, but also underlines the predominance of discourses of service to an ethnic nation or local community, albeit outwardly linked by common gender and youth. These discourses emphasised leadership but replicated colonial trickle-down models of education and modernity, dominating but never fully consuming individual expressions of belonging and friendship.

Scripting: Tracing intertextual critique

A focus on translated fiction further illuminates intertextual discursive formation. Literary fiction was a popular genre of consumption, some written expressly for newspapers and some adapted and serialised to encourage repeat purchases.[78] Extant copies of the monthly periodical *Minangkabau* (1918) suggest that Fatimah Rasad translated two stories, 'The Empty Drum' (titled 'Emelyan the Day Labourer') by Leo Tolstoy and 'The Story of Kuprin's Mother', attributed to a Muslim woman named Moesafir. The microfilm copies I accessed did not contain either story in full, so I have chosen to analyse the more complete, 'The Empty Drum'.[79]

---

77   Perret, 'Ethnicity and Colonization in Northeast Sumatra', 158.
78   Joachim Nieβ, 'Telling and Selling: Literary Fiction in Early Malay Language Newspapers in Colonial Indonesia', *Wacana: Journal of the Humanities of Indonesia* 17, no. 3 (2017): 377–403, doi.org/10.17510/wacana.v17i3.453, at 383.
79   Extracts of 'The Story of Kuprin's Mother' demonstrate a similar concern for the international situation and maternal themes.

This section offers a speculative reading of Fatimah's translation of this 1891 short story based on a Volga region folktale. The story follows the poor labourer Emelyan, who meets an otherworldly, beautiful woman, who suggests that they marry despite Emelyan's hesitation because of his limited means. The tsar, glimpsing the beauty of Emelyan's wife, desires her as his own and seeks to work Emelyan to death, yet Emelyan survives and eventually prevails by summoning the tsar's soldiers and destroying the drum of war. Although Fatimah did not directly write of herself or her world, an intertextual analysis of her translation reveals worlding that connected local discourses on capitalist injustice to global literary flows.

Fatimah's translation was published in *Minangkabau*, a periodical that promoted self-sufficiency. Under Netherlands-educated agriculturalist Bagindo Djamaloeddin Rasjad, the monthly attracted subscribers in Pariaman, the West Sumatran highlands and Aceh.[80] While studying in Wageningen in 1910, Djamaloeddin wrote about the obligation to work with Dutch officials as equals: '[W]hile these matters [progress] are incredibly large, they can in fact become light if we, the children of the earth and government officials, white and black, see each other as carrying it together.'[81] Correspondingly, the 1918 publication *Minangkabau* positioned itself as upholding justice, couched in a colonial humanist position of improving conditions to achieve welfare—somewhat symptomatic of the Ethical Policy but with an emphasis on local leadership.[82] The August editorial stressed how agriculture underpinned the lives of all, 'from the day labourer to the Governor General'.[83] Some writers, however, emphasised that to become knowledgeable and skilled, farmers needed to learn from Indonesian agriculturalists, as 'agriculturalists in the Netherlands [provide examples] for farmers native to the Netherlands, or German agricultural officials in Germany'.[84] *Minangkabau*'s focus on self-sufficiency also reflects wartime economic shifts.[85] Fakih suggested that the war resulted in the expansion of credit and the employment of Indonesian men in administrative positions,

---

80 Adam, *Minangkabau Voices*, 148.
81 Djamaloeddin Rasad, *Boeah-Pikiran* [*Essays*] (The Hague: Luyendijk, 1910), 44.
82 See also Joel S. Kahn, *Constituting the Minangkabau: Peasants, Culture and Modernity in Colonial Indonesia* (Providence: Berg, 1993), 122.
83 'Pembatja-pembatja j.t. [Dear Readers]', *Minangkabau*, August 1918: 3.
84 '6. Aniaja jang Didatangkan oleh Wang Pindjaman kepada Sipeladang [6. The Suffering Brought About by Money Lent to Farmers]', *Minangkabau*, October 1918: 35.
85 In the case of copra, in 1915, 17,000 tonnes passed through Padang's Telukbayur (Emmahaven) port, steeply declining to 8,000 in 1917 and 692 in 1918, before rebounding to 30,000 tonnes in 1919. John A. Fowler, 'Copra and Coconut Oils in the Netherlands Indies and British Malaya', *Trade Information Bulletin Foodstuffs Division*, no. 34 (9 June 1922), 8.

which exposed Indonesians to racial discrimination, while *Minangkabau* underlines its influence in cementing a commitment to self-help.[86] More seismic yet was the deepening of a cash economy. While in 1905 only 4.5 per cent of West Sumatra's male agricultural population did not own their land, by 1920, 20 per cent engaged in wage labour.[87] *Minangkabau*'s opening editorial stated that wartime disruptions had altered perspectives: 'We understand even more because we have felt the difficulties and ill-fortune of this world war that farming is the mother of all industries on earth.'[88]

Fatimah and her colleagues sought to serve farmers. She had recently graduated from the King's School in Bukittinggi and worked at the Minangkabau Cooperative Bank run by Sarekat Minangkabau in Pariaman.[89] This bank provided loans to farmers. Sarekat Minangkabau established itself as a bridge between colonial agricultural offices and farmers, in contrast to Mohammad Hatta's later conception of cooperatives carving out autonomous economic spaces to free Indonesian capabilities and energies from colonial structures of dependence.[90] Advertisements to join the bank and association addressed both women and men. Beyond bringing together village (*nagari*) heads in Pariaman to develop training in agriculture with the district government, the association advanced more forthright political agendas, including women petitioning to replace a district head[91] and the association advocating for autocratic rules to be replaced with democracy in 1919.[92] The association imagined an inherently racialised local (*bumiputera*, 'son of the earth') solidarity with lower-class farmers, positioning them as

---

86   Farabi Fakih, 'The Bolshevik Infection: European Perspectives on Communism in the Netherlands East Indies Press', in *The Russian Revolution in Asia: From Baku to Batavia*, eds Sabine Dullin, Étienne Forestier-Peyrat, Yuexin Rachel Lin, and Naoko Shimazu (London: Routledge, 2022), 91–107, doi.org/10.4324/9780429352195, at 92.

87   Pim de Zwart, 'Globalisation, Inequality and Institutions in West Sumatra and West Java, 1800–1940', *Journal of Contemporary Asia* 51, no. 4 (2021): 564–90, doi.org/10.1080/00472336.2020.1765189, at 574.

88   *Minangkabau*, August 1918: 4, Microfilm, 33168134992318 (Melbourne: Monash University).

89   The first female graduate of the King's School was Sjarifah in 1907. See Hadler, *Muslims and Matriarchs*, 95.

90   Suzanne Moon, 'Building from the Outside In: Sociotechnical Imaginaries and Society in New Order Indonesia', in *Dreamscapes of Modernity: Sociotechnical Imaginaries and the Fabrication of Power*, eds Sheila Jasanoff and Sang-Hyun Kim (Chicago: University of Chicago Press, 2015), 174–98, doi.org/10.7208/chicago/9780226276663.003.0008, at 78; see also John Ingleson, 'Mutual Benefit Societies in Indonesia', *International Social Security Review* 46, no. 3 (1993): 69–77, doi.org/10.1111/j.1468-246X.1993.tb00384.x, at 70.

91   'Perskroniek Inlandsche Bladen. Sarikat Minangkabau [Press Chronicle, Native Newspapers. Minangkabau Association]', *Bataviaasch Nieuwsblad* [Batavia Newspaper], 9 May 1919: 1, resolver.kb.nl/resolve?urn=ddd:011038568:mpeg21:p001.

92   'Uit Ai Maleische -pers [From the Malay Press]', *Sumatra Post*, 25 April 1919: 10, resolver.kb.nl/resolve?urn=ddd:010367809:mpeg21:p01.

victims of capitalist exploitation and government ineptitude that inhibited higher crop grades and more advantageous supply chains. *Minangkabau* framed the Cooperative Bank as helping farmers navigate traders, who were their 'whole world' (*bumi langit*), yet the publication set about increasing awareness among agricultural officials rather than engaging directly with farmers.[93] *Minangkabau*'s emphasis on local and global interconnectedness frames Fatimah's translation of Tolstoy's short story 'The Empty Drum', published in the August and September issues.

Fatimah's translation scripted local grievances with economic modernity into global circuits of moral literature. Analysing contemporaneous Korean translators of Tolstoy, Heekyoung Cho argued that translators idealised Tolstoy and minimised the citation of influential Japanese texts to craft an image of a nationalist-resisting intellectual.[94] Why this story was selected for *Minangkabau* and by whom cannot be definitively stated. Equally, it can only be presumed that Fatimah translated from Dutch. Significantly, Fatimah did not vernacularise 'The Empty Drum' by adapting it to her local context. Apart from one addition of '*Bismillah*' (*Basmala*) and an emphasis on divine fate, her translation resembles widely accessible English-language translations of Tolstoy's work.[95] This contrasts with Hoogervorst's work on Chinese Indonesian translators who, he argued, attempted to 'de-Europeanise' short stories by staging narratives for 'a more forward-looking, ethnically heterogeneous readership'.[96] Instead, Fatimah's translation extended the geography of *Minangkabau*, appealing to a belief that the ingenuity of the oppressed would overcome unjust labour relations. The dually fatalistic and agentive world view of 'The Empty Drum' is captured by Emelyan's wife, who, having presented an evening meal, reassures her husband, 'Don't look before or behind to see how much you have done or how much there is left to do; only keep on working and all will be alright.'[97] The story emphasises women's strength through the characters of Emelyan's

---

93 *Minangkabau*, October 1918: 31, August–October, Microfilm, 33168134992318 (Melbourne: Monash University).
94 Heekyoung Cho, *Translation's Forgotten History: Russian Literature, Japanese Mediation, and the Formation of Modern Korean Literature* (Cambridge: Harvard University Asia Center, 2016), doi.org/10.1163/9781684175697, 48.
95 In contrast to Maier's analysis of novels and serialised fiction in *We Are Playing Relatives*, 147.
96 Tom G. Hoogervorst, 'Gained in Translation: The Politics of Localising Western Stories in Late-Colonial Indonesia', in *Translational Politics in Southeast Asian Literatures: Contesting Race, Gender, and Sexuality*, ed. Grace V.S. Chin (New York: Routledge, 2021), 100–31, doi.org/10.4324/9781003036128, at 123; Nieβ, 'Telling and Selling Literary Fiction', 388.
97 Leo Tolstoy, 'Tjerita Sipeladang Koeli Hari Emeljan [Story of the Day Labouring Farmer]', trans. Fatimah Rasad, *Minangkabau*, August 1918, 9–10.

wife and a grandmother, who enables Emelyan's survival by completing seemingly impossible tasks, but it also reinscribes gendered scripts of conjugal service, domesticity and objectifying patriarchal competition.

The positioning of Fatimah's translation underneath essays in *Minangkabau* perhaps invited parallels to be drawn between Emelyan and the tsar, who attempts to work the man to death to marry his wife, and farmers perceived to be exploited by a cash economy. Titling the story 'The Day Labouring Farmer' (*sipeladang koeli hari*), Fatimah scripted it into *Minangkabau*'s emerging anti-capitalist, anticolonial vernacular about the exploitation of farmers (*peladang*) and day labourers (*koeli beroesaha tanah*). The publication repeatedly critiqued Dutch and Chinese Indonesian agents who bought crops in advance at reduced prices, which supported the consumption aspirations of farmers and entered them into inescapable cycles of financial uncertainty, calling them those 'who are unashamed of enriching themselves with the sweat of the farmer'.[98] This critique was positioned above a passage of 'The Empty Drum' describing the tsar's obsession with exploiting Emelyan. Similarly, the tsar's cunning plan to make Emelyan guess the one object he desires was positioned below a letter decrying how practices of advance payment to purchase lifestyle products marketed as necessary to be modern conveyed a cycle of suffering with a smile. The page included the caustic critique of traders and lenders who 'will help until' the farmer 'is diminished and broken'—a helplessness compounded by Fatimah's translation of the impossibility of Emelyan guessing correctly.[99] Although the deliberate or accidental nature of layout decisions remains unclear, read intertextually, the translation appealed to a global sense of the inevitable overthrow of exploitative relations, with Emelyan's destruction of the symbol of the tsar's legitimacy, the empty drum of war.

The reaction of three girl readers to Fatimah's translation underlines how her work conveyed female utility. Tjajadani Saleh, Alidjah Rasjid and Noermali Latif were students at a *HIS* in Pariaman and wrote to *Soenting Melajoe* to celebrate Fatimah Rasad as shaping a new progressivism and enlarged world. They stated that Fatimah 'found examples [of] how progress is in other lands, to provide lessons to us women in Sumatra'.[100] These girls interpreted Fatimah's employment as wanting not to serve the Netherlands East Indies

---

98 'Tanaman Teroetama [Primary Crops]', *Minangkabau*, September 1918: 26.
99 Tolstoy, 'Story of the Day Labouring Farmer', 37.
100 Tjajadani Saleh, Alidjah Rasjid, and Noermali Latif, 'Soerat Kiriman dari Periaman [Letter from Pariaman]', *Soenting Melajoe* [*Malay Headdress*], 11 October 1918: 1.

Government but to serve *the* girls of Pariaman. 'Because she loves us women she does not want to be employed by the government, Uni Fatimah Rasad intends to advance girls of Pariaman to the field of progress.'[101] They located Fatimah at the centre of a map linking their local context to global circuits of knowledge. Building off Jedamski's claim that '*pribumi* [native Indonesian] writers did not recognise the political potential of translated or adapted fiction' in her account of colonial-era Chinese-Malay and Eurasian translators, for these girl readers, the political potential was a female translator rather than her translation.[102] Their praise reinscribed the purpose of education as 'sharpening minds in the way of the Dutch'.[103] Yet, at the same time, they emphasised how Fatimah, a King's School graduate, chose to work outside the state education system.[104] Notwithstanding an inability to precisely identify Fatimah's intentions, Tjajadani, Alidjah and Noermali's interpretation of her community service demonstrates the significance of her labour in creating a desirable imagined world.

Conclusion: Reading selves and worlds in letters

For the elite girl writers in this chapter, modernity promised opportunities to be educated, work and serve their community, ethnic nation and gender. Their diverse self-making and world-making efforts—bridging forms of knowledge, meeting common goals and scripting local critiques into global circuits—coalesce in discourses of service that positioned the education of privileged girls as a societal good. These discourses conformed to the coloniality of power by presenting Western education and wage employment as the means to achieve modernity. The hierarchy and singularity inherent within coloniality are echoed in Siti Hafasah's identification of her Tapanuli community as being 'behind' in multiple political and economic ways. This chapter extends an understanding of print culture's role in demarcating collective identities (see Ricci's Chapter 3 in this volume), revealing ambiguous visions about who could embody modernity. Retna imagined

---

101 ibid. *Uni* is a Minang term of address for a (older) sister.
102 Doris Jedamski, 'Translation in the Malay World: Different Communities, Different Agendas', in *Asian Translation Traditions*, eds Eva Tsoi Hung and Judy Wakabayashi (London: Routledge, 2005), 211–45, at 223.
103 Saleh et al., 'Letter from Pariaman'.
104 Many Sumatran elite nationalists later attended the King's School. See Hadler, *Muslims and Matriarchs*, 97.

herself and other elite girls across borders, while Fatimah Rasad worked for agendas of Pariaman *bumiputera* self-help that defined them against what they perceived as economic exploitation through moneylending and brokerage. These self-making and world-making efforts are more complex than appropriation, erasure and replication.[105] Tjajadani, Alidjah and Noermali's interpretation of Fatimah's translation and employment as community rather than government service opens the possibility of desires and engagement that both cohered with forms of colonial knowledge production and critiqued the colonial state.

Visibility was a cornerstone of elite-dominated textual communities. Decolonially reading girls' writing recognises them as products of privileged subjectivities reliant on rendering invisible lower-class girls, who were not seen to embody a Dutch-speaking modernity sketched by Retna and were not necessarily materially served by elite girls' educational advancement through exclusive systems. These case studies underline the contingency of engaging responsibly with girls in print culture.[106] Claiming historical subjectivity for elite girl writers by reading their words, seeking to understand their perspectives and influences and growing an analysis with them must be advanced with attention to limitations and silences as symptoms of the structures in which their agency operated. Such ambivalences were shaped by their privileged life worlds but are also characteristic of their youthful always-in-formation selves. Making visible multiple processes of self-making and world-making lays claim to girls' production, adaptation and consumption within local and global circuits of ideas that shaped the worlds of far more girls than those who signed their names into these print culture archives.

References

Primary sources

Bataviaasch Nieuwsblad. 1913. 'Gouvernements Onderwijs voor Inlandsche Meisjes [Government Education for Native Girls].' *Bataviaasch Nieuwsblad* [*Batavia Newspaper*], 16 June: 5. resolver.kb.nl/resolve?urn=ddd:011036306:mpeg21:p005.

---

105 Stoler and Cooper, 'Between Metropole and Colony', 6.
106 Saraswati and Beta, 'Knowing Responsibly', 771.

Bataviaasch Nieuwsblad. 1919. 'Perskroniek Inlandsche Bladen. Sarikat Minangkabau' [Press Chronicle, Native Newspapers. Minangkabau Association].' *Bataviaasch Nieuwsblad* [*Batavia Newspaper*], 9 May: 1. resolver.kb.nl/resolve?urn=ddd: 011038568:mpeg21:p001.

Fowler, John A. 1922. 'Copra and Coconut Oils in the Netherlands Indies and British Malaya.' *Trade Information Bulletin Foodstuffs Division*, no. 34 (9 June).

Lekkerkerker, C. 1914. *Meisjesonderwijs, Coeducatie en Meisjesscholen voor de Inlandsche Bevolking in Nederlandsch-Indië, 1914* [*Girls' Education, Co-Education and Girls' Schools for the Native Population of the Netherlands Indies, 1914*]. Padangpanjang: Pusat Dokumentasi dan Informasi Minangkabau [Minangkabau Documentation and Information Centre].

Minangkabau. 1918. August–October. Microfilm, 33168134992318. Melbourne: Monash University.

Oetoesan Melajoe [*Malay Messenger*]. 1915–26. Vols 5–16. Microfilm, 33168179 290909. Melbourne: Monash University.

Rasad, Djamaloeddin. 1910. *Boeah-Pikiran* [*Essays*]. The Hague: Luyendijk.

Soenting Melajoe [*Malay Headdress*]. 1912–16. Vol. 1, no. 2 (1912) – vol. 5, no. 51 (1916). Microfilm, 33168008944775. Melbourne: Monash University.

Soenting Melajoe [*Malay Headdress*]. 1917–21. Vol. 6, no. 1 (1917) – vol. 10, no. 4 (1921). Microfilm, 33168008944734. Melbourne: Monash University.

Sumatra Post. 1919. 'Uit Ai Maleische -pers [From the Malay Press].' *Sumatra Post*, 25 April: 10. resolver.kb.nl/resolve?urn=ddd:010367809:mpeg21:p010.

Secondary sources

Abdullah, Taufik. 2009 [1971]. *Schools and Politics: The Kaum Muda Movement in West Sumatra (1927–1933)*. Jakarta: Equinox Publishing.

Adam, Ahmat. 1995. *Sejarah Awal Pers dan Kebangkitan Kesadaran Keindonesiaan* [*The Vernacular Press and the Emergence of Modern Indonesian Consciousness*]. Jakarta: Hasta Mitra.

Adam, Ahmat. 2012. *Suara Minangkabau: Sejarah dan Bibliografi Akhbar dan Majalah di Sumatera Barat* [*Minangkabau Voices: A History and Bibliography of Newspapers and Magazines in West Sumatra*]. Kuala Lumpur: University of Malaysia Press.

Anderson, Benedict. 2006. *Imagined Communities: Reflections on the Origin and Spread of Nationalism*. 2nd edn. London: Verso.

Arivia, Gadis. 2022. 'Menumbuhkan Analisis Dekolonialisasi di Indonesia: Studi Pemikiran Toety Heraty, Kartini, dan Siti Roehana, Sebuah Refleksi Kritis Filosofis dan Feminis [A Philosophical and Feminist Analysis of Decoloniality in Indonesia: A Critical Study of Toeti Heraty, Kartini, and Siti Roehana].' *Jurnal Perempuan* [*Women's Journal*] 27, no. 2: 93–102.

Asmaradana, Aura. 2021. 'Di Bawah Bayang-bayang Adat: Sebuah Pembacaan atas Hidup, Pemikiran, dan Karya Saadah Alim [Under the Shadow of *Adat*: A Reading of the Life, Thought, and Works of Saadah Alim].' In *Yang Terlupakan dan Dilupakan: Membaca Kembali Sepuluh Penulis Perempuan Indonesia* [*Those Accidentally Forgotten and Those Forgotten: Rereading Ten Indonesian Women Writers*], edited by Ruang Perempuan dan Tulisan, 150–60. Jakarta: Marjin Kiri.

Beech Jones, Bronwyn Anne. 2020. 'Narrating Intimate Violence in Public Texts: Women's Writings in the Sumatran Newspaper *Soenting Melajoe*.' In *Gender, Violence and Power in Indonesia: Across Time and Space*, edited by Katharine McGregor, Ana Dragojlovic, and Hannah Loney, 1–38. London: Routledge. doi.org/10.4324/9781003022992-1.

Beech Jones, Bronwyn Anne. 2021. '"The Age of Women Adept at Writing": Female Voices from the Dutch East Indies in the Early Twentieth Century.' *Agora* 56, no. 1: 69–75.

Beech Jones, Bronwyn Anne. 2021. 'Crafting Community.' *Inside Indonesia* [SI], no. 144 (April–June). www.insideindonesia.org/crafting-community.

Beech Jones, Bronwyn Anne. 2023. 'Textual Worlds: Rethinking Self, Community and Activism in Colonial-Era Sumatran Women's Newspapers.' PhD diss., University of Melbourne.

Bellacasa de la, María Puig. 2017. *Matters of Care: Speculative Ethics in More than Human Worlds*. Minneapolis: University of Minnesota Press. www.jstor.org/stable/10.5749/j.ctt1mmfspt.

Bijl, Paul. 2017. 'Legal Self-Fashioning in Colonial Indonesia: Human Rights in the Letters of Kartini.' *Indonesia* 103: 51–71. doi.org/10.1353/ind.2017.0002.

Blackburn, Susan. 2004. *Women and the State in Modern Indonesia*. Cambridge: Cambridge University Press. doi.org/10.1017/CBO9780511492198.

Blackwood, Evelyn. 2001. 'Representing Women: The Politics of Minangkabau *Adat* Writings.' *The Journal of Asian Studies* 60, no. 1: 125–49. doi.org/10.2307/2659507.

Chaniago, Danil. 2014. 'Perempuan Bergerak: Surat Kabar Soenting Melajoe 1912–1921 [Women Agitating: The Newspaper *Soenting Melajoe* 1912–21].' *Kafa'ah: Journal of Gender Studies* 4: 80–99. doi.org/10.15548/jk.v4i1.90.

Cho, Heekyoung. 2016. *Translation's Forgotten History: Russian Literature, Japanese Mediation, and the Formation of Modern Korean Literature*. Cambridge: Harvard University Asia Center. doi.org/10.2307/j.ctv47w7v7.

de Zwart, Pim. 2021. 'Globalisation, Inequality and Institutions in West Sumatra and West Java, 1800–1940.' *Journal of Contemporary Asia* 51, no. 4: 564–90. doi.org/10.1080/00472336.2020.1765189.

Dick, Murray. 2020. *The Infographic: A History of Data Graphics in News and Communications*. Cambridge: MIT Press. doi.org/10.7551/mitpress/11379.001.0001.

Fakih, Farabi. 2022. 'The Bolshevik Infection: European Perspectives on Communism in the Netherlands East Indies Press.' In *The Russian Revolution in Asia: From Baku to Batavia*, edited by Sabine Dullin, Étienne Forestier-Peyrat, Yuexin Rachel Lin, and Naoko Shimazu, 91–107. London: Routledge. doi.org/10.4324/9780429352195.

Hadler, Jeffrey. 2008. *Muslims and Matriarchs: Cultural Resilience in Indonesia through Jihad and Colonialism*. Ithaca: Cornell University Press.

Hanani, Silfia. 2018. 'Women's Newspapers as Minangkabau Feminist Movement Against Marginalization in Indonesia.' *Global Journal Al-Thaqafah* 8, no. 2: 75–83.

Hoogervorst, Tom G. 2021. 'Gained in Translation: The Politics of Localising Western Stories in Late-Colonial Indonesia.' In *Translational Politics in Southeast Asian Literatures: Contesting Race, Gender, and Sexuality*, edited by Grace Chin, 100–31. New York: Routledge. doi.org/10.4324/9781003036128.

Hoogervorst, Tom, and Henk Schulte Nordholt. 2017. 'Urban Middle Classes in Colonial Java (1900–1942): Images and Language.' *Bijdragen Tot de Taal-, Land- en Volkenkunde [Journal of the Humanities and Social Sciences of Southeast Asia]* 173, no. 4: 442–74. doi.org/10.1163/22134379-17304002.

Ingleson, John. 1993. 'Mutual Benefit Societies in Indonesia.' *International Social Security Review* 46, no. 3: 69–77. doi.org/10.1111/j.1468-246X.1993.tb00384.x.

Jedamski, Doris. 2005. 'Translation in the Malay World: Different Communities, Different Agendas.' In *Asian Translation Traditions*, edited by Eva Tsoi Hung and Judy Wakabayashi, 211–45. London: Routledge.

Kahn, Joel S. 1993. *Constituting the Minangkabau: Peasants, Culture and Modernity in Colonial Indonesia*. Providence: Berg.

Karagiannis, Nathalie. 2007. 'Multiple Solidarities: Autonomy and Resistance.' In *Varieties of World-Making: Beyond Globalization*, edited by Nathalie Karagiannis and Peter Wagner, 154–72. Liverpool: Liverpool Scholarship Online. doi.org/10.5949/UPO9781846314346.009.

Karagiannis, Nathalie, and Peter Wagner, eds. 2007. *Varieties of World-Making: Beyond Globalization*. Liverpool: Liverpool Scholarship Online. doi.org/10.5949/UPO9781846310201.

Kato, Tsuyoshi. 1982. *Matriliny and Migration: Evolving Minangkabau Traditions in Indonesia*. Ithaca: Cornell University Press.

Lewis, Su Lin. 2016. *Cities in Motion: Urban Life and Cosmopolitanism in Southeast Asia, 1920–1940*. Cambridge: Cambridge University Press. doi.org/10.1017/CBO9781316257937.

Maier, H.M.J. 2004. *We Are Playing Relatives: A Survey of Malay Writing*. Singapore: ISEAS. doi.org/10.1163/9789004454606.

Mariana, Anna. 2021. 'Memikirkan Ulang Historiografi Sejarah Perempuan [Rethinking the Historiography of Women's History].' *Jurnal Sejarah* [*History Journal*] 4: i–iv.

Mignolo, Walter D., and Catherine E. Walsh. 2018. *On Decoloniality: Concepts, Analytics, Praxis*. Durham: Duke University Press. doi.org/10.1215/9780822371779.

Milner, Anthony. 2002. *The Invention of Politics in Colonial Malaya: Contesting Nationalism and the Expansion of the Public Sphere*. Cambridge: Cambridge University Press.

Moon, Suzanne. 2015. 'Building from the Outside In: Sociotechnical Imaginaries and Society in New Order Indonesia.' In *Dreamscapes of Modernity: Sociotechnical Imaginaries and the Fabrication of Power*, edited by Sheila Jasanoff and Sang-Hyun Kim, 174–98. Chicago: University of Chicago Press. doi.org/10.7208/chicago/9780226276663.003.0008.

Nieβ, Joachim. 2017. 'Telling and Selling: Literary Fiction in Early Malay Language Newspapers in Colonial Indonesia.' *Wacana: Journal of the Humanities of Indonesia* 17, no. 3: 377–403. doi.org/10.17510/wacana.v17i3.453.

Perret, Daniel. 2009. 'Ethnicity and Colonization in Northeast Sumatra: Bataks and Malays.' In *From Distant Tales: Archaeology and Ethnohistory in the Highlands of Sumatra*, edited by Dominik Bonatz, John Miksic, J. David Neidel, and Mai Lin Tjoa-Bonatz, 143–68. Newcastle upon Tyne: Cambridge Scholars Publishing.

Rodgers, Susan. 2012. 'Sutan Pangurabaan Rewrites Sumatran Language Landscapes: The Political Possibilities of Commercial Print in the Late Colonial Indies.' *Bijdragen tot de Taal-, Land en Volkenkunde [Journal of the Humanities and Social Sciences of Southeast Asia]* 168, no. 1: 26–54. doi.org/10.1163/22134379-90003568.

Ruang Perempuan dan Tulisan, ed. 2021. *Yang Terlupakan dan Dilupakan: Membaca Kembali Sepuluh Penulis Perempuan Indonesia* [*Those Accidentally Forgotten and Those Forgotten: Rereading Ten Indonesian Women Writers*]. Jakarta: Marjin Kiri.

Samry, Wannofri, and Rahilah Omar. 2012. 'Gagasan dan Aktiviti Wartawan Wanita Minangkabau pada Masa Kolonial Belanda [Concepts and Activities of Minangkabau Women Journalists in the Dutch Colonial Period].' *Jebat: Malaysian Journal of History, Politics and Strategy* 39, no. 2: 24–47.

Saraswati, L. Ayu. 2013. *Seeing Beauty, Sensing Race in Transnational Indonesia*. Honolulu: University of Hawai`i Press. doi.org/10.21313/hawaii/9780824 836641.001.0001.

Saraswati, Marissa, and Annisa R. Beta. 2021. 'Knowing Responsibly: Decolonizing Knowledge Production of Indonesian Girlhood.' *Feminist Media Studies* 21, no. 5: 758–74. doi.org/10.1080/14680777.2020.1763418.

Sari, Sartika. 2018. *Seroean Kemadjoean: Puisi Pergerakan Perempuan di Sumatra Utara 1919–1941* [*Ideas of Gender Equality in Poetry Published in North Sumatran Newspapers, 1919–1941*]. Yogyakarta: CV Arti Bumi Intaran.

Setiadarma, Eunike G. 2021. 'Hoedjin: Eksplorasi Metode Penulisan Sejarah Perempuan [Hoedjin: A Methodological Exploration for Writing Women's History].' *Jurnal Sejarah* [*History Journal*] 4, no. 1: 1–13. msi.or.id/journal/index.php/js/article/download/49/47/112.

Spivak, Gayatri Chakravorty. 2009. 'The Politics of Translation.' In *Outside in the Teaching Machine*, 200–25. 2nd edn. New York: Routledge Classics.

Stoler, Ann Laura, and Frederick Cooper. 1997. 'Between Metropole and Colony: Rethinking a Research Agenda.' In *Tensions of Empire: Colonial Cultures in a Bourgeois World*, edited by Frederick Cooper and Ann Laura Stoler, 1–56. Berkeley: University of California Press. doi.org/10.1525/9780520918085-003.

Suwignyo, Agus. 2014. 'The Making of Politically Conscious Indonesian Teachers in Public Schools, 1930–42.' *Southeast Asian Studies* 3: 119–49.

Taylor, Jean Gelman. 2012. 'The Sewing-Machine in Colonial-Era Photographs: A Record from Dutch Indonesia.' *Modern Asian Studies* 46, no. 1: 71–95. doi.org/10.1017/s0026749x11000576.

Tuhiwai Smith, Linda. 2012. *Decolonizing Methodologies: Research and Indigenous Peoples*. 2nd edn. London: Zed Books.

van Dijk, Kees. 2007. *The Netherlands Indies and the Great War, 1914–1918*. Leiden: KITLV Press. doi.org/10.26530/OAPEN_389234.

Vreede-de Stuers, Cora. 1960. *The Indonesian Woman: Struggles and Achievements*. The Hague: Mouton.

Wieringa, Saskia. 1995. 'Matrilinearity and Women's Interests: The Minangkabau of Western Sumatra.' In *Subversive Women: Women's Movements in Africa, Asia, Latin America and the Caribbean*, edited by Saskia Wieringa, 241–68. London: Zed Books.

Wink, André. 2002. *Al-Hind: The Making of the Indo-Islamic World. Volume 2*. Leiden: Brill.

Witsen Geysbeek, P.G. n.d. *Algemeen Noodwendig Woordenboek der Zamenleving* [*General Essential Dictionary of Society*]. *Volume 6*. Gouda: Witsen G.B. van Goor en D. Noothoven van Goor.

Zed, Mestika. 2017. *Saudagar Pariaman: Menerjang Ombak Membangun Maskapai* [*Pariaman Trader: Riding the Waves, Building a Fleet*]. Depok: LP3ES.

5

Dealing with modernities: East Java's plantation society in colonial times and the revolution

Grace T. Leksana

In 1934 the Dutch East Indies Government completed four years of construction work on the South Semeru Road (*Zuid-Smeroeweg*)—a project that had been planned since 1913. The new road connected Malang and Lumajang, which made possible travel by car in this southern part of East Java. A famous part of this road was a bridge across the Besoek Koboan River that was difficult to construct due to the contours of the hills at each end of the bridge.[1] The road was so important for East Java that a large ceremony was held for its opening, as reported by the Dutch-language Surabaya newspaper *Soerabaiasch Handelsblad* ('*Surabaya Commercial Paper*') on 2 November 1934. In an array of speeches, Mr Schmidt, a surveyor from

---

1 This bridge in Lumajang is currently known as Jembatan Gladak Perak and is no longer used. It is preserved as cultural heritage and managed by the Lumajang district government. The colonially built Gladak Perak bridge was destroyed in the 1947 military actions by republican soldiers, but was rebuilt in the 1950s.

Kooy and Co., one of the plantation companies operating in Malang and Lumajang, stated that 'the planters felt somewhat like parents of the Zuid Smeroeweg' and were proud of how 'the baby' had grown.[2]

Figure 5.1 Bridge on the South Semeru Road from Malang to Bondowoso, 1939
Source: Leiden University Library digital collection.

---

2   '*Spr.gaf een terugblik naar den tijd, nu 25 jaar geleden, toen men te paard de ondernemingen bereikte en de auto wegens gebrek aan wegen nog van weinig nut was … doch diezelfde auto liet niet met zich sollen en zoo was en er weldra op uit, haar de noodige wegen te verschaffen. Spr.noemde den heer Andriessen, van "Soember Telogo", die de eerste auto kocht, en herinnerde aan de heeren Onderwater en Van de Sandt, welke de eerste plannen smedden voor aan leg van een weg. De heer Schmidt, landmeter van Kooyen Co., deed destijds de eerste metingen, en zoo werd in 1913 deze weg reeds voorbereid. De planters gevoelden zich dus eenigszins als ouders van den Zuid-Smeroeweg en spr.voegde hier een geestig woord aan toe over den uitgroei van hun "baby"* [Spr. recalled 25 years ago, when one reached the enterprises on horseback and the car was of little use because of the lack of roads … but that same car was not to be trifled with and so soon people were eager to provide it with the necessary roads. Spr. mentioned Mr Andriessen, from "Soember Telogo", who bought the first car, and recalled Mr Onderwater and Mr Van de Sandt, who made the first plans for the construction of a road. Mr Schmidt, surveyor for Kooyen Co., took the first measurements at the time, and that is how this road was prepared in 1913. So the planters felt somewhat like parents of the South Meroe Road and Spr. added a witty comment about the growth of their "baby"].' 'Feestelijke Opening Zuid-Smeroeweg: Plantershulde Aan "Kennis Den Bruggebouwer" [Festive Opening of South Semeru Road: Planters' Tribute to Acknowledge the Bridge Builder]', *Soerabaiasch Handelsblad* [*Surabaya Commercial Paper*], 3 November 1934, resolver.kb.nl/resolve?urn=ddd:011110054:mpeg21:p009.

The report on the opening ceremony indicates that the construction of the South Semeru Road was driven by the business agendas of plantation companies in East Java. The road connected different plantations in Malang and Lumajang that were previously only accessible with horses and carts. This meant that crops produced on those plantations, such as rubber and coffee, could be more easily and quickly distributed. While the South Semeru Road project fulfilled the agenda of the plantation owners, the surrounding villagers were supposed to join in and celebrate the road during the ceremony. The villagers were instructed to prepare the roadside in advance to welcome the guests at the opening ceremony. They hoisted flags as a welcoming gesture, but the result was not as expected. The *Soerabaiasch Handelsblad* reporter wrote specifically about these flags:

> The flags fluttered happily in the village of Soemberrowo next to the houses. We could see countless variations of our national flag ... purple-white-brown, bright red-white-lilac, amber-white-green, etc. The white colour was always in order, in any case, after 300 years of colonisation people are already starting to approach our tricolour [flag] nicely, another 300 years and they will understand it perfectly.[3]

In this cynical comment, the journalist suggests that the locals were unable to follow instructions and simply display the tricoloured Dutch flag of red, white and blue. Instead, the villagers prepared and displayed flags of a mix of colours—far from what was intended. This could have been for several reasons, including that the villagers did not have cloth of the required colours or it was an act of local subversion. Either way, without trying to understand the causes, the journalist adopted a highly colonial tone, emphasising the need for 300 more years of colonisation for the villagers to properly understand the Dutch national symbol. The journalist harshly implies that Indonesians were slow learners and in need of further education.

---

3   'Vroolijk wapperden in het dorpje Soemberrowo de vlaggen naast de huisjes; we ontwaarden ontelbare variaties op onze nationale vlag ... paars-wit-terra cotta, cerise-wit-lila, amber-wit-groen, enz. De witte kleur was steeds in orde; in ieder geval begint men na 300 jaar kolonisatie onze drie-kleur al aardig te benaderen, nog eens 300 jaar en men is er glad achter [Merrily, in the village of Soemberrowo, the flags fluttered next to the houses; we discovered countless variations on our national flag ... purple-white-terra cotta, cerise-white-lilac, amber-white-green, etc. The white colour was always in order; in any case, after 300 years of colonisation, they are starting to get pretty close to our three-colour, another 300 years and they will be smoothly behind it].' 'Festive Opening of South Semeru Road', *Soerabaiasch Handelsblad* [*Surabaya Commercial Paper*].

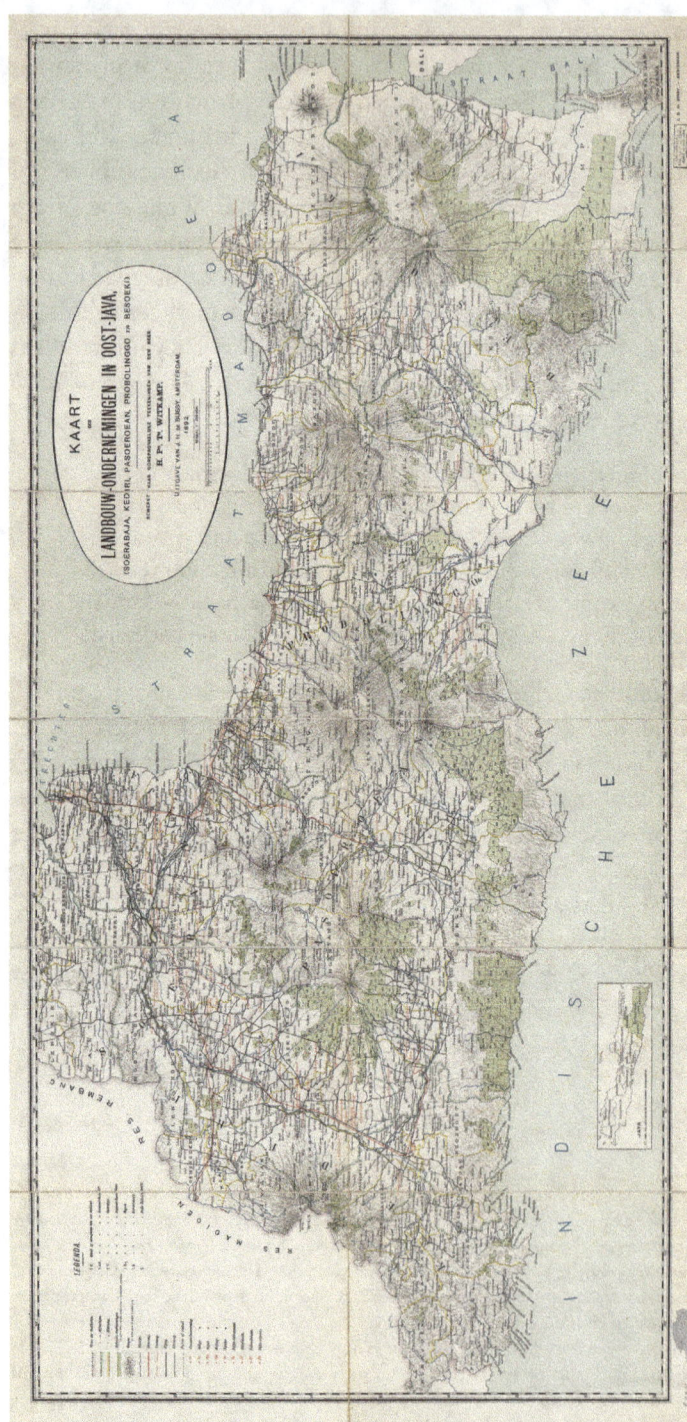

Map 5.1 Agricultural enterprises in East Java (Surabaya, Kediri, Pasuruan, Probolinggo and Besuki), adapted from original drawings by Mr H. P{}^h. T{}^h. Witkamp, 1892

Source: Leiden University Library digital collections.

Nevertheless, the newspaper article about the opening of South Semeru Road was not just a report on a successful Dutch infrastructure project. The article presents the new road and flags as symbols that differentiate Dutch advancement and modernity (the high technology of road construction) from local 'backwardness' (the inability to understand the colour of a Dutch flag). As in other colonial states, infrastructure projects were built to pave the way for modernity—a process within which locals were expected to become educated and advanced.[4] But, as Khusyairi and Colombijn have argued, modernity serves particular groups while excluding others.[5] The South Semeru Road was built to accommodate the plantation economy in East Java, but along the way the effects of the road on local residents—those who could not put up the correct-coloured Dutch flag— were never considered.

The main aim of this chapter is not to add to the extensive literature on the injustice or exclusion of colonial modernities.[6] What I intend to do is examine how the marginalised—in this case, the Indonesians—interpret, imagine and utilise modernity, and for what reasons. In other words, my aim is to scrutinise colonial modernisation not merely as a system imposed by the colonisers, but also in terms of the desires and agency of the colonised. For this aim, I chose to delve into the lives of local people working in the plantation society in South Malang. As Ann Stoler argues, modernity projects within plantation societies are part of a 'larger effort of colonising bodies and minds in a sustained, systemic, and incomplete political project'.[7] This chapter focuses on two plantations in the districts of Donomulyo and Dampit in Malang, East Java. To bring forward the agency of plantation workers and their interpretations of modernity, I provide a critical reading

---

4   For example, Vatthana Pholsena shows how the Tonkin–Yunnan railway construction project (between what is now Vietnam and China) was part of broader and more complex factors of imperial rivalry (particularly between France and Britain), the *mise en valeur* ideology of the French (colonisation must be cheap yet profitable) and the motive of introducing modernity with the hope that it would create a greater appreciation of the French's presence. See Vatthana Pholsena, 'Technology and Empire: A Colonial Narrative of the Construction of the Tonkin–Yunnan Railway', *Critical Asian Studies* 47, no. 4 (2015): 537–57, doi.org/10.1080/14672715.2015.1079985, at 538–40.
5   Johny A. Khusyairi and Freek Colombijn, 'Moving at a Different Velocity: The Modernization of Transportation and Social Differentiation in Surabaya in the 1920s', in *Cars, Conduits, and Kampongs: The Modernization of the Indonesian City, 1920–1960*, eds Freek Colombijn and Joost Coté (Leiden: Brill, 2015), 249–71, doi.org/10.1163/9789004280724_011.
6   See, for example, Paul Gillen and Devleena Ghosh, *Colonialism & Modernity* (Sydney: UNSW Press, 2007); Tani Barlow, 'Debates Over Colonial Modernity in East Asia and Another Alternative', *Cultural Studies* 26, no. 5 (2012): 617–44, doi.org/10.1080/09502386.2012.711006.
7   Ann Stoler, *Carnal Knowledge and Imperial Power: Race and the Intimate in Colonial Rule* (Berkeley: University of California Press, 2010), 10.

of archival sources from the colonial period, such as plantation reports and newspaper articles between 1900 and the 1930s, and combine these with oral sources collected during my fieldwork in 2017–18 from the second generation of plantation workers.

Modern plantations, modernising lives

The rapid investment of capital in plantations, particularly in the nineteenth century, transformed local society. This can be seen through the boom of plantation companies that was related to the establishment of the 1870 Agrarian Law. The law enabled European entrepreneurs to lease *sawah* ('wet rice') land from the local population on an annual basis. Moreover, allegedly uncultivated lands known as 'waste' lands could be leased from the colonial government under hereditary leases (*erfpacht*) for up to 75 years.[8] The law soon contributed to the rise of private, European-owned plantation companies throughout the archipelago, including in Malang. From 1881 to 1884, almost one-third of the coffee production in Java came from Malang and, in 1922, the regency contributed 19.6 per cent of the total coffee production in Java and Madura.[9]

Following the extensive growth of plantation companies, infrastructure was developed to support the mobilisation of crops and people, such as the South Semeru Road. In 1879, a new railway was opened, connecting Surabaya, Pasuruan and, later, Malang. In 1901, the tramway in Malang City was opened, carrying people and crops from the plantation areas into the city and vice versa.[10] Newly built residential areas and other infrastructure such as a market, slaughterhouse and water plant marked Malang's new status as a modern city.[11] These developments characterised what Anthony Reid refers

---

8   Vincent J.H. Houben, 'Java in the 19th Century: Consolidation of a Territorial State', in *The Emergence of a National Economy: An Economic History of Indonesia, 1800–2000*, eds Howard Dick, Vincent J.H. Houben, J. Thomas Lindblad, and Thee Kian Wie (Sydney: Allen & Unwin, 2002), 56–81, at 65–66.
9   Hiroyoshi Kano, *Pagelaran: Anatomi Sosial Ekonomi Pelapisan Masyarakat Tani Di Sebuah Desa Jawa Timur* [*Pagelaran: The Anatomy of Social-Economic Layering Amongst Farmers in an East Java Village*] (Yogyakarta: Gadjah Mada University Press, 1990), 13.
10 Nawiyanto, *Dari Rimba Menjadi Kota: Bank Indonesia Dalam Evolusi Malang Raya* [*From Forest to City: The Indonesian Bank in Malang's Evolution*] (Jakarta: Bank Indonesia Institute, 2020), 65.
11 Malang was inaugurated as a *gementee* (town, city or district with its own government) in 1914. Reza Hudiyanto, 'Between Modernization and Capitalization: Commercialization of Malang in the Early Twentieth Century', *Paramita: Historical Studies Journal* 31, no. 1 (2021): 45–55, doi.org/10.15294/paramita.v31i1.20463, at 50.

5. DEALING WITH MODERNITIES

to as the 'high colonial period' between 1870 and 1930, when increasing colonial capital was used for the extensive development of infrastructure: railways, roads, harbours and port cities.[12]

Moving away from cities towards plantation areas, modernisation manifested in the use of technology. One example is NV Kali Tello, a rubber and coffee company that was established in 1895 in Donomulyo, South Malang. In 1922, the company occupied 1,465 *bouw*[13] (1,026 hectares) of land, of which 207 *bouw* (145 hectares) was used for the factory, houses, *kampongs* ('villages') and roads, while the remainder was given over to the coffee and rubber plantations. The rubber factory can be considered modern, for example, because of the use of machines and running freshwater to produce latex.[14] A further sign of modernisation was the use of electricity in the factory, which also opened access for the neighbouring *kampong*.[15] After the acquisition of the adjacent Poerwodadie plantation, NV Kali Tello established a special crop transportation system, in 1926, between these two plantations, comprising 2.6 kilometres of electric cable car (*kabelbaan*).[16]

Growing infrastructure such as roads and train systems also facilitated mobility, which led to an increased supply of labour. The 1907 Dutch government report *Research on Declining Welfare* (*Mindere Welvaart Onderzoek*) recorded that, between 1880 and 1885 and the opening of the plantations and the train connection from Surabaya to Malang, the population in Pagak subdistrict, South Malang, had tripled. There were thousands of new labourers from Central Java working for the plantation companies.[17] People also travelled from Madura to the plantations,

---

12   Anthony Reid, *A History of Southeast Asia: Critical Crossroads* (Chichester: Wiley Blackwell, 2015), 295–319.
13   1 *bouw* equals 0.7 hectare.
14   *Verslag Over Het Boekjaar 1902–1949* [Report on the Financial Year 1902–1949], Internationaal Instituut voor Sociale Geschiedenis [International Institute of Social History], Inv. ZK 60163 (Amsterdam: Nederlandsch Economisch-Historisch Archief [Netherlands Economic History Archive]), 1920.
15   ibid., 1919.
16   ibid., 1926.
17   Dutch East Indies Welvaartcommissie [Dutch East Indies Welfare Commission], Batavia, *Onderzoek Naar de Mindere Welvaart Der Inlandsche Bevolking Op Java En Madoera. [IX, Economie van de Desa]: Samentrekking van de Afdeelingsverslagen over de Uitkomsten Der Onderzoekingen* [Inquiry into the Declining Prosperity of the Domestic Population in Java and Madura. (IX, Economy of the Village): Merging of the Departmental Reports about the Outcomes of the Inquiries], Ministerie van Koloniën: Collectie Grijs [Ministry of the Colonies: Grijs Collection], Inv. 2.10.64, Box 21, folder 21.4 (The Hague: Nationaal Archief [National Archives], 1907).

particularly in the regions of Pakis, Sengguruh, Gondanglegi and Turen. Plantation managers and owners preferred these workers to local people, who apparently had higher demands for their labour.[18]

Migration led to a surplus of contract labour in the South Malang area. However, this does not necessarily mean that labour recruitment was easy for the companies. NV Kali Tello's yearly report described competition with other industries, particularly sugar factories, which offered better pay, which led to ongoing difficulties in recruiting labourers for their plantation. Furthermore, during planting seasons, locals opted to work on their own lands instead of for the plantation companies. To overcome this situation, plantations competed by offering alluring salaries and facilities to recruit labour. For example, Kali Tello plantation strove to bind its permanent workforce to the company by providing good housing.[19] Health services were also established, particularly as a response to outbreaks of disease. When the bubonic plague hit Malang between 1910 and 1916, Kali Tello plantation provided vaccination for workers and converted their dwellings into rat-free houses *by force*.[20] NV Kali Tello also provided free medicines, sent critically ill patients to the clinic in Malang and established an outpatient clinic in the plantation area. The residents of the plantations could also be treated by a doctor, who came from Malang once a week.

As well as health care, plantation companies provided entertainment for their workers. This is illustrated by Prambodo (pseudonym), the son of a former middle-level overseer in Gladakan Pancur plantation in Dampit. Born in 1930 on the plantation, Prambodo explained that, every week, the company organised shows for their workers:

> The wage was given every week, on Saturdays. The lower-level overseer reported to the higher level, and the records were submitted to the factory, to another overseer, who was responsible for wages. So all work was reported every Saturday, and the workers received their payments ... The Dutch were smart. Workers lived in the plantation area, a remote area. So they gave us entertainment. Every Saturday, there was entertainment, with *tandak*, or dancing. People

---

18 ibid.
19 *Report on the Financial Year 1902–49*, 1910.
20 For example, they did this by changing bamboo poles to solid teak poles so that rats would not hide in the cavity of the bamboo. Authorised personnel were assigned to villages to enforce the hygiene of houses. See Martina Safitry, 'Dukun Dan Mantri Pes: Praktisi Kesehatan Lokal Di Jawa Masa Epidemi Pes 1910–1942 [Shamans and Health Care Workers: Local Health Care Practitioners in Java during the Bubonic Plague Epidemic 1910–42]' (Master's thesis, Universitas Gadjah Mada, Depok, 2016).

also played with dice [a form of gambling]. From my observations, workers became occupied with this entertainment, while the Dutch went to Malang. They went to bowling centres, hotels, while the workers drank. They gladly joined in *tandak*, and other activities, that drained their money. And when their money was gone, they would work again on Monday.[21]

Prambodo's experience shows how the plantation managers used entertainment as a strategy to keep their workers within the compound. Prambodo added that Chinese and Arab merchants also came to the plantation every week on payday to offer their merchandise. This further enticed workers to quickly spend their wages. The plantation was turned into an isolated compound full of facilities that were there not to support the workers' welfare, but to maintain the capitalist production of the plantation.

It is important to note that, although modern plantation life was created to ensure the continuity of the company's production, the drive towards modernity was not the monopoly of the colonisers. Prambodo illustrates this drive in his family's motivation for education:

> The Dutch would organise large events, such as art shows. Of course, the workers were happy. But on the top of that was colonialism … I witnessed those things. But I went to school, in Malang. And I return[ed] during vacations. So, how to describe it … I lived in the plantation, but I did not work there, in a sense I was a child of the plantation. No, I went to school [Rooms-Katholieke Hollandsch

---

21 '*Upahnya per minggu, tiap hari sabtu. Apa yang dikerjakan oleh mandor-mandor kecil dikumpulkan sama mandor besar, lalu datanya disetorkan ke pabrik. Ke sinder, yang bagian upah. Jadi semua hasil kerja Sabtu dilaporkan, lalu dia terima gajian … Itulah pintarnya Belanda. Mereka tinggal di perkebunan, daerah terpencil, sehingga dikasih hiburan. Tiap Sabtu dikasih hiburan, ada tandak, menari itu. ada orang main dadu. Sehingga saya amati, pekerja-pekerja itu disibukkan dengan kesenangan itu. Belandanya pergi ke Malang. Ke kamar bola, ke hotel, tapi pekerjanya dengan mabuk-mabuk, dengan senang hati dia senang main-main begitu, ada tandak, ada macam-macam, uangnya kan habis. Karena habis, dia semangat lagi Senin cari duit lagi* [The wages are paid weekly, every Saturday. What the small foremen do is collected by the big foreman, then the data is submitted to the factory. To the *sinder* [office supervisor], the wage department. So all the results of Saturday's work were reported, then he received his pay cheque … That's how clever the Dutch were. They lived in plantations, remote areas, so they were given entertainment. Every Saturday they were given entertainment, there was *tandak*, dancing, people playing dice. So I observed that the workers were occupied with this fun. The Dutch went to Malang. He went to the ballroom, to the hotel, but the workers got drunk, they were happy to play around like that, there was *tandak*, there were all kinds of things, and the money ran out. Because he ran out, he was excited again on Monday to make more money].' Interview with Prambodo, Malang, 29 July 2016, #14.04–15.57. This interview is also cited in Grace T. Leksana, *Memory Culture of the Anti-Leftist Violence in Indonesia: Embedded Remembering* (Amsterdam: Amsterdam University Press, 2023), doi.org/10.5117/9789463723565.

Inlandsche School, Dutch Roman Catholic School for Natives]. Why did my father send me to school? Because my father mingled with the plantation staff who graduated from *HBS, AMS, HIK*.[22] This is where plantation staff usually came from. My father mingled with those people, so he thought of his children's improvement, by sending us to school in Malang so that we wouldn't work in the factory. But all the kids my age worked in the factory, some in the plantation, others on the road ... My father was given a position as a middle level overseer, so he did not directly tend the crops. But he was also considered an elder, someone who took care of residents in the plantation. Like a community leader.[23]

Prambodo realised his family's distinct position in the plantation society. His father envisioned education as the path to social change for his family, which was inspired by a circle of highly educated personnel in the plantation. Prambodo's access to education was a result of his father's position in the plantation, which was different from other Indonesians, most of whom were labourers. Prambodo's family was middle class with certain privileges. This shows that individuals within the plantation society were never equal and, therefore, access to modernity also depended on class differentiation.

---

22   The *Hoogere burgerschool* (*HBS*) or middle school was specifically for Dutch, Europeans and limited Chinese and Indonesian elites. The *algemeene middelbare school* (*AMS*) was a form of high school for Indonesians. The *Hollandse indische kweekschool* (*HIK*) was a school for teachers who would go on to teach in Indonesian schools.

23   'Dibikinkan rame-rame sama Belanda. Ya kesenian, ya senang orang. Tapi sesungguhnya di balik itu ya menjajah ... Saya menyaksikan itu. Tapi saya sekolah, sekolah di Malang. Kalau vakansi pulang. Jadi agak gimana ya, saya hidup di perkebunan, tapi saya gak ikut kerja di perkebunan, dalam arti anak-anak perkebunan. Ndak, saya sekolah. Kenapa bapak nyekolahkan saya? Karena bapak bergaul sama itu, sama staf-staf perkebunan yang lulusan HBS, AMS, HIK, itu kan staf perkebunan kan itu. Bapak bergaul sama orang-orang itu, sehingga punya pikiran untuk anaknya maju, disekolahkan ke malang. Jadi ndak ikut kerja di pabrik. Tapi anak-anak sebangsa saya kerjanya ke pabrik, ada yang kebun, ada yang ke jalan ... Bapak diberi jabatan wakilnya sinder, dan dia tidak ada urusan kebun. Tapi dia juga sebagai sesepuh, orang yang ngopeni yang tinggal di kampung itu. Seperti tokoh masyarakat [It was made by the Dutch. Yes art, yes people were happy. But actually behind it is colonising ... I witnessed that. But I went to school, to school in Malang. When I travelled, I went home. So it was a bit like, I lived on a plantation, but I didn't work on the plantation, in the sense of the plantation children. No, I went to school. Why did you send me to school? Because you hang out with the plantation staff who graduated from *HBS, AMS, HIK*, that's the plantation staff. You hang out with those people, so you have the idea that your children should progress, so you send them to school in Malang. So they didn't work in the factory. But the children of my countrymen went to the factory, some to the plantation, some to the road ... My father was given the position of deputy sinder, and he had nothing to do with the plantation. But he is also an elder, someone who takes care of the people who live in the village. Like a community leader].' Interview with Prambodo, Malang, 29 July 2016, #18.18–21.25.

Implementing security and law, but whose justice?

Modernity also created new concepts of ownership: a strict line between what belonged to the plantation owners and what did not. The 1920 annual report of Kali Tello company stated that it built a long wall more than 2.5 metres high to surround the plantation area. The main purpose of the wall was to protect the plantation against coffee theft.[24] Thefts were conducted by groups whose members had familial connections with plantation labourers and were a growing concern in the early 1900s in this area.[25] As a response to these cases, the government established the *koffiepassen stelsel* ('coffee pass system') in the 1920s—a pass that local owners in Malang were required to possess, process or transport coffee. The pass was considered necessary because of the frequent coffee theft, caused by the boom in prices for coffee in the 1920s and insufficient security on plantations.[26] However, when coffee prices fell dramatically during the Great Depression in 1929–30, and the security system had been improved, the passes were abolished.

Coffee thefts seem to have involved different modus operandi. Some were cross-border district operations, while others were quite local. For example, *Soerabaiasch Handelsblad* on 23 June 1934 reported that a group of five farmers from Donomulyo village stole 60 *katti*[27] (30 kilograms) of coffee and sold it to another farmer in the village for a total of 86 cents.[28] Another thief, named Karim, who was imprisoned for three weeks in 1933, stole 0.5 *picol*[29] (31 kilograms) of coffee beans, which he sold to his niece in the same village. It was not uncommon for women to be involved in these activities. For example, the *Soerabaiasch Handelsblad* on 22 September 1939 recorded that two women were caught stealing coffee from Poerwodadi plantation. One had already been sentenced three times for the same act and the other received additional punishment for using a fake name during

---

24 *Report on the Financial Year 1902–49*, 1920.
25 Dutch East Indies Welfare Commission, *Inquiry into the Declining Prosperity of the Domestic Population in Java and Madura*.
26 'De Nieuwe Koffie Ordonantie [The New Coffee Regulation]', *Soerabaiasch Handelsblad* [*Surabaya Commercial Paper*], 13 July 1931.
27 One *katti* equals 0.5 kilogram.
28 'Koffiediefstallen [Coffee Thefts]', *Soerabaiasch Handelsblad* [*Surabaya Commercial Paper*], 23 June 1934.
29 One *picol* equals 61.7 kilograms.

her arrest. In another incident, five women plantation workers in Kali Tello were caught stealing 2–3.5 kilograms of coffee. These women were arrested in their homes and sentenced to one month in prison.[30]

Of course, for the plantation companies, these acts were considered harmful. They used different security forces to guard the plantations from theft, which entailed high costs. In 1922, the Kali Tello administrator estimated that 20 per cent of coffee beans were lost to theft. This drove the management to ask for protection from the head of the regional administration, who sent 40 infantry men under the command of an officer. However, the presence of the infantry was not very useful because they had no authority to arrest the thieves.[31] In 1924, the head of the military was stationed on company land and authorised to conduct house searches.[32] The expenses related to the military and police were charged to the company. However, because these security forces were still considered inadequate, the company employed their own plantation guards and established a barbed-wire fence to increase security.[33] The company guards possessed police equipment and cooperated with security forces from other companies and the village heads. The company spent ƒ4,300 a year on security alone.[34] It was only in 1939 that the thefts began to decrease.

The colonial state and the plantation owners regarded these thefts as criminal acts. Cases were brought to the district court, with sentences that ranged from weeks to six months. However, this is a one-sided view of criminality. As illustrated by the police and justice report *Research on Declining Welfare*, laws concerning ownership were interpreted differently by the colonial government and local people. While theft of coffee was considered a 'heavy' criminal act by the government, workers and those living adjacent to the plantations did not think of the act of taking coffee in the same way.[35] In another example, the newspaper *De Avondpost* ('*The Evening Post*') reported that although coffee thefts were spreading 'like cancer' in South

---

30 'De Koffiediefstallen in Zuid Malang [The Coffee Thefts in South Malang]', *Soerabaiasch Handelsblad [Surabaya Commercial Paper]*, 22 September 1939.
31 *Report on the Financial Year 1902–1949*, 1922.
32 ibid., 1924.
33 ibid., 1929.
34 ibid., 1930.
35 Dutch East Indies Welfare Commission, *Inquiry into the Declining Prosperity of the Domestic Population in Java and Madura*.

Malang, the act was not considered as a misdeed by the thieves.[36] There was never a unified conception of law in the colonial period, because the law was constructed and imposed by colonial authorities to sustain their power rather than being a mechanism to establish justice. Even if laws such as those used to prosecute coffee theft functioned as mechanisms of justice, we are left with the question: whose justice?

Going further than conceptions of law, these thefts point to a more substantial problem than mere criminality. This problem emerged as an effect of the 1870 Agrarian Law, which enabled private companies to directly rent land from landowners (in a system known as *erfpacht*). For large farms, a maximum of 250 hectares of land could be leased for 75 years.[37] In reality, implementation of the law involved a certain degree of manipulation, such as forcing villagers to convert their tilled land into *erfpacht* land, therefore leasable to companies. In the long run, as plantation companies began to grow, the amount of good-quality tilled land was reduced and became inaccessible to local farmers.[38] This is what Tania Li points to as the process of dispossession—a condition in which people can no longer sustain their own lives through either direct access to the means of production or access to a living wage.[39] In the case of plantations in South Malang, incidents of coffee theft are presumably related closely to the effect of this dispossession of land. This could explain why coffee thieves did not consider their acts as misdeeds. For them, it was a strategy and implementation of their agency to tackle their dispossession.

Claiming modernity in the revolution

In general, plantations in Indonesia experienced massive transformation during the Japanese occupation of 1942–45. The Japanese rapidly took control of Java and started to exploit the island's economic resources to

---

36 'Het oude zeer der koffielanden heeft aan het bestuur reeds heel wat hoofdbrekens gekost; het is tot een ingekankerd misbruik geworden en in vele streken voelt men het confiskeeren van koffiebes niet eens als misdrijf aan. Koffiepluk—koffiediefstal is er voldoende bewaking [The old pain of the coffee lands has already cost the administration many headaches; it has become an ingrained abuse and in many regions confiscating coffee berries does not even feel like a crime. Coffee picking—coffee theft is there enough surveillance]?' *De Avondpost* [*The Evening Post*], [The Hague], 19 April 1933: 9.
37 Noer Fauzi, *Petani & Penguasa: Dinamika Perjalanan Politik Agraria Indonesia* [*Farmers and Rulers: The Dynamic Processes of Agrarian Politics in Indonesia*] (Yogyakarta: INSIST, KPA, Pustaka Pelajar, 1999), 36.
38 ibid., 36–41.
39 Tania Murray Li, 'To Make Live or Let Die? Rural Dispossession and the Protection of Surplus Populations', *Antipode* 41, no. s1 (2010): 66–93, doi.org/10.1111/j.1467-8330.2009.00717.x, at 67.

support their military operations during the war. Farmers had almost no freedom to choose the crops planted on their land.[40] Most of the plantation areas owned by Dutch companies were transferred to Japanese enterprises, such as the case of 80 Dutch-owned sugar companies in Java that were distributed among six Japanese corporations.[41] Although the Imperial Japanese Government in Indonesia launched a massive campaign to increase food production, output in fact dropped sharply, in part because the amount of land for growing food crops decreased when the land was used for the production of non-edible crops.[42] Another factor that contributed to a decrease in food production was the insufficient number of labourers to work the land, because most had been mobilised for defence and the production of military-related resources.[43]

After the Japanese surrendered, Indonesians were forced to defend their independence in the revolution of 1945–49. In this period, Dutch companies tried to reclaim their plantations. They put much effort into securing their properties—for example, by forming plantation guards comprising indigenous and a few European personnel under the companies' direct management.[44] However, on the republican side, plantations were also highly prized, which can be seen in several different functions of plantations in this period. First, crops were used to finance the war. Instead of giving employees a salary, they were paid with crops that were collected through compulsory donations from farmers. Regular farmers had to give up 20 per cent of their crops, half of which was given to the army and half to the civilian government.[45] Every district was given the responsibility to provide food, money and travel funds for the military division within their

---

40   Aiko Kurosawa, *Kuasa Jepang Di Jawa: Perubahan Sosial Di Pedesaan 1942–1945* [*Japanese Power in Java: Social Transformation in Villages 1942–1945*] (Depok: Komunitas Bambu, 2015), 4.
41   However, not all the sugar companies continued to produce sugar under the Japanese government. Of the 85 companies, only 13 continued their operations, while at least 17 were converted into cement factories and nine into spinning mills. ibid., 52, 61.
42   Shigeru Sato, 'Relocation of Labor and the Romusha Issue', in *The Encyclopedia of Indonesia in the Pacific War*, eds Peter Post, William Bradley Horton, and Didi Kwartanada (Leiden: Brill, 2010), 245–61, at 257.
43   Defence in this context included a range of military and semi-military activities. Production involved producing strategic resources such as oil, minerals, transport and clothing. ibid., 245.
44   See Roel Frakking. '"Who Wants to Cover Everything, Covers Nothing": The Organization of Indigenous Security Forces in Indonesia, 1945–50', in *Colonial Counterinsurgency and Mass Violence: The Dutch Empire in Indonesia*, eds Bart Luttikhuis and A. Dirk Moses (London: Routledge, 2014), 111–32, doi.org/10.4324/9781315767345-6.
45   See Ari Sapto, *Republik Dalam Pusaran Elite Sipil Dan Militer* [*Republic in the Vortex of Military and Civilian Elites*] (Yogyakarta: Matapadi Pressindo, 2018).

area.⁴⁶ This policy was very hard to control and often led to the military arbitrarily taking state-owned crops.⁴⁷ Second, plantation lands were taken over by republican state forces and continued to produce crops. In some cases, the republican forces also divided this plantation land into farmland for incoming war refugees. Third, republican soldiers destroyed plantations as a tactic to prevent the return of the Dutch. Former plantation labourers then converted these ex-plantation lands into residential areas and farmland. These residential areas were called *desa darurat* ('emergency villages') because they sprang up in the emergency context of the revolution. While some of these villages were later formalised and included in the administrative government arrangements, in other cases, their inhabitants became a continuous focus of disputes between villagers and the state, such as the case of the current land dispute in Sumbermanjing Wetan, Malang.

The experiences of people living within plantation societies during the revolution were very different from the heroic depiction of this period in Indonesian historiography. Returning to Prambodo, the plantation overseer's son in Dampit, he described the rubber plantation's situation during the revolution as follows:

> The plantations were strategically seized at that time, to support the guerrilla fighters in the mountains … The people planted [crops]. It was to support them. Besides the army, also to support the refugees. People from the city, from Malang, who migrated to the plantation area … After the transfer of sovereignty, they continued [to cut down the rubber trees] until everything was finished. Now it became the plantation village … It was scorched to the ground in the period of the second clash, in 1948. All the plantations were scorched … [T]he army brought bombs to the factory. The people who lived in the plantation were told to move away because they were going to blow it up. After the destruction, the people who lived in the mountains, that was it. Law was not working. The factory was destroyed, stripped down. Gosh, how can our people behave like this? All of it, the machines, the iron sheeting, were taken to build houses in the plantation … People took whatever they wanted, sold, or used them to build houses. Our family also built a house. The roof was previously reeds, but after the scorched earth, it was changed into iron sheet. Everybody took it.⁴⁸

---

46   ibid.
47   ibid.
48   'Terus ditebangi jaman revolusi. Sehingga akhirnya kebun-kebun itu di samping juga jaman itu menguntungkan untuk menghidupi para pejuang yang bergerilya di daerah gunung-gunung itu …

This experience in Dampit was replicated in Kali Tello plantation in Donomulyo. Marwono (a pseudonym), a farmer whose parents and grandparents worked in the plantation, described the revolution, saying it happened

> [b]ecause people didn't have land. The Dutch had already been sent home. It was the Dutch who had the right [to the plantation]. If we didn't destroy it, they would return. That's what they said, people said that. [Plants] were destroyed, everything was cut down to be planted [with] food crops. Some people walked around and burnt the factory ... I didn't really understand, but there was somebody who managed [the action]. My uncle was a guard at that time, a security guard. [Our family received] one farm, if I'm not mistaken, one hectare. The size depended on the number of family members.[49]

Rakyat itu nanam itu. Itu untuk menghidupi mereka-mereka itu. di samping untuk menghidupi tentara, juga menghidupi pengungsi. Orang dari kota, dari Malang, yang mengungsi ke perkebunan dari jaman penjajahan Belanda ... dia hidupnya dari mana? Padahal dia ndak ada gaji. Ya hidupnya dari rakyat yang nanam kebun itu ... hingga akhirnya berlanjut, sehabis penyerahan kedaulatan itu, ditingkatkan sehingga habis. Sekarang jadi desa perkebunan itu ... Bumi hangus periode clash II, [19]48. Semua kebun-kebun itu dibumi hangus ... dari tentara membawa bom ke pabrik. Rakyat yang tinggal di perkebunan disuruh menjauh karena itu diledakkan. Habis itu setelah diledakkan dan rakyat itu tinggal di pegunungan, ya udah, hukum tidak berjalan, sudah, dihabiskan pabrik itu. Diteteli. Aduh, kok bangsa kita begitu ya. Semua, mesinnya, sengnya diambili, karena untuk kepentingan rumah-rumah penduduk yang di kebun-kebun itu. Diambili, habis. Penduduk mengambil seenaknya sendiri untuk kepentingannya sendiri, ya dijual, dipakai untuk rumah. Habis. Ya gimana, jaman seperti itu. termasuk saya sendiri bikin rumah ... Dulu atapnya dari alang-alang, tapi dengan adanya bumi hangus, bisa berubah jadi seng. Semua ngambili [Then it was cut down during the revolutionary era. So in the end, the gardens were also profitable at that time to support the fighters who were guerrilla warriors in the mountains ... The people planted them. In addition to supporting soldiers, they also supported refugees. People from the city, from Malang, who fled to the plantations from the Dutch colonial era ... where do they live? He has no salary. He lived off the people who planted the plantation ... Until finally it continued, after the transfer of sovereignty, it was increased until it was exhausted. Now it is a plantation village ... The scorched earth of the second clash period, [19]48. All the plantations were scorched ... from the army bringing bombs to the factory. The people who lived on the plantation were told to stay away because it was blown up. After that, after it was blown up and the people lived in the mountains, that's it, the law didn't work, that's it, the factory was destroyed. That's it. Ouch, how come our nation is like that. Everything, the machine, the zinc was taken away, because it was for the benefit of the houses of the people in the gardens. Taken away, exhausted. The people take whatever they want for their own use, they sell it, use it for their houses. It's gone. I myself built a house ... The roof used to be made of reeds, but with the scorched earth, it was turned into zinc. Everyone took.' Interview with Prambodo, Malang, 29 July 2016, #45.27–51.03.

49 '*Karena rakyat gak punya tanah, Belanda sudah diusir pulang. Dulu yang haknya kan belanda. Yang berhak sudah pulang ke negaranya. Kalau ndak dibabat, nanti pulang ke sini kembali. Katanya gitu, orang-orang ngomong gitu. [Tanaman] dihancurkan, babat semua. Untuk tanaman polowijo. Untuk tanaman makanan bagi rakyat, gitu. Sebagian mlayu-mlayu mbakar pabrik itu ... Saya juga gak tau, tapi ada yang ngatur itu. [Paklik] jaman semonten njogo. Njogo keamanan ... [Dapat] 1 kebon, kalo ndak keliru 1 hektar. Lihat banyak kecilnya anggota keluarga* [Because the people didn't have land, the Dutch had been driven home. In the past, it was the Dutch who had the rights. The rightful ones have returned to their countries. If you don't clear it, you will come back here again. They say that, people say that. [Crops] were destroyed, cut down. For *polowijo* plants. For food crops for the people, that is. Some people

Marwono was a schoolboy at that time. Although he could not recognise the people who carried out these acts, he remembered the chaos in the plantation where his family had worked. Moreover, both Marwono's and Prambodo's families benefited from this chaos, for example, by obtaining land and materials for their houses. From both accounts, it seems that some plantation workers used the revolution to dismantle the colonial capitalists' control of modernity—an opportunity to reverse their dispossession.

Perceiving modernity

The case of plantations in South Malang shows the proximity of colonialism, capitalism and modernity. Underlying the transformation of South Malang into a plantation society was systematic repression, the imposition of the ruler's own knowledge production and, at the same time, the impeding of the cultural production of the dominated and the establishment of social and cultural control over them.[50] In extreme cases of European cultural colonisation, peasant subcultures were condemned and replaced with formalised and objectivised expressions, through the cultural patterns of the rulers.[51] Walter Mignolo goes even further by arguing that 'there is no modernity without coloniality'.[52] He argues that modernity is 'a complex narrative that builds Western civilization by celebrating its achievements while hiding at the same time its darker side, "coloniality"'.[53]

I agree that colonialism is inseparable from modernity, but to perceive modernity merely in this way assumes that the concept itself is one dimensional: modernity is imposed and the colonised have no agency in its construction. According to Dipesh Chakrabarty, this unidimensional assumption stems from the tendency to perceive modernity as a binary. Tropes such as 'premodern', 'backward' and 'medieval' are used to define

---

burned down the factory … I don't know either, but someone arranged it. My uncle at that time was guarding. As a security … [you received] one garden, if I'm not mistaken, 1 hectare. See how many family members there are.' Interview with Marwono, Donomulyo, 16 September 2016, #14.42–22.10. This interview is also cited Leksana, *Memory Culture of the Anti-Leftist Violence in Indonesia*.
50   Aníbal Quijano, 'Coloniality and Modernity/Rationality', *Cultural Studies* 21, nos 2–3 (2007): 168–78, doi.org/10.1080/09502380601164353.
51   ibid.
52   Walter D. Mignolo, *The Darker Side of Western Modernity: Global Futures, Decolonial Options* (Durham: Duke University Press, 2011), doi.org/10.1215/9780822394501, 3.
53   ibid., 2–3.

modernity itself.⁵⁴ Chakrabarty then illustrates how the conception of modern versus backwardness or traditional is often not strict or clear in postcolonial India. Today's India is more democratic (and, in that sense, more modern), enabling people to challenge older hierarchies of power and status.⁵⁵ But this does not necessarily mean it is more civil. Chakrabarty writes: 'Verbal, physical, and symbolic violence underwriting relations of domination and subordination are to be seen in every department of life: from relations of production to relationships in the family.'⁵⁶ Modern democracy does not automatically diminish so-called traditional elements: local conflicts, patronage relations, family ties, factions, and so on. To define modernity in contrast to the traditional, then, is insufficient to understand the concept itself, because modernity is permeable, historically constructed, multifaceted and sometimes messy. Modernity is also mobilised and constructed by different people, both the colonised and the oppressed, and, as such, it encompasses what Susie Protschky describes as the 'historical imagination' of the Indies people.⁵⁷

Therefore, to talk about colonial modernity is to look at how the concept is shaped, through what means and by whom. To do this, it is not enough to interpret modernity as an imposed act of colonialism. It is also necessary to interrogate how it is articulated and contested by the colonised themselves. According to Frederick Cooper, to elevate messy histories that shaped modernity into a consistent project underplays the efforts of colonised people to deflect and appropriate elements of colonising policies.⁵⁸ Furthermore, Carol Gluck noted that, despite condemnation of colonial modernity, it also possessed a magnetism for reformers and revolutionaries, workers and peasants, elites and ordinary people who reached for modern ways of living and being.⁵⁹ The Indonesian nationalist movement, the *pribumi pangreh praja* (native officials/government officers)⁶⁰ and the urban middle class in

---

54   Dipesh Chakrabarty, *Habitations of Modernity: Essays in the Wake of Subaltern Studies* (Chicago: University of Chicago Press, 2002), xx.
55   ibid.
56   ibid., xxii.
57   Susie Protschky, *Photography, Modernity and the Governed in Late-Colonial Indonesia* (Amsterdam: Amsterdam University Press, 2014), doi.org/10.1515/9789048523382.
58   Frederick Cooper, *Colonialism in Question: Theory, Knowledge, History* (Berkeley: University of California Press, 2005), doi.org/10.1525/9780520938618.
59   Carol Gluck, 'The End of Elsewhere: Writing Modernity Now', *The American Historical Review* 116, no. 3 (2011): 676–87, doi.org/10.1086/ahr.116.3.676, at 677.
60   Heather Sutherland, 'Pangreh Pradja: Java's Indigenous Administrative Corps and Its Role in the Last Decades of Dutch Colonial Rule' (PhD diss., Yale University, New Haven, 1973).

the 1930s who were highly motivated to participate in a modern lifestyle[61]—all are examples of how modernity was also utilised for the agendas of Indonesians. Indonesian 'wild literature' of the 1930s is another example of how locals offered alternative versions of being modern, in which ideas of freedom were central.[62] The life histories of plantation families, such as Prambodo's, also illustrate how modern education was desired by middle-class overseer families. By glossing over such processes of engagement with modernity, we will have an incomplete understanding of colonial modernity. Furthermore, the violence and chaos in plantations during the Indonesian revolution show us yet another element of modernity. As Colombijn notes, a counter-colonial process of defining modernity did not reject the fundamental ingredients of modernity but challenged the assumption of its exclusive ownership.[63] The cases of coffee thefts, destruction of plantations and land squatting during the revolution point to another dimension of modernity. These acts confronted the function of modernity as a catalyst of colonial capitalism through claims of property (be it coffee beans or land) and to shatter the monopoly of modernity that was once in the hands of the elites. Looking at the life history accounts of plantation communities, the revolution offered an opportunity to give a new meaning to modernity, which relates to the equality and agency of the Indonesians.

Conclusion

This chapter has articulated diverse interpretations of modernity not through the binary opposition between the colonisers and the colonised, but through their interactions and contestations. Plantation companies set the standards of modernity through the establishment of technology, facilities, housing, health care and security systems geared towards sustaining colonial capitalism. Health care and entertainment, for example, were provided to sustain workers within the plantation areas. At the same time, modernity

---

61 Henk Schulte Nordholt, 'Modernity and Middle Classes in the Netherlands Indies: Cultivating Cultural Citizenship', in *Photography, Modernity and the Governed in Late-Colonial Indonesia*, ed. Susie Protschky (Amsterdam: Amsterdam University Press, 2018), 223–54, doi.org/10.1515/9789048523382-009.
62 Hilmar Farid and Razif, '*Batjaan Liar* in the Dutch East Indies: A Colonial Antipode', *Postcolonial Studies* 11, no. 3 (2008): 277–92, doi.org/10.1080/13688790802226694.
63 Freek Colombijn and Joost Coté, eds, *Cars, Conduits, and Kampongs: The Modernization of the Indonesian City, 1920–1960* (Leiden: Brill, 2014), doi.org/10.1163/9789004280724, 11.

created dispossession and exacerbated class differences. The case of coffee thefts indicates that the conception of property and legality that modernity brought was interpreted differently by plantation owners and locals.

However, this is not a complete picture of what modernity means. Focusing on the agency of the colonised, modernity is also the desires and goals of the locals or the colonised, which enable them to move towards social change. This move manifested in different forms, from ideas of independence to access to education. Nevertheless, this drive for modernity among the colonised does not necessarily mean that every group has equal access to achieve it. The opportunity to claim this equality emerged with the revolution. The destruction of plantations as a republican war tactic presented the chance for villagers to claim land or materials that once belonged to the colonial elites. In this case, violence became an extreme means to assert modernity.

References

Primary sources

Dutch East Indies Welvaartcommissie [Dutch East Indies Welfare Commission], Batavia. 1907. *Onderzoek Naar de Mindere Welvaart Der Inlandsche Bevolking Op Java En Madoera. [IX, Economie van de Desa]: Samentrekking van de Afdeelingsverslagen over de Uitkomsten Der Onderzoekingen [Inquiry into the Declining Prosperity of the Domestic Population in Java and Madura. (IX, Economy of the Village): Merging of the Departmental Reports about the Outcomes of the Inquiries]*. Ministerie van Koloniën: Collectie Grijs [Ministry of the Colonies: Grijs Collection]. Inv. 2.10.64. Box 21, folder 21.4. The Hague: Nationaal Archief [National Archives].

Dutch East Indies Welvaartcommissie [Dutch East Indies Welfare Commission], Batavia. 1907. *Onderzoek Naar de Mindere Welvaart Der Inlandsche Bevolking Op Java En Madoera. [Recht En Politie]: Samentrekking van de Afdeelingsverslagen over de Uitkomsten Der Onderzoekingen [Inquiry into the Declining Prosperity of the Domestic Population in Java and Madura. (Law and Police): Merging of the Departmental Reports about the Outcomes of the Inquiries]*. Ministerie van Koloniën: Collectie Grijs [Ministry of the Colonies: Grijs Collection]. Inv. 2.10.64. Box 21, folder 21.4. The Hague: Nationaal Archief [National Archives].

Soerabaiasch Handelsblad. 1931. 'De Nieuwe Koffie Ordonantie [The New Coffee Regulation].' *Soerabaiasch Handelsblad [Surabaya Commercial Paper]*, 13 July.

Soerabaiasch Handelsblad. 1934. 'Koffiediefstallen [Coffee Thefts].' *Soerabaiasch Handelsblad* [*Surabaya Commercial Paper*], 23 June.

Soerabaiasch Handelsblad. 1934. 'Feestelijke Opening Zuid-Smeroeweg: Plantershulde Aan "Kennis Den Bruggebouwer" [Festive Opening of South Semeru Road: Planters' Tribute to Acknowledge the Bridge Builder].' *Soerabaiasch Handelsblad* [*Surabaya Commercial Paper*], 3 November. resolver.kb.nl/resolve?urn=ddd:011110054:mpeg21:p009.

Soerabaiasch Handelsblad. 1939. 'De Koffiediefstallen in Zuid Malang [The Coffee Thefts in South Malang].' *Soerabaiasch Handelsblad* [*Surabaya Commercial Paper*], 22 September.

Verslag Over Het Boekjaar 1902–1949 [*Report on the Financial Year 1902–1949*]. Internationaal Instituut voor Sociale Geschiedenis [International Institute of Social History]. Inv. ZK 60163. Amsterdam: Nederlandsch Economisch-Historisch Archief [Netherlands Economic History Archive].

Secondary sources

Barlow, Tani. 2012. 'Debates Over Colonial Modernity in East Asia and Another Alternative.' *Cultural Studies* 26, no. 5: 617–44. doi.org/10.1080/09502386.2012.711006.

Chakrabarty, Dipesh. 2002. *Habitations of Modernity: Essays in the Wake of Subaltern Studies*. Chicago: University of Chicago Press.

Colombijn, Freek, and Joost Coté, eds. 2014. *Cars, Conduits, and Kampongs: The Modernization of the Indonesian City, 1920–1960*. Leiden: Brill. doi.org/10.1163/9789004280724.

Cooper, Frederick. 2005. *Colonialism in Question: Theory, Knowledge, History*. Berkeley: University of California Press. doi.org/10.1525/9780520938618.

Farid, Hilmar, and Razif. 2008. '*Batjaan Liar* in the Dutch East Indies: A Colonial Antipode.' *Postcolonial Studies* 11, no. 3: 277–92. doi.org/10.1080/13688790802226694.

Fauzi, Noer. 1999. *Petani & Penguasa: Dinamika Perjalanan Politik Agraria Indonesia* [*Farmers and Rulers: The Dynamic Processes of Agrarian Politics in Indonesia*]. Yogyakarta: INSIST, KPA, Pustaka Pelajar.

Frakking, Roel. 2014. '"Who Wants to Cover Everything, Covers Nothing": The Organization of Indigenous Security Forces in Indonesia, 1945–50.' In *Colonial Counterinsurgency and Mass Violence: The Dutch Empire in Indonesia*, edited by Bart Luttikhuis and A. Dirk Moses, 111–32. London: Routledge. doi.org/10.4324/9781315767345-6.

Gillen, Paul, and Devleena Ghosh. 2007. *Colonialism & Modernity*. Sydney: UNSW Press.

Gluck, Carol. 2011. 'The End of Elsewhere: Writing Modernity Now.' *The American Historical Review* 116, no. 3: 676–87. doi.org/10.1086/ahr.116.3.676.

Houben, Vincent J.H. 2002. 'Java in the 19th Century: Consolidation of a Territorial State.' In *The Emergence of a National Economy: An Economic History of Indonesia, 1800–2000*, edited by Howard Dick, Vincent J.H. Houben, J. Thomas Lindblad, and Thee Kian Wie, 56–81. Sydney: Allen & Unwin. doi.org/10.1163/9789004486454_012.

Hudiyanto, Reza. 2021. 'Between Modernization and Capitalization: Commercialization of Malang in the Early Twentieth Century.' *Paramita: Historical Studies Journal* 31, no. 1: 45–55. doi.org/10.15294/paramita.v31i1.20463.

Kano, Hiroyoshi. 1990. *Pagelaran: Anatomi Sosial Ekonomi Pelapisan Masyarakat Tani di Sebuah Desa Jawa Timur* [*Pagelaran: The Anatomy of Social-Economic Layering Amongst Farmers in an East Java Village*]. Yogyakarta: Gadjah Mada University Press.

Khusyairi, Johny A., and Freek Colombijn. 2015. 'Moving at a Different Velocity: The Modernization of Transportation and Social Differentiation in Surabaya in the 1920s.' In *Cars, Conduits, and Kampongs: The Modernization of the Indonesian City, 1920–1960*, edited by Freek Colombijn and Joost Coté, 249–71. Leiden: Brill. doi.org/10.1163/9789004280724_011.

Kurosawa, Aiko. 2015. *Kuasa Jepang Di Jawa: Perubahan Sosial Di Pedesaan 1942–1945* [*Japanese Power in Java: Social Transformation in Villages 1942–1945*]. Depok, West Java: Komunitas Bambu.

Leksana, Grace T. 2023. *Memory Culture of the Anti-Leftist Violence in Indonesia: Embedded Remembering*. Amsterdam: Amsterdam University Press. doi.org/10.5117/9789463723565.

Li, Tania Murray. 2010. 'To Make Live or Let Die? Rural Dispossession and the Protection of Surplus Populations.' *Antipode* 41, no. s1: 66–93. doi.org/10.1111/j.1467-8330.2009.00717.x.

Mignolo, Walter D. 2011. *The Darker Side of Western Modernity: Global Futures, Decolonial Options*. Durham: Duke University Press. doi.org/10.1215/97808 22394501.

Nawiyanto. 2020. *Dari Rimba Menjadi Kota: Bank Indonesia Dalam Evolusi Malang Raya [From Forest to City: The Indonesian Bank in Malang's Evolution]*. Jakarta: Bank Indonesia Institute.

Nordholt, Henk Schulte. 2018. 'Modernity and Middle Classes in the Netherlands Indies: Cultivating Cultural Citizenship.' In *Photography, Modernity and the Governed in Late-Colonial Indonesia*, edited by Susie Protschky, 223–54. Amsterdam: Amsterdam University Press. doi.org/10.1515/9789048523382-009.

Pholsena, Vatthana. 2015. 'Technology and Empire: A Colonial Narrative of the Construction of the Tonkin–Yunnan Railway.' *Critical Asian Studies* 47, no. 4: 537–57. doi.org/10.1080/14672715.2015.1079985.

Protschky, Susie. 2014. *Photography, Modernity and the Governed in Late-Colonial Indonesia*. Amsterdam: Amsterdam University Press. doi.org/10.1515/9789048 523382.

Quijano, Aníbal. 2007. 'Coloniality and Modernity/Rationality.' *Cultural Studies* 21, nos 2–3: 168–78. doi.org/10.1080/09502380601164353.

Reid, Anthony. 2015. *A History of Southeast Asia: Critical Crossroads*. Chichester: Wiley Blackwell.

Safitry, Martina. 2016. 'Dukun Dan Mantri Pes: Praktisi Kesehatan Lokal Di Jawa Masa Epidemi Pes 1910–1942 [Shamans and Health Care Workers: Local Health Care Practitioners in Java during the Bubonic Plague Epidemic 1910–1942].' Master's thesis, Universitas Gadjah Mada, Depok.

Sapto, Ari. 2018. *Republik Dalam Pusaran Elite Sipil Dan Militer [Republic in the Vortex of Military and Civilian Elites]*. Yogyakarta: Matapadi Pressindo.

Sato, Shigeru. 2010. 'Relocation of Labor and the Romusha Issue.' In *The Encyclopedia of Indonesia in the Pacific War*, edited by Peter Post, William Bradley Horton, and Didi Kwartanada, 245–61. Leiden: Brill.

Stoler, Ann. 2010. *Carnal Knowledge and Imperial Power: Race and the Intimate in Colonial Rule*. Berkeley: University of California Press. doi.org/10.1525/ 9780520946194.

Sutherland, Heather. 1973. 'Pangreh Pradja: Java's Indigenous Administrative Corps and Its Role in the Last Decades of Dutch Colonial Rule.' PhD diss., Yale University, New Haven.

6

Rethinking histories of military atrocity, ethnic violence and photography, from the Aceh War to the Indonesian national revolution

Susie Protschky

Introduction

The subjugation campaigns of the colonial army in the Netherlands East Indies at the turn of the twentieth century produced one of the most substantial photographic records of military atrocities committed by a European colonial regime anywhere in Southeast Asia before World War II.[1] We do not see its like again in Indonesia until the surfeit of photographs by Dutch soldiers during the Indonesian national revolution (1945–49). While a few studies have examined the visual culture of specific wars in

---

1 Research for this essay was funded by an Australian Research Council Future Fellowship (FT200100597). I am grateful to the editors and two anonymous peer reviewers for their feedback on earlier versions. Thanks to Melle van Maanen for remote research assistance during the Covid-19 pandemic, and John Klein Nagelvoort for advice at Bronbeek.

colonial Indonesia,[2] scholars have neglected the longer history of war photography, military atrocity and ethnic violence across the period bracketed by the Aceh War (1873–1942) and the revolution. This chapter attempts to begin such a history.

Only a few studies link the Dutch colonial army's wars in the nineteenth and twentieth centuries to form a coherent overview of colonial military conflict across the period, and most are in Dutch.[3] Drawing continuities is complicated by the fact that the colonial Royal Netherlands East Indies Army (Koninklijk Nederlandsch-Indisch Leger, KNIL) was joined on Indonesian soil by the Netherlands' national forces (the Royal Netherlands Army or Koninklijke Landmacht, and the Royal Netherlands Navy or Koninklijke Marine) for the first and last time between 1946 and 1950. New research argues that the colonial army strongly influenced the leadership, training and tactics of the Dutch armed forces throughout the revolution.[4] As the introduction in Chapter 1 of this volume explains, recent work on 'extreme violence' perpetrated by Dutch soldiers against Indonesian combatants and civilians during the revolution prompted fresh questions in the Netherlands and Indonesia about whether this focus occludes a broader discussion of *colonial* violence and its longer history.[5] Put differently for my purposes

---

2   James T. Siegel, 'The Curse of the Photograph: Atjeh 1901', in *Photographies East: The Camera and its Histories in East and Southeast Asia*, ed. Rosalind C. Morris (Durham: Duke University Press, 2009), 57–78, doi.org/10.1215/9780822391821-003; Louis Zweers, 'Atjeh-Oorlog', in *Sumatra: Kolonialen, Koelies en Krijgers [Sumatra: Colonials, Coolies and Combatants]* (Houten: Fibula, 1988), 38–58; Louis Zweers, *De Gecensureerde Oorlog: Militairen versus Media in Nederlands-Indië [The Censored War: Military Personnel Versus Media in the Netherlands Indies]* (Zutphen: Walburg Pers, 2013); Liesbeth Ouwehand, 'Militaire Albums [Military Albums]', in *Herinneringen in Beeld: Fotoalbums uit Nederlands-Indië [Recollections in Pictures: Photo Albums from the Netherlands Indies]* (Leiden: KITLV Press, 2009), 87–110; Paul Bijl, *Emerging Memory: Photographs of Colonial Atrocity in Dutch Cultural Remembrance* (Amsterdam: Amsterdam University Press, 2015), doi.org/10.1515/9789048522019; René Kok, Erik Somers, and Louis Zweers, *Koloniale Oorlog 1945–1949: Van Indië naar Indonesië [Colonial War 1945–1949: From the Indies to Indonesia]* (Amsterdam: Uitgeverij Carrera, 2015).
3   Piet Hagen, *Koloniale Oorlogen in Indonesië: Vijf Eeuwen Verzet Tegen Vreemde Overheersing [Colonial Wars in Indonesia: Five Centuries of Resistance Against Foreign Domination]* (Amsterdam: Uitgeverij De Arbeiderspers, 2018); Petra Groen, Anita van Dissel, Mark Loderichs, Rémy Limpach, and Thijs Brocades Zaalberg, *Krijgsgeweld en Kolonie: Opkomst en Ondergang van Nederland als Koloniale Mogendheid, 1816–2010 [Military Violence and the Colony: The Netherlands' Rise and Fall as a Colonial Power, 1816–2010]* (Amsterdam: Boom, 2021); Henk Schulte Nordholt, 'A Genealogy of Violence', in *Roots of Violence in Indonesia: Contemporary Violence in Historical Perspective*, eds Freek Colombijn and J. Thomas Lindblad (Leiden: KITLV Press, 2002), 33–62, doi.org/10.1163/9789004489561_004.
4   Gert Oostindie and Rémy Limpach, 'The War in Indonesia 1945–1949: The Military-Historical Context', in *Beyond the Pale: Dutch Extreme Violence in the Indonesian War of Independence, 1945–1949*, eds Gert Oostindie, Ben Schoenmaker, and Frank van Vree (Amsterdam: Amsterdam University Press, 2022), 69–106, at 83.
5   See also Setiawan's Chapter 14 in this volume.

6. RETHINKING HISTORIES OF MILITARY ATROCITY, ETHNIC VIOLENCE AND PHOTOGRAPHY

here, we know that 'colonial history is military history',[6] but what, if anything, made Dutch military violence in Indonesia *colonial* over the longer period? And how can a historical analysis of war photography help answer this question?

This chapter considers the photographers who accompanied KNIL campaigns in Aceh and Bali at the turn of the twentieth century as the first practitioners in Indonesia of 'embedded' photography—a genre that scholars more typically date to the 1940s. For example, Hugo Wilmar (1923–57), one of the best-known accredited Dutch military photographers deployed to Indonesia during the revolution, is usually compared with the American cameramen among whom he trained during World War II and the Dutch soldiers with whom he served in 1946–47, rather than with the photographers who accompanied the bloody wars of the KNIL before 1942.[7] Wilmar and his ilk were preceded by C.B. Nieuwenhuis, who photographed the Sigli and Samalanga (Aceh) 'expeditions' in 1897 and 1901, respectively; H.M. Neeb, who photographed the Gayo and Alas (Aceh) campaigns of 1904; and H.M. van Weede, who photographed the KNIL's role in a Badung *puputan* (dynastic 'ending') in 1906 (Bali).

I will examine two aspects of these embedded photographers' works that place war photography, and its relationship to military *and* colonial violence, in historical context. The first aspect is the prominence of ethnic violence in photographs of Dutch colonial military atrocities. Comprehension of the KNIL's hierarchical organisation along ethnic lines remains largely confined to the subfield of (Dutch) military history.[8] The KNIL's renowned 'martial race'—the so-called Ambonese soldiers, who were in fact men recruited from throughout present-day Maluku and the Minahasa Peninsula—have attracted special attention.[9] Colonial photographs reveal the importance of the Aceh War for valorising the reputed ferocity of 'Ambonese' soldiers. Such images arguably formed a historical foundation for an enduring colonial stereotype—one that informed white Dutch accounts of 'extreme' violence during the Indonesian national revolution. However, in a novel extension

---

6   Backcover blurb to Groen et al., *Military Violence and the Colony*.
7   Louis Zweers, *Front Indië: Hugo Wilmar, Ooggetuig van een Koloniale Oorlog* [*The Indies Front: Hugo Wilmar, Eyewitness to a Colonial War*] (Zutphen: Walburg Pers, 1994), 11; Kok et al., *Colonial War*, 52; see the Stichting Hugo Wilmar [Hugo Hilmar Foundation], online at: hugowilmar.nl/en/biografie/nederlands-indie/, hugowilmar.nl/en/biografie/.
8   See Groen et al., *Military Violence and the Colony*.
9   See Richard Chauvel, *Nationalists, Soldiers and Separatists: The Ambonese Islands from Colonialism to Revolt* (Leiden: KITLV Press, 2008), doi.org/10.1163/9789004253957.

of Karl Hack and Tobias Rettig's notion of 'martial Orientalism',[10] I argue here that the entire spectrum of the KNIL hierarchy—from the European officers to the lowest convict auxiliaries from Java—must be brought into a critical historical analysis of how ethnic differences were theorised and mobilised for warfare within the Dutch colonial army.

My second purpose is to move beyond the massacre images that made certain indigenous soldiers' reputations for ferocity iconic. I explain how a broader body of work by photographers embedded within the KNIL captured modes of 'approved violence'.[11] Paul Bijl, in his brilliant work on H.M. Neeb's Aceh photographs, first used this term to signify the realpolitik of the 'Ethical Policy'—a period of liberal imperial reforms coinciding with intensive Dutch military expansion across the Indonesian archipelago.[12] I develop his concept here to explain how forms of colonial violence that were widespread across civilian society in the Netherlands East Indies also supported military structures. In so doing, I aim to nuance a contemporary Dutch scholarship on wartime atrocities in Indonesia that remains fixated on the breach of judicial and military *upper* limits to violence. I attend equally to how a *baseline* of what was considered acceptable violence in fact derived from peacetime civilian practices under colonial rule.[13] Recognising the colonial genealogy of embedded war photography thus places revolution-era dynamics in historical context and reveals what I will call the 'double-embeddedness' of war photographers: the productive synergy between their certified interloper status in the army, whose interests they ostensibly served, and their positions as men *of* colonial societies who valorised forms of violence that permeated both civilian and military institutions.

---

10   Karl Hack, with Tobias Rettig, 'Imperial Systems of Power, Colonial Forces and the Making of Modern Southeast Asia', in *Colonial Armies in Southeast Asia*, eds Karl Hack and Tobias Rettig (London: Routledge, 2006), 3–38, doi.org/10.4324/9780203414668_chapter_1, at 14.
11   On nomenclature: I use 'indigenous' from here on to signify diverse ethnic groups local to Indonesia, as distinct from 'Indonesians', since the history of the KNIL reveals how contested that category was for some of its soldiers before and across independence.
12   Paul Bijl, 'Saving the Children? The Ethical Policy and Photographs of Colonial Atrocity during the Aceh War', in *Photography, Modernity and the Governed in Late-Colonial Indonesia*, ed. Susie Protschky (Amsterdam: Amsterdam University Press, 2015), 103–32, doi.org/10.1515/9789048523382-005, at 111.
13   I use a similar approach, focused on the topic of violence against women and children who worked inside Dutch military barracks, in Susie Protschky, 'Home at the Front: Violence Against Indonesian Women and Children in Dutch Military Barracks during the Indonesian National Revolution', in *Gender, Violence and Power in Indonesia: Across Time and Space*, eds Katharine McGregor, Ana Dragojlovic, and Hannah Loney (London: Routledge, 2020), 59–83.

The first embedded war photographers in colonial Indonesia

During the Indonesian national revolution, officially embedded photographers consistently self-censored or were censored by Dutch authorities.[14] It was the amateur frontline Dutch soldier-photographers ostensibly making 'private' images who produced a much larger, more explicit record of atrocities during the mid to late 1940s. Their prints circulated widely among comrades and military institutions during the war and among veterans and their supporters for decades afterwards but remained out of the media until recently.[15] During the revolution, embedded photographers were technically trained and equipped for their roles. Large numbers of self-taught amateurs were also able to operate because small handheld cameras and roll film had become standard by the 1940s. By contrast, the embedded photographers who had accompanied KNIL expeditions in the early twentieth century monopolised skills that were relatively rare before the advent of mass photography, and contended with very different technology—slower shutter speeds, fragile or volatile materials and cumbersome equipment—such that an element of staging was still necessary to their practice.[16] For these reasons, embedded photographers, and not combatants themselves, provided the most comprehensive record of KNIL atrocities at the turn of the twentieth century.

Christiaan Benjamin Nieuwenhuis (1863–1922) was a successful commercial photographer active on Sumatra and best known for his landscapes and ethnographic portraits[17] but, given the militarisation of large parts of the island at the turn of the twentieth century, it is impossible to separate his practice from war photography. He took his camera on at least two KNIL campaigns in Aceh, to Sigli in 1897 and Samalanga in 1901. Nieuwenhuis probably met Lieutenant Colonel Joannes Benedictus van Heutsz, the highest military authority in the Netherlands East Indies,

---

14   Zweers, *The Censored War*.
15   Susie Protschky, 'Burdens of Proof: Photography and Evidence of Atrocity during the Dutch Military Actions in Indonesia (1945–50)', *Bijdragen tot de Taal-, Land- en Volkenkunde* [*Journal of the Humanities and Social Sciences of Southeast Asia*] 176, nos 2–3 (2020): 240–78, doi.org/10.1163/22134379-bja10015.
16   Bijl, *Emerging Memory*, 50–51; H.M. van Weede, *Indische Reisherinneringen* [*Indies Travel Memories*] (Haarlem: H.D. Tjeenk Willink & Zoon, 1908), 501.
17   Anneke Groeneveld, 'C.B. Nieuwenhuis' View of Sumatra', in *Toward Independence: A Century of Indonesia Photographed*, ed. Jane Levy Reed (San Francisco: Friends of Photography, 1991), 65–71.

during the Sigli 'expedition' he commanded. It was van Heutsz who later sanctioned Nieuwenhuis's official attendance at Samalanga. Nieuwenhuis was self-conscious of his authorised position as an 'eyewitness' (*ooggetuige*) to events. 'Although I am known by many,' he proclaimed in his Samalanga account, 'here in the Indies it has never been known for a professional photographer [*vakfotograaf*] to be granted such an excursion.'[18]

Hendricus Marinus Neeb (1870–1933) was a non-combatant in the colonial army, who was primarily employed as a medic. Born in the Indies and trained in Leiden, Neeb joined the KNIL in 1893 and first went to Aceh as an army doctor 10 years later.[19] Neeb's interest in photography was welcomed by an institution that routinely combined topographic, anthropological and scientific work with military campaigns. He produced 173 photographs, including landscapes and ethnographic portraits, from the KNIL 'expedition' to the Gayo, Alas and Batak lands between 8 February and 23 July 1904 under Lieutenant Colonel Gotfried Coenraad Ernst van Daalen. Copies were given to the Royal Military Academy in Breda, two Dutch ethnographic museums and the Batavian Society for Arts and Sciences, which exhibited them in 1905.[20] That same year, van Daalen's aide, J.C.J. Kempees, reproduced 29 of Neeb's photographs as plates in his book-length account of the expedition.[21]

Hendrik Maurits van Weede (1879–1912) was a *jonkheer* ('young lord', lower nobility) and only son of a former diplomat, chamberlain to Queen Wilhelmina of the Netherlands and, briefly, foreign minister in the Dutch Parliament. Van Weede's career and hobbies were typical of aristocratic Dutchmen. He was a reserve officer in a cavalry brigade of the Netherlands Royal Army. After completing his studies at Utrecht University, he took

---

18   C.B. Nieuwenhuis, *De Expeditie naar Samalanga (Januari 1901): Dagverhaal van een Fotograaf te Velde* [*The Expedition to Samalanga (January 1901): Tales of a Photographer in the Field*] (Amsterdam: Van Holkema & Warendorf, 1901), vii, 1.
19   Anneke Groeneveld, 'H.M. Neeb: A Witness of the Aceh War', in *Toward Independence: A Century of Indonesia Photographed*, ed. Jane Levy Reed (San Francisco: Friends of Photography, 1991), 72–77, at 73.
20   Bilj, *Emerging Memory*, 43–44.
21   J.C.J. Kempees, *De Tocht van Overste Van Daalen door de Gajo, Alas- en Bataklanden 8 Februari tot 23 Juli 1904* [*The March of Commander van Daalen through the Gayo, Alas and Batak Lands, 8 February to 23 July 1904*] (Amsterdam: J.C. Dalmeijer, 1905). Van Daalen and Neeb also produced reports on the campaign in the *Indisch Militair Tijdschrift* [*Indies Military Journal*] in 1905, but these were not illustrated.

6. RETHINKING HISTORIES OF MILITARY ATROCITY, ETHNIC VIOLENCE AND PHOTOGRAPHY

a 14-month grand tour of British India and the Netherlands East Indies.[22] His published account of this journey indulged his two passions: hunting (which killed him, by way of an accident, in 1912) and photography (which has arguably given him a longer 'afterlife'). Van Weede's published travelogue included more than 200 of his own photographs, including those taken after the Badung *puputan*. He saw this as the guest of Major General Marinus Bernardus Rost van Tonningen, commander of the Seventh Bali Expedition, with whom he became acquainted via a letter of introduction from his father. Like Nieuwenhuis, van Weede invoked his status not as a soldier or an aristocrat, but as an eyewitness—'I was present at the spot'—to two massacres on 20 September 1906, the first at the *puri* ('royal court') of Denpasar and the second, a few hours later, at Pemecutan.[23]

Across four separate campaigns in Aceh and Bali, Nieuwenhuis, Neeb and van Weede produced 14 explicit photographs between them showing the grisly aftermath of KNIL massacres, most taken by Neeb.[24] Nieuwenhuis's 1897 photograph of the massacre at Kuta Sukun (Figure 6.1) was not reproduced in a published expedition account, but was consumed as a commercial print that could be purchased from his studio.[25] His 1901 photograph of the massacre at Batu Iliq (Figure 6.2) was published in his own account of the Samalanga campaign and circulated in other contemporary Dutch media.[26] Some (not all) of Neeb's 1904 photographs from massacres in the Gayo and Alas lands were published in Kempees' account and, as Bijl has shown, became the subject of parliamentary debate and public

---

22 'Genealogie van Weede [Genealogy van Weede]', in *Nederland's Adelsboek* [*Netherlands' Book of Nobility*], 97 (The Hague: Centraal Bureau voor Genealogie [Central Bureau for Genealogy], 2012), 204–31, at 222–23; *Inventaris van de Dienststaten en Stamboeken van Officieren van de Koninklijke Landmacht en van de Koloniale Troepen in Nederland* [*Inventory of the Service Records and Registers of Officers of the Royal Netherlands Army and Colonial Troops in the Netherlands*] (1715) 1814–1940 (1945), 2.13.04, no. 763 (The Hague: Nationaal Archief [National Archives]), 64–65.
23 van Weede, *Indies Travel Memories*, 1, 5, 371, 407, 448, quote at 477.
24 Nieuwenhuis: two from Kuta Sukun (1897), one from Batu Iliq (1901); Neeb: three from Kuta Rih, four from Likat, one from Rékét Göïp (all 1904); van Weede: three from Badung (all 1906).
25 See the copies held at: the Wereldmuseum [World Museum], Leiden (RV-A78), 'Sold by A. Kaulfuss, Penang'; the Wereldmuseum [World Museum] Amsterdam, in the album of Serge Sergeivitch Grigorieff (TM-ALB-1991); the album in the archive of the NV Deli Maatschappij [Deli Company], Nationaal Archief [National Archives], The Hague, 2.20.46, *Inventaris van het archief van de NV Deli Maatschappij, Dochtermaatschappijen en Gefuseerde Bedrijven* [*Inventory of the Archives of NV Deli Maatschappij, Subsidiaries and Merged Companies*] (ca. 1700) 1869–1989 (1994), 850; and at Museum Bronbeek, 2005/00-654 (unknown owner), 2011/06/03-1-4/18 (Collection of J.C. Lamster [1872–1954], filmmaker and former major in the Topographical Service of the KNIL, 2021/04/20-3 (descendant of an officer in the *Korps Marechausee*).
26 Nieuwenhuis, *The Expedition to Samalanga*, Plate 19; Bijl, *Emerging Memory*, 68.

controversy (Figures 6.3 and 6.4).²⁷ Van Weede's 1906 photograph showing mounds of dead men, women and children in a Badung palace forecourt circulated privately in albums, but was omitted from his book (Figure 6.5).²⁸ The image was not published until after Indonesian independence and has rarely been acknowledged let alone critically examined in scholarship on KNIL atrocities.²⁹

Thus, between 1897 and 1906, photographs celebrating KNIL atrocities circulated openly, through various channels, in Dutch colonial society. The captions for published versions of these photographs were originally more euphemistic than those I reformulate here. They adopted military perspectives and referred to locations where the battle turned in favour of the Dutch, for example, rather than to 'massacres'. The language of the time framed these outcomes as victories rather than atrocities. Until at least 1906, the KNIL leadership readily approved embedded photographers to 'witness' these military campaigns and relay the nature of colonial warfare to the Dutch public.

---

27 Kempees, *The March of Commander van Daalen*; Bijl, *Emerging Memory*, 91–92.
28 Leiden University Library Special Collections, KITLV Album 3; Wereldmuseum [World Museum] Amsterdam, TM-60050657–TM-60050669; Bronbeek Museum, 1973/04/09-2-2/32.
29 Works that published the image without acknowledging the photographer are: Pierre Heijboer, *Klamboes, Klewangs, Klapperbomen: Indië Gewonnen en Verloren* [*Mosquito Nets, Swords, Coconut Trees: The Indies Won and Lost*] (Haarlem: De Haan, 1977), 85; Helen Creese, Darma Putra, and Henk Schulte Nordholt, *Seabad Puputan Bali: Perspektif Belanda dan Bali* [*Centenary of the Bali Puputan: Dutch and Balinese Perspectives*] (Jakarta: KITLV Press, 2006). He is named in Petra Groen, 'Koortsachtig imperialisme 1894–1914 [Feverish Imperialism 1894–1914]', in *Krijgsgeweld en Kolonie: Opkomst and Ondergang van Nederland als Koloniale Mogendheid, 1816–2010* [*Military Violence and the Colony: The Netherlands' Rise and Fall as a Colonial Power, 1816–2010*], eds Petra Groen, Anita van Dissel, Mark Loderichs, Rémy Limpach, and Thijs Brocades Zaalberg (Amsterdam: Boom, 2021), 135–60, at 156; and discussed in Anne-Lot Hoek, *De strijd om Bali: Imperialisme, verzet en onafhankelijkheid, 1846–1950* [*The Battle for Bali: Imperialism, Resistance and Independence, 1846–1950*] (Amsterdam: De Bezige Bij, 2021), 57–65.

6. RETHINKING HISTORIES OF MILITARY ATROCITY, ETHNIC VIOLENCE AND PHOTOGRAPHY

Figure 6.1 Aftermath of the KNIL massacre at Kuta Sukun, Sigli (Aceh), 6 August 1897
Photo: C.B. Nieuwenhuis, Nationaal Museum van Wereldculturen (National Museum of World Cultures) Collection, RV-A78-189.

Figure 6.2 Aftermath of the KNIL massacre at Batu Iliq, Samalanga (Aceh), 3 February 1901
Photo: C.B. Nieuwenhuis, Leiden University Library Special Collections, KITLV 27179.

Figure 6.3 Aftermath of the KNIL massacre at Kuta Rih (1), Alas (Aceh), 14 June 1904
Photo: H.M. Neeb, Leiden University Library Special Collections, KITLV 503098.

Figure 6.4 Aftermath of the KNIL massacre at Kuta Rih (2), Alas (Aceh), 14 June 1904
Photo: H.M. Neeb, Nationaal Museum van Wereldculturen (National Museum of World Cultures) Collection, TM-60001244.

Figure 6.5 Aftermath of the KNIL massacre at the puri Pemecutan, Badung (south Bali), 20 September 1906
Photo: H.W. van Weede, Leiden University Library Special Collections, KITLV A3, 10084.

Martial orientalism and KNIL atrocities in colonial sources

The photographs of Nieuwenhuis, Neeb and van Weede show the immediate aftermath of KNIL massacres of civilians killed in the attempt to resist Dutch conquest (Figures 6.1–6.5). These can be described as 'massacres' because the casualties were markedly asymmetric: the KNIL had guns and artillery capable of causing mass deaths and soldiers took no prisoners, killing the fleeing, wounded and unarmed.[30] At Kuta Sukun and its nearby fortification, 110 people were killed, while the KNIL lost a single soldier.[31] At the mountain stronghold of Batu Iliq (Baté Ilië) in 1901, Nieuwenhuis counted five KNIL deaths against 71 enemy casualties, not including the scores of people felled in skirmishes during the army's advance on the *benteng* ('fortification') or, indeed, in the preceding naval

---

30 J.B. van Heutsz, 'Expeditie naar Segli [Expedition to Segli]', 3 Oktober 1897, NIMH Collectie 511, f. 19r (The Hague: Nederlands Instituut voor Militaire Historie [Netherlands Institute of Military History]); Nieuwenhuis, *The Expedition to Samalanga*, 17, 20; Kempees, *The March of Commander van Daalen*, 158, 160, 161; van Weede, *Indies Travel Memories*, 463–64, 467–68.
31 van Heutsz, 'Expedition to Segli'.

bombardment of coastal villages.³² The people killed at Kuta Rih (Koetö Réh) in 1904 outnumbered KNIL casualties across van Daalen's entire campaign—313 men, 189 women and 59 children, not counting fatalities along the march to the fortification—versus 35 men killed in the colonial army. KNIL soldiers fired 4,400 rounds of ammunition into the enclosed space of this *benteng* against a group armed with 75 guns, bladed weapons, stones and lances. 'Among these dense ranks,' Kempees wrote, 'each bullet made several targets, and in a very short time the bloody drama was played out.'³³ Van Weede gave no casualty figures from south Bali in 1906, but it is estimated that at least 1,000 people died in the Badung *puputan*.³⁴

Neeb's photographs (Figures 6.3 and 6.4) and several others he took at Kuta Rih have received the most sustained attention, both during his own lifetime and in the postcolonial period.³⁵ However, it is Nieuwenhuis's earlier image of the slaughter at the fortified village of Kuta Sukun on 6 August 1897 (Figure 6.1) that has arguably come to represent KNIL military atrocities in recent museum and scholarly representations, perhaps because it expresses the 'horrifying, necrotic' theatricality viewers register when a photographer inserts themselves into a violent scene and asks killers to pose with their victims.³⁶ J.B. van Heutsz's report of the attack during the Sigli expedition under his command remains unpublished³⁷ and historians have sometimes omitted or incorrectly identified Nieuwenhuis's photograph from Kuta Sukun in favour of having it speak more generally for KNIL atrocities.³⁸ The latter recently featured as the banner to an editorial titled 'The Evil of Colonialism is Unforgivable' in the Dutch daily newspaper of record *NRC Handelsblad*. Award-winning journalist Goenawan Mohamad, co-founder and editor of the Indonesian politics journal *TEMPO*, begins this piece with a childhood memory from shortly after the conclusion

---

32   Nieuwenhuis, *The Expedition to Samalanga*, vii, 11, 13, 17, 18, 20, 25.
33   Kempees, *The March of Commander van Daalen*, 156–57, 163, 243, quote at 159–60.
34   Henk Schulte Nordholt, *The Spell of Power: A History of Balinese Politics, 1650–1940* (Leiden: KITLV Press, 1996), 213–14; Hoek, *The Battle for Bali*, 60.
35   See Paul van 't Veer, *De Atjeh-Oorlog* [*The Aceh War*] (Amsterdam: Uitgeverij De Arbeiderspers, 1969); Siegel, 'The Curse of the Photograph'; Groeneveld, 'H.M. Neeb'; Bijl, *Emerging Memory*; Bijl, 'Saving the Children?'.
36   Sean Willcock, 'Aesthetic Bodies: Posing on Sites of Violence in India, 1857–1900', *History of Photography* 39, 2 (2015): 142–59, doi.org/10.1080/03087298.2015.1038108, at 153, 157–58.
37   van Heutsz, 'Expedition to Segli'.
38   See Gerke Teitler, 'The Mixed Company: Fighting Power and Ethnic Relations in the Dutch Colonial Army, 1890–1920', in *Colonial Armies in Southeast Asia*, eds Karl Hack and Tobias Rettig (London: Routledge, 2006), 154–68, doi.org/10.4324/9780203414668_chapter_6, at 162; Bijl (*Emerging Memory*, 16) says the photograph was taken during the 1898 Pidie expedition.

of the Renville Agreement, in February 1948.[39] He recounts a day in his neighbourhood that began with jubilation at the ceasefire but ended with Dutch soldiers shooting four local men in a rice field. Mohamad also refers to the atrocities committed under Raymond Westerling's command in South Sulawesi (1946–47) and the execution of his own father in 1947.[40] Nowhere, however, does the article attempt any connection between the pictured KNIL massacre half a century earlier and the 'extreme violence' committed by Dutch soldiers against Indonesians during the late 1940s. The photograph is burdened with working solo to demonstrate a longer history of Dutch military violence. The contrast between Mohamad's description of revolution-era atrocities committed by white Dutch soldiers and the visual dominance of indigenous men as both perpetrators and victims in the 1897 image is a complication that goes unaddressed.

At the Wereldmuseum (World Museum) Amsterdam, a copy of the 1897 photograph at original print size features in the new '*Onze Koloniale Erfenis*' ('Our Colonial Inheritance') exhibition with text that acknowledges the ethnic diversity of the KNIL. Before 2022, an enlarged version covered a whole wall of the long-standing '*Oostwaarts!*' ('Eastwards!') exhibition (Figure 6.6). The caption acknowledged 'Indonesian soldiers with their European officers' in a display about 'colonial wars', but a cropped, reoriented version of the photograph centred the European figures and cut out half the indigenous soldiers. At Bronbeek, the official museum of the KNIL in the Netherlands, an even narrower focus prevailed for more than a decade in the reproduction of a tightly cropped image behind a display of historical weapons. In the new permanent exhibition, opened in June 2024,[41] the photograph remains cropped behind a display of weapons, but now enlarged to fill an entire wall.

---

39   The January 1948 Renville Agreement was a ceasefire agreement that confirmed Dutch territorial gains in return for a plebiscite in Dutch-occupied parts of Java, Madura and Sumatra as to whether they would join the Republic of Indonesia or become separate states.
40   Goenawan Mohamad, 'Het Kwaad van het Kolonialisme is Onvergeeflijk [The Evil of Colonialism is Unforgivable]', *NRC Handelsblad*, [Amsterdam], 25 March 2022, www.nrc.nl/nieuws/2022/03/25/het-kwaad-van-het-kolonialisme-is-onvergeeflijk-a4104979 [first published as Goenawan Mohamad, 'Maaf (Sorry)', *Majalah Tempo*, (Jakarta), 19 February 2022].
41   *Door de ogen van … Over kolonisatie, oorlog en onafhankelijkheid van Indonesië* [*Through the Eyes of … About Colonisation, War and Independence of Indonesia*], Museum Bronbeek, Netherlands.

Figure 6.6 C.B. Nieuwenhuis's photograph of the massacre at Kuta Sukun from the '*Oostwaarts!*' ('Eastwards!') exhibition
Source: Tropenmuseum (Museum of the Tropics), now Wereldmuseum (World Museum), part of the Nationaal Museum van Wereldculturen (National Museum of World Cultures), 2018.

Vague contextualisations and, in the case of some museum displays, cropping and reorientations of the 1897 Nieuwenhuis photograph are ironically at odds with the aim of addressing colonial violence, since such manipulations elide or minimise important aspects of KNIL warfare under Dutch rule. From the Aceh War onwards, Javanese, Moluccan and Minahasan troops were not just prominent but also numerically dominant among the soldiers the Dutch deployed to conquer not just territory, but also other ethnic, language and (sometimes) religious groups in Aceh, Bali and elsewhere in the so-called Outer Provinces (*Buitengewesten*) of the Indonesian archipelago.[42] That is why indigenous soldiers crowd the frame and swarm the borders of the massacre sites photographed by Nieuwenhuis, Neeb and van Weede.

Although excluded from the commanding ranks of the KNIL, which were reserved for European and Eurasian men, indigenous soldiers and a small number of men from West Africa—known colloquially as *Belanda Hitam* ('Black Dutchmen')—made up the majority of the infantry and,

---

42 Recruitment of soldiers from Ambon to Dutch forces in the Indies had already begun in the period of the Dutch East India Company. See Chauvel, *Nationalists, Soldiers and Separatists*, 40.

significantly, the *marechaussees* ('military police').⁴³ The *Korps Marechaussee* of Aceh, founded in 1890 and considered one of van Heutsz's great military innovations, was a multi-ethnic brigade specialised in counter-guerilla warfare. It was frequently deployed for punitive expeditions and to exact exemplary violence as a deterrent against further rebellion.⁴⁴

Despite the clear presence of indigenous soldiers in the photographs examined here, a persistent blindness to the ethnic violence involved in colonial expansion characterises present-day historical presentations of KNIL warfare. This is true of not just recent Dutch museum displays, but also a historiography that recognises the ethnically mixed nature of the colonial army while often failing to critically explore the historical dynamics and implications of indigenous soldiers as perpetrators of military violence.⁴⁵ The lacuna perhaps originates in conflicting narratives within key colonial sources. Nieuwenhuis's Samalanga account, for example, is transparent on the *marechaussees*' role as a special force deployed to 'finish off' resistance worn down by KNIL artillery fire and infantry regiments.⁴⁶ But the photographs in his book tell a different story. One image showing an artillery installation foregrounds a throng of European soldiers, relegating Ambonese infantry to a mass of staffage in the rear (Figure 6.7). Indeed, most of Nieuwenhuis's camp portraits and battle scenes visually centred European officers, whom he diligently named in his captions and text.⁴⁷ Van Weede's photographs from the Seventh Bali Expedition similarly focus on the European military leadership. However, like Neeb in Aceh, van Weede captured the significant role of indigenous troops in Badung's subjugation.⁴⁸

---

43 Teitler, 'The Mixed Company', 155. Indonesians outnumbered Europeans in the infantry and *marechaussees* for the period 1861–1918, while Europeans slightly outnumbered Indonesians in the cavalry, artillery and engineering regiments.

44 *Gedenkboek van het Korps Marechaussee van Atjeh en Onderhoorigheden: 1890–2 April 1940* [*Commemorative Book of the Military Police Corps of Aceh and Dependencies: 1890 – 2 April 1940*] (Korps Marechaussee [Military Police Corps], 1940); Kempees, *The March of Commander van Daalen*, 157; Teitler, 'The Mixed Company', 161, 164.

45 See Teitler, 'The Mixed Company', 160; Siegel, 'The Curse of the Photograph'; Kees van Dijk, 'The Fears of a Small Country with a Big Colony: The Netherlands Indies in the First Decades of the Twentieth Century', in *Armies and Societies in Southeast Asia*, eds Volker Grabowsky and Frederik Rettig (Chiang Mai: Silkworm Books, 2019), 87–122. Notable exceptions are Jean Gelman Taylor, 'Aceh Histories in the KITLV Images Archive', in *Mapping the Acehnese Past*, eds R. Michael Feener, Patrick Daly, and Anthony Reid (Leiden: KITLV Press, 2011), 199–239, doi.org/10.1163/9789004253599_011, at 202–3, 218; Mark Loderichs and Anita van Dissel, 'Militaire Instrumenten van de Koloniale Macht 1816–1941 [Military Instruments of Colonial Power 1816–1941]', in *Krijgsgeweld en Kolonie; Opkomst en Ondergang van Nederland als Koloniale Mogendhied 1816–2010* [*Military Violence and the Colony: The Netherlands' Rise and Fall as a Colonial Power, 1816–2010*], eds Petra Groen, Anita van Dissel, Mark Loderichs, Rémy Limpach, and Thijs Brocades Zaalberg (Amsterdam: Boom, 2021), 171–206, at 180–84.

46 Nieuwenhuis, *The Expedition to Samalanga*, 25.

47 ibid., Plates 4, 5, 8, 10, 20.

48 van Weede, *Indies Travel Memories*, 431–33, 435–36, 438–40, 442–44, 451, 455, 457–59, 474, 479.

Figure 6.7 'Mountain gun in position on the Glé Risa Poenggoeng', Samalanga (Aceh), 1901
Photo: C.B. Nieuwenhuis, Nationaal Museum van Wereldculturen (National Museum of World Cultures) Collection, RV-A78-20.

Where van Weede, Nieuwenhuis and Kempees differ markedly is in their textual acknowledgement of the indigenous soldiers who carried out the massacres they photographed. Ever the Dutch aristocrat, van Weede vigorously name-dropped the European officers among whom he was accommodated, but was almost silent on the indigenous troops who did the killing at Denpasar and Pemecutan. By contrast, Kempees, a KNIL insider (he was van Daalen's aide), explicitly lauded the 'martial character' of the Ambonese, whose *landaard* ('ethnicity'), in his opinion, made their impact at Alas disproportionate to their relatively small numbers.[49] At Samalanga, the night before the main attack on Batu Iliq, Nieuwenhuis found the piety and docility of the Ambonese troops while they were led in prayer by their Christian pastor difficult to reconcile with what he had already seen of their 'turbulent' (*woelig*) and 'passionate' (*hartstochtelijk*) nature in battle.[50] In Dutch military discourse, both these characteristics, their

---

49 Kempees, *The March of Commander van Daalen*, 233.
50 Nieuwenhuis, *The Expedition to Samalanga*, 19.

6. RETHINKING HISTORIES OF MILITARY ATROCITY, ETHNIC VIOLENCE AND PHOTOGRAPHY

Christianity and their ferocity, made 'the Ambonese' an effective martial race—a typology common to many European colonial armies that valued particular ethnic groups for local warfare.

Hack and Rettig's notion of 'martial Orientalism' acknowledges the wider practice of ethnic profiling within colonial armies,[51] and thus has the capacity to illuminate the competitive racial hierarchies forming an entire organisational spectrum, from the European command to subaltern auxiliaries. Kempees' soldierly account of the 1904 van Daalen campaign reflected at length on how ethnic divisions in the KNIL were best instrumentalised. His description of Neeb's *marechaussees* lining the broken parapets of Kuta Rih (Figure 6.4) signified a military ideal of the best fighting unit to wage guerilla wars of subjugation within the Indies, and he recommended their widespread replication across the KNIL. Van Daalen's *marechaussees* in Gayo and Alas comprised two European sergeants (first class), two Ambonese sergeants (second class) and a mixed company of about 20 Ambonese and Javanese soldiers, each directed by their own 'representatives' but working together 'as a family'.[52] The shortcomings and benefits of such mixed units—particularly pertaining to the large-scale recruitment of Muslim Javanese soldiers—were hotly debated among military authorities until the end of World War I.[53] For Kempees, however, their virtues were clear. Significantly, he considered Javanese soldiers unjustly maligned relative to their Ambonese counterparts. In his view, mixing promoted a competition useful to the army. He wrote:

> The mutual jealousy, not towards the whites, whom the Javanese have learned to see as their betters, but rather, with respect to their colleagues of the same skin colour, inspires the inferior one [the Javanese] to strive to set his best foot forward.

Kempees valued *all* 'Native' troops for their fitness, endurance and strength in tough mountain terrain, where they proved themselves capable of long marches on meagre rations of 'rice and dried fish' (or less) while bearing heavy loads.[54]

---

51 Hack and Rettig, 'Imperial Systems of Power', 14.
52 Kempees, *The March of Commander van Daalen*, 234–35.
53 Teitler, 'The Mixed Company'; van Dijk, 'The Fears of a Small Country with a Big Colony'.
54 Kempees, *The March of Commander van Daalen*, 233–34.

In fact, Kempees' account, read against the grain, suggests a culture of deprivation, struggle and suffering among indigenous troops in the KNIL.[55] This context is directly pertinent to understanding the army's moral and material economy, which fostered internal competition between soldiers *and* ruthlessness towards their common external enemies. Kees van Dijk has shown that, by 1914, tensions between Ambonese and Javanese soldiers over differential pay, conditions and privileges frequently erupted in complaint, strike action and defection. It was not until 1918 that cruel punishments within the KNIL were abolished, under protest from the high command. These included rattan (bamboo) canings and the dreaded *kromsluiten* ('close') restraint, which involved shackling a person tightly in a contorted position for hours.[56] Martial Orientalism and competitive ethnic hierarchies within the KNIL made for brutal conditions among indigenous soldiers whose material and moral rewards, controlled by their European commanding officers, derived from not only how much pain they could endure, but also, significantly, how viciously they were able to mete it out. 'Savage warfare' in this schema was not exclusively the consequence of white soldiers dehumanising indigenous Others,[57] but also the outcome of carefully graded ethnic typologies integrated within a military ranking system that produced indigenous perpetrators and allies, as well as victims and enemies.

The ferocity valorised in Nieuwenhuis's Sigli photograph (Figure 6.1), which foregrounds an 'Ambonese' corps, was perhaps the most explicit articulation of the martial identity that van Heutsz and his successors actively cultivated for this group in Aceh. In more innocuous photographs of KNIL activities from the period, such as group portraits of soldiers (Figure 6.8), we see *marechaussees* use the same distinctive gestures and props—*klewangs* ('swords') brandished, carbines cocked (at comrades!)—in visual rehearsal of the association between 'Ambonese' and the bloodlust on which their reputations and privileges depended. Of course, we cannot know whether KNIL photographers demanded or simply captured such poses and, therefore, whether they recorded or created the stereotype of 'the' battle-hungry Ambonese. The contemporary written sources demand that historians make no assumptions about the innateness of such traits but acknowledge the role of the military leadership in fostering them. We should arguably follow the archival grain more closely to examine how theories and practices of martial Orientalism were (co-)constructed within the KNIL and by its close observers.

---

55 See also Veer, *The Aceh War*, 235, 268–69.
56 van Dijk, 'The Fears of a Small Country with a Big Colony', 110, 112.
57 Kim A. Wagner, 'Savage Warfare: Violence and the Rule of Colonial Difference in Early British Counterinsurgency', *History Workshop Journal* 85 (Spring 2018): 217–37, doi.org/10.1093/hwj/dbx053.

Figure 6.8 'Marechaussee brigade from Samagani at Pasar Sibreuë', Aceh, c. 1897–1901
Photo: Photographer unknown, Nationaal Museum van Wereldculturen (National Museum of World Cultures) Collection, TM-ALB-1991.

Approved violence and the double-embeddedness of colonial war photographers

Scholarship on embedded photography emphasises the integration of soldiers into the military and their managed adoption of military ways of seeing.[58] Equally important, but frequently overlooked, is the embedded photographer's entanglement in civilian society, on which their effectiveness as interlocutor

---

58 See Fay Anderson, 'Australians, Allies and Enemies', in *Shooting the Picture: Press Photography in Australia*, by Fay Anderson and Sally Young (Melbourne: The Miegunyah Press, 2016), 88–116, at 89. The concept arises from Anglophone theorists who foreground the recent wars in Iraq and Afghanistan or, at the very earliest, World War II: Judith Butler, 'Photography, War, Outrage', *Publications of the Modern Language Association of America* 120, no. 3 (2005): 822–27, doi.org/10.1632/003081205X63886; Susan L. Carruthers, *The Media at War*, 2nd edn (London: Red Globe Press, 2011); Christopher Paul and James J. Kim, *Reporters on the Battlefield: The Embedded Press System in Historical Context* (Santa Monica: RAND Corporation, 2004); Liam Kennedy, 'Photojournalism and Warfare in the Postphotographic Age', *Photography and Culture* 8, no. 2 (2015): 159–71, doi.org/10.1080/17514517.2015.1076242.

relies. What authorised Nieuwenhuis's and van Weede's accounts was their status not just as embeds with the KNIL, but also as respected members of a colonial society to whom they reported and returned 'from' war. Van Weede and Nieuwenhuis can thus be productively reconceived as *doubly* embedded: as interlopers among combatant forces *and* as deeply imbricated in communities in which approved colonial violence was widespread.

These men's war accounts obscured the fluid boundaries between militarised and civilian spaces in motifs of travel from 'somewhere else' that artificially differentiate the terrains of war and peace. Van Weede's book was in the hallowed tradition of a Dutch *reisverhaal* ('travelogue') about the Indies. Nieuwenhuis similarly took a journey by boat from civilian territory to a battlefront.[59] The notion of travelling in and out of a war 'front' was a uniquely European perspective on late-colonial conflict in Indonesia—one viewed differently by mobile Sumatran communities moving to negotiate survival under violent, sustained and expanding occupation.[60] However, even the European framing of colonial wars of conquest as 'over there' and *always already over*—as the Aceh War was many times prematurely declared, including by Nieuwenhuis himself in his 1901 Samalanga account—was a fragile fiction. Through Nieuwenhuis's eyes, for example, we glimpse how the civil context 'apart from' war in Sumatra was in fact profoundly militarised. His Samalanga account contained a portrait of two KNIL soldiers from his Padang circle of acquaintances whom he unexpectedly met on the campaign.[61] In fact, among the 80,000 or so Europeans who resided in the Netherlands East Indies at the turn of the twentieth century, a staggering 30 per cent were employed in the KNIL.[62] Although the proportion of soldiers per population was much smaller for Indonesians, from a civilian perspective, military conflicts were ubiquitous. As Henk Schulte Nordholt has shown, within the space of a generation, during a period roughly contemporaneous with the Aceh War, the KNIL *additionally* subjugated Lombok, central and south Sumatra, Borneo, central and south Sulawesi (Celebes), Seram, Flores, Timor and Bali. He counted a total of 32 'wars' between 1874 and 1910.[63] Piet Hagen's more recent book examines, in addition to 'wars', 'expeditions', 'actions' and responses to 'resistance' and 'rebellion' from the

---

59 Nieuwenhuis, *The Expedition to Samalanga*, 1–5.
60 David Kloos, 'Dis/connection: Violence, Religion, and Geographic Imaginings in Aceh and Colonial Indonesia, 1890s–1920s', *Itinerario* 45, no. 3 (2021): 389–412, doi.org/10.1017/S0165115321000255.
61 Nieuwenhuis, *The Expedition to Samalanga*, 16, Plate 13.
62 Teitler, 'The Mixed Company', 155–56.
63 Schulte Nordholt, 'A Genealogy of Violence', 36–37.

6. RETHINKING HISTORIES OF MILITARY ATROCITY, ETHNIC VIOLENCE AND PHOTOGRAPHY

colonial army, navy and local police across the Netherlands East Indies. He tallies at least 160 armed encounters across the century from 1840 to 1940, with barely a year passing unmarked by conflict.[64] Thus, in the last 100 years of Dutch rule in Indonesia, there was always a military campaign or armed skirmish between colonial authorities and local civilians or militias taking place somewhere.

Furthermore, throughout the entire period of Dutch colonial rule in Indonesia, repressive, unfree labour regimes upheld colonial authority, particularly on plantations and in the burgeoning mining sector, as well as in public works. Exploitative corvée labour regimes were sources of local unrest and brutal military reprisal across the archipelago.[65] Roel Frakking has explained how the plantation system, 'from its inception to its violent demise in 1949, functioned as the space in which indigenous populations were classified, deconstructed and rearranged according to the needs of an extractive economy backed by the threat of violence'.[66] During the Indonesian national revolution, plantations became deeply contested sites of conflict between the Dutch military, local police, the TNI (Indonesian National Armed Forces) and *laskar* ('paramilitary') forces precisely because of their centrality to Dutch legitimacy, the colonial economy and strategic control of both land and labour. On estates, rebellious workers enacting arson or isolated attacks on planters rarely achieved organised or enduring effects. Colonial retribution, however, was swift and exemplary, including police fire on demonstrators, corporal punishment and death sentences.[67] As the Edwards Collection of luxury albums at the Leiden University Library reveals, European planters visually fetishised the regimes of punishment that instilled fear and discipline on estates (Figure 6.9).[68]

---

64   Hagen, *Colonial Wars in Indonesia*, 889–905.
65   Geoffrey Robinson, *The Dark Side of Paradise: Political Violence in Bali* (Ithaca: Cornell University Press, 1995), 59–69; Jan Breman, *Mobilizing Labour for the Global Coffee Market: Profits from an Unfree Work Regime in Colonial Java* (Amsterdam: Amsterdam University Press, 2015), doi.org/10.1515/9789048527144; Hagen, *Colonial Wars in Indonesia*, 439–80.
66   Roel Frakking, 'The Plantation as Counter-Insurgency Tool: Indonesia 1900–50', in *Decolonization and Conflict: Colonial Comparisons and Legacies*, eds Martin Thomas and Gareth Curless (London: Bloomsbury Academic, 2017), 57–78, at 70. See also Leksana's Chapter 5 in this volume; Marieke Bloembergen, *De Geschiedenis van de Politie in Nederlands-Indië: Uit Zorg en Angst* [*The History of the Police in the Netherlands Indies: Out of Concern and Fear*] (Amsterdam & Leiden: Boom & KITLV Press, 2009), 109–36.
67   Frakking, 'The Plantation as Counter-Insurgency Tool', 58, 62, 64, 68–69.
68   First published in Jan Breman, *Taming the Coolie Beast: Plantation Society and the Colonial Order in Southeast Asia* (New Delhi: Oxford University Press, 1990).

Figure 6.9 Stafhell & Kleingrothe, 'Execution on a Deli plantation', Sumatra, c. 1880–1901
Source: Leiden University Library, Geoffrey Allan Edwards Collection, Or. 27.389, 44.

Nieuwenhuis, Neeb and van Weede could not have taken their war photographs without the systems of unfree labour that permeated civilian society. Coolies ported their photographic equipment on the march from camp to battlefront, sometimes under fire.[69] Nieuwenhuis recounted how, before the main attack on Batu Iliq:

> I, alas, was able to take no photos. My servants and coolies who carried my equipment were nowhere to be found; frightened by the rattling gunfire, they sought shelter behind a protected spot, and not without great effort was I finally able to bring my device into position, although only shortly after the storming [of the target].[70]

---

69 Bijl, *Emerging Memory*, 51. Van Weede had several coolies and a manservant named Karemin: van Weede, *Indies Travel Memories*, 407–8.
70 Nieuwenhuis, *The Expedition to Samalanga*, 27.

Van Weede's and Nieuwenhuis's war photography additionally reveals the army's widespread use of non-uniformed auxiliaries from throughout the Indonesian archipelago, including convict labourers (*dwangarbeiders*). Colonial courts reserved the criminal sentence of forced labour for 'natives', who were allocated to public works like road construction and repair, in mines and as expedition porters.[71] The Aceh War generated such demand for convict labour that legislators in the 1870s and 1880s endlessly debated and delayed planned reforms to the statutes governing *dwangarbeid* in deference to the KNIL's insatiable needs.[72] To allay government concerns that convicts might join local rebellions rather than support the colonial army, from the early 1870s, those assigned to military expeditions had to serve their sentences away from the region where they had committed their crimes.[73] Such provisions built ethnic differences between army staff and 'enemies' into the very lowest levels of the KNIL.

Nieuwenhuis noted how, on the Samalanga campaign, the KNIL employed 955 'indispensable forced labourers'—a number almost equal to the combat personnel.[74] He photographed some of these men, working with the draught animals among whom he listed them, carrying water to the KNIL encampment 'under the guidance of several armed *jantjes*' ('little Jans': ordinary soldiers) (Figure 6.10).[75] 'I found this convoy such a typical sight that I could not resist taking a snapshot,' he wrote.[76] Although he made light of it, manning supply columns was among the most dangerous military work in the Aceh War.[77] Convicts died in such numbers—tens of thousands—building the rail, road and fort infrastructure on which the KNIL relied to subjugate Aceh that the Director of Justice, in the mid-1880s, held that transport there constituted a 'type of suspended death sentence'.[78]

---

71 Robert Cribb, 'Convict Exile and Penal Settlement in Colonial Indonesia', *Journal of Colonialism and Colonial History* 18, no. 3 (2017), doi.org/10.1353/cch.2017.0043, 7.
72 *Historische Nota Betreffende de Regeling der Wijze van Toepassing van de Straf van Dwangarbeid* [*Historical Note Concerning the Regulations on the Method of Application of the Penalty of Forced Labour*] (Batavia: Landsdrukkerij, 1897), 29–32.
73 ibid., 11.
74 Nieuwenhuis, *The Expedition to Samalanga*, 6.
75 ibid., 10, 21.
76 ibid., 11.
77 Emmanuel Kreike, 'Genocide in the Kampongs? Dutch Nineteenth Century Colonial Warfare in Aceh, Sumatra', in *Colonial Counterinsurgency and Mass Violence: The Dutch Empire in Indonesia*, eds Bart Luttikhuis and A. Dirk Moses (London: Routledge, 2014), 45–63, doi.org/10.4324/9781315767345-3, at 49.
78 *Historical Note Concerning the Regulations*, 42. See also Veer, *The Aceh War*, 168–69.

Figure 6.10 'Water transport to the Glé Nang Roë', Samalanga (Aceh), 29 January 1901
Photo: C.B. Nieuwenhuis, Nationaal Museum van Wereldculturen (National Museum of World Cultures) Collection, RV-A78-12.

Van Weede's and Nieuwenhuis's many photographs of auxiliaries demonstrate their fascination with the masses of labour required to support KNIL logistics, from the porting of war matériel to the formation of human chains at river crossings (Figures 6.11–6.13). Their photographs show an unfree, largely immigrant workforce produced by penal judiciaries and indentured labour systems that underpinned every major sector of the colonial economy. Military accounts may have alluded to these mobile workers primarily as resources, but they were as pertinent to the conquest of ethnically 'Other' populations as the soldiering rank and file. Photographs of these militarised personnel, many of them brought to Aceh from far away, must equally be integrated into understandings of how martial Orientalism in the KNIL conceived and instrumentalised a hierarchy—differentiated by ethnicity as well as class—of indigenous men who were both subject to and agents of colonial violence, in peacetime and in war.

Figure 6.11 'Coolies and military police assemble before the attack on Kuta Sukun', Sigli (Aceh), August 1897
Photo: C.B. Nieuwenhuis, Nationaal Archief (National Archives), The Hague, 2.20.46 Album 850, p. 14.

Figure 6.12 'Convict labourers assist soldiers with a river crossing', Samalanga (Aceh), February 1901
Photo: C.B. Nieuwenhuis, Leiden University Library Special Collections, KITLV 43051.

Figure 6.13 'The draught horse convoy on the plain before the *puri* Denpasar', Badung (south Bali), September 1906
Photo: H.M. van Weede, Leiden University Library Special Collections, KITLV A3 10078.

Conclusions

In a recent article on what Dutch soldiers of the KNIL and Royal Army thought of their 'Ambonese' comrades' reputation for ferocity during the Indonesian national revolution, Gert Oostindie and Fridus Steijlen canvassed veterans' ego-documents for testimonies. Some might have served as captions to the photographs by Nieuwenhuis, Neeb and van Weede from almost half a century earlier. 'The Ambonese were wild and blood-thirsty after this massacre. They kicked and beat the prisoners until there was nothing but blood,' wrote one. '[T]hey attacked with the *klewang* [sword] and then licked the enemy's blood from the blade,' wrote another.[79] Other Dutch soldiers expressed gratitude for the unfailing courage and loyalty of their Ambonese brothers-in-arms. The authors describe a 'bias' in the Dutch sources—one they rightly suspect abrogated responsibility for 'extreme' violence to ethnic Others within the Dutch forces. Peculiarly, they conclude

---

79   Gert Oostindie and Fridus Steijlen, 'Ethnic "Ferociousness" in Colonial Wars: Moluccans in the Dutch Army in Indonesia, 1945–1949', *Bijdragen tot de Taal-, Land- en Volkenkunde* [*Journal of the Humanities and Social Sciences of Southeast Asia*] 177, no. 4 (2021): 491–523, doi.org/10.1163/22134379-bja10032, at 504.

that, '[a]lthough Moluccans themselves contributed to the longevity of the "martial race" myth, explaining Moluccan attitudes and behaviour through Orientalist frames of ethnicity remains a dead end'.[80]

Contra Oostindie and Steijlen, and following this volume's attention to coloniality, I have argued that historians must take seriously the colonial genealogy of such frames and trace their mobilisation during earlier wars in Indonesia. I have shown how Dutch war photographers embedded within the KNIL in Aceh and Bali at the turn of the twentieth century captured modes of approved colonial violence, like unfree labour and rule by racialised difference, which not only underpinned the colonial army, but also permeated and were produced by civilian institutions in peacetime. These photographers' visual works and the narrations containing them reveal racialised practices of divide and rule *within* military ranks, with consequences for recognising how ethnic violence figured in military atrocities *against* enemies defined in advance as 'internal' to the borders of the colonial state and as recalcitrant Others.[81] Such findings should caution historians against dismissing 'quotidian' forms of colonial violence in the pursuit of understanding European motives in perpetrating atrocities.[82] From Indonesian perspectives, approved forms of violence *conditioned* civilian and military experiences of war. The KNIL replicated and concentrated the racial and class hierarchies on which Dutch colonialism in the East Indies was built.

For certain groups of soldiers and militarised Indonesian personnel deemed loyal or useful to the colonial army, opportunities for survival or even advancement were predicated on participating in atrocities against ethnic Others. Rethinking histories of colonialism in Indonesia therefore demands critical examination of genealogies of military violence within as well as by the KNIL and requires further research on the origins of ethnic violence perpetrated by members of the colonial army long before the Indonesian national revolution.

---

80   ibid., 519. The authors use 'Moluccan' instead of 'Ambonese' following the conventions of the contemporary diaspora community in the Netherlands.
81   An emerging historiography of racialised warfare in colonial Southeast Asia is captured in Farish A. Noor and Peter Carey, 'Why Race Mattered: Racial Difference, Racialised Colonial Capitalism and the Racialised Wars of Nineteenth-Century Colonial Southeast Asia', in *Racial Difference and the Colonial Wars of 19th Century Southeast Asia*, eds Farish A. Noor and Peter Carey (Amsterdam: Amsterdam University Press, 2021), 9–30, doi.org/10.2307/j.ctv1dc9kb3.3.
82   Kim A. Wagner, '"Calculated to Strike Terror": The Amritsar Massacre and the Spectacle of Colonial Violence', *Past and Present* 233, no. 1 (2016): 185–225, doi.org/10.1093/pastj/gtw037, at 190.

References

Primary sources

'Genealogie van Weede [Genealogy van Weede].' 2012. In *Nederland's Adelsboek [Netherlands' Book of Nobility]* 97, 204–31. The Hague: Centraal Bureau voor Genealogie [Central Bureau for Genealogy].

Historische Nota Betreffende de Regeling der Wijze van Toepassing van de Straf van Dwangarbeid [Historical Note Concerning the Regulations on the Method of Application of the Penalty of Forced Labour]. 1897. Batavia: Landsdrukkerij.

Indisch Militair Tijdschrift [Indies Military Journal]. 1902, 1905, 1906.

Inventaris van de Dienststaten en Stamboeken van Officieren van de Koninklijke Landmacht en van de Koloniale Troepen in Nederland [Inventory of the Service Records and Registers of Officers of the Royal Netherlands Army and Colonial Troops in the Netherlands]. (1715) 1814–1940 (1945), 2.13.04, no. 763. The Hague: Nationaal Archief [National Archives].

Kempees, J.C.J. 1905. *De Tocht van Overste Van Daalen door de Gajo, Alas- en Bataklanden 8 Februari tot 23 Juli 1904 [The March of Commander van Daalen through the Gayo, Alas and Batak Lands, 8 February to 23 July 1904]*. Amsterdam: J.C. Dalmeijer.

Korps Marechaussee [Military Police Corps]. 1940. *Gedenkboek van het Korps Marechaussee van Atjeh en Onderhoorigheden: 1890–2 April 1940 [Commemorative Book of the Military Police Corps of Aceh and Dependencies: 1890 – 2 April 1940]*.

Nieuwenhuis, C.B. 1901. *De Expeditie naar Samalanga (Januari 1901): Dagverhaal van een Fotograaf te Velde [The Expedition to Samalanga (January 1901): Tales of a Photographer in the Field]*. Amsterdam: Van Holkema & Warendorf.

van Heutsz, J.B. 1897. 'Expeditie naar Segli [Expedition to Segli].' 3 Oktober 1897, NIMH Collectie 511, f. 19r. The Hague: Nederlands Instituut voor Militaire Historie [Netherlands Institute of Military History].

van Weede, H.M. 1908. *Indische Reisherinneringen [Indies Travel Memories]*. Haarlem: H.D. Tjeenk Willink & Zoon.

Secondary sources

Anderson, Fay. 2016. 'Australians, Allies and Enemies.' In *Shooting the Picture: Press Photography in Australia*, by Fay Anderson and Sally Young, 88–116. Melbourne: The Miegunyah Press.

Bijl, Paul. 2015. *Emerging Memory: Photographs of Colonial Atrocity in Dutch Cultural Remembrance*. Amsterdam: Amsterdam University Press. doi.org/10.1515/9789048522019.

Bijl, Paul. 2015. 'Saving the Children? The Ethical Policy and Photographs of Colonial Atrocity during the Aceh War.' In *Photography, Modernity and the Governed in Late-Colonial Indonesia*, edited by Susie Protschky, 103–32. Amsterdam: Amsterdam University Press. doi.org/10.1515/9789048523382-005.

Bloembergen, Marieke. 2009. *De Geschiedenis van de Politie in Nederlands-Indië: Uit Zorg en Angst* [*The History of the Police in the Netherlands Indies: Out of Concern and Fear*]. Amsterdam & Leiden: Boom & KITLV Press.

Breman, Jan. 1990. *Taming the Coolie Beast: Plantation Society and the Colonial Order in Southeast Asia*. New Delhi: Oxford University Press.

Breman, Jan. 2015. *Mobilizing Labour for the Global Coffee Market: Profits from an Unfree Work Regime in Colonial Java*. Amsterdam: Amsterdam University Press. doi.org/10.1515/9789048527144.

Butler, Judith. 2005. 'Photography, War, Outrage.' *Publications of the Modern Language Association of America* 120, no. 3: 822–27. doi.org/10.1632/003081205X63886.

Carruthers, Susan L. 2011. *The Media at War*. 2nd edn. London: Red Globe Press.

Chauvel, Richard. 2008. *Nationalists, Soldiers and Separatists: The Ambonese Islands from Colonialism to Revolt, 1880-1950*. Leiden: KITLV Press. doi.org/10.1163/9789004253957.

Creese, Helen, Darma Putra, and Henk Schulte Nordholt. 2006. *Seabad puputan Bali: Perspektif Belanda dan Bali* [*Centenary of the Bali Puputan: Dutch and Balinese Perspectives*]. Jakarta: KITLV Press.

Cribb, Robert. 2017. 'Convict Exile and Penal Settlement in Colonial Indonesia.' *Journal of Colonialism and Colonial History* 18, no. 3. doi.org/10.1353/cch.2017.0043.

Frakking, Roel. 2017. 'The Plantation as Counter-Insurgency Tool: Indonesia 1900–50.' In *Decolonization and Conflict: Colonial Comparisons and Legacies*, edited by Martin Thomas and Gareth Curless, 57–78. London: Bloomsbury Academic.

Groen, Petra. 2021. 'Koortsachtig imperialisme 1894–1914 [Feverish Imperialism 1894–1914].' In *Krijgsgeweld en Kolonie: Opkomst and Ondergang van Nederland als Koloniale Mogendheid, 1816–2010* [*Military Violence and the Colony: The Netherlands' Rise and Fall as a Colonial Power, 1816–2010*], edited by Petra Groen, Anita van Dissel, Mark Loderichs, Rémy Limpach, and Thijs Brocades Zaalberg, 135–60. Amsterdam: Boom.

Groen, Petra, Anita van Dissel, Mark Loderichs, Rémy Limpach, and Thijs Brocades Zaalberg. 2021. *Krijgsgeweld en Kolonie: Opkomst and Ondergang van Nederland als Koloniale Mogendheid, 1816–2010* [*Military Violence and the Colony: The Netherlands' Rise and Fall as a Colonial Power, 1816–2010*]. Amsterdam: Boom.

Groeneveld, Anneke. 1991. 'C.B. Nieuwenhuis' View of Sumatra.' In *Toward Independence: A Century of Indonesia Photographed*, edited by Jane Levy Reed, 65–71. San Francisco: Friends of Photography.

Groeneveld, Anneke. 1991. 'H.M. Neeb: A Witness of the Aceh War.' In *Toward Independence: A Century of Indonesia Photographed*, edited by Jane Levy Reed, 72–77. San Francisco: Friends of Photography.

Hack, Karl, with Tobias Rettig. 2006. 'Imperial Systems of Power, Colonial Forces and the Making of Modern Southeast Asia.' In *Colonial Armies in Southeast Asia*, edited by Karl Hack and Tobias Rettig, 3–38. London: Routledge. doi.org/10.4324/9780203414668_chapter_1.

Hagen, Piet. 2018. *Koloniale Oorlogen in Indonesië: Vijf Eeuwen Verzet Tegen Vreemde Overheersing* [*Colonial Wars in Indonesia: Five Centuries of Resistance Against Foreign Domination*]. Amsterdam: Uitgeverij De Arbeiderspers.

Haks, Leo, and Paul Zach. 1987. *Indonesia: Images from the Past*. Singapore: Times Editions.

Heijboer, Pierre. 1977. *Klamboes, Klewangs, Klapperbomen: Indië Gewonnen en Verloren* [*Mosquito Nets, Swords, Coconut Trees: The Indies Won and Lost*]. Haarlem: De Haan.

Hoek, Anne-Lot. 2021. *De strijd om Bali: Imperialisme, verzet en onafhankelijkheid, 1846–1950* [*The Battle for Bali: Imperialism, Resistance and Independence, 1846–1950*]. Amsterdam: De Bezige Bij.

Kennedy, Liam. 2015. 'Photojournalism and Warfare in the Postphotographic Age.' *Photography and Culture* 8, no. 2: 159–71. doi.org/10.1080/17514517.2015.1076242.

Kloos, David. 2021. 'Dis/connection: Violence, Religion, and Geographic Imaginings in Aceh and Colonial Indonesia, 1890s–1920s.' *Itinerario* 45, no. 3: 389–412. doi.org/10.1017/S0165115321000255.

Kok, René, Erik Somers, and Louis Zweers. 2015. *Koloniale Oorlog 1945–1949: Van Indië naar Indonesië* [*Colonial War 1945–1949: From the Indies to Indonesia*]. Amsterdam: Uitgeverij Carrera.

Kreike, Emmanuel. 2014. 'Genocide in the Kampongs? Dutch Nineteenth Century Colonial Warfare in Aceh, Sumatra.' In *Colonial Counterinsurgency and Mass Violence: The Dutch Empire in Indonesia*, edited by Bart Luttikhuis and A. Dirk Moses, 45–63. London: Routledge. doi.org/10.4324/9781315767345-3.

Loderichs, Mark, and Anita van Dissel. 2021. 'Militaire Instrumenten van de Koloniale Macht 1816–1941 [Military Instruments of Colonial Power 1816–1941].' In *Krijgsgeweld en Kolonie; Opkomst en Ondergang van Nederland als Koloniale Mogendhied, 1816–2010* [*Military Violence and the Colony: The Netherlands' Rise and Fall as a Colonial Power, 1816–2010*], edited by Petra Groen, Anita van Dissel, Mark Loderichs, Rémy Limpach, and Thijs Brocades Zaalberg, 171–206. Amsterdam: Boom.

Mohamad, Goenawan. 2022. 'Het Kwaad van het Kolonialisme is Onvergeeflijk [The Evil of Colonialism is Unforgivable].' *NRC Handelsblad*, [Amsterdam], 25 March. www.nrc.nl/nieuws/2022/03/25/het-kwaad-van-het-kolonialisme-is-onvergeeflijk-a4104979.

Nieuwenhuys, Rob. 1988. 'Oorlogen, opstanden, tuchtigen [Wars, Rebellions, Chastisements].' In *Met Vreemde Ogen. Tempo Doeloe—Een Verzonken Wereld. Fotografische Documenten uit het Oude Indië* [*With Fresh Eyes: The Good Old Days—A Sunken World. Photographic Documents from the Former Indies*], 148–63. Amsterdam: Querido.

Noor, Farish A., and Peter Carey. 2021. 'Why Race Mattered: Racial Difference, Racialised Colonial Capitalism and the Racialised Wars of Nineteenth-Century Colonial Southeast Asia.' In *Racial Difference and the Colonial Wars of 19th Century Southeast Asia*, edited by Farish A. Noor and Peter Carey, 9–30. Amsterdam: Amsterdam University Press. doi.org/10.2307/j.ctv1dc9kb3.3.

Oostindie, Gert, and Rémy Limpach. 2022. 'The War in Indonesia 1945–1949: The Military-Historical Context.' In *Beyond the Pale: Dutch Extreme Violence in the Indonesian War of Independence, 1945–1949*, edited by Gert Oostindie, Ben Schoenmaker, and Frank van Vree, 69–106. Amsterdam: Amsterdam University Press.

Oostindie, Gert, and Fridus Steijlen. 2021. 'Ethnic "Ferociousness" in Colonial Wars: Moluccans in the Dutch Army in Indonesia, 1945–1949.' *Bijdragen tot de Taal-, Land- en Volkenkunde* [*Journal of the Humanities and Social Sciences of Southeast Asia*] 177, no. 4: 491–523. doi.org/10.1163/22134379-bja10032.

Ouwehand, Liesbeth. 2009. 'Militaire Albums [Military Albums].' In *Herinneringen in Beeld: Fotoalbums uit Nederlands-Indië [Recollections in Pictures: Photo Albums from the Netherlands Indies]*, 87–110. Leiden: KITLV Press.

Paul, Christopher, and James J. Kim. 2004. *Reporters on the Battlefield: The Embedded Press System in Historical Context*. Santa Monica: RAND Corporation.

Protschky, Susie. 2020. 'Burdens of Proof: Photography and Evidence of Atrocity during the Dutch Military Actions in Indonesia (1945–50).' *Bijdragen tot de Taal-, Land- en Volkenkunde [Journal of the Humanities and Social Sciences of Southeast Asia]* 176, nos 2–3: 240–78. doi.org/10.1163/22134379-bja10015.

Protschky, Susie. 2020. 'Home at the Front: Violence Against Indonesian Women and Children in Dutch Military Barracks during the Indonesian National Revolution.' In *Gender, Violence and Power in Indonesia: Across Time and Space*, edited by Katharine McGregor, Ana Dragojlovic, and Hannah Loney, 59–83. London: Routledge.

Robinson, Geoffrey. 1995. *The Dark Side of Paradise: Political Violence in Bali*. Ithaca: Cornell University Press.

Schulte Nordholt, Henk. 1996. *The Spell of Power: A History of Balinese Politics, 1650–1940*. Leiden: KITLV Press.

Schulte Nordholt, Henk. 2002. 'A Genealogy of Violence.' In *Roots of Violence in Indonesia: Contemporary Violence in Historical Perspective*, edited by Freek Colombijn and J. Thomas Lindblad, 33–62. Leiden: KITLV Press. doi.org/10.1163/9789004489561_004.

Siegel, James T. 2009. 'The Curse of the Photograph: Atjeh 1901.' In *Photographies East: The Camera and its Histories in East and Southeast Asia*, edited by Rosalind C. Morris, 57–78. Durham: Duke University Press. doi.org/10.1215/9780822391821-003.

Taylor, Jean Gelman. 2011. 'Aceh Histories in the KITLV Images Archive.' In *Mapping the Acehnese Past*, edited by R. Michael Feener, Patrick Daly, and Anthony Reid, 199–239. Leiden: KITLV Press. doi.org/10.1163/9789004253599_011.

Teitler, Gerke. 2006. 'The Mixed Company: Fighting Power and Ethnic Relations in the Dutch Colonial Army, 1890–1920.' In *Colonial Armies in Southeast Asia*, edited by Karl Hack and Tobias Rettig, 154–68. London: Routledge. doi.org/10.4324/9780203414668_chapter_6.

van Dijk, Kees. 2019. 'The Fears of a Small Country with a Big Colony: The Netherlands Indies in the First Decades of the Twentieth Century.' In *Armies and Societies in Southeast Asia*, edited by Volker Grabowsky and Frederik Rettig, 87–122. Chiang Mai: Silkworm Books.

Veer, Paul van 't. *De Atjeh-Oorlog* [*The Aceh War*]. Amsterdam: Uitgeverij De Arbeiderspers.

Wagner, Kim A. 2016. '"Calculated to Strike Terror": The Amritsar Massacre and the Spectacle of Colonial Violence.' *Past and Present* 233, no. 1: 185–225. doi.org/10.1093/pastj/gtw037.

Wagner, Kim A. 2018. 'Savage Warfare: Violence and the Rule of Colonial Difference in Early British Counterinsurgency.' *History Workshop Journal* 85 (Spring): 217–37. doi.org/10.1093/hwj/dbx053.

Willcock, Sean. 2015. 'Aesthetic Bodies: Posing on Sites of Violence in India, 1857–1900.' *History of Photography* 39, no. 2: 142–59. doi.org/10.1080/03087298.2015.1038108.

Zweers, Louis. 1988. 'Atjeh-Oorlog [Aceh War].' In *Sumatra: Kolonialien, Koelies en Krijgers* [*Sumatra: Colonials, Coolies and Combatants*], 38–58. Houten: Fibula.

Zweers, Louis. 1994. *Front Indië: Hugo Wilmar, Ooggetuig van een Koloniale Oorlog* [*The Indies Front: Hugo Wilmar, Eyewitness to a Colonial War*]. Zutphen: Walburg Pers.

Zweers, Louis. 2013. *De Gecensureerde Oorlog: Militairen versus Media in Nederlands-Indië* [*The Censored War: Military Personnel Versus Media in the Netherlands Indies*]. Zutphen: Walburg Pers.

7

Francisca Fanggidaej: A decolonial perspective on colonial elites and the Indonesian revolution

Katharine McGregor[1]

Introduction

Growing up in the late colonial era as the daughter of a colonial official cocooned in an environment in which she was allowed to speak only Dutch, Francisca Fanggidaej (1925–2013) became increasingly critical of the hierarchies she observed both in the colony of the Netherlands East Indies and in global politics as the Indonesian revolution of 1945–49 unfolded. Her memoir, written in 2006, offers unique insights into this period of colonial history, stretching from the late 1930s to 1949, due to her Eastern Indonesian background, her upbringing in Java, her political orientation as a revolutionary and her gender—all of which gave her a marginal position in Indonesian society.

---

1   I would like to thank Rika Theo and Willy Alfarius for their research assistance in preparation for the writing of this chapter. I would also like to thank Vannessa Hearman for her detailed comments on an earlier draft of this paper and all the workshop participants and reviewers for additional comments, particularly Ken M.P. Setiawan, Sadiah Boonstra, Susie Protschky, Jim Fox, and Bronwyn Anne Beech Jones.

Fanggidaej was born on Timor Island, but, due to her father's work as a colonial official, the family moved to Java during her childhood, where she attended a Dutch-language school from the age of nine. Her family's position as privileged elites changed with the onset of the Japanese occupation in 1942 due to her father's closeness to the Dutch. It was during this period that Fanggidaej met some Indonesian nationalists who exposed her to new ideas that caused her to radically rethink her cultural and political orientation. Following the August 1945 Indonesian declaration of independence, when the British attacked Surabaya to enable a restoration of Dutch control, she joined several organisations dedicated to defending independence. In 1948, as a member of Pesindo (Pemuda Sosialis Indonesia, Socialist Youth of Indonesia), she attended the infamous Southeast Asian Youth and Students Conference in Calcutta and then returned to Indonesia and became embroiled in the fallout from the Madiun Affair.

The Calcutta conference, an anticolonial gathering of youths concerned with achieving independence for nations such as India and Vietnam, became the subject of intense political speculation, which lasted for decades. The Cold War theory was that instructions had been passed in Calcutta from the Soviet Union to Southeast Asian delegates to engage in revolutions once they returned home. Fanggidaej was even accused in the 1950s by the journalist Rosihan Anwar of having carried such instructions.[2] In September 1948, Pesindo members joined those of the broader Front Demokrasi Rakyat (People's Democratic Front) to oppose the republican army in the so-called Madiun Affair. This was related to the proposed rationalisation of leftist troops, but also included the proclamation of a popular sovereign state. The army and the republican government dubbed the movement a communist revolt and carried out a violent crackdown on the political left and all associated organisations, including Pesindo. Despite the Cold War theory, the link between Calcutta and Madiun has never been proven.[3]

After the revolution and the recovery of the political left, Fanggidaej continued to work with the communist party's youth organisation, Pemuda Rakyat (People's Youth), becoming a chairwoman in 1950 and then serving from 1957 as a member of the Foreign Affairs Committee of the Indonesian parliament. Her work as a political revolutionary was disrupted by the

---

2   On the history wars over Madiun, see Katharine McGregor, 'A Reassessment of the Significance of the 1948 Madiun Uprising to the Cold War in Indonesia', *Kajian Malaysia* 26, no. 1 (2009): 86–119.
3   Larisa Efimova, 'Did the Soviet Union Instruct Southeast Asian Communists to Revolt? New Russian Evidence on the Calcutta Youth Conference February 1948', *Journal of Southeast Asian Studies* 40, no. 3 (2009): 449–69, www.jstor.org/stable/27751581.

7. FRANCISCA FANGGIDAEJ

army's second violent attack on the political left, known as the Indonesian genocide, which began in October 1965. To avoid this repression, she was forced to seek exile—first, in China and then in the Netherlands for a total of almost four decades.

Although Fanggidaej's background as an elite nationalist woman fits with a problematic emphasis in Indonesian history to date on women who were part of the colonial *pribumi*,[4] Fanggidaej is unique because of her highly critical attitude towards elite privilege, which was influenced in turn by the fact that she joined organisations on the political left from the mid-1940s. Her participation in these organisations led her to critique multiple forms of domination in the colonial era, including feudal and colonial traditions and continuing inequalities in diplomatic negotiations following the declaration of independence. Her background further enabled her to critique racist colonial ideology, because it often targeted people of Eastern Indonesian heritage. Throughout this chapter, I use Walter Mignolo's ideas about decolonial thinking to consider how Fanggidaej engaged with colonialism. Mignolo argues that:

> decolonial thinking and doing focus on enunciation, engaging in epistemic disobedience and delinking from the colonial matrix [of power] in order to open up decolonial options—a vision of life and society that requires decolonial subjects, decolonial knowledges and decolonial institutions.[5]

He uses 'decolonial thinking' to refer to a mode of critical action. Through close attention to Fanggidaej's memoir, I examine how she demonstrates decolonial thinking by reflecting on the colonial categories and practices that reproduced notions of difference and hierarchy in the late colonial period and why she became attracted to a revolutionary version of Indonesian nationalism.

Fanggidaej offers a rare example of the thinking of an Indonesian revolutionary. I argue that the way in which she imagined the Indonesian revolution offers a novel way of understanding the differing meanings of the

---

4   *Pribumi* ('native of the soil') is a term used to refer to local Indonesians and is sometimes also used to exclude those considered to be of migrant descent. Ruth Indiah Rahayu, 'Konstrusksi Historiografi Feminisme dari Tutur Perempuan [The Construction of Feminist Historiography from Women's Perspectives]', Presented to Indonesia Historiografi Indonesia: di Antara Historiografi Nasional dan Alternatif, Pusat Studi Sosial Asia Tenggara [Indonesian Historiography: Between National and Alternative Historiography, Center for Southeast Asian Social Studies] and ARC, Yogyakarta, 2–4 July 2007.
5   Walter D. Mignolo, *The Darker Side of Western Modernity: Global Futures, Decolonial Options* (Durham: Duke University Press, 2001), 9.

revolution. She describes her path to embracing *merdeka* ('independence'), for example, as 'going home' or 'finding a home'. Yet, the sense of home she felt was also challenged after 1948 when she was suddenly deemed an enemy of the republic. I ask what her opposition to colonialism, within and outside Indonesia, tells us about differing versions of *merdeka* and related struggles against multiple forms of coloniality along the axis also of class.

Her experiences offer important insights into the last decade of colonialism and alternative visions of the Indonesian revolution that are not part of mainstream nationalist recollections of this period due to the general trend that began in the New Order (1966–98) period of erasing people from the political left from Indonesian history.[6] They provide an excellent starting point for rethinking the history of colonialism and paying attention to the structures of power around ethnicity and class in late colonial society through to the revolution. Yet, despite her many probing critiques of inequalities in society, Fanggidaej is sometimes silent about other forms of societal division. This includes divisions that resulted in violence against different communities, including Eastern Indonesians due to assumed histories of collaboration with the Dutch. She is also noticeably silent about gender and related structures of power.

The primary sources used for my analysis are Francisca Fanggidaej's 2006 narrated memoir[7] and accounts of different parts of her life that she wrote and are held in the International Institute of Social History archive in the Netherlands. Her memoir can be contextualised alongside other memoirs written by people with complicated relationships with colonial structures of power and similarly complex identities relating to their experiences of the Dutch colony. The memoirs of Indo-European women, for example, who, like Fanggidaej, experienced privilege, discrimination and forced migration to the Netherlands (under different circumstances), provide interesting points of contrast because of their shared experiences of growing up between two cultures.[8] At the time Fanggidaej's memoir was written,

---

6   Katharine E. McGregor, *History in Uniform: Military Ideology and the Construction of Indonesia's Past* (Singapore: NUS Press, 2007).

7   Hersri Setiawan, *Memoar Perempuan Revolusioner: Francisca Fanggidaej* [*Memoirs of a Woman Revolutionary: Francisca Fanggidaej*] (Yogyakarta: Galang Press, 2006).

8   For an interesting discussion of two such memoirs, see Susie Protschky, 'The Flavour of History: Food, Family and Subjectivity in Two Indo-European Women's Memoirs', *The History of the Family* 14, no. 4 (2009): 369–85, doi.org/10.1016/j.hisfam.2009.08.006.

she was 81 years old and had lived in the Netherlands for just over 20 years after 20 years living in China, after her Indonesian passport was cancelled in 1966.[9]

The fact that Fanggidaej's memoir was narrated to Indonesian and fellow political exile Hersri Setiawan influences what has been recorded on the page and the framing throughout the text. Hersri Setiawan is a famous literary writer of the political left, who has penned several memoirs about his experiences as a political prisoner of the Suharto regime.[10] Because of the persecution of leftists in Indonesia, narrating her story to a friend, fellow exile and leftist would presumably have enabled Fanggidaej to more freely express her political ideas but may at the same time have led her to emphasise critiques of class and elitism. Hersri Setiawan recorded, published and disseminated the stories of several former political prisoners and exiles and created the Fanggidaej archive.[11] Fanggidaej's memoir was based on interviews collected by Setiawan with Fanggidaej in 1995 and forms part of a series called 'In Search of Silenced Voices' housed at the International Institute of Social History. The series title reflects the fact that the voices of people from the political left were heavily censored throughout the Suharto regime due to intense anticommunism.

Fanggideaj's memoir belongs to a genre of memoirs from the political left published after the end of the Suharto regime in 1998.[12] The book is one of a smaller number of memoirs written by political exiles who were not imprisoned and one of very few by women on the political left.[13]

---

9   On the experiences of Indonesian exiles in China, see David Hill, 'Indonesia's Exiled Left as the Cold War Thaws', *RIMA* 44, no. 1 (2010): 21–51, at 31–32; Hersri Setiawan, 'Some Thoughts on Indonesian Exilic Literature', *RIMA* 44, no. 1 (2010): 9–20; and Taomo Zhou, 'Passports to the Post-Colonial World: Space and Mobility in Francisca Fanggidaej's Afro-Asian Journeys', in *The Lives of Cold War Afro-Asianism*, eds Carolien Stolte and Su Lin Lewis (Amsterdam: Amsterdam University Press, 2022), 309–26, doi.org/10.1515/9789400604346-017.
10 Hersri Setiawan, *Diburu di Pulau Buru* [*Hunted on Buru Island*] (Yogyakarta: Galang Press, 2006); Hersri Setiawan, *Aku Eks-Tapol* [*I Am an Ex-Political Prisoner*] (Yogyakarta: Galang Press, 2003); Hersri Setiawan, *Memoar Pulau Buru* [*Memoir of Buru Island*] (Jakarta: Gramedia, 2016).
11 Hersri Setiawan, *Kidung Para Korban: Dari Tutur Sepuluh Narasumber Eks-Tapol seperti Diceritakan kepada Hersri Setiawan* [*A Victims' Ballad: Testimonies of 10 Ex-Political Prisoners as Told to Hersri Setiawan*] (Yogyakarta: Pakorba and Pustaka Pelajar, 2006).
12 Vannessa Hearman, 'The Uses of Memoirs and Oral History Works in Researching the 1965–1966 Political Violence in Indonesia', *International Journal of Asia Pacific Studies* 5, no. 2 (2009): 21–42.
13 These include Sulami, *Perempuan, Kebenaran dan Penjara: Kisah Nyata Wanita Dipenjara 20 Tahun karena Tuduhan Makar dan Subversi* [*Women, Truth, and Prison: The True Story of a Woman Imprisoned for 20 Years because of Accusations of Treason and Subversion*] (Jakarta: Cipta Lestari, 1999); Sudjinah, *Terempas Gelombang Pasang* [*Crushed by a Tidal Wave*] (Jakarta: Pustaka Utan Kayu, 2003); Mia Bustam, *Sudjono dan Aku* [*Sudjono and I*] (Jakarta: Pustaka Utan Kayu, 2006); and Mia Bustam, *Dari Kamp ke Kamp: Cerita Seorang Perempuan* [*From Camp to Camp: A Woman's Story*] (Jakarta: Kerja Sama Spasi, VHR Book and Institut Studi Arus Informasi, 2008).

Women revolutionaries imprisoned by the Suharto regime have focused on rehabilitating their political image.[14] Women's memoirs that deal with the pre-1965 period also seek to reclaim a place for the Indonesian left in the struggle against colonialism and imperialism, especially during the 1945–49 revolution, because their roles have largely been erased from the historical record.[15] The reason for the erasure is that those on the political left were cast as traitors to the nation in standard interpretations of both the 1948 Madiun Affair and the Thirtieth of September Movement of 1965—a movement during which the top army leadership was kidnapped and killed.[16] The army blamed the Thirtieth of September Movement on the hugely popular Indonesian Communist Party and used this event as a pretext for the 1965 genocide against the Indonesian left.

In recent years, there has been increased attention to the histories and contributions of Indonesian women on the political left. This has included new attention to Francisca Fanggidaej, especially her experiences after the Indonesian revolution, as well as to key leaders within the left progressive Indonesian Women's Movement (Gerakan Wanita Indonesia, or Gerwani), such as Umi Sardjono.[17] This has led to new understanding of some of the most critical positions held by Indonesian women on the incomplete processes of decolonisation.[18] Fanggidaej's memoir has further significance as the only memoir of a non-Javanese revolutionary woman.

Thinking about the distance in time between the late colonial era and when she was interviewed, it is more difficult to trace how Fanggidaej's experiences of living in the Netherlands as a migrant and part of a minority

---

14   Katharine McGregor and Vannessa Hearman, 'Challenges of Political Rehabilitation in Post–New Order Indonesia: The Case of Gerwani (the Indonesian Women's Movement)', *South East Asia Research* 15, no. 3 (2007): 355–84, doi.org/10.5367/000000007782717759.
15   McGregor and Hearman, 'Challenges of Political Rehabilitation in Post–New Order Indonesia'.
16   McGregor, *History in Uniform*.
17   This includes new research by Dr Taomo Zhou into Francisca Fanggidaej and her activism during her time in exile and her relationship with her children as an exiled mother. See Zhou, 'Passports to the Post-Colonial World'. See also research by Ita Nadia into Francisca's life experiences and by Widya Fitria Ningsih into her engagement with nation and state-building. On another key revolutionary Indonesian woman, see Katharine McGregor and Ruth Indiah Rahayu, 'Umi Sardjono (1923–2011) and the Quest to Build a New Society for Indonesian Women', in *The Palgrave Handbook of Communist Women Activists from Around the World*, ed. Francisca de Haan (London: Palgrave Macmillan, 2023), 377–97, doi.org/10.1007/978-3-031-13127-1_15.
18   See also Katharine McGregor, 'Indonesian Women, the Women's International Democratic Federation and the Struggle for "Women's Rights", 1946–1965', *Indonesia and the Malay World* 40, no. 117 (2012): 193–208, doi.org/10.1080/13639811.2012.683680; and Katharine McGregor, 'The Cold War, Indonesian Women and the Global Anti-Imperialist Movement 1946–1965', in *De-Centring Cold War History*, eds Jadwiga E. Pieper Mooney and Fabio Lanza (London: Routledge, 2013), 31–51.

influenced her feelings about the legacies of colonialism. She did not write directly about this topic and instead seemed to have focused most of her attention on developments in Indonesia. Fanggidaej was a member of the Netherlands-based Indonesia Committee whose members campaigned for the release of Indonesian political prisoners of the Suharto regime and against its authoritarian practices. Fanggidaej described the committee as 'a place where Indonesians could work for our country and people and for the liberation from the regime'.[19] The chair of the Indonesia Committee Wim Wertheim, a retired Dutch professor who had worked in the colony, was a firm critic of colonial and ongoing racism in the Netherlands.[20] Noting her birth in West Timor, it is curious that Fanggidaej also critiqued forms of coloniality practised by the Suharto government particularly against the East Timorese. In 1992, for example, she signed a public letter commemorating the East Timorese who were shot by the Indonesian army in the 1991 Dili Massacre.[21] This massacre took place in the context of the three-decade occupation of East Timor (now Timor-Leste) from 1975 to 1999. In her memoir, looking back at her experiences of the last decades of Dutch colonialism, she offers sharp critiques of how coloniality functioned.

Reflections on the era of late colonialism: Rethinking the meanings of coloniality

Francisca Fanggidaej was born on 15 August 1925. In her memoir, she reflects a strong awareness of how her life was shaped by colonialism. She explains, for example, that she 'came from a family that was a political product of the Dutch'.[22] Her father was employed in the Burgerlijke Openbare Werken (Department for Civil Public Works) in the position of *hoofdopzichter* ('chief superintendent') and also in the Department van Verkeer en Waterstaat (Department of Traffic and Water Management),

---

19 Francisca Fanggidaej, 'Cisca Fanggidaej voor IFM [Speech for the 55th Indonesian Independence Anniversary, A Celebratory Event Held by the Indonesia Friendship Organization, An Organisation of Indonesian Exiles in Amsterdam, 2000]', Francisca Fanggidaej Papers, Box 12, Folder 9, Pics 74–78, ARCH04303 (Amsterdam: International Institute of Social History), 5.
20 Wim F. Wertheim, 'Netherlands-Indian Colonial Racism and Dutch Home Racism', in *Imperial Monkey Business: Racial Supremacy in Social Darwinist Theory and Colonial Practice*, eds Jan Breman, Piet de Rooy, Ann Stoler, and Wim F. Wertheim, CASA Monographs 3 (Amsterdam: VU University Press, 1990), 71–88.
21 'Familieberichten [Family Announcements]', *Trouw*, [Meppel], 12 November 1992, resolver.kb.nl/resolve?urn=ABCDDD:010822191:mpeg21:p008.
22 Setiawan, *Memoir of a Revolutionary Woman*, 13.

with an echelon three position just below that of *bupati* ('regent').²³ He was part of the colonial elite civil service. The branch of the civil service staffed by locals was called the Pangreh Praja and was dominated by the sons of *priyayi*, elite Javanese with lineage to Javanese sultans.²⁴ Fanggidaej's father, Gottlieb Fanggidaej, by contrast, came from the eastern island of Rote, and her mother, Magda Mael, from the eastern island of Timor, where Francisca was born. The Rotenese were recognised as intellectual elites due to the early establishment of Malay schools on the island in 1769.²⁵ The islands of Rote and Timor neighbour one another and form part of the Lesser Sunda Islands. Kupang, the capital of Timor, was the administrative centre of Dutch colonial power in this region.²⁶

Eastern elites played a key role in the colony particularly because this part of the archipelago experienced the longest and most penetrating effects of Dutch influence. The Dutch East India Company (Vereenigde Oostindische Compagnie, or VOC), set up harbour towns and early settlements across the central Moluccas due to the company's monopoly production of the in-demand spices of cloves and nutmeg. This included the longest-established areas of Ambon, Makassar and the Banda Islands. After 1860, the Dutch recruited people from eastern islands, especially the central Moluccas, for positions in all levels of government and the army.²⁷ They took up occupations as 'clerks, teachers, ministers and soldiers'.²⁸ Despite the different cultures and languages across this region, the people of Eastern Indonesia generally referred to themselves and were referred to by the Dutch as Moluccans.

---

23 Norman Joshua Soelias, *Pesindo, Pemuda Sosialis Indonesia, 1945–1950* [*Pesindo: Indonesian Socialist Youth, 1945–1950*] (South Tangerang: Marjin Kiri, 2016), 130; and Setiawan, *Memoir of a Revolutionary Woman*, 15–18.
24 Heather Sutherland, *The Making of the Bureaucratic Elite: The Colonial Transformation of the Javanese Priyayi* (Singapore: Heineman Educational Books, 1979).
25 James J. Fox, *Explorations in Semantic Parallelism* (Canberra: ANU Press, 2014), doi.org/10.22459/ESP.07.2014, 318. Exemplifying this trend, Francisca's grandfather produced the first Rotenese translation of the Bible (Fox, pp. 321–22).
26 Hans Hägerdal, 'The Native as *Exemplum*: Missionary Writings and Colonial Complexities in Eastern Indonesia, 1819–1860', *Itinerario* 37, no. 2 (2013): 73–99, doi.org/10.1017/S0165115313000478, at 73. For more on the history of Rote and Timor, see James J. Fox, *Harvest of the Palm: Ecological Change in Eastern Indonesia* (Cambridge: Harvard University Press, 1977), doi.org/10.4159/harvard.9780674331884.
27 Ulbe Bosma and Remco Raben, *Being Dutch in the Indies: A History of Creolisation and Empire, 1500–1920*, trans. Wendy Schaffer (Singapore: NUS Press, 2008), 144.
28 Wim Manuhutu, 'Moluccans in the Netherlands: A Political Minority', in *L'émigration Politique en Europe aux XIXe et XXe siècles. Actes du colloque de Rome (3–5 Mars 1988)* [*Political Emigration in Europe in the Nineteenth and Twentieth Centuries. Proceedings of the Rome Conference, 3–5 March 1988*] (Rome: École Française de Rome, 1991), 498.

The first chapter of Francisca Fanggidaej's memoir, entitled 'My Father Who was a Black Dutch', offers a reflection on her family's positionality in the colony of the Netherlands East Indies. The Dutch used the term *Belanda Hitam* ('Black Dutchmen') to refer to soldiers of African background in the colonial army whose ancestors were brought to the Indies as enslaved persons from the Gold Coast (modern-day Ghana).[29] These men often intermarried with Indonesian women, spoke Dutch and were considered Dutch. The term was also used, however, to refer to Moluccans to whom the Dutch similarly awarded European status. Holding 'European' status entailed special treatment in terms of the law and the courts to which one was subjected in civil and criminal matters as well as access to better education and jobs.[30] Fanggidaej explains that her family carried Dutch status as far back as her grandfather, who was a Christian pastor and a descendent of a well-known elite family known locally as a *raja*, from Baubau, but also because of her father's status as a colonial official. She offers far less information on her mother's family, perhaps because she was less elite and because the memoir focuses on dismantling the elite privilege of her father's family.

Fanggidaej reflects critically on her father's cooperation with the Dutch and his embrace of Dutch culture, claiming he denied his identity as a *pribumi*. She explained that 'denying does not mean betraying', but it took the form of 'hiding his own black skin'. She remembers her father often said, 'We are not *Inlanders* ['Native']. We are Dutch!'[31] The term 'Inlanders' was the lowest racial categorisation in the colony. It was below 'Foreign Orientals', with Europeans or Dutch at the apex. Fanggidaej's memoir was undoubtedly influenced by her exposure across her lifespan to new ways of framing her experiences. Her choice to emphasise her father's insistence on being Dutch mirrors, for example, the observations of the Martinique-born Frantz Fanon about how the colonised can internalise racial hierarchies to the extent that they try to be like the coloniser. In a scathing critique of this practice, Fanon argued in his 1952 work, *Black Skin, White Masks*, that 'the black man who wants to turn his race white is as miserable as he

---

29   Ineke van Kessel, 'Belanda Hitam: The Indo-African Communities on Java', *African and Asian Studies* 6, no. 3 (2007): 243–70, doi.org/10.1163/156920907X212222, at 258.
30   Susie Protschky, 'The Colonial Table: Food, Culture and Dutch Identity in Colonial Indonesia', *Australian Journal of Politics and History* 54, no. 3 (2008): 346–57, doi.org/10.1111/j.1467-8497.2008.00501.x, at 348.
31   Setiawan, *Memoir of a Revolutionary Woman*, 17.

who preaches hatred for the whites'.[32] By the time Fanggidaej's memoir was written, Fanon's work had become part of a canon on decolonial thinking with which Fanggidaej was presumably familiar.

In her memoir, Fanggidaej highlights the process of alienation she felt growing up in a household as the second youngest child in which she and her four siblings were forbidden to speak Malay and forced to speak Dutch. These anecdotes, combined with mentions of her parents' preference for elite pastimes and sports such as tennis and bridge and the fact that they mostly ate Dutch food and had seven household servants,[33] indicate that her parents had assimilated into elite Dutch culture. As Susie Protschky notes, the granting of European status depended on 'performing Europeanness' or 'cultural affiliation and social connections'.[34] This included the ability to speak Dutch and fit into Dutch social circles. Her family's religious status as Protestants, which was also a product of Dutch influence in the central Moluccas, also made this easier.[35]

Fanggidaej critiques not only her father's embrace of Dutch culture, but also his adoption of feudal Javanese customs as a way of marking out his status in colonial society. She remembers that when she accompanied her father in his jeep on inspections throughout Java, the workers would immediately '*duduk berjongkok*' (or crouch) as her father approached.[36] This feudal custom of lowering oneself to those of higher status was originally only practised by Javanese of lower birth status in greeting sultans and *priyayi*, but over time, Dutch officials became '*gila hormat*' ('crazy for respect'), requiring the same expressions of deference to be extended to them.[37] Arnout van de Meer argues that, for the Dutch, these acts constituted a 'scripted performance of power' whereby colonialists sought to 'affirm, uphold, and strengthen colonial hierarchies of race, class, and gender'.[38] Dating from 1913, however, Indonesian nationalists protested against these mandated forms of deference on the basis that they were 'humiliating', which led to bans on such practices.[39] Indonesian nationalists critiqued the traditions of *sembah*

---

32 Frantz Fanon, *Black Skin, White Masks*, trans. Charles Lam Markmann (London: Pluto Books, 2008 [1952]), 2.
33 Setiawan, *Memoir of a Revolutionary Woman*, 24.
34 Protschky, 'The Colonial Table', 349.
35 Manuhutu, 'Moluccans in the Netherlands', 497.
36 Setiawan, *Memoir of a Revolutionary Woman*, 19.
37 Sutherland, *The Making of the Bureaucratic Elite*, 36.
38 Arnout van der Meer, *Performing Power: Cultural Hegemony, Identity, and Resistance in Colonial Indonesia* (Ithaca: Cornell University Press, 2020), doi.org/10.1515/9781501758607, 2.
39 ibid., 9–12.

(the practice of making a sign of worship with one's hands towards someone else) and *jongkok*, calling instead for 'a more egalitarian national identity' and one not based on Javanese traditions.[40] Fanggidaej must have observed her father using such practices in the 1930s to early 1940s, well after these critiques. She comments on the strangeness of this mimicry of Javanese customs, yet these experiences gave her an acute awareness of social status.[41] Her attention to class hierarchies in her memoir reflects her position as a leftist revolutionary who also wants to present herself to readers as highly attentive to class and critical of feudal traditions.

Fanggidaej communicates an awareness that despite their legal status as 'Europeans', the colonial categorisation of her family as *Belanda Hitam* also implied inferiority. She reports that her family made two trips to the Netherlands for vacations during her childhood. On their way when they stopped in the British territory of Penang, her father chose to swim in a 'whites only' swimming pool. A Dutch man approached her father and patronisingly 'patted him from his stomach to head', sarcastically asking: 'So Black fatso, are you having a good time?'[42] She felt a temptation to attack the conceited man but was held back by her father, who remained silent. It is clear from this recounting of racial vilification that the term 'black' was used derogatively. Fanggidaej questioned why the term 'dark' was always associated with something bad.[43] Ayu Saraswati argues that during the colonial era 'the boundary of who could be considered racially white and white skinned was unclear; racial projects that were implemented in colonial Indonesia actually produced a white racial category that only partially relied on skin colour as its signifier'.[44] There was, however, a hierarchy of desirability according to which being 'black' was undesirable. Laurie Sears argues, for example, that in colonial-era literary texts references to darker skin generally took the form of 'racial slurs and whispers that reveal colonial aversions to racial others'.[45] Further to this, people from Eastern Indonesia, including the Ambonese, Timorese and Papuans, were often characterised as 'the darker people with frizzy hair of the East'.[46] According to the racist

---

40 ibid., 104–6.
41 Setiawan, *Memoir of a Revolutionary Woman*, 21, 25.
42 Original: '*Zo, zwarte* [sic] *dikkertje! Heb je lekker gezwommen?*'. ibid., 22.
43 Zhou, 'Passports to the Post-Colonial World', 312.
44 L. Ayu Saraswati, *Seeing Beauty, Sensing Race in Transnational Indonesia* (Honolulu: University of Hawai`i Press, 2013), 37.
45 Laurie Sears, 'Racial Slurs and Whispers in Situated Testimonies in Dutch Imperial Fiction', *Positions: Asia critique* 29, no. 1 (2021): 67–91, doi.org/10.1215/10679847-8722784, at 71.
46 Fenneke Sysling, *Racial Science and Human Diversity in Colonial Indonesia* (Singapore: NUS Press, 2016), doi.org/10.2307/j.ctv9hj794, 104.

social Darwinist ideas of British and Dutch explorers and scientists, these physical attributes were associated with being less advanced.[47] These racist stereotypes of Papuans in particular have persisted in modern-day Indonesia. In 2019, for example, Papuan students and others protested following racial slurs made against them by civil militia and police in the city of Surabaya.[48]

Fanggidaej explains that the experience as a 10-year-old girl of witnessing her father be racially vilified was so transformative that it became a *leidstar* ('guiding star'). This was so much so, she argues, that 'if there had not been a revolution in Indonesia' in which she could involve herself, this experience of racism 'could have become a life-long trauma'.[49]

Reflecting on having grown up as the daughter of a colonial official, she states that her identity was almost as different as 'the earth from the sky, to that of her father'.[50] For her, the legal status of being equalised with Europeans, *gelijkstelling*, meant taking 'on the character of an oppressor'.[51] In her mind, the influence and effects of the *gelijkstelling* were that, without being aware, she and her family had joined the Dutch in 'sucking and oppressing' the people.[52] In her memoir, she positions her experiences of elite colonial society and related social hierarchies as critical to her commitment to transformative change and hence to the Indonesian revolution.[53] In this narration of her early life experiences on the cusp of the Indonesian revolution, Fanggidaej reflects on the complex dimensions of the 'colonial matrix' of power.[54] She rejects inequality across the colonial divide between Dutch and local people, but also the inequality imposed by local elites on other Indonesians.

As a daughter of a colonial official, rather than a son, she potentially had greater insights into colonial inequalities. By virtue of her gender, she had an alternative perspective on society because she faced gender-based restrictions that her brothers would not have. She could not, for example, easily imagine a career in the colonial bureaucracy for there were few Indonesian women in

---

47 ibid., 104–8.
48 Sophie Chao, 'West Papua and Black Lives Matter', *Inside Indonesia*, 17 June 2020, www.insideindonesia.org/west-papua-and-black-lives-matter. For more on this topic, see Suryawan's Chapter 15 in this volume.
49 Setiawan, *Memoir of a Revolutionary Woman*, 22.
50 ibid., 24.
51 ibid., 24.
52 ibid., 26.
53 ibid., 25.
54 Mignolo, *The Darker Side of Western Modernity*, 9.

these roles. Yet, her critique of coloniality in the memoir does not go so far as to reflect on the relationship between gender and coloniality. In one chapter devoted to her mother, she acknowledges the gender divide in terms of elite access to education by expressing admiration for her mother's adaptability given she, unlike her husband, was not given an education and had to learn Dutch and European customs.[55] In the chapters dealing with her role in the revolution, Fanggidaej similarly offers little reflection on gender relations.

The Indonesian revolution and decolonisation

During the Japanese occupation, Fanggidaej's family was in danger because of her father's position. He was interrogated by the Japanese and suffered a fatal heart attack a year into the occupation.[56] In this period, members of some ethnic groups, such as the Ambonese and Chinese, became the targets of violence carried out by the Japanese and other Indonesians on the basis that members of these groups had previously collaborated with or worked alongside the Dutch.[57]

Despite the danger, Fanggidaej claims the Japanese occupation was transformative for her. It was during this time she first met nationalists from Eastern Indonesia. She was influenced especially by her niece, who moved in with Francisca's family after returning from the Netherlands, where she had studied to be a headteacher. Fanggidaej was impressed that her niece rejected Western dress and instead wore the traditional Javanese dress of a sarong and kebaya. This sartorial choice reflected the general direction of Indonesian nationalism according to which many Indonesian men dropped traditional Javanese clothing and donned Western dress, while women were encouraged by men to wear traditional clothing. The rationale for women wearing traditional dress was that they were supposed to preserve both

---

55 Setiawan, *Memoir of a Revolutionary Woman*, 40.
56 ibid., 45. See also Fanggidaej, 'Cisca Fanggidaej voor IFM [Speech for the 55th Indonesian Independence Anniversary]'.
57 In his memoir, the Ambonese doctor and nationalist Gerrit Siwabessy reflects that he donned a *peci* (cone-shaped hat) and his wife a head scarf to look less identifiably Ambonese during this period. Gerrit Siwabessy, *Upuleru: Memoar Dr G.A. Siwabessy* [*Upuleru: Memoir of Dr G.A. Siwabessy*] (Jakarta: Gunung Agung, 1979), 19. On violence against the Chinese Indonesians in this period, see Ravando and Harsono's Chapter 8 in this volume.

their dignity and 'Indonesian'—but in this case, really Javanese—cultural traditions.[58] Despite her Moluccan background, Fanggidaej seems to read this choice of clothing as firmly nationalist.

Through her niece's links, Fanggidaej was exposed to nationalist thinking.[59] She recalls that the gatherings of her niece's friends at their home caused her great confusion:

> When they sang together in Indonesian, I couldn't understand. I felt left out, displaced. I started to wonder: where do I actually belong? I didn't feel at home anywhere anymore. I came to realise that something was missing. But I didn't know what.[60]

This sense of displacement was most likely accentuated by the ban on the use of Dutch language during the Japanese occupation.[61] A Moluccan teacher offered to teach Fanggidaej Indonesian. She recollected that he told her tales from Ambon that prompted a discovery of her own culture. Previously such stories had been dismissed in her home 'as uninteresting and common folklore'.[62] Her comment reflects her awareness of the colonial privileging of certain forms of knowledge. Connecting to her niece and other Moluccans made this period 'a very meaningful time' because she began to feel a greater sense of belonging.[63]

The feelings of displacement expressed by Fanggidaej mirror the thinking that was taking place within elite Ambonese political circles dating back to the 1920s. Within the increasingly politicised organisation Sarekat Ambon, for example, there was questioning of the place of the Ambonese and whether they were really fully accepted 'into the Dutch family'.[64] The writer Kayadoe, for example, writing in Sarekat Ambon's journal, *Mena Moeria*, mocked the Ambonese who had become legal Europeans and those who had tried to disown their origins.[65] In 1938 a prominent doctor, Gerrit Siwabessy, who was a distant relative of Francisca's, established the Advance Moluccan Culture organisation as one way to address the identity

---

58 On these patterns concerning gender and national dress, see the interesting discussion in van der Meer, *Performing Power*, 129–44.
59 Fanggidaej, 'Cisca Fanggidaej voor IFM [Speech for the 55th Indonesian Independence Anniversary]'.
60 ibid.
61 Siwabessy, *Upuleru*, 25.
62 Fanggidaej, 'Cisca Fanggidaej voor IFM [Speech for the 55th Indonesian Independence Anniversary]'.
63 ibid.
64 Richard Chauvel, *Nationalists, Soldiers and Separatists: The Ambonese Islands from Colonialism to Revolt, 1880–1950* (Leiden: KITLV Press, 2008), doi.org/10.1163/9789004253957, 77.
65 ibid., 78.

crisis within this community in relation to the extent to which they were Indonesian or Dutch.[66] Francisca connected with Siwabessy and other Moluccan intellectuals in Surabaya when selling cakes door to door to help support her family during the Japanese occupation. Through these people, she was introduced to new political ideas and learnt new words such as *'penjajah'* ('colonists') and about concepts like fascism and Nazism.[67] She recalls: 'I became aware how refined the cruel system of colonialism was. Little by little the poison was administered gradually such that people did not notice the poison running through their brains and breath.'[68]

If the Japanese occupation was a period of political and cultural awakening for Fanggidaej, the Indonesian revolution that followed the 1945 declaration of independence was an extension of this process. Coming from the strictures of her family's adherence to Dutch culture and their dismissal of Eastern Indonesian culture, she notes:

> [F]or me the path of national independence felt like the path to my own independence. With the arrival of independence, I felt freed by it. Free from what, I did not understand. But I felt that I had come home to my own home.[69]

In her memoir, she makes repeated references to finding a home, finding an identity and a new *'lingkungan'* ('environment') during the revolution, by which she also meant a new political community.[70] The sense of transitioning from living between two worlds, quickly learning the Indonesian language and embracing Indonesian nationalism is something Fanggidaej shared with other Dutch-educated elite nationalists,[71] but there were specific dimensions to this transition for her due to the complex politics within the Moluccan community.

Fanggidaej refers here to her separation from the colonial world as part and parcel of her separation from her mother, who decided to leave Indonesia in 1947 for the Netherlands,[72] among a cohort of Moluccan elites who chose to emigrate. Others, especially those who were attacked during the Japanese

---

66   ibid., 146.
67   Setiawan, *Memoir of a Revolutionary Woman*, 51.
68   ibid., 54.
69   ibid., 44.
70   ibid., 57.
71   See the discussion in Frances Gouda with Thijs Brocades Zaalberg, *American Visions of the Netherlands East Indies/Indonesia: US Foreign Policy and Indonesian Nationalism, 1920–1949* (Amsterdam: Amsterdam University Press, 2002), library.oapen.org/handle/20.500.12657/35075, 132–34.
72   Setiawan, *Memoir of a Revolutionary Woman*, 57.

occupation or in the early years of the revolution by other Indonesians, chose to stay on in Indonesia and support the Dutch. What this meant is that, for the Ambonese, the Indonesian revolution entailed 'members of one family not infrequently fighting on opposing sides'.[73] Fanggidaej was in a similar position to Ambonese elites due to her family background. In her memoir, she mentions these fractures in her own family, but not the violence that accompanied such political choices. One organisation which she joined, the Pemuda Republik Indonesia Maluku (Moluccan Youths of the Indonesian Republic), for example, led by Gerrit Siwabessy and Sam Malessy, focused on spreading news among Moluccan people in Surabaya of the values underlying the Indonesian proclamation, while at the same time protecting the Ambonese from attacks from other Indonesians due to their perceived loyalty to the Dutch.[74]

Fanggidaej became more politically active during the revolution. In a brief reflection on her life, she stated that '17 August 1945 not only changed the path of my life, but also my identity and mentality'.[75] She joined a branch of Pemuda Republik Indonesia in the city of Surabaya in which there were many Moluccan youths.[76] She stressed their egalitarian attitudes, exemplified by the terms of address they used such as '*bung*' and '*zus*' ('brother' and 'sister') to refer to comrades.[77] This was a marked contrast to the hierarchies and categorisations that permeated colonial society. She does not, however, comment on the gendered hierarchies at work during the revolution and how these affected her. Gouda notes, for example, that within the circles of male nationalists, there was a new emphasis on 'hyper-masculinity' and a rejection of femininity.[78] On this point it is interesting to reflect on how this emphasis on hyper-masculinity may have carried forward into narratives of the revolution, including this memoir.[79] Years later, reflecting on why

---

73 Chauvel, *Nationalists, Soldiers and Separatists*, 203.
74 Siwabessy, *Upuleru*, 31.
75 Francisca Fanggidaej, 'Pernilaian terhadap Masakini atas Dasar Pengalamanku Masalampau [An Examination of the Present Based On My Past Experiences]', Francisca Fanggidaej Papers, Box 5, Folder 6, Pics 46–49, 2005, ARCH04303 (Amsterdam: International Institute of Social History), 1.
76 Setiawan, *Memoir of a Revolutionary Woman*, 65.
77 ibid., 68. While *bung* is a Malay word, *zus* is, interestingly, a Dutch word.
78 Frances Gouda, 'Gender and "Hyper-Masculinity" as Post-Colonial Modernity During Indonesia's Struggle for Independence, 1945 to 1949', in *Gender, Sexuality and Colonial Modernities*, ed. Antoinette Burton (London: Routledge, 1999), 163–76.
79 See, for example, my review of the strong emphasis in the 2022 Rijksmuseum exhibition entitled '*Revolusi!*' on Indonesian men as the key agents of the revolution. Katharine McGregor, 'Review: "Revolusi", An Exhibition', *Inside Indonesia*, 11 February 2023, www.insideindonesia.org/editions/edition-150-oct-dec-2022/review-revolusi.

she sought out and joined these groups and why she embraced the new revolutionary language of the revolution including terms such as *merdeka*, Fanggidaej suggests she was drawn to their ideas and mission.[80]

Fanggidaej was chosen by leading Indonesian nationalists including president Sukarno to participate in the 8–10 November 1945 Youth Congress in Yogyakarta.[81] It was at this conference that Pesindo was created as an amalgamation of 40 youth organisations. Attending the conference, Fanggidaej felt united with others by the pursuit of *kemerdekaan* ('independence'). She enjoyed being part of this 'new and welcoming world' and felt a shared sense of identity with fellow participants.[82] Taomo Zhou describes Fanggidaej's awakening at this conference, when she began to fully imagine Indonesian self-determination, as her 'Wilsonian Moment'.[83] While the conference was under way the British bombarded the city of Surabaya, which made a deep impression on her.[84] In her mind and that of many other Indonesian nationalists, this was an attack on a sovereign country. In response, the congress delegates decided they should disband and instead go and fight.[85]

The global revolution against colonialism

Fanggidaej worked in the information division of Pesindo spreading information about the revolution especially through her radio broadcasts in Dutch and English for Radio Gelora Pemuda Indonesia. When Pesindo received an invitation to two congresses in Europe in 1947, she was chosen to go, together with Suripno, who had been an underground member of the Dutch Communist Party until his return to Indonesia in 1946. Harry Poeze suggests Fanggidaej was chosen primarily because of her ability to speak the international language of English.[86] The two congresses were those of the International Union of Students, in which Suripno had already participated, and the World Federation of Democratic Youth in Prague. At these congresses, Fanggidaej argued that she represented all Indonesian

---

80 Fanggidaej, 'An Evaluation of the Present Based on My Experiences of the Past', 1.
81 Setiawan, *Memoir of a Revolutionary Woman*, 69.
82 ibid., 134–35.
83 Zhou, 'Passports to the Post-Colonial World', 314.
84 Setiawan, *Memoir of a Revolutionary Woman*, 76.
85 ibid., 76.
86 Harry Poeze, 'The Cold War in Indonesia, 1948', *Journal of Southeast Asian Studies* 40, no. 3 (2009): 497–517, doi.org/10.1017/S002246340999004X, at 507n.12.

youth, not just socialist youth. She stressed that her most important mission was to look for sources of support for the Indonesian struggle.[87] She appealed at these congresses for delegates to campaign to 'stop the war', meaning a Dutch withdrawal.[88]

Fanggidaej travelled via India on her way to and from Europe and spent three months there. She used these opportunities to spread news about the Indonesian proclamation and the struggle against the Dutch.[89] There she received an invitation to attend the 1948 Southeast Asian Youth and Students Conference in Calcutta and helped to organise the conference.[90] She became a key speaker in the main program and in the general meeting. For many years, the Cold War conspiracy theory regarding the Calcutta conference, noted above, overshadowed its significance as a united expression of opposition by Asian peoples to imperialism at a time when several European powers, including the Dutch, British and French, were attempting to take back their former colonies. Fanggidaej offers another view of the conference, claiming the Indonesian delegation was a focus because Indonesia was the first Southeast Asian country after the war to declare independence and 'free itself from colonialism' and because Indonesians were continuing to defend that independence.[91] In a recent study of Indian–Indonesian connections in the 1940s, Heather Goodall confirms that 'the Indonesian Revolution seemed—for a while—to be everybody's revolution', noting that it 'sent waves of hope and fear across many borders'.[92] Indeed, at the Calcutta conference, delegations from Vietnam, Malaya, China, Burma and the Philippines joined with large delegation of Indians and Pakistanis as hosts.[93]

Reflecting on the conference, Fanggidaej says it 'was the first time after the Second World War when the youths of Asia could gather as representatives of their respective countries who were in the midst of rising up to oppose colonialism'.[94] She claims that 'the spirit of Calcutta was the embryo for the spirit of Bandung'.[95] What precisely did Fanggidaej mean by the Bandung spirit? Recent scholarship on the 1955 Bandung Conference has begun to

---

87   Setiawan, *Memoir of a Revolutionary Woman*, 109.
88   ibid., 115.
89   ibid., 109.
90   ibid., 119.
91   ibid., 120.
92   Heather Goodall, *Beyond Borders: Indians, Australians and the Indonesian Revolution, 1939 to 1950* (Amsterdam: Amsterdam University Press, 2019), doi.org/10.1515/9789048531103, 1.
93   Setiawan, *Memoir of a Revolutionary Woman*, 119.
94   ibid., 123.
95   ibid., 124.

unpack the multiple meanings of Bandung and to move beyond a narrow understanding of this conference as the root of the non-aligned movement.[96] South African scholar Ndlovu-Gatsheni, for example, uses the concept of the Bandung spirit to refer to 'a melange of resistance and struggles against colonial encounters, colonialism, and coloniality—going as far back as the time of the Haitian Revolution (1791–1804)'.[97] In this conceptualisation, the Bandung spirit refers to a long global process of contesting colonialism and coloniality.

This process of contesting coloniality for the political left extended to a critique of how the international order and related political inequalities continued to influence the diplomatic negotiations that took place throughout the revolution. In a recent study of some of the major agreements made during the revolution, Nila Ayu Utami argues that Indonesia was forced to contend with 'remnants of colonial practices' for years, as signified by the Linggadjati Agreement of 1946, within which the Republic of Indonesia was considered only one constituent of the future Dutch-created political unit of the United States of Indonesia.[98] During the revolution, Fanggidaej was outraged at the apparent unequal status of the Republic of Indonesia in diplomatic negotiations and used her speaking platform at the Calcutta conference and related press interviews to critique the premises of the 1948 Renville Agreement. This agreement, brokered by the UN Security Council, recognised all territories gained by the Dutch until this stage of the revolution as Dutch controlled until the formation of the United States of Indonesia.[99] Fanggidaej objected to the fact that in this agreement the republic was given the same status as what she referred to as Dutch 'puppet states' like the State of East Sumatra, which, for her, symbolised that 'the Republic has fallen from the status of being a sovereign

---

96   See, for example, Katharine McGregor and Vannessa Hearman, 'Challenging the Lifeline of Imperialism: Reassessing Afro-Asian Solidarity and Related Activism in the Decade 1955–1965', in *Bandung, Global History, and International Law: Critical Pasts and Pending Futures*, eds Luis Eslava, Michael Fakhri, and Vasuki Nesiah (Cambridge: Cambridge University Press, 2017), 161–76, doi.org/10.1017/9781316414880.012; and Carolien Stolt and Su Lin Lewis, eds, *The Lives of Cold War Afro-Asianism* (Amsterdam: Amsterdam University Press, 2022).
97   Sabelo Ndlovu-Gatsheni, 'When Did the Masks of Coloniality Begin to Fall: Decolonial Reflections on the Bandung Spirit of Decolonisation', *Bandung: Journal of the Global South* 6, no. 2 (2019): 210–32, at 210.
98   Nila Ayu Utami, 'Revisiting the Bandung Conference: *Berbeda Sejak dalam Pikiran*', *Inter-Asia Cultural Studies* 17, no. 1 (2016): 140–47, doi.org/10.1080/14649373.2016.1134045, at 142.
99   'Pemuda di Awal Perang Kemerdekaan kisah seperti dituturkan pada Hersri Setiawan [The Youth Movement at the Beginning of the War of Independence, a Story as Told to Hersri Setiawan]', Francisca Fanggidaej Papers, Box 3, Folder 4, Pics 33–37, ARCH04303 (Amsterdam: International Institute of Social History, n.d.), 3.

state to a state that had no power whatsoever'.[100] She claims that she felt betrayed by the republic for making this agreement because it did not honour the sacrifices made by the Indonesian people during the revolution. She received backlash at the time from the republic for her criticism and for highlighting the inequality of this deal. Her criticisms remind us of the highly contested political agreements negotiated throughout the revolution and the ongoing influence of coloniality and power in negotiations about its resolution—a theme that is further explored in Boonstra's Chapter 9 and Karabinos and Theo's Chapter 10 in this volume.

Fanggidaej returned to Indonesia just four days before the outbreak of the Madiun Affair, which began on 18 September 1948.[101] In her memoir, she notes that she was preparing to socialise the messages of the Calcutta conference about opposing colonialism in Indonesia. Due to the theory that the Soviets had passed on instructions at the Calcutta conference for Southeast Asians to revolt in their own countries and the timing of the Madiun Affair, her political position suddenly became dangerous. She admits in her memoir to carrying a secret letter but claims it did not contain instructions. She emphasises that all she could do was run given she was wanted for questioning by the republic about the Calcutta conference and the related conspiracy theory. She witnessed the brutal repression by republican forces of members of Pesindo, including the killing of her husband. Fanggidaej was imprisoned but released. Following the recovery of the political left, as noted above, she went on to play a major role in Indonesian politics, challenging ongoing forms of imperialism until the 1965 repression.

Conclusions

Fanggidaej's life experiences as narrated in her memoir provide rare insights into the thinking of an Indonesian revolutionary. The memoir traces her transformation from being raised in Dutch cultural traditions in the colonial era through to discovering her cultural identity and her political home among Pesindo, which made her a firm critic of colonialism in its many forms. Because of Fanggidaej's unique position as a revolutionary and an exile locked out of her country for many years, her memoir, written

---

100 Setiawan, *Memoir of a Revolutionary Woman*, 126.
101 The Madiun Affair (*Peristiwa Madiun*) began when factions in the Indonesian military seized control of the City of Madiun in East Java, which was declared an illegal uprising by the republican government.

many years after her experiences, offers unique insights into coloniality and marginality and efforts to dismantle and challenge different forms of coloniality in daily life, through to international relations. Her decolonial perspectives allow insights into different visions of the Indonesian nation that have been marginalised in Indonesia.

Perhaps due to her status as an exile and the need to prove her nationalist credentials, her memoir is framed very much within a nationalist paradigm such that differences across the relatively fragile political community of the Indonesian nation, especially between ethnic groups and including those between men and women, are not addressed. The silences of her memoir mean that it does not fully engage with how the coloniality of power continued to negatively impact the experiences of both women and ethnic minorities from the late colonial period through to the Indonesian revolution. Yet, the work remains an important decolonial text.

References

Primary sources

Fanggidaej, Francisca. n.d. 'Pemuda di Awal Perang Kemerdekaan kisah seperti dituturkan pada Hersri Setiawan' [The Youth Movement at the Beginning of the War of Independence, a Story as Told to Hersri Setiawan].' Francisca Fanggidaej Papers, Box 3, Folder 4, Pics 33–37, ARCH04303. Amsterdam: International Institute of Social History.

Fanggidaej, Francisca. 2000. 'Cisca Fanggidaej voor IFM [Speech for the 55th Indonesian Independence Anniversary, a Celebratory Event Held by the Indonesia Friendship Organization, An Organisation of Indonesian Exiles in Amsterdam].' Francisca Fanggidaej Papers, Box 12, Folder 9, Pics 74–78, ARCH04303. Amsterdam: International Institute of Social History.

Fanggidaej, Francisca. 2005. 'Pernilaian terhadap Masakini atas Dasar Pengalamanku Masalampau [An Evaluation of the Present Based on My Experiences of the Past].' Francisca Fanggidaej Papers, Box 5, Folder 6, Pics 46–49, ARCH04303. Amsterdam: International Institute of Social History.

Setiawan, Hersri. 2006. *Memoar Perempuan Revolusioner: Francisca Fanggidaej* [*Memoir of a Revolutionary Woman: Francisca Fanggidaej*]. Yogyakarta: Galang Press.

Siwabessy, Gerrit. 1979. *Upuleru: Memoar Dr G.A. Siwabessy* [*Upuleru: Memoir of Dr G.A. Siwabessy*]. Jakarta: Gunung Agung.

Secondary sources

Bosma, Ulbe, and Remco Raben. 2008. *Being Dutch in the Indies: A History of Creolisation and Empire, 1500–1920*. Translated by Wendy Schaffer. Singapore: NUS Press.

Bustam, Mia. 2006. *Sudjono dan Aku* [*Sudjono and I*]. Jakarta: Pustaka Utan Kayu.

Bustam, Mia. 2008. *Dari Kamp ke Kamp: Cerita Seorang Perempuan* [*From Camp to Camp: The Story of a Woman*]. Jakarta: Kerja Sama Spasi, VHR Book and Institut Studi Arus Informasi.

Chao, Sophie. 2020. 'West Papua and Black Lives Matter.' *Inside Indonesia*, 17 June. www.insideindonesia.org/west-papua-and-black-lives-matter.

Chauvel, Richard. 2008. *Nationalists, Soldiers and Separatists: The Ambonese Islands from Colonialism to Revolt, 1880–1950*. Leiden: KITLV Press. doi.org/10.1163/9789004253957.

Efimova, Larisa. 2009. 'Did the Soviet Union Instruct Southeast Asian Communists to Revolt? New Russian Evidence on the Calcutta Youth Conference of February 1948.' *Journal of Southeast Asian Studies* 40, no. 3: 449–69. doi.org/10.1017/S0022463409990026.

Fanon, Frantz. 2008 [1952]. *Black Skin, White Masks*. Translated by Charles Lam Markmann. London: Pluto Books.

Fox, James J. 1977. *Harvest of the Palm: Ecological Change in Eastern Indonesia*. Cambridge: Harvard University Press. doi.org/10.4159/harvard.9780674331884.

Fox, James J. 2014. *Explorations in Semantic Parallelism*. Canberra: ANU Press. doi.org/10.22459/ESP.07.2014.

Goodall, Heather. 2019. *Beyond Borders: Indians, Australians and the Indonesian Revolution, 1939 to 1950*. Amsterdam: Amsterdam University Press. doi.org/10.1515/9789048531103.

Gouda, Frances. 1999. 'Gender and "Hyper-Masculinity" as Post-Colonial Modernity During Indonesia's Struggle for Independence, 1945 to 1949.' In *Gender, Sexuality and Colonial Modernities*, edited by Antoinette Burton, 163–76. London: Routledge.

Gouda, Frances, with Thijs Brocades Zaalberg. 2002. *American Visions of the Netherlands East Indies/Indonesia: US Foreign Policy and Indonesian Nationalism, 1920–1949*. Amsterdam: Amsterdam University Press. library.oapen.org/handle/20.500.12657/35075.

Hägerdal, Hans. 2013. 'The Native as *Exemplum*: Missionary Writings and Colonial Complexities in Eastern Indonesia, 1819–1860.' *Itinerario* 37, no. 2: 73–99. doi.org/10.1017/S0165115313000478.

Hearman, Vannessa. 2009. 'The Uses of Memoirs and Oral History Works in Researching the 1965–1966 Political Violence in Indonesia.' *International Journal of Asia Pacific Studies* 5, no. 2: 21–42.

Hill, David. 2010. 'Indonesia's Exiled Left as the Cold War Thaws.' *RIMA* 44, no. 1: 21–51.

Manuhutu, Wim. 1991. 'Moluccans in the Netherlands: A Political Minority.' In *L'émigration politique en Europe aux XIXe et XXe siècles. Actes du colloque de Rome (3–5 mars 1988)* [*Political Emigration in Europe in the Nineteenth and Twentieth Centuries. Proceedings of the Rome Conference, 3–5 March 1988*]. Rome: École Française de Rome.

McGregor, Katharine. 2007. *History in Uniform: Military Ideology and the Construction of Indonesia's Past*. Singapore: NUS Press.

McGregor, Katharine. 2009. 'A Reassessment of the Significance of the 1948 Madiun Uprising to the Cold War in Indonesia.' *Kajian Malaysia* 26, no. 1: 86–119.

McGregor, Katharine. 2012. 'Indonesian Women, the Women's International Democratic Federation and the Struggle for "Women's Rights", 1946–1965.' *Indonesia and the Malay World* 40, no. 117: 193–208. doi.org/10.1080/13639811.2012.683680.

McGregor, Katharine. 2013. 'The Cold War, Indonesian Women and the Global Anti-Imperialist Movement 1946–1965.' In *De-Centring Cold War History*, edited by Jadwiga E. Pieper Mooney and Fabio Lanza, 31–51. London: Routledge.

McGregor, Katharine. 2018. 'The Making of a Transnational Activist: The Indonesian Human Rights Campaigner Carmel Budiardjo.' In *The Transnational Activist: Transformations and Comparisons from the Anglo-World Since the Nineteenth Century*, edited by Stefan Berger and Sean Scalmer, 165–91. London: Palgrave Macmillan. doi.org/10.1007/978-3-319-66206-0_7.

McGregor, Katharine. 2023. 'Review: "Revolusi", An Exhibition.' *Inside Indonesia*, 11 February. www.insideindonesia.org/editions/edition-150-oct-dec-2022/review-revolusi.

McGregor, Katharine, and Vannessa Hearman. 2007. 'Challenges of Political Rehabilitation in Post–New Order Indonesia: The Case of Gerwani (the Indonesian Women's Movement).' *South East Asia Research* 15, no. 3: 355–84. doi.org/10.5367/000000007782717759.

McGregor, Katharine, and Vannessa Hearman. 2017. 'Challenging the Lifeline of Imperialism: Reassessing Afro-Asian Solidarity and Related Activism in the Decade 1955–1965.' In *Bandung, Global History, and International Law: Critical Pasts and Pending Futures*, edited by Luis Eslava, Michael Fakhri, and Vasuki Nesiah, 161–76. Cambridge: Cambridge University Press. doi.org/10.1017/9781316414880.012.

McGregor, Katharine, and Ruth Indiah Rahayu. 2023. 'Umi Sardjono (1923–2011) and the Quest to Build a New Society for Indonesian Women.' In *The Palgrave Handbook of Communist Women Activists from Around the World*, edited by Francisca de Haan, 377–97. London: Palgrave Macmillan. doi.org/10.1007/978-3-031-13127-1_15.

Mignolo, Walter D. 2001. *The Darker Side of Western Modernity: Global Futures, Decolonial Options*. Durham: Duke University Press.

Ndlovu-Gatsheni, Sabelo. 2019. 'When Did the Masks of Coloniality Begin to Fall: Decolonial Reflections on the Bandung Spirit of Decolonisation.' *Bandung: Journal of the Global South* 6, no. 2: 210–32.

Poeze, Harry. 2009. 'The Cold War in Indonesia, 1948.' *Journal of Southeast Asian Studies* 40, no. 3: 497–517. doi.org/10.1017/S002246340999004X.

Protschky, Susie. 2008. 'The Colonial Table: Food, Culture and Dutch Identity in Colonial Indonesia.' *Australian Journal of Politics and History* 54, no. 3: 346–57. doi.org/10.1111/j.1467-8497.2008.00501.x.

Protschky, Susie. 2009. 'The Flavour of History: Food, Family and Subjectivity in Two Indo-European Women's Memoirs.' *The History of the Family* 14, no. 4: 369–85. doi.org/10.1016/j.hisfam.2009.08.006.

Rahayu, Ruth Indiah. 2007. 'Konstruksksi Historiografi Feminisme dari Tutur Perempuan [The Construction of Feminist Historiography from Women's Perspectives].' Presented to Historiografi Indonesia: di Antara Historiografi Nasional dan Alternatif, Pusat Studi Sosial Asia Tenggara [Indonesian Historiography: Between National and Alternative Historiography, Center for Southeast Asian Social Studies] and ARC, Yogyakarta, 2–4 July.

Saraswati, L. Ayu. 2013. *Seeing Beauty, Sensing Race in Transnational Indonesia*. Honolulu: University of Hawai'i Press.

Sears, Laurie. 2021. 'Racial Slurs and Whispers in Situated Testimonies of Dutch Imperial Fiction.' *positions: Asia critique* 29, no. 1: 67–91. doi.org/10.1215/ 10679847-8722784.

Setiawan, Hersri. 2003. *Aku Eks-Tapol* [*I Am an Ex-Political Prisoner*]. Yogyakarta: Galang Press.

Setiawan, Hersri. 2006. *Diburu di Pulau Buru* [*Hunted on Buru Island*]. Yogyakarta: Galang Press.

Setiawan, Hersri. 2006. *Kidung Para Korban: Dari Tutur Sepuluh Narasumber Eks-Tapol seperti Diceritakan kepada Hersri Setiawan* [*A Victims' Ballad: As Told by Ten Ex-Political Prisoners to Hersri Setiawan*]. Yogyakarta: Pakorba and Pustaka Pelajar.

Setiawan, Hersri. 2010. 'Some Thoughts on Indonesian Exilic Literature.' *RIMA* 44, no. 1: 9–20.

Setiawan, Hersri. 2016. *Memoar Pulau Buru* [*Memoir of Buru Island*]. Jakarta: Gramedia.

Soelias, Norman Joshua. 2016. *Pesindo, Pemuda Sosialis Indonesia, 1945–1950* [*Pesindo: Indonesian Socialist Youth, 1945–1950*]. South Tangerang: Marjin Kiri.

Stolt, Carolien, and Su Lin Lewis, eds. 2022. *The Lives of Cold War Afro-Asianism*. Amsterdam: Amsterdam University Press.

Sudjinah. 2003. *Terempas Gelombang Pasang* [*Crushed by a Tidal Wave*]. Jakarta: Pustaka Utan Kayu.

Sulami. 1999. *Perempuan, Kebenaran dan Penjara: Kisah Nyata Wanita Dipenjara 20 Tahun karena Tuduhan Makar dan Subversi* [*Women, Truth, and Prison: The True Story of a Woman Imprisoned for 20 Years because of Accusations of Treason and Subversion*]. Jakarta: Cipta Lestari.

Sutherland, Heather. 1979. *The Making of the Bureaucratic Elite: The Colonial Transformation of the Javanese Priyayi*. Singapore: Heineman Educational Books.

Sysling, Fenneke. 2016. *Racial Science and Human Diversity in Colonial Indonesia*. Singapore: NUS Press. doi.org/10.2307/j.ctv9hj794.

Utami, Nila Ayu. 2016. 'Revisiting the Bandung Conference: *Berbeda Sejak dalam Pikiran*.' *Inter-Asia Cultural Studies* 17, no. 1: 140–47. doi.org/10.1080/1464 9373.2016.1134045.

van der Meer, Arnout. 2020. *Performing Power: Cultural Hegemony, Identity, and Resistance in Colonial Indonesia*. Ithaca: Cornell University Press. doi.org/10.1515/9781501758607.

van Kessel, Ineke. 2007. 'Belanda Hitam: The Indo-African Communities on Java.' *African and Asian Studies* 6, no. 3: 243–70. doi.org/10.1163/156920907X212222.

Wertheim, Wim F. 1990. 'Netherlands-Indian Colonial Racism and Dutch Home Racism.' In *Imperial Monkey Business: Racial Supremacy in Social Darwinist Theory and Colonial Practice*, edited by Jan Breman, Piet de Rooy, Ann Stoler, and Wim F. Wertheim, 71–88. CASA Monographs 3. Amsterdam: VU University Press.

Zhou, Taomo. 2022. 'Passports to the Post-Colonial World: Space and Mobility in Francisca Fanggidaej's Afro-Asian Journeys.' In *The Lives of Cold War Afro-Asianism*, edited by Carolien Stolte and Su Lin Lewis, 309–26. Amsterdam: Amsterdam University Press. doi.org/10.1515/9789400604346-017.

8

Giving voice to the voiceless: 'Sin Po' and the Chinese massacres during the revolutionary period

Ravando and F.X. Harsono

Between 2009 and 2019, F.X. Harsono, one of the authors of this chapter, performed pilgrimages to various cemeteries in Java to locate the mass graves of Chinese victims of violence during the Indonesian war of independence (1945–49).[1] Harsono's curiosity about this topic was sparked during his childhood. As a primary school student, he often flipped through an album belonging to his father that contained more than 60 photographs of the exhumed remains of Chinese victims from several villages in Blitar, East Java. It is highly likely that these people perished at the hands of Indonesian militia during the Second Dutch Military Aggression (19 December 1948 – 5 January 1949).[2] Harsono's father, Oh Hok Tjoe, was appointed by the Blitar branch of Chung Hua Tsung Hui (CHTH, the Federation of Chinese Organisations in Indonesia) to photograph the exhumation event

---
1 This period is also widely known as the Indonesian national revolution (*Revolusi Nasional Indonesia*).
2 The First Dutch Military Aggression ('*Operatie Product*') began on 21 July 1947 and concluded on 5 August 1947, whereas the Second Dutch Military Aggression ('*Operatie Kraai*') began on 19 December 1948 and ended in January 1949.

(see Figure 8.1).³ Although the massacre occurred between December 1948 and January 1949, the process of exhuming the remains could not begin until mid-1951 when CHTH considered the situation safe.

Figure 8.1 Photograph of the exhumation of Chinese remains in Karangbendo, Ponggok and Blitar, taken in 1951 by Harsono's father, Oh Hok Tjoe

Source: F.X. Harsono's collection.

---

3   Harsono's father, Oh Hok Tjoe, who subsequently changed his name to Hendro Subagio, was a photographer in Blitar. In the 1950s, he owned the Atom Photo Studio, the most popular photo studio in town at that time. In 1951, together with the CHTH, Hendro helped document the number of victims, contact the victims' family members and ensure that the victims were properly buried.

8. GIVING VOICE TO THE VOICELESS

On 26 April 1951, the Committee for Exhuming Chinese Corpses (Panitia Penggalian Jenazah Tionghoa) was established in Blitar. This committee endeavoured to collect information and map the locations of Chinese mass graves, which were scattered on the outskirts of the city of Blitar. The location of these graves indicates that most of the executions occurred in areas under the authority of pro-republican militias, whose operations were outside the supervision of the official republican army or Dutch soldiers.[4] The exhumation process was conducted in multiple phases across areas near Blitar, including in Karangbendo, Jajar and Sanankulon. Over eight months, the committee exhumed 191 bodies from multiple graves. Of these victims, half were men, more than 70 were women and the remainder were children.[5]

Subsequently, all the exhumed remains were placed at Jalan Garum 1 before being put in a coffin measuring 5 x 2 x 2.5 metres. On 9 December 1951, representatives from the Government of the Republic of Indonesia, the Indonesian Communist Party (Partai Komunis Indonesia), the Indonesian Women's Association (Persatuan Wanita Republik Indonesia) and others attended a reburial procession at Karangsari, Mbamban. As a sign of mourning, Chinese merchants in Blitar also briefly suspended their business activities.[6]

The anti-Chinese violence that occurred at Blitar was one of several violent crimes against ethnic Chinese Indonesians during the Indonesian war of independence (1945–49). From his research and pilgrimages throughout Java, Harsono has pinpointed several other locations of Chinese mass graves across the island of Java, such as in Nganjuk, Pare, Tulungagung, Kediri, Purwokerto, Wonosobo, Muntilan, Yogyakarta and Banjar.

This chapter argues that the existence of the Chinese mass graves is essential for reconstructing narratives of anti-Chinese violence that have generally been silenced or forgotten in popular and scholarly accounts of the history

---

4   During the war of independence, various regions in Indonesia, particularly in Java, were divided into two territories: one controlled by the Dutch and one by the Republic of Indonesia. Many areas were also under the control of Indonesian paramilitary forces and local youths due to the inability of the armies of both sides to control all their territory. See Robert Cribb, *Gangsters and Revolutionaries: The Jakarta People's Militia and the Indonesian Revolution, 1945–1949* (Sydney: ASAA, 1991).
5   This number does not include the 10 additional victims that were reported missing after this exhumation. 'Pemakaman Djenazah Korban2 Tionghoa di Blitar [Burial of Chinese Victims in Blitar]', *Sin Po*, [Jakarta], 3 December 1951.
6   'Pemakaman Kembali Para Korban Tionghoa di Blitar [Reburial of Chinese Victims in Blitar]', *Sin Po*, [Jakarta], 13 December 1951.

of the Indonesian war of independence.[7] We argue that these sites are a crucial missing link to identifying and understanding the roots of violence against ethnic Chinese communities, who frequently have become prime targets amid political crises. Without intending to reopen these painful old wounds for Chinese Indonesian communities, we chose this topic so that we could gain a better understanding of the nature of anti-Chinese violence and how Dutch colonialism contributed to hostilities between Chinese and Indonesian groups, which culminated during the war.

In this chapter, we ask, why were ethnic Chinese often targeted by the succession of violent atrocities during the period? To what extent did Dutch colonialism contribute to this sequence of atrocities? How do Chinese mass graves convey information about these atrocities? To address these questions, we primarily rely on information about Chinese mass graves scattered over Central and East Java as well as reports from the newspaper *Sin Po* (1910–65).[8] In contrast to pro-republican newspapers that often portrayed the ethnic Chinese at that time as Dutch collaborators, *Sin Po* provides a counter-narrative from the perspective of the victims of targeted violence. Alongside these sources, the search for Chinese mass graves that Harsono has been conducting for many years has also led him to meet people who either witnessed the violence or were themselves victims and these perspectives have contributed to this chapter, as well as Harsono's broader study. This chapter also draws on several other key primary sources

---

7   A few scholars have examined this violence in detail, such as Mary Somers, Taomo Zhou and Geza Surya Pratiwi. Their research, however, focused on the violent events and barely touched on their aftermath. Thus, the exhumation and reburial processes are barely mentioned in these texts. See Mary Somers Heidhues, 'Anti-Chinese Violence in Java during the Indonesian Revolution, 1945–49', *Journal of Genocide Research* 14, nos 3–4 (2012): 381–401, doi.org/10.1080/14623528.2012.719371; Taomo Zhou, *Migration in the Time of Revolution: China, Indonesia, and the Cold War* (Ithaca: Cornell University Press, 2019), doi.org/10.1515/9781501739941; Geza Surya Pratiwi, 'Kekerasan Terhadap Golongan Tionghoa pada Masa Revolusi di Malang, 1945–1949 [Violence Against the Chinese during the Revolution in Malang, 1945–1949]', *Lembaran Sejarah* [*History Gazette*] 18, no. 1 (2022): 78–94, doi.org/10.22146/lembaran-sejarah.80455.

8   *Sin Po* was the largest Chinese publication during the war for independence, with a combined circulation of 30,253 copies for its Indonesian and Chinese editions as of early 1949. This newspaper was founded on 1 October 1910 by Lauw Giok Lan and Yoe Sin Gie, who adhered to Chinese nationalism but were very sympathetic to the Indonesian independence movement. *Sin Po*, whose publication was banned during the Japanese occupation, was reborn on 25 October 1945, amid turmoil. The paper often criticised the Government of the Republic of Indonesia because of the wartime violence against the Chinese. Due to its political stance, *Sin Po* became a prime target for pro-republican periodicals such as *Merdeka* ('*Independence*') and *Soeloeh Merdeka* ('*Torch of Independence*'). See Central Intelligence Agency (CIA), 'Indonesian Newspapers', General CIA Records, CIA-RDP79T01049A000200020010-3, Publication date: 27 April 1950, Document release date: 4 January 2000 (Langley: Central Intelligence Agency).

and archives from the Dutch Algemeene Secretarie (General Secretariat),[9] which are crucial to develop a broader understanding of anti-Chinese violence during the period.

The Indonesian war of independence: Sharper friction

The Indonesian war of independence is often remembered as a moment of unified struggle in Indonesian history, but it was also the darkest period for minority groups, particularly Indo-Europeans and Chinese. According to historian Sartono Kartodirdjo, the crisis of the war and high levels of political tension at the beginning of this period contributed to the emergence of countless frictions and divisions between groups. At the same time, the new Indonesian State, due to various shortcomings at the time, was unable to assure the safety of its people, and this resulted in minority groups commonly being made scapegoats and targets of the economic and political crises.[10] In addition to these fissures during the decolonisation process, the war of independence was also characterised by social and political conflict between classes.[11] Leo Suryadinata has argued that modern anti-Chinese movements in Indonesia arose during the revolutionary period. He particularly emphasises that, although the 'indigenous' population now ruled the government, the economic factors that had constituted the core of previous conflicts persisted.[12]

To identify the historical roots of violence and discriminatory sentiments against the ethnic Chinese, it is critical that we trace antecedent cases of colonial classification and division. After the 1740 Chinese massacre in Batavia, the Dutch East India Company (Vereenigde Oostindische Compagnie, VOC) government realised how precarious could be collaboration between the Chinese and ethnic groups classified as 'indigenous' (*Bumiputera*). After the massacre, the Chinese were required to reside in a specific area (*wijk*)

---

9   These documents originated from the confidential archives of the General Secretariat of the Netherlands Indies Government and the Cabinet of the Governor-General.
10   Sartono Kartodirdjo, 'Wajah Revolusi Indonesia Dipandang dari Perspektivisme Struktural [The Nature of the Revolution from a Structural Perspective]', *Prisma* X, no. 8 (August 1981): 3–13, at 3.
11   Soejatno and Benedict Anderson, 'Revolution and Social Tensions in Surakarta 1945–1950', *Indonesia*, no. 17 (April 1974): 99–111, doi.org/10.2307/3350775, at 104.
12   Leo Suryadinata, 'Anti-Chinese Actions in Southeast Asia: In Search of Causes and Solutions', in *Violent Internal Conflicts in Asia Pacific: Histories, Political Economies and Policies*, ed. Dewi Fortuna Anwar (Jakarta: Yayasan Obor Indonesia, 2005), 151–62, at 155.

that became known as 'Pecinan' (Chinatown).¹³ They were not permitted to leave the *wijk* without a valid travel permit (*pas*). In this way, the mobility of the Chinese community was restricted.¹⁴ This policy of segregation implemented in Batavia also served as a model for subsequent Dutch colonies in other areas.

Segregation was first legally regulated and implemented in 1818, based on *regeeringsreglement* ('government regulations').¹⁵ The term *Vreemde Oosterlingen* ('Foreign Orientals') was coined to classify Chinese, Arab and Indian communities. As a result of this regulation, colonial society became more and more divided. Inhabitants were classified not only by ethnicity (European or non-European), but also by religion (Christian or non-Christian).¹⁶ These discriminatory laws also led to division between each ethnic group, particularly between the Chinese and the *Bumiputera*. The ethnic Chinese were undeniably crucial to the Dutch colonial economy. They obtained numerous economic privileges, including opium concessions, pawnshops, toll gates and the like.¹⁷ However, the collapse of the revenue-farming system at the end of the nineteenth century, followed by the implementation of the 'Ethical Policy' by the Dutch colonial government in 1901, ended the Chinese economic monopoly that had lasted for centuries.¹⁸

Systems of classification further complicated the position of the ethnic Chinese in colonial Indonesian society. The Dutch colonial government officially recognised and classified the Japanese as European in 1899, which was regarded as an insult to the ethnic Chinese, who were classified as *Bumiputera*. In the eyes of the law, they were equivalent to the *Bumiputera* category despite being subject to a variety of taxes similar to those applying

---

13 See also Kusno's Chapter 11 in this volume.
14 Benedict Anderson, *The Spectre of Comparison: Nationalism, Southeast Asia and the World* (London: Verso, 1998), 13–14.
15 See *Staatsblad van Nederlandsch-Indie* [*Official Gazette of the Netherlands Indies*], no. 622 (1919).
16 Mona Lohanda, *Growing Pains: The Chinese and the Dutch in Colonial Java, 1890–1942* (Jakarta: Yayasan Cipta Loka Caraka, 2002), 78–79.
17 Mona Lohanda, *The Kapitan Cina of Batavia, 1837–1942: A History of Chinese Establishment in Colonial Society* (Jakarta: Djambatan, 1996), 179; John Butcher and Howard Dick, eds, *The Rise and Fall of Revenue Farming: Business Elites and the Emergence of the Modern State in Southeast Asia* (London: Macmillan, 1993), doi.org/10.1007/978-1-349-22877-5.
18 The prime objective of ethical policies was to improve the living conditions of the *Bumiputera* by fostering native awakening through advancements in the education, irrigation and transmigration sectors. In practice, however, this policy often alienated the Chinese. See Lea E. Williams, 'The Ethical Program and the Chinese of Indonesia', *Journal of Southeast Asian History* 2, no. 2 (1961): 35–42, at 35–36.

to Europeans in their daily lives.[19] In essence, following this classification, the Chinese no longer served as a buffer between the rulers and the ruled. They were merely ordinary subjects without significant privileges.[20]

The end of Dutch colonialism with the Japanese invasion of the Indonesian archipelago in 1942 did not necessarily bring an end to the sentiments shared by the two groups. In fact, the Japanese military government took advantage of these hostilities by enacting discriminatory policies that exacerbated tensions between ethnic Chinese and Indonesians. Along with the European population, the Chinese community comprised the lowest strata of the population structure during the occupation. The Chinese community was also subjected to the strict implementation of the re-Sinification process, which mandated the daily use of the Chinese language. In addition, they were permitted to attend only Chinese schools, even though most no longer spoke their ancestral language.[21] The social divide between the Chinese and Indonesian populations was further widened by these discriminatory regulations. During this period, prejudices against Chinese as 'foreigners' (*orang asing*), 'outsiders' (*orang luar*) and 'immigrants' (*pendatang*) intensified.

Tjamboek Berdoeri (Kwee Thiam Tjing) referred to the three and a half years of Japanese occupation as the 'crazy era' (*zaman gendeng-gendengan*) and regarded this period as a major contributor to the outbreak of violence against ethnic Chinese during the Indonesian war of independence.[22] A series of atrocities in Indonesia began following the Japanese capitulation

---

19   After their status was equated with that of Europeans, a Japanese prisoner had the right to be tried by the Dutch colonial court known as the Raad van Justitie (Higher Court). Meanwhile, *Bumiputera* and Chinese communities were dealt with in a Landraad (Native Court) hearing. According to *Sin Po*, the treatment received in the two courts significantly differed because the prosecutors and justices used 'two scales' (*doea timbangan*). In a similar case, a person might be released by the Raad van Justitie, but it was highly probable that they would be imprisoned by the Landraad. See 'Memake Doea Timbangan [Using Two Scales]', *Sin Po: Oost-Java Editie* [*East Java edition*], 23 January 1923; 'Diborgol [Handcuffed]', *Sin Po: Oost-Java Editie* [*East Java edition*], 25 January 1923; 'Apa Sebab Tida Dibekoek [Why Was It Not Prevented]?', *Sin Po: West-Java Editie* [*West Java edition*], 12 July 1924.
20   Kwee Tek Hoay, 'Atsal Moelanja Timboel Pergerakan Tionghoa jang Modern di Indonesia [The Origins of the Modern Chinese Movement in Indonesia]', *Moestika Romans* (February 1937), 58; Johann-Friedrich Scheltema, *De Opiumpolitiek der Regeering en de Vrijheid der Drukpers in Nederlandsch-Indie* [*The Opium Policy of the Government and Freedom of the Press in the Netherlands Indies*] (The Hague: W.P. van Stockum en Zoon, 1903), 9.
21   Didi Kwartanada, 'Kolaborasi dan Resinifikasi: Komunitas Cina Kota Yogyakarta pada Jaman Jepang, 1942–1945 [Collaboration and Re-Sinification: The Chinese Community of Yogyakarta during the Japanese Era, 1942–1945] (Undergraduate thesis, Universitas Gadjah Mada, Yogyakarta, 1997).
22   Tjamboek Berdoeri [Kwee Thiam Tjing], *Indonesia dalem Api dan Bara* [*Indonesia in Flames and Embers*] (Jakarta: Elkasa, 2004), 261.

to the Allies on 15 August 1945, which created a power vacuum. Countless incidents of atrocities erupted in regions abandoned by the Dutch and the local *pangreh pradja* (colonial aristocratic bureaucrats). In addition to robbery, arson and the widespread destruction of property, there were also cases of forced circumcision perpetrated against ethnic Chinese in Tangerang, Bekasi and Pekalongan, as well as in various regions of South Sumatra and East Java. Just a few days before the proclamation of Indonesian independence, it was estimated that the Chinese community had sustained losses of up to $100 million.[23]

After Sukarno and Mohammad Hatta proclaimed the independence of Indonesia on 17 August 1945, the situation of the Chinese population did not immediately improve. Japan, which was tasked with maintaining security and order in Indonesia until the arrival of Allied forces, was unable to prevent attacks by youth groups (*pemuda*) and other armed militias.[24] Numerous criminal acts, including kidnappings, enforced disappearances, shootings, robberies and even assassinations, occurred nearly every day. Mary Somers Heidhues described how areas of Java and Sumatra became 'stateless societies' (*masyarakat tanpa negara*) in which youths and paramilitary groups assaulted anyone they suspected to be an enemy spy or Dutch informant.[25]

Most of the Chinese population lacked the capacity and resources to defend themselves against violent assaults, making them convenient scapegoats and easy targets. As the majority were merchants, Chinese Indonesians were frequently victims of robbery and racketeering, which often led to other atrocities. According to Victor Purcell, incidents typically started with the looting of one or two Chinese houses in an area. When there was

---

23 Twang Peck Yang, *The Chinese Business Elite in Indonesia and the Transition to Independence, 1940–1950* (Kuala Lumpur: Oxford University Press, 1998), 71.
24 The early stages of the Indonesian war of independence were marked by the emergence of various militia groups across Indonesia. At least 17 militias declared war on behalf of the Republic of Indonesia, including Laskar Hizbullah, Sabilillah, Laskar Rakjat, Partai Rakjat Djelata and the Barisan Banteng Hitam ('Black Bull Front'). According to *Sin Po*, these groups had their own armies and frequently operated independently without official command from the Indonesian republican army. They often perpetrated atrocities against Chinese citizens and other civilians. Consequently, their legitimacy was frequently disregarded by the Government of the Republic of Indonesia. *Sin Po* had warned the republican government to maintain control over these militias once the war began. The newspaper also predicted an increase in the kidnapping and murder of civilians, along with their increasingly uncontrolled movements. See 'Indonesia Kaja Partij [Indonesia is Rich with Political Parties]', *Sin Po*, [Jakarta], 25 September 1946; Cribb, *Gangsters and Revolutionaries*.
25 Heidhues, 'Anti-Chinese Violence in Java during the Indonesian Revolution'.

no resistance or the authorities prevented it, locals then joined the assault. In the absence of social control, these robberies frequently led to sexual violence and homicide.[26]

Historian Robert Cribb describes the early years of Indonesian independence as a period of *bersiap* ('be ready'), which was marked by the outbreak of violence against minority groups, such as the Chinese, Indo-Europeans and Ambonese, who were accused of being enemy spies.[27] Despite the fact that a significant number of the Chinese population was subjected to violence during this period, the number of casualties was not as high as in European and Indo-European communities.[28] However, as 1946 began, violent incidents against European groups subsided. In contrast, the situation for the Chinese community was becoming increasingly uncertain. On 4 April 1946, the republican government resolved to relocate the capital of the republic to Yogyakarta because it could no longer defend Jakarta.[29] This situation deteriorated after the Netherlands East Indies Civil Administration (NICA) released a new currency. The Chinese traders caught conducting transactions with this new money were easily accused of being Dutch collaborators or 'NICA's dogs'. Conversely, the Dutch harboured suspicions that the Chinese were aiding the Indonesians, resulting in frequent intimidation from both sides.[30]

Even though most of the Chinese population initially supported Indonesian independence, the violence they experienced and witnessed at the beginning of the war made many sceptical about the future of the new Indonesian

---

26   Victor Purcell, *The Chinese in Southeast Asia* (Oxford: Oxford University Press, 1966), 472.
27   For a discussion of recent controversy about this term in the Netherlands, see Chapter 1 in this volume; Robert Cribb, 'The Brief Genocide of Eurasians in Indonesia, 1945/46', in *Empire, Colony, Genocide: Conquest, Occupation and Subaltern Resistance in World History*, ed. Dirk Moses (New York: Berghahn Books, 2008), 424–39, doi.org/10.1515/9781782382140-019.
28   For more information related to the *bersiap* period, see Esther Captain and Onno Sinke, *Het Geluid van Geweld: Bersiap en de Dynamiek van Geweld tijdens de Eerste Fase van de Indonesische Revolutie, 1945–1946* [*The Sound of Violence: Bersiap and Dynamics of Violence during the First Phase of the Indonesian Revolution, 1945–1946*] (Amsterdam: Amsterdam University Press, 2022); Herman Bussemaker, *Bersiap! Opstand in het paradijs. De Bersiap-periode op Java en Sumatra 1945–1946* [*Bersiap! Revolt in Paradise: The Bersiap Period on Java and Sumatra 1945–1946*] (Zutphen: Walburg Pers, 2005); Elly-Touwen Bouwsma and Petra Groen, *Tussen Banzai en Bersiap: De Afwikkeling van de Tweede Wereldoorlog in Nederlands-Indië* [*Between Banzai and Bersiap: The Settlement of the Second World War in the Netherlands Indies*] (The Hague: SDU Publishers, 1996); Mary C. van Delden, *Bersiap in Bandoeng: Een Onderzoek naar Geweld in de Periode van 17 Augustus 1945 tot 24 Maart 1946* [*Bersiap in Bandung: Research into Violence in the Period from 17 August 1945 to 24 March 1946*] (Kockengen: van Delden, 1989).
29   Adrian Vickers, *A History of Modern Indonesia* (Cambridge: Cambridge University Press, 2005), doi.org/10.1017/CBO9780511801020, 99.
30   Purcell, *The Chinese in Southeast Asia*, 157.

State. As a result, many became dependent on the assistance of the Allies and/or Dutch for their survival. One solution was to flee to Allied territory, where they believed their families and businesses would be safer, but this had consequences. The pro-republican militia viewed relocation as treasonous and they frequently used this as an excuse to persecute Chinese people.[31] In June 1946, the massacre of Chinese in Tangerang was the culmination of anti-Chinese violence that had occurred during the war. More than 700 Chinese, including 200 women and children, were killed by the Laskar Rakyat ('People's Warriors') militia, a further 200 were proclaimed missing, between 40 and 50 villages were destroyed and 1,200 homes were ransacked or burned.[32]

Even though president Sukarno and several other Indonesian republican officials vehemently condemned this atrocity, the situation for the Chinese did not immediately improve. Militias and pro-republican youth continued to target Chinese citizens with violence. Hundreds of Chinese civilians were intimidated, robbed and murdered in Bekasi, as well as Bagansiapiapi in Riau and Padang in West Sumatra.[33] This resurgence of violence was followed by the First and Second Dutch Military Aggressions, which resulted in the death of thousands of Chinese civilians.[34]

The First Dutch Military Aggression

On Sunday, 20 July 1947, at 11 pm, under the pretext of restoring 'security and order', the Dutch military initiated '*Operatie Product*' ('Operation Product'), a major military invasion of republican areas. In Indonesia, this became known as *Agresi Militer Belanda* ('Dutch Military Aggression') or 'Clash I', while the Dutch referred to their action as a '*politionele actie*' ('police action').

---

31   'Hoakiauw di Sumatra [Chinese in Sumatra]', *Sin Po*, [Jakarta], 22 April 1946.
32   *Star Weekly*, [Jakarta], 9 June 1946. See also Ravando, 'Now is the Time to Kill All Chinese: Social Revolution and the Massacre of Chinese in Tangerang, 1945–1946' (Master's thesis, Leiden University, Netherlands, 2014).
33   See, for instance, 'Banjak Orang Tionghoa dari Padang Mengoengsi ka Laen Tempat Lantaran Keadahan Semingkin Genting [Many Chinese from Padang Fled to Other Places Due to Increasing Tension]', *Sin Po*, [Jakarta], 16 August 1946; 'Kasengsarahan dan Kamelaratan di Bagan Siapi-Api [Suffering and Hardship in Bagansiapiapi]', *Sin Po*, [Jakarta], 8 November 1946.
34   The term '*Politionele Actie*' ('Police Action') is commonly used in Dutch historiography to refer to these events. The Dutch considered Indonesia's proclamation of independence illegitimate, so police action was required to eliminate extremist elements and restore order.

8. GIVING VOICE TO THE VOICELESS

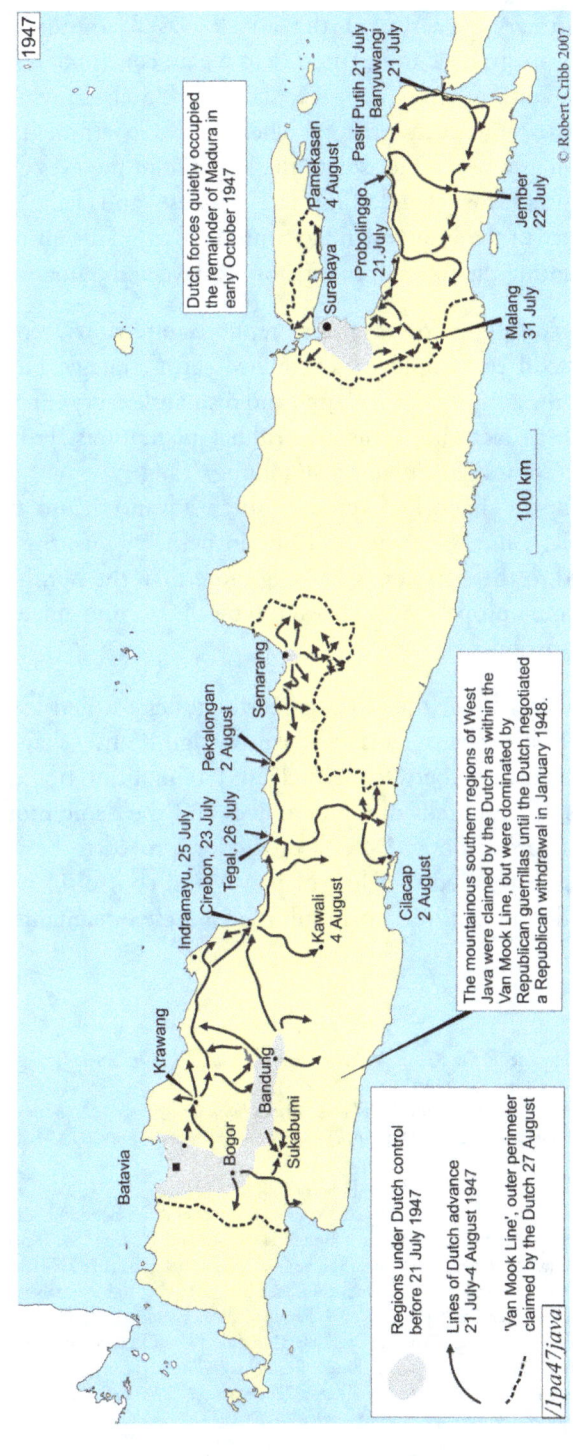

Map 8.1 Map of the First Dutch Military Aggression in Java, July–August 1947

Source: Robert Cribb, *Digital Atlas of Indonesian History* (Copenhagen: NIAS Press, 2010). Reproduced with permission.

The primary objective of the attack was to capture and demolish all republican strategic infrastructure to regain control of resource-rich regions in Java and Sumatra. The next day, the Dutch army and marines began to invade republican territory. The Dutch Government used this military invasion as a pretext to isolate the republic in the eyes of the international community for abandoning the Chinese and failing to suppress the influence of the Indonesian Communist Party. This invasion was successful in shrinking the republican territory to Java and Sumatra.[35]

As soon as Dutch forces entered republican territory, republican forces and their auxiliaries employed a scorched-earth strategy. The objective was to hinder the advance of the Dutch and dismantle everything that could benefit it, such as factories, mills and rubber plantations. From the experiences of the Chinese in Surabaya, Bandung, Tangerang and Palembang, it was well known that whenever the Dutch advanced into the interior of the republic, Chinese safety would be in peril.[36] Thus, the newspaper *Sin Po* referred to these tactics as nothing more than the burning and destruction of Chinese property, which were typically accompanied by looting, arson and extortion.[37]

Sin Po feared that the scorched-earth strategy would lead to the massacre of Chinese civilians. This concern was significantly shaped by the fact that previous battles between Dutch and republican troops had resulted in the loss of hundreds of Chinese lives and the demolition of thousands of Chinese properties.[38] *Sin Po*'s prediction proved to be valid. The military aggression resulted in a loss of power and control in several areas, which enabled armed militias to assault the Chinese inhabitants.[39]

---

35   George McTurnan Kahin, *Nationalism and Revolution in Indonesia* (Ithaca: Southeast Asia Program Publications, Cornell University, 2003), 27.
36   *Memorandum Outlining Acts of Violence and Inhumanity Perpetrated by Indonesian Bands on Innocent Chinese Before and After the Dutch Police Action was Enforced on July 21, 1947* (Jakarta: Zhonghua Zong Hui, 1947), 10.
37   'Merdeka [Freedom]', *Sin Po*, [Jakarta], 29 July 1947.
38   The Battle of Surabaya (19–26 November 1945) and the Bandung Sea of Fire incident (March 1946) both resulted in substantial Chinese casualties and damage. See 'Koendjoengan pada Medan Pertempoeran Soerabaja (I) [Visit to the Surabaya Battlefield (I)]', *Sin Po*, [Jakarta], 3 December 1945; 'Koendjoengan pada Medan Pertempoeran Soerabaja (II) [Visit to the Surabaya Battlefield (II)]', *Sin Po*, [Jakarta], 4 December 1945. See also 'Pendoedoekan Bandoeng Selatan Soeda Seleseh Dilakoeken: Karoegian Sanget Besar Dari Pendoedoek Tionghoa [The Occupation of South Bandung Has Been Completed: Huge Losses for the Chinese Residents]', *Sin Po*, [Jakarta], 27 March 1946.
39   Kwee Kek Beng, *Doea Poeloe Lima Tahon Sebagi Wartawan* [*Twenty-Five Years as a Journalist*] (Batavia: Kuo, 1948), 96; Zhou, *Migration in the Time of Revolution*, 18.

Even though these incidents appeared to have occurred coincidentally, various reports indicate that the violence was meticulously planned and involved multiple parties, such as paramilitary groups, local religious leaders and the Indonesian military. *Sin Po* suspected that the Dutch were also negligent in protecting Chinese communities during the countless anti-Chinese incidents that occurred mostly in Java and Sumatra. Despite having sufficient soldiers and armaments to prevent such incidents, Dutch forces would only emerge as 'heroes' or 'liberators' when there were already many casualties. According to *Sin Po*, the objective of permitting violence before intervening was to tarnish the image of the Indonesian republic in the eyes of the international community and convince the League of Nations that the republic was incapable of governing and protecting its own people.[40]

During the First Dutch Military Aggression, Malang in East Java was among the regions that sustained the most damage. On 22 July 1947, a series of robberies and violent acts erupted on the outskirts of the city, which swiftly expanded into the downtown area. In Kayutangan and Kota Lama, Chinese and European residences and businesses were looted and destroyed by mobs who were strongly suspected of having been provoked by the Laskar Hizbullah ('Army of God'). The following week, arson attacks against government buildings and enterprises began. Even the CHTH's Malang building was not spared from this violent assault.[41]

Based on the accounts of several eyewitnesses published in *Sin Po*, up to 30 Chinese residents of Kotalama were gathered at the militia headquarters in the Mergosono area under the pretence of being 'secured' (*diamankan*). The order was issued by Prawiro, the local militia leader, who had accused the Chinese of being Dutch informants. However, before their arrival, they were detained in a meat-grinding factory at Gadang. The victims were subsequently tortured, mutilated and burned. Identification and autopsy

---

40 See 'Kakedjeman Terhadap Bangsa Tionghoa [Cruelty Towards the Chinese People]', *Sin Po*, [Jakarta], 25 August 1947; '36 Hari Dalem Sarangnja Kaoem Extremist [Thirty-Six Days in the Extremists' Nest]', *Sin Po*, [Jakarta], 5 September 1947; '1178 Kiaopao Kita jang Ditoeloeng [1,178 Fellow Chinese People Assisted]', *Sin Po*, [Jakarta], 19 November 1947.

41 'Malang Sasoeda Dibikin Antjoer [Malang After Being Destroyed]', *Sin Po*, [Jakarta], 6 August 1947. See also 'Verklaring [Declaration]', NEFIS/CMI [Netherlands Forces Intelligence Service/Central Military Intelligence Service], 1942–1949, Inv. no. 02022 (The Hague: Archief van het Ministerie van Buitenlandse Zaken [Archives of the Ministry of Foreign Affairs]); 'Moorden door de TNI Troepen Gepleegd op Chinese Ingezetenen te Malang [Murders Committed by TNI Troops on Chinese Residents in Malang]', NEFIS/CMI [Netherlands Forces Intelligence Service/Central Military Intelligence Service], 1942–1949, Inv. no. 02022 (The Hague: Archief van het Ministerie van Buitenlandse Zaken [Archives of the Ministry of Foreign Affairs]).

procedures performed by the Chinese Red Cross and CHTH Malang confirmed the victims had been subjected to extreme violence before their deaths.[42]

The situation remained volatile in Malang for several weeks. As soon as things began to improve following the acceptance of a ceasefire proposal from the Security Council of the League of Nations on 17 August 1947, CHTH Malang ordered the exhumation of the victims who had been hastily buried in Mergosono and its surrounds. All these victims were later reburied en masse in a large hole at the Kutobedah cemetery, following the instruction of the CHTH Malang leader, Liem Bian Sioe. In his speech, Liem begged the Chinese not to hold grudges against the Indonesians.[43] Based on a preliminary report issued by CHTH Malang, at least 25 Chinese in the city and its surroundings were victims of this violence, of whom 20 were massacred in Kutobedah and Buring. However, the real number of casualties was likely much higher, as hundreds of victims remained missing. Meanwhile, the total material losses were very difficult to estimate. In the Singosari area alone, for instance, losses due to property damage there were estimated at $f7$ million.[44]

Various pro-republican militia groups also utilised similar patterns to perform anti-Chinese violence in other areas, targeting businesses, property and lives. In Krawang and Cikampek (both in West Java), for instance, on the evening of 21 July 1947, the local militia assembled all Chinese residents on the football field before looting and burning their dwellings. The Chinese were falsely accused of being Dutch collaborators—an accusation that was never proven in a court of law. Many people believed these allegations were fabricated to justify the heinous crimes. In other regions of West Java, such as Rengasdengklok, Cibadak, Jatiwangi and Sukabumi, hundreds of Chinese-owned factories, rice mills and homes were also targeted by locals. Chinese communities strongly suspected that youths and local religious leaders provoked the assaults on Chinese-owned property, which they perceived as a symbol of 'foreign' capitalism. In comparison with Dutch-owned properties, Chinese Indonesian properties typically lacked

---

42   See 'Pembakaran, Perampokan dan Pemboenoean di Lawang [Arson, Robbery and Murder in Lawang]', *Sin Po*, [Jakarta], 26 July 1947; 'Pembakaran dan Perampokan di Singosari [Arson and Robbery in Singosari]', *Sin Po*, [Jakarta], 31 July 1947; 'Malang After Being Destroyed', *Sin Po*.
43   Berdoeri, *Indonesia in Flames and Embers*, 394.
44   *Memorandum Outlining Acts of Violence and Inhumanity*, 16–17.

security, making them more vulnerable. While the local CHTH reported no casualties despite the deplorable conditions in these areas, the loss of property was estimated to be worth millions of guilders.[45]

Several areas of Cirebon, also in West Java, such as Jatitujuh and Cilimus, witnessed a far more perilous situation and killings following the Dutch reoccupation on 23 July 1947. At that time, CHTH Cirebon reported that the Chinese population was generally safe. However, a few days later, the situation became tense after the Dutch withdrew some of their troops and refocused their security measures on only a few areas, including Losari, Kadipaten and Sumedang. This power vacuum was abused by militias and locals to launch attacks against the powerless Chinese. According to CHTH reports, 36 of the 616 Chinese residents of Jatitujuh were executed by local militia, which was likely Laskar Hizbullah. This number did not include the 12 victims who were declared missing.

In Jatitujuh, according to several eyewitness testimonies, men and women were separated after being driven into the forest near Kedung Maung. The women were sexually assaulted in groups and their belongings were seized. The men were instructed to form a line before being stabbed or shot to death. According to a report issued by CHTH Jakarta, at least eight women were also executed in Jatitujuh, indicating that the executions were carried out without regard for gender. The youngest victim was one year old and the oldest was 60.

In Cilimus, about 20 kilometres from the city of Cirebon, similarly extreme violence was carried out. It was reported that of a total Chinese population of 820 people, more than 50 were brutally executed by the Laskar Hizbullah paramilitary group in collaboration with the Indonesian army and several other militias. As well as the 50 confirmed dead, 21 victims remained missing, 14 were severely wounded and three people were reportedly circumcised against their will. Circumcision signified that they had been forcefully converted to Islam, which was one of the conditions for avoiding execution. This illustrates how vulnerable the Chinese position was as they were targeted not only due to their physical differences but also because of their religion. In a matter of days, anti-Chinese violence continued to spread to various areas of Cirebon, including Rajagaluh, Babakan, Maja and Parapatan, causing a mass exodus of Chinese residents from the city.[46]

---

45 ibid., 11.
46 ibid., 12.

At the end of 1947, CHTH Jakarta tried to compile a report of the violence suffered by the Chinese during the war, particularly after the First Dutch Military Aggression. The report was subsequently submitted to Dr Ching-lin Hsia, the representative of the Chinese Delegation to the League of Nations, with the intention of attracting international attention to the issue of violence against Chinese people. The CHTH also urged the League of Nations to take a more proactive role in resolving issues between the Netherlands and Indonesia. In its 31-page English-language report, the CHTH divided the acts of violence into seven categories: extortion (*pemerasan*), plundering (*penjarahan*), destruction of property (*penghancuran properti*), deprivation of freedom (*perampasan kemerdekaan*), kidnapping (*penculikan*), rape (*pemerkosaan*) and massacres (*pembantaian*).[47] The pattern of anti-Chinese violence that occurred during the First Dutch Military Aggression met at least one of these criteria.

The interim report of the CHTH stated that, between 21 July and 21 August 1947, 293 Chinese residents were murdered, 6,453 were declared missing and 912 Chinese-owned homes and businesses were destroyed. The incidents of anti-Chinese violence discussed above are only a few of the many during this period. *Sin Po* and the CHTH also documented widespread atrocities in some Central and East Java regencies, including Bumiayu, Tegal, Pekalongan, Purwokerto, Banyumas, Purbalingga, Gombong, Salatiga, Karanganyar, Lumajang and Jember.[48] As conditions progressively improved, many Chinese decided to return home—unaware that a few months later, with the commencement of the Second Dutch Military Aggression, they would face an even more dire situation.

The Second Dutch Military Aggression

After the cessation of the First Dutch Military Aggression, the situation in Indonesia did not significantly improve. Between April and June 1948, the United Nations (successor to the League of Nations) exerted pressure on the Dutch Government to negotiate with the Republic of Indonesia so that both parties would stop violating the ceasefire and settle disputes

---

47   ibid., 6–9.
48   ibid., 10–31. See also 'Boemiajoe Mendjadi Boemiangoes [Bumiayu Becomes Scorched Earth]', *Sin Po*, [Jakarta], 21 August 1947; '23 Orang Tionghoa Disembeleh di Soerdjo dan Bawang [23 Chinese Slaughtered in Surjo and Bawang]', *Sin Po*, [Jakarta], 15 September 1947; 'Korban Pemboenoehan, Pembakaran dan Perampokan dari Hoakiauw di Indramajoe [Victims of Murder, Arson and Robbery of Chinese in Indramayu]', *Sin Po*, [Jakarta], 19 September 1947.

over plantations and market commodities in the custody of republican and irregular insurgent movements. A stalemate ensued, paving the way for '*Operatie Kraai*' ('Operation Crow') on 19 December 1948, which lasted until 15 January 1949. In this brief period, the Dutch were able to invade Yogyakarta, Solo, Parakan, Secang and Wonosobo, as well as other significant republican territories.[49]

Yogyakarta, the temporary Indonesian capital, was effectively captured by the Dutch. All significant republican-held cities in Java and Sumatra were conquered by the Dutch in just under two weeks. Meanwhile, Sukarno, Hatta and six other republican ministers were arrested and exiled to Bangka Island, off the coast of Sumatra. Republican forces, however, declined to surrender and instead fought a guerilla war under the command of General Sudirman.

Several weeks before the outbreak of the war, *Sin Po* had predicted that unsuccessful negotiations between the Netherlands and Indonesia in Kaliurang, Yogyakarta, would ignite another crisis. The paper used what had occurred during the First Dutch Military Aggression to illustrate how a stalemate could result in a bloody war. Even though the Dutch always claimed that their 'police actions' were intended to eradicate criminals and restore peace and order in Java and Sumatra, *Sin Po* persisted in viewing them as invasive military actions. The paper also predicted that if another battle were to occur, the Chinese would be victimised again.[50]

Sin Po's prediction proved to be accurate. On 19 December 1948, the Netherlands launched the Second Dutch Military Aggression. To prevent the Dutch from seizing strategic facilities, republican soldiers and militias employed a scorched-earth strategy in multiple locations. *Sin Po* describes the atmosphere as extremely tense, akin to 'returning to the *kempeitai* [Japanese military police] era' (*kombali ka djeman kempeitai*).[51] The circulation of various forms of propaganda, such as slogans like 'The Netherlands go, the Chinese suffer' (*Landa loengo, Tjina tjiloko*) and 'The Netherlands withdraw, the Chinese are devastated' (*Landa moendoer, Tjina hantjoer*), made the situation even tenser.[52]

---

49 'Solo, Tjepoe dan Laen-Laen Djato [Solo, Cepu and Other Areas Fall]', *Sin Po*, [Jakarta], 22 December 1948.
50 'Kandasnja Pembitjarahan [Negotiations Fail]', *Sin Po*, [Jakarta], 9 December 1948.
51 'Kombali ka Djeman Kempeitai [Return to the Kempeitai Era]', *Sin Po*, [Jakarta], 21 February 1949.
52 'Wonogiri dan Patjitan [Wonogiri and Pacitan]', *Sin Po*, [Jakarta], 21 October 1949.

It cannot be denied that the fall of Yogyakarta as the capital of the Republic of Indonesia ignited a series of atrocities in urban areas and on the outskirts of the city. *Sin Po* reported how armed gangs were caught in the act of ransacking and burning Chinese houses in Gondomanan—acts that quickly spread to Sosrowijayan, Kemetiran, Jogonegaran, Gandekan and Pajeksan.[53] The scorched-earth action was followed by a series of massacres in multiple districts in Yogyakarta. The identities of several victims were recorded, such as The Soo Hwa from Wonosari, who was slain alongside two other Chinese in Cepor Village, which is close to Kalasan. Similarly, five Chinese people in Prambanan were murdered by armed gangs. *Sin Po* also recorded the identities of five Chinese whose fate is uncertain: Liem Khing Liem (Ngampilan), Sie Tjing Hian, Liem Ing Sing (Wirobrajan), Lie Gee Oe and his son, (Pathuk). It is highly likely that they were killed.

Sie Joe Ging, one of the Chinese adolescents who survived the massacre in Groso Village, described the chronology of the atrocities to *Sin Po*. On 24 December 1948, Police Commander Soediman gathered all Chinese residents of the village of Kedaton Plered, 12 kilometres from Yogyakarta, on one of the village's soccer fields. Soediman then demanded their house keys, vowing to safeguard their belongings. However, the opposite occurred: their homes were looted, and all the residents were transported to Groso Village, 2 kilometres away. A total of 29 Chinese were confined there, along with six members of a Swiss family and an Indo-Dutch individual. On their arrival, they were rounded up, taken to the edge of a cliff on a mountain and executed at close range. Oey Ging Tjwan, Sie Kiem Tjing, M.J. Thomas (who was Indo-Dutch) and R.O. Long (from the Swiss family) were among the casualties who could be identified.[54]

Nganjuk, East Java, was one of the regions that experienced the most severe anti-Chinese violence during the Second Dutch Military Aggression. A day after the Groso Village violence, on 25 December 1948, at approximately 1 pm, Laskar Hizbullah troops in Wirojayeng rounded up and detained as many as 70 Chinese people. On 31 December, they were transported to Karangseneh Village, then Ngujung and finally Rejoso. They were then taken to a forest in the vicinity of Jetis, along with hundreds of other refugees from Nganjuk, Gondang, Lengkong and Berbek who were en route to Rejoso. Up to 800 were then confined to a single building and fired on with machine

---

53 'Kegelisahan Dalem Masjarakat Tionghoa Memoentjak [Anxiety in the Chinese Community is Peaking]', *Sin Po*, [Jakarta], 21 October 1949.
54 'Pemboenoehan Setjara Besar-Besaran di Desa Groso [Mass Murder in the Groso Village]', *Sin Po*, [Jakarta], 1 February 1949.

8. GIVING VOICE TO THE VOICELESS

guns from the perimeter. According to *Sin Po*, only five individuals survived the massacre.[55] According to the testimony of an eyewitness published in the newspaper, between 700 and 800 Chinese residents of Nganjuk and Waujung were gathered in one building in Ngluyu by Laskar Hizbullah. Only 67 individuals were documented as having escaped the massacre.[56]

Comparable patterns of violence occurred in other locations in Central Java—for instance, in the Wonosobo region. There, 70 Chinese residents of the Sapuran district were taken to Bakalan Village in Banyumudal on 21 December 1948, for no evident reason. All their belongings were confiscated and their homes were burned down. Oey Tjie Hiang, the commander of CHTH Wonosobo, who attempted to negotiate with the kidnappers, was executed by a Laskar Hizbullah soldier. At the same time, as many as 700 Chinese residents of Kertek were abducted by Laskar Hizbullah and transported to Kalikajar Village, where 79 were executed on suspicion of spying for Dutch soldiers. Fortunately, most of the remainder were eventually rescued by republican Siliwangi soldiers.[57]

Based on these examples, we can conclude that the pattern of violence experienced by the Chinese during this period was comparable with that of the First Dutch Military Aggression. The perpetrators of the violence were strongly suspected of belonging to the same pro-republican militias, such as Laskar Rakyat, Laskar Hizbullah and Barisan Pelopor, whose actions were frequently supported by both the Indonesian military and agitated mobs of residents. In addition to the locations listed above, anti-Chinese atrocities also occurred in Sukoharjo, Magelang, Tulungagung, Pare, Ponorogo and other places, indicating the massive scale of anti-Chinese sentiment during the war.

Sin Po cited a report from CHTH Yogyakarta that suggested that up to 1,025 Chinese people were executed during the Second Dutch Military Aggression. While 115 were gravely injured, 9,050 were reported missing and 31,497 others were forced to evacuate to safer locations.[58] It should be noted that *Sin Po* emphasised that these numbers were preliminary and

---

[55] 'Pemboenoehan Besar-Besaran di Redjoso [Mass Murder in Rejoso]', *Sin Po*, [Jakarta], 25 January 1949.
[56] 'Ratoesan Pendoedoek Tionghoa Dikoempoel dan Dibakar [Hundreds of Chinese Residents Are Rounded Up and Burnt]', *Sin Po*, [Jakarta], 1 February 1949.
[57] 'Pendoedoek Tionghoa di Kertek Diboenoeh [Chinese Residents in Kertek Killed]!', *Sin Po*, [Jakarta], 11 January 1949.
[58] 'Hoakiauw di Daerah Pendoedoekan Baroe [Chinese in New Settlement Area]', *Sin Po*, [Jakarta], 12 February 1949.

the real number of victims was likely to be significantly higher. Neither the CHTH nor the Government of the Republic of Indonesia has ever disclosed the official victim statistics, even though their mass graves still exist.

A committee to exhume Chinese mass graves

In early 1950, just a few weeks after the Dutch recognised Indonesian sovereignty, the central CHTH association in Jakarta instructed all its branches in Java and Sumatra to exhume the mass graves of Chinese people who were killed during the First and Second Dutch Military Aggressions. The exhumation of the victims' bodies began with the formation of the Committee for Relocating the Graves of Chinese Victims (Panitia Pemindahan Makam Korban Tionghoa) in various regions. By using the testimonies of residents and reports from victims' families, this committee tried to pinpoint the locations of the mass graves, which were usually far from the city centre.

The CHTH in Magelang, Central Java, was most likely the first to exhume and rebury remains. This reburial was carried out in two stages. The first step occurred at the end of March 1950 at Blabak, Magelang. According to the accounts of several eyewitnesses, the bodies of victims were found in the vicinity of Muntilan and Magelang. Most were bound and naked, which implies that they had been subjected to extreme violence before they were executed. Fifty-two corpses were then buried in an unmarked mass grave. At the same time, CHTH Magelang extended the search for bodies to other areas, such as Pucang, Pakis, Rejosari and Tegalrejo. This proved successful, as an additional 90 corpses were discovered and later reburied in a mass grave in Blabak on 26 May 1950.[59]

Meanwhile, in Nganjuk, East Java, CHTH Nganjuk, with the assistance of locals, from 26 December 1950, mapped dozens of Chinese mass graves, including at Gondang-Gowar (two graves, 40 victims), Wedekan (three graves, 50 victims), Bingungan (one grave, 17 victims), Ngangkatan (one grave, one victim), Sumberkepuh (eight graves, 16 victims), Sambong (12 graves, 30 victims), Jambe (three graves, 43 victims), Ngrongot (one grave, 22 victims), Kelurahan (one grave, nine victims), Desa Ketandan (one grave, two victims),

---

59 'Pemakaman Kembali Korban-Korban Tionghoa [Reburial of Chinese Victims]', *Sin Po*, [Jakarta], 20 May 1950.

Logawe (one grave, four victims) and a grave containing nine victims in a place identified by the newspaper only as a 'subdistrict' (*kelurahan*)—likely a proofreading error. Just like in Magelang, most of the corpses had been buried carelessly and were in horrendous conditions, which showed that they had been subjected to severe torture before being executed.[60]

The Committee for Relocating the Graves of the Chinese Victims in Nganjuk was established to manage the funeral arrangements for the victims. It coordinated fundraising and organised the victims' funeral procession. On 26 August 1951, a funeral procession for the victims was conducted at a Chinese cemetery in Manyung Village. More than 600 corpses were reburied in a single pit. The search for victims continued, and CHTH Nganjuk discovered dozens of additional bodies from Senggowar, Gondang, Lengkong, Cabean Village, Sambong Village (Warujayeng) and other villages. These were then buried alongside hundreds of others in the same hole.[61] Figure 8.3 shows this mass grave in Manyung, Nganjuk, where more than 700 Chinese were buried together. The two marble reliefs on the left bear the names of the victims in Indonesian, while the marble on the right is written in Chinese.

Meanwhile, in Wonosobo in 1951, after the violence ceased, CHTH Wonosobo established a group called the Corpse Excavation Committee (Panitia Penggalian Majat) to exhume the victims' bodies. Ten corpses were discovered in Bojong Village (Kepel), all of which belonged to Tio Eng Tiauw's family. Meanwhile, the group also found 18 victims in Lempuyang Village (Kalikajar); all 16 victims in Sapuran were relatives of Ong Mo An. On 14 January 1951, a funeral was conducted in Jelegang, Pagerkukuh, and was preceded by a prayer at the CHTH Wonosobo building. The funeral for 154 people, whose remains were put in 25 coffins, was attended by more than 1,000 people.[62] Tombstones from this mass grave (see Figure 8.4) list the names and ages of the victims at the time of their execution. The youngest victim listed on the tombstones is a one-year-old baby named Tjie Tjing Nio, who was executed in Sapuran alongside his parents.

---

60 'Untuk Penguburan Korban2 Tionghoa di Ngandjuk [For the Burial of Chinese Victims in Nganjuk]', *Sin Po*, [Jakarta], 10 January 1951.
61 'Penguburan Kembali Djenazah Tionghoa [Reburial of Chinese Corpses]', *Sin Po*, [Jakarta], 11 August 1951; 'Pemakaman Djinazah Korban2 Tionghoa di Ngandjuk [Burial of Chinese Victims in Nganjuk]', *Sin Po*, [Jakarta], 13 August 1951.
62 The Kertek area had the highest number of victims (110 people), followed by Sapuran (27), Semayu (11), Kaliwiro (3), Wonosobo (2) and Kejajar (1). See 'Korban2 Clash Kedua Di Daerah Wonosobo [Victims of the Second Clash in the Wonosobo Area]', *Sin Po*, [Jakarta], 30 December 1950; 'Penguburan Djenasah Korban2 Clash II [Burial of Victims of the Second Clash]', *Sin Po*, [Jakarta], 27 January 1951.

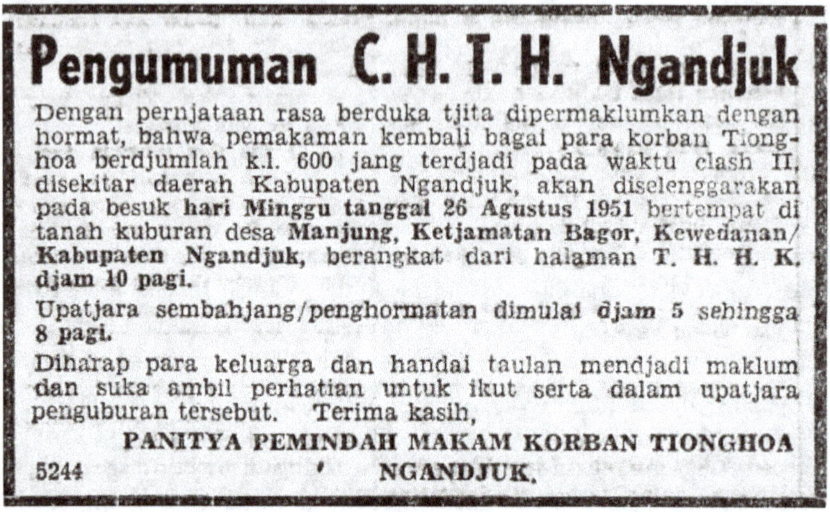

Pengumuman C.H.T.H. Ngandjuk

Dengan pernjataan rasa berduka tjita dipermaklumkan dengan hormat, bahwa pemakaman kembali bagai para korban Tionghoa berdjumlah k.l. 600 jang terdjadi pada waktu clash II, disekitar daerah Kabupaten Ngandjuk, akan diselenggarakan pada besuk **hari Minggu tanggal 26 Agustus 1951** bertempat di tanah kuburan desa **Manjung, Ketjamatan Bagor, Kewedanan/ Kabupaten Ngandjuk**, berangkat dari halaman T. H. H. K. djam 10 pagi.

Upatjara sembahjang/penghormatan dimulai djam 5 sehingga 8 pagi.

Diharap para keluarga dan handai taulan mendjadi maklum dan suka ambil perhatian untuk ikut serta dalam upatjara penguburan tersebut. Terima kasih,

PANITYA PEMINDAH MAKAM KORBAN TIONGHOA

5244 NGANDJUK.

Figure 8.2 An announcement in *Sin Po* made by CHTH Nganjuk on 26 August 1951 regarding the reburial of Chinese victims in Manyung Village

Source: *Sin Po*, 18 August 1951.

Figure 8.3 A Chinese mass grave in Manyung, Nganjuk
Source: Ravando.

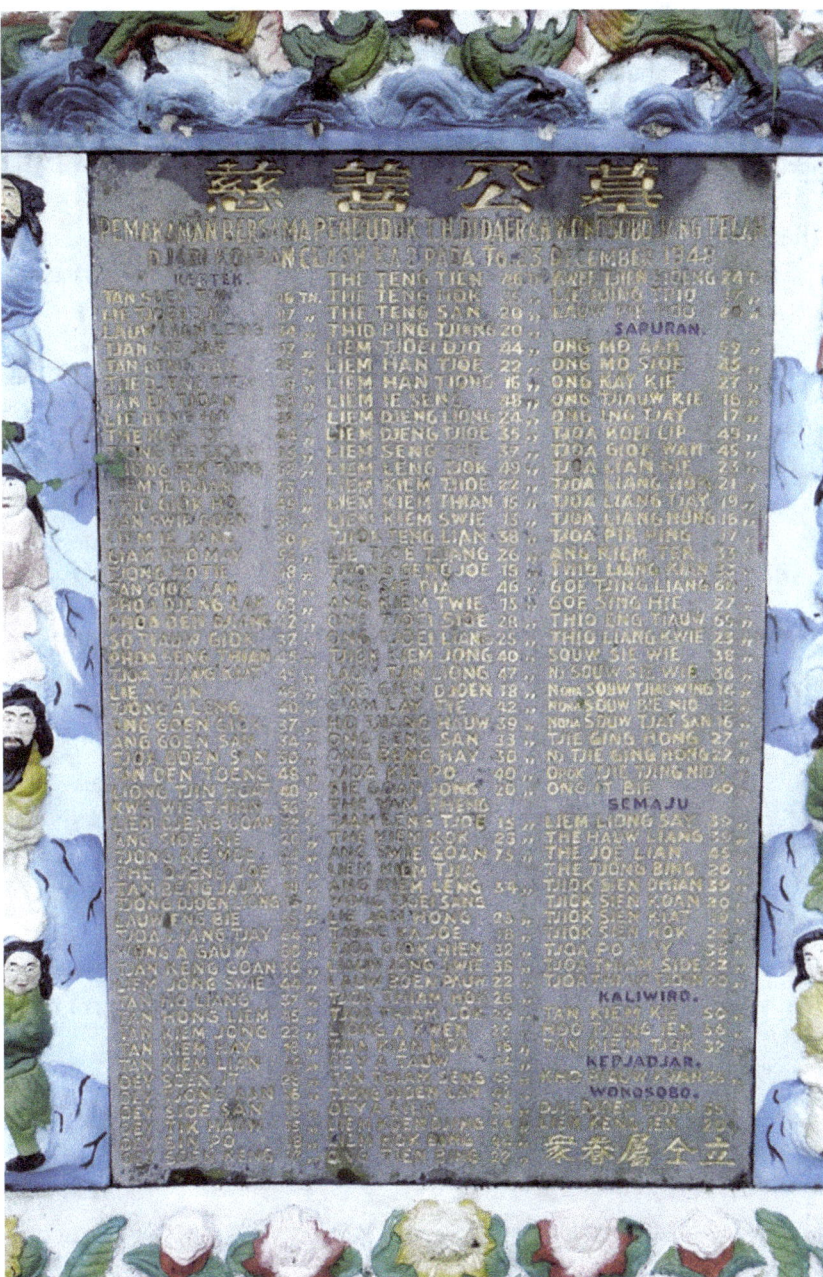

Figure 8.4 Inscribed tombstones from the Chinese mass grave in Bojong Village, Wonosobo

Source: Ravando.

In most areas, exhumations could only be carried out within a few years of the executions. On 30 September 1951, for instance, a reburial ceremony was conducted for the bodies of approximately 170 Chinese who had been slaughtered in Maja during the First Dutch Military Aggression. They were buried in a mass grave in Bandung's Cikadut cemetery at the initiative of Hua Chiao Lien Ho Hui, one of the largest Chinese organisations in West Java.[63] The tombstones on this mass grave, however, indicate the date 1 December 1952. Thus, it was highly probable that another reburial process was carried out after the discovery of new bodies.

It is also highly probable that the Chinese mass grave in Yogyakarta is the only one that contains victims from other ethnic groups. On 2 August 1953, the victims of the Yogyakarta atrocity were reburied in a mass pit in Pingit. In addition to dozens of Chinese victims, there were reburials of the aforementioned Indo-Dutch man, M.J. Thomas, and the Swiss R.O. Long and his wife and children. As a marker for the grave, a monument bearing the names of the victims stands tall.

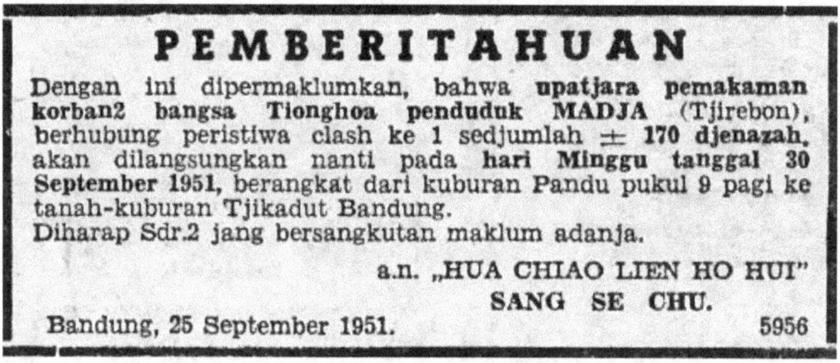

PEMBERITAHUAN

Dengan ini dipermaklumkan, bahwa **upatjara pemakaman korban2 bangsa Tionghoa penduduk MADJA** (Tjirebon), berhubung peristiwa clash ke 1 sedjumlah ± 170 djenazah, akan dilangsungkan nanti pada **hari Minggu tanggal 30 September 1951**, berangkat dari kuburan Pandu pukul 9 pagi ke tanah-kuburan Tjikadut Bandung.
Diharap Sdr.2 jang bersangkutan maklum adanja.

a.n. „HUA CHIAO LIEN HO HUI"
SANG SE CHU.

Bandung, 25 September 1951.   5956

Figure 8.5 A notice in *Sin Po* announcing the reburial of the bodies of the Chinese massacred in Maja
Source: *Sin Po*, 25 September 1951.

---

63   'Pemberitahuan [Announcement]', *Sin Po*, [Jakarta], 25 September 1951.

Figure 8.6 The mass grave of Chinese massacre victims in Maja
Source: Sugiri Kustedja.

Figure 8.7 The Yogyakarta Chinese mass grave in the Pingit area, Bumijo
Source: F.X. Harsono.

After the 1965 tragedy and the rise of the Suharto regime, this grave visiting tradition stopped. All Chinese institutions were shut by force, and the Chinese language and characters were also deemed 'threatening' (*berbahaya*) and were thus prohibited. Such discriminatory state regulations were tightened by also prohibiting the practice of Chinese customs and beliefs. Members of the Chinese community were compelled to assimilate by adopting Indonesian names.[64]

The Chinese community was terrified by this tumultuous political atmosphere. During this period, they no longer had the courage to make pilgrimages to the mass graves from the revolutionary period, which had been an annual occurrence. Visits were resumed, however, after the collapse of the Suharto regime in 1998. The families of the Wonosobo victims, for instance, gather every year to clean the grave collectively and console one another. This gathering typically occurs on *Ching Ming* ('Tomb-Sweeping Day'), which is the time when all Chinese graves are cleaned.

---

64 Leo Suryadinata, 'Indonesian Policies Toward the Chinese Minority Under the New Order', *Asian Survey* 16, no. 8 (1976): 770–87, doi.org/10.2307/2643578, at 776–82.

Figure 8.8 The vandalised Chinese mass grave in Grogolan Village, Pekalongan
Source: F.X. Harsono.

In addition to the mass graves we have already discussed, Harsono has located Chinese mass graves in Caruban (69 victims), Purwokerto (78 victims), Tulungagung (73 victims), Pare (68 victims) and Kediri (300 victims). However, there are still many mass graves of Chinese individuals the location of which remains unknown. In the name of 'development' (*pembangunan*), some of these graves have been destroyed or vandalised irreparably. In Grogolan Village (Pekalongan), for instance, not only is the grave covered with bushes, but also it has been vandalised and the tombstone stolen, making it difficult to identify. The absence of a plaque also conceals the fact that the site is a Chinese mass grave.

A similar situation occurred in Malang, where to the time of writing, we have not been able to locate the mass graves that existed in the Kutobedah area. In 1951, it was reported that eight individuals had vandalised this mass grave, even removing the headstone and additional marble from it.[65] Rumours circulated that this mass grave had been destroyed by building projects and the remains relocated to Sentong, Lawang. Our investigation of the area was fruitless.

---

65   See 'Graven Geschonden [Graves Violated]', *De Vrije Pers* [*The Free Press*], 12 March 1951; 'Niets Meer Heilig [Nothing Is Sacred Anymore]', *De Nieuwsgier* [*The Curious*], [Jakarta], 14 March 1951.

Conclusion

This chapter has demonstrated that Chinese mass graves are more than just a final resting place for victims; they also serve as an integral component of the local landscape. Rather than being merely a pile of stones, these mass graves are a crucial starting point for unearthing and reconstructing information about the violence against ethnic Chinese during the Indonesian war of independence—a period that has always been glorified as a conflict between the Dutch and Indonesia, with little effort to elaborate on the various atrocities committed against minority groups such as the Chinese, Indo-Europeans and Ambonese.

The process of exhumation and reburial of the remains of Chinese victims, which was carried out in various areas throughout the 1950s, was crucial to the project of reconstructing what occurred, as it became an indirect source for deconstructing, rethinking and identifying the root causes of discrimination against ethnic Chinese in Indonesia. Moreover, by revisiting the roots of discrimination against ethnic Chinese during the colonial period, we learn that prejudice against this group was a recurring phenomenon, and the end of Dutch colonialism did not instantaneously eradicate this sentiment. Powerful actors have used these embedded anti-Chinese sentiments for their own interests, particularly during moments of political crisis.

This study has revealed that the Indonesian war of independence was marked not only by discrimination, but also by the inability of the governing authorities to protect vulnerable minority groups, impunity and forgetfulness about the series of violent atrocities during that period. After the transfer of sovereignty from the Netherlands to the Republic of Indonesia on 27 December 1949, the government of the republic never attempted to resolve the animosity between militia, Chinese Indonesians and their neighbours of other ethnicities. Most of the perpetrators of this violence were never brought to justice. It was believed that some occupied strategic positions within the post-independence government. The hostility between ethnic groups was allowed to fester, becoming a ticking time bomb that could detonate at any moment.

References

Primary sources

Central Intelligence Agency (CIA). 1950. 'Indonesian Newspapers.' General CIA Records, CIA-RDP79T01049A000200020010-3, Publication date: 27 April 1950, Document release date: 4 January 2000. Langley: Central Intelligence Agency.

De Nieuwsgier. 1951. 'Niets Meer Heilig [Nothing Is Sacred Anymore].' *De Nieuwsgier* [*The Curious*], [Jakarta], 14 March.

De Vrije Pers. 1951. 'Graven Geschonden [Graves Violated].' *De Vrije Pers* [*The Free Press*], 12 March.

Kwee, Kek Beng. 1948. *Doea Poeloe Lima Tahon Sebagi Wartawan* [*Twenty-Five Years as a Journalist*]. Jakarta: Kuo.

Kwee, Tek Hoay. 1937. 'Atsal Moelanja Timboel Pergerakan Tionghoa jang Modern di Indonesia [The Origins of the Modern Chinese Movement in Indonesia].' *Moestika Romans*, February.

Memorandum Outlining Acts of Violence and Inhumanity Perpetrated by Indonesian Bands on Innocent Chinese Before and After the Dutch Police Action was Enforced on July 21, 1947. 1947. Jakarta: Zhonghua Zong Hui.

Netherlands Forces Intelligence Service/Central Military Intelligence Service (NEFIS/CMI). 1942–49. 'Moorden door de TNI Troepen Gepleegd op Chinese Ingezetenen te Malang [Murders Committed by TNI Troops on Chinese Residents in Malang].' NEFIS/CMI [Netherlands Forces Intelligence Service/Central Military Intelligence Service], 1942–1949, Inv. no. 02022. The Hague: Archief van het Ministerie van Buitenlandse Zaken [Archives of the Ministry of Foreign Affairs].

NEFIS/CMI. 1942–49. 'Verklaring [Declaration].' NEFIS/CMI [Netherlands Forces Intelligence Service/Central Military Intelligence Service], 1942–1949, Inv. no. 02022. The Hague: Archief van het Ministerie van Buitenlandse Zaken [Archives of the Ministry of Foreign Affairs].

Sin Po. 1923. 'Memake Doea Timbangan [Using Two Scales].' *Sin Po: Oost-Java Editie* [East Java edition], 23 January.

Sin Po. 1923. 'Diborgol [Handcuffed].' *Sin Po*, [East Java edition], 25 January.

Sin Po. 1924. 'Apa Sebab Tida Dibekoek [Why Was It Not Prevented]?' *Sin Po*, [West Java edition], 12 July.

Sin Po. 1945. 'Koendjoengan pada Medan Pertempoeran Soerabaja (I) [Visit to the Surabaya Battlefield (I)].' *Sin Po*, [Jakarta], 3 December.

Sin Po. 1945. 'Koendjoengan pada Medan Pertempoeran Soerabaja (II) [Visit to the Surabaya Battlefield (II)].' *Sin Po*, [Jakarta], 4 December.

Sin Po. 1946. 'Pendoedoekan Bandoeng Selatan Soeda Seleseh Dilakoeken: Karoegian Sanget Besar Dari Pendoedoek Tionghoa [The Occupation of South Bandoeng Has Been Completed: Huge Losses for the Chinese Residents].' *Sin Po*, [Jakarta], 27 March.

Sin Po. 1946. 'Hoakiauw di Sumatra [Chinese in Sumatra].' *Sin Po*, [Jakarta], 22 April.

Sin Po. 1946. 'Banjak Orang Tionghoa dari Padang Mengoengsi ka Laen Tempat Lantaran Keadahan Semingkin Genting [Many Chinese from Padang Fled to Other Places Due to Increasing Tension].' *Sin Po*, [Jakarta], 16 August.

Sin Po. 1946. 'Indonesia Kaja Partij [Indonesia is Rich with Political Parties].' *Sin Po*, [Jakarta], 25 September.

Sin Po. 1946. 'Kasengsarahan dan Kamelaratan di Bagan Siapi-Api [Suffering and Hardship in Bagansiapiapi].' *Sin Po*, [Jakarta], 8 November.

Sin Po. 1947. 'Pembakaran, Perampokan dan Pemboenoean di Lawang [Arson, Robbery and Murder in Lawang].' *Sin Po*, [Jakarta], 26 July.

Sin Po. 1947. 'Merdeka [Freedom].' *Sin Po*, [Jakarta], 29 July.

Sin Po. 1947. 'Pembakaran dan Perampokan di Singosari [Arson and Robbery in Singosari].' *Sin Po*, [Jakarta], 31 July.

Sin Po. 1947. 'Malang Sasoeda Dibikin Antjoer [Malang After Being Destroyed].' *Sin Po*, [Jakarta], 6 August.

Sin Po. 1947. 'Boemiajoe Mendjadi Boemiangoes [Bumiayu Becomes Scorched Earth].' *Sin Po*, [Jakarta], 21 August.

Sin Po. 1947. 'Kakedjeman Terhadap Bangsa Tionghoa [Cruelty Towards the Chinese People].' *Sin Po*, [Jakarta], 25 August.

Sin Po. 1947. '36 Hari Dalem Sarangnja Kaoem Extremist [Thirty-Six Days in the Extremists' Nest].' *Sin Po*, [Jakarta], 5 September.

Sin Po. 1947. '23 Orang Tionghoa Disembeleh di Soerdjo dan Bawang [Twenty-Three Chinese Slaughtered in Surjo and Bawang].' *Sin Po*, [Jakarta], 15 September.

Sin Po. 1947. 'Korban Pemboenoehan, Pembakaran dan Perampokan dari Hoakiauw di Indramajoe [Victims of Murder, Arson and Robbery of Chinese in Indramajoe].' *Sin Po*, [Jakarta], 19 September.

Sin Po. 1947. '1178 Kiaopao Kita jang Ditoeloeng [1,178 Fellow Chinese People Assisted].' *Sin Po*, [Jakarta], 19 November.

Sin Po. 1948. 'Kandasnja Pembitjarahan [Negotiations Fail].' *Sin Po*, [Jakarta], 9 December.

Sin Po. 1948. 'Solo, Tjepoe dan Laen-Laen Djato [Solo, Cepu and Other Areas Fall].' *Sin Po*, [Jakarta], 22 December.

Sin Po. 1949. 'Pendoedoek Tionghoa di Kertek Diboenoeh [Chinese Residents in Kertek Killed]!' *Sin Po*, [Jakarta], 11 January.

Sin Po. 1949. 'Pemboenoehan Besar-Besaran di Redjoso [Mass Murder in Rejoso].' *Sin Po*, [Jakarta], 25 January.

Sin Po. 1949. 'Pemboenoehan Setjara Besar-Besaran di Desa Groso [Mass Murder in the Groso Village].' *Sin Po*, [Jakarta], 1 February.

Sin Po. 1949. 'Ratoesan Pendoedoek Tionghoa Dikoempoel dan Dibakar [Hundreds of Chinese Residents Are Rounded Up and Burnt].' *Sin Po*, [Jakarta], 1 February.

Sin Po. 1949. 'Hoakiauw di Daerah Pendoedoekan Baroe [Chinese in New Settlement Area].' *Sin Po*, [Jakarta], 12 February.

Sin Po. 1949. 'Kombali ka Djeman Kenpeitai [Return to the Kempeitai Era].' *Sin Po*, [Jakarta], 21 February.

Sin Po. 1949. 'Kegelisahan Dalem Masjarakat Tionghoa Memoentjak [Anxiety in the Chinese Community is Peaking].' *Sin Po*, [Jakarta], 21 October.

Sin Po. 1949. 'Wonogiri dan Patjitan [Wonogiri and Pacitan].' *Sin Po*, [Jakarta], 21 October.

Sin Po. 1949. 'Sesoedah Dirampok, Diboenoeh [After Being Robbed, Killed].' *Sin Po*, [Jakarta], 15 November.

Sin Po. 1950. 'Pemakaman Tongpao Korban-Korban Blabak [Burial of Chinese Compatriots in Blabak].' *Sin Po*, [Jakarta], 6 April.

Sin Po. 1950. 'Pemakaman Kembali Korban-Korban Tionghoa [Reburial of Chinese Victims].' *Sin Po*, [Jakarta], 20 May.

Sin Po. 1950. 'Korban2 Clash Kedua Di Daerah Wonosobo [Victims of the Second Clash in the Wonosobo Area].' *Sin Po*, [Jakarta], 30 December.

Sin Po. 1951. 'Untuk Penguburan Korban2 Tionghoa di Ngandjuk [For the Burial of Chinese Victims in Nganjuk].' *Sin Po*, [Jakarta], 10 January.

Sin Po. 1951. 'Penguburan Djenasah Korban2 Clash II [Burial of Victims of the Second Clash].' *Sin Po*, [Jakarta], 27 January.

Sin Po. 1951. 'Penguburan Kembali Djenazah Tionghoa [Reburial of Chinese Corpses].' *Sin Po*, [Jakarta], 11 August.

Sin Po. 1951. 'Pemakaman Djinazah Korban2 Tionghoa di Ngandjuk [Burial of Chinese Victims in Nganjuk].' *Sin Po*, [Jakarta], 13 August.

Sin Po. 1951. 'Pemberitahuan [Announcement].' *Sin Po*, [Jakarta], 25 September.

Sin Po. 1951. 'Pemakaman Djenazah Korban2 Tionghoa di Blitar [Burial of Chinese Victims in Blitar].' *Sin Po*, [Jakarta], 3 December.

Sin Po. 1951. 'Pemakaman Kembali Para Korban Tionghoa di Blitar [Reburial of Chinese Victims in Blitar].' *Sin Po*, [Jakarta], 13 December.

Staatsblad van Nederlandsch-Indie [*Official Gazette of the Netherlands Indies*]. 1919. No. 622.

Star Weekly. [Jakarta]. 9 June 1946.

Secondary sources

Anderson, Benedict. 1998. *The Spectre of Comparison: Nationalism, Southeast Asia and the World*. London: Verso.

Berdoeri, Tjamboek [Kwee Thiam Tjing]. 2004. *Indonesia dalem Api dan Bara* [*Indonesia in Flames and Embers*]. Jakarta: Elkasa.

Bouwsma, Elly-Touwen, and Petra Groen. 1996. *Tussen Banzai en Bersiap: De Afwikkeling van de Tweede Wereldoorlog in Nederlands-Indië* [*Between Banzai and Bersiap: The Settlement of the Second World War in the Netherlands Indies*]. The Hague: SDU Publishers.

Bussemaker, Herman. 2005. *Bersiap! Opstand in het Paradijs: de Bersiap-periode op Java en Sumatra 1945–1946* [*Bersiap! Revolt in Paradise: The Bersiap Period on Java and Sumatra 1945–1946*]. Zuthpen: Walburg Pers.

Butcher, John, and Howard Dick, eds. 1993. *The Rise and Fall of Revenue Farming: Business Elites and the Emergence of the Modern State in Southeast Asia*. London: Macmillan. doi.org/10.1007/978-1-349-22877-5.

Captain, Esther, and Onno Sinke. 2022. *Het Geluid van Geweld: Bersiap en de Dynamiek van Geweld tijdens de Eerste Fase van de Indonesische Revolutie, 1945–1946* [*The Sound of Violence: Bersiap and Dynamics of Violence during the First Phase of the Indonesian Revolution, 1945–1946*]. Amsterdam: Amsterdam University Press.

Cribb, Robert. 1991. *Gangsters and Revolutionaries: The Jakarta People's Militia and the Indonesian Revolution, 1945–1949*. Sydney: ASAA.

Cribb, Robert. 2000. *Historical Atlas of Indonesia*. Copenhagen: NIAS Press. doi.org/10.4324/9780203824610.

Cribb, Robert. 2008. 'The Brief Genocide of Eurasians in Indonesia, 1945/46.' In *Empire, Colony, Genocide: Conquest, Occupation and Subaltern Resistance in World History*, edited by Dirk Moses, 424–39. New York: Berghahn Books. doi.org/10.1515/9781782382140-019.

Cribb, Robert. 2010. *Digital Atlas of Indonesian History*. Copenhagen: NIAS Press.

Heidhues, Mary Somers. 2012. 'Anti-Chinese Violence in Java during the Indonesian Revolution, 1945–49.' *Journal of Genocide Research* 14, nos 3–4: 381–401. doi.org/10.1080/14623528.2012.719371.

Kahin, George McTurnan. 2003. *Nationalism and Revolution in Indonesia*. Ithaca: Southeast Asia Program Publications, Cornell University.

Kartodirdjo, Sartono. 1981. 'Wajah Revolusi Indonesia Dipandang dari Perspektivisme Struktural [The Nature of the Revolution from a Structural Perspective].' *Prisma* X, no. 8 (August): 3–13.

Kwartanada, Didi. 1997. 'Kolaborasi dan Resinifikasi: Komunitas Cina Kota Yogyakarta pada Jaman Jepang, 1942–1945 [Collaboration and Re-Sinification: The Chinese Community of Yogyakarta during the Japanese Era, 1942–45].' Undergraduate thesis, Universitas Gadjah Mada, Yogyakarta.

Lohanda, Mona. 1996. *The Kapitan Cina of Batavia, 1837–1942: A History of Chinese Establishment in Colonial Society*. Jakarta: Djambatan.

Lohanda, Mona. 2002. *Growing Pains: The Chinese and the Dutch in Colonial Java, 1890–1942*. Jakarta: Yayasan Cipta Loka Caraka.

Pratiwi, Geza Surya. 2022. 'Kekerasan Terhadap Golongan Tionghoa pada Masa Revolusi di Malang, 1945–1949 [Violence Against the Chinese during the Revolution in Malang, 1945–49].' *Lembaran Sejarah* [*History Gazette*] 18, no. 1: 78–94. doi.org/10.22146/lembaran-sejarah.80455.

Purcell, Victor. 1966. *The Chinese in Southeast Asia*. Oxford: Oxford University Press.

Ravando. 2014. 'Now is the Time to Kill All Chinese: Social Revolution and the Massacre of Chinese in Tangerang, 1945–1946.' Master's thesis, Leiden University, Netherlands.

Scheltema, Johann-Friedrich. 1903. *De Opiumpolitiek der Regeering en de Vrijheid der Drukpers in Nederlandsch-Indie* [*The Opium Policy of the Government and Freedom of the Press in the Netherlands Indies*]. The Hague: W.P. van Stockum en Zoon.

Soejatno, and Benedict Anderson. 1974. 'Revolution and Social Tensions in Surakarta 1945–1950.' *Indonesia*, no. 17 (April): 99–111. doi.org/10.2307/3350775.

Suryadinata, Leo. 1976. 'Indonesian Policies Toward the Chinese Minority Under the New Order.' *Asian Survey* 16, no. 8: 770–87. doi.org/10.2307/2643578.

Suryadinata, Leo. 2005. 'Anti-Chinese Actions in Southeast Asia: In Search of Causes and Solutions.' In *Violent Internal Conflicts in Asia Pacific: Histories, Political Economies and Policies*, edited by Dewi Fortuna Anwar, 151–62. Jakarta: Yayasan Obor Indonesia.

Twang Peck Yang. 1998. *The Chinese Business Elite in Indonesia and the Transition to Independence, 1940–1950*. Kuala Lumpur: Oxford University Press.

van Delden, Mary C. 1989. *Bersiap in Bandoeng: Een Onderzoek naar Geweld in de Periode van 17 Augustus 1945 tot 24 Maart 1946* [*Bersiap in Bandung: Research into Violence in the Period from 17 August 1945 to 24 March 1946*]. Kockengen: van Delden.

Vickers, Adrian. 2005. *A History of Modern Indonesia*. Cambridge: Cambridge University Press. doi.org/10.1017/CBO9780511801020.

Williams, Lea E. 1961. 'The Ethical Program and the Chinese of Indonesia.' *Journal of Southeast Asian History* 2, no. 2: 35–42.

Zhou, Taomo. 2019. *Migration in the Time of Revolution: China, Indonesia, and the Cold War*. Ithaca: Cornell University Press. doi.org/10.1515/9781501739941.

Part 2.
Colonial legacies: The persistence of and attempts to dismantle coloniality

9

Beyond the point of no return: The re-emergence of Indonesian debates about concepts of the return of cultural objects

Sadiah Boonstra

Introduction

The shift towards systemic and structural criticism as represented by decolonial and anti-racist paradigms includes worldwide calls to decolonise the museum. These calls have fuelled demands for the return of cultural objects acquired in colonial situations and held in museum collections around the world, especially, but not limited to, looted objects. Formerly colonised peoples no longer accept the historical injustices and ongoing inequalities created by colonialism that continue to be reflected in museum collections and exhibitions. Indonesians, for example, are thinking more critically about the display and place of Indonesian objects in museum collections in the Netherlands. The topic is also receiving increasing scholarly attention to the extent that there now exists an extensive body of research that has meticulously mapped the historical development of the political discourse on restitution of cultural objects from the Netherlands to Indonesia.[1]

Early work in this field was published at the start of the 2000s but debates really gained momentum from the mid-2010s. The findings of the 2020 Dutch report *Guidance on the Way Forward for Colonial Collections: Colonial Collection—A Recognition of Injustice*[2] were implemented on 15 July 2022[3] and led to the appointment of an advisory committee to the Dutch Government on the return of cultural objects from colonial contexts.[4] In Indonesia,

---

1   Susan Legêne and Els Postel-Coster, 'Isn't It All Culture? Culture and Dutch Development Policy in the Post-Colonial Period', in *Fifty Years of Dutch Development Cooperation, 1949–1999*, eds Peter Malcontent and Jans Nekker (The Hague: SDU Publishing, 2000), 271–88; Jos van Beurden, *The Return of Cultural and Historical Treasures: The Case of the Netherlands* (Amsterdam: KIT Publishers, 2012); Jos van Beurden, *Treasures in Trusted Hands: Negotiating the Future of Colonial Cultural Objects* (Leiden: Sidestone Press, 2017); Jos van Beurden, 'Returns by the Netherlands to Indonesia in the 2010s and the 1970s', in *Returning Southeast Asia's Past: Objects, Museums, and Restitution*, eds Louise Tythacott and Panggah Ardiyansyah (Singapore: NUS Press, 2021), 187–209, doi.org/10.2307/j.ctv1r4xctd.13; Cynthia Scott, *Cultural Diplomacy and the Heritage of Empire: Negotiating Postcolonial Returns* (New York: Routledge, 2020); Cynthia Scott, 'Renewing the "Special Relationship" and Rethinking the Return of Cultural Property: The Netherlands and Indonesia, 1949–79', *Journal of Contemporary History* 52, no. 3 (2017): 646–68, doi.org/10.1177/0022009416658698; Cynthia Scott, 'Sharing the Divisions of the Colonial Past: An Assessment of the Netherlands–Indonesia Shared Cultural Heritage Project, 2003–2006', *International Journal of Heritage Studies* 20, no. 2 (2012): 181–95, doi.org/10.1080/13527258.2012.73 8239; Cynthia Scott, 'Negotiating the Colonial Past in the Age of European Decolonization: Cultural Property Return between the Netherlands and Indonesia' (PhD diss., Claremont Graduate University, California, 2014); Marieke Bloembergen and Martijn Eickhoff, 'Exchange and the Protection of Java's Antiquities: A Transnational Approach to the Problem of Heritage in Colonial Java', *The Journal of Asian Studies* 72, no. 4 (2013): 893–916, doi.org/10.1017/S0021911813001599; Hari Budiarti, 'The Sulawesi Collections: Missionaries, Chiefs and Military Expeditions', in *The Discovery of the Past*, eds Endang Sri Hardiati and Pieter ter Keurs (Amsterdam: KIT Publishers, 2006), 160–72; Caroline Drieënhuizen, 'Mirrors of Time and Agents of Action: Indonesia's Claimed Cultural Objects and Decolonisation, 1947–1978', *BMGN* 133, no. 2 (2018): 79–90, doi.org/10.18352/bmgn-lchr.10552; Panggah Ardiyansyah, 'Restitution and National Heritage: (Art) Historical Trajectories of Raden Saleh's Paintings', in *Returning Southeast Asia's Past: Objects, Museums, and Restitution*, eds Louise Tythacott and Panggah Ardiyansyah (Singapore: NUS Press, 2021), 163–86, doi.org/10.2307/j.ctv1r4xctd.12; Wieske Sapardan, 'The Return of Cultural Property and National Identity in Postcolonial Indonesia', in *Returning Southeast Asia's Past: Objects, Museums, and Restitution*, eds Louise Tythacott and Panggah Ardiyansyah (Singapore: NUS Press, 2021), 213–34, doi.org/10.2307/j.ctv1r4xctd.14.
2   Advisory Committee on the National Policy Framework for Colonial Collections, *Guidance on the Way Forward for Colonial Collections: Colonial Collection—A Recognition of Injustice* (The Hague: Council for Culture, 2020), www.raadvoorcultuur.nl/documenten/adviezen/2021/01/22/colonial-collection-and-a-recognition-of-injustice.
3   House of Representatives of the States General, 'Brief van de Staatssecretaris van Onderwijs, Cultuur en Wetenschap: Nieuwe Visie Cultuurbeleid [Letter from the State Secretary of Education, Culture and Science: New Cultural Policy Vision]', *Kamerstuk* [*Parliamentary Paper*], Session Year 2021–2022, 32820, No. 480, 29 July 2022, zoek.officielebekendmakingen.nl/kst-32820-480.html.
4   Government of the Netherlands, 'Benoeming Leden Adviescommissie Teruggave Cultuurgoederen uit Koloniale Context [Appointment of Members of the Advisory Committee on the Return of Cultural Objects from a Colonial Context]', News release (The Hague, 17 November).

the Committee for the Repatriation of Collections from Indonesia in the Netherlands (Tim Repatriasi Koleksi Asal Indonesia di Belanda) was set up in 2021 to advise the government on object repatriation.⁵ In 2024 a Dutch report, *Omgaan met Gedeelde Bronnen van het Koloniale Verleden* (*Dealing with Shared Sources of the Colonial Past*),⁶ advised conditional return of archival materials to source countries on a case-by-case basis.

While discussions about object return and provenance research have recently gained momentum,⁷ the history of return in the context of Indonesia can be traced back to the colonial period. As such, and as set out in Chapter 1 of this volume, these discussions can be understood as an ongoing process of decolonisation, which will be discussed below.⁸ Within this longer history, the Draft Cultural Agreement developed during the Dutch–Indonesian Round Table Conference (RTC; or Konferensi Meja Bundar) held in The Hague in 1949 is generally regarded as a turning point in the discourse of restitution. Legêne and Postel-Coster, van Beurden and Scott refer to Clause 19 of this agreement as evidence that restitution matters were already on the political agenda during the RTC negotiations. Clause 19 states:

> Objects of cultural value, originating from Indonesia and which otherwise than by transfer of private law have come in the possession of the Netherlands Government or of the former Netherlands-Indies Government, shall be transferred to the Government of R.I.S. [Republik Indonesia Serikat, United States of Indonesia] in result of the transfer of sovereignty from the Kingdom of the Netherlands to the R.I.S.
>
> For the effectuation of the provision in the first paragraph, the joint Committee shall propose on the footing of article 5 a separate regulation, in which provisions shall be included concerning

---

5   'Keputusan Menteri Pendidikan dan Kebudayaan Nomor 18/P/2021, 24 Februari 2021 [Decree of the Minister of Education and Culture Number 18/P/2021, 24 February 2021]', [Electronic copy seen by the author].
6   Council for Culture, *Omgaan met Gedeelde Bronnen van het Koloniale Verleden. Advies voor Herstel en Restitutie in Relatie tot Koloniale Archiven* [*Dealing with Shared Sources of the Colonial Past. Advice on Recovery and Restitution in Relation to Colonial Archives*] (The Hague: Council for Culture, 2024), www.raadvoorcultuur.nl/documenten/adviezen/2024/03/25/omgang-met-gedeelde-bronnen-van-het-koloniale-verleden.
7   Between 2019 and 2022, the Netherlands Institute for War, Holocaust and Genocide Studies and its in-house Expert Centre Restitution led a joint initiative with the Rijksmuseum Amsterdam and the National Museum of World Cultures called the Pilot Project Provenance Research on Objects of the Colonial Era, which aimed to develop a research methodology for determining the provenance of colonial collections to advise policymakers in the Netherlands.
8   van Beurden, *Treasures in Trusted Hands*, 144–49; van Beurden, 'Returns by the Netherlands to Indonesia'.

a possible exchange of objects of cultural or historical value, being the property or in the possession of the one country and originating from or of importance to the other country.[9]

Legêne and Postel-Coster view the Draft Cultural Agreement as the basis for Dutch cultural policy and Dutch–Indonesian cultural relations after 1949. They point out that the Dutch Government 'had considered the idea of returning objects of particular value as a goodwill gesture to mark the transfer of sovereignty in 1949'.[10] Scott echoes this viewpoint and signals that the Dutch considered a return of cultural objects as 'spare change' in the political negotiations and an opportunity to build goodwill in the relationship with Indonesia during the RTC in 1949.[11]

Ironically, during negotiations about the return of objects, the Dutch shipped off the archives of the Netherlands Forces Intelligence Service (NEFIS) containing documents of the Indonesian Government before the signing of the sovereignty transfer agreement on 27 December 1949. The so-called Djogdja Documenten, which hold records of the Indonesian republican state institutions and leaders that the NEFIS seized during the Second Dutch Military Aggression in Yogyakarta, were sent to the National Archives of the Netherlands (Nationaal Archief, NA) in The Hague (see Karabinos and Theo's Chapter 10 in this volume).

The fact that debates about restitution of cultural objects have largely been discussed from the Dutch perspective is chiefly due to the accessibility of the NA, which contains the complete archives of the RTC. However, given the nature of the RTC—and the moment of decolonisation—in which the terms of the independence agreement were negotiated, Indonesian discourses on the return of cultural objects deserve more attention. Therefore, this chapter, in the words of Rolando Vázquez, intends to 'listen to the colonial difference'[12] by foregrounding Indonesian voices, which is

---

9   Arsip Nasional Republik Indonesia [National Archives of the Republic of Indonesia; hereinafter ANRI], *Draft Cultural Agreement between the Kingdom of the Netherlands and the Republic of the United States of Indonesia in English and Dutch*, DI 1281, Document No. GS 701/RTC, Guide Arsip Diplomasi Indonesia [Guide to Indonesian Diplomatic Archives] 1945–2009 (Jakarta: National Archives of the Republic of Indonesia, n.d.); ANRI, *Draft Cultural Agreement in Bahasa Indonesia, 28 October 1949*, DI 1281, Guide Arsip Diplomasi Indonesia [Guide to Indonesian Diplomatic Archives] 1945–2009 (Jakarta: National Archives of the Republic of Indonesia, 1949).
10 Legêne and Postel-Coster, 'Isn't It All Culture?', 274.
11 Scott, *Cultural Diplomacy and the Heritage of Empire*.
12 Rolando Vázquez, 'The Museum, Decoloniality and the End of the Contemporary', in *The Future of the New: Artistic Innovation in Times of Social Acceleration*, ed. Thijs Lijster (Amsterdam: Valiz, 2018), 181–95.

also a key theme of this volume. This chapter focuses on the development of the Draft Cultural Agreement from an Indonesian perspective over about two months during the RTC, and its finalisation on 28 October 1949. As Dutch discussions have been extensively documented, this chapter asks how Indonesian delegates discussed culture and how Clause 19 ended up in the Draft Cultural Agreement. What did the Indonesian delegates discuss in the subcommittee for cultural affairs? How was culture understood and interpreted, and how do Clause 19 and the return of cultural objects fit within this larger discussion of culture? How did Indonesian delegates' conversations and attitudes change over the course of negotiations? Zooming in on the discussions of the Indonesian side during the RTC provides a better understanding of discourses of the return of objects and how these fit into the larger context of discussions about culture.

Although it was decided that no official records would be kept of the meetings of the Cultural Committee during the RTC, the NA holds copies of this committee's reports, predominantly in Dutch and English,[13] while the UN Archives have mostly English copies. Reports primarily in Indonesian can be found in the Arsip Nasional Republik Indonesia (ANRI, National Archives of the Republic of Indonesia) in Jakarta.[14] As this chapter will show, language and translation play a crucial role in our understanding of the discussions of Clause 19 of the Draft Cultural Agreement. By examining the archives available at ANRI and the United Nations, this chapter aims to reconstruct the Indonesian debates about cultural objects before, during and after the Draft Cultural Agreement was formulated. In so doing, I seek to examine early Indonesian efforts to decolonise cultural objects and cultural rights and attempts to equalise relations between the former coloniser and the formerly colonised, while also paying attention to how ideas developed during the period of political decolonisation have evolved over time and persist today.

Colonial collection practices

The current call for the return of cultural objects can be regarded as a reaction to colonial collection practices that emerged in the mid-eighteenth century as a result of the European urge to map the world through the collection and

---

13 Rivka Baum (Researcher at NA), Email exchange, 22 June 2022.
14 I would like to thank Siti Zaenatul Umaroh and Sukiato Khurniawan for their research assistance. I would also like to thank all workshop participants and reviewers for their valuable comments.

display of objects. Colonial, ethnographic and anthropological museums attempted to understand and display the world and its inhabitants beyond Europe through a European lens. Benedict Anderson pointed to the role of the museum in empire-building in his seminal 1983 work, *Imagined Communities*.[15] Tony Bennett describes in *The Birth of the Museum* how the museum became one of the major institutions that facilitated the development of new sets of knowledge such as geology, biology, archaeology and anthropology, but also history and art history. Crucial for each of these new disciplines was the selection and ordering of objects in evolutionary sequence to map human progress and development.[16] As one of the core institutions of modernity, in addition to the university, the museum can thus be viewed as implicated in coloniality. The formation of collections, narratives and peoples presented to European audiences lay at the core of the establishment of normative cultural archives, world views and subject formations[17] that facilitated the separation of Europeans from other peoples and worlds through the process of 'othering' and the formation of ways of knowing and, as such, has become a 'cultural archive'.[18]

Through such colonial practices, large numbers of Indonesian objects were collected and shipped to Europe, especially the Netherlands (see also Isabella's Chapter 13 in this volume). These objects included but were not limited to art, religious and historical objects, jewellery, natural history objects and utensils. Human and ancestral remains also ended up in Dutch museum collections as ethnographic objects. The Tropenmuseum (Museum of the Tropics) and Museum of Ethnology (both now part of the Wereldmuseum, or World Museum), Museum Bronbeek and the Rijksmuseum hold the largest collections of cultural objects, amounting to hundreds of thousands of artefacts acquired in colonial contexts. Many smaller museums also own collections of Indonesian objects, as do private individuals.[19] Cultural objects were obtained by many different people and institutions in a multitude of ways. Pieter ter Keurs points to six different contexts in which objects were acquired: scientific expeditions, archaeological sites, individual collectors,

---

15 Benedict Anderson, *Imagined Communities: Reflections on the Origin and Spread of Nationalism* (London: Verso, 1983).
16 Tony Bennett, *The Birth of the Museum* (New York: Routledge, 1995).
17 Vázquez, 'The Museum, Decoloniality and the End of the Contemporary', 183–85.
18 Gloria Wekker, *White Innocence: Paradoxes of Colonialism and Race* (Durham: Duke University Press, 2016), doi.org/10.1515/9780822374565, 2. See also Isabella's Chapter 13 in this volume for further reflection on the coloniality of museums.
19 Advisory Committee on the National Policy Framework for Colonial Collections, *Guidance on the Way Forward for Colonial Collections*, 30.

colonial exhibitions, gifts and military expeditions. Individual collectors can subsequently be divided into subcategories, such as members of the civil service and the military, scientists, missionaries, private traders and art lovers.[20] Some objects were stolen and some came to the Netherlands as war loot or booty, were taken from temples and shrines or were 'given to' or purchased by Dutch people during collecting expeditions.[21] It is crucial to consider the fact that practices of colonial collecting took place in the context of unequal power relations. For instance, 'gifts' might in fact have been coerced from their owners and, as a result, these objects certainly differ from those that were given under equal circumstances.

Ownership, value and collection practices were already points of discussion during the colonial period in Indonesia, which in some cases led to the return of objects to their original location or owners. An early case of return is the three Ramayana reliefs of the Prambanan Temple that were returned from Siam (now Thailand) to their original location in 1926. The reliefs had come into the possession of King Chulalongkorn of Siam in 1896, after the Dutch colonial government, the Archaeological Society, local colonial civil servants and princes collaborated to gift five Buddha statues of the Borobudur Temple, four Ramayana reliefs from Prambanan and two Ganesha statues from the Singosari Temple to the king when he visited Java. Chulalongkorn, as king of independent Siam, had expressed his religious and scholarly interest in his request for the objects, which in turn became popular for Buddhist worship in Siam. In 1926, however, when indignation arose in Dutch public discourse in both the Indonesian archipelago and the Netherlands about the loss of and harm from the removal of Javanese antiquities from their original site, three of the four Prambanan reliefs were returned to the Dutch colonial government. Nonetheless, one Prambanan relief and the Borobudur statues had gained such popular status in Thailand that they remained there.[22]

Another case of return during the colonial period concerns the regalia of the Bone and Gowa kingdoms in South Sulawesi in 1931 and 1938, respectively. The museum of the Batavian Society for Art and Sciences (Bataviaasch Genootschap voor Kunsten en Wetenschappen) in Jakarta

---

20 Pieter ter Keurs, 'Introduction: Theory and Practice of Colonial Collecting', in *Colonial Collections Revisited*, ed. Pieter ter Keurs (Leiden: Leiden University Press, 2007): 1–15, at 2–3.
21 Advisory Committee on the National Policy Framework for Colonial Collections, *Guidance on the Way Forward for Colonial Collections*, 39.
22 Bloembergen and Eickhoff, 'Exchange and the Protection of Java's Antiquities', 899–904.

returned the regalia to the rulers of Bone and Gowa, who had argued that they were powerless without them.[23] These two examples of return indicate that, during the 1920s and 1930s, disputes about the ownership and value of cultural objects had begun to emerge.

Principles for a cultural future: Equality and voluntariness

A little more than a decade after the return of the Gowa regalia, the RTC began, on 23 August 1949, in The Hague. The RTC followed a tumultuous and violent period of struggle between Indonesians and the Dutch, who attempted to retake their former colony in what became known as the Indonesian revolution. The Dutch favoured and pursued a federal system that would unite the Republic of Indonesia (RI)—dominant in Java and Sumatra—with six autonomous or non-republican *negara* ('states') into the so-called United States of Indonesia (Republik Indonesia Serikat, RIS). The RIS in turn would be part of the Netherlands–Indonesian Union, after which the Dutch would formally 'transfer sovereignty' to the RIS.[24] During the RTC, the non-republican states (see Map 9.1) unified in the Dutch-sponsored Bijeenkomst voor Federaal Overleg (BFO, Federal Consultative Assembly) together with the republic started to negotiate the terms of the independence agreement with the Kingdom of the Netherlands under the supervision of the United Nations. The Dutch State and the republican government dominated the negotiations, which focused largely on political, economic and military matters, while the BFO played a relatively minor role. Even though culture was considered of minor importance to the negotiations, a subcommittee was formed to discuss cultural matters.

---

23   Budiarti, 'The Sulawesi Collections', 168–70; Hari Budiarti, 'Taking and Returning Objects in a Colonial Context: Tracing the Collections Acquired during the Bone–Gowa Military Expeditions', in *Colonial Collections Revisited*, ed. Pieter ter Keurs (Leiden: Leiden University Press, 2007), 123–44.
24   For more detailed information, see Robert Cribb, *Historical Atlas of Indonesia* (London: Routledge, 2000), doi.org/10.4324/9780203824610, 160–61.

9. BEYOND THE POINT OF NO RETURN

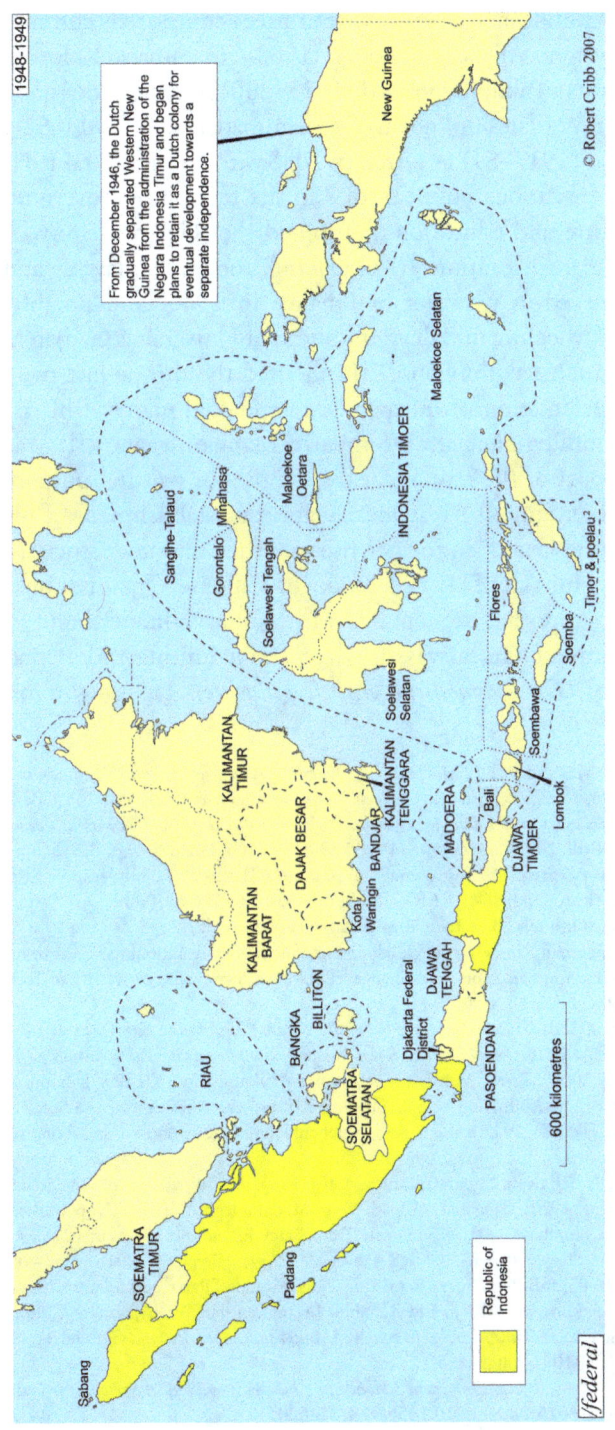

Map 9.1 Federal Indonesia, 1948–1949

Source: Robert Cribb, *Digital Atlas of Indonesian History* (Copenhagen: NIAS Press, 2010). Reproduced with permission.

The republican Cultural Committee comprised cultural and political heavyweights Ali Sastroamidjojo (1903–76), Sunarjo Kolopaking (1906–72), Susuhunan Pakubuwono XII (1925–2004), Mangkunegara VIII (1925–87), Sim Ki Ay (dates unknown), Mohammad Yamin (1903–62) and Soesilo H. Prakoso (1917–81) as secretary. Ali Sastroamidjojo, trained as a lawyer, had served in various political roles in the republican government in the field of culture and education and joined the RTC as deputy chairman of the republican delegation.[25] Kolopaking, too, was a lawyer and a sociologist, who served as Minister of Finance in 1945, and notably held the first sociology lecture in Bahasa Indonesia at Universitas Gadjah Mada in 1948.[26] Susuhunan Pakubuwono XII inherited the throne just two months before the proclamation of independence and sold many of his assets to support the republic financially.[27] Similarly, Mangkunegara VIII ceded all his assets in support of the republic, except those for cultural purposes.[28] Trained in medicine, Sim Ki Ay advocated for the establishment of higher education in Indonesia and led the newly established Chinese association Chung Hwa Tsung Hui (CHTH; Federation of Chinese Organisations in Indonesia), which supported the republic with military, financial and logistic means.[29] Mohammad Yamin was an advocate for uniting Indonesian language and identity (*De Indonesische eenheidsgedachte*). He fought for the inclusion

---

25 C.L.M. Penders, ed., *Milestones on My Journey: The Memoirs of Ali Sastroamijoyo, Indonesian Patriot and Political Leader* (Brisbane: University of Queensland Press, 1979); Tod Jones, *Culture, Power, and Authoritarianism in the Indonesian State: Cultural Policy across the Twentieth Century to the Reform Era* (Leiden: Brill, 2013), doi.org/10.1163/9789004255104; Hendi Johari, 'Kisah Sunyi Ali Sastroamidjojo [The Silent Story of Ali Sastroamidjojo]', *Historia*, [Jakarta], 11 July, historia.id/politik/articles/kisah-sunyi-ali-sastroamidjojo-P1RMO; 'Profil Ali Sastroamidjojo [Profile Ali Sastroamidjojo]', *Tirto.id*, [Jakarta], [Online], 2024, tirto.id/m/ali-sastroamidjojo-Dh.
26 Hanneman Samuel, 'The Development of Sociology in Indonesia: The Production of Knowledge, State Formation and Economic Change' (PhD diss., Swinburne University of Technology, Melbourne, 1999), 146.
27 Bram Setiadi, *Raja Di Alam Republik: Keraton Kesunanan Surakarta dan Pakubuwono XII [King in the Realm of the Republic: The Royal Palace of Surakarta and Pakubuwono XII]* (Jakarta: Bina Rena Pariwara, 2001); Petrik Matanasi, 'Penculikan Pakubuwono XII dan Dihapusnya Daerah Istimewa Surakarta [The Abduction of Pakubuwono XII and the Abolition of the Surakarta Special Region]', *Tirto.id*, [Jakarta], 29 December, tirto.id/penculikan-pakubuwono-xii-dan-dihapusnyadaerah-istimewa-surakarta-f8aC.
28 Dody Setiawan, 'Biografi Kanjeng Gusti Pangeran Adipati Aryo Mangkunegoro VIII [Biography of Kanjeng Gusti Pangeran Adipati Aryo Mangkunegoro VIII]' (Unpublished thesis, Universitas Airlangga, Surabaya, 2013); Sunarmi, 'Democracy in Indonesia Towards Mangkunegaran: The Fade of Javanese Royal Palace's Political Power', *Al-Ulum* 18, no. 1 (2018): 231–46, doi.org/10.30603/au.v18i1.285; Adi Putra Surya Wardhana, Titis Srimuda Pitana, and Susanto, 'Revivalisme Kebudayaan Jawa Mangkunegara VIII di Era Republik [Mangkunegara VIII: Javanese Cultural Revivalism in the Republic Era]', *Mudra Jurnal Seni Budaya [Mudra Journal of Arts and Culture]* 34, no. 1 (2019): 105–15, doi.org/10.31091/mudra.v34i1.568.
29 Leo Suryadinata, *Prominent Indonesian Chinese: Biographical Sketches*, 4th edn (Singapore: ISEAS Publishing, 2015), doi.org/10.1355/9789814620512.

of regional representatives within the *Volksraad* ('People's Council') and promoted collaboration between Indonesia and the Netherlands in the cultural field.[30] Notably, Sastroamidjojo and Yamin were also members of the Committee for State Administration, which dealt with matters of nationality and citizenship, as well as sovereignty. Sastroamidjojo was also a member of the Committee for Foreign Affairs and Kolopaking was on the Committee of Financial and Economic Affairs.[31] This suggests that culture was viewed in relation to the politics of state, foreign affairs and economic matters. The perspectives of these men—there were notably no women serving on the cultural committee—would shape the ideas about Indonesia's cultural future.

Looking at Indonesian cultural discussions, three strands emerge from the archives. There is material from the republican delegation, as well as information on internal coordination meetings between the republic and the BFO, which operated as one front in the negotiations with the Netherlands. Third, there are reports of the negotiations between the Indonesians (the RI and the BFO) and the Netherlands. From the reconstruction of these meetings, we learn that the principles as formulated at the end of the second session of the Inter-Indonesian Conference, on 2 August 1949, were leading throughout the negotiations.

During the first internal meeting of the republican Cultural Committee on 21 August, Sastroamidjojo, Kolopaking, Yamin and Soesilo crucially determined that the principles of the Inter-Indonesian Conference and 'whatever was set/decided by UNESCO' (the UN Educational, Scientific and Cultural Organization) would serve as guidelines for cultural negotiations with the Netherlands but were not further specified.[32] The Inter-Indonesian Conference had been held between the republic and the BFO before the RTC. The BFO was formed on 15 July 1948 to coordinate the autonomous non-republican states such as Negara Indonesia

---

30　Restu Gunawan, *Muhammad Yamin dan Cita-Cita Persatuan Indonesia [Mohammad Yamin and the Ideals of Indonesian Unity]* (Jakarta: Ombak, 2005).
31　ANRI, 'Document Containing a List of All Members of the Indonesian Delegation, 11 October 1949', DI 1278, Document No. GS 703/RTC (Jakarta: National Archives of the Republic of Indonesia, 1949). See also United Nations Archives and Records Management System [hereinafter UNARMS], 'List of Committee Members of the Netherlands Delegation to the R.T.C.', S-0681-0004-09-00002, Document Master Files, R.T.C.—Cultural Committee (New York: UNARMS, n.d.).
32　ANRI, *Panitia Kebudajaan (Delegasi R.I. ke K.M.B.), Tjatatan rapat ke-1, 21 August 1949 [Cultural Committee (Delegation of the Republic of Indonesia to Roundtable Conference), Minutes of the First Meeting, 21 August 1949]*, DI 1268, Guide Arsip Diplomasi Indonesia [Guide to Indonesian Diplomatic Archives] 1945–2009. Jakarta: National Archives of the Republic of Indonesia.

Timur (State of East Indonesia), Negara Sumatra Timur (State of East Sumatra), Negara Pasundan (State of Pasundan) and Negara Jawa Timur (State of East Java). Initially, the BFO opposed the republic as they feared and rejected the 'Javanisation' of the entire Indonesian archipelago, while the republicans viewed the BFO as Dutch marionettes who supported Dutch imperialism. This opposition started to decrease when Ide Anak Agung Gde Agung (1921–99) was appointed Prime Minister of Negara Indonesia Timur. In his drive for Indonesian unity, he proposed the Inter-Indonesian Conference to coordinate the positions of the republic and the BFO in the leadup to the RTC.[33]

During the first session of the Inter-Indonesian Conference (20–22 July), several committees convened,[34] but no cultural committee gathered, for reasons unknown. Outstanding issues were discussed during the second session of the Inter-Indonesian Conference (31 July – 2 August). This time a cultural committee formulated 10 mutual starting points for the BFO and the republic in their negotiations with the Netherlands. These included the development of an Indonesian National Culture for all Indonesian people, being a 'synthesis' of the cultures of various areas throughout the United States of Indonesia, based on 'godliness, humanitarianism and democracy' with Bahasa Indonesia as the uniting language to be used for education and culture. International cultural cooperation was considered beneficial for the development of an Indonesian National Culture but must be based on the principles of equality and voluntariness,[35] in contrast with the unequal power relations in, and coerced nature of, colonialism. Sovereignty thus was considered crucial for cultural collaboration. Notably, the return of cultural objects was not mentioned in the reports of the Second Inter-Indonesian Conference.

---

[33] Ide Anak Agung Gde Agung, *From the Formation of the State of East Indonesia towards the Establishment of the United States of Indonesia* (Jakarta: Yayasan Obor Indonesia, 1996), 560; Widhi Setyo Putro, 'Konferensi Inter-Indonesia Tahun 1949: Wujud Konsensus Nasional antara Republik Indonesia dengan Bijeenkomst voor Federaal Overleg [The Inter-Indonesian Conference of 1949: Formation of National Consensus between the Republic of Indonesia and the Federal Consultative Assembly]', *Jurnal Sejarah Citra Lekha* [*Citra Lekha History Journal*] 3, no. 1 (2018): 34–42, doi.org/10.14710/jscl.v3i1.17341.
[34] Ide Anak Agung, *From the Formation of the State of East Indonesia*, 595–99.
[35] ibid., 611–13.

During the first internal meeting of the republican cultural delegation, representatives reiterated what the principles of the inter-Indonesian conferences meant for negotiations with the Netherlands. Culture was understood very broadly and must be based on education and knowledge to build a 'national spirit–character', expressed in Dutch as '*nationale geest–karakter*', which could support a sovereign republic. Kolopaking emphasised that sovereignty must be the basis for cultural collaboration with the Netherlands, while Sastroamidjojo added that cultural collaboration with any foreign country had to be based on the principles of 'equality/ voluntariness' (*gelijkwaardigheid/vrijwilligheid*).[36] In the spirit of the Inter-Indonesian Conference, they decided to contact the BFO's cultural committee as well as distinguished, 'especially progressive' people (*terutama jang progressif*) in Indonesia and the Netherlands.

Discussing the return of cultural objects

In the first introductory meeting between the republic, the BFO and the Netherlands on 26 August 1949, the negotiation agenda was discussed. Susuhunan Pakubuwono XII, Mangkunegara VIII and Sim Ki Ay joined the republican Cultural Committee from this meeting. Importantly, the three parties agreed that meetings would be conducted in Dutch and no records would be made; only short notes would be drawn up in Dutch, Indonesian and English. It was also acknowledged that none of the delegations had a proposal ready.[37] Negotiations thus started with a clean slate.

The republic and the BFO met on 5 September to coordinate and agreed that the mutual starting points formulated during the Second Inter-Indonesian Conference would serve as guidelines for the cultural negotiations with the Netherlands. Culture was to be understood in close connection with education and religion. Cultural collaboration with the Netherlands was considered beneficial for the development of an Indonesian culture and would focus on teaching and education, the exchange of experts and professors, as well as performing arts, knowledge and economics. The republic and the

---

36   Sastroamidjojo used Dutch to articulate these principles. ANRI, *Cultural Committee (Delegation of the Republic of Indonesia to Roundtable Conference)*.
37   UNARMS, 'Record of the First Meeting of the Committee for Cultural Affairs on Friday, 26th of August 1945 at 10.00 Hours in the State Hall (Ministry of Transport and Waterways), 21 Binnenhof, The Hague', S-0681-0004-03-00002, Document Master Files, R.T.C.—Cultural Committee (New York: UNARMS, 1945.).

BFO also discussed that any cultural collaboration with the Netherlands must be regulated through a bilateral cultural agreement (Indonesian: *perdjandjian kebudajaan*; Dutch: *bilateraal cultureel verdrag*).[38]

During this first coordination meeting, the republican and BFO delegates discussed the return of cultural objects for the first time. Point II of the results of this meeting states that there was agreement to:

> [The] transfer of assets and liabilities to the R.I.S. as a consequence of the transfer of sovereignty, the Delegations jointly take this position that transfer must take place of: a. all cultural property [*segala harta-benda*], buildings for education, bodies for science and art and other bodies for science and art both inside Indonesia and outside Indonesia.[39]

The return of '*harta-benda*' (translated as 'material assets' in the English report) was the priority, followed by the transfer of property and liabilities and assets. In other words, the return of cultural objects was high on the list of demands.

On 9 September, the Indonesians met with the Dutch for the second time to discuss the form and nature of cultural collaboration. The Indonesian principles for collaboration—freedom, voluntariness and mutuality—were unanimously adopted. It was also agreed that the cultural relations should have a 'universal character' and focus on 'the democratic principle of the

---

38   ANRI, *Putusan jang Diambil dalam Rapat Panitya2 Kebudajaan dari Delegasi Republik dan B.F.O. untuk Menghadapi Pembitjaraan dengan Delegasi Belanda dan K.M.B jang Mengenai Soal Kebudajaan* [*Decisions Taken at the Meeting of the Cultural Committee of the Delegation of the Republic and the BFO to Talk with the Dutch Delegation in Roundtable Conference about Cultural Matters*], DI 1272, Guide Arsip Diplomasi Indonesia [Guide to Indonesian Diplomatic Archives] 1945–2009 (Jakarta: National Archives of the Republic of Indonesia, n.d.); ANRI, *Laporan Mingguan No. 2. 12 September 1949* [*Weekly Report No. 2. 12 September 1949*], DI 1274, Guide Arsip Diplomasi Indonesia [Guide to Indonesian Diplomatic Archives] 1945–2009 (Jakarta: National Archives of the Republic of Indonesia, 1949); ANRI, *Results Arrived at the Meeting between the Cultural Sections of the Delegations of the BFO and the Republic of Indonesia Preliminary to the Discussions with the Netherlands Delegation to the RTC Regarding Cultural Matters*, DI 1286, Guide Arsip Diplomasi Indonesia [Guide to Indonesian Diplomatic Archives] 1945–2009 (Jakarta: National Archives of the Republic of Indonesia, n.d.).

39   ANRI, *Weekly Report No. 2, 12 September 1949*; ANRI, *Laporan Rahasia, Sekretariat Uni Indonesia Nederland Djakarta, 5 September 1949* [*Confidential Report, Secretariat of the Indonesian Netherlands Union Jakarta, 5 September 1949*], DI 1272, Guide Arsip Diplomasi Indonesia [Guide to Indonesian Diplomatic Archives] 1945–2009 (Jakarta: National Archives of the Republic of Indonesia, 1949).

realisation of the free development of the free human spirit in a free society'.[40] An informal report of the meeting in English paraphrases Sastroamidjojo's delivery of the outcomes of the internal Indonesian meeting:

> As soon as Indonesia became an independent sovereign state it were [sic] to take *cultural affairs* into its own hands, which had not been the case so far. If this fundamental principle were accepted, matters would be considerably simplified, and the question would be how further to organise co-operation.[41]

The English terms 'material assets', 'cultural affairs' or 'cultural riches' and the Dutch *'culturele rijkdommen'*, as used in the Dutch reports,[42] are very broad and can refer to general matters of culture. *'Culturele rijkdommen'* can also refer to multiple forms of cultural heritage, including movable objects and immovable forms like heritage sites. These translations suggest a very general interpretation of culture.

An amendment to the report of 9 September that appeared five days later provides clarity on what Sastroamidjojo had meant by 'cultural riches':

> Even now he [Sastroamidjojo] would like to raise the reminder that, as a result of the transfer of sovereignty, cultural property in Indonesia must also be handed over to the R.I.S. After that, the cooperation in the cultural field between R.I.S. and Holland can be built.[43]

Notably, in the Indonesian amendments, the word *'harta-benda'* is used, which refers to cultural objects with societal and historical value. *Harta-benda* can also designate places such as heritage sites. For the first time in

---

40   ANRI, *Konferensi Medja Bundar Panitia Urusan Kebudajaan. Laporan Mingguan no. 3 Sesuai Fasal 32 Peraturan Tata-Tertib, untuk Minggu 4–10 September 1949* [Roundtable Conference. Committee on Cultural Affairs. Weekly Reports No. 3 According to Article 32 of the Rules of Conduct, for the Week of 4–10 September 1949], DI 1278, RTC/Versl./CIV/3, Guide Arsip Diplomasi Indonesia [Guide to Indonesian Diplomatic Archives] 1945–2009 (Jakarta: National Archives of the Republic of Indonesia, 1949).
41   UNARMS, 'Informal Report Prepared by the Secretariat for the Information of the Members of the Commission. Informal Meeting of the Cultural Committee Held on 9 September at 11.30 in the State Hall, 21 Binnenhof, The Hague, page 3', S-0681-0004-03-00002, 9 September 1949, Document Master Files, R.T.C.—Cultural Committee (New York: UNARMS, 1949) [emphasis added].
42   ANRI, *Konferensi Medja Bundar Panitia Urusan Kebudajaan, 15 September 1949* [Roundtable Conference Committee on Cultural Affairs, 15 September 1949], DI 1518, RTC/Not/CIV/2, Verb.1 (Off), Guide Arsip Diplomasi Indonesia [Guide to Indonesian Diplomatic Archives] 1945–2009 (Jakarta: National Archives of the Republic of Indonesia, 1949).
43   ibid. The transcript in Indonesian is as follows: *'Sekarangpun ia [Sastroamidjojo] hendak memperingatkan, bahwa, sebagai akibat dari penjerahan kedaulatan, harta-benda kebudajaan di Indonesia harus diserahkan dijuga kepada R.I.S. Sesudah itu barulah kerdjasama dilapangan kebudajaan antara R.I.S. dan Nederland dapat dibangun.'*

the negotiations with the Netherlands, Sastroamidjojo had raised the return of cultural property located within Indonesia as a condition for cultural collaboration.

During the third meeting, on the morning of Wednesday, 14 September, a small working committee was appointed, as per Sastroamidjojo's suggestion, with three members of each delegation to discuss a concept drafted by the Netherlands delegation that was confidentially and informally distributed to the Indonesians. The republican delegation comprised Sastroamidjojo, Kolopaking and Yamin; the BFO delegation was chair Abdul Malik (1912–?), Head of State and Representative of the State of South Sumatra, Jan Engelbert Tatengkeng (1907–68), Minister of Education of the State of East Indonesia, and K.H.M. Wilmers (dates unknown), Member of Parliament of the State of East Indonesia. Malik commented that the Dutch draft offered many points of connection but needed further consideration. The Indonesians were allowed to make (counter) proposals in writing and the results of the meetings would be reported to the central steering committee of the RTC.[44]

On the same day, Sastroamidjojo reported in a confidential memorandum on the progress of the cultural committee to Mohammad Hatta (1902–80), head of the overall republican delegation. Sastroamidjojo warned Hatta that 'there may also be some difficulties regarding the confiscation of "all cultural property [*harta-benda*], college buildings, scientific and artistic bodies and other scientific and artistic bodies in Indonesia and outside Indonesia"'.[45] Furthermore, Sastroamidjojo set out the main 'point of disagreement' (*verschilpunt*) was the Dutch concept of cultural collaboration, which he deemed overly formalistic and regulated. He emphasised the importance of the two main principles for collaboration in line with the results of the Second Inter-Indonesian Conference: sovereignty (independence) and the notion of voluntariness.[46] Sastroamidjojo's pencilled notes (Figure 9.1) in Dutch show that 'voluntariness' was a condition for 'smooth' collaboration that should be based on universal 'human rights' (*peri kemanusiaan*),

---

44 ANRI, *Wekelijks Verslag nr. 4 Ingevolge Artikel 32 Reglement van Orde, over de Week van 11–17 September 1949* [*Weekly Report No. 4 Pursuant to Rule 32 of the Rules of Procedure, for the Week of 11–17 September 1949*], DI 1278, RTC/Versl./CIV/4, Guide Arsip Diplomasi Indonesia [Guide to Indonesian Diplomatic Archives] 1945–2009 (Jakarta: National Archives of the Republic of Indonesia, 1949).
45 ANRI, DI 1277, *Panitia Kebudayaan (Delegasi Republik Indonesia). Memorandum Ali Sastroamidjojo, 14 September 1949* [*Committee on Cultural Affairs (Delegation of the Republic of Indonesia). Memorandum of Ali Sastroamidjojo, 14 September 1949*], DI 1277, Guide Arsip Diplomasi Indonesia [Guide to Indonesian Diplomatic Archives] 1945–2009 (Jakarta: National Archives of the Republic of Indonesia, 1949).
46 ibid.

9. BEYOND THE POINT OF NO RETURN

while democracy meant the 'free development of the free spirit in a free fatherland'.[47] Equality and freedom were thus considered the basis for cultural collaboration.

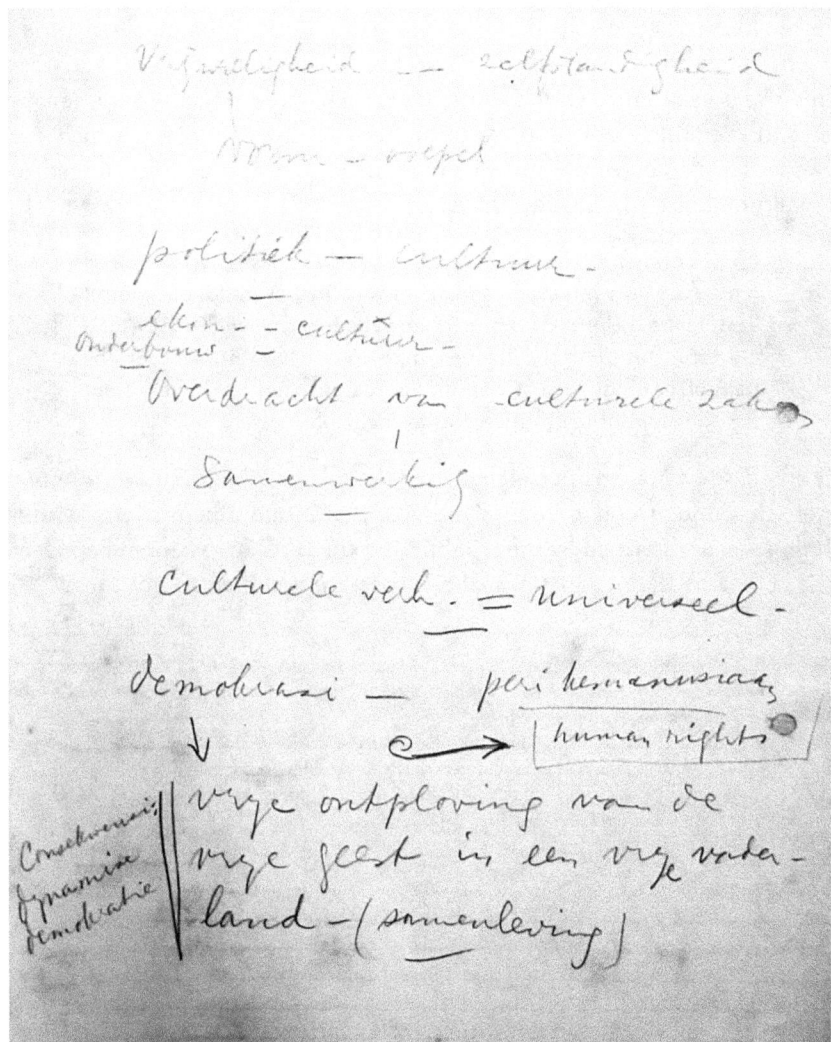

Figure 9.1 Pencilled notes by Ali Sastroamidjojo
Source: ANRI, DI 1277 (1949).

---

47   ibid. Ali Sastroamidjojo's memorandum is reported in the minutes: ANRI, *Periodiek Verslag van het Secretariaat-Genereaal der RTC van 7 tot en met 16 September 1949* [*Periodic Report of the Secretariat General of the RTC from 7 to 16 September 1949*], DI 1219, Guide Arsip Diplomasi Indonesia [Guide to Indonesian Diplomatic Archives] 1945–2009 (Jakarta: National Archives of the Republic of Indonesia, 1949).

Two days later, on 16 September, the working committee gathered to discuss the cultural agreement drafted by the Dutch delegation and agreed on the principles as previously discussed between the republic and the BFO. By 22 September, two versions of the Draft Cultural Agreement were circulated. In one, Clause 19 details that 'the joint committee will annually compile a written report on work for the respective Governments'.[48] It is likely that this was the original Dutch draft. Later that same day, the Indonesians met to coordinate and drafted a counter-concept agreement, which the Netherlands accepted on 23 September, including a request for the return of cultural objects in Clause 19:[49]

> *Cultural goods originating from Indonesia other than those for which rights have been transferred* and are now owned or under the control of the Dutch Royal Government and the former Dutch East Indies Government, must be handed over to the Government of the Republic of Indonesia, as a result of the transfer of sovereignty from the Kingdom of the Netherlands to the R.I.S.[50]

From these events, we can conclude that the cultural objects and their return were first understood as part of movable and immovable property within Indonesia, as discussed by the republic and the BFO on 5 September. Over the course of the negotiations, the conversation shifted to encompass all

---

48   ANRI, *Konferensi Medja Bundar. Panitia Kebudajaan. Lapuran Minggu No. 4 Menurut Fasal 32 Peraturan Tata Tertib, dari Minggu 11–17 September 1949* [Roundtable Conference. Committee on Cultural Affairs. Weekly Reports No. 4 According to Article 32 of the Rules of Conduct, from the Week of 11–17 September 1949], DI 1278, RTC/Verls./CIV/4, Guide Arsip Diplomasi Indonesia [Guide to Indonesian Diplomatic Archives] 1945–2009 (Jakarta: National Archives of the Republic of Indonesia, 1949). Also see: UNARMS, 'Survey of the Activities of the Committee for Cultural Affairs Reported in the Meeting of the Steering Committee of 11th October 1949', S-0681-0004-02-00001, Document No. GS 701/RTC (New York: UNARMS, 1949).

49   ANRI, *Weekly Report No. 2, 12 September 1949*; ANRI, *Laporan Pekerdjaan Panitya Kebudajaan dari Delegasi Republik Indonesia ke Konperensi Medja Bundar Selama 2 minggu Mulai dari Tg 11-Tg 24 September* [Work Report of the Cultural Committee from the Delegation of the Republic of Indonesia to the Roundabout Conference for 2 Weeks Starting from 11–24 September], 26 September, Sekneg [State Secretary] 862 (Jakarta: National Archives of the Republic of Indonesia, 1949).

50   ANRI, *Weekly Report from Ali Sastroamidjojo to the President of the Republic of Indonesia, Dated 26 September 1949 with the Draft of Cultural Agreement from the Republic and BFO*, Sekneg [State Secretary] 862, Arsip Sekretariat Negara Republik Indonesia [Archives of the Ministry of State Secretariat] 1945–1949 (Jakarta: National Archives of the Republic of Indonesia, 1949) [emphasis added]. The Indonesian text reads as follows: '*Barang² kebudajaan jang berasal dari Indonesia selain dari pada jang telah berlaku pemindahan-hak atasnja dan sekarang dimiliki atau ada dalam penguasaan Pemerintah Keradjaan Belanda dan Pemerintah Hindia-Belanda dahulu, harus diserahkan kepada Pemerintah R.I.S. sebagai akibat daripada penjerahan kedaulatan dari Keradjaan Belanda kepada R.I.S. Untuk melaksanakan apa jang tersebut di ajat 1, Panitia-Bersama akan mengusulkan, menurut tjara tersebut dalam fasal 6 suatu peraturan chusus, dalam mana diadakan pula ketentuan² berhubung dengan kemungkinan adanja penukaran barang² jang berharga bagi kebudajaan atau sedjarah, jang dimiliki atau diakuasai oleh negeri jang satu dan berasal dari atau penting bagi negeri jang lain.*'

cultural objects originating from Indonesia that were now both within and outside the archipelago. The clause specified that it applied to all objects *except* those 'for which rights have been transferred' or, in other words, all objects looted or taken without permission. Further, the issue was considered important enough that it received a separate clause.

The Draft Cultural Agreement reached

On 11 October, the cultural committee reported to the steering committee a 'provisional result' 'regarding the editing of the Draft Cultural Agreement'[51] and, by 28 October 1949, the Draft Cultural Agreement was reached, containing 20 articles. The Indonesian principles for cultural collaboration ended up in Article 1 as:

> Cultural relations between the Kingdom of the Netherlands and the R.I.S. are based on complete freedom, free will and mutuality. These cultural relations between the Kingdom of the Netherlands and the R.I.S. bear a universal character and aim at the realisation of the free development of the free human mind.[52]

The Draft Cultural Agreement reflected the outcomes of the Second Inter-Indonesia Conference as discussed throughout the negotiations. Culture was important for the development of an Indonesian spirit based on education, and cultural collaboration was believed to contribute to building this new spirit. Radio broadcasts, cultural and educational institutions and recognition of certificates, books and translations were identified as tools to develop culture and cultural collaboration. Education in Indonesia was

---

51   ANRI, *Ronde Tafel Conferentie. Commissie voor Culturele Aangelegenheden, 10 October 1949* [*Round Table Conference. Commission on Cultural Affairs, 10 October 1949*], DI 1289, RTC/Versl/CIV/7, Guide Arsip Diplomasi Indonesia [Guide to Indonesian Diplomatic Archives] 1945–2009. (Jakarta: National Archives of the Republic of Indonesia, 1949); ANRI, *Draft Cultural Agreement between the Kingdom of the Netherlands and the Republic of the United States of Indonesia*, Kabinet Presiden RIS 1945–1950, No. 339 (Jakarta: National Archives of the Republic of Indonesia, n.d.); ANRI, *Rentjana Perdjanjian tentang Kerdja-sama Kebudajaan antara Republik Indonesia Serikat dan Keradjaan Belanda* [*Draft Cultural Agreement between the Republic of the United States of Indonesia and the Kingdom of the Netherlands*], DI 1282, Guide Arsip Diplomasi Indonesia [Guide to Indonesian Diplomatic Archives] 1945–2009 (Jakarta: National Archives of the Republic of Indonesia, n.d.); ANRI, *Ichtisar Pekerdjaan2 Panitia Urusan Kebudajaan Diadjukan dalam Rapat Panitia Pusat dari 11 Oktober 1949* [*The Summary of the Work of the Committee on Cultural Affairs, Presented at the Central Committee Meeting of 11 October 1949*], DI 1282, Guide Arsip Diplomasi Indonesia [Guide to Indonesian Diplomatic Archives] 1945–2009 (Jakarta: National Archives of the Republic of Indonesia, 1949).
52   ANRI, *Draft Cultural Agreement between the Kingdom of the Netherlands and the Republic of the United States of Indonesia* [No. 339]; ANRI, *Draft Cultural Agreement between the Republic of the United States of Indonesia and the Kingdom of the Netherlands* [DI 1282]; ANRI, *The Summary of the Work of the Committee on Cultural Affairs*.

expected to benefit from the exchange of knowledge through the unlimited and free sharing of books, newspapers and periodicals published in both countries, as well as teachers, experts and scholarship programs for students.

Also on 28 October, republican secretary Soesilo sent 'an improved Indonesian version of the Draft Cultural Agreement' (Figure 9.2), which finalised the agreement. His corrections further specified the requested objects as those obtained by means other than 'private law'.[53] This shows that the republic requested the return of *all* cultural objects except those acquired under private law, which narrows the requested objects to those of cultural and historical value and excludes any that were exchanged in horizontal relationships between citizens. With Soesilo's legal addition, Clause 19 was finalised as the clause quoted in the introduction and approved by the three cultural delegations. The Draft Cultural Agreement was reported to the steering committee for formalisation on 1 November.[54]

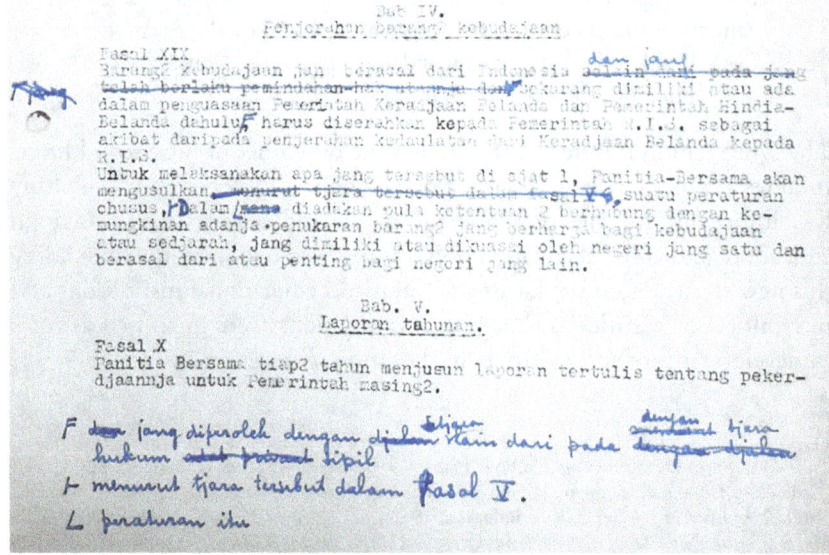

Figure 9.2 Corrections made by Soesilo to the final Draft Cultural Agreement
Source: ANRI, DI 1531 (1949).

---

53   ANRI, 'Letter from Soesilo H. Prakoso to Mr. J. de Bruyn, 29 October 1949', DI 1531, Guide Arsip Diplomasi Indonesia [Guide to Indonesian Diplomatic Archives] 1945–2009 (Jakarta: National Archives of the Republic of Indonesia, 1949).
54   UNARMS, 'Record of the Fourth Meeting (First Formal Meeting) in the State Hall, 20 Binnenhof, The Hague, Held on Tuesday 1st November 1949 at 11.15 Hours', S-0681-0004-03-00001, 3 November 1949, Document No. RTC/Not/CIV/4, Document Master Files, R.T.C.—Cultural Committee (New York: UNARMS, 1949).

The Draft Cultural Agreement was, however, never ratified. After several attempts to keep it alive in the years after the RTC, the agreement was finally withdrawn in a 1954 protocol, apart from Clause 19.[55] The point of disagreement—a too formalistic Dutch approach to cultural collaboration, raised by Sastroamidjojo earlier in the drafting process—seemed to have been the stumbling block for ratification. In 1950, the Dutch rigidity was characterised by former education minister Ki Hadjar Dewantara[56] as 'cultural imperialism' in a speech delivered at the Taman Siswa Congress in Yogyakarta.[57] Nevertheless, the Draft Cultural Agreement of 1949 put the issue of restitution of colonial cultural objects on the political agenda for decades to come, even laying the groundwork for discussions today.

Legacies of the Draft Cultural Agreement

As Jennifer Lindsay has noted, after 1949, nationhood was negotiated 'on the wide cultural front' for Indonesia as a new nation-state.[58] The Indonesian requests for the return of objects from the Netherlands persisted in the following decades, but amounted to nothing until the 1970s. The palm-leaf manuscript *Nagarakratagama* (1365) was given back in 1971 and, when the two countries reached the Joint Cultural Agreement in 1975, several objects, manuscripts and archives were returned. Some objects related to the Indonesian resistance hero Prince Diponegoro (1785–1855), including his umbrella, spear and the saddle of his horse, were returned (on 7 October 1977), and the thirteenth-century Buddhist statue Prajnaparamita also came back, in 1978. In this period, the so-called Djogdja Documenten—356 documents from the NEFIS archive—were returned as well.[59] It then became quiet on the cultural object return front until, in 2015, the descendants of

---

55   Legêne and Postel-Coster, 'Isn't It All Culture?', 272.
56   Ki Hadjar Dewantara was a leading activist in the Indonesian independence movement and Indonesia's first Minister of Education, in 1945. As an educational pioneer, he founded the Taman Siswa schools that provided education for common Indonesians, which had been limited to the Javanese aristocracy and Dutch colonials. He is perhaps most famous for his writing as Soewardi Soerjaningrat, 'If I Were a Dutchman [*Als ik eens Nederlander was*]', printed in *De Expres* newspaper on 13 July 1913, in which he fiercely criticised the colonial government of the Dutch East Indies.
57   ANRI, *Ki Hadjar Dewantara Menolak K.M.B. tentang Kerdja-sama soal Kebudajaan* [*Ki Hadjar Dewantara Refuses Roundtable Conference About Cultural Cooperation*], Djawatan Kepolisian Negara Bagian [State Police Department] P.A.M. Yogyakarta, 13 March 1950, KPM RI Jogja, No. 107 (Jakarta: National Archives of the Republic of Indonesia, 1950).
58   Jennifer Lindsay, 'Heirs to World Culture 1950–1965: An Introduction', in *Heirs to World Culture: Being Indonesian, 1950–1965*, eds Jennifer Lindsay and Maya Liem (Boston: Brill, 2012), 1–30, doi.org/10.26530/OAPEN_403204, at 5–9.
59   See Karabinos and Theo's Chapter 10 in this volume.

Governor-General Jean Chrétien Baud (1789–1859) returned Diponegoro's staff to the Museum Nasional Indonesia (MNI). In 2019, 1,500 objects from the collection of the former Museum Nusantara in Delft were returned to the MNI after an arduous three-year process. On 20 March 2020, the first day of the state visit to Indonesia by Dutch King Willem-Alexander and Queen Máxima, the *keris* ('ritual dagger') belonging to Prince Diponegoro, which for more than 200 years had been untraceable in the collections of the National Museum of Ethnology in Leiden, was returned.

In recent years, both Indonesia and the Netherlands have created restitution committees, as discussed in the introduction to this chapter, which indicates that both countries intend to pursue more actively issues of ownership of Indonesian objects of (contested) cultural and historical value from colonial contexts in Dutch museum collections. This has led to the transfer and return of 472 objects: 355 from the Lombok collection looted in 1894, four statues from the thirteenth-century Singosari Temple, a *keris* from Klungkung and 132 items known as the Pita Maha collection in 2023.[60]

While during the RTC negotiations cultural objects were understood as part of culture and embedded in the quest to build an Indonesian culture, the return of significant Indonesian icons in the late 1970s was interpreted and implemented as identity politics. A similar approach was also discernible in the exhibition '*Repatriasi: Kembalinya Saksi Bisu Peradaban Nusantara*' ('Repatriation: The Return of the Silent Witnesses of the Archipelago's Civilisation'), held from 28 November to 10 December 2023 at the National Gallery of Indonesia. In a press release accompanying the exhibition, Director-General of Culture Hilmar Farid emphasised the importance of knowledge production about the objects.[61] Farid, historian Sri Margana, members of the Indonesian repatriation committee and others

---

60 Ministry of Education, Culture, Research and Technology, 'Indonesia Terima 472 Koleksi Benda Bersejarah dari Pemerintah Belanda [Indonesia Receives 472 Historical Objects from the Dutch Government]', News release (Jakarta: Government of the Republic of Indonesia, 11 July 2023), www.kemdikbud.go.id/main/blog/2023/07/indonesia-terima-472-koleksi-benda-bersejarah-dari-pemerintah-belanda.

61 Ministry of Education, Culture, Research and Technology, 'Kemendikbudristek Gelar Pameran REPATRIASI: Kembalinya Saksi Bisu Peradaban Nusantara [Ministry of Education and Culture Holds REPATRIATION Exhibition: The Return of the Silent Witnesses to Indonesian Civilisation]', News release (Jakarta: Government of the Republic of Indonesia, 28 November 2023), www.kemdikbud.go.id/main/blog/2023/11/kemendikbudristek-gelar-pameran-repatriasi-kembalinya-saksi-bisu-peradaban-nusantara.

have repeatedly spoken in public forums[62] about the importance of research, knowledge-building and exchange regarding the cultural objects collected in colonial contexts held in the Netherlands. Their comments suggest that as well as nation-building efforts, in which returned Indonesian objects are instrumentalised in political schemes, a desire to develop knowledge-building and exchange for a meaningful cultural future can be discerned once again.

References

Primary sources

Arsip Nasional Republik Indonesia (ANRI). n.d. *A List of All Members of the Indonesian Delegation*. DI 1278. Guide Arsip Diplomasi Indonesia [Guide to Indonesian Diplomatic Archives] 1945–2009. Jakarta: National Archives of the Republic of Indonesia.

ANRI. n.d. *Draft Cultural Agreement between the Kingdom of the Netherlands and the Republic of the United States of Indonesia*. Kabinet Presiden RIS 1945–1950, No. 339. Jakarta: National Archives of the Republic of Indonesia.

ANRI. n.d. *Draft Cultural Agreement between the Kingdom of the Netherlands and the Republic of the United States of Indonesia in English and Dutch*. DI 1281, Document No. GS 701/RTC. Guide Arsip Diplomasi Indonesia [Guide to Indonesian Diplomatic Archives] 1945–2009. Jakarta: National Archives of the Republic of Indonesia.

ANRI. n.d. *Draft Cultural Agreement in Bahasa Indonesia*. DI 1282. Guide Arsip Diplomasi Indonesia [Guide to Indonesian Diplomatic Archives] 1945–2009. Jakarta: National Archives of the Republic of Indonesia.

---

62   Hilmar Farid's presentation to the webinar 'The Politics of Restitution', organised by the Centre of South East Asian Studies and Southeast Asian Art Academic Programme, SOAS University of London, 20 May 2021, is available on YouTube: www.youtube.com/watch?v=aOF0tMOHnf4&t=2763s, at 46:03 mins. Sri Margana presented to the webinar 'Decolonizing Museums: The Long and Winding Road of the Restitution Process of the Colonial Collection' (6 April 2021) organised by PCI Nahdatul Ulama Belanda. I Gusti Agung Wesaka Puja's speech in reaction to the PPROCE results presentation (17 March 2022) is available on YouTube: www.youtube.com/watch?v=omtStMtVhTM.

ANRI. n.d. *Putusan jang Diambil dalam Rapat Panitya2 Kebudajaan dari Delegasi Republik dan B.F.O. untuk Menghadapi Pembitjaraan dengan Delegasi Belanda dalam K.M.B. jang Mengenai soal Kebudajaan* [*Decisions Taken at the Meeting of the Cultural Committee of the Delegation of the Republic and the BFO to Talk with the Dutch Delegation in Roundtable Conference About Cultural Matters*]. DI 1272. Guide Arsip Diplomasi Indonesia [Guide to Indonesian Diplomatic Archives] 1945–2009. Jakarta: National Archives of the Republic of Indonesia.

ANRI. n.d. *Rentjana Perdjanjian tentang Kerdja-sama Kebudajaan antara Republik Indonesia Serikat dan Keradjaan Belanda* [*Draft Cultural Agreement between the Republic of the United States of Indonesia and the Kingdom of the Netherlands*]. DI 1282. Guide Arsip Diplomasi Indonesia [Guide to Indonesian Diplomatic Archives] 1945–2009. Jakarta: National Archives of the Republic of Indonesia.

ANRI. n.d. *Results Arrived at the Meeting between the Cultural Sections of the Delegations of the BFO and the Republic of Indonesia Preliminary to the Discussions with the Netherlands Delegation to the RTC Regarding Cultural Matters*. DI 1286. Guide Arsip Diplomasi Indonesia [Guide to Indonesian Diplomatic Archives] 1945–2009. Jakarta: National Archives of the Republic of Indonesia.

ANRI. 1949. *Panitia Kebudajaan (Delegasi RI ke KMB). Tjatatan Rapat ke-1, 21 August 1949* [*Cultural Committee (Delegation of the Republic of Indonesia to Roundtable Conference). Minutes of the First Meeting, 21 August 1949*]. DI 1268. Guide Arsip Diplomasi Indonesia [Guide to Indonesian Diplomatic Archives] 1945–2009. Jakarta: National Archives of the Republic of Indonesia.

ANRI. 1949. *Laporan Rahasia, Sekretariat Uni Indonesia Nederland Djakarta, 5 September 1949* [*Confidential Report, Secretariat of the Indonesian Netherlands Union Jakarta, 5 September 1949*]. DI 1272. Guide Arsip Diplomasi Indonesia [Guide to Indonesian Diplomatic Archives] 1945–2009. Jakarta: National Archives of the Republic of Indonesia.

ANRI. 1949. *Konferensi Medja Bundar Panitia Urusan Kebudajaan. Lapuran Mingguan no. 3 Sesuai Fasal 32 Peraturan Tata-Tertib, untuk Minggu 4–10 September 1949* [*Roundtable Conference. Committee on Cultural Affairs. Weekly Reports No. 3 According to Article 32 of the Rules of Conduct, for the Week of 4–10 September 1949*]. DI 1278, RTC/Versl./CIV/3. Guide Arsip Diplomasi Indonesia [Guide to Indonesian Diplomatic Archives] 1945–2009. Jakarta: National Archives of the Republic of Indonesia.

ANRI. 1949. *Konferensi Medja Bundar. Panitia Kebudajaan. Laporan Minggu no. 4 Menurut Fasal 32 Peraturan Tata Tertib, dari Minggu 11–17 September 1949* [*Roundtable Conference. Committee on Cultural Affairs. Weekly Reports No. 4 According to Article 32 of the Rules of Conduct, from the Week of 11–17 September 1949*]. DI 1278, RTC/Verls./CIV/4. Guide Arsip Diplomasi Indonesia [Guide to Indonesian Diplomatic Archives] 1945–2009. Jakarta: National Archives of the Republic of Indonesia.

ANRI. 1949. *Wekelijks Verslag nr. 4 Ingevolge Artikel 32 Reglement van Orde, over de week van 11–17 September 1949* [*Weekly Report No. 4 Pursuant to Rule 32 of the Rules of Procedure, for the Week of 11–17 September 1949*]. DI 1278, RTC/Versl./ CIV/4. Guide Arsip Diplomasi Indonesia [Guide to Indonesian Diplomatic Archives] 1945–2009. Jakarta: National Archives of the Republic of Indonesia.

ANRI. 1949. *Laporan Mingguan No. 2. 12 September 1949* [*Weekly Report No. 2. 12 September 1949*]. Sekneg [State Secretary] 862. Arsip Sekretariat Negara Republik Indonesia [Archives of the Ministry of State Secretariat] 1945–1949. Jakarta: National Archives of the Republic of Indonesia.

ANRI. 1949. *Laporan Mingguan No. 2. 12 September 1949* [*Weekly Report No. 2. 12 September 1949*]. DI 1274. Guide Arsip Diplomasi Indonesia [Guide to Indonesian Diplomatic Archives] 1945–2009. Jakarta: National Archives of the Republic of Indonesia.

ANRI. 1949. *Panitia Kebudajaan (Delegasi Republik Indonesia). Memorandum Ali Sastroamidjojo, 14 September 1949* [*Committee on Cultural Affairs (Delegation of the Republic of Indonesia). Memorandum of Ali Sastroamidjojo, 14 September 1949*]. DI 1277. Guide Arsip Diplomasi Indonesia [Guide to Indonesian Diplomatic Archives] 1945–2009. Jakarta: National Archives of the Republic of Indonesia.

ANRI. 1949. *Konferensi Medja Bundar Panitia Urusan Kebudajaan, 15 September 1949* [*Roundtable Conference Committee on Cultural Affairs, 15 September 1949*]. DI 1518, RTC/Not/CIV/2, Verb.l (Off). Guide Arsip Diplomasi Indonesia [Guide to Indonesian Diplomatic Archives] 1945–2009. Jakarta: National Archives of the Republic of Indonesia.

ANRI. 1949. *Periodiek Verslag van het Secretariaat-Genereaal der RTC van 7 tot en met 16 September 1949* [*Periodic Report of the Secretariat General of the RTC from 7 to 16 September 1949*]. DI 1219. Guide Arsip Diplomasi Indonesia [Guide to Indonesian Diplomatic Archives] 1945–2009. Jakarta: National Archives of the Republic of Indonesia.

ANRI. 1949. *Laporan Pekerdjaan Panitya Kebudajaan dari Delegasi Republik Indonesia ke Konperensi Medja Bundar Selama 2 minggu Mulai dari Tg 11-Tg 24 September* [*Work Report of the Cultural Committee from the Delegation of the Republic of Indonesia to the Roundabout Conference for 2 Weeks Starting from 11– 24 September*], 26 September. Sekneg [State Secretary] 862. Jakarta: National Archives of the Republic of Indonesia.

ANRI. 1949. *Weekly Report from Ali Sastroamidjojo to the President of the Republic of Indonesia, Dated 26 September 1949 with the Draft of Cultural Agreement from the Republic and BFO.* Sekneg [State Secretary] 862. Arsip Sekretariat Negara Republik Indonesia [Archives of the Ministry of State Secretariat] 1945–1949. Jakarta: National Archives of the Republic of Indonesia.

ANRI. 1949. *Ronde Tafel Conferentie. Commissie voor Culturele Aangelegenheden, 10 October 1949 [Round Table Conference. Commission on Cultural Affairs, 10 October 1949].* DI 1289, RTC/Versl/CIV/7. Guide Arsip Diplomasi Indonesia [Guide to Indonesian Diplomatic Archives] 1945–2009. Jakarta: National Archives of the Republic of Indonesia.

ANRI. 1949. 'Document Containing a List of All Members of the Indonesian Delegation, 11 October 1949.' DI 1278, Document No. GS 703/RTC. Jakarta: National Archives of the Republic of Indonesia.

ANRI. 1949. *Ichtisar Pekerdjaan2 Panitia Urusan Kebudajaan Diadjukan dalam Rapat Panitia Pusat dari 11 Oktober 1949 [The Summary of the Work of the Committee on Cultural Affairs, Presented at the Central Committee Meeting of 11 October 1949].* DI 1282. Guide Arsip Diplomasi Indonesia [Guide to Indonesian Diplomatic Archives] 1945–2009. Jakarta: National Archives of the Republic of Indonesia.

ANRI. 1949. *Draft Cultural Agreement in Bahasa Indonesia, 28 October 1949.* DI 1281. Guide Arsip Diplomasi Indonesia [Guide to Indonesian Diplomatic Archives] 1945–2009. Jakarta: National Archives of the Republic of Indonesia.

ANRI. 1949. 'Letter from Soesilo H. Prakoso to Mr. J. de Bruyn, 29 October 1949.' DI 1531. Guide Arsip Diplomasi Indonesia [Guide to Indonesian Diplomatic Archives] 1945–2009. Jakarta: National Archives of the Republic of Indonesia.

ANRI. 1950. *Ki Hadjar Dewantara menolak K.M.B. tentang Kerdja-sama soal Kebudajaan [Ki Hadjar Dewantara Refuses Roundtable Conference About Cultural Cooperation].* Djawatan Kepolisian Negara Bagian [State Police Department] P.A.M. Yogyakarta, 13 March 1950. KPM RI Jogja, No. 107. Jakarta: National Archives of the Republic of Indonesia.

House of Representatives of the States General. 2022. 'Brief van de Staatssecretaris van Onderwijs, Cultuur en Wetenschap: Nieuwe Visie Cultuurbeleid [Letter from the State Secretary for Education, Culture and Science: New Cultural Policy Vision].' *Kamerstuk [Parliamentary Paper].* Session Year 2021–2022, 32820, No. 480, 29 July. zoek.officielebekendmakingen.nl/kst-32820-480.html.

United Nations Archives and Records Management System (UNARMS). n.d. 'List of Committee Members of the Netherlands Delegation to the R.T.C.' S-0681-0004-09-00002, Document Master Files, R.T.C.—Cultural Committee. New York: United Nations Archives and Records Management System.

UNARMS. 1945. 'Record of the First Meeting of the Committee for Cultural Affairs on Friday, 26th of August 1945 at 10.00 Hours in the State Hall (Ministry of Transport and Waterways), 21 Binnenhof, The Hague.' S-0681-0004-03-00002, Document Master Files, R.T.C.—Cultural Committee. New York: United Nations Archives and Records Management System.

UNARMS. 1949. 'Informal Report Prepared by the Secretariat for the Information of the Members of the Commission. Informal Meeting of the Cultural Committee Held on 9 September at 11.30 in the State Hall, 21 Binnenhof, The Hague, Page 3.' S-0681-0004-03-00002, 9 September 1949. Document Master Files, R.T.C.—Cultural Committee. New York: United Nations Archives and Records Management System.

UNARMS. 1949. 'Survey of the Activities of the Committee for Cultural Affairs Reported in the Meeting of the Steering Committee of 11th October 1949.' S-0681-0004-02-00001, Document No. GS 701/RTC. New York: United Nations Archives and Records Management System.

UNARMS. 1949. 'Round Table Conference Results as Accepted in the Second Plenary Meeting Held on 2 November 1949 in the "Ridderzaal" at The Hague.' S-0681-0025-04-00002, R.T.C.—Various Booklets Round Table Conference (in Dutch and English). New York: United Nations Archives and Records Management System.

UNARMS. 1949. 'Record of the Fourth Meeting (First Formal Meeting) in the State Hall, 20 Binnenhof, The Hague, Held on Tuesday 1st November 1949 at 11.15 Hours.' S-0681-0004-03-00001, 3 November 1949, Document No. RTC/Not/CIV/4. Document Master Files, R.T.C.—Cultural Committee. New York: United Nations Archives and Records Management System.

Secondary sources

Advisory Committee on the National Policy Framework for Colonial Collections. 2020. *Guidance on the Way Forward for Colonial Collections: Colonial Collection—A Recognition of Injustice*. The Hague: Council for Culture. www.raadvoorcultuur.nl/documenten/adviezen/2021/01/22/colonial-collection-and-a-recognition-of-injustice.

Anderson, Benedict. 1983. *Imagined Communities: Reflections on the Origin and Spread of Nationalism*. London: Verso.

Ardiyansyah, Panggah. 2021. 'Restitution and National Heritage: (Art) Historical Trajectories of Raden Saleh's Paintings.' In *Returning Southeast Asia's Past: Objects, Museums, and Restitution*, edited by Louise Tythacott and Panggah Ardiyansyah, 163–86. Singapore: NUS Press. doi.org/10.2307/j.ctv1r4xctd.12.

Bennett, Tony. 1995. *The Birth of the Museum*. New York: Routledge.

Bloembergen, Marieke, and Martijn Eickhoff. 2013. 'Exchange and the Protection of Java's Antiquities: A Transnational Approach to the Problem of Heritage in Colonial Java.' *Journal of Asian Studies* 72, no. 4: 893–916. doi.org/10.1017/S0021911813001599.

Budiarti, Hari. 2006. 'The Sulawesi Collections: Missionaries, Chiefs and Military Expeditions.' In *The Discovery of the Past*, edited by Endang Sri Hardiati and Pieter ter Keurs, 160–72. Amsterdam: KIT Publishers.

Budiarti, Hari. 2007. 'Taking and Returning Objects in a Colonial Context: Tracing the Collections Acquired during the Bone–Gowa Military Expeditions.' In *Colonial Collections Revisited*, edited by Pieter ter Keurs, 123–44. Leiden: Leiden University Press.

Council for Culture. 2024. *Omgang met Gedeelde Bronnen van het Koloniale Verleden. Advies voor Herstel en Restitutie in Relatie tot Koloniale Archieven* [Dealing with Shared Sources of the Colonial Past. Advice on Recovery and Restitution in Relation to Colonial Archives]. The Hague: Council for Culture. www.raadvoorcultuur.nl/documenten/adviezen/2024/03/25/omgang-met-gedeelde-bronnen-van-het-koloniale-verleden.

Cribb, Robert. 2000. *Historical Atlas of Indonesia*. London: Routledge. doi.org/10.4324/9780203824610.

Cribb, Robert. 2010. *Digital Atlas of Indonesian History*. Copenhagen: NIAS.

Drieënhuizen, Caroline. 2018. 'Mirrors of Time and Agents of Action: Indonesia's Claimed Cultural Objects and Decolonisation, 1947–1978.' *BMGN* 133, no. 2: 79–90. doi.org/10.18352/bmgn-lchr.10552.

Government of the Netherlands. 2022. 'Benoeming Leden Adviescommissie Teruggave Cultuurgoederen uit Koloniale Context [Appointment of Members of the Advisory Committee on the Return of Cultural Objects from a Colonial Context].' News release, 17 November. The Hague: Government of the Netherlands.

Gunawan, Restu. 2005. *Muhammad Yamin dan Cita-Cita Persatuan Indonesia* [Mohammad Yamin and the Ideals of Indonesian Unity]. Jakarta: Ombak.

Handler, Richard. 1988. *Nationalism and the Politics of Culture in Quebec*. Madison: University of Wisconsin Press.

Ide, Anak Agung Gde Agung. 1996. *From the Formation of the State of East Indonesia towards the Establishment of the United States of Indonesia*. Jakarta: Yayasan Obor Indonesia.

Johari, Hendi. 2020. 'Kisah Sunyi Ali Sastroamidjojo [The Silent Story of Ali Sastroamidjojo].' *Historia*, [Jakarta], 11 July. historia.id/politik/articles/kisah-sunyi-ali-sastroamidjojo-P1RMO.

Jones, Tod. 2013. *Culture, Power, and Authoritarianism in the Indonesian State: Cultural Policy across the Twentieth Century to the Reform Era*. Leiden: Brill. doi.org/10.1163/9789004255104.

Keurs, Pieter ter. 2007. 'Introduction: Theory and Practice of Colonial Collecting.' In *Colonial Collections Revisited*, edited by Pieter ter Keurs, 1–15. Leiden: Leiden University Press.

Legêne, Susan, and Els Postel-Coster. 2000. 'Isn't It All Culture? Culture and Dutch Development Policy in the Post-Colonial Period.' In *Fifty Years of Dutch Development Cooperation, 1949–1999*, edited by Peter Malcontent and Jans Nekker, 271–88. The Hague: SDU Publishing.

Lindsay, Jennifer. 2012. 'Heirs to World Culture 1950–1965: An Introduction.' In *Heirs to World Culture: Being Indonesian, 1950–1965*, edited by Jennifer Lindsay and Maya H.T. Liem, 1–30. Boston: Brill. doi.org/10.26530/OAPEN_403204.

Matanasi, Petrik. 2020. 'Pencuplikan Pakubuwono XII dan Dihapusnya Daerah Istimewa Surakarta [The Abduction of Pakubuwono XII and the Abolition of the Surakarta Special Region].' *Tirto.id*, [Jakarta], 29 December. tirto.id/penculikan-pakubuwono-xii-dan-dihapusnyadaerah-istimewa-surakarta-f8aC.

Ministry of Education, Culture, Research and Technology. 2023. 'Indonesia Terima 472 Koleksi Benda Bersejarah dari Pemerintah Belanda [Indonesia Receives 472 Historical Objects from the Dutch Government].' News release, 11 July. Jakarta: Government of the Republic of Indonesia. www.kemdikbud.go.id/main/blog/2023/07/indonesia-terima-472-koleksi-benda-bersejarah-dari-pemerintah-belanda.

Ministry of Education, Culture, Research and Technology. 2023. 'Kemendikbudristek Gelar Pameran REPATRIASI: Kembalinya Saksi Bisu Peradaban Nusantara [Ministry of Education and Culture Holds REPATRIATION Exhibition: The Return of the Silent Witnesses to Indonesian Civilisation].' News release, 28 November. Jakarta: Government of the Republic of Indonesia. www.kemdikbud.go.id/main/blog/2023/11/kemendikbudristek-gelar-pameran-repatriasi-kembalinya-saksi-bisu-peradaban-nusantara.

Penders, C.L.M., ed. 1979. *Milestones on My Journey: The Memoirs of Ali Sastroamijoyo, Indonesian Patriot and Political Leader*. Brisbane: University of Queensland Press.

Putro, Widhi Setyo. 2018. 'Konferensi Inter-Indonesia Tahun 1949: Wujud Konsensus Nasional antara Republik Indonesia dengan Bijeenkomst voor Federaal Overleg [The Inter-Indonesian Conference of 1949: Formation of National Consensus between the Republic of Indonesia and the Federal Consultative Assembly].' *Jurnal Sejarah Citra Lekha* [*Citra Lekha History Journal*] 3, no. 1: 34–42. doi.org/10.14710/jscl.v3i1.17341.

Samuel, Hanneman. 1999. 'The Development of Sociology in Indonesia: The Production of Knowledge, State Formation and Economic Change.' PhD diss., Swinburne University of Technology, Melbourne.

Sapardan, Wieske. 2021. 'The Return of Cultural Property and National Identity in Postcolonial Indonesia.' In *Returning Southeast Asia's Past: Objects, Museums, and Restitution*, edited by Louise Tythacott and Panggah Ardiyansyah, 213–34. Singapore: NUS Press. doi.org/10.2307/j.ctv1r4xctd.14.

Scott, Cynthia. 2014. 'Negotiating the Colonial Past in the Age of European Decolonization: Cultural Property Return between the Netherlands and Indonesia.' PhD diss., Claremont Graduate University, California.

Scott, Cynthia. 2014. 'Sharing the Divisions of the Colonial Past: An Assessment of the Netherlands–Indonesia Shared Cultural Heritage Project, 2003–2006.' *International Journal of Heritage Studies* 20, no. 2: 181–95. doi.org/10.1080/13527258.2012.738239.

Scott, Cynthia. 2017. 'Renewing the "Special Relationship" and Rethinking the Return of Cultural Property: The Netherlands and Indonesia, 1949–79.' *Journal of Contemporary History* 52, no. 3: 646–68. doi.org/10.1177/0022009416658698.

Scott, Cynthia. 2020. *Cultural Diplomacy and the Heritage of Empire: Negotiating Post-Colonial Returns*. New York: Routledge.

Setiadi, Bram. 2001. *Raja Di Alam Republik: Keraton Kesunanan Surakarta dan Pakubuwono XII* [*King in the Realm of the Republic: The Royal Palace of Surakarta and Pakubuwono XII*]. Jakarta: Bina Rena Pariwara.

Setiawan, Dody. 2013. 'Biografi Kanjeng Gusti Pangeran Adipati Aryo Mangkunegoro VIII [Biography of Kanjeng Gusti Pangeran Adipati Aryo Mangkunegoro VIII].' Unpublished thesis, Universitas Airlangga, Surabaya.

Sunarmi. 2018. 'Democracy in Indonesia Towards Mangkunegaran: The Fade of Javanese Royal Palace's Political Power.' *Al-Ulum* 18, no. 1: 231–46. doi.org/10.30603/au.v18i1.285.

Suryadinata, Leo. 2015. *Prominent Indonesian Chinese: Biographical Sketches*. 4th edn. Singapore: ISEAS Publishing. doi.org/10.1355/9789814620512.

Tirto.id. 2024. 'Profil Ali Sastroamidjojo [Profile Ali Sastroamidjojo].' *Tirto.id*, [Jakarta]. [Online]. tirto.id/m/ali-sastroamidjojo-Dh.

van Beurden, Jos. 2012. *The Return of Cultural and Historical Treasures: The Case of the Netherlands*. Amsterdam: KIT Publishers.

van Beurden, Jos. 2017. *Treasures in Trusted Hands: Negotiating the Future of Colonial Cultural Objects*. Leiden: Sidestone Press.

van Beurden, Jos. 2021. 'Returns by the Netherlands to Indonesia in the 2010s and the 1970s.' In *Returning Southeast Asia's Past: Objects, Museums, and Restitution*, edited by Louise Tythacott and Panggah Ardiyansyah, 187–209. Singapore: NUS Press. doi.org/10.2307/j.ctv1r4xctd.13.

Vázquez, Rolando. 2018. 'The Museum, Decoloniality and the End of the Contemporary.' In *The Future of the New: Artistic Innovation in Times of Social Acceleration*, edited by Thijs Lijster, 181–95. Amsterdam: Valiz.

Wardhana, Adi Putra Surya, Titis Srimuda Pitana, and Susanto. 2019. 'Revivalisme Kebudayaan Jawa Mangkunegara VIII di Era Republik [Mangkunegara VIII: Javanese Cultural Revivalism in the Republic Era].' *Mudra Jurnal Seni Budaya [Mudra Journal of Arts and Culture]* 34, no. 1: 105–15. doi.org/10.31091/mudra.v34i1.568.

Wekker, Gloria. 2016. *White Innocence: Paradoxes of Colonialism and Race*. Durham: Duke University Press. doi.org/10.1515/9780822374565.

10

How to liberate the colonised archives? Describing the Djogdja Documenten after their return

Michael Karabinos and Rika Theo

Introduction

When it comes to archival descriptions, words matter. When dealing with colonial collections, the terminology used to describe records is increasingly seen as important to reconsider and evaluate as part of a larger project of decolonising knowledge. What we have seen is a prevalence of research into descriptions provided within colonial archives in former settler colonies and the archives of indigenous communities in Canada, Australia, the United States and New Zealand.[1] What is missing are studies that look at descriptions of colonial collections in institutions of the former coloniser

---

1 See, for instance, Trish Luker, 'Decolonising Archives: Indigenous Challenges to Record Keeping in "Reconciling" Settler Colonial States', *Australian Feminist Studies* 32, nos 91–92 (2017): 108–25, doi.org/10.1080/08164649.2017.1357011; Kimberly Christen, 'Tribal Archives, Traditional Knowledge, and Local Contexts: Why the "s" Matters', *Journal of Western Archives* 6, no. 1 (2015): Art. 3, doi.org/10.26077/78d5-47cf; Hannah Turner, 'Decolonizing Ethnographic Documentation: A Critical History of the Early Museum Catalogs at the Smithsonian's National Museum of Natural History', *Cataloging & Classification Quarterly* 53, nos 5–6 (2015): 658–76, doi.org/10.1080/01639374.2015.1010112; Sue McKemmish, Shannon Faulkhead, and Lynette Russell, 'Distrust in the Archive: Reconciling Records', *Archival Science* 11, no. 3 (2011): 211–39, doi.org/10.1007/s10502-011-9153-2; Siobhan Senier, 'Digitizing Indigenous History: Trends and Challenges', *Journal of Victorian Culture* 19, no. 3 (2014): 396–402, doi.org/10.1080/13555502.2014.947188.

as well as in former colonies. Museums appear to be ahead of archives in terms of re-evaluating and changing the text they use. This chapter provides one example of why it is also important to critically evaluate archival descriptions. Such descriptions are the first interactions users have with an archive, so the word choices can be the difference between someone requesting a record and leaving it unread.

This chapter takes a unique example, the so-called Djogdja Documenten, a collection of archives that bear witness to a sliver of the Indonesian independence war of 1945–49 between the newly proclaimed Republic of Indonesia and the Dutch colonial power. This collection is now housed at both the national archives of the former colonial power and that of the former colony. This collection is, to use the term from Jeurgens and Karabinos, a 'colonised archive'—one 'originally created, owned, and used by local institutions and people' using items 'that were collected, looted, bought or copied, and shipped to the coloniser'.[2] By examining the descriptions of this 'colonised' archive in the national archives of both places, we will show how the repatriated records are represented in each country.

The subject of this chapter is not the history of the Djogdja Documenten or how they came to be found within the collections of each national archive; this information can be found in more detail elsewhere.[3] The focus here is on the descriptions provided for these records. However, part of our interest is the fact that the Djogdja Documenten are held at both the National Archives of Indonesia (Arsip Nasional Republik Indonesia; hereinafter ANRI) and the National Archives of the Netherlands (Nationaal Archief, or NA), so it is worth highlighting part of the custodial history of this archive.

---

2   Charles Jeurgens and Michael Karabinos, 'Paradoxes of Curating Colonial Memory', *Archival Science* 20 (2020): 199–220, doi.org/10.1007/s10502-020-09334-z, at 207.

3   Michael Karabinos, 'Displaced Archives, Displaced History: Recovering the Seized Archives of Indonesia', *Bijdragen Tot de Taal-, Land- En Volkenkunde* [*Journal of the Humanities and Social Sciences of Southeast Asia*] 169, nos 2–3 (2013): 279–94, doi.org/10.1163/22134379-12340027; Michael Karabinos, 'The Djogdja Documenten: The Dutch–Indonesian Relationship Following Independence through an Archival Lens', *Information & Culture* 50, no. 3 (2015): 372–91, doi.org/10.7560/IC50304; Michael Karabinos, 'Indonesian National Revolution Records in the National Archives of the Netherlands', in *Displaced Archives*, ed. James Lowry (London: Routledge, 2017), 60–73, doi.org/10.4324/9781315577609-5; Rika Theo, 'The Djogdja Documenten Revisited: Repatriation, Silence, and the Seized Archives of the Decolonization War' (Master's thesis, University of Amsterdam, 2021), scripties. uba.uva.nl/search?id=c4364542; Okeu Yulianasari, 'Deciphering the NEFIS Archives: Investigating Dutch Information Gathering in Indonesia 1945–1949' (Master's thesis, Leiden University, Netherlands).

10. HOW TO LIBERATE THE COLONISED ARCHIVES?

The Djogdja Documenten are primarily government archives that were created during the turbulence of the Indonesian war of independence against the Netherlands in 1945–49. Materials from this period are unsurprisingly scarce in Indonesia. Most have been disposed of, burned or scattered; much is now held only in various individual collections and archives. The war resulted in the destruction not only of lives and places, but also of archives. The description of ANRI's inventory of 1945–50 static archives says that information about events in the early years of independence is incomplete. For instance, ANRI has only three boxes of archives for the Indonesian Ministry of Internal Affairs in this period.[4]

On top of the scarcity of the records from this period, the importance of the seized archives lies more in the fact that these records bear witness to a defining period of decolonisation—the very process of liberation that shaped the new nation-state. They provide evidence of not only the early dynamics of the new republic, but also the conflicts and dissonances that the Dutch faced in their attempt to recolonise Indonesia. Unfortunately, even though in the NA there are many seized documents, such as in the archives of the Procureur-Generaal (Attorney-General) and the Ministry of Defence, only the small portion referred to as the Djogdja Documenten were deemed by the Netherlands to legally belong to the Republic of Indonesia and it was thus only these records that were returned. The NA's other material includes a wealth of records seized from various individuals, organisations and sociopolitical movements.

Eric Ketelaar states that records 'may be instruments of power, but, paradoxically, the same records can also become instruments of empowerment and liberation, salvation and freedom'.[5] What we see in the case of the Djogdja Documenten is that this paradox applies not only to records, but also to archival institutions. While repatriation may seem to be the undoing of archival seizure, there are lingering traces of instruments of power in archival descriptions, which can similarly become places of 'empowerment and liberation'. Ketelaar uses the example of Nazi registry

---

4   Kris Hapsari and Neneng Ridayanti, *Layanan Akses Arsip Statis Di ANRI* [*ANRI's Static Archive Access Services*], Subdirektorat Layanan Arsip Direktorat Layanan dan Pemanfaatan Arsip Nasional RI [Subdirectorate of Archives Services, Directorate of Services and Utilisation of the National Archives of the Republic of Indonesia, 2019].

5   Eric Ketelaar, 'Archival Temples, Archival Prisons: Modes of Power and Protection', *Archival Science* 2, nos 3–4 (2002): 221–38, doi.org/10.1007/BF02435623, at 229.

records of Jews becoming instruments of liberation as they are used in the restitution of and compensation for Nazi seizures.[6] We can also see that restructured descriptions produce similar liberatory effects.

Despite the return of the Djogdja Documenten being marked as a rare successful archival collaboration between a former colony and its coloniser, silences and gaps remain. For instance, information on the selection criteria used to determine which archives were returned is unknown and cannot be found in the archival descriptions at the NA. This is important to know because there are still many Indonesian Government archives captured in Yogyakarta (and beyond) that remain in the Netherlands. If the legal basis of the return was only 'Indonesian republican government archives', why were many other seized Indonesian Government records left unreturned? The situation is such that Indonesians must travel to the Netherlands to view the archives that record part of this crucial period in Indonesian history. Access to the records of the struggle against recolonisation, which were created by the formerly colonised, is hindered because these archives remain in the hands of the former coloniser and are catalogued in the colonial language, Dutch.

For the pursuit of decoloniality, an archival institution should aim to do more than just provide access to records. Archival repatriation has been positively seen as a step towards decolonialising the archives, but, through our analysis of the Djogdja Documenten, this chapter will show that further steps must be taken to liberate the archives from the persistent legacy of colonial archival infrastructure. The homecoming of colonised archives should entail not only exposing, redressing and reconciling the past violence of colonialism, but also a process of contesting and dismantling the colonial logic that remains in the archival practices and infrastructures of the present.[7] This is a process that has not yet happened for the Djogdja Documenten. As noted by Nurjaman: 'The decolonisation that was done is only to restore the physical form of the archive, without changing the system and archive structure.'[8]

---

6 ibid., 229.
7 Jeurgens and Karabinos, 'Paradoxes of Curating Colonial Memory'; Michael Karabinos, 'The Shadow Continuum: Testing the Records Continuum Model through the Djogdja Documenten and the Migrated Archives' (Doctoral thesis, Leiden University, Netherlands, 2015), hdl.handle.net/1887/33293; Ann Laura Stoler, *Along the Archival Grain: Epistemic Anxieties and Colonial Common Sense* (Princeton: Princeton University Press, 2010).
8 Jajang Nurjaman, 'Dekolonisasi Arsip Sebagai Warisan Budaya: Kajian Awal Pengembalian Arsip Statis Era Hindia Belanda [Decolonisation of Archives as Cultural Heritage: A Preliminary Study of the Return of Static Archives from the Netherlands East Indies Era]', *Khazanah: Jurnal Pengembangan Kearsipan* [*Khazanah: Journal of Archival Development*] 13, no. 1 (2020): 75–90, doi.org/10.22146/khazanah.55713, at 83.

10. HOW TO LIBERATE THE COLONISED ARCHIVES?

This chapter focuses on the description of the Djogdja Documenten as it is the most visible interface that shows us how the archives are represented to users,[9] where content and context are told. While the content of the Djogdja Documenten is not the focus of this chapter, it is impossible to tell this story without devoting some time to it, as it was this that led to their seizure by the Netherlands East Indies Forces Intelligence Service (NEFIS).[10] This is especially important when considering the terminology chosen for archival descriptions. We will also spend considerable time discussing the context of the archive—its creation, seizure, return and current situation. After this we will begin our analysis of the descriptions at both the NA and ANRI, paying particular attention to how the contents and contexts of the records are portrayed in each place. We believe the context provided for their content is minimal at best in the descriptions of both archives, while any context of their seizure is missing from both institutions. We therefore see a need to impose a new praxis on these descriptions that can better express the history of the Djogdja Documenten. We will present a liberatory praxis for description that, we argue, can play a role in the decolonialisation process of these archives. This will be done by looking at the Djogdja Documenten as a community of records—to borrow a phrase from Jeannette Bastian[11]—and exploring the potential for a smarter digitisation plan that would allow for the (re)linking of records to add and reignite contextual layers and remove imposed layers of coloniality.

Layers of provenance

The Djogdja Documenten are not a 'colonial collection', but rather a 'colonised' archive. They are records originally created, owned and used by Indonesian institutions and people that were collected, looted, bought or copied and shipped to the coloniser's home country.[12] They were created, seized, re-created, displaced, re-created, returned and re-created again. Each time these records are activated, they are being contextualised and

---

9 Margaret Hedstrom, 'Archives, Memory, and Interfaces with the Past', *Archival Science* 2, nos 1–2 (2002): 21–43, doi.org/10.1007/BF02435629.
10 The full name of this organisation is clouded with ambiguity. While the Netherlands Institute for Military History and other sources refer to it as the Netherlands East Indies Forces Intelligence Service, the National Archives (NA) and more refer to it as the Netherlands Forces Intelligence Service.
11 Jeannette Allis Bastian, 'Reading Colonial Records Through an Archival Lens: The Provenance of Place, Space and Creation', *Archival Science* 6, nos 3–4 (2007): 267–84, doi.org/10.1007/s10502-006-9019-1.
12 Jeurgens and Karabinos, 'Paradoxes of Curating Colonial Memory', 207.

recontextualised—or, in other words, changed. This shows how archives may have multilayered contexts, defying the old notion of single, static and linear provenance of traditional archival principles. To understand the context and content of the Djogdja Documenten, one must follow its genealogy, which we will soon be doing.

The creators of the original documents in the Djogdja Documenten were, for the most part, ministries and institutions of the Indonesian Government. The records were created in the context of a newly independent country that, while facing internal dynamics and dissonances, resisted Dutch recolonisation after World War II and the Japanese capitulation. In December 1948, amid the war of independence, the Dutch military invaded the Republic of Indonesia's then capital, Yogyakarta (Djogdja). The military not only arrested senior republican officials, but also seized their archives. All these seized archives were collected, arranged and processed by the Netherlands East Indies Forces Intelligence Service.

NEFIS was a large-scale operation, a military intelligence service that was founded by the Dutch colonial government-in-exile in Australia after the Japanese invasion in 1942 during World War II.[13] In 1943 it became an independent agency focused on gathering intelligence on the situation in Japanese-occupied Indonesia. In 1945, following the Japanese capitulation, NEFIS relocated to Dutch-controlled areas of Indonesia. Its central focus also shifted to gathering intelligence on active independence movements across the newly declared independent Republic of Indonesia. Its archive contains not only the records created by the institution, but also the thousands of documents 'collected' in the former Dutch East Indies over the course of the colony's existence. NEFIS was renamed the Centrale Militaire Inlichtingendienst (CMI; Central Military Intelligence Service) in 1948.

The records that NEFIS seized as part of its intelligence mission after the invasion of Yogyakarta in 1948 were especially important resources for the Dutch colonial government and were used for reports to influence international opinion and diplomacy towards the Dutch recolonisation effort. Furthermore, as researched by Okeu Yulianasari[14] and later expanded by Michael Karabinos,[15] the seized archives served as documentary evidence to support Dutch accusations about the incapacity and dysfunctionality

---

13   Yulianasari, 'Deciphering the NEFIS Archives'.
14   ibid.
15   Karabinos, 'The Shadow Continuum'.

of the Indonesian republican government. Records relating especially to the opium trade, insurgency and communism were used, for example, to play to international and often colonial perceptions of a threatening Asia. During talks with international delegations, the Dutch officials felt their claims were being ignored while Indonesian claims were unfairly supported.[16] Recorded evidence was then sought, leading to archival seizure.[17] A report was written by Dutch officials using such seized archives in February 1949, but international pressure to draw the war to a close led to the paper going unpublished.[18] In other words, the records were recontextualised and repurposed during the Dutch recolonisation effort. To that aim, the reports containing the original, copied or translated versions of these raw documents were sent to various Dutch and international bodies. This is one of the reasons the seized records can be found in multiple places across the world and not just the NEFIS/CMI archives. For instance, they were scattered in the archives of the Algemeene Secretarie (General Secretariat), Procureur Generaal (Attorney-General), Rapportage Indonesia and other international bodies and countries outside the Netherlands.

At the end of the independence struggle, the transfer of archives and cultural objects was discussed at the United Nations–sponsored final negotiations on issues related to Indonesia's sovereignty, the Dutch–Indonesian Round Table Conference (RTC) in 1949. Article 19 of the Draft Cultural Agreement signed at this conference stipulated that cultural objects of Indonesian origin were to be handed over to the Indonesian Government.[19] However, the NEFIS archives had already been transported to the Netherlands by boat before the Dutch signed the agreement recognising a sovereign and independent Republik Indonesia Serikat (United States of Indonesia) on 27 December 1949. Thereafter, in the Netherlands, they were appraised and transferred many times between various ministries while remaining closed to the public. The archives were finally placed at the NA and made available for public viewing only from 1990. In the current NA catalogue, the entire NEFIS archive covers 75.5 metres and contains more than 7,300

---

16 Oey Hong Lee, *War and Diplomacy in Indonesia, 1945–1950* (Townsville: James Cook University of North Queensland, 1981), 193.
17 Karabinos, 'The Djogdja Documenten', 375.
18 ibid., 375–76. The report can be found at Collectie S.H. Spoor, Nummer toegang [Access number] 2.21.036.01 (The Hague: National Archives of the Netherlands, 1946–49).
19 Susan Legêne and Els Postel-Coster, 'Isn't It All Culture? Culture and Dutch Development Policy in the Post-Colonial Period', in *Fifty Years of Dutch Development Cooperation 1949–1999* (The Hague: SDU Publishing, 2000), 271–88, research.vu.nl/en/publications/abaab046-a28c-466d-ad21-0c1671e52038, at 272.

inventory numbers. A subsection of these collected documents includes the 4,100 files labelled 'seized, found and stolen' ('*inbeslaggenomen, gevonden en buitgemaakte*')—what we have referred to as the seized archives. Within this seized archive—but by no means constituting the majority of it—are the so-called Djogdja Documenten. They comprise only 356 inventory numbers—a small number compared with the thousands in the NEFIS seized archives.

This selection of seized documents, inscribed by the state institutions and leaders of the Republic of Indonesia, was returned to Indonesia in two batches in 1976. The NA transferred another batch of archives in 1987, including the papers of Abdul Gaffar Pringgodigdo, who recorded the making of Indonesia's Constitution. Though archival cooperation between Indonesia and the Netherlands was discussed in the 1950s in the form of a Dutch microfilming project, the bilateral work stalled because of strained relations after president Sukarno's 'Guided Democracy' period and disputes over the control of Papua. The opportunity for the two national archives to work together would not come again until the rise of Suharto in the late 1960s.[20]

The return itself originated from an unprecedented request from Indonesia, made rather informally during the early microfilm exchange project between the two national archives. The state archivists of both countries played a substantial role in advancing the return amid political instabilities between the two countries. The return was continuously pushed for by Raden Adjeng Soemartini, ANRI's director from 1970 to 1990, with her many attempts beginning in 1970. Soemartini, who studied in the Netherlands, kickstarted and sustained the former coloniser–colonised archival cooperation by accepting the colonial nature of archives and working with the former colonial power.[21] She stressed the cooperation fulfilled the 'mutual interests' of both countries and offered numerous Dutch colonial documents held in Jakarta to be microfilmed in exchange. These actions imply that her outreach to her Dutch counterparts used a framework of archives as a shared colonial heritage. Soemartini's persistence was not the only factor that determined the success of the return. Her counterpart, the NA's head archivist Ton Ribberink played a substantial role in locating and procuring a further return in 1987 after protracted negotiations and disagreement between Dutch ministries on this matter.

---

20 Karabinos, 'The Djogdja Documenten', 376–78.
21 Karabinos, 'Displaced Archives, Displaced History'.

For this return, records in the NEFIS seized archives were reappraised and selected to meet certain Dutch Government criteria for repatriation. At the time, this meant only the Indonesian Government archives seized in Yogyakarta. Each record was checked and arranged into a new collection called the Djogdja Documenten on approval by the related Dutch Government bodies. Returning the seized archive to Indonesia as the 'Djogdja Documenten' essentially meant narrowing the return to just the records captured in the Yogyakarta invasion. This re-creation of the Djogdja Documenten, even though it was for repatriation purposes, was decided largely through a political process by the former coloniser. It resembles exactly what Trouillot[22] calls a silence in the moment of fact assembly. This silence lies not only in the process that delayed archival repatriation, but also in the lack of transparency about the repatriation process itself. The brief descriptions in both national archives' catalogues of the Djogdja Documenten do not cover the repatriation history, including the criteria for selection.

This section has shown how the Djogdja Documenten were created, shaped and reactivated, and the silences therein. There are at least three layers of context of the Djogdja Documenten: their original creation in Indonesia, the re-creation and repurposing of the archives in NEFIS's intelligence work and the selection of the archives for repatriation. These layers, however, remain obscure in the current descriptions of this collection provided at each archive. The next section explains this obscurity and the consequences for the content and then suggests what should be done to liberate these repatriated archives.

When multiple contexts are obscured

Viewed from the context of their creation by NEFIS, the Djogdja Documenten are records created for and from intelligence activities. A major portion of this intelligence gathering involved the procurement of records, which was done extensively by NEFIS. As well as being a records gatherer, NEFIS was a prolific records creator. After it collected documents from both informants and the seizure of property, each was processed according to its importance to the colonial government's purposes. NEFIS comprised various divisions and translation and documentation were the jurisdiction of *Afdeling* ('Division') V. Each document that passed through Division V

---

22 Michel-Rolph Trouillot, *Silencing the Past: Power and the Production of History*, 20th anniversary edn (Boston: Beacon Press, 2015).

was combined with a *geleidebrief* ('routing slip') that contained metadata such as the date and location of procurement, material, form, language, where it was to be distributed and a NEFIS-supplied document number.

The routing slip created during NEFIS procurements always accompanies the original Indonesian documents in each record folder; however, the original metadata are not always present due to the nature of the seizure and the fact that NEFIS often divided and transferred documents to other government departments for their intelligence purposes. We therefore see more of the imprint of NEFIS in the Djogdja Documenten in both the returned records at ANRI and the 'copies' at the NA. The only difference is that, in most cases, ANRI has the original Indonesian documents and the copy of NEFIS procurement records, while the NA has the copy of Indonesian documents and the original NEFIS procurement records.

The consequence is that NEFIS metadata dominantly describe and introduce these seized Indonesian records. Without adequate description, the dominant context of NEFIS intelligence gathering and procurement overshadows the Indonesian context. More importantly, the colonial perspective embedded in NEFIS metadata is stronger in the archival description.

This is obvious in the archival description of the NEFIS seized archives at the NA prior to 2016. The online inventory simply listed the NA's inventory number, which ranged from 1 to 4,100. No additional information was provided to researchers through the finding aid. This is a perfect example of an insufficient inventory that hindered access to the archive. For such a unique collection—one created in the wake of war and fought over by two countries—it was incredibly lacking. A researcher on the subject had to know that a paper inventory with more detailed descriptions could be requested from the reference desk.

The inventory at the NA received a major boost in 2016 when Dutch scholar of Indonesia Harry Poeze expanded on the descriptions for each record. As the inventory now states, 'in these new descriptions, attempts have been made to refer as much as possible to personal names, organisation names, placenames and dates'.[23] Along with the brief descriptions (generally

---

23   Nationaal Archief [hereinafter NA], *Inventaris van het archief van de Marine en Leger Inlichtingendienst, de Netherlands Forces Intelligence Service en de Centrale Militaire Inlichtingendienst in Nederlands-Indië* [*Inventory of the Archives of the Navy and Army Intelligence Service, the Netherlands Forces Intelligence Service and the Central Military Intelligence Service in the Dutch East Indies*], No. 2.10.62 (The Hague: National Archives of the Netherlands, 1942–45), www.nationaalarchief.nl/onderzoeken/archief/2.10.62.

10. HOW TO LIBERATE THE COLONISED ARCHIVES?

one or two sentences) are the NEFIS number, the date received by NEFIS, the location where it was found and whether it is an original or a copy. The location where it was found can be a place or an archive, if seized from a Republic of Indonesia ministry or official. With the search function, researchers can find much more than in the original, more restricted descriptions. The Poeze descriptions, and their online availability, therefore came as a welcome addition to the inventory for researchers wanting to consult the archive. However, we will now compare these new descriptions with the inventory at ANRI, revised in 2004 by Eni Yuliastuti and Isye Djumenar and still used by that institution.[24]

First, the new inventory descriptions of the NEFIS archive at the NA, while certainly more informative than before, still run into linguistic issues and problems of historical perspective. Most of these seized archives are in either Bahasa Indonesia or a local Indonesian language. The inventory of the NEFIS archive does state that knowledge of the Indonesian language is required to read many of the stolen, found and seized records. Given that they were created by groups within the Indonesian independence movement for original distribution within Indonesia, this makes sense. Until the end of 2023, this note and the inventory in its entirety were written in Dutch, which constitutes a linguistic barrier for Indonesian-reading researchers. One must know Dutch to know there are archives in Indonesian. Unlike English in many former British colonies or even Dutch in Suriname, there is very little of a Dutch linguistic legacy in Indonesia. At the National Archives of the Netherlands, therefore, certain Dutch terms for Indonesian events and groups must be known—for instance, *Republikeinse Luchtmacht* ('Republican Air Force') is used in place of *Tentara Nasional Indonesia Angkatan Udara* ('Indonesian National Military–Air Force') or the Republican (Indonesian) Airforce mentioned in NEFIS document number 5392.[25]

---

24   Arsip Nasional Republik Indonesia [hereinafter ANRI], *Daftar Arsip Djogdja Documenten [List of Djogdja Documenten Archives] 1945–1949* (Jakarta: National Archives of the Republic of Indonesia, 2004).
25   NA, 'Algemeen Rijksarchief (ARA), Tweede Afdeling, nummer toegang 2.14.04, inventarisnummer 201. NL-HaNA, Netherland Forces Intelligence Service en Centrale Militaire Inlichtingendienst in Nederlandsch-Indië, nummer toegang 2.10.62, inventarisnummer 6702 [General State Archives (ARA), Second Department, Access Number 2.14.04, Inventory Number 201. NL-HaNA, Netherland Forces Intelligence Service and Central Military Intelligence Service in Dutch-India, Access Number 2.10.62, Inventory Number 6702]' (The Hague: National Archives of the Netherlands, n.d.).

In 2024, the NA added an automatic translator to the online finding aid on its website, so the description can be read in several languages, including Bahasa Indonesia. While it is a first step in improving access, the machine-based translation can only make literal translations of the available text. It cannot capture language nuances and contains translation mistakes due to lack of context or spelling errors. In some cases, the translated Indonesian terms are confusing; they have different meanings as the machine cannot capture context. For instance, '*militaire intelligentie*' is translated as '*kecerdasan militer*' as the term 'intelligence' in Bahasa Indonesia has two contexts. In this translation, intelligence means intellectual ability, while the correct translation should be '*intelijen militer*'. The term '*inventaris*' is translated into '*persediaan*', which means 'stock' or 'supply', while translation is not needed as Indonesian archives use the same term, '*inventaris*'. Furthermore, the Dutch description contains terms and abbreviations for which literal translation does not work, such as '*Archief Rep. Min. van BuZa*' and '*Archief Rep. Min. van Voorl*'. For those unfamiliar with Dutch ministerial abbreviations, the machine translation does not help at all, as they become '*Arsip Rep. Minimal Buza*' and '*Arsip Rep. Minimal dari Voorl*'. These are simple translation problems; the principal issue is that the problematic terms are translated literally, without any explanation. '*Politioneele actie*' is '*aksi polisionil*', showing that colonial perspective is reproduced even after translation. This kind of machine translation might improve access to a slight extent but does not work to decolonise the archives. Daniela Agostinho states that digital archives must 'interrogate and disassemble, rather than repeat, the inherited structure of colonial archives'.[26] We argue that the same is true in the presentation of archival information online, whether digitised archives or the online translations of descriptions.

Second, while the new NA inventory mentions that the Djogdja Documenten are within inventory numbers 3013 and 7112, it does not mention which records form the Djogdja Documenten or that they were returned to Indonesia and can be found at ANRI. A trip to Jakarta, and a peek at the Djogdja Documenten there, would reveal that what has been given that title amounts to 356 records. Most of the seized material from NEFIS is therefore still held in the Netherlands. Given the size of the NEFIS archive and its scope, the archival context of the Djogdja Documenten is stronger at the NA.

---

26 Daniela Agostinho, 'Archival Encounters: Rethinking Access and Care in Digital Colonial Archives', *Archival Science* 19, no. 2 (2019): 141–65, doi.org/10.1007/s10502-019-09312-0.

Third, comparing the inventory lists of ANRI and NA, we can see that some records are registered as 'original' by both institutions. While this is not only confusing, it also highlights the fact that there is no gap in the NEFIS archive in The Hague since the NA has all the copies of the Djogdja Documenten and the original NEFIS routing slips. At ANRI, however, the Djogdja Documenten sit removed from the larger NEFIS archive.

Fourth, though ANRI's description of the Djogdja Documenten is in Bahasa Indonesia, the arrangement of the records follows the arrangement of the NEFIS archive. The Western archival principle of respect for original order—first codified in the 1898 'Dutch Manual' (or the *Manual for the Arrangement and Description of Archives*) by Dutch archivists Samuel Muller, Johan Feith and Robert Fruin—requires records to be arranged in the order in which they were originally found by the archival institution. The main purpose is to preserve the relationship between records that inform the context and, hence, maintain evidential significance inferred from it.[27] NEFIS, however, arranged the seized archives based on its intelligence operations in supporting the Dutch recolonisation attempt. Slivers of context from the Indonesian creation can be seen in the routing slips—for instance, from where the records came—but the structure of the records is defined by how NEFIS processed them. This complete restructuring that delinks the seized records from their Indonesian creators shows that they are treated as the property of NEFIS. Not only the structure but also the original purpose and function of the records were altered to follow NEFIS's own purpose as a colonial agency. In short, the seized records have been colonised.

The NA maintains this re-created NEFIS order as it was the order of the archive when they received it. The NEFIS context is preserved, as is the NEFIS colonial logic. Original ordering can, therefore, obscure layers of context when the colonial order is preserved by the archival institution. In the case of the Djogdja Documenten, ANRI follows the original NEFIS order, and, unfortunately, in so doing, obscures the original order of the Indonesian creators and, consequently, its context. While highlighting the context of seizure, the context of their initial creation is ignored. In choosing this arrangement, ANRI is regarding NEFIS as the creator of the *archive*, though not the creator of the individual records.

---

27 Society of American Archivists, *Dictionary of Archives Terminology* [Online] (Chicago: Society of American Archivists, 2005–24), dictionary.archivists.org/.

The disorder of Indonesian documents is now even more severe at ANRI than at the NA. In the NA's revised descriptions, the place where each record was seized, found or received is mentioned, while it is unavailable in ANRI's descriptions. As a result, the user can only know about the record from the available description of the content, which is often brief and administerial.

We underline the fact that the multiple layers of context of the Djogdja Documenten are their distinctive feature, thus, preserving and revealing all these layers in the descriptions are imperative if they are to be liberated. The original Indonesian documents were seized because of their context and content, the context of the seizure makes us research them and the context of repatriation brings the Djogdja Documenten into 'being'. Is it even possible to see them at ANRI and the NA if one lacks an understanding or awareness of the context? The multiple layers of context are still greatly lacking in the inventory descriptions of the Djodgja Documenten in both state archives.

Understanding the Indonesian context

The description and arrangement of the Djogdja Documenten in both national archives deprive users of the Indonesian context, even though knowledge of the Indonesian context is essential to understanding these records. The current description, especially at ANRI, offers little help for one not equipped with extra knowledge about the Indonesian context.

The Djogdja Documenten are records created during and providing evidence of the independence struggle of the new republic against the Dutch recolonisation campaign. This is the general context that we know. But, within this, the records provide traces of the struggles of different Indonesians: the government and its parties, the sociopolitical movements, different military divisions and individuals throughout a turbulent period that was also affected by the Cold War. Most records in the Djogdja Documenten date from 1948–49, when internal divisions in Indonesia intensified among various groups—namely, the nationalists, the right-wing and left-wing groups, parties and figures.

After the result of the Renville Agreement on 17 January 1948, which Indonesians highly criticised for its detrimental effect on them, the then left-wing prime minister Amir Sjarifuddin had to resign. Mohammad Hatta, who was also the Minister of Defence, replaced him and led a centrist cabinet

10. HOW TO LIBERATE THE COLONISED ARCHIVES?

without incorporating any left-wing representatives. It is unsurprising, then, that during the Dutch invasion of the capital of the republic, Yogyakarta, many archives were seized from Hatta and the Ministry of Defence. In this archive are records of Hatta's policies and decisions during defining events of Indonesian history. Not all these archives were returned to Indonesia; some remain in the NA.

For the records returned to ANRI, they are scattered throughout the Djgodja Documenten because they are still arranged according to the NEFIS document numbers. In addition, the descriptions sometimes obscure the content of these files. For example, the content description of records in NEFIS inventory number 5722 at ANRI says merely: '*Berkas bulan Oktober–November 1948 tentang organisasi dan susunan Komando Djawa* [October–November 1948 file on the organisation and composition of the Javanese Command].' The description of the same records at the NA states: '*Documenten over de organisatie van het Republikeinse leger; met besluit Hatta over rationalisatie/reconstructie Komando Djawa TNI, Jogjakarta, 28-8-1948; met richtlijnen over uitvoering besluit; met organieke samenstelling; met reorganisatie ministerie van defensie, Jogjakarta, 4-11-1948* [Documents on the organisation of the Republican Army; with Hatta's decision about rationalisation/reconstruction of Javanese Command TNI [Indonesian military], Yogyakarta, 28-8-1948; with guidelines on implementation decision; with organic composition; with reorganisation Ministry of Defence, Yogyakarta, 4-11-1948].' The NA's description gives far more information on the *Program Rekonstruksi dan Rasionalisasi* (RERA; Reconstruction and Rationalisation Program), Hatta's policy of restructuring the Indonesian army from 460,000 to only 160,000 soldiers, which brought social and political consequences.[28] Other documents about RERA in the Djogdja Documenten are the records with NEFIS number 5328, described by ANRI thus: '*Catatan singkat rapat informal di Tjode tanggal 31 Agustus 1948 tentang perubahan organisasi* [Brief notes of the informal meeting in Tjode on 31 August 1948 regarding organisational change]', without mentioning this related to the army. The description at the NA gives more clues on the content: '*Verslag van een vergadering van hoge officieren over de reorganisatie van het Republikeinse leger, 31-8-1948* [Report on a meeting of high officers on the reorganisation of the Republican army, 31-8-1948].'

---

28 Frances Gouda and Thijs Brocades Zaalberg, *American Visions of the Netherlands East Indies/Indonesia: US Foreign Policy and Indonesian Nationalism, 1920–1949* (Amsterdam: Amsterdam University Press, 2002).

These documents also include information on pivotal events in Indonesia that are not clearly indicated in the labelling at ANRI. In 1948, for example, Indonesia faced various internal revolts, the most prominent of which was the Madiun Affair—a left-wing uprising in September 1948. This and other events before and after are recorded in the seized archives, since one of NEFIS's interests was to prove communist influence in Indonesia. Various records belonging to the Indonesian Communist Party (Partai Komunis Indonesia, PKI), the Socialist Youth of Indonesia (Pemuda Sosialis Indonesia, known as Pesindo) and the People's Democratic Front (Front Demokrasi Rakyat, or FDR), as well as military and government documents, can be found here. But, again, the descriptions at ANRI obscure the content of these records.

In some instances, the PKI is not mentioned at all. For example, records with NEFIS number 5324 are described by ANRI as: '*Surat dari Sutjiono kepada Jaksa Agung Tentara tanggal 10 November 1948 tentang laporan singkat daerah pendudukan pendapat organisasi Barisan Terpendam, dengan lampiran* [Letter from Sutjiono to the Attorney-General of the Army dated 10 November 1948 regarding a brief report on the occupied areas, the opinion of the Barisan Terpendam organisation, with attachments].' Meanwhile, the NA mentions the content of the report in detail: '*Rapport over activiteiten Barisan Terpendam in bezet gebied Semarang, na arrestatie van zijn leider luitenant-kolonel S. Sudiarto, betrokken bij de PKI opstand; met resolutie Barisan Terpendam met verzoek Soediarto vrij te laten, 7-11-1948* [Report on Barisan Terpendam's activities in occupied Semarang territory, after arrest of its leader Lieutenant Colonel S. Sudiarto, involved in the PKI uprising; with resolution Barisan Terpendam with a request to release Soediarto, 7-11-1948].'

These are examples of how descriptions obscure the context and content of the records. Other than this, the descriptions in both state archives are problematic in relation to the terminology used. For instance, we found the term '*politionele actie*' ('police action') is still used without any explanation by either institution. This term was used by the Netherlands and represents the Dutch perspective of the conflict as a domestic conflict needing policing rather than a war with military engagements. In contrast, the general term used in Indonesia to refer to what happened in the 1945–49 period is '*revolusi kemerdekaan*' ('independence revolution') or '*perang kemerdekaan*' ('war of independence'), while the Dutch military attacks are called '*agresi militer*' ('military aggression').

Liberatory praxis in decolonialising the archives

In 2022 a new layer of context was added to the NEFIS archive—and, by extension, to the Djogdja Documenten—because of the use of selected original documents held only at the NA in the *'Revolusi!'* exhibition at the Rijksmuseum in Amsterdam. The chosen records offer us a glimpse of some of the *unreturned* NEFIS archive, including photographs, photo albums, pamphlets, posters, drawings and written records. Their inclusion has highlighted archival seizure and the vast looted cultural heritage held at Dutch institutions. This led to intense discussions of the NEFIS archive in the Dutch press.[29]

The publicisation of these seized archives (photographs, diaries, political posters) was presented in relation to the 2022 implementation of a 2020 advisory report on colonial collection policy that stated that seized colonial art would be returned in cooperation with former colonies, including Suriname and Indonesia.[30] The decision did not include archival material, however, and a gallery full of looted material at the Rijksmusem highlighted the need for further debate on seized material held in Dutch archives. In March 2024, the Dutch Raad voor Cultuur (Council for Culture) published *Dealing with Shared Sources from Colonial History*, an advisory report to the Ministry of Education, Culture and Science on 'redress and restitution in relation to colonial archives'.[31] This report, which was meant to fill the archival void in the 2021 decree, focused not only on repatriation of seized archives, but also on restorative justice through the management of archives. Though the final report does not provide explicit recommendations on the NEFIS case, it mentions a 2023 parliamentary motion to return the archive. The NEFIS

---

29 See 'Geroofde objecten te zien in Rijksmuseum-tentoonstelling Revolusi [Looted Objects on Display in Rijksmuseum Exhibition Revolusi]', *NOS Nieuws* [*Dutch Broadcasting Foundation News*], 11 February 2022, nos.nl/artikel/2416790-geroofde-objecten-te-zien-in-rijksmuseum-tentoonstelling-revolusi; Jan Kleinnijenhuis, 'Nationaal Archief worstelt met roofkunst in collectie bij Indonesiëtentoonstelling [National Archive Struggles with Looted Art in Collection of Indonesia Exhibition]', *Trouw*, [Amsterdam], 11 February 2022, www.trouw.nl/binnenland/nationaal-archief-worstelt-met-roofkunst-in-collectie-bij-indonesie-tentoonstelling-b9477780/; Afran Groenewoud, 'Tentoonstelling Revolusi! in Rijksmuseum bevat geroofde eigendommen [Exhibition Revolusi! in Rijksmuseum Contains Looted Property]', *DPG Media*, [Antwerp], 11 February 2022, www.nu.nl/binnenland/6183271/tentoonstelling-revolusi-in-rijks museum-bevat-geroofde-eigendommen.html.
30 See also Boonstra's Chapter 9 in this volume for further reflection on the advice and its consequences.
31 Council for Culture, *Dealing with Shared Sources from Colonial History: Advice on Recovery and Restitution in Relation to Colonial Archives* (The Hague: Council for Culture, 2024), www.raadvoorcultuur.nl/documenten/adviezen/2024/03/25/dealing-with-shared-sources-from-colonial-history.

archive is featured in the report as an outstanding case of colonial archives from Indonesia and their use in the '*Revolusi!*' exhibition can be seen as one of the catalysts for the report, as it highlighted the omission of archives from the 2021 report.

Inclusion of the NEFIS archives in the '*Revolusi!*' exhibition further delineates repatriated archives (the Djogdja Documenten) from those that were not returned. But, as we have seen, the reasoning behind repatriation and continued custody at the NA is unclear and the differences in the records of each are negligible. So, while there is a clear new context added to the exhibited records—these records have been shown in the Rijksmuseum, they were chosen by curators, they morphed from archival records to museum objects—we also see through this exhibition a new context for the Djogdja Documenten. The records at ANRI are historically connected to those still at the NA. By having the NEFIS archive spark a debate about displaced and seized archives in the Netherlands, the return of the Djogdja Documenten represents one aspect of what could be done for the rest. Without a change in how the Djogdja Documenten are described and contextualised, however—at both the NA and ANRI—their repatriation means that the records are only slightly altered from those still in the Netherlands and displayed at the Rijksmuseum.

Our analysis has shown that neither the NA nor ANRI contextualises the Djogdja Documenten in a way that successfully conveys its nuances and unique history. The fact that even ANRI's descriptions hide or obscure layers of context leads us to believe that any process of archival decolonisation cannot end at repatriation. There is a deeper coloniality of archives at work—one rooted in the recordkeeping system that was passed down from coloniser to colonised and lingers within the structure and work processes at ANRI.

Jeurgens and Karabinos[32] wrote of archival coloniality in two ways: colonial archives (such as those of the Dutch East India Company or the colonial administration) and colonised archives (seized local archives such as the Djogdja Documenten). What we see on display on a deeper level in the Djogdja Documenten is a third archival coloniality—one of archival structures, which can manifest even in archives that superficially have no connection to colonial history. It is *how* we archive, not what, that

---

32 Jeurgens and Karabinos, 'Paradoxes of Curating Colonial Memory', 207.

has an entrenched coloniality. In the case of the Djogdja Documenten, its coloniality is therefore twofold: as a colonised archive that was seized and with structural coloniality due to how it has been archived, along with the insufficient contextual descriptions.

By focusing on seizure as the main source of an archive's coloniality, repatriation is seen as a way towards an archive's decolonialisation. But rather than speaking of only decolonialising the Djogdja Documenten, we instead must propose a new structure—one that is not merely decolonialised, but also exists outside the colonial system and is noncolonial in nature.

Therefore, we seek a liberatory archival praxis that liberates the Djogdja Documenten from the coloniality of its archival structures. Digital repatriation or simple digitisation will not dismantle the colonial logic and system inherent in this colonised archive, especially if the same archival structure—its description and arrangement—is reproduced.

Liberatory archival practices treat records not only as mere traces from the past that are preserved for a vague potential future use, but also as sources to be reactivated and connected to current liberation struggles.[33] Instead of featuring a single provenance of the NEFIS seizure and colonial perspective, the noncolonial structure provides descriptions with multilayered context that attends to the interests and benefits of the community to whom the records belong.

References

Primary sources

Arsip Nasional Republik Indonesia (ANRI). 2004. *Daftar Arsip Djogdja Documenten [List of Djogdja Documenten Archives] 1945–1949*. Jakarta: National Archives of the Republic of Indonesia.

Collectie S.H. Spoor. 1946–49. Nummer toegang [Access number] 2.21.036.01. The Hague: National Archives of the Netherlands.

---

33 Michelle Caswell, *Urgent Archives: Enacting Liberatory Memory Work* (London: Routledge, 2021), doi.org/10.4324/9781003001355.

Nationaal Archief (NA). n.d. 'Algemeen Rijksarchief (ARA), Tweede Afdeling, nummer toegang 2.14.04, inventarisnummer 201. NL-HaNA, Netherland Forces Intelligence Service en Centrale Militaire Inlichtingendienst in Nederlands-Indië, nummer toegang 2.10.62, inventarisnummer 6702 [General State Archives (ARA), Second Department, Access Number 2.14.04, Inventory Number 201. NL-HaNA, Netherland Forces Intelligence Service and Central Military Intelligence Service in Dutch-India, Access Number 2.10.62, Inventory Number 6702].' The Hague: National Archives of the Netherlands.

NA. 1942–45. *Inventaris van het archief van de Marine en Leger Inlichtingendienst, de Netherlands Forces Intelligence Service en de Centrale Militaire Inlichtingendienst in Nederlands-Indië* [*Inventory of the Archives of the Navy and Army Intelligence Service, the Netherlands Forces Intelligence Service and the Central Military Intelligence Service in the Dutch East Indies*]. No. 2.10.62. The Hague: National Archives of the Netherlands. www.nationaalarchief.nl/onderzoeken/archief/2.10.62.

Secondary sources

Agostinho, Daniela. 2019. 'Archival Encounters: Rethinking Access and Care in Digital Colonial Archives.' *Archival Science* 19, no. 2: 141–65. doi.org/10.1007/s10502-019-09312-0.

Bastian, Jeannette Allis. 2007. 'Reading Colonial Records Through an Archival Lens: The Provenance of Place, Space and Creation.' *Archival Science* 6, nos 3–4: 267–84. doi.org/10.1007/s10502-006-9019-1.

Caswell, Michelle. 2021. *Urgent Archives: Enacting Liberatory Memory Work*. London: Routledge. doi.org/10.4324/9781003001355.

Christen, Kimberly. 2015. 'Tribal Archives, Traditional Knowledge, and Local Contexts: Why the "s" Matters.' *Journal of Western Archives* 6, no. 1: Art. 3. doi.org/10.26077/78d5-47cf.

Council for Culture. 2024. *Dealing with Shared Sources from Colonial History: Advice on Recovery and Restitution in Relation to Colonial Archives*. The Hague: Council for Culture. www.raadvoorcultuur.nl/documenten/adviezen/2024/03/25/dealing-with-shared-sources-from-colonial-history.

Gouda, Frances, and Thijs Brocades Zaalberg. 2002. *American Visions of the Netherlands East Indies/Indonesia: US Foreign Policy and Indonesian Nationalism, 1920–1949*. Amsterdam: Amsterdam University Press.

Groenewoud, Afran. 2022. 'Tentoonstelling Revolusi! in Rijksmuseum bevat geroofde eigendommen [Exhibition Revolusi! in Rijksmuseum Contains Looted Property].' *DPG Media*, [Antwerp], 11 February. www.nu.nl/binnenland/6183271/tentoonstelling-revolusi-in-rijksmuseum-bevat-geroofde-eigendommen.html.

Hapsari, Kris, and Neneng Ridayanti. 2019. *Layanan Akses Arsip Statis Di ANRI [ANRI's Static Archive Access Services]*. Subdirektorat Layanan Arsip Direktorat Layanan dan Pemanfaatan Arsip Nasional RI [Subdirectorate of Archives Services, Directorate of Services and Utilisation of the National Archives of the Republic of Indonesia]. anri.go.id/storage/attachment/Layanan%20Akses%20 Arsip%20Statis.pdf.pdf.pdf [page discontinued].

Hedstrom, Margaret. 2002. 'Archives, Memory, and Interfaces with the Past.' *Archival Science* 2, nos 1–2: 21–43. doi.org/10.1007/BF02435629.

Jeurgens, Charles, and Michael Karabinos. 2020. 'Paradoxes of Curating Colonial Memory.' *Archival Science* 20: 199–220. doi.org/10.1007/s10502-020-09334-z.

Karabinos, Michael. 2013. 'Displaced Archives, Displaced History: Recovering the Seized Archives of Indonesia.' *Bijdragen Tot de Taal-, Land- En Volkenkunde [Journal of the Humanities and Social Sciences of Southeast Asia]* 169, nos 2–3: 279–94. doi.org/10.1163/22134379-12340027.

Karabinos, Michael. 2015. 'The Djogdja Documenten: The Dutch–Indonesian Relationship Following Independence through an Archival Lens.' *Information & Culture* 50, no. 3: 372–91. doi.org/10.7560/IC50304.

Karabinos, Michael. 2015. 'The Shadow Continuum: Testing the Records Continuum Model through the Djogdja Documenten and the Migrated Archives.' Doctoral thesis, Leiden University, Netherlands. hdl.handle.net/1887/33293.

Karabinos, Michael. 2017. 'Indonesian National Revolution Records in the National Archives of the Netherlands.' In *Displaced Archives*, edited by James Lowry, 60–73. London: Routledge. doi.org/10.4324/9781315577609-5.

Ketelaar, Eric. 2002. 'Archival Temples, Archival Prisons: Modes of Power and Protection.' *Archival Science* 2, nos 3–4: 221–38. doi.org/10.1007/BF02435623.

Kleinnijenhuis, Jan. 2022. 'Nationaal Archief worstelt met roofkunst in collectie bij Indonesiëtentoonstelling [National Archive Struggles with Looted Art in Collection of Indonesia Exhibition].' *Trouw*, [Amsterdam], 11 February. www.trouw.nl/binnenland/nationaal-archief-worstelt-met-roofkunst-in-collectie-bij-indonesie-tentoonstelling~b9477780/.

Lee, Oey Hong. 1981. *War and Diplomacy in Indonesia, 1945–1950*. Townsville: James Cook University of North Queensland.

Legêne, Susan, and Els Postel-Coster. 2000. 'Isn't It All Culture? Culture and Dutch Development Policy in the Post-Colonial Period.' In *Fifty Years of Dutch Development Cooperation 1949–1999*, 271–88. The Hague: SDU Publishing. research.vu.nl/en/publications/abaab046-a28c-466d-ad21-0c1671e52038.

Luker, Trish. 2017. 'Decolonising Archives: Indigenous Challenges to Record Keeping in "Reconciling" Settler Colonial States.' *Australian Feminist Studies* 32, nos 91–92: 108–25. doi.org/10.1080/08164649.2017.1357011.

McKemmish, Sue, Shannon Faulkhead, and Lynette Russell. 2011. 'Distrust in the Archive: Reconciling Records.' *Archival Science* 11, no. 3: 211–39. doi.org/10.1007/s10502-011-9153-2.

NOS Nieuws. 2022. 'Geroofde objecten te zien in Rijksmuseum-tentoonstelling Revolusi [Looted Objects on Display in Rijksmuseum Exhibition Revolusi].' *NOS Nieuws* [*Dutch Broadcasting Foundation News*], 11 February. nos.nl/artikel/2416790-geroofde-objecten-te-zien-in-rijksmuseum-tentoonstelling-revolusi.

Nurjaman, Jajang. 2020. 'Dekolonisasi Arsip Sebagai Warisan Budaya: Kajian Awal Pengembalian Arsip Statis Era Hindia Belanda [Decolonisation of Archives as Cultural Heritage: A Preliminary Study of the Return of Static Archives from the Netherlands East Indies Era].' *Khazanah: Jurnal Pengembangan Kearsipan* [*Khazanah: Journal of Archival Development*] 13, no. 1: 75–90. doi.org/10.22146/khazanah.55713.

Senier, Siobhan. 2014. 'Digitizing Indigenous History: Trends and Challenges.' *Journal of Victorian Culture* 19, no. 3: 396–402. doi.org/10.1080/13555502.2014.947188.

Society of American Archivists (SAA). 2005–24. *Dictionary of Archives Terminology*. [Online]. Chicago: Society of American Archivists. dictionary.archivists.org/.

Stoler, Ann Laura. 2010. *Along the Archival Grain: Epistemic Anxieties and Colonial Common Sense*. Princeton: Princeton University Press.

Theo, Rika. 2021. 'The Djogdja Documenten Revisited: Repatriation, Silence, and the Seized Archives of the Decolonization War.' Master's thesis, University of Amsterdam. scripties.uba.uva.nl/search?id=c4364542.

Trouillot, Michel-Rolph. 2015. *Silencing the Past: Power and the Production of History*. 20th anniversary edn. Boston: Beacon Press.

Turner, Hannah. 2015. 'Decolonizing Ethnographic Documentation: A Critical History of the Early Museum Catalogs at the Smithsonian's National Museum of Natural History.' *Cataloging & Classification Quarterly* 53, nos 5–6: 658–76. doi.org/10.1080/01639374.2015.1010112.

Yulianasari, Okeu. 2012. 'Deciphering the NEFIS Archives: Investigating Dutch Information Gathering in Indonesia 1945–1949.' Master's thesis, Leiden University, Netherlands.

11
The rise and fall of Glodok

Abidin Kusno

Introduction

This chapter discusses issues of space, politics and identity formation among ethnic Chinese from a historical perspective. In so doing, it speaks to a key theme of this volume, which is understanding how colonial categories were constructed, the extent to which these were repurposed in the organisation of urban space over time and how colonial categories persist into the present. This chapter consists of two parts. The first part explores the ways in which Glodok, an area in present-day Jakarta known as a *Pecinan* (or 'Chinatown') since the Dutch colonial era, was historically constructed and subsequently transformed in relation to ethnic Chinese identities. The aim of this part is to dislodge stereotypes assigned to ethnic Chinese and Glodok in the mainstream history of Jakarta.

The second part considers the voices of *pedagang* ('merchants' or 'traders') in Glodok as represented by the daily newspaper *Sinar Glodok* (*'Light of Glodok'*), which emerged in 1998 during the political turmoil of the early post-Suharto era. Through an analysis of reporting in *Sinar Glodok*, I tease out *pedagang*'s sense of time in relation to politics and to Glodok and ask how Chinese Indonesian identity was produced in the aftermath of anti-Chinese violence in 1998. Overall, this chapter seeks to problematise some dominant misconceptions about ethnic Chinese, by considering the spatial effects of colonial and postcolonial production of identity.

By reflecting on issues of space and identity, this chapter seeks to contribute to discussions of decolonising the history of Chinese Indonesians (see Chapter 1 of this volume), focusing on urban space in Batavia/Jakarta. The chapter complements other contributions to this volume, by Abdul Wahid on ethnic Chinese and the colonial tax regimes in Java in the 1910s to 1940s (Chapter 2), and Ravando and F.X. Harsono on the massacre of ethnic Chinese during the Indonesian revolutionary period, 1945–49 (Chapter 8).

Part I: History matters

How Dutch was the colonial city?

The dominant history of Jakarta gives little or no reference to the role of ethnic Chinese in building the city.[1] Historian Leonard Blussé was among the first to write about the Chinese legacy of building what was then called Batavia under the Dutch East India Company (Vereenigde Oostindische Compagnie, VOC). He uses 'Chinese Batavia' to refer to Batavia as essentially a 'Chinese colonial town under Dutch protection' that was shaped by the Chinese presence and influence.[2] Instead of seeing Batavia as a seventeenth-century European castle town, Blussé describes the city as a node in a Chinese maritime network that facilitated Chinese settlers and contractors, who constructed canals, walls and houses.[3] Therefore, the designs of the seventeenth and eighteenth-century Dutch Batavian townhouses 'clearly point to Chinese influence'.[4] In terms of expenditure, the Chinese 'paid five times as much as the other town people did for Batavia's fortifications. For the construction of the town hall, they paid three times as much as all

---

1   Leonard Blussé indicates that 'some Indonesian historians write about the history of their capital with little or no reference to its important Chinese heritage'. See Leonard Blussé, *Strange Company: Chinese Settlers, Mestizo Women and the Dutch in VOC Batavia* (Dordrecht: Foris Publications, 1986), 8. Other major works on Batavia, however, include very little about ethnic Chinese—see, for instance: Jean Gelman Taylor, *The Social World of Batavia: European and Eurasian in Dutch Asia* (Madison: University of Wisconsin Press, 1983); and Susan Abeyasekere, *Jakarta: A History* (Singapore: Oxford University Press, 1987). Several works came out in the 1990s and 2000s with a particular focus on Chinese Batavia, such as Mona Lohanda, *The Kapitan Cina of Batavia, 1837–1942: History of Chinese Establishment in Colonial Society* (Jakarta: Djambatan, 1996); Mona Lohanda, *The Chinese and the Dutch in Colonial Java, 1890–1942* (Jakarta: Yayasan Cipta Loka Caraka, 2002); Monique Erkelens, 'The Decline of the Chinese Council of Batavia' (PhD diss., Leiden University, Netherlands, 2013).
2   Blussé, *Strange Company*, 8.
3   ibid., 79–80.
4   ibid., 80.

other groups did together.'⁵ And, in little more than a decade after the city's founding (in 1619), taxes collected from the Chinese amounted to more than half the VOC's total income.⁶

The Chinese were just too important, so the Dutch chose to live with them *inside* the walled city. Such a dependency produced a 'rather unique kind of cooperation', which Blusse aptly calls 'strange company'. 'Strange' in the eyes of the Dutch, as, while the Chinese in Batavia were crucial in many respects to the VOC, the Dutch continued to warn one another that 'the Chinese are so full of deceit that we cannot trust them at all'.⁷

Yet, there was much for the Dutch to learn from the Chinese. First, not all the Chinese who came to live in Batavia were merchants. Many were farmers or land cultivators and many had various other occupations. François Valentijn, a religious minister whom the VOC employed to serve in Java, recorded (in his *Oud en Nieuw Oost-Indiën* [*Old and New East Indies*]) the activities of the ethnic Chinese in the 1720s, which covered everything from trade and crafts to restaurants and transportation. He wrote: '[T]he entire agriculture of Batavia also depends on them, because they are extraordinarily ingenious and diligent … There is nothing that one can imagine that they do not undertake and in which they do not practice.'⁸

Indonesian historian Mona Lohanda similarly points out that 'all agriculture around Batavia depended upon the Chinese' and the VOC relied on ethnic Chinese market-gardeners, labourers and artisans.⁹ Jan Hooyman's account in *Bataviaasch Genootschap* (*Batavian Society*) even pondered whether the Dutch could ever manage the colony without the Chinese:

> The Jung from China that arrived every year for trading brought about 1,200 to 1,300 people … It is hard to understand how they could work with *such* diligence and eagerness. Without them it would be difficult if not impossible for us to have all the farms in the Ommelanden ['hinterland'].¹⁰

---

5   ibid., 80.
6   ibid., 81.
7   As stated by Governor-General Brouwer in 1633 (cited in ibid., 81).
8   François Valentijn, *Oud en Nieuw Oost-Indien* [*Old and New East Indies*]. Volume 3 (The Hague: H.C. Susan, 1856), archive.org/details/franoisvalentij00valegoog/page/n6, 533. Translated by and cited in Kimberly Wilhelmina Wells, 'The Batavia Massacre: The Tragic End to a Century of Cooperation' (Master's thesis, Missouri State University, United States, 2019), 37–38.
9   Lohanda, *The Kapitan Cina of Batavia*, 12.
10 As cited in Denys Lombard, *Nusa Jawa: Silang Budaya* [*Between Islands: Cultural Crossroads*]. Volume II (Jakarta: Gramedia, 1990) [Originally published as *Le Carrefour Javanais: Essai d'histoire globale*, Paris: Editions de l'Ecole des hautes etudes en sciences sociales, 1990], 245.

Apparently, the Chinese were everywhere, inside and outside the walled city.

Who were the Chinese?

Race and space are contextually constructed and racial segregation has often been the basis of colonial organisation of space. Yet, in contrast to the Dutch citizenry, the Chinese, once they rendered themselves financially independent, had no hesitation in staying and marrying—in many cases, Balinese women who had been brought to the city as slaves.[11] It is not surprising then that, unlike the Dutch who lived inside the walls of Batavia, 'the houses of the Chinese were scattered throughout the city'.[12] This shows that the history of the ethnic Chinese in the city is marked by a long integration into Indonesian society, yet no matter their origins, they were recognised in VOC records only under a single category: *Chinees* or *Chinezen*.

Benedict Anderson offers the following explanation for the VOC's classification:

> Oblivious of the heterogenous populations of the Middle Kingdom; of the mutual incomprehensibility of many of their spoken languages; and of the peculiar social and geographic origins of their diaspora across coastal Southeast Asia, the company imagined, with its transoceanic eye, an endless series of *Chinezen* ... And on the basis of this inventive census it began to insist that those under its control whom it categorised as *Chinezen* dress, reside, marry, be buried, and bequeath property according to that census.[13]

The stereotype that the Chinese were a community of merchants whose identity was organised around profit generation from overseas trade indicates the construction of the *pedagang* or Chinese trading class as a category, but such a construct has concealed the fact that many came to the colony alone as labourers and remained poor for most of their lives. Their lengthy stay created bonds with local women with whom they produced children, most of whom grew up to marry other 'mixed' or local people, thus producing more and more 'mixed people'. Within an environment surrounded by one's local wife and relatives, it was extremely hard for the 'Chinese'

---

11 Largely Balinese women due to culinary habits, including eating pork. As cited in Blussé, *Strange Company*, 81.
12 ibid., 84.
13 Benedict Anderson, *Imagined Communities: Reflections on the Origins and Spread of Nationalism* (London: Verso, 1990), 168.

fathers to keep their children 'Chinese'. Instead, distinctive subcultures emerged, which came to be termed *peranakan*. *Peranakan* Chinese cultures were heavily influenced by Javanese, Sundanese, Balinese and even various Muslim cultures. Left alone, such *peranakan* and their complex cultural practices would have gradually disappeared into the general population to the point where people who thought of themselves as 'Chinese' would have been mixed race.

But the colonial apparatus of power recognised no such category of *peranakan*. It gave no space for racial ambiguity as it looked only for idealised racial definition. Despite the profound mixture of ethnicities and cultures, the Arabs, the Chinese and the Indians were all framed under the category of *Vreemde Oosterlingen*—a term institutionalised by the colonial state in 1855.[14] One could translate this term as either 'Foreign Orientals' or 'Foreign Easterners', which effectively distinguished *Vreemde Oosterlingen* from other Asians—most notably, 'Indonesians'. It also seemed to give a context for the Europeans to be seen as non-foreigners while erasing the Asian history of precolonial migration, interaction and integration.

How was the ethnic Chinese community territorialised?

The stereotype that the ethnic Chinese formed an exclusive community of walls has underplayed the fact that they were at once scattered and localised. When the Dutch built Batavia Castle on the coast, ethnic Chinese had already spread to the interior. They worked land in the countryside with the locals and these relations, while discursive and multilayered, were deeper and more extensive than those of the Dutch. Over time, such practices served to facilitate trust and relations with locals that in turn smoothed the enterprises run by the ethnic Chinese. When the Dutch eventually acquired agricultural land in Batavia's *Ommelanden* ('hinterland'), they had to rely on the ethnic Chinese to work it with indigenous labourers.

More contrasts could be teased out between the ethnic Chinese and the Dutch. The latter occupied land through an administrative machine that was slow but territorially fixed and exclusive. The Chinese, by contrast, moved rapidly everywhere, neither attended by their officers nor accompanied

---

14   Rosy Antons-Sutanto and Christoph Antons, 'The Construction of Ethnicity in Colonial Law and its Legacy: The Example of the Peranakan Chinese in Indonesia', in *Routledge Handbook of Asian Law*, ed. Christoph Antons (London: Routledge, 2016), 398–420, doi.org/10.2139/ssrn.3205090.

by an administrative apparatus. They often did not bother to officially register the land on which they worked.[15] They ran into trouble when signs of 'economic depression and gross ineptitude' among both the Dutch authorities and the Chinese *kapitein*[16] (chiefs given power by the colonial state to take care of the Chinese community) began to be strongly felt in the first quarter of the eighteenth century.

As many Chinese labourers continued to enter the *Ommelanden* without registering with the VOC or the Chinese *kapitein*, 'the *Ommelanden* had grown into a kind of Wild West avant la lettre'.[17] Uncounted (for tax purposes) and unemployed, the newly arrived Chinese, in the eyes of the Dutch, became a 'dangerous class' and rumours circulated about the threat posed by the 'menacing Chinese'. Dutch authorities soon decided to use force to deal with what they considered to be a Chinese uprising in the *Ommelanden*. In 1740, this resulted in the massacre of 10,000 Chinese people in Batavia. The massacre, which clearly reflected the VOC's fears of Chinese dominance in Batavia, changed the relationship between the Dutch and the Chinese, and the Dutch authorities banned the Chinese survivors from living within Batavia's walls. On 3 March 1741, the VOC issued a new policy sanctioning the Chinese survivors to live in the Chineesche Kamp in an area called Diestpoort, south of Batavia—today's Glodok.[18]

In this chapter, I suggest that fears of the Chinese intermingling with locals might have contributed to the VOC's decision after the massacre to territorialise Chinese in Glodok and keep them under the eyes of Dutch-approved chiefdoms. To control and restrict movement, the colonial rulers implemented a residential system and its *passenstelsel* ('pass system').[19] This set of restrictive and repressive policies was in place until 1916— long enough for Glodok to become recognised as the exclusive 'ghetto' of ethnic Chinese. The production of racialised city space was followed by sociocultural practices, all of which contributed to the formation of a signifier called 'Chinese.'

---

15 Lohanda, *The Kapitan Cina of Batavia*, 13.
16 Blussé, *Strange Company*, 96.
17 ibid., 88.
18 ibid., 96; Wells, 'The Batavia Massacre', 93; Lohanda, *The Kapitan Cina of Batavia*, 19.
19 See Lohanda, *The Kapitan Cina of Batavia*, 19.

How successful was the colonial racial ordering of space?

Through spatial containment, the Dutch sought to re-establish the previous Sino-European 'strange company' relations. The Dutch appointed a Chinese *kapitein* and restored the Chinese Council to organise Chinese communities. What was new was the Chineesche Kamp.

Yet, while this marking of space created a social category, the policy also encouraged the concentration of socioeconomic activities and, perhaps unintendedly, the formation of political identities. It brought rich and poor Chinese into close contact, enabling them to share experiences and work together. The Chineesche Kamp, including Glodok, ironically articulated stories not of isolation, but of connection and of ways of building a centre for activities that were at once social, economic and political. It was a place where modern political consciousness developed and traditions were debated; Glodok gave birth to Chinese political figures, activists, journalists and their social associations. It was always bound up with modern political development in faraway China, but such a connection need not be confined to identification with China alone. Instead, it led to various strands of globalised anticolonialism, including pan-Asianism and Indonesian nationalism.[20] Racialised spatial exclusion thus failed to marginalise Glodok.

From Glodok, the ethnic Chinese claimed their right to participate in city life, in association with broader political movements while producing 'Chinese cultures'. In 1755 the Chinese Council set up a school called Beng Seng Sie Wan.[21] This self-supporting education facility developed into the Sekolah Tjina[22] Tiong Hoa Hwee Koan (THHK), which was opened in 1901. The THHK, formed in response to the rise of consciousness among ethnic Chinese of being part of a Chinese 'modern' nation ('*bangsa Tionghoa*'),[23] played a pioneering role in education and became a model for modern sociopolitical movements like the Djamiat'ul Chair (1905) for the

---

20   Rebecca Karl, *Staging the World: Chinese Nationalism at the Turn of the Twentieth Century* (Durham: Duke University Press, 2002), doi.org/10.2307/j.ctv11cw4rg; Benedict Anderson, *Under Three Flags: Anarchism and the Anti-Colonial Imagination* (London: Verso, 2007): Su Lin Lewis, *Cities in Motion: Urban Life and Cosmopolitanism in Southeast Asia, 1920–1940* (Cambridge: Cambridge University Press, 2016), doi.org/10.1017/CBO9781316257937.
21   Lohanda, *The Kapitan Cina of Batavia*, 114–15.
22   Also known as Tiong Hoa Hak Tong; see also Ravando and Harsono's Chapter 8 in this volume.
23   Lea E. Williams, *Overseas Chinese Nationalism: The Genesis of the Pan-Chinese Movement in Indonesia, 1900–1916* (Glencoe: The Free Press, 1960). See also Leo Suryadinata, 'Pre-War Indonesian Nationalism and the Peranakan Chinese', *Indonesia*, no. 11 (1971): 83–94, doi.org/10.2307/3350745.

Arab community and, possibly, Budi Utomo (or Boedi Oetomo, 'Noble Endeavour'; 1908).[24] By the time the government removed residential restrictions and the rigid travel pass system in 1911, Glodok was already a centre of Chinese cultural production. Pioneers of news media set up their offices in Glodok and publishing houses produced an enormous corpus of writing in Sino-Malay, which contributed to the formation of modern literature in the language now known as Bahasa Indonesia.

How was postcolonial Glodok depoliticised?

The construct of the ethnic Chinese as the 'middle' subject served the function of the colonial apparatus. As the go-betweens for the colonial administration, the ethnic Chinese carried out the dirty work of extracting payments from people, which often involved coercion. This 'privilege' left an impression that the ethnic Chinese were close to the Dutch power elite even though they were not any higher in status than the natives.[25] This exceptional treatment was tied to the divide-and-rule strategy, but it did contribute to the strengthening of the economic position of ethnic Chinese. It also produced an identity and identification for the ethnic Chinese as the class of *pedagang*. Working for the colonial state, *pedagang* were not always confined by the boundary of Glodok. For instance, to increase state opium revenues in the nineteenth century, the ethnic Chinese who ran opium farms were not subject to Dutch-imposed travel and residential restrictions.[26] This helped the expansion of Chinese commercial activities in rural areas and strengthened further the image of Chinese as *pedagang*. The ethnic Chinese thus benefited from their 'middle' position even though it also left them vulnerable to victimhood.

The departure of the Dutch after independence generated profound uncertainty among ethnic Chinese, including those who had sided with the nationalists. Leaders such as Liem Koen Hian (1896–1952), who was formally involved in preparing for Indonesia's independence through the Investigating Committee for Preparatory Work for Independence

---

24   Suggested by Benedict Anderson in a conversation in July 2000. See also Asvi Warman Adam, 'The Chinese in the Collective Memory of the Indonesian Nation', *Kyoto Review of Southeast Asia* no. 3 (March 2003), kyotoreview.org/issue-3-nations-and-stories/the-chinese-in-the-collective-memory-of-the-indonesian-nation/.

25   Dewi Anggraeni, 'Does Multicultural Indonesia Include its Ethnic Chinese?', *Wacana: Journal of the Humanities of Indonesia* 13, no. 2 (2011): 256–78, doi.org/10.17510/wjhi.v13i2.23, at 266.

26   James R. Rush, *Opium to Java: Revenue Farming and Chinese Enterprise in Colonial Indonesia, 1860–1910* (Ithaca: Cornell University Press, 1990).

(Badan Penyelidikan Usaha Persiapan Kemerdekaan Indonesia), requested his fellow Indonesian nationalists that all ethnic Chinese be automatically granted Indonesian citizenship without having to go through an application process.[27] His request indicated that welcoming the Indonesian nation and its struggle for independence did not guarantee acceptance by the new nation. Years of colonial divide and rule had produced a 'general mental landscape' of the non-Chinese community towards the ethnic Chinese, who were regarded as 'disloyal and swaying where the wind (of power) blew'.[28] The ethnic Chinese knew perfectly well that they had to live under such a (mental) perception regardless of official policies, including that of assimilation. Many therefore found 'Chinese ethnicity' to be an identity or identifier that posed no contradiction with being Indonesian. Siaw Giok Tjhan, for instance, led the Consultative Council for Indonesian Citizenship (Badan Permusjawaratan Kewarganegaraan Indonesia) (from 1954 to 1965) to fight against racism by proposing a concept of 'integration' (rather than assimilation), which recognised Chinese ethnicity while accepting Indonesia as the homeland. In this case, ethnic Chinese would be considered one of the Indonesian *suku* ('ethnic groups').[29]

The citizenship of most Chinese remained ambiguous until 1960 when the Citizenship Law was implemented. The law required ethnic Chinese to submit an official statement rejecting Chinese citizenship, before they could apply for Indonesian citizenship.[30] This process registered ethnic Chinese as outsiders who still needed to be incorporated into the nation, regardless of their deeply rooted historical experiences in Indonesia.[31]

---

27 Anggraeni, 'Does Multicultural Indonesia Include its Ethnic Chinese?', 270.
28 ibid., 268.
29 Siauw Giok Tjhan, *G30S dan Kejahatan Negara* [*G30S and the Crimes of the State*] (Bandung: Ultimus, 2015).
30 Chong Wu Ling, 'Rethinking the Position of Ethnic Chinese in Southeast Asia', in *Contesting Chineseness: Ethnicity, Identity, and Nation in China and Southeast Asia*, eds Chang-Yau Hoon and Ying-kit Chan (Singapore: Springer, 2021), 125–47, doi.org/10.1007/978-981-33-6096-9_7.
31 Before the Citizenship Law, the postcolonial government had issued two economic policies that sought to dislodge the economic power of ethnic Chinese, the Benteng Program (1950) and the Presidential Decree No. 10/1959. These policies were based on the colonial assumption that ethnic Chinese were a separate category and not Indonesian enough to be treated equally. For the economic policy during this era, see: Thee Kian Wie, 'The Indonesian Government's Economic Policies Towards the Ethnic Chinese: Beyond Economic Nationalism?', in *Southeast Asia's Chinese Businesses in an Era of Globalization: Coping with the Rise of China*, ed. Leo Suryadinata (Singapore: Institute of Southeast Asian Studies, 2006), 76–101, doi.org/10.1355/9789812306531-006, at 88.

The ethnic Chinese played a range of active roles in the sociopolitical life of the city and the nation under the Sukarno government,[32] but the new nation-state was founded on claims over a territorially based identity. After eliminating the old colonial system of classification, all 'Chinese' had to decide on their citizenship: Indonesian or Chinese (the People's Republic of China in Beijing or the Republic of China in Taipei). The territorial nation-state demanded the Chinese be either 'foreign' or 'Indonesian', regardless of the long history of *peranakan Tionghoa* ('rooted Chinese') that belies such a simple dichotomy. The state, in principle, demanded complete assimilation to 'non-ethnic', even though many ethnic Chinese saw no contradiction in deepening local ties and maintaining linkages to places of origin.[33]

Yet, the idea of 'assimilation' into 'non-ethnic' Indonesian proved deceptive. The authorities were quick to learn that, once 'nationalised', ethnic Chinese could be used to manage economic enterprises and serve as the domestic motor for capitalist modernisation in the interests of the ruling elite. This scenario played out most perfectly under Suharto's New Order (1966–98). Backed by the army, the Suharto regime used the Chinese minority to ensure personal control of the country's domestic wealth. Ethnic Chinese were encouraged to focus on economic activities to the point that a select number (such as Liem Sioe Liong and Bob Hasan) became major cronies of the Suharto family. The state apparatus carried out its mission by narrowing the 'public sphere' of ethnic Chinese while enlarging the participation of Suharto's cronies in the economic sphere. Under the pretext of speeding up assimilation, the state closed Chinese schools and newspapers, effectively erasing the memories of Chinese roles in city and nation-building. The Suharto clique, insisting that the People's Republic of China had supported the 'communist coup' in 1965, prohibited Chinese language and culture and officially used the pejorative term '*Cina*' (that is, 'the Qing of China') for ethnic Chinese. They could be recognised as *Warga Negara Indonesia* ('citizens of Indonesia'), but not Indonesians. This policy can in some ways be understood as a return to the *Vreemde Oosterlingen* of colonial times. The assimilation policy of the Suharto era was essentially a restoration of the politics of 'divide and rule', with the Chinese separately

---

32 Leo Suryadinata, 'The State and Chinese Minority in Indonesia', in *Chinese Adaptation and Diversity: Essays on Society and Literature in Indonesia, Malaysia & Singapore*, ed. Leo Suryadinata (Singapore: Singapore University Press, 1993), 77–99, at 88.
33 For a discussion of this aspect of Chinese migration, see Henry Yu, 'Then and Now: Trans-Pacific Ethnic Migrants in Historical Context', in *The World of Transnational Asian Americans*, ed. Daizaburō Yui (Tokyo: Centre for Pacific and American Studies, University of Tokyo, 2006), 53–64.

integrated under 'citizens of Indonesia'. The social and political implications of such policies were consequential as they left ethnic Chinese 'alone' as easy targets for any violence.[34]

How about Glodok under the New Order? All Chinese signage was erased or Romanised under Indonesian terms. Temples were renamed with Hindu-Buddhist–sounding terms. The social organisation Sin Ming Hui was renamed Candra Naya and, since then, the memories of Glodok and Sin Ming Hui's social activism have faded, replaced with images of heritage architecture. In the mid-1990s, the organisation's headquarters was almost demolished when a developer targeted the location to build a new superblock, comprising shops, offices and apartments. What happened to Candra Naya was symptomatic of the transformation of Glodok under the New Order into a centre of commodity—a *pusat perdagangan* associated only with the economic activities of the ethnic Chinese community.

For much of its life under the New Order, Glodok was promoted as a 'Chinatown' where 'Chinese cultures' were represented largely by Chinese medicine, food and shops. It was portrayed as a space of consumption. Meanwhile, the political Glodok disappeared from public consciousness. What was left in Glodok was not only the representation of a *pusat pedagangan* ('trading centre'), but also a reduction of *Tionghoa* ('Chinese') into *Homo economicus* and, not less, a perfect ground for racist scapegoating in a time of political and economic crises.

For instance, when the economic crisis hit in 1998, orchestrated racial violence against ethnic Chinese, including sexual violence against women, broke out in several cities throughout Indonesia—most notably, Medan, Jakarta and Solo.[35] Glodok was shattered and torched. While casualties included both Chinese and non-Chinese, the violence pointed to deep discrimination and cultural suppression of ethnic Chinese under the Suharto regime.

On 26 May 1998, two weeks after the orchestrated riots that destroyed more than 4,500 shops in the Glodok area, Suharto's successor, president B.J. Habibie, visited Glodok and met with victims. He said: 'I suggest that

---

34 For instance, the anticommunist military takeover on 1 October 1965 took a strong anti-Chinese turn. For violence against ethnic Chinese before the Suharto era, see Ravando and Harsono's Chapter 8 in this volume; and J.A.C. Mackie, 'Anti-Chinese Outbreaks in Indonesia, 1959–68', in *The Chinese in Indonesia: Five Essays*, ed. J.A.C. Mackey (Melbourne: Thomas Nelson, 1976), 77–138, at 95.

35 See Jemma Purdey, *Anti-Chinese Violence in Indonesia, 1996–1999* (Leiden: Asian Studies Association of Australia in Association with KITLV Press, 2006), doi.org/10.1163/9789004486560.

we all work together to uphold peace, unity and work together to restore and upgrade the order of the *economy* that we had enjoyed before.' A Glodok resident responded:

> [B]ut how are we going to deal with trauma, Mr President? I don't understand how the looting could take place for two days in the daylight. We cried. But what we cried for was not even clear to us. The military commander and the head of the police had repeatedly said that they would guarantee security, but the looting still took place. How can we build up a new image, a new economy in Glodok with an Indonesian spirit?[36]

This response referred to the shocking scale of destruction and the truth about gang rapes (expressed in the language of 'trauma'), the sense that the state apparatus was unreliable and that fellow Indonesians were unpredictable. In this context, how could one trust the proposal to reconstruct the previous economy-centred order that had subjected the Chinese to attack and racial prejudice?

Part II. The restless *pusat pedagangan*: Critical reflexivity in 'Sinar Glodok'

In the early 2000s, I collected some bundles of *Sinar Glodok*, a daily newspaper for readers interested in the Chinese business areas of Glodok. I was intrigued by the newspaper's geographical focus on Glodok, the various locales identified as *pusat perdagangan Tionghoa* ('Chinese trading centre') in the Kota ('old town') area of Jakarta. Is *Sinar Glodok* just a medium for the revitalisation of the 'previous economic order', for 'peace and unity', as president Habibie suggested? How might it be involved in transmitting the *dagang* ('trade') tradition, which might in turn reproduce the stereotype of Chinese people? Could we look at *Sinar Glodok* as a voice of the *pedagang* in the post-riot, post-Suharto era? Could it be a medium for social change and hence an apolitical *political* struggle to redefine Chinese identity in this period?

---

36   'Habibie Temui Pedagang [Habibie Met Traders]', *Kompas*, [Jakarta], 27 May 1998: 1 [emphasis added].

G.L.O.D.O.K
70% UANG BEREDAR DISANA

LODOK adalah kawasan bisnis paling sibuk di Jakarta, bahkan melebihi kesibukan kawasan manapun di Indonesia. Seluruh jenis perdagangan beraktivitas disana : mulai elektronik, ponsel, garmen, sampai mobil dan perbankan. Tak heran kalau orang memperkirakan 70% peredaran uang di Indonesia berpusat di Glodok.

Kini telah hadir Harian Pagi SINAR GLODOK, sebagai koran pertama komunitas kawasan Kota yang meliputi, Glodok, Roxy, Mangga Dua, Pluit, Cempaka Putih dan Kelapa Gading.

Menyajikan informasi-informasi penting yang dibutuhkan para pelaku bisnis dan ekonomi. Aktal dan terpercaya berkat dukungan Grup Jawa Pos yang telah terbukti sukses mengelola lebih 80 koran diseluruh Indonesia.

Harian Pagi Sinar Glodok benar-benar siap menjadi lokomotif bisnis dan ekonomi sekaligus kepercayaan masyarakat kawasan Kota.

"Raihlah potensi yang luar biasa ini melalui Harian Pagi Sinar Glodok"

Harian Pagi SINAR G GLODOK
KORAN KEBANGGAAN KAWASAN KOTA

KANTOR PUSAT :
Komplek P. Jayakarta Center Blok D1 No. 8. (Jl. Tiangseng, P. Jayakarta No. 73) - Jakarta 10730.
Telpon : 6244876, 6288359, Fax : 6246858

Figure 11.1 *Sinar Glodok* advertisement at Jakarta Fair
Source: *Sinar Glodok*, 2001.

With the fall of Suharto's authoritarian regime in 1998, Indonesia entered a period of political transition (known as the Reformasi era) that was marked by a more open political and social environment. In contrast to the pervasive censorship under the New Order, the process of *reformasi* resulted in a higher degree of freedom of speech, of which *Sinar Glodok* was essentially a product. The newspaper circulated at the time when no government permit was required to publish newspapers (under president Habibie). It was a division of *Jawa Pos*'s newspapers after its mid-1990s restructuring by the journalism entrepreneur Dahlan Iskan, who considered *Sinar Glodok* a medium for voicing the interests of ethnic Chinese communities in Jakarta. *Sinar Glodok* was the only daily newspaper of the five Indonesian-language 'Chinese' publications that emerged in post-1998 Jakarta. For reasons that are not yet clear, it existed only for six (or seven) years, which still gives it one of the longest lifespans of a newspaper of this kind. As suggested by the name, *Sinar Glodok* ('*Light of Glodok*') offered information about businesses in Glodok, where it claimed 70 per cent of Indonesia's money circulated.

Figure 11.2 Graphic slogan in *Sinar Glodok*
Source: *Sinar Glodok*, 2001.

Yet, while commercially motivated, *Sinar Glodok* headlined national news and consistently published commentaries about the changing social and political climate at the time. In a study of the Chinese press in the post-Suharto era, media scholar Chang-Yau Hoon argues that *Sinar Glodok* contributed to perpetuating the idea that 'all Chinese people are traders'.[37] Indeed, about one-quarter of *Sinar Glodok*'s content was ads for sales of electronic goods, mobile phones and services in the areas of Glodok, Mangga Dua and Roxy. The press was also seen as carrying out a cultural mission to re-Sinicise Chinese Indonesians. Hoon observed that there were special sections on

---

37 Chang-Yau Hoon, *Chinese Identity in Post-Suharto Indonesia: Culture, Politics and Media* (Brighton: Sussex Academic Press, 2008), 102.

Chinese-language lessons, medicine, cultural values and work ethics. Indeed, the front page of one issue features a graphic image of a giant snake chasing a man. The caption reads: 'The Year of Snake 2001: Stay away from Politics: Follow *Sinar Glodok*: work … work … work' (Figure 11.2).

Perhaps because of such representations, Hoon considered *Sinar Glodok* as reproducing the stereotypes of ethnic Chinese as 'disloyal, exclusive and economic animals'.[38] Hoon concluded that *Sinar Glodok* reinforced the image of Chinese Indonesians as 'once a Chinese, always a Chinese',[39] and that the newspaper 'is the product of 32 years of internalising the stereotypes and essentialist views that have been held by mainstream society',[40] with little or no attention given to 'hybridisation and localisation of Chinese-Indonesians'.[41]

Pedagang's perspectives on politics

Hoon's valuable study encourages us to consider *Sinar Glodok* more deeply. In this section, I read *Sinar Glodok* as attempting to combine the economistic concerns of *pedagang* with a campaign to promote political consciousness. The term *pedagang* ('trader') has been associated with the ethnic Chinese,[42] but, as discussed earlier, this association should be understood as a sociohistorical construction rooted in the colonial social structure. In the colonial economy, the ethnic Chinese functioned as a *commercial* middle class, situated between the Dutch ruling class and the local population. This notion of '*pedagang*' continued in the postcolonial era. At the same time, it has also become a term used to blame the ethnic Chinese for any economic downturn, harbouring foreign allegiances and refusing to assimilate. The term could also be associated with discrimination against the ethnic Chinese as being a *pedagang* is due to the limited opportunities to develop other skills. In any case, *pedagang* is a problematic term, but it is used by *Sinar Glodok* to refer to shop-owners in Glodok.

---

38 ibid., 108.
39 ibid., 108.
40 ibid., 109.
41 ibid., 108.
42 For instance, see: 'Benarkah Orang Tionghoa Terlahir sebagai Pedagang/Pengusaha? [Is It True That Chinese Are Born as Traders?]', *Kompasiana.com: Beyond Blogging*, 7 June 2017, www.kompasiana.com/bocah_ngapak/59381d86a223bd4e5ade2308/benarkah-orang-cina-terlahir-sebagai-pedagang-pengusaha.

Rather than largely apolitical, *Sinar Glodok* occasionally featured interviews with researchers to tease out issues of minorities, discrimination and nation-building. It also featured a regular social commentary column called '*Corong*' ('funnel to amplify the voice'), which encouraged readers to speak up:

> Today is the era of *reformasi* and transparency. So as citizens of a sovereign country, we are free to speak up. Come on ... pour your complaints and praise on anything including public services such as those of telephone, electricity, land certificate, water, bazaar, traffic, roads, etc.; even topics on political issues are welcome.[43]

This statement indicates that *pedagang* in Glodok had issues with the quality of public services. Glodok falls under the jurisdiction of the local municipality. As an area that is not in any exclusive, privatised or gated neighbourhood or town, its fate depends on city government–provided services, including public security, which is tied to state politics. *Pedagang* in Glodok had to confront the situation in the streets since they shared space with street vendors, who dominated their storefronts, parking lots and the streets themselves. They had to deal with the effects of political instability, which manifested in various forms—from street demonstrations to potential riots. *Pedagang* thus had to turn their attention to politics as much as to the quality of public security and services. Their political consciousness is tied not only to their interests as *pedagang*, but also, more importantly, to their identity as traders and the spatiality of Glodok as a *pusat pedagangan Tionghoa* ('Chinese trading centre'). Glodok is accessible to everyone, which is good for business, yet this also makes it politically vulnerable as a *pusat pedagangan Tionghoa*.

'*Corong*', however, was quite reflective in its observations of *pedagang* and their sense of vulnerability:

> As a place associated with trading [*aktivitas niaga*], people have in mind only the volume of transactions and flow of money. This has led to potential crime in the area. So, if Mangga Dua [one of the trading centres] is known as a crime-prone area, it is due to us representing the area as a centre of business. In this sense, we are partly responsible for our vulnerability to crime.[44]

Such a reflection locates *pedagang* within, rather than outside, the space of 'crime' (*kejahatan*). '*Corong*' suggests that the line that divides *pusat pedagangan* and *pusat kejahatan* is not clear, as one serves to reinforce the other. But one

---

43 'Jangan Takut Bicara [Don't Be Afraid to Speak Up]', *Sinar Glodok* [*Light of Glodok*], [every issue]: 4.
44 '*Corong*', 'M-2 Rawan Kriminalitas [Mangga Dua, Crime-Prone Area]?', *Sinar Glodok* [*Light of Glodok*], [Jakarta], 22 June 2001: 4.

cannot blame *pedagang* for *kejahatan* and vice versa, as such a formulation leaves out the government's responsibility. From the perspective of '*Corong*', it is poverty that causes crime. And poverty is due in large measure to the government's failure to take care of the city's poor (*rakyat*).

'*Corong*' occasionally launched critiques of government officers (*pejabat*) for incompetency, mishandling cases and ignoring the needs of the *rakyat*. For instance, during the fuel hike in the early 2000s, a letter from a reader stated that 'the government lives on exploitation of its own *rakyat*, rather than supporting them'.[45] '*Corong*' explained that 'the fuel hike is squeezing the economic life of the middle lower income population. Under such circumstances, theoretically, crime rates will move up as people will do anything to survive.'[46] Responding to the police department's intention to mobilise snipers in places considered to be crime prone,[47] '*Corong*' said that such a tough measure was not at all a solution to crime. Instead, *Sinar Glodok* proposed economic adjustment. To the bus drivers going on strike against a hike in oil prices, a *pedagang* wrote, 'Please don't go on strike! The government should adjust bus fares to match the hike in oil prices, but buses must offer a better service and perform safer rides.'[48]

Sinar Glodok was quite upfront in voicing its critical perspectives on politics. For instance, in the early 2000s, during the presidencies of Abdurrahman Wahid (also known as Gus Dur) (1999–2001) and Megawati Sukarnoputri (2001–04), many headlines were about issues of political instability. For the ethnic Chinese, Abdurrahman Wahid was recognised as the defender of various marginalised groups. When he served as president, he revoked the discriminatory laws against the ethnic Chinese and issued a presidential decree in 2001 that made Chinese New Year (*Imlek*) a holiday for those who celebrate it.[49] Wahid's successor, Megawati Sukarnoputri, then declared *Imlek* a national holiday, in 2003. The *pedagang* at Glodok appreciated Abdurrahman Wahid and sought to help in the economic recovery effort by working and working ('*kerja … kerja … kerja*'), but they also knew perfectly well that the president

---

45   Yohanes Leo, 'Harga Jangan Naik, Dong [Don't Raise the (Fuel) Price, Please]!', *Sinar Glodok* [*Light of Glodok*], [Jakarta], 15 June 2001: 4.
46   '*Corong*', 'Penundaan Kenaikan BBM dan Gangguan Kamtibnas [Delay the Fuel Hike and National Security]', *Sinar Glodok* [*Light of Glodok*], [Jakarta], 15 June 2001: 4.
47   'Polda Tempatkan 100 Sniper di 17 Titik Rawan [Police Put 100 Snipers in 17 Crime-Prone Locations]', *Sinar Glodok* [*Light of Glodok*], [Jakarta], 15 June 2001: 8.
48   'Aduh, Jangan Mogok Dong [Alas, Please Don't Go on Strike]', *Sinar Glodok* [*Light of Glodok*], [Jakarta], 20 June 2001: 4.
49   Leo Suryadinata, 'Chinese Politics in Post-Suharto's Indonesia: Beyond the Ethnic Approach?', *Asian Survey* 41, no. 3 (2005): 502–24, doi.org/10.1525/as.2001.41.3.502, at 521.

continued to be challenged by other politicians. *Sinar Glodok* suggested that *pedagang* were aware that politicians who were only interested in gaining power or advancing their careers caused political instability. Political elites often mobilised these interests through street demonstrations. The political dramas involving presidents Gus Dur and Megawati were routinely covered. In 'Amien [Rais] is Not Ethical', the editorial page took aim at the then speaker of the People's Consultative Assembly (Majelis Permusyawaratan Rakyat) and chairperson of the National Mandate Party (Partai Amanat Nasional), who orchestrated the downfall of Gus Dur, even though *pedagang* had doubts about his ability to serve as president.[50] The political instability that elite manoeuvres caused made *pedagang* in Glodok 'very annoyed by the behaviour of the political elites'.[51]

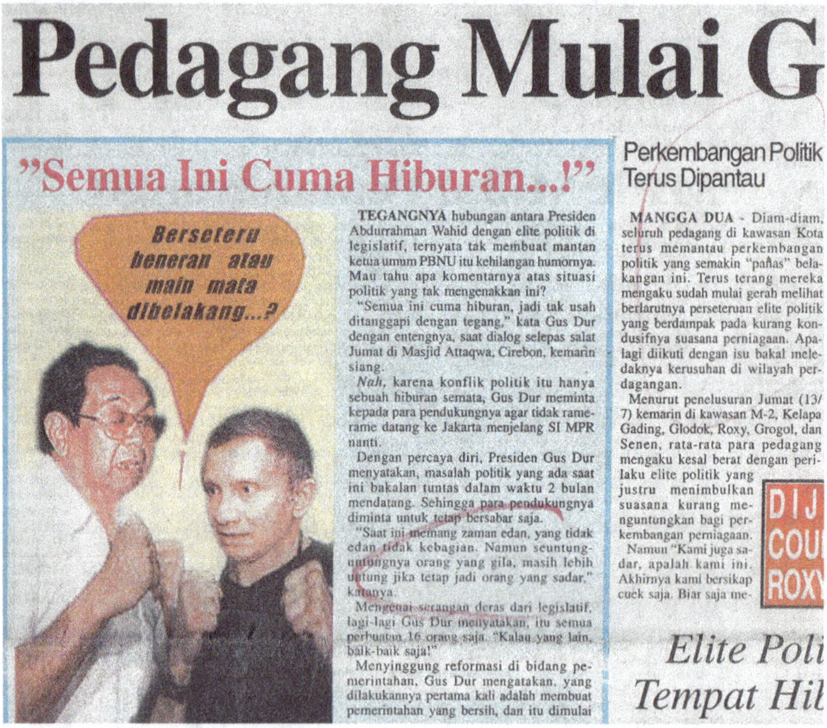

Pedagang Mulai G

"Semua Ini Cuma Hiburan...!"

TEGANGNYA hubungan antara Presiden Abdurrahman Wahid dengan elite politik di legislatif, ternyata tak membuat mantan ketua umum PBNU itu kehilangan humornya. Mau tahu apa komentarnya atas situasi politik yang tak mengenakkan ini?

"Semua ini cuma hiburan, jadi tak usah ditanggapi dengan tegang," kata Gus Dur dengan entengnya, saat dialog selepas salat Jumat di Masjid Attaqwa, Cirebon, kemarin siang.

Nah, karena konflik politik itu hanya sebuah hiburan semata, Gus Dur meminta kepada para pendukungnya agar tidak rame-rame datang ke Jakarta menjelang SI MPR nanti.

Dengan percaya diri, Presiden Gus Dur menyatakan, masalah politik yang ada saat ini bakalan tuntas dalam waktu 2 bulan mendatang. Sehingga para pendukungnya diminta untuk tetap bersabar saja.

"Saat ini memang zaman edan, yang tidak edan tidak kebagian. Namun seuntung-untungnya orang yang gila, masih lebih untung jika tetap jadi orang yang sadar," katanya.

Mengenai serangan deras dari legislatif, lagi-lagi Gus Dur menyatakan, itu semua perbuatan 16 orang saja. "Kalau yang lain, baik-baik saja!"

Menyinggung reformasi di bidang pemerintahan, Gus Dur mengatakan, yang dilakukannya pertama kali adalah membuat pemerintahan yang bersih, dan itu dimulai

Perkembangan Politik Terus Dipantau

MANGGA DUA - Diam-diam, seluruh pedagang di kawasan Kota terus memantau perkembangan politik yang semakin "panas" belakangan ini. Terus terang mereka mengaku sudah mulai gerah melihat berlarutnya perseteruan elite politik yang berdampak pada kurang kondusifnya suasana perniagaan. Apalagi diikuti dengan isu bakal meledaknya kerusuhan di wilayah perdagangan.

Menurut penelusuran Jumat (13/7) kemarin di kawasan M-2, Kelapa Gading, Glodok, Roxy, Grogol, dan Senen, rata-rata para pedagang mengaku kesal berat dengan perilaku elite politik yang justru menimbulkan suasana kurang menguntungkan bagi perkembangan perniagaan.

Namun "Kami juga sadar, apalah kami ini. Akhirnya kami bersikap cuek saja. Biar saja me-

DIJ
COU
ROXY

Elite Poli
Tempat Hil

Figure 11.3 Reporting politics in *Sinar Glodok*

Source: *Sinar Glodok*, 14 July 2001.

50 'Amien Tak Beretika [Amien is Not Ethical]', *Sinar Glodok* [*Light of Glodok*], [Jakarta], 28 Maret 2000; 2.

51 'Pedagang Mulai Gerah [Traders Are Getting Restless]', *Sinar Glodok* [*Light of Glodok*], [Jakarta], 14 July 2001: 1.

Pedagang's apolitical stance and the decline of Glodok

Not all *pedagang*, however, were interested in party politics. Some ignored politics all together and were mainly concerned with how to safely open their businesses. They welcomed the government to mobilise police or snipers around crime-prone areas. These are the *pedagang* who were tired of politics:

> We are tired of political issues as they tend to lead to riots [*kerusuhan*] … [W]e are actually immune to such a situation … [W]e no longer need to fear as we are sure that nothing could be worse than the past May 98. Moreover, snipers are around riot-prone areas.[52]

They asked their *pedagang* peers to stay focused on their *dagang*: 'Let the politicians be noisy, but business should go as usual.'[53]

These *pedagang* were no longer alarmed, even when rumours of mass rallies and demonstrations spread in the city after president Wahid's resignation in July 2001. They secured their business interests by ignoring the threats of political instability. 'They were no longer affected by such issues,' '*Corong*' recorded: 'Demo? People are tired of this old call which has brought no change.'[54] For '*Corong*', the indifferent attitude of *pedagang* to political matters stemmed not so much from ignorance, as from fatigue of fear about riots. They had lived in and through repeated fear and trauma to the point where they had become numb to street demonstrations. These *pedagang* generally were no longer affected. 'What does this indicate?' asked the reflective '*Corong*': 'Does this mean that the world of commerce has transcended the effects of political turmoil thanks to *pedagang*'s own capacity?'[55] '*Corong*' concluded:

> What is clear is that in the world of commerce, a strong sense of pride as *pedagang* has finally been attained—so strong that it can't be played [*dipermainkan*] … The *pedagang* have developed their consciousness through their experiences and determination to not … be bullied. They no longer wish to be puppets. Who they are is simple. Their mind is focus[ed] and their program is clear: *dagang*

---

52 ibid., 11.
53 ibid.
54 '*Corong*', 'Acuan Jempol pada Suasana Perniagaan [Thumbs Up for the Conducive Trading Environment]', *Sinar Glodok* [*Light of Glodok*], [Jakarta], 29 March 2001: 4.
55 ibid.

for profit to raise their family with dignity. Such a consciousness has been formed. Unaffected by political turmoil, it brings calmness to society. I think they are right. Through commerce we restore [a] relaxed atmosphere, conducive environment, and promises of a better tomorrow. This is a mission we give to *pedagang* today.[56]

In the view of '*Corong*', in the aftermath of May 1998, these *pedagang* assumed their *pedagang* subjectivity, not by the power of the state, but by their own agency. After years of experiencing subjection to power, *pedagang* had gained their autonomous agency in and through their experiences of anti-Chinese riots. Instead of leaving their profession for fear of another riot, they embraced it as the core of their identity and even saw redemption in *dagang*. These *pedagang* believed that their devotion to business and family would ultimately restore order and create a better future for a nation shaken by political strife.

Yet, it is worth noting that while *Sinar Glodok* found in *pedagang* a strong confidence in their identity as *pedagang*, and while they were largely ignorant (*cuek*) of the impacts of street demonstrations, traders in fact suffered from economic decline due to the vulnerability of Glodok's location. In other words, the space of Glodok is not autonomous. No matter how much agency *pedagang* invest in themselves, they cannot ignore, or control, the space within which they are embedded. They saw reduced numbers of customers and declining sales levels. They could ignore politics and disregard security, but they could not ignore the diminishing profits and dwindling number of customers visiting their stores. Visitors declined by about 30 to 40 per cent in 2000, *Sinar Glodok* reported.[57]

Soon, *pedagang* also realised that Glodok was not the only place on which to rely. In *Sinar Glodok*, they saw reports about and advertisements for new towns—most notably, Kelapa Gading, which by then was aggressively promoting a new shopping mall and other real estate in the northeast of Jakarta. There was the option for *pedagang* in Glodok to consider a new kind of *pusat perdagangan* safely contained in a new town, managed not by the city government, but by a private real estate company that oversaw not only the streets, but the whole built environment.

---

56 ibid.
57 'Pedagang GMP Cuek [Traders in Gajah Mada Plaza Don't Care]', *Sinar Glodok* [*Light of Glodok*], [Jakarta], 28 March 2001: 1.

The new enclosure: The rise of Kelapa Gading

> It turns out that at the end of [the] Monetary Crisis, capital gains earned from the rent were very good and there were a lot of requests for space. Potential store tenants instantly offered [a] down payment because they knew that there will be a lot of shoppers coming to the mall.[58]

The statement above was recorded in the memoir of Soetjipto Nagaria, the founder of Kelapa Gading new town, most of whose residents are ethnic Chinese. Nagaria recalls that in 2001, many *pedagang* showed interest in the new town and he decided to extend the square footage of his Kelapa Gading Mall. *Sinar Glodok* indeed often featured Kelapa Gading in its pages as an exceptionally safe area. Commentaries such as the one below consistently appeared on the page dedicated to the town: 'I am sure that this area is out of reach by rioters who seek to disrupt the social and economic life of *pedagang* ... Even though crime rates have surged in Jakarta, none of the *pedagang* in Kelapa Gading are worried.'[59] *Sinar Glodok* compared different locations and asked *pedagang* in Kelapa Gading what they thought about the security situation:

> Why should I use firearms? It is safe here. Since I opened my store here, there has not been a single incident that harms my business. At any rate, it is always safe here, because authorities are consistently on standby. And, we always pray.[60]

Furthermore: 'Kelapa Gading offers complete facilities, from residential, business centres to shopping mall, and it is free from flooding and crime.'[61]

Be that as it may, what we know is that, in October 2001, Nagaria decided to expand his Kelapa Gading Mall with the aim of creating the largest shopping mall in Jakarta. The rise of Kelapa Gading in the post-

---

58   Soetjipto Nagaria, in Li Zhuo Hui, *Pancaran Cahaya Tujuh Generasi: Kisah Perjalanan Keluarga Soetjipto Nagaria dalam Dunia Bisnis dan Social* [*The Radiance of Seven Generations: The Story of the Soetjipto Nagaria's Family Journey in the Business and Social World*] (Jakarta: PT Menaravisi Commerce, 2012), 268.
59   'Pedagang Kelapa Gading Bebas Senpi [Traders in Kelapa Gading Free of Firearms]', *Sinar Glodok* [*Light of Glodok*], [Jakarta], 15 June 2001: 8.
60   ibid. *Sinar Glodok*, however, reported that such security was due to the shopping mall's manager mobilising 100 security guards (*satpam*) and 20 soldiers (from the TNI, or Indonesian National Armed Forces). In addition, 'security personnel were privately hired by shop owners'. 'Andalkan Satpam Swasta [Relying on Private Security]', *Sinar Glodok* [*Light of Glodok*], [Jakarta], 28 March 2001: 1.
61   'Melongok Komunitas Kelapa Gading: Kawasan Terlengkap dan Nyaman [Observing Kelapa Gading's Communities: A Complete and Comfortable Neighbourhood]', *Sinar Glodok* [*Light of Glodok*], [Jakarta], 16 June 2001: 8.

Suharto era was due in no small measure to the decline of Glodok as a *pusat perdagangan*, due to the political anxieties recorded in *Sinar Glodok*. It also reflected a paradigm shift: the *pusat perdagangan* had increasingly come to be understood as a 'shopping mall', contained safely in a new town managed by a real estate company.

The shift from public city to private town is underscored by the creation of spaces for 'ABG' (*Anak Baru Gede*)—a slang term for teenagers, literally translating to 'new grown-ups'. This new young consumer class looked for a 'European lifestyle', including a 'bowling alley of 24 lanes, Time Zone and Cineplex'.[62] None of these facilities was part of the Glodok world. Kelapa Gading Mall is not the only shopping mall that transformed the *pusat perdagangan* of Glodok into a remnant of the past. It was just one among several new *pusat perdagangan* safely contained in new towns and airconditioned superblocks: self-contained multiplexes of office, residential and commercial space in Jakarta.

But Kelapa Gading did more than other shopping malls in its displacement of Glodok; in fact, it was meant to replace Glodok. Nagaria's Summarecon team promoted Kelapa Gading, in the northeast of Jakarta, as the head of the dragon (whereas Glodok was the dragon's tail). Temporally, its location signified the arrival of the dragon's head, which would lead *pedagang* into the future. However, this brought a number of issues into focus, such as whether Kelapa Gading could be seen as a new Chinese habitus in which the memories of May 1998 served as an unspoken framework for the town's securitisation.[63] Furthermore, in Kelapa Gading, we see the formation of class distinctions (in the ABG) as well as the promotion of the theme of *Nusantara* (the Indonesian archipelago) in various festivals to showcase the diversity of Indonesian culture, ranging from food to fashion. Yet, in as much as Kelapa Gading seeks to represent a variety of *Nusantara* cultures, it recalls the trope of ghettoisation, of the Chineesche Kamp that prevailed in colonial times or the gated communities of Suharto's New Order when the Chinese were encouraged to reproduce only their economic identity. It remains to be seen whether Kelapa Gading will replicate old Glodok in producing a generation of human rights lawyers, activists and progressive intellectuals.

---

62   Li Zhou Hui, *The Radiance of Seven Generations*, 270.
63   For an exploration of this theme in Kelapa Gading, see Charlotte Setijadi, *Memories of Unbelonging: Ethnic Chinese Identity Politics in Post-Suharto Indonesia* (Honolulu: University of Hawai`i Press, 2023), doi.org/10.1515/9780824896058, 68–96.

In our capacities as citizens and urban professionals, we owe a debt to Glodok and its histories. No text, however, can provide all the stories we need. We hope nevertheless that in debating the history of Glodok and orienting ourselves to the world of the present, we begin the work of refining the unresolved questions of decolonisation, discrimination and democracy—precisely what people of ethnic Chinese background ask of us. Responses to such questions are indeed our responsibility.

References

Abeyasekere, Susan. 1987. *Jakarta: A History*. Singapore: Oxford University Press.

Adam, Asvi Warman. 2003. 'The Chinese in the Collective Memory of the Indonesian Nation.' *Kyoto Review of Southeast Asia*, no. 3 (March). kyotoreview.org/issue-3-nations-and-stories/the-chinese-in-the-collective-memory-of-the-indonesian-nation/.

Anderson, Benedict. 1990. *Imagined Communities: Reflections on the Origins and Spread of Nationalism*. London: Verso.

Anderson, Benedict. 2007. *Under Three Flags: Anarchism and the Anti-Colonial Imagination*. London: Verso.

Anggraeni, Dewi. 2011. 'Does Multicultural Indonesia Include Its Ethnic Chinese?' *Wacana: Journal of the Humanities of Indonesia* 13, no. 2: 256–78. doi.org/10.17510/wjhi.v13i2.23.

Antons-Sutanto, Rosy, and Christoph Antons. 2016. 'The Construction of Ethnicity in Colonial Law and its Legacy: The Example of the Peranakan Chinese in Indonesia.' In *Routledge Handbook of Asian Law*, edited by Christoph Antons, 398–420. London: Routledge. doi.org/10.2139/ssrn.3205090.

Blussé, Leonard. 1986. *Strange Company: Chinese Settlers, Mestizo Women and the Dutch in VOC Batavia*. Dordrecht: Foris Publications.

Chong, Wu-Ling. 2021. 'Rethinking the Position of Ethnic Chinese in Southeast Asia.' In *Contesting Chineseness: Ethnicity, Identity, and Nation in China and Southeast Asia*, edited by Chang-Yau Hoon and Ying-kit Chan, 125–47. Singapore: Springer. doi.org/10.1007/978-981-33-6096-9_7.

Erkelens, Monique. 2013. 'The Decline of the Chinese Council of Batavia.' PhD diss., Leiden University, Netherlands.

Hoon, Chang-Yau. 2008. *Chinese Identity in Post-Suharto Indonesia: Culture, Politics and Media*. Brighton: Sussex Academic Press.

Karl, Rebecca. 2002. *Staging the World: Chinese Nationalism at the Turn of the Twentieth Century.* Durham: Duke University Press. doi.org/10.2307/j.ctv11cw4rg.

Kompas. 1998. 'Habibie Temui Pedagang [Habibie Met Traders].' *Kompas*, [Jakarta], 27 May: 1.

Kompasiana.com. 2017. 'Benarkah Orang Tionghoa Terlahir sebagai Pedagang/Pengusaha [Is It True That Chinese Are Born as Traders]?' *Kompasiana.com: Beyond Blogging*, 7 June. www.kompasiana.com/bocah_ngapak/59381d86a223bd4e5ade2308/benarkah-orang-cina-terlahir-sebagai-pedagang-pengusaha?page=all#section1.

Leo, Yohanes. 2001. 'Harga Jangan Naik, Dong [Don't Raise the (Fuel) Price, Please]!' *Sinar Glodok*, [*Light of Glodok*], [Jakarta], 15 June: 4.

Lewis, Su Lin. 2016. *Cities in Motion: Urban Life and Cosmopolitanism in Southeast Asia, 1920–1940.* Cambridge: Cambridge University Press. doi.org/10.1017/CBO9781316257937.

Li, Zhuo Hui. 2012. *Pancaran Cahaya Tujuh Generasi: Kisah Perjalanan Keluarga Soetjipto Nagaria dalam Dunia Bisnis dan Social* [*The Radiance of Seven Generations: The Story of the Soetjipto Nagaria's Family Journey in the Business and Social World*]. Jakarta: PT Menaravisi Commerce.

Lohanda, Mona. 1996. *The Kapitan Cina of Batavia, 1837–1942: History of Chinese Establishment in Colonial Society.* Jakarta: Djambatan.

Lohanda, Mona. 2002. *The Chinese and the Dutch in Colonial Java, 1890–1942.* Jakarta: Yayasan Cipta Loka Caraka.

Lombard, Denys. 1990. *Nusa Jawa: Silang Budaya* [*Between Islands: Cultural Crossroads*]. *Volume II.* Jakarta: Gramedia. [Originally published as *Le Carrefour Javanais: Essai d'histoire globale*, Paris: Editions de l'Ecole des hautes etudes en sciences sociales, 1990.]

Mackie, J.A.C. 1976. 'Anti-Chinese Outbreaks in Indonesia, 1959–68.' In *The Chinese in Indonesia: Five Essays*, edited by J.A.C. Mackey, 77–138. Melbourne: Thomas Nelson.

Purdey, Jemma. 2006. *Anti-Chinese Violence in Indonesia, 1996–1999.* Leiden: Asian Studies Association of Australia in Association with KITLV Press. doi.org/10.1163/9789004486560.

Rush, James R. 1990. *Opium to Java: Revenue Farming and Chinese Enterprise in Colonial Indonesia, 1860–1910.* Ithaca: Cornell University Press.

Setijadi, Charlotte. 2023. *Memories of Unbelonging: Ethnic Chinese Identity Politics in Post-Suharto Indonesia*. Honolulu: University of Hawai'i Press. doi.org/10.1515/9780824896058.

Siauw Giok Tjhan. 2015. *G30S dan Kejahatan Negara* [*G30S and the Crimes of the State*]. Bandung: Ultimus.

Suryadinata, Leo. 1971. 'Pre-War Indonesian Nationalism and the Peranakan Chinese.' *Indonesia*, no. 11 (April): 83–94. doi.org/10.2307/3350745.

Suryadinata, Leo. 1976. *Peranakan Chinese Politics in Java, 1917–1942*. Singapore: Institute of Southeast Asian Studies.

Suryadinata, Leo. 1993. 'The State and Chinese Minority in Indonesia.' In *Chinese Adaptation and Diversity: Essays on Society and Literature in Indonesia, Malaysia & Singapore*, edited by Leo Suryadinata, 77–99. Singapore: Singapore University Press.

Suryadinata, Leo. 2005. 'Chinese Politics in Post-Suharto's Indonesia: Beyond the Ethnic Approach.' *Asian Survey* 41, no. 3: 502–24. doi.org/10.1525/as.2001.41.3.502.

Taylor, Jean Gelman. 1983. *The Social World of Batavia: European and Eurasian in Dutch Asia*. Madison: University of Wisconsin Press.

Thee Kian Wie. 2006. 'The Indonesian Government's Economic Policies Towards the Ethnic Chinese: Beyond Economic Nationalism?' In *Southeast Asia's Chinese Businesses in an Era of Globalization: Coping with the Rise of China*, edited by Leo Suryadinata, 76–101. Singapore: Institute of Southeast Asian Studies. doi.org/10.1355/9789812306531-006.

Toer, Pramoedya Ananta, and Stanley Adi Prasetyo, eds. 1995. *Memoar Oei Tjoe Tat: Pembantu Presiden Soekarno* [*The Memoir of Oei Tjoe Tat: Assistant to President Sukarno*]. Jakarta: Hasta Mitra.

Valentijn, François. 1856. *Oud en Nieuw Oost-Indien* [*Old and New East Indies*]. Volume 3. The Hague: H.C. Susan. archive.org/details/franoisvalentij00vale goog/page/n6.

Wells, Kimberly Wilhelmina. 2019. 'The Batavia Massacre: The Tragic End to a Century of Cooperation.' Master's thesis, Missouri State University, United States.

Williams, Lea E. 1960. *Overseas Chinese Nationalism: The Genesis of the Pan-Chinese Movement in Indonesia, 1900–1916*. Glencoe: The Free Press.

Yu, Henry. 2006. 'Then and Now: Trans-Pacific Ethnic Migrants in Historical Context.' In *The World of Transnational Asian Americans*, edited by Daizaburō Yui, 53–64. Tokyo: Centre for Pacific and American Studies, University of Tokyo.

12

Decolonising a colonial fort? The case of Fort Rotterdam, Makassar

Ajeng Ayu Arainikasih

Introduction

Fort Rotterdam in Makassar, South Sulawesi, was first named Fort Ujung Pandang. It was built in 1545 by the Sultan of Gowa, I Manriwagau Daeng Bonto Karaeng Lakiung, who was widely known as Tunipalangga Ulaweng. The rectangular fort was Portuguese in style. Its outer wall was a mixture of stone and clay, and inside the fort were Makassar-style wooden houses.[1]

In the sixteenth and seventeenth centuries, the Kingdom of Gowa, affiliated with the Makassarese people—and located in present-day South Sulawesi—was a strong maritime power. Its capital, Makassar, was a free multicultural port city. However, this kingdom competed with another strong maritime power in the area, the Kingdom of Bone, of the Bugis people.[2] Therefore, to protect his kingdom, Tunipalangga Ulaweng decided to continue his father's

---

1 Muhammad Ramli, 'Peran dan Penamaan Benteng Ujungpandang dari Masa ke Masa [The Role and Naming of Fort Ujung Pandang from Time to Time]', in *Fort Rotterdam. Benteng di Simpang Masa* [*Fort Rotterdam: Fort at the Junction of Time*], ed. Iwan Sumantri (Makassar: Balai Pelestarian Cagar Budaya Sulawesi Selatan [South Sulawesi Cultural Heritage Conservation Centre], 2021), 79–102, at 84–90.
2 Hari Budiarti, 'Taking and Returning Objects in a Colonial Context: Tracing the Collections Acquired during the Bone–Gowa Military Expeditions', in *Colonial Collections Revisited*, ed. Pieter ter Keurs (Leiden: Leiden University Press, 2007), 123–44, at 123–26.

initiative to build several European-style forts throughout Gowa.³ In 1607, the Dutch East India Company (Vereenigde Oostindische Compagnie, VOC), like many other foreign traders, obtained permission to establish a trading office in Makassar. The VOC understood that the location of the Kingdom of Gowa, particularly its capital, Makassar, was very strategic (for the spice trade). The intention of the VOC was to create a monopoly over this trade.⁴

From the sixteenth to the twentieth centuries, conflict and wars over the spice trade occurred between the VOC and the Kingdom of Gowa, including the Makassar War, which broke out in 1666–67. The VOC secured help from Arung Palakka, a Bone nobleman, as well as from other local kingdoms in Sulawesi and the Moluccas, such as Buton, Ternate and Ambon.⁵

In 1667, to end the war, Sultan Hasanuddin of Gowa (1631–70) signed the Treaty of Bongaya. The terms of the treaty were that all Gowa's forts would be destroyed by the VOC except Fort Ujung Pandang, which would be seized and used by the Dutch for their own purposes. In 1673 the fort was redesigned into a modern European fortification: a turtle-shaped pentagonal fort with five bastions. The fort was renamed Fort Rotterdam to commemorate the birthplace of Cornelis Janszoon Speelman (1628–84), the Dutch commander (and the VOC Governor-General from 1680 to 1684) who oversaw the conquest of Gowa.⁶

According to *Forts in Indonesia* (2012) published by the Indonesian Ministry of Education and Culture, in 2010 Indonesia had approximately 400 'colonial forts', 'Nusantara forts' and World War II defence structures. The authors categorise colonial forts as those built by former European colonisers to defend their trading posts and warehouses and for military purposes. Meanwhile, forts built by communities or local rulers of the Indonesian archipelago, including those built by Europeans by request of the locals, are defined as Nusantara forts.⁷

---

3   Ramli, 'The Role and Naming of Fort Ujung Pandang', 84–90.
4   Budiarti, 'Taking and Returning Objects in a Colonial Context', 123–26.
5   ibid.
6   Yadi Mulyadi, 'Bermula dari Benteng Ujung Pandang: Telisik Nilai Penting Dibalik Fort Rotterdam [Starting from Fort Ujung Pandang: Explore the Important Values of Fort Rotterdam]', in *Fort Rotterdam. Benteng di Simpang Masa [Fort Rotterdam: Fort at the Junction of Time]*, ed. Iwan Sumantri (Makassar: Balai Pelestarian Cagar Budaya Sulawesi Selatan [South Sulawesi Cultural Heritage Conservation Centre], 2021), 103–34, at 103–4.
7   Ministry of Education and Culture, *Forts in Indonesia* (Jakarta: Ministry of Education and Culture of the Republic of Indonesia, 2012), 20–21.

After Indonesia's declaration of independence (in 1945), colonial forts were commonly regarded as undesirable heritage—representations of Indonesia's dark past. Therefore, some believed that conserving and preserving colonial forts were unnecessary. Others argued that the forts symbolised Indonesian resistance against colonial power and their preservation was therefore important.[8]

Today, some forts, such as Fort Legok Jawa in West Java, are empty and in ruins. Some are still used for military purposes by the Indonesian Government—for example, Fort Kuto Besak in Palembang and Fort Victoria in Ambon. Others have been repurposed as government office buildings and/or museums, such as Fort Marlborough in Bengkulu, Fort Vredeburg in Yogyakarta and Fort Rotterdam in Makassar. These forts have become popular tourist destinations.

The book *Forts in Indonesia* declares Fort Rotterdam the most successful example of the repurposing of a colonial fort in Indonesia.[9] Today the fort is a popular tourist destination for Makassar city locals, as well as other domestic and foreign tourists. Fort Rotterdam also plays an important role in the social and cultural life of the people of Makassar. It has become a public place for people to socialise and spend their spare time, attending cultural and/or community events or using the fort as background for photos and videos.[10] The fort also houses the provincial museum of South Sulawesi, La Galigo Museum.[11]

This chapter discusses the transformations of Fort Rotterdam across different political eras, from the colonial to the present. This chapter asks to what extent this fort was decolonised, and analyses to what extent, over time, La Galigo Museum's permanent exhibitions have shown evidence of decolonisation.

As discussed in Chapter 1 of this book, decolonisation is not merely the removal of a colonial power when a local ruler reclaims power and creates a new nation. Rather, decolonisation is an ongoing process of dismantling

---

8   M.D. Sagimun, *Benteng Ujung Pandang* [*Fort Ujung Pandang*] (Jakarta: Departemen Pendidikan dan Kebudayaan [Department of Education and Culture], 1992–93), 1–4.
9   Ministry of Education and Culture, *Forts in Indonesia*, 195.
10 Anggi Purnamasari, 'Benteng Rotterdam Sebagai Public Space [Fort Rotterdam as a Public Space]', in *Fort Rotterdam. Benteng di Simpang Masa* [*Fort Rotterdam: Fort at the Junction of Time*], ed. Iwan Sumantri (Makassar: Balai Pelestarian Cagar Budaya Sulawesi Selatan [South Sulawesi Cultural Heritage Conservation Centre], 2021), 283–312, at 302–11.
11 Ministry of Education and Culture, *Forts in Indonesia*, 187–95.

colonial legacies and colonial ways of thinking that have influenced almost all aspects of society.[12] There has been recent attention to the work of decolonising museums in the Netherlands (see Isabella's Chapter 13 in this volume). According to Mirjam Shatanawi, what this means for the Netherlands—as a former colonising power—is repatriating colonial collections, rewriting colonial vocabularies, sharing authority with the source communities and acknowledging the cultural diversity of Dutch society in museums.[13]

But there is also critical museum and heritage work to do in Indonesia. I argue that decolonising museums in Indonesia—a formerly colonised nation—means presenting narratives from local perspectives, as well as challenging colonial forms of knowledge-making that remain embedded in Indonesian museums.

The information in this chapter forms part of my PhD dissertation and is based on archival research, interviews and observations of Fort Rotterdam and La Galigo Museum's permanent exhibitions. The main written sources are La Galigo Museum's guidebooks published in different years, unpublished reports and newspaper articles. The interviews for this research were conducted with the current and former curators of the museum, as well as with employees of the Office for Cultural Preservation in Region XIX (South and Southeast Sulawesi provinces).

Decolonising Fort Rotterdam?

After being seized and redesigned by the Dutch in the seventeenth century, Fort Rotterdam became a trading post that the VOC sought to defend as well as a government and military headquarters for the company. It became the centre of the company's control over Sulawesi and the eastern part of modern-day Indonesia. The interior of the fort complex included the houses of the VOC governor and high-ranking officials, military barracks, a church, offices, ammunition storage buildings, a prison, a military hospital and

---

12 Aníbal Quijano, 'Coloniality and Modernity/Rationality', *Cultural Studies* 21, nos 2–3 (2007): 168–78, doi.org/10.1080/09502380601164353; Walter D. Mignolo and Catherine E. Walsh, *On Decoloniality: Concepts, Analytics, Praxis* (Durham: Duke University Press, 2018), doi.org/10.1215/9780822371779, 17.
13 Mirjam Shatanawi, 'Making and Unmaking Indonesian Islam: Legacies of Colonialism in Museums' (PhD diss., University of Amsterdam, Netherlands 2022), 14.

12. DECOLONISING A COLONIAL FORT?

warehouses.[14] After more than two centuries, by 1908, the Dutch no longer used Fort Rotterdam as a fortification[15] or as the centre for governmental affairs as the government offices were moved outside the fort complex.[16]

There were several reasons for the loosening of Dutch control over the fort. The VOC declared bankruptcy in 1799. In 1816, after the French and British interregnum (1806–16), the Indonesian archipelago became a colony of the Kingdom of the Netherlands and was known as the Dutch East Indies. Over time, the territory under Dutch control expanded.

By 1905, all of South Sulawesi had been annexed by the Dutch after a military expedition.[17] It is possible, therefore, that, by 1908, the role of colonial forts (particularly in South Sulawesi) was not as important as before because there were no more territories to conquer or protect.

By the 1930s, as reported by the *Bataviaasch Nieuwsblad* ('*Batavia Newspaper*') and the *Nieuwe Apeldoornsche Courant*, Fort Rotterdam was decaying and its outer walls had turned black. In 1937 the colonial government handed Fort Rotterdam over to the (presumably Makassar-based) Fort Rotterdam Foundation (Fort Rotterdam Stichting) and it was restored between 1937 and 1939.[18] The fort was officially declared a heritage site on 23 May 1940 (No. 1010 *Monumenten Ordonnantie* [Monuments Ordinance] *Stbld*. 1931 No. 238)[19] and deemed a historical landmark for Makassar.[20]

Various government offices were housed within the fort after its restoration and these organisations worked to prevent further deterioration of the structures. In a 1938 report in *Het Vaderland* ('*The Fatherland*'), it was stated that the Matthes Stichting (Matthes Foundation) had completely restored a building in the fort's northeast bastion for its own use.[21] According to

---

14   Adang Sujana and Nafsiah Aswawi, 'Arsitektur Fort Rotterdam [The Architecture of Fort Rotterdam]', in *Fort Rotterdam. Benteng di Simpang Masa* [*Fort Rotterdam: Fort at the Junction of Time*], ed. Iwan Sumantri (Makassar: Balai Pelestarian Cagar Budaya Sulawesi Selatan [South Sulawesi Cultural Heritage Conservation Centre], 2021), 189–224, at 199–213.
15   Ministry of Education and Culture, *Forts in Indonesia*, 192.
16   Mulyadi, 'Starting from Fort Ujung Pandang', 104.
17   Budiarti, 'Taking and Returning Objects in a Colonial Context', 126–32.
18   'Restauratie Fort Rotterdam [Restoration of Fort Rotterdam]', *Bataviaasch Nieuwsblad* [*Batavia Newspaper*], 27 May 1938; 'Het Historische Fort Rotterdam [The Historic Fort Rotterdam]', *Nieuwe Apeldoornsche Courant*, 29 November 1938.
19   Mulyadi, 'Starting from Fort Ujung Pandang', 104.
20   'Restoration of Fort Rotterdam', *Batavia Newspaper*; 'The Historic Fort Rotterdam', *Nieuwe Apeldoornsche Courant*.
21   'Het fort Rotterdam en de Matthes stichting [Fort Rotterdam and the Matthes Foundation]', *Het Vaderland* [*The Fatherland*], 4 August 1936.

Dr F.D.K. Bosch (1887–1968), the head of the colonial-era Archaeological Service (1916–36), the Matthes Foundation had a library and collections of ethnographic objects and manuscripts.[22]

The foundation was named after Benjamin Frederik Matthes (1818–1908), a Dutch linguist and missionary who arrived in Makassar in 1848 and worked in South Sulawesi for 23 years.[23] Matthes studied Makassar and Bugis literature, translated the Bible into Makassar and Bugis languages, published a Makassar–Bugis–Dutch dictionary and grammar books, wrote down local poetry and legends and collected manuscripts.[24] Matthes collaborated with Retna Kencana Colliq Pujie Arung Pancana Toa Matinroe ri Tucae (1812–76), the exiled Queen of Tanete Kingdom, to write and compile the manuscript *Sureq I La Galigo*.[25] The name of the manuscript was later adopted—in post-independent Indonesia—as the name of the provincial museum of South Sulawesi, previously called the Celebes Museum.

Celebes was the colonial-era name for the entire island of what is today known as Sulawesi. The colonial Celebes Museum, established in 1938, was an ethnographic museum housed within the Fort Rotterdam complex in the former house of VOC Governor-General Speelman.[26]

During the late colonial era, Fort Rotterdam became an important heritage site for the Dutch. By restoring and declaring the fort a historical site, as well as reusing it for government offices and the museum, the fort's role was transformed from a headquarters for VOC trade and military purposes into a site of significance (particularly for the Dutch in colonial Indonesia). It was preserved by the Dutch to demonstrate colonial power over Sulawesi (and the eastern part of the Indonesian archipelago).

---

22 'Het museumwezen in Indie [Museums in the Indies]', *De Indische Courant*, 11 November 1935.
23 'Benjamin Frederik Matthes', *Tirto.id*, [Jakarta], tirto.id/m/benjamin-frederik-matthes-pM.
24 Johann Christoph Gerhard Jonker, 'Levensbericht van B.F. Matthes [Biography of B.F. Matthes]', in *Jaarboek van de Maatschappij der Nederlandse Letterkunde, 1909* [*Yearbook of the Society of Dutch Literature, 1909*] (Leiden: Society of Dutch Literature, 1909), 254–72, www.dbnl.org/tekst/_jaa003190901_01/_jaa003190901_01_0018.php.
25 Ach. Hidayat Alsair, 'Perjuangan Gigih BF Matthes dan Colliq Pujie Bukukan I La Galigo [B.F. Matthes and Colliq Pujie's Persistent Struggle to Write I La Galigo]', *IDN Times Sulsel* [*IDN Times South Sulawesi*], 5 September 2019, sulsel.idntimes.com/life/education/ahmad-hidayat-alsair/perjuangan-gigih-bf-matthes-dan-colliq-pujie-bukukan-i-la-galigo.
26 Harun Kadir and M. Yamin Data, *Petunjuk Museum Negeri La Galigo Ujung Pandang* [*The Guidebook of Provincial Museum La Galigo Ujung Pandang*] (Makassar: Departemen Pendidikan dan Kebudayaan Direktorat Jenderal Kebudayaan Proyek Pengembangan Permuseuman Sulawesi Selatan [Department of Education and Culture, Directorate General of Culture, South Sulawesi Museum Development Project], 1985–86), 28–29; Wall text in the lobby of the permanent exhibition, Museum La Galigo, Makassar, Indonesia.

I argue that it was only in the 1930s that the Dutch started to realise the importance of preserving their 300-year history in and domination of the colony. Various art historians, archaeologists and historians, such as Pauline Lunsingh Scheurleer, Marieke Bloembergen, Martijn Eickhoff and Sri Margana, have argued that European interest in, research into and preservation of (Javanese) antiquities and cultural heritage began in the early nineteenth century.[27] As described by Margana, the need to more deeply understand the history and cultures of the colony's peoples was driven by the Dutch ambition to build an empire after the British interregnum.[28] It was only in the late colonial era, however, that attention to preserving colonial heritage increased. There are several examples of this.

In Surabaya, a locally born man of German descent, G.H. von Faber (1899–1955), established the Provincial en Stedelijk Historisch Museum (Provincial and Municipal Historical Museum) in 1933. The museum's exhibitions related the role of the Europeans in developing the modern city of Surabaya and displayed a Chinese altar and local ethnographic objects, particularly from East Java and Madura.[29]

In Koetaradja (present-day Banda Aceh), the Dutch Korps Marechaussee ('Military Police') established the Atjehsch Legermuseum (Aceh Army Museum) in 1937, which illustrated the 'successful' Dutch colonisation of Aceh.[30] Aceh was one of the last territories to be violently conquered by the Dutch, in the Aceh War (1873–1913). The museum's collections included mementos of that war: photographs, maps, memoirs, weapons, medals, uniforms, flags and parts of war vehicles. The Atjehsch Legermuseum was also financially supported by major Dutch companies.[31]

---

27   Pauline Lunsingh Scheurleer, 'Collecting Javanese Antiquities: The Appropriation of a Newly Discovered Hindu–Buddhist Civilization', in *Colonial Collections Revisited*, ed. Pieter ter Keurs (Leiden: Leiden University Press, 2007), 73–114, at 85–97; Sri Margana, 'Sana Budaya: Dari Orientalisme hingga Nasionalisme [Sana Budaya: From Orientalism to Nationalism]', in *Sonobudoyo: Sejarah dan Identitas Keistimewaan* [*Sonobudoyo: History and Special Identity*], ed. Herry Mardianto (Yogyakarta: Museum Sonobudoyo, 2018), 1–14; Marieke Bloembergen and Martijn Eickhoff, *The Politics of Heritage in Indonesia: A Cultural History* (Cambridge: Cambridge University Press, 2020), doi.org/10.1017/9781108614757, 22–60.
28   Margana, 'Sana Budaya'.
29   G.H. von Faber, *Korte Handleiding Provinciaal en Stedelijk Museum* [*Short Guide to the Provincial and Municipal Museum*] (Surabaya: Provinciaal en Stedelijk Historisch Museum [Provincial and Municipal History Museum], 1939), 7–9.
30   Tristan Broos, 'Het Atjehsch Legermuseum 1937–1942, waar de herinnering aan den Atjehkrijg aanschouwelijk werd bewaard [The Aceh Army Museum 1937–42, Where the Memory of the Aceh War Was Clearly Preserved]', *Armamentaria* 45 (2010–11): 6–29.
31   'Atjehsch Legermuseum [The Aceh Army Museum]', *De Tijd* [*The Time*], 30 March 1938.

Meanwhile in Batavia (present-day Jakarta), the Oud Batavia Museum was established in 1939 by the Museum of the Royal Batavian Society of Arts and Science—also funded by major Dutch companies—to celebrate the legacy and 350th birthday of Jan Pieterszoon Coen (1587–1629). Coen was admired as the founder of Batavia and later became the VOC Governor-General, between 1618–23 and 1627–29. The facade of the Oud Batavia Museum was purposely designed to resemble a typical Dutch house. The museum also housed the tombs of VOC governors-general, including Coen.[32] These three examples demonstrate that the move to preserve the fort in Makassar was part of a broader shift towards saving Dutch colonial heritage in the Indonesian archipelago.

During the Japanese occupation and the Indonesian revolution, Fort Rotterdam was used for more practical purposes. During the Japanese occupation (1942–45), it was home to the office of the Japanese Navy Administration in Eastern Indonesia and a centre for agricultural and language studies.[33] During the Indonesian revolution (1945–49), the fort became a military base for the Royal Netherlands East Indies Army (Koninklijk Nederlandsch-Indisch Leger, or KNIL). At that time, the fort served as the home of 1,200 Ambonese KNIL soldiers. By 1950, the fort was used as a residence for members of the Indonesian Army and their families. Consequently, the condition of the fort once again deteriorated. In 1953 the Archaeological Office claimed the fort should be used only for cultural purposes, however, it was only in 1970 that members of the Indonesian Army and their families living inside the fort were relocated by the Government of South Sulawesi to new homes outside the fort.[34]

By 1970, Indonesians were being ruled by an authoritarian regime, known as the New Order (1966–98), under president Suharto (1921–2008), who remained in power for 32 years. During the New Order, the regime paid new attention to culture and heritage. Its policy towards archaeology and museums was to safeguard cultural heritage and build a national identity based on the ideological slogan of 'unity in diversity'. One means of achieving this was to establish museums in every Indonesian province, each of which would present similar storylines about the region's contribution

---

32 'Het Graf van Coen. Het plan-Blankenberg Goedgekeurd [Coen's Grave. The Blankenberg Plan Approved]', *Sumatra Post*, 17 November 1937; 'Het Coen-Monument en Museum [The Coen Monument and Museum]', *De Indische Courant*, 18 November 1939; 'Museum Oud Batavia [Old Batavia Museum]', *Algemeen Handelsblad*, 13 December 1939.
33 Ministry of Education and Culture, *Forts in Indonesia*, 192.
34 Ramli, 'The Role and Naming of Fort Ujung Pandang', 94–95.

to the resistance to colonialism. The regime also worked closely with the UN Educational, Scientific and Cultural Organization (UNESCO) in developing and restoring cultural heritage.[35]

After the army vacated, between 1970 and 1976, Fort Rotterdam was restored by the Indonesian Government and the buildings inside—like in the colonial era—were used as government offices for the cultural sector, including for the regional archives, the Cultural Preservation Office of South Sulawesi Region and La Galigo Museum.[36]

Furthermore, in the 1970s, the original name, Fort Ujung Pandang, was reinstated.[37] In fact, in 1971 the city of Makassar was also renamed, as Ujung Pandang—chosen because it originated from the name of a *kampong* ('village') near the fort (as well as being the original name of the fort). 'Ujung Pandang' was considered more neutral than Makassar because it was not related to one specific ethnicity.[38] The Makassarese are just one ethnic group among the population of South Sulawesi Province, which includes the Buginese, Torajans and Mandarese.[39]

Figure 12.1 Fort Rotterdam, Makassar
Source: Ajeng Ayu Arainikasih.

---

35 Tod Jones, *Culture, Power, and Authoritarianism in the Indonesian State: Cultural Policy across the Twentieth Century to the Reform Era* (Boston: Brill, 2013), doi.org/10.1163/9789004255104, 162–69.
36 Ramli, 'The Role and Naming of Fort Ujung Pandang', 94–95.
37 Sagimun, *Fort Ujung Pandang*, 4.
38 Nurhadi, 'Inilah Alasan Nama Ujung Pandang Berganti Jadi Makassar [This is the Reason Ujung Pandang's Name Changed to Makassar]', *Tempo.co*, [Jakarta], 7 July 2022, nasional.tempo.co/read/1609468/inilah-alasan-nama-ujung-pandang-berganti-jadi-makassar.
39 Budiarti, 'Taking and Returning Objects in a Colonial Context', 123–26.

The name Ujung Pandang was changed back to Makassar in 1999 after the demise of the New Order government and the shift towards decentralisation.[40] As for the fort, Rotterdam is today widely used as both the official and the popular names for the fort.

The status of Fort Rotterdam as a heritage site continued in post-independent and post–New Order Indonesia, recognised for its municipal heritage related to the city of Makassar as well as Indonesian national heritage. Indeed, as argued by Indonesian archaeologist Yadi Mulyadi, one reason Fort Rotterdam became important for Indonesians is because it was a Nusantara fort before being transformed into a colonial fort.[41] I will now consider more carefully the museum within the fort and how the histories of the fort and the region have been presented to audiences over time. In so doing, I will consider the critical question of the extent to which the fort has been decolonised.

The Celebes Museum

The Celebes Museum, established in 1938 inside the Fort Rotterdam complex, was a colonial-era ethnographic museum. In the early twentieth century, museums (particularly ethnographic museums) mushroomed throughout the Indonesian archipelago. Their establishment was related to the Dutch imperial mission of the previous century. At that time, as argued by Indonesian historian Sri Margana, the Dutch realised that to build an empire within their colonies, it was important to understand the languages, customs, laws and cultures of the local population. They therefore introduced policies encouraging the study of local cultures, which increased the interest of both Europeans and local elites in studying and preserving cultural heritage.[42]

Consequently, by the early twentieth century, about 25 museums had been established in colonial Indonesia, by both European and local Indonesian actors through learned societies, the colonial government, missionaries and private initiatives. The museums were mostly ethnographic, although there were also institutions dedicated to archaeology, antiquity, city history and natural history.[43]

---

40 Nurhadi, 'This is the Reason Ujung Pandang's Name Changed to Makassar'.
41 Mulyadi, 'Starting from Fort Ujung Pandang', 103–6.
42 Margana, 'Sana Budaya', 1–14.
43 Ajeng Ayu Arainikasih, 'Heritage Politics and Museums during Japanese Occupation Period, 1942–1945', *International Review of Humanities Studies* 6, no. 1 (2021): 138–56, at 140–42.

The main purposes of these ethnographic museums (in the colony) were to collect, preserve and study cultural objects of an area and its peoples—as completely as possible—before the objects were consumed by modernisation or sold abroad.[44] Indeed, at that time, ethnographic objects (and antiquities) were extensively transported overseas.[45]

The colonial-era ethnographic museum, both in Europe and in the colony, was a tool to promote and legitimise colonialism.[46] Museums were also a tool of empire. They attempted to represent a visual encyclopedia of knowledge through exploration, collecting and classification of the natural and cultural worlds. Museums displayed European possession of the lands and cultures of 'Others' in the colonies, and also tried to show the great achievements and progress made in the colonies to justify European domination.[47] The arrangement of collections clearly showed that the cultures of Others were considered primitive, rare or exotic—and inferior to that of the superior Europeans.[48] Colonial-era ethnographic museums were, indeed, works of political representation that produced specific knowledge.[49]

The Celebes Museum is one such example. Its collection included ceramics, coins and ethnographic objects from South Sulawesi: kitchen utensils, traditional clothes, children's games, musical instruments, weapons, wooden boats, agricultural tools and jewellery.[50] Through this museum, the Dutch colonisers not only occupied the land but also attempted to show that they had mastered the local culture. At that time, the Dutch presented themselves as preserving the culture of Others from extinction. This belief was based on the racist social Darwinist idea that so-called primitive cultures would die out.

---

44 Bloembergen and Eickhoff, *The Politics of Heritage in Indonesia*, 171.
45 C. van Dijk, 'Gathering and Describing: Western Interest in Eastern Nature and Culture', in *Treasure Hunting? Collectors and Collections of Indonesian Artefacts*, eds Reimar Schefold and Hans F. Vermeulen (Leiden: CNWS Publications and the National Museum of Ethnology, 2002), 23–46, at 36; Scheurleer, 'Collecting Javanese Antiquities', 85–97.
46 Robert Aldrich, 'Colonial Museums in a Postcolonial Europe', in *Museums in Postcolonial Europe*, ed. Dominic Thomas (London: Routledge, 2010), 12–31, doi.org/10.4324/9781315875453, at 12–18.
47 John M. Mackenzie, *Museums and Empire: Natural History, Human Cultures and Colonial Identities* (Manchester: Manchester University Press, 2009), 1–17; Susan Legêne, 'Museums, Empire Utopias and Connected Worlds', in *Museums and the Idea of Historical Progress*, eds Rooksana Omar, Bongani Ndhlovu, Laura Gibson, and Shahid Vawda (Cape Town: Iziko Museums and ICOM South Africa, 2014), 15–30.
48 Aldrich, 'Colonial Museums in a Postcolonial Europe', 14.
49 Henrietta Lidchi, 'The Poetics and the Politics of Exhibiting Other Cultures', in *Representation: Cultural Representations and Signifying Practices*, ed. Stuart Hall, Jessica Evans, and Sean Nixon, 2nd edn (London: Sage Publications, 2013), 168–84.
50 Kadir and Data, *The Guidebook of the Provincial Museum La Galigo Ujung Pandang*, 28–29.

The fate of the Celebes Museum during the Japanese occupation (1942–45) and World War II is unclear. However, as described above, the book *Forts in Indonesia* claims Fort Rotterdam was used as offices for the Japanese Navy Administration as well as a centre for agricultural and language studies.[51] It is possible that the centre for agricultural and language studies was actually a continuation of the work of the colonial era's Matthes Foundation and Celebes Museum. Based on my research on museums during the Japanese occupation, it is known that museums in Java remained opened during the occupation and continued to be used as a tool of empire—this time, by the Japanese—as well as serving Japanese war propaganda.[52] According to Australian historian Adrian Vickers, during the Japanese occupation, the Bali Museum in Denpasar also remained opened and continued its activities.[53]

News reports about the Celebes Museum reappeared in 1948. At that time, *De Heerenveensche Koerier* ('*Heerenveen Courier*') and *Nieuwsblad van Friesland* ('*Newspaper of Friesland*') reported that the Mayor of Makassar Abdul Hamid Daeng Magassing (in office 1946–49) visited the Princessehof Museum in Leeuwarden, the Netherlands. During the visit, Magassing saw the fragment of a wood carving from a destroyed Makassar Chinese temple. Magassing and the Dutch museum's curator made a promise to exchange collections between their two museums.[54] These newspaper reports show that the Celebes Museum still existed in 1948 and was actively seeking collaborations with at least one museum in the Netherlands. It is unknown whether any exchanges of objects took place. The museum's fate in the 1950s also remains unknown due to a dearth of sources.

La Galigo Museum

What is known is that in 1966 Abdul Rahim Daeng Mone, an Indonesian linguist and the head of cultural inspection for South and Southeast Sulawesi, initiated the re-establishment of the museum in the fort. La Galigo Museum

---

51 Ministry of Education and Culture, *Forts in Indonesia*, 192.
52 Arainikasih, 'Heritage Politics and Museums during Japanese Occupation Period'.
53 Adrian Vickers, 'Dugas Jepangé/The Japanese Period: Bali under the Japanese', in *The Encyclopedia of Indonesia in the Pacific War*, eds Peter Post, William H. Frederick, Iris Heidebrink, and Shigeru Sato (Boston: Brill, 2010), 86–92, at 92.
54 'Uitwisseling Museumstukken Leeuwarden–Makassar [Exchange of Museum Pieces Leeuwarden–Makassar]', *De Heerenveensche Courier* [*Heerenveen Courier*], 28 August 1948; 'Makassar's burgemeester te Leeuwarden, 27 Aug [Makassar's Mayor in Leeuwarden, 27 August]', *Nieuwsblad van Friesland* [*Newspaper of Friesland*], 30 August 1948.

was officially inaugurated on 26 February 1974 and, in 1979, it became the provincial museum of South Sulawesi.[55] Its early collections were similar to those of the Celebes Museum and included ethnographic objects that were part of a bequest from the Matthes Foundation and the Eastern Indonesia Cultural Foundation (Yayasan Pusat Kebudayaan Indonesia Timur).[56]

As mentioned above, the name La Galigo refers to South Sulawesi's legendary ancestral figure and the ancient manuscript *Surek I La Galigo*, written in the thirteenth to fifteenth centuries. It is a name widely known in South Sulawesi. I La Galigo was believed to be the ancestor of the kings of all South Sulawesi's kingdoms.[57] The name is an inclusive one and an effort to represent all South Sulawesi's ethnicities and local kingdoms in a postcolonial context.

However, it seems that the decision to change the name of the museum (and the fort in the 1970s) was the only attempt at decolonisation. Because there have only been very slight changes to the museum's permanent exhibition and narratives, I argue that La Galigo Museum is a continuation of the colonial museum concept, particularly the colonial-era ethnographic museum.

Indeed, as argued by Katharine McGregor, the formal end of colonial rule in Indonesia did not include an end to colonial ways of thinking, as seen through the displays of museums. For instance, McGregor (2004) argued that the National Museum of Indonesia continuously used colonial concepts and values previously embedded in its permanent exhibition but creatively adapted these to suit the needs of postcolonial Indonesia, particularly as a tool for nation-building and to stimulate national pride.[58] As discussed in the Introduction, the Indonesian postcolonial local governments (and museums) failed to fully overthrow 'coloniality' and continued to replicate patterns used by the colonisers—this time, for the sake of national sovereignty.

---

55   Unit Pelaksana Teknis Daerah [Regional Technical Implementation Unit] (UPTD) Museum La Galigo, *Buku Petunjuk UPTD Museum La Galigo* [*La Galigo Museum Regional Technical Implementation Unit Manual*] (Makassar: Pemerintah Provinsi Sulawesi Selatan Dinas Kebudayaan dan Pariwisata UPTD Museum La Galigo [South Sulawesi Provincial Government Culture and Tourism Service UPTD La Galigo Museum], 2008), 17.
56   Kadir and Data, *The Guidebook of the Provincial Museum La Galigo Ujung Pandang*, 28–29.
57   *Museum La Galigo* (Makassar: PT Gramajapa Bersaudara Mandiri, 2011), 4.
58   Katharine E. McGregor, 'Museums and the Transformation from Colonial to Post-Colonial Institutions in Indonesia: A Case Study of the Indonesian National Museum, Formerly the Batavia Museum', in *Performing Objects: Museums, Material Culture and Performance in Southeast Asia*, ed. Fiona Kerlogue (London: The Horniman Museum and Gardens, 2004), 15–29.

This was very clear during president Suharto's New Order, when the colonial-era ethnographic museums within the capital of a province were nationalised into provincial museums (including the Celebes Museum). New provincial museums were also established and all were managed under the Directorate of Museums in the Ministry of Culture.[59]

Under Mohammad Amir Sutaarga (1928–2013) as the Director of Museums (1966–84), these provincial museums were standardised. Sutaarga trained under Dutch museum curator Dr A.N.J.Th. à Th. van Der Hoop (1893–1969) and was strongly influenced by the colonial-era Archaeological Service's F.D.K. Bosch. Following Bosch, Sutaarga believed Indonesia was in the middle of modernisation and acculturation processes that included the penetration of Western culture. Therefore, the existence of museums was necessary to safeguard Indonesian traditional cultures, which were about to become extinct; museums were important to minimise—as both Bosch and Sutaarga phrased it—'cultural impoverishment'.[60]

This view is clearly seen in a paper presented by the Department of Museums, History and Culture of the Regional Office of the Ministry of Education and Culture of South Sulawesi Province (Bidang Permuseuman Sejarah dan Kebudayaan Kantor Wilayah Departemen Pendidikan dan Kebudayaan Provinsi Sulawesi Selatan) to a seminar on architecture and museum exhibitions held in Bogor in 1975. The paper stated that Makassar was seen as an exit gate for cultural heritage leaving South Sulawesi, as well as an entry point for foreign culture. Therefore, local culture was believed to be in danger of extinction, potentially causing cultural impoverishment. Thus, La Galigo Museum was established to inform the public about the nature and historical events of South Sulawesi, as well as to safeguard the cultures of the Makassarese, Buginese, Torajan and Mandarese peoples as the ethnic groups of the province.[61]

---

59 Jones, *Culture, Power, and Authoritarianism in the Indonesian State*, 166.
60 Moh. Amir Sutaarga, *Persoalan Musium di Indonesia* [*The Problems of Indonesian Museums*] (Jakarta: Djawatan Kebudajaan Departemen PD dan K [Directorate of Museums, Directorate General of Culture, Department of Education and Culture], 1962), 11–45.
61 Bidang Permuseuman, Sejarah dan Kepurbakalaan [Museums, History and Antiquities Section], *Sebuah Laporan: Proyek Rehabilitasi dan Perluasan Museum La Galigo Sulawesi Selatan di Ujung Pandang* [*A Report: Rehabilitation and Expansion Project for La Galigo Museum South Sulawesi in Ujung Pandang*] (Bogor: Kantor Wilayah Departemen Pendidikan dan Kebudayaan Propinsi Sulawesi Selatan [Regional Office of the Department of Education and Culture, South Sulawesi Province], 1975), 1–4.

12. DECOLONISING A COLONIAL FORT?

These moves were also strongly influenced by the suggestions of John Irwin, a UNESCO delegate who came to Indonesia in the late 1950s to give recommendations on how to develop Indonesian museums. Sutaarga used the concept of what he called the ethnographic museum as the core model for the provincial museums.[62] The idea was reflected within the *Pedoman Pembakuan Museum Umum Tingkat Propinsi* (*Guidebook to Standardise Provincial Museums*) published by the Directorate of Museums in 1979–80.

The book stated that provincial museums should collect and display natural history specimens, paleontological and prehistoric objects, archaeological artefacts, historical objects, manuscripts, numismatic and heraldic collections, ceramics, art and craft objects and ethnographic objects.[63] The collections should represent the province's natural history, science, technological and historical development and cultural heritage, as well as representing Indonesia in general.[64] Their purpose was to promote national integration.[65]

Therefore, since the 1980s, all provincial museums have followed a similar 'template' for their permanent exhibitions. They commonly begin with a description of the natural resources of the province, continue to the prehistoric era, the Hindu/Buddhist kingdoms, the Islamic kingdoms and the colonial era—here, documenting local resistance to colonial power. The exhibitions usually conclude with ethnographic displays of the material culture of each province's ethnic groups.[66]

The New Order era's La Galigo Museum followed exactly this kind of storyline. Its permanent exhibition is housed within two buildings inside the Fort Rotterdam complex, Buildings D and M. Building D is the three-storey former governor-general's quarters and former home of Cornelis J. Speelman. This building was also the location of the 1938 Celebes Museum. The three-storey Building M was once used as a spice warehouse (first floor), VOC army barracks (second floor) and snipers' post (third floor).[67]

---

62   Sutaarga, *The Problems of Indonesian Museums*, 81.
63   Departemen Pendidikan dan Kebudayaan [Department of Education and Culture], *Pedoman Pembakuan Museum Umum Tingkat Propinsi* [*Guidelines for Standardisation of Provincial Museums*] (Jakarta: Proyek Pengembangan Permuseuman Jakarta [Jakarta Museum Development Project], 1979–80), 8.
64   Department of Education and Culture, *Guidelines for Standardisation of Provincial Museums*, 25.
65   Moh. Amir Sutaarga, 'Perspektif Pembinaan Museum di Indonesia [Perspectives on Museum Development in Indonesia]', *Museografia* V, nos 3–4 (1974): 105–10, at 110.
66   Department of Education and Culture, *Guidelines for Standardisation of Provincial Museums*, 25.
67   Sujana and Aswawi, 'The Architecture of Fort Rotterdam', 209.

From an examination of the museum's guidebooks over time, it can be concluded that the permanent exhibitions in La Galigo Museum experienced only minor changes from the 1970s and 1980s to 2010. After the New Order ended in 1998, the government passed a series of decentralisation policies. In 2002 provincial governments began to take over management of the provincial museums that had been managed by the central government. As argued by US anthropologist Christina Kreps, the authoritarian, top-down, centralised approach of the New Order towards provincial museums disempowered museum employees. Managers were unprepared to handle the museums without guidance from the central government. Furthermore, the New Order's policies meant that community members were unfamiliar with the management of the museums.[68] As a result of their transfer to provincial control in 2002, museums suffered decay and under-management.

In 2010 president Susilo Bambang Yudhoyono planned a revitalisation program for Indonesia's museums to cover their physical rejuvenation, management, programs, networking, policy development and branding.[69] La Galigo Museum was a target of the revitalisation project, although its storyline has not substantially changed.

Before and after the 2010 revitalisation, the museum's permanent exhibition within Building D showed the history of the conflicts between South Sulawesi kingdoms and the VOC. Although the current display regarding the conflict between Gowa–Bone and the VOC is simplified compared with the previous one, the museum seems to have tried to present a different historical perspective.

The extended object label for a painting depicting Bone nobleman Arung Palakka states: 'During his reign, Arung Palakka succeeded in liberating the Kingdom of Bone from the dominance of the Sultanate of Gowa and made the Buginese one of the largest maritime forces in the Indonesian archipelago at that time.'[70] This statement is different to the narrative typically used in Indonesian history books. Arung Palakka is usually considered a traitor, who worked with the VOC; and Sultan Hasanuddin of Gowa is usually

---

68   Christina F. Kreps, *Museums and Anthropology in the Age of Engagement* (New York: Routledge, 2020), doi.org/10.4324/9780203702208, 153–84.
69   UNESCO Office in Jakarta, *Panduan Praktis untuk Revitalisasi Museum di Indonesia* [*The Practical Guide for Indonesian Museum Revitalisation*] (Jakarta: UNESCO Office in Jakarta and Ministry of Culture and Tourism of the Republic of Indonesia, 2011), unesdoc.unesco.org/ark:/48223/pf0000192097, 2.
70   Object label, 'Simbol Kekuasaan dan Kekuatan [Symbol of Power and Strength]', Permanent Exhibition, Museum La Galigo, Makassar, Indonesia.

presented as a hero (although some people of Bugis Bone consider Arung Palakka the real hero).[71] This version represents the museum's attempt to offer different perspectives on history.

The trend of telling other versions of history flourished in the immediate post–New Order period. As argued by Dutch historian Henk Schulte Nordholt, during the New Order, regional histories and perspectives were marginalised in nationalist accounts. If regional histories were presented, they had to fit into the larger narrative of Indonesian history.[72] Schulte Nordholt's theory is strengthened by the omission from museum narratives of the fact that Ambonese KNIL soldiers lived within Fort Rotterdam during the *Revolusi* period. The story of the Ambonese soldiers did not fit into the national history narrative, so it was given no space within the museum's exhibit.

Schulte Nordholt further argued that, during the New Order, there was very little attention given to ordinary people as historical actors. National heroes were predominantly men, born on Java and belonged to the elite.[73] However, interestingly, the story of Bendara Pangeran Harya Dipanegara, widely known as Pangeran Diponegoro (1785–1855), a Javanese prince and Indonesian national hero who spent his time as a Dutch political prisoner inside Fort Rotterdam (1834–55), was not mentioned at all within La Galigo Museum's permanent exhibition.

The story of Prince Diponegoro does appear, however, in Building N of the fort complex. Building N is managed by the Office for Cultural Preservation of Region XIX and not by La Galigo Museum.[74] Indeed, many buildings inside the fort complex are managed by different governmental institutions.

The absence of Prince Diponegoro from La Galigo's permanent exhibition suggests continuity with both a colonial point of view and a New Order view. As a former New Order provincial museum, La Galigo only presents the culture and history of South Sulawesi and its people. Because local museums are supposed to present the history of local colonial resistance, the

---

71   Iswara N. Raditya, 'Arung Palakka diantara Gelar Pahlawan dan Pengkhianat [Arung Palakka between the Titles of Hero and Traitor]', *Tirto.id*, [Jakarta], 5 April 2019, tirto.id/arung-palakka-di-antara-gelar-pahlawan-dan-pengkhianat-cmej.
72   Henk Schulte Nordholt, *De-Colonizing Indonesian Historiography*, Working Paper No. 6 (Lund: Lund University, 2004), 7–8.
73   ibid., 7–8.
74   Purnamasari, 'Fort Rotterdam as a Public Space', 299.

stories of Sultan Hasanuddin of Gowa and Arung Palakka of Bone were the ones profiled. Although Diponegoro was a Javanese royal and national hero, his story does not fit into the museum's narrative.

After the 2010 revitalisation, illustrations of scenes from *Sureq I La Galigo* were put on display. The story of Retna Kencana Colliq Pujie Arung Pancana Toa Matinroe ri Tucae, the Queen of Tanete Kingdom, is mentioned in passing in a nearby moveable panel label. As noted, the queen collaborated with Matthes to compile the manuscript for *Sureq I La Galigo* and her story represents a viable option in attempts to decolonise the history of South Sulawesi.

Before and after the 2010 revitalisation, Building M displayed ethnographic objects. The permanent exhibition on the first and second floors currently illustrates the history and culture of South Sulawesi's ethnic groups thematically. The museum presents the civilisations of South Sulawesi in chronological order, from the prehistoric to the Hindu/Buddhist era, Islamic kingdoms and the colonial era. In some places the museum employs a thematic approach, concentrating on the agrarian and maritime cultures of the local peoples. Traditional farming tools, miniature traditional houses, wedding ceremonies and funeral customs are illustrated under this theme, as well as miniatures of boats and fishing equipment. The museum is focused on the Makassarese, Buginese and Torajans.

Presenting only the material culture of the local ethnic groups and ignoring other Indonesians who lived within the province are a colonial legacy. This idea can be traced back to the nineteenth and early twentieth centuries, when physical anthropology reached its peak. Physical anthropology is concerned with the study of evolution and human diversity. At that time, physical anthropologists preferred to conduct research on hinterland rather than coastal areas as they were not interested in mixed-race peoples.[75] After independence, provincial museums continued to focus on preserving the cultures of the peoples believed to be indigenous to each province.

---

75 Fenneke Sysling, *Racial Science and Human Diversity in Colonial Indonesia* (Singapore: NUS Press, 2016), 10.

Figure 12.2 La Galigo Museum's permanent exhibition in Building M, 2019
Source: Ajeng Ayu Arainikasih.

In the concluding sections of Building M's permanent exhibition, the museum illustrates the development of colonial cities in South Sulawesi such as Makassar, Watampone, Pare-Pare and Palopo. Information about the cities' development is displayed in wall-mounted labels inside glass vitrines, together with some objects. Although the museum has tried to present Makassar as a multicultural city, there is a sentence about Chinese Indonesians that, once again, illustrates a colonial legacy. The label explains that Makassar was a multicultural city where Malays, Javanese, Ambonese, Chinese, Arabs and Europeans resided. However, when explaining Makassar's Chinatown, La Galigo Museum's curator has written (in Bahasa Indonesia) that 'the gate in Makassar's China Town symbolises the friendship between the *pribumi* [native Indonesians] and the Chinese as non-*pribumi*'.[76]

In colonial Indonesia, the Dutch divided the population into a social hierarchy of three classes: the Europeans and the Indo-Eurasians (mixed descent), the Foreign Orientals (the Chinese and the Arabs) and the

---

76 Wall text, 'Pertumbuhan dan Perkembangan Kota [City Growth and Development]', Permanent Exhibition, Museum La Galigo, Makassar, Indonesia.

Inlanders or *Pribumi* (native Indonesians).[77] The Chinese themselves were divided into two groups: the *Totok* and the *Peranakan*. The *Totok* were the newly arrived Chinese, while the *Peranakan* were Chinese who were born in the Indonesian archipelago to families who had lived there for generations. Under the leadership of president Sukarno (1945–65), the Citizenship Law of 1958 forced Chinese Indonesians to choose between Chinese and Indonesian citizenship. As argued by Thung Ju Lan, an Indonesian Sinologist, the *Peranakan* were rendered foreigners. The situation worsened after the 1965 incident.[78] Moreover, in 1967, the New Order prohibited Chinese rituals and cultural customs. Consequently, Indonesian Chinese continued to be considered as 'outsiders', 'foreigners' or 'non-*Pribumi*' until president Abdurrahman Wahid reformed the law in 2006.[79]

Although the museum's statement emphasises friendship, it highlights the social segregation of the 'locals' and the Indonesian Chinese that is definitely a legacy of the colonial era as well as both Sukarno's and Suharto's reigns. My interview with La Galigo Museum's curator in 2019 revealed that the text was unintentionally written in this way.[80]

Conclusion

This chapter shows that coloniality still exists in the cultural heritage and museum sector in postcolonial Indonesia. Although Fort Rotterdam changed in different political periods and is considered important because it was once a Nusantara fort, the work of decolonising the site requires more than merely changing its name to Fort Ujung Pandang in the 1970s. While this act nationalised the Celebes Museum and tried to re-establish it as a provincial museum called La Galigo, it did not entail decolonisation. Colonial points of view and knowledge-making were adapted by the New Order elites for the sake of nation-building. This legacy is still strongly embedded in the museum to the present day.

---

77 Bart Luttikhuis, 'Beyond Race: Constructions of "Europeanness" in Late-Colonial Legal Practice in the Dutch East Indies', *European Review of History: Revue Européenne d'histoire* 20, no. 4 (2013): 539–58, doi.org/10.1080/13507486.2013.764845.
78 The aborted coup known as the Thirtieth of September Movement and subsequent anticommunist mass violence.
79 Thung Ju Lan, 'Contesting the Post-Colonial Legal Construction of Chinese Indonesians as "Foreign Subjects"', *Asian Ethnicity* 13, no. 4 (2012): 373–87, doi.org/10.1080/14631369.2012.710075, at 375–77.
80 Lenora (curator of La Galigo Museum), Interviewed by Ajeng Ayu Arainikasih, Makassar, 7 October 2019.

References

Primary sources

Bidang Permuseuman, Sejarah dan Kepurbakalaan [Museums, History and Antiquities Section]. 1975. *Sebuah Laporan: Proyek Rehabilitasi dan Perluasan Museum La Galigo Sulawesi Selatan di Ujung Pandang* [*A Report: Rehabilitation and Expansion Project for La Galigo Museum South Sulawesi in Ujung Pandang*]. Bogor: Kantor Wilayah Departemen Pendidikan dan Kebudayaan Propinsi Sulawesi Selatan [Regional Office of the Department of Education and Culture, South Sulawesi Province].

Departemen Pendidikan dan Kebudayaan [Department of Education and Culture]. 1979–80. *Pedoman Pembakuan Museum Umum Tingkat Propinsi* [*Guidelines for Standardisation of Provincial Museums*]. Jakarta: Proyek Pengembangan Permuseuman Jakarta [Jakarta Museum Development Project].

Kadir, Harun, and M. Yamin Data. 1985–86. *Petunjuk Museum Negeri La Galigo Ujung Pandang* [*The Guidebook of the Provincial Museum La Galigo Ujung Pandang*]. Makassar: Departemen Pendidikan dan Kebudayaan Direktorat Jenderal Kebudayaan Proyek Pengembangan Permuseuman Sulawesi Selatan [Department of Education and Culture, Directorate General of Culture, South Sulawesi Museum Development Project].

Ministry of Education and Culture. 2012. *Forts in Indonesia*. Jakarta: Ministry of Education and Culture of the Republic of Indonesia.

Mulyadi, Yadi. 2021. 'Bermula dari Benteng Ujung Pandang: Telisik Nilai Penting Dibalik Fort Rotterdam [Starting from Fort Ujung Pandang: Explore the Important Values of Fort Rotterdam].' In *Fort Rotterdam. Benteng di Simpang Masa* [*Fort Rotterdam: Fort at the Junction of Time*], edited by Iwan Sumantri, 103–34. Makassar: Balai Pelestarian Cagar Budaya Sulawesi Selatan [South Sulawesi Cultural Heritage Conservation Centre].

Museum La Galigo. 2011. *Museum La Galigo*. Makassar: PT Gramajapa Bersaudara Mandiri.

Ramli, Muhammad. 2021. 'Peran dan Penamaan Benteng Ujungpandang dari Masa ke Masa [The Role and Naming of Fort Ujung Pandang from Time to Time].' In *Fort Rotterdam. Benteng di Simpang Masa* [*Fort Rotterdam: Fort at the Junction of Time*], edited by Iwan Sumantri, 79–102. Makassar: Balai Pelestarian Cagar Budaya Sulawesi Selatan [South Sulawesi Cultural Heritage Conservation Centre].

Sagimun, M.D. 1992–93. *Benteng Ujung Pandang* [*Fort Ujung Pandang*]. Jakarta: Departemen Pendidikan dan Kebudayaan [Department of Education and Culture].

Sutaarga, Moh. Amir. 1962. *Persoalan Musium di Indonesia* [*The Problems of Indonesian Museums*]. Jakarta: Djawatan Kebudajaan Departemen PD dan K [Directorate of Museums, Directorate General of Culture, Department of Education and Culture].

Sutaarga, Moh. Amir. 1974. 'Perspektif Pembinaan Museum di Indonesia [Perspectives on Museum Development in Indonesia].' *Museografia* V, nos 3–4: 105–10.

UNESCO Office in Jakarta. 2011. *Panduan Praktis untuk Revitalisasi Museum di Indonesia* [*The Practical Guide for Museum Revitalisation in Indonesia*]. Jakarta: UNESCO Office in Jakarta and Ministry of Culture and Tourism of the Republic of Indonesia. unesdoc.unesco.org/ark:/48223/pf0000192097.

Unit Pelaksana Teknis Daerah [Regional Technical Implementation Unit] (UPTD) Museum La Galigo. 2008. *Buku Petunjuk UPTD Museum La Galigo* [*La Galigo Museum Regional Technical Implementation Unit Manual*]. Makassar: Pemerintah Provinsi Sulawesi Selatan Dinas Kebudayaan dan Pariwisata UPTD Museum La Galigo [South Sulawesi Provincial Government Culture and Tourism Service UPTD La Galigo Museum].

von Faber, G.H. 1939. *Korte Handleiding Provinciaal en Stedelijk Museum* [*Short Guide to the Provincial and Municipal Museum*]. Surabaya: Provinciaal en Stedelijk Historisch Museum [Provincial and Municipal History Museum].

Secondary sources

Aldrich, Robert. 2010. 'Colonial Museums in a Postcolonial Europe.' In *Museums in Postcolonial Europe*, edited by Dominic Thomas, 12–31. London: Routledge. doi.org/10.4324/9781315875453.

Alsair, Ach. Hidayat. 2019. 'Perjuangan Gigih BF Matthes dan Colliq Pujie Bukukan I La Galigo [B.F. Matthes and Colliq Pujie's Persistent Struggle to Write I La Galigo].' *IDN Times Sulsel* [*IDN Times South Sulawesi*], 5 September. sulsel.idntimes.com/life/education/ahmad-hidayat-alsair/perjuangan-gigih-bf-matthes-dan-colliq-pujie-bukukan-i-la-galigo.

Arainikasih, Ajeng Ayu. 2021. 'Heritage Politics and Museums during Japanese Occupation Period, 1942–1945.' *International Review of Humanities Studies* 6, no. 1: 138–56.

Bloembergen, Marieke, and Martijn Eickhoff. 2020. *The Politics of Heritage in Indonesia: A Cultural History*. Cambridge: Cambridge University Press. doi.org/10.1017/9781108614757.

Broos, Tristan. 2010–11. 'Het Atjehsch Legermuseum 1937–1942, waar de herinnering aan den Atjehkrijg aanschouwelijk werd bewaard [The Aceh Army Museum 1937–42, Where the Memory of the Aceh War Was Clearly Preserved].' *Armamentaria* 45: 6–29.

Budiarti, Hari. 2007. 'Taking and Returning Objects in a Colonial Context: Tracing the Collections Acquired during the Bone–Gowa Military Expeditions.' In *Colonial Collections Revisited*, edited by Pieter ter Keurs, 123–44. Leiden: Leiden University Press.

Jones, Tod. 2013. *Culture, Power, and Authoritarianism in the Indonesian State: Cultural Policy Across the Twentieth Century to the Reform Era*. Boston: Brill. doi.org/10.1163/9789004255104.

Jonker, Johann Christoph Gerhard. 1909. 'Levensbericht van B.F. Matthes [Biography of B.F. Matthes].' In *Jaarboek van de Maatschappij der Nederlandse Letterkunde, 1909* [*Yearbook of the Society of Dutch Literature, 1909*], 254–72. Leiden: Society of Dutch Literature. www.dbnl.org/tekst/_jaa003190901_01/_jaa003190901_01_0018.php.

Kreps, Christina Faye. 2020. *Museums and Anthropology in the Age of Engagement*. New York: Routledge. doi.org/10.4324/9780203702208.

Lan, Thung Ju. 2012. 'Contesting the Post-Colonial Legal Construction of Chinese Indonesians as "Foreign Subjects".' *Asian Ethnicity* 13, no. 4: 373–87. doi.org/10.1080/14631369.2012.710075.

Legêne, Susan. 2014. 'Museums, Empire Utopias and Connected Worlds.' In *Museums and the Idea of Historical Progress*, edited by Rooksana Omar, Bongani Ndhlovu, Laura Gibson, and Shahid Vawda, 15–30. Cape Town: Iziko Museums and ICOM South Africa.

Lidchi, Henrietta. 2013. 'The Poetics and the Politics of Exhibiting Other Cultures.' In *Representation: Cultural Representations and Signifying Practices*, edited by Stuart Hall, Jessica Evans, and Sean Nixon, 168–84. 2nd edn. London: Sage Publications.

Luttikhuis, Bart. 2013. 'Beyond Race: Constructions of "Europeanness" in Late-Colonial Legal Practice in the Dutch East Indies.' *European Review of History: Revue Européenne d'Histoire* 20, no. 4: 539–58. doi.org/10.1080/13507486.2013.764845.

Mackenzie, John M. 2009. *Museums and Empire: Natural History, Human Cultures and Colonial Identities*. Manchester: Manchester University Press.

Margana, Sri. 2018. 'Sana Budaya: Dari Orientalisme hingga Nasionalisme [Sana Budaya: From Orientalism to Nationalism].' In *Sonobudoyo: Sejarah dan Identitas Keistimewaan [Sonobudoyo: History and Special Identity]*, edited by Herry Mardianto, 1–14. Yogyakarta: Museum Sonobudoyo.

McGregor, Katharine E. 2004. 'Museums and the Transformation from Colonial to Post-Colonial Institutions in Indonesia: A Case Study of the Indonesian National Museum, Formerly the Batavia Museum.' In *Performing Objects: Museums, Material Culture and Performance in Southeast Asia*, edited by Fiona Kerlogue, 15–29. London: The Horniman Museum and Gardens.

Mignolo, Walter D., and Catherine E. Walsh. 2018. *On Decoloniality: Concepts, Analytics, Praxis*. Durham: Duke University Press. doi.org/10.1215/9780822371779.

Nordholt, Henk Schulte. 2004. *De-Colonizing Indonesian Historiography*. Working Paper No. 6. Lund: Lund University.

Nurhadi. 2022. 'Inilah Alasan Nama Ujung Pandang Berganti Jadi Makassar [This is the Reason Ujung Pandang's Name Changed to Makassar].' *Tempo.co*, [Jakarta], 7 July. nasional.tempo.co/read/1609468/inilah-alasan-nama-ujung-pandang-berganti-jadi-makassar.

Purnamasari, Anggi. 2021. 'Benteng Rotterdam Sebagai Public Space [Fort Rotterdam as a Public Space].' In *Fort Rotterdam. Benteng di Simpang Masa [Fort Rotterdam: Fort at the Junction of Time]*, edited by Iwan Sumantri, 283–312. Makassar: Balai Pelestarian Cagar Budaya Sulawesi Selatan [South Sulawesi Cultural Heritage Conservation Centre].

Quijano, Aníbal. 2007. 'Coloniality and Modernity/Rationality.' *Cultural Studies* 21, nos 2–3: 168–78. doi.org/10.1080/09502380601164353.

Raditya, Iswara N. 2019. 'Arung Palakka diantara Gelar Pahlawan dan Pengkhianat [Arung Palakka between the Titles of Hero and Traitor].' *Tirto.id*, [Jakarta], 5 April. tirto.id/arung-palakka-di-antara-gelar-pahlawan-dan-pengkhianat-cmej.

Scheurleer, Pauline Lunsingh. 2007. 'Collecting Javanese Antiquities: The Appropriation of a Newly Discovered Hindu–Buddhist Civilization.' In *Colonial Collections Revisited*, edited by Pieter ter Keurs, 73–114. Leiden: Leiden University Press.

Shatanawi, Mirjam. 2022. 'Making and Unmaking Indonesian Islam: Legacies of Colonialism in Museums.' PhD diss., University of Amsterdam.

Sujana, Adang, and Nafsiah Aswawi. 2021. 'Arsitektur Fort Rotterdam [The Architecture of Fort Rotterdam].' In *Fort Rotterdam. Benteng di Simpang Masa [Fort Rotterdam: Fort at the Junction of Time]*, edited by Iwan Sumantri, 189–224. Makassar: Balai Pelestarian Cagar Budaya Sulawesi Selatan [South Sulawesi Cultural Heritage Conservation Centre].

Sysling, Fenneke. 2016. *Racial Science and Human Diversity in Colonial Indonesia*. Singapore: NUS Press.

van Dijk, C. 2002. 'Gathering and Describing: Western Interest in Eastern Nature and Culture.' In *Treasure Hunting? Collectors and Collections of Indonesian Artefacts*, edited by Reimar Schefold and Hans F. Vermeulen, 23–46. Leiden: CNWS Publications and the National Museum of Ethnology.

Vickers, Adrian. 2010. 'Dugas Jepangé/The Japanese Period: Bali under the Japanese.' In *The Encyclopedia of Indonesia in the Pacific War*, edited by Peter Post, William H. Frederick, Iris Heidebrink, and Shigeru Sato, 86–92. Boston: Brill.

13

After recognition: Decolonial re-affect outside/within the museum

Brigitta Isabella

Introduction

The more ubiquitous the word 'decolonisation' becomes, the more it triggers disquiet and suspicion. When established institutions such as schools, universities and museums adopt the word 'decolonisation', we must ask what motivations and political logic underlie these decisions. Institutional decolonisation is generally presented by way of official apologies to acknowledge dark histories or inclusion programs for subjects who are recognised as victims of the past. Here, performances of the politics of recognition have a central role in symbolically producing historical breaks. This politics has a problematic linear temporal logic because it assumes that the history of colonialism can be separated from structures of coloniality that still dominate our lives today (see Chapter 1 of this volume). As a result, many activists and researchers believe that we must be wary of the foundational assumptions of a model of institutional decolonisation that invites us to recognise past problems only to soon forget them to move into the future.

Ethnographic museums, which until now have functioned as a bourgeois public sphere to promote the epistemology underlying nationalism and European imperialism, have become a most productive site to contest the basis of the politics of recognition. In the past two decades, museologists, inspired by postcolonial critiques and decolonial activism, have developed repertoires of recognition practices to include 'source communities',[1] engage in dialogues on processes of historical reconciliation and position the museum as a site for the redemption of history.[2] Museologist Mary Stevens even imagines that ethnographic museums can be 'authorities of recognition', which will contribute to the settlement of colonial debts.[3] Ethnographic museums have attempted to redefine themselves, supported by theories associated with 'the reflective turn' in the discipline of anthropology. In critical museum studies that developed in academia since the 1980s, ethnographic museums have been theorised as 'contact zones'[4] and democratic sites for contesting the ownership of cultural heritage. Parallel developments have taken place in modern art museums with the emergence of discourses about the simultaneity and coevalness of history, which have dismantled barriers and temporal hierarchies between the art categories 'primitive', 'traditional' and 'modern'.[5] Both the tearing down of this temporal hierarchy and the reflective turn in scholarship have opened new doors and encouraged encounters between critical ethnographic discourses and contemporary art. One such encounter is the phenomenon of contemporary artists from formerly colonised nations being invited to create interventions in the colonial order of ethnographic museums. For instance, Walter Mignolo has convincingly argued for the 'decolonial option' in his analysis of works by the Black artist Fred Wilson in the exhibition 'Mining the Museum' (1992), which used museum collections from the Maryland Historical Society to challenge widely held beliefs about history and race politics in the United States of America.[6]

---

1   Laura Peers and Alison Brown, eds, *Museum and Source Communities* (London: Routledge, 2003).
2   Wayne Modest, 'Introduction: Ethnographic Museums and the Double Bind', in *Matters of Belonging: Ethnographic Museums in a Changing Europe*, eds Wayne Modest, Nicholas Thomas, Doris Prlić, and Claudia Augustat (Leiden: Sidestone Press, 2019), 9–21, at 14.
3   Mary Stevens, 'Museums, Minorities and Recognition: Memories of North Africa in Contemporary France', *Museum and Society* 5, no. 1 (2007): 29–43.
4   James Clifford, 'Museums as Contact Zones', *Routes: Travel and Translation in the Late Twentieth Century* (Cambridge: Harvard University Press, 1997), 188–219.
5   Johannes Fabian, *Time and the Other: How Anthropology Makes Its Object* (New York: Columbia University Press, 2014), doi.org/10.7312/fabi16926.
6   Walter Mignolo, 'Museums in the Colonial Horizons of Modernity: Fred Wilson's Mining the Museum', in *Globalization and Contemporary Art*, ed. Jonathan Harris (Malden: Blackwell Publishing, 2011), 71–85.

Nevertheless, the presence of this increasingly trendy ethical practice raises valid concerns from practitioners who are positioned as subjects to be included and recognised by museum authorities. 'Will I become a "native informant"? A shaman to exorcise feelings of guilt carried by the ethnographic museum? Will I become a neoliberal art cheerleader to add value to the museum's brand?' asked contemporary artist Rajkamal Kahlon, who held a residency at Weltmuseum Wien (World Museum Vienna) in 2016.[7] 'The museum will not be decolonised', declared curator Sumaya Kassim, who rejects instant reconciliation programs that merely provide space for practitioners of colour, non-Western practitioners and those from formerly colonised countries to participate in the colonial structures of museums.[8] Having had similar experiences and been in a critical position similar to Kahlon and Kassim, I find this concern is not one of nihilistic pessimism but, rather, offers a healthy scepticism and radical hope that demand structural change. Recognition should not necessarily be assumed to automatically erase power imbalances in present-day colonial relations. On the contrary, recognition can even be a colonial tool to reproduce power imbalances, especially when it is created with terms and conditions that merely reconcile the guilt and complicity of the coloniser in contemporary colonial structures.

Departing from critiques of the politics of recognition,[9] the first and second parts of this chapter argue that recognition alone is not sufficient to transform colonial relations in museums. So, what can be offered after recognition? I offer re-affect: a relational practice based on a nonlinear temporal logic that mediates decolonial subjects' claims to self-recognition to create new narratives, contacts and relationships outside and within museums. This proposition departs from the observation that artists occupy

---

7   Rajkamal Kahlon, 'Love and Loss in the Ethnographic Museum', in *Matters of Belonging: Ethnographic Museums in a Changing Europe*, eds Wayne Modest, Nicholas Thomas, Doris Prlić, and Claudia Augustat (Leiden: Sidestone Press, 2019), 101–10, at 104.
8   Sumaya Kassim, 'The Museum Will Not be Decolonised', *Media Diversified*, 15 November 2017, mediadiversified.org/2017/11/15/the-museum-will-not-be-decolonised/.
9   Frantz Fanon, *Black Skin, White Masks*, trans. Charles Markman (London: Pluto Press, 1986); Elizabeth A. Povinelli, *The Cunning of Recognition: Indigenous Alterities and the Making of Australian Multiculturalism* (Durham: Duke University Press, 2002), doi.org/10.2307/j.ctv116895z; Nancy Fraser and Axel Honneth, *Redistribution or Recognition? A Political Philosophical Exchange* (New York: Verso, 2003); Glen Sean Coulthard, *Red Skin, White Masks: Rejecting the Colonial Politics of Recognition* (Minneapolis: University of Minnesota Press, 2014), doi.org/10.5749/minnesota/9780816679645.001.0001.

a unique position as guests of ethnographic museums, because they reflect on their complex position *outside/within the museum* that subverts the one-way processes of a politics of recognition.[10]

To demonstrate the artistic side of re-affect work, I will examine case studies of two art and research collectives from Yogyakarta, Indonesia, Kunci and Lifepatch, who accepted invitations to 'decolonise' ethnographic museums in Europe in 2017. Kunci, a collective of which I am a member, held a residency at the Tropenmuseum (Museum of the Tropics) in Amsterdam and created an audio guide titled *Outside Within Colonial Theater* to redistribute counter-positions and create new affective routes for the museum's permanent collection. Lifepatch, in their solo exhibition 'The Tiger and the Lion' at the Museum of Contemporary Art Antwerp, within the performance framework of Europalia Indonesia in Belgium, attempted to build a contact zone by interweaving colonial artefacts and oral stories about the Batak War in Belgium, the Netherlands and Tanah Batak (the land of the Batak peoples) in North Sumatra. By examining these two artistic research projects, I will offer some thoughts about re-affect work as a process outside and within the museum that dismantles colonial binarism in the politics of recognition and seeks to facilitate decolonial aspirations for social justice activism that goes beyond the walls of the museum.

Theorising recognition

> For Hegel there is reciprocity [in the master–slave dialectic]; here the master laughs at the consciousness of the slave. What he wants from the slave is not recognition but work.[11]
>
> —Frantz Fanon, *Black Skin, White Masks*

The roots of theories of recognition can be traced to the thinking of the nineteenth-century German philosopher Georg Wilhelm Friedrich Hegel, who developed the idea of a 'struggle for recognition' in *Phenomenology of Spirit* (1807). To answer the philosophical question of human consciousness, Hegel argues that recognition constitutes a central requirement for the formation of subjectivity and, further, that this process is inherently intersubjective. His most famous premise is 'self-consciousness exists in

---

10   The term 'outside/within' is not mine, but rather was collectively coined by Kunci members as we titled the audio guide *Outside Within Colonial Theater*. Ideas presented in this chapter are also indebted to the collective learning and reflexive conversations shared among Kunci members.
11   Fanon, *Black Skin, White Masks*, 172.

itself and for itself, in that and by the fact that it exists for another self-consciousness; that is to say, it is only by being acknowledged or recognised'.[12] In contrast with previous classical liberal thought, Hegel's theory considers self-consciousness as something born not from the introspection of individual moral consciousness but instead through its mediation with the consciousness of other people.

Hegel's theory grew into a normative political theory and an institutional practice among twentieth-century human rights movements, which claimed differences based on ethnicity, nationality, religion, sexuality or gender minority status, with the fundamental assumption that recognition and institutional accommodation on the basis of difference would have implications for the improvement of social justice.[13] State institutions were expected to become the mediators of intersubjective relationships and guarantee the liberties of all parties so that mutual recognition could form. This paradigm was also central to postcolonial activism that construed history as the site of political contestation, with demands for recognition as the starting point for processes of historical reconciliation.

At the same time as this approach's popularity, multiple critiques emerged and presented a serious challenge to the motivation and orientation of the politics of recognition. Decolonial perspectives that successfully show the limitations of a Hegelian politics of recognition commonly cite the thinking of anticolonial activist Frantz Fanon, who developed his critique in *Black Skin, White Masks* (1952). If neo-Hegelian thinkers assume that misrecognition is always a problem and recognition is always a solution, Fanon argues that in the context of colonial relations recognition in fact can have a negative effect on the colonised subject. For Fanon, normative Hegelian recognition can never become a source of freedom and self-worth for the colonised. Conversely, recognition reproduces the domination of the coloniser over the colonised and creates dependency as, 'not only must the black man be black; he must be black in relation to the white man'.[14] Fanon situates race relations within Hegel's master–slave dialectic; however, in contrast to Hegel, for Fanon, the self-consciousness of the White master *needs* to recognise the Black slave so that he can acquire his moral status as a good human being.

---

12   Georg Wilhelm Friedrich Hegel, *Phenomenology of Spirit* (Oxford: Oxford University Press, 1977), 178.
13   Fraser and Honneth, *Redistribution or Recognition?*, 8.
14   Fanon, *Black Skin, White Masks*, 82–83.

Thinking through Fanon's critique, recognition from the White master causes the Black slave to be in a position that must always undertake emotional work, by thanking the master and even latently making his self-consciousness dependent on the kindness of the master. This dependency creates relations of colonial recognition wherein the moral position of the White master is superior and the Black slave is subordinate because the slave is in danger of being trapped in an inferior mentality.[15] These are the colonial relations that mean that 'the master laughs at the consciousness of the slave'.[16]

Fanon's critique is evidently very valuable for contemporary decolonial thinkers, especially in an era in which we witness the politics of recognition as a common response of state institutions to the demands of decolonial activists. Elizabeth Povinelli argues that recognition from the state has the potential to depoliticise the critical consciousness of the colonial subject because it is always conditional, with the goal of assimilating the colonial subject into the dominant culture of the coloniser instead of fundamentally changing colonial relations.[17] Glen Coulthard elaborates on Fanon's critique as the radical conclusion to fully reject a politics of recognition. For Coulthard, contemporary recognition in the form of affirmative politics and institutional accommodation of the Other is 'the field of power through which colonial relations are produced and maintained'.[18] Consequently, even if demands for recognition are met by dominant institutions, this will only bring about symbolic change that accrues the moral capital of those who provide the recognition, instead of structurally changing relations of power.

After recognition in the museum

In the context of postcolonial relations, European and American ethnographic museums that are haunted by their colonial legacies occupy a central position in the articulation of demands as well as the recognition of histories of colonial subjugation and plunder. For the museologist Mary Stevens, ethnographic museums today have a share in 'the authority of recognition' because they have legitimacy as a state apparatus as well as a public sphere

---

15 ibid., 171–72.
16 ibid., 171–72.
17 Povinelli, *The Cunning of Recognition*.
18 Coulthard, *Red Skin, White Masks*, 17.

to mediate multiple interpretations of history. Stevens' perspective coheres with an institutional politics of recognition supported by neo-Hegelian thinkers, in so far as she suggests that museums as state institutions have a central role in guaranteeing Hegel's ideal of reciprocal recognition. Based on the model of recognition of the Holocaust theorised by anthropologist Stephan Feuchtwang, Stevens contends that the experiences of victims who undergo suffering and immense loss because of past colonial violence can be framed as a debt and, by the same token, the recognition of museums is a form of atonement for colonial sins.[19]

For Feuchtwang, recognition is a cycle whereby an increasing amount of recognition is given by institutions and is accompanied by an increasing number of interventions and counterclaims from different groups as well as internal rivals within groups. Here Stevens' opinion deviates from Feuchtwang's, as she is concerned that this cycle negates the possibility of resolution and closure.[20] Notwithstanding this, I think Stevens' hope for the resolution of historical mass violence *within* the museum fails to recognise the interwovenness of claims to recognition with the redistribution of power, access and resources *within and outside* the museum. Framing recognition as a debt implies a transactional process that can be concluded with a payment or settlement. The payment of such a debt, if read through a Fanonian critique, can only accumulate the symbolic capital of the museum as a moral authority and repeats the same old story, reproducing the museum's position as a paternal figure with a progressive and inclusive face.

In fairness to Stevens, she does not assume that recognition constitutes a method to create instant resolution because, as she states, a museum 'needs to consider recognition as a multi-stage process, not a singular event'.[21] However, instead of considering recognition as a cycle (Feuchtwang) or a script for resolution (Stevens), I suggest we can turn to Fanon's concept of self-recognition as a way out of the unequal binarism in institutional recognition. Indeed, in his critique of a Hegelian model of recognition, Fanon does not abandon the paradigm of recognition entirely. In accordance with Coulthard's reading of Fanon, he advocated for colonised subjects to direct attention to practices of personal and collective self-recognition to free themselves from the coloniser's misrecognition of themselves. For Fanon, instead of demanding recognition from the coloniser and tying

---

19   Stevens, 'Museums, Minorities and Recognition', 32.
20   ibid., 38.
21   ibid., 37.

self-worth to institutional acceptance, the colonised achieve freedom by affirming themselves and recognising fellow colonised people to strengthen one another.[22]

Self-recognition contains what Fanon termed 'psycho-affective elements' in colonial relations. In the context of museums, many studies have shown that our understanding of colonial heritage is always mediated by affective articulation, such as feelings of suffering, loss, pride, shame, anger and nostalgia.[23] Affect is an important source of knowledge because coloniality regulates not only what we think (the cognitive sphere) but also what we feel (the affective sphere). More than that, affect also contains within it the most intimate resistance of subjectivity and personal and collective agency, or what Ferdiansyah Thajib has called the 'affective dynamics of agency'.[24] In other words, affect is a site of simultaneous control and resistance. Affective agency here is not taken to mean an individual mental consciousness, but rather such agency is relational between two or more individuals and is closely related to the material conditions that encompass it. This relational aspect is important in practices of self-recognition because, as stated by antiracist feminist theorist bell hooks, a project of self-recognition means ceasing to find 'recognition in the Other' and choosing to recognise 'ourselves and make contact with all who would engage us in a constructive manner'.[25]

In my discussion of the two case studies of Kunci and Lifepatch, I will argue that artistic practices, as they may be adept at articulating feelings, sentiments and embodied experiences, are strategies of personal and collective self-recognition that can be used to forge new relationships, both between museums and communities and between different communities which are regarded as constituents of the museum. I call this process of creating new contacts and relationships wrapped in affective dynamics 're-affect'—a term of which I propose to provoke a notion after recognition. Affect is also about love and solidarity and is an ethical practice that, while it might sound clichéd, is nevertheless central to our efforts to rebuild social relations and emotional ties that were destroyed by colonialism. I use the prefix 're-' in 're-affect' to emphasise the relational nature of affect as ongoing work and an alternative to a binary frame of recognition. Moreover, in the context of

---

22 Fanon via Coulthard, *Red Skin, White Masks*, 43.
23 Divya P. Tolia-Kelly, Emma Waterton, and Steve Watson, eds, *Heritage, Affect and Emotion: Politics, Practices and Infrastructures* (London: Routledge, 2016), doi.org/10.4324/9781315586656, 1–11.
24 Ferdiansyah Thajib, 'Inhabiting Difference: The Affective Lives of Indonesian Muslim Queers' (PhD diss., Freie Universität Berlin, Germany, 2019), 22.
25 bell hooks, *Yearning: Race, Gender and Cultural Politics* (Boston: South End Press, 1990), 22.

affective relations and colonial heritage, 're-' does not suggest moving back to the past but rather a temporal-political relationship that looks to the past and connects it to present political aims. In the next section, I will explain how re-affect work is carried out in the artistic practices of artists in museums and how this work interacts with key practices that are critical for a politics of recognition: redistribution (Nancy Fraser) and resurgence (Coulthard).

Outside within the colonial theatre: Re-affect and redistribution after recognition

> Follow my voice ... I will take you through some detours, my reveries. I will introduce you to some of my friends here: other mannequins, the paintings, the writings. We are all brought here to give life to a theater of colonialism, a play staged in a museum structure which was built to enclose the institution's property claim on a territory far far away, a land which is now called Indonesia. Who owns the stories of Indonesia? Who owns its history? Who owns the knowledge on Indonesia?

The above quote is enunciated by the mannequin Sulastri, the central character and intellectual avatar in the audio guide *Outside Within the Colonial Theater* produced by Kunci.[26] The 'detours' and 'reveries' of Sulastri navigate the listener on an alternative interpretation of and journey through the permanent collection 'Netherlands East Indies: A Colonial History' (hereinafter NEI) at the Tropenmuseum, which has now closed. Unlike the official Tropenmuseum guide that must be listened to through a museum device, Kunci's audio guide can be accessed on our website or a visitor's smartphone. Kunci's physical presence at the Tropenmuseum was temporary and we mitigated this by making our intervention permanent without relying on the museum. Moreover, Kunci's audio guide can be listened to without one being present at or ever having directly viewed the Tropenmuseum exhibition.[27] Kunci's interest in audio practices during the residency started

---

26   The dual-language audio guide (English and Indonesian) can be accessed online at: radio.kunci.or.id/di-luar-dalam-teater-kolonial-sebuah-audio-guide/.
27   In her residency in Taiwan in December 2017, Kunci member Syafiatudina (Dina) introduced the audio guide *Outside Within the Colonial Theater*, which was then later partly translated into Mandarin. During this residency, Dina also produced an audio guide for a public space in Taipei. For Dina's reflections on listening and decolonial practices, see Syafiatudina, 'Something About Nusantara, the Listening, and the Project of Decolonization', *No Man's Land*, 28 December 2017, www.heath.tw/nml-article/something-about-nusantara-the-listening-and-the-project-of-decolonization/?lang=en.

as our method of research to interview various activists and academics about alternative archival practices in the Netherlands, including political exile Sarmadji, anthropologist Chiara De Cesari and archivist Michael Karabinos (who also writes in this volume, see Chapter 10).[28]

We open an opportunity for visitors, by adopting an embodied and affective approach through listening to an audio guide, to take part in and form a relationship with museum objects. The theatrical position we offer is always a political one. The Kunci audio guide spoken through the mannequin Sulastri does not eschew her subjectivity and recognises political positions that were excluded or sidelined in the NEI exhibition. The mannequin Sulastri was located on the second floor of the museum, in the middle of an exhibition zone that presented fragments of the history of education systems and the Ethical Policy in the Netherlands East Indies. It is a wax statue of a brown-skinned woman with her hair in a neat bun, wearing a white *kebaya* (long-sleeved blouse) with a small floral pattern and a batik material that appears a little shabby. The name Sulastri denotes the character of a 'wild school' (nationalist independent school) teacher in the semi-autobiographical novel *Out of Bounds* (*Manusia Bebas* or *Buiten het Gareel*, 1946) written by Soewarsih Djojopoespito (1912–77). The figure of Sulastri drew Kunci's attention because of our long-held interest in alternative education.[29]

Sulastri is a new role that museum curators assigned to this mannequin on the opening of the permanent exhibition in 2003. Before this, she was an unnamed wax statue that had played many roles in the colonial theatre through the years: as a tobacco worker displayed at the World Exhibition in Paris in 1931, a *warung* ('kiosk') seller in an exhibition on food and hygiene in Amsterdam in 1933 and, finally, in the Tropenmuseum as a *jamu* ('herbal medicine') seller and batik maker.[30] In the 1970s, wax statues like the mannequin Sulastri were considered outdated and embarrassing for critical Dutch curators. Most of these statues were thrown away as they were

---

28 We published this interview as a podcast and Kunci members Fiky Daulay and Nuraini Juliastuti had a central role in its production and conceptualisation. Access the podcast online at: radio.kunci.or.id.

29 Since 2016, Kunci has developed the Sekolah Salah Didik (School of Improper Education) to experiment with collective learning methods, online at: sekolah.kunci.or.id. See also the collective's writings in Kunci Study Forum & Collective, *Letters: The Classroom is Burning, Let's Dream about a School of Improper Education* (New York: Ugly Duckling Presse, 2020).

30 Willem Westerkamp, 'Ethnicity or Culture: The Career of Mannequins in (Post)Colonial Displays', in *Sites, Bodies and Stories: Imagining Indonesian History*, eds Susan Legêne, Bambang Purwanto, and Henk Schulte Nordholt (Singapore: NUS Press, 2015), 89–112, doi.org/10.2307/j.ctv1nth6b.9, at 105.

regarded as no longer fitting with the Tropenmuseum's postcolonial renewal concept, although some were kept in a storage facility and eventually exhibited in the NEI exhibition.[31]

The multiple identities assigned to and changes in the material status of Sulastri's mannequin make it a colonial ethnographic object that has stored the history of Dutch knowledge of colonialism or, to be precise, a history of misrecognition through the colonial gaze that classifies colonial subjects into ethnic types and works within the hierarchy of colonial society. Here, the colonial museum is a site of misrecognition that performs epistemic violence by denying the individual and collective agency and knowledge of colonial subjects. In a wave of decolonial demands, museums have moved in droves to revise this history of misrecognition by presenting narratives of anticolonial thought and resistance that are excluded from the hegemonic colonial gaze. Curators of the NEI exhibition, Susan Legêne and Janneke van Dijk, interestingly chose to practice self-recognition of the colonial gaze that shaped the objects and information in the Tropenmuseum's collection, trying to self-criticise the institutional practices of the museum. They articulated this institutional self-recognition by presenting nine new mannequins representing archetypes of colonial identities and the collector community that shaped the museum's collection and titled this part of the exhibition 'The Colonial Theater'.

'The Colonial Theater' attempts to shift attention from objects of colonial collections to subjects of colonial collectors. The characters showcased are a Koninklijk Nederlandsch-Indisch Leger (KNIL, Royal Netherlands East Indies Army) soldier, the wife of a missionary, a governor, a housewife, an artist, a plantation owner, an explorer, a civil servant and an academic. Some of these mannequin characters were based on those in colonial novels. For instance, Himpies, the KNIL soldier, is from the novel *The Ten Thousand Things* (*De Tienduizend Dingen*, 1955), written by Marie Dermoût and Tuan Anwar, and the civil servant is from the novel *The Advisor* (*De Raadsman*, 1958) by H.J. Friedericy. Others were based on real people, such as the blind scientist Georgius Everhardus Rumphius (1627–1702) and former Dutch East Indies governor-general Bonifacius Cornelis de Jonge (1875–1958). The curators stated that their conceptual decision was intended to centre 'an interpretation of the colonizers' perspective on colonial society during

---

31 Susan Legêne and Janneke van Dijk, 'Introduction: The Netherlands East Indies, A Colonial History', in *The Netherlands East Indies at Tropenmuseum*, eds Susan Legêne and Janneke van Dijk (Amsterdam: KIT Publishers, 2006), 20.

the era of the Ethical Policy'. Colonial voices were *intentionally* privileged precisely to 'weaken the authority of the institution [Tropenmuseum] by making it vulnerable for critique and offer possibilities for counter narratives and a dialogue on history'.[32] The voices of nationalist groups and Indonesian independence fighters appeared in the exhibition, but the curators stated that they intentionally treated them only as an insertion within it.[33] This decision is reflected in how the mannequin Sulastri was treated as a minor character and not physically refurbished. In contrast, the nine new mannequins feature highly detailed skin texture and eyes, while some parts of their limbs are made from transparent fibreglass materials that disrupt the mimetic effect of realist sculpture. The hyperrealist impression that was deliberately given to the new mannequins made their appearance contrast with the stiff and caricatured nature of the colonial heritage mannequins like Sulastri.

It is because of this curatorial choice that, unlike Sulastri's voiceless mannequin, each new mannequin has a fragment of a personal story and an individual voice that museum visitors can listen to through headphones. In the NEI exhibition, body and voice are metaphors as well as important material elements for rereading the museum's colonial history. Through their material embodiment, the new mannequins have more opportunities to express their human agency and individual voice as ambivalent figures entangled in colonial structures. Here, affect plays a role as an important pedagogical element because the platform of the new mannequins' bodies and voices has been presented to invite visitors to listen to the feelings and sentiments of the figures represented.

Kunci 'brought to life' Sulastri's voice and body to decentre the perspectives and affect privileged by the curators. Kunci arrived 14 years after the NEI exhibition opened and our involvement was facilitated by Heterotropics, an independent platform based in Amsterdam founded by curator Sara Giannini.[34] Giannini submitted Kunci's residency proposal to the research wing of the Tropenmuseum, the Research Centre for Material Culture, which at the time was led by Wayne Modest. The presentation of new mannequins was a courageous choice with the potential to break a cycle of colonial recognition through self-recognition of the colonial gaze in the history of the Tropenmuseum as an institution. However, self-recognition

---

32   ibid., 24–25.
33   ibid., 24–25.
34   See: heterotropics.com/.

always risks becoming a practice of domination when it is centred on only one perspective and does not weave contacts and connectedness with other articulations of self-recognition outside oneself or one's group. In the exhibition's material structure, the curators did not offer a permanent platform for subjects excluded by the centrality of the colonial gaze to speak back and articulate moments of self-recognition. Despite the good intentions of the curators to weaken the authority of the colonial gaze through the NEI exhibition project, during its 14 years on show, it materially failed to provide the promised space for criticism and ongoing dialogue. This shortcoming was caused by the narrative and concept of the exhibition that were too dependent on the curators' authority, instead of making the exhibition a growing, open platform to invite the participation of the museum public.

Kunci borrowed the anticolonial body of the Sulastri mannequin as a semifictitious actor to practise self-recognition and express a voice of disobedience to talk back to the theatre of coloniality. Sulastri recognises herself as a subject who is perceived by, and perceives, others, who is spoken of as well as speaking back to the exhibition that has construed her as having a part in the colonial theatre. The audio guide *Outside Within the Colonial Theater* can be interpreted as an intervention that proposes the de-identification of the supremacy of a white gaze and decentring the museum's single voice. Kunci's re-affect work attempts to create a new position through which a relationship with the museum can be forged and enable a plurality of role choices and affective routes within the theatricality of a journey through the museum. More than that, in Kunci's audio guide, the impacts of re-affect work are projected not only to the outside but also within us, as a process of self-reflection—a position 'outside within' that Kunci adopted when working with the museum.

Kunci's Sulastri mannequin looks within and speaks from within Kunci's subjective layers to decentre the colonial perspective that was curatorially privileged by the NEI exhibition. However, it is important to note that Sulastri's voice does not present a stable and intact narrative that is all-knowing and free of bias. As Fanon reminds us, self-recognition to affirm an anticolonial subjectivity is important but always risks being trapped in essentialism and elite nationalism. The identity of the colonised is plural and fragmented, so 'it is impossible for them to claim a single unity'.[35]

---

35 Fanon, *Black Skin, White Masks*, 133.

Recognition of the limitations of Sulastri's voice and critical gaze emerged at the end of the voice-guided tour, at the point where an exhibition depicts the history of missionaries in Papua and Papua New Guinea. Between the juxtaposition of the Bible and the missionary's white robes with totems and traditional Papuan clothing, Sulastri's mannequin ponders distance—an abyss—and finally runs out of words:

> The distance between Java and Papua is not as far as between Java and the Netherlands. Yet, the distance between me, as someone who was born and lives in Java, feels so far away. I feel so separated from Papua. The history and culture of Papua seems to be much more foreign to me compared to Dutch history and culture … The Javanese become new missionaries who bring enlightenment to the darkness on Papuan land. I feel like I'm starting to lose my voice here. I feel like I have to stop my ranting now before I speak as if I know anything about Papuan people.

Instead of talking for a Papuan subject who until this day is still subaltern-ised by Indonesian-Javanese–centric colonialism (also see Suryawan's Chapter 15 in this volume), Sulastri's mannequin ends her journey by recognising her privileged position as a Javanese subject within the constellation of the postcolonial theatre. Like the NEI exhibition curators, Kunci also undertakes a process of self-recognition that privileges a certain perspective. However, unlike the voices of the new mannequins, the voice of Sulastri's mannequin explicitly invites the listener to step outside the colonial theatre and advocates for the redistribution of discursive space for subjects other than herself within the structures of the attention economy in the museum. This is because self-recognition risks becoming neoliberal identity politics if it is proclaimed solely for the sake of an individual identity's status, which will eventually compete for the status of victim, instead of claiming collective agency to fight for shared rights through demands for the redistribution of access and resources. As Nancy Fraser reminds us, not all claims of self-recognition are automatically progressive. As a result, to justify a claim of self-recognition, one must be able to show how the desired change will redistribute and work towards participatory parity.[36] If the physical space of the museum is confined within the concrete and walls that surround it, Kunci claims that the aural space of the museum is infinite in which one can intervene to encourage more participation.

---

36 Fraser and Honneth, *Redistribution or Recognition?*, 38.

It is in this space that self-recognition as an ethical position enacts not only the courage to speak but also the humility to be quiet and listen. The audio guide wants us to share such experiences of listening. The practice of 'decolonial listening' that we propose is not a passive act but rather an actualisation of the redistribution of discursive space, because it is precisely by letting go of our right to speak that a privileged subject can contribute to efforts to undo colonial silencing and erasure. Active listening requires an intention to shift from the centrality of the author, admit bias, reposition oneself and establish relationships with subjects who have been silenced and excluded by modernity and coloniality. The re-affect work voiced by Sulastri is not satisfied in the comfort of self-recognition, but instead opens a niche of discomfort towards her own position and proposes work to redistribute discursive space within the structure of the museum's economy of attention. Re-affect work within a museum puts into practice self-recognition that is oriented both internally and externally to move beyond the stable binary between the acts of recognising and of being recognised, as well as decentring the museum as an authority of recognition.

The tale of the tiger and the lion: Re-affect and resurgence after recognition

> Must the truth be evidenced by the presentation of objects? Or can truth be equated to a lived belief without the need for physical proof? Which version is more reliable? Is the narrative constructed by the museum more believable than the stories told by people in North Sumatra?[37]

This reflection on the relationship between objects, narration and institutional politics was put forth by Sita Magfira, a member of Lifepatch, after her collective came face to face with the history of the Batak War (1878–1907) and two contrasting models of preserving memories—in Antwerp, Belgium, and Tanah Toba, North Sumatra, Indonesia. Lifepatch's exhibition, 'The Tale of Tiger and Lion', at the Museum of Contemporary Art Antwerp (M HKA), focused on links between two important figures in the saga of the Batak War, Hans Christoffel (1865–1962) and

---

37 Sita Magfira, 'Si Singamangaraja, Christoffel, dan Hal-Hal yang Terserak [Si Singamangaraja, Christoffel, and Scattered Things]', in *Pameran Seni Kontemporer Europalia Arts Festival Indonesia [Europalia Arts Festival Indonesian Contemporary Art Exhibition]*, eds Alia Swastika and Irham Nur Ansari (Jakarta: Kementerian Pendidikan dan Kebudayaan [Ministry of Education and Culture], 2017), 83.

Si Singamangaraja XII (1845–1907). In Antwerp, at the Museum aan de Stroom (MAS), Lifepatch found hundreds of collections of objects from Tanah Toba, such as war banners, weapons, jewellery and heirlooms donated to the museum by Christoffel, a Swiss-born military captain of the *Colonnie Matjan* (Tiger Brigade) that was decisive in the Dutch victory in the Batak War. Soon after military operations ceased, Christoffel moved to Antwerp and married the daughter of governor Jan van Rijswijk, Adolphine, who was known as a pacifist. His marriage to Adolphine changed Christoffel's view of war. Adolphine is credited with donating Christoffel's collection of items to the MAS.[38] These findings prompted Lifepatch to travel to Tanah Batak in North Sumatra—itself a 'living museum', which is a term used by Lifepatch member Agung 'Geger' Firmanto—which also holds memories of the Batak War and Si Singamangaraja XII.

In Belgium, Christoffel is a minor historical figure whose name is quite foreign to the public. The current occupants of the villa where Christoffel and his wife once lived in the Kalmthout district only came to know of Christoffel when Lifepatch members visited. Indeed, Christoffel himself did not seem to want to remember his past as a military officer. Archival research conducted by Lifepatch highlights a journalist's interview with Christoffel for the newspaper *De Telegraaf* in 1940. In it, the captain of the Tiger Brigade said: 'Thirty years ago, I dropped a curtain about everything that had happened. I shook off all my time in the jungle, started a new life, thought about the past as little as possible, searched for and found peace.'[39] Christoffel's anxiety about his past suggests that the Batak archives and artefacts in Belgium can act not only as sources of historical knowledge ripe for information to be extracted, but also as affective subjects that contain mixed emotions with ever-changing meanings—from trophies of pride to monuments of guilt. The MAS building, which houses the collection of objects donated by Christoffel, can thus no longer be regarded as a gallery of the glory of colonialism but as a warehouse where historical objects that generate trauma and inconvenience are packed away and hidden. The museum is paradoxically a place of care and abandonment, a site of recognising and forgetting history. Christoffel's gesture of donating objects

---

38 All information about Christoffel is drawn from Lifepatch's research, which is accessible on their website: lifepatch.id/Air_Antwerpen_Residency_Program_2017.

39 This quote was highlighted by Lifepatch in their video installation 'Lucid Memories', which was shown as part of the exhibition. See: www.youtube.com/watch?v=RmOtpMKp0Y0.

from his past to 'close the curtains' on history is arguably an articulation of a politics of recognition partial to colonial bias, wherein its main function is to save Christoffel from guilt.

In the living museum of the Tanah Batak, Lifepatch attempted to reopen the curtains of history and was confronted with the reality of the enormous popularity of Si Singamangaraja XII, who was installed as a national hero of Indonesia in 1961. Although there are no photographic records depicting Si Singamangaraja XII, Indonesians alive in the 1980s recognised the drawing of his face from 1,000-rupiah banknotes. Lifepatch conducted fieldwork for a month using a trail method to follow the route of the guerillas led by Si Singamangaraja XII when they were chased by the Tiger Brigade around the Lake Toba area, in Bakkara, Balige, Parlilitan, Silindung and Pangururan. The collective walked, stopping when tired, chatted to people they met along the road and stayed in the houses of people they met. Their research was full of coincidences and unanticipated encounters. With the hospitality and enthusiasm of communities around Lake Toba who positively welcomed Lifepatch's research, they collected memories preserved by older generations and traces of narratives in folktales and songs. This artistic research method was developed collectively by Lifepatch, which is framed as a 'citizen initiative'. Since its foundation in 2012, Lifepatch has operated at the intersection of art, science and technology to democratise access to shared knowledge-production processes.

The absence of script-based archives in Tanah Batak is inversely proportional to the fact that the history of Si Singamangaraja's resistance survives as a force in identity politics among Batak communities today. It could be suggested that Lifepatch's artistic research is part of a methodological shift in understanding archives, from extractive to ethnographic work. In this shift, in coherence with Ann Stoler's notion, an archive is a 'messy space between reason and sentiment' where critical historical reformulations can take place by destabilising a hierarchy of credibility between ratio and affect, which generally regards hard archives (documents, artefacts) as primary sources and soft archives (oral histories, traces of memories) merely as secondary data. The push to reformulate the way we construct historical narratives was similarly conveyed by 'The Tale' exhibition's curator, Alia Swastika, who stated that Lifepatch's artistic research method invites us to rethink the meaning of 'collecting' in the context of museums, which are typically obsessed with the acquisition of artefacts or archives. For Alia, Lifepatch's journey to these sites stressed the practice of gathering, which produces a collection of stories from various sources and perspectives so that history becomes a space for the contestation of versions of truth that sometimes intersect and sometimes contradict.[40]

For me, this practice of gathering is contingent on Lifepatch's role as facilitators of a process of collective self-recognition and mediators of re-affect work. The art exhibitions presented by Lifepatch in the exhibition space were not just illustrations that extracted findings from their research, but also a tool to drive conversations connecting stories and activating the 'messy space between reason and sentiment' as a place where sources of decolonial political affect could come together. There is much that can be discussed in detail about each work in the exhibition 'The Tale'. Due to the limited space in this chapter, I will focus only on three works that I think successfully demonstrate the complexity involved in practices of self-recognition and that set in motion decolonial re-affect work.

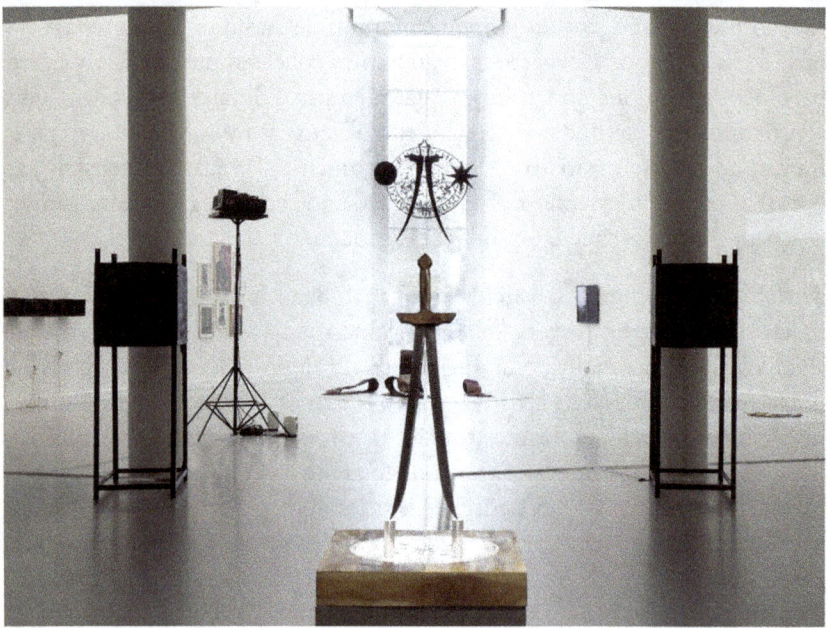

Figure 13.1 Replica of Gajah Dompak sword, 2017
Source: Lifepatch/Museum of Contemporary Art Antwerp.

---

40 Alia Swastika, 'The Tale of Tiger and Lion: Lifepatch at M HKA', in *Pameran Seni Kontemporer Europalia Arts Festival Indonesia* [*Europalia Arts Festival Indonesian Contemporary Art Exhibition*], eds Alia Swastika and Irham Nur Ansari (Jakarta: Kementerian Pendidikan dan Kebudayaan [Ministry of Education and Culture], 2017), 77.

The first is a replica of the *pedang* ('sword') Gajah Dompak (Figure 13.1), which visitors see immediately as they enter the exhibition space. The Gajah Dompak sword belonged to Si Singamangaraja and has been passed down through the generations. Our understanding of its previous whereabouts is cloudy. The National Museum of Indonesia has a collection of Gajah Dompak swords whose authenticity has been questioned by several people Lifepatch met in Tanah Batak. These interlocutors stated that the swords in the National Museum are different from visual images that have been circulating in the community. The shape of the sword in the National Museum is more like a Japanese Samurai sword, while communities believe that the Gajah Dompak blade has two branches like elephant tusks, meaning that it cannot be used for killing and therefore symbolises peace rather than war.[41] Ownership of historical artefacts does not guarantee the veracity of the authority of recognition. By presenting a replica of the Gajah Dompak sword produced from the visual speculation of Toba communities, Lifepatch alludes to the unclear whereabouts of the sword, and these questions about its authenticity strengthen a narrative of the supernatural powers of Si Singamangaraja. According to local stories, Si Singamangaraja always carried this sword and it can only be revealed to and used by his descendants. The existence of this story contradicts colonial military reports that Si Singamangaraja was killed by a bullet from one of the Tiger Brigade soldiers.

The narrative that Si Singamangaraja died from a bullet from a modern weapon is incongruous with the belief in Batak culture that he had supernatural powers of invulnerability ('*ilmu kebal*') due to the purity of his soul as a priest-king. Lifepatch heard this oral history account circulating in communities articulated in many versions and accents, all of which, it can be said, commonly apply moral and occult glosses to death, humanity and Si Singamangaraja's anticolonial heroism. When one says that Si Singamangaraja was killed by a bullet fired by the corporal of the Tiger Brigade, there is no explanation that can adequately bridge the terror of the modern colonial weapons they wielded with the dignity of Si Singamangaraja's anticolonial heroism and spiritual strength. The various accounts told and kept alive by communities as articulations of their self-recognition fill the void in the above explanation with the close relationship between fact and fiction and realism and surrealism in 'the space of death' to narrate colonial violence during the Batak War.

---

41   Magfira, 'Si Singamangaraja, Christoffel, and Scattered Things', 86.

I borrow the term 'the space of death' from the conceptualisation of anthropologist Michael Taussig, who researches the relationship between capitalism, colonialism and shamanic practices in Colombia in Latin America. Death is a space for the growth of imagination and social metaphors in the verge between the tenacity to survive and the reality of colonial violence. Paradoxically, the space of death is a symbolic sphere in which to fight against death, which is so close to daily lives full of terror—from not only past colonial violence but also colonial violence that is ongoing today.[42] In the context of reformulating archives, memories and history, we can add to this definition that the space of death is a place of political relationships between reason and sentiment, drawing on Stoler's conceptualisation mentioned above. Therefore, instead of allowing a secular Enlightenment world view to deny the fantastical and mystical aspects of the oral narratives that circulate about the death of Si Singamangaraja, we must see the transformative power of reimagining and historical speculation about the figure of Si Singamangaraja as a political metaphor that speaks back to histories of colonialism and the coloniality of history. Holding onto and claiming collective self-recognition in the sphere of death are an effort to protect anticolonial consciousness for people who, within a script-centric historical method, are regarded as 'a people without history'.[43]

Historian of Southeast Asia Anthony Reid stated that those in the Batak highlands are 'a people without history', according to the premise that 'history' equates to professional academic research and there are very few written sources that 'speak directly from the past that has been lost', such as artefacts, inscriptions and the records of pre–nineteenth-century colonial travellers. While Reid thickens a construction of Batak historiography by detailing travel records and archaeological evidence that can be excavated, Lifepatch deepens the complexity of modes of historical storytelling by collecting personal and collective narratives of self-recognition from people they met during their journey. The space of death in the history of the Batak War is a space for the resurgence, or revival, of memories and narratives that have been marginalised by the structures of colonial history. The resurgence of cultural practices, languages, ways of thinking and collective memories is an articulation of the dynamism of tradition that is given life once more not as nostalgic gestures to the past, but as a presentation of the past as a source of political knowledge that can change the colonial relations that dominate life until the present.[44]

---

42 Michael Taussig, *Shamanism, Colonialism, and the Wild Man: A Study in Terror and Healing* (Chicago: University of Chicago Press, 1987), doi.org/10.7208/chicago/9780226790114.001.0001, 5–7.
43 Anthony Reid, *Imperial Alchemy: Nationalism and Political Identity in Southeast Asia* (New York: Cambridge University Press, 2010), doi.org/10.1017/CBO9780511691829, 146.
44 Coulthard, *Red Skin, White Masks*, 157–58.

Working in the historical space of death, artists are positioned as political mediators between colonial archives and oral history, between narratives of the lethal colonial terror of the past and the afterlife of anticolonialism today. These cultural resurgence efforts were pursued by Lifepatch through the postcard project (see Figure 13.2) 'My Message to Tana Toba', initiated by Geger. Lifepatch asked community members whom they met to write messages on postcards that were then displayed in the exhibition space. Through these dozens of short messages, we see the variety of community members' agency for self-recognition that awakens their passion and embodied cultural knowledge as well as revokes an essentialist viewpoint of a narrow, singular political identity. Some of the messages demanded that artefacts in Belgium be returned to Batak communities, some wanted villages burned by the Dutch during the war to be rebuilt and others articulated a vision of the history of Si Singamangaraja as global heritage. Claims of identity and cultural ownership, whether mediated by national, regional or ethnic identities, always risk creating essentialist imaginations, so artists, as agents who facilitate collective processes of self-recognition, must provide a platform where a plurality of visions and aspirations can exist simultaneously notwithstanding the impossibility of it being whole.

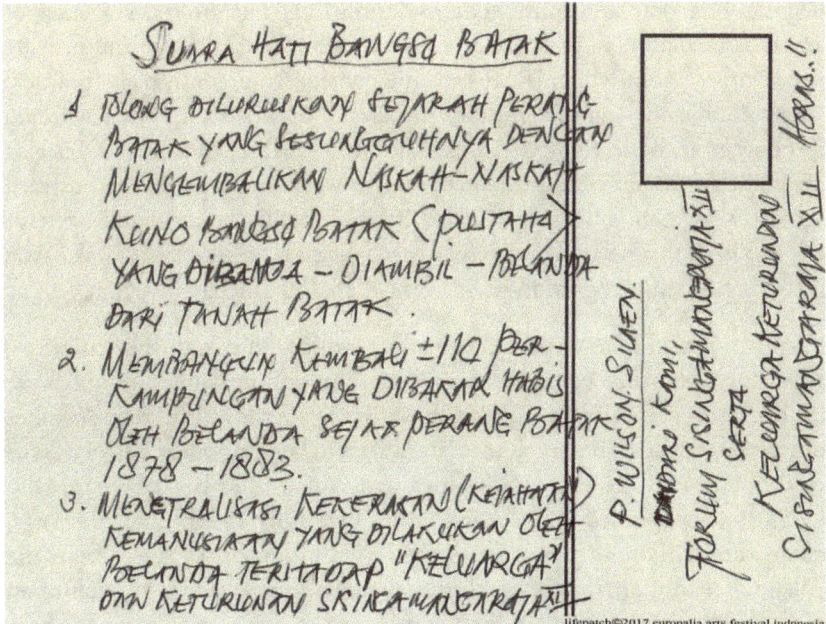

Figure 13.2 One of the postcards from 'My Message to Tana Toba'
Source: Lifepatch.

At the outset of their project, Lifepatch planned to produce a speculative proposal for the return to Tanah Batak of Batak cultural objects (*pusaka*) from the Christoffel collection. After the exhibition, the MAS curator even contacted Lifepatch to consult about this wish. There has so far been no meaningful follow-up and, in my conversations with Sita and Geger, both expressed Lifepatch's doubts. First and foremost, as an artistic collective operating in Yogyakarta, they do not feel they have the right to represent 'the Batak community' to talk about an issue as complicated as repatriation. Indeed, the repatriation of colonial heritage is the most complex area of negotiation in recognition and ethnographic re-affect (see Boonstra's Chapter 9 in this volume). This complexity is intensified if we acknowledge that the framework of international diplomatic relations has the potential to reduce the diversity of individual agency and entanglements of power in the community of those who are the main stakeholders in the repatriation process. In repatriation, processes of personal and collective self-recognition confront national identity politics and, as Fanon repeatedly warned, have the potential to be abused by the political elite. Of course, the aspirations of one or a handful of community members do not give them full rights to determine the political and contextual fate of a cultural heritage object. Whether we like it or not, a democratic solution must be forged through negotiations that are contingent and political. The political agency of artists as mediators of re-affect processes is important to centre and provide perspectives about which issues must be considered urgent. In the political arena of collective self-recognition, the agency of artists cannot be assumed to be neutral. Reflecting on the exhibition 'The Tale', Sita and Geger also realised that 90 per cent of the people who wrote messages in the postcard project were men. This gender disparity is easily identifiable, and we have not explored the internal hierarchies based on class or inherited status in the gathering of self-recognition narratives collated by Lifepatch.

I want to return here to connect re-affect work with practices of collective self-recognition and cultural resurgence. The performance piece 'Tribute to Boru Lopian' (Figure 13.3), initiated by Ferial Affif, demonstrates processes of resurgence that mediate affect in an embodied history. This work focuses on the story of Si Singamangaraja's child Boru Lopian, who fought and was killed in the Batak War. This story is kept alive in songs, dances and children's games performed by a group of teenagers from the village of Parlilitan, where Si Singamangaraja and several of his children died. Ferial recorded the Parlilitan youth performances and projected them in the M HKA exhibition space. She then invited four teenage white girls from Antwerp to follow the Parlilitan teenagers' choreography as a gesture symbolising the transfer of embodied knowledge across cultural boundaries.

13. AFTER RECOGNITION

Figure 13.3 Performance piece 'Tribute to Boru Lopian', Museum HKA, Antwerp
Source: Lifepatch.

This cross-cultural knowledge transfer is important because a spectacular performance of a cultural practice implies a position 'inside' and 'outside', where the performer puts forth an insider identity they are playing and the audience becomes an outsider or a distant consumer. By provoking the synchronisation of movement between teenagers in Parlilitan and Antwerp, Lifepatch blurs inner and outer boundaries so that cultural performance practices can become a metaphor for regenerative engagements that dispel the terror of the Batak War to work towards processes of peace today. The performativity of this work invites us to consider the issue of repatriation not just as a transactional process of returning objects to those entitled to them in a one-way move and state-to-state framework. Transactional repatriation will only accumulate moral capital for colonial authorities who return the objects and accrue the capital of narrow identity politics for the postcolonial national authorities who accept them. Because of this, repatriation as re-affect work requires processes to reconnect and form new, more equal relationships. In so doing, the politics of re-affect work clearly does not come to an end in the field of artistic practice and museology, but also is something we work through together in spaces of social justice activism.

Conclusion: Decolonial re-affect outside and within the museum

Speaking analytically towards artists who are invited by museums as authorities of recognition, I suggest that the terms and conditions when accepting invitations for such work should be used not to seek recognition from institutions but as an opportunity to decentre the authority of the museum and practise personal and collective self-recognition. In a decentred framework, artists exist strategically outside the museum. Artists are not just subjects who receive recognition to enter the museum; they also problematise power relations in the politics of recognition and mediate decolonial demands from outside the museum so that recognition does not become merely an instant solution to save the moral position of an institution.

Artists play a role as agents of self-recognition to articulate, reflect and mediate relational matters such as conflicts, tensions and negotiations between a variety of positions outside and within the museum's colonial heritage. Self-recognition is a relational process that dismantles the binary of the giver and receiver of recognition. Critical personal and collective self-recognition must be able to redistribute space for balanced participation, showcase a plurality of positions and agencies to safeguard us from cultural identity essentialism and undertake a process of self-critique of internal colonialism among groups in postcolonial societies. Self-recognition practices that are productive for decolonial activism will be directed not with a desire to create a mutual relationship with the coloniser, but with a desire to reawaken the dignity of cultural knowledge (resurgence), to be in solidarity with and mutually affirm the rights, experiences, feelings and aspirations of those who have been marginalised by present-day coloniality. Because of the centrality of psycho-affective elements in the process of relational self-recognition, the method offered by this chapter is re-affect work that values feelings, sentiments and embodied experiences.

Black feminist Audre Lorde long ago cautioned that recognition and institutional inclusion must be approached critically. She wrote that 'an old and primary tool of all oppressors' is a mental framework that ensures that the oppressed subject must always be preoccupied with the issues of concern and existential interests of the oppressor alone.[45] Will artists

---

45 Audre Lorde, 'The Master's Tools Will Never Dismantle the Master's House', in *This Bridge Called My Back: Writings by Radical Women of Color*, eds Cherrie Moraga and Gloria Anzaldua (Watertown: Persephone Press, 1981), 100–3, at 100.

become like Marie Kondo, helping to reorganise and clean the excesses of colonial consumerism that no longer 'spark joy'? That is not an impossible implication of re-affect work funded by museums, and it is our choice to not be absorbed by colonial anxiety that requires the atonement of guilt through the politics of recognition. However, it is also not impossible—and is something that must be fought for—that when artists receive an invitation to enter the museum, they break down the boundaries of property, redistribute museum resources and use them for the resurgence of anticolonial knowledge to be brought outside, to the field of social justice solidarity, which is far vaster than the European colonial fort.

References

Clifford, James. 1997. 'Museums as Contact Zones.' In *Routes: Travel and Translation in the Late Twentieth Century*, 188–219. Cambridge: Harvard University Press.

Coulthard, Glen Sean. 2014. *Red Skin, White Masks: Rejecting the Colonial Politics of Recognition*. Minneapolis: University of Minnesota Press. doi.org/10.5749/minnesota/9780816679645.001.0001.

Fabian, Johannes. 2014. *Time and the Other: How Anthropology Makes Its Object*. New York: Columbia University Press. doi.org/10.7312/fabi16926.

Fanon, Frantz. 1986. *Black Skin, White Masks*. Translated by Charles Markman. London: Pluto Press.

Fraser, Nancy, and Axel Honneth. 2003. *Redistribution or Recognition? A Political Philosophical Exchange*. New York: Verso.

Hegel, Georg Wilhelm Friedrich. 1977. *Phenomenology of Spirit*. Oxford: Oxford University Press.

hooks, bell. 1990. *Yearning: Race, Gender and Cultural Politics*. Boston: South End Press.

Kahlon, Rajkamal. 2019. 'Love and Loss in the Ethnographic Museum.' In *Matters of Belonging: Ethnographic Museums in a Changing Europe*, edited by Wayne Modest, Nicholas Thomas, Doris Prlić, and Claudia Augustat, 101–10. Leiden: Sidestone Press.

Kassim, Sumaya. 2017. 'The Museum Will Not be Decolonised.' *Media Diversified*, 15 November. www.mediadiversified.org/2017/11/15/the-museum-will-not-be-decolonised/.

Kunci Study Forum & Collective. 2020. *Letters: The Classroom is Burning, Let's Dream about a School of Improper Education*. New York: Ugly Duckling Presse.

Legêne, Susan, and Janneke van Dijk. 2006. 'Introduction: The Netherlands East Indies, A Colonial History.' In *The Netherlands East Indies at Tropenmuseum*, edited by Susan Legêne and Janneke van Dijk. Amsterdam: KIT Publishers.

Lorde, Audre. 1981. 'The Master's Tools Will Never Dismantle the Master's House.' In *This Bridge Called My Back: Writings by Radical Women of Color*, edited by Cherrie Moraga and Gloria Anzaldua, 100–3. Watertown: Persephone Press.

Magfira, Sita. 2017. 'Si Singamangaraja, Christoffel, dan Hal-Hal yang Terserak [Si Singamangaraja, Christoffel, and Scattered Things].' In *Pameran Seni Kontemporer Europalia Arts Festival Indonesia* [*Europalia Arts Festival Indonesian Contemporary Art Exhibition*], edited by Alia Swastika and Irham Nur Ansari. Jakarta: Kementerian Pendidikan dan Kebudayaan [Ministry of Education and Culture].

Mignolo, Walter. 2011. 'Museums in the Colonial Horizons of Modernity: Fred Wilson's Mining the Museum.' In *Globalization and Contemporary Art*, edited by Jonathan Harris, 71–85. Malden: Blackwell Publishing.

Modest, Wayne. 2019. 'Introduction: Ethnographic Museums and the Double Bind.' In *Matters of Belonging: Ethnographic Museums in a Changing Europe*, edited by Wayne Modest, Nicholas Thomas, Doris Prlić, and Claudia Augustat, 9–21. Leiden: Sidestone Press.

Peers, Laura, and Alison Brown, eds. 2003. *Museum and Source Communities*. London: Routledge.

Povinelli, Elizabeth A. 2002. *The Cunning of Recognition: Indigenous Alterities and the Making of Australian Multiculturalism*. Durham: Duke University Press. doi.org/10.2307/j.ctv116895z.

Reid, Anthony. 2010. *Imperial Alchemy: Nationalism and Political Identity in Southeast Asia*. New York: Cambridge University Press. doi.org/10.1017/CBO 9780511691829.

Stevens, Mary. 2007. 'Museums, Minorities and Recognition: Memories of North Africa in Contemporary France.' *Museum and Society* 5, no. 1: 29–43.

Swastika, Alia. 2017. 'The Tale of Tiger and Lion: Lifepatch at M HKA.' In *Pameran Seni Kontemporer Europalia Arts Festival Indonesia* [*Europalia Arts Festival Indonesian Contemporary Art Exhibition*], edited by Alia Swastika and Irham Nur Ansari. Jakarta: Kementerian Pendidikan dan Kebudayaan [Ministry of Education and Culture].

Syafiatudina. 2017. 'Something About Nusantara, the Listening, and the Project of Decolonization.' *No Man's Land*, 28 December. www.heath.tw/nml-article/something-about-nusantara-the-listening-and-the-project-of-decolonization/?lang=en.

Taussig, Michael. 1987. *Shamanism, Colonialism, and the Wild Man: A Study in Terror and Healing*. Chicago: University of Chicago Press. doi.org/10.7208/chicago/9780226790114.001.0001.

Thajib, Ferdiansyah. 2019. 'Inhabiting Difference: The Affective Lives of Indonesian Muslim Queers.' PhD diss., Freie Universität Berlin, Germany.

Tolia-Kelly, Divya P., Emma Waterton, and Steve Watson, eds. 2016. *Heritage, Affect and Emotion: Politics, Practices and Infrastructures*. London: Routledge. doi.org/10.4324/9781315586656.

Westerkamp, Willem. 2015. 'Ethnicity or Culture: The Career of Mannequins in (Post)Colonial Displays.' In *Sites, Bodies and Stories: Imagining Indonesian History*, edited by Susan Legêne, Bambang Purwanto, and Henk Schulte Nordholt, 89–112. Singapore: NUS Press. doi.org/10.2307/j.ctv1nth6b.9.

14

Confronting coloniality through the courts? Reconsidering the Rawagede case

Ken M.P. Setiawan[1]

Introduction

In the morning of 9 December 1947 in the village of Rawagede[2] in West Java, Cawi binti Baisa's husband left home to work in the rice fields. He would never return. He was one of the hundreds of men and boys[3] executed by Dutch troops who had come to the village searching in vain for the republican army captain Lukas Kustaryo. Sixty-four years later, in September 2011, a Dutch civil court ruled that the Dutch State was responsible for the massacre and ordered it to pay compensation to eight widows, including Cawi, and one male survivor. The court also demanded the Dutch State apologise. The Dutch Ambassador to Indonesia, Tjeerd de Zwaan, delivered this apology at the memorial site for the massacre in the

---

1   I would like to thank Hellena Souisa for her research assistance. Many thanks also to Eveline Buchheim for her detailed feedback on an earlier draft of this chapter, as well as all workshop participants and reviewers for their additional comments.
2   Rawagede is presently known as Balongsari. In this chapter, I use Rawagede to refer to the village in line with public debates and reporting on the court case.
3   According to Dutch internal correspondence, 120 men were killed, while Indonesian counts claimed 430 deaths. See Gert Oostindie and Rémy Limpach, 'The War in Indonesia 1945–1949: The Military-Historical Context', in *Beyond the Pale: Dutch Extreme Violence in the Indonesian War of Independence, 1945–1949*, eds Gert Oostindie, Ben Schoenmaker, and Frank van Vree (Amsterdam: Amsterdam University Press, 2022), 69–106, doi.org/10.1515/9789048557172-002, at 102.

presence of hundreds of villagers. Cawi welcomed the apology and said that 'it makes me feel that my struggle was not useless', while another widow, Lasmi binti Kasilan, added that 'we never wanted vengeance. We wanted an apology and compensation, and in the end, we got it.'[4]

The Rawagede case has been regarded as pathbreaking. Historian Nicole Immler argued that the verdict changed 'Dutch perceptions'[5] of the 1945–49 revolution in which Indonesians were forced to fight to defend their declaration of independence, leading to a new conceptualisation of the Dutch colonisers as 'perpetrators'.[6] Furthermore, legal scholar Larissa van den Herik argued the case was 'a catalyst for the Dutch state and society to revisit its colonial past'.[7] Indeed, the Rawagede case opened avenues for other survivors and relatives of victims of violence perpetrated during the Indonesian revolution to initiate civil proceedings against the Dutch State.[8] The cases heard in the Dutch courts follow developments elsewhere in the world where increased attention to colonial injustices has led, among other things, to former colonising nations being held to account through the courts.[9] Nonetheless, even successful efforts remain exceptions, rather than the norm, and former colonising powers are careful 'to avoid creating precedent that could potentially apply to other colonial abuses, much less to the act of colonisation itself'.[10]

---

4   Niniek Karmini, 'Dutch State Apologizes for 1947 Indonesia Massacre', *Boston Globe*, 9 December 2011, archive.boston.com/news/world/europe/articles/2011/12/09/dutch_state_apologizes_for_1947_indonesia_massacre/.
5   Nicole L. Immler, 'Hoe Koloniaal Onrecht te Erkennen? De Rawagede-zaak Laat Kansen en Grenzen van Rechtsherstel Zien [How to Acknowledge Colonial Injustices? The Rawagede Case Shows Opportunities and Limitations of the Restoration of Rights]', *BMGN–Low Countries Historical Review* 133, no. 4 (2018): 57–87, doi.org/10.18352/bmgn-lchr.10613, at 58.
6   Nicole L. Immler and Stef Scagliola, 'Seeking Justice for the Mass Execution in *Rawagede*/Probing the Concept of "Entangled History" in a Postcolonial Setting', *Rethinking History* 24, no. 1 (2020): 1–28, doi.org/10.1080/13642529.2019.1693134, at 2.
7   Larissa van den Herik, 'Addressing Colonial Crimes through Reparations? Adjudicating Dutch Atrocities Committed in Indonesia', *Journal of International Criminal Justice* 10, no. 3 (2012): 693–706, doi.org/10.1093/jicj/mqs033, at 694.
8   For an overview, see Eefje de Volder and Anne-Marie de Brouwer, *The Impacts of Litigation in Relation to Systematic and Large-Scale Atrocities Committed by the Dutch Military Forces in the 'Dutch East Indies' between 1945–1949* (Amsterdam: Nuhanovic Foundation, 2019).
9   For instance, in 2012, victims of the suppression of the Mau Mau rebellion in Kenya were given the right to claim compensation from the UK Government, which the next year agreed to pay £19.9 million in damages. In 2021, Germany officially acknowledged it committed genocide during its occupation of Namibia. In addition to an apology, Germany also pledged €1.1 billion in financial aid for development projects.
10 Max Fisher, 'The Long Road Ahead for Colonial Reparations', *New York Times*, 27 August 2022, www.nytimes.com/2022/08/27/world/americas/colonial-reparations.html.

Court cases related to colonial violence can have a significant impact on both those directly affected by that violence and broader society. For instance, in Australia—a settler colony where decolonisation remains an ongoing and contested process—the verdict in the Mabo Case (1982–92) delivered by the High Court is widely regarded as a landmark decision.[11] In this case, the panel of judges acknowledged the history of Indigenous dispossession by colonial settlers and abolished the legal doctrine of *terra nullius* (or 'land belonging to no-one'). Before this, the application of *terra nullius* had effectively denied Indigenous peoples' ownership of and connection to the land. As such, the rejection of *terra nullius* opened a legal pathway for Indigenous Australians to put forward claims to native title. Perhaps more importantly, the Mabo Case generated more knowledge about settler dispossession of, and violence against, Indigenous peoples. In so doing, the case helped shift societal perceptions and attitudes, suggesting that court proceedings can play a role in rectifying past wrongs.

At the same time, it is important to not overstate the significance of court processes. In fact, one limitation of court cases on historical violence is that they tend to address these matters in the context only of the case that is being examined, thereby giving insufficient attention to the deeper socioeconomic and structural causes and consequences of colonialism that enabled these violations in the first place.[12] In addition, it is necessary to be critical of the mechanisms through which changes take place. Indigenous feminist and author-activist Aileen Moreton-Robinson has pointed out that while the Mabo Case had important consequences for Indigenous Australians and broader society, the judgement was delivered by a court established by the oppressors of Indigenous peoples.[13] As such, she argues, the decision was not only shaped and determined through a system controlled by the (former) oppressor but also based on 'a possessive investment in patriarchal whiteness',[14] prioritising the protection of the oppressor's interests rather

---

11   The case is formally known as *Mabo v Queensland (No. 2)*.
12   Chris Cunneen, 'Colonialism and Historical Injustice: Reparations for Indigenous Peoples', *Social Semiotics* 15, no. 1 (2005): 59–80, doi.org/10.1080/10350330500059130; Bill Rolston and Fionnuala Ní Aoláin, 'Colonialism, Redress and Transitional Justice: Ireland and Beyond', *State Crime Journal* 7, no. 2 (2018): 329–48, doi.org/10.13169/statecrime.7.2.0329.
13   The High Court of Australia, for example, was established in 1901 for the purpose of making decisions regarding the settler colony within which Indigenous peoples had virtually no rights and were subjected to special laws based on racist, paternalistic assumptions about the need to 'protect' this community, which in practice meant forced assimilation and control.
14   Aileen Moreton-Robinson, *The White Possessive: Property, Power, and Indigenous Sovereignty* (Minneapolis: University of Minnesota Press, 2015), doi.org/10.5749/minnesota/9780816692149.001. 0001, 69.

than bringing justice to those oppressed. On this note it is important to recognise that while the Mabo Case enabled the passing of the 1993 *Native Title Act*, establishing a process for claiming and recognising native title, in practice, it remains very difficult for Indigenous communities to claim these rights. One issue is that Indigenous communities must prove their continuing connection to land and water, which is difficult in the absence of written traditions, while records made by European settlers are limited by their ethnocentric views and limited understanding of Indigenous languages and cultures.[15] Noongar man Glenn Kelly, chief executive of the South West Aboriginal Land and Sea Council, stated that the *Native Title Act* is 'a white fella legal construct and what it is actually designed to do, in my view, is not to enliven traditional law and custom but to control traditional law and custom'.[16]

Moreton-Robinson's critical appraisal of the Mabo Case and the ongoing challenges for Indigenous peoples to claim native title reminds us that courts are a manifestation of coloniality: colonial structures of power and control that persist in the present. In drawing attention to the entrenched continuities between colonial pasts and present-day structures of governance, as well as the administration of so-called justice, Moreton-Robinson's work aligns with Quijano's theory on the coloniality of power or the entrenched relationship between practices and legacies of European colonialism in contemporary societies.[17] This, then, raises the question of to what extent court cases can contribute to decolonial ways of thinking and being.

In this chapter, I seek to answer this question through examining public discussions on the court case relating to the 1947 Rawagede Massacre, as represented through newspaper reports in both Dutch and Indonesian media. Departing from this volume's premise that to decolonise there must be an acknowledgement of coloniality,[18] in examining these texts, I focus on three themes. First, I explore the extent to which these public discussions contextualise the violence broadly in the longer history of colonialism, as 'the main cause of the wave of violence [was] the return of the Dutch, who wanted to restore colonial rule. The violence was not unexpected at the

---

15   Australian Law Reform Commission, *Connection to Country: Review of the* Native Title Act 1993 *(Cth): Final Report* (Sydney: Australian Government, 2015), www.alrc.gov.au/wp-content/uploads/2019/08/alrc_126_final_report.pdf, 213.
16   Darren Mara, 'The Native Title Act, 20 Years On', [Transcript], *SBS World News Radio*, 28 February 2014, www.sbs.com.au/news/article/the-native-title-act-20-years-on/2iqilg3jo.
17   Aníbal Quijano, 'Coloniality of Power and Eurocentrism in Latin America', *International Sociology* 15, no. 2 (2000): 215–32, doi.org/10.1177/0268580900015002005.
18   See Chapter 1 of this volume.

time.'[19] Second, I consider the extent to which these public discussions seek to centre subaltern voices and thus, in particular, how the female claimants are portrayed. Third, in my analysis, I focus on the extent to which, and how, the legal framework (that is, Dutch courts and laws) that applies to the case is discussed.

This chapter will start with a background, in which I discuss the various steps that have been taken to address colonial violence over time, tracing this back to the revolution. The chapter then moves to the Rawagede case and surrounding public discussions on the three themes outlined above. This analysis will show that while the Rawagede case has certainly intensified the debate about colonial violence and, to some extent, has rendered more visible the voices and experiences of those affected, the legal process itself has not repositioned Rawagede in broader contexts of colonialism and colonial policy.

Seeking justice for colonial crimes

The 2011 decision of the Civil Court in The Hague may have resulted in renewed attention to colonial violence during the revolution, but Indonesian advocacy for such violence to be addressed dates to the 1940s. The Rawagede Massacre itself is an example of this. At the time, the government of the republic appealed to the United Nations Committee of Good Offices on the Indonesian Question about the massacre. This committee then undertook an investigation and concluded that the actions of the Dutch military were 'deliberate and ruthless'.[20] The United Nations, however, did not issue sanctions. This reflected the United Nations' reluctance to actively push for the dismantling of colonialism[21] to the point that the organisation acted as an instrument in upholding coloniality.

---

19   Hilmar Farid, 'Dealing with the Legacies of a Violent Past', in *Beyond the Pale: Dutch Extreme Violence in the Indonesian War of Independence, 1945–1949*, eds Gert Oostindie, Ben Schoenmaker, and Frank van Vree (Amsterdam: Amsterdam University Press, 2022), 473–86, at 476.
20   Chris Lorenz, 'Can a Criminal Event in the Past Disappear in a Garbage Bin in the Present? Dutch Colonial Memory and Human Rights: The Case of Rawagede', in *Afterlife of Events: Perspectives of Mnemohistory*, ed. Marek Tamm (London: Palgrave Macmillan, 2014), 219–42, doi.org/10.1057/ 9781137470188_12, at 224.
21   The time of the establishment of the United Nations saw both the development of supervisory mechanisms for colonised territories and efforts of colonial governments to justify imperialism at the international level. See Jessica Lynne Pearson, 'Defending Empire at the United Nations: The Politics of International Colonial Oversight in the Era of Decolonisation', *The Journal of Imperial and Commonwealth History* 45, no. 3 (2017): 525–49, doi.org/10.1080/03086534.2017.1332133.

Notwithstanding the severity of the massacre, Rawagede was only one event during the 1945–49 revolution. Scholars have described this period as one of 'extreme violence',[22] in which Dutch forces committed 'structural and excessive violence' against the civilian population.[23] It has been estimated that, during this four-year period, about 100,000 Indonesians serving in the republican forces died, compared with 5,000 Dutch soldiers, while estimates range between 25,000 and 100,000 civilian deaths.[24] Chapter 8 of this volume, by Ravando and F.X. Harsono, documents Chinese Indonesian deaths and experiences of violence. Moreover, although recent debates have focused on the violence that occurred during the revolution, prior to this period there were other colonial wars that have largely been ignored in discussions about claims, including the Aceh War (see Protschky's Chapter 6 in this volume). Indeed, it has been estimated that because of armed conflicts and wars waged, first, by the Dutch East India Company (Vereenigde Oostindische Compagnie, VOC) and, subsequently, by the Kingdom of the Netherlands, hundreds of thousands became victims of the establishment, expansion and consolidation of the colonial state.[25]

At the time of the transfer of sovereignty in 1949, however, the issue of violence during the colonial period was not pursued: both Dutch and Indonesian representatives agreed on a reciprocal amnesty,[26] thereby closing off possibilities to prosecute those responsible for the violence. Despite this amnesty, some Indonesian claims against the Dutch State emerged. In 1950, the Indonesian Government unsuccessfully requested the extradition of Captain Raymond Westerling, under whose command thousands of civilians in South Sulawesi were killed.[27] Following the revolution, Westerling had escaped to Singapore, however, the Singapore Supreme Court—then still under British control—denied the Indonesian Government's extradition

---

22   de Volder and de Brouwer, *The Impacts of Litigation*, 9.
23   Rémy Limpach, *De Brandende Kampongs van General Spoor* [*The Burning Kampongs of General Spoor*] (Amsterdam: Boom, 2016), 737–46.
24   'Indonesian War of Independence (In Numbers)' (Amsterdam: NIOD Institute for War, Holocaust and Genocide Studies, n.d.), [Online], www.niod.nl/en/frequently-asked-questions/indonesian-war-independence-numbers.
25   Gert Oostindie, 'The Netherlands and Indonesia 1945–1949: The Political-Historical Context', in *Beyond the Pale: Dutch Extreme Violence in the Indonesian War of Independence, 1945–1949*, eds Gert Oostindie, Ben Schoenmaker, and Frank van Vree (Amsterdam: Amsterdam University Press, 2022), 35–68, at 36.
26   Immler and Scagliola, 'Seeking Justice for the Mass Execution in *Rawagede*', 2.
27   Westerling led elite commando units (Depot Speciale Troepen, DST, later known as Korps Speciale Troepen, KST) that were notorious for their systematic use of extreme violence. These troops were responsible for the killing of at least 3,500 unarmed Indonesians between mid-December 1946 and late February 1947. See Oostindie and Limpach, 'The War in Indonesia', 85, 94.

request.²⁸ The refusal of the Singapore court thus also illustrated how global inequalities and structures of coloniality (see McGregor's Chapter 7 in this volume) shielded perpetrators from being held to account.

In the same year, Adriana Nasoetion-van der Have claimed compensation from the Dutch State for the December 1948 execution by a group of Dutch officers of her husband, Masdoelhak Nasoetion, who was the government secretary of the Indonesian Republic. The Dutch State initially rejected her claim. However, in 1953, the Dutch Civil Court used the state's rejection of the claim as evidence that the killing had occurred, ruled that the state was liable and ordered compensation. While the Dutch State appealed the decision and continued to deny its liability, it eventually agreed to pay Adriana Nasoetion-van der Have a sum of ƒ149,000. However, there was no criminal prosecution of those involved in the murder of Masdoelhak Nasoetion.²⁹

Nasoetion-van der Have's successful claim was an exception, with accountability for colonial violence remaining largely absent because of the political climate in both Indonesia and the Netherlands. Although both the Sukarno (1945–66) and the Suharto (1966–98) governments paid significant attention to the revolution as part of nation-building processes,³⁰ there was far less interest in holding the perpetrators of violence to account. Particularly during Suharto's New Order, priorities shifted to re-establishing political and economic relations with the Netherlands.³¹

Meanwhile, in the Netherlands, there certainly was awareness of colonial violence. In fact, the Rawagede Massacre was debated among senior army officials shortly after it occurred and the general of the Dutch army at the time, Simon Spoor, even went so far as to recommend the prosecution of Alphons Wijnen, who headed the army unit involved in Rawagede. The Dutch Attorney-General, however, refused and did not open a criminal

---

28   'Indonesia is Rebuffed; Bid for Westerling's Extradition is Denied in Singapore', *New York Times*, 4 August 1950.
29   'Hoe een Weduwe de Nederlandse Staat Deed Buigen [How a Widow Made the Dutch State Bow]', *NRC*, [Amsterdam], 27 January 2017, www.nrc.nl/nieuws/2017/01/27/hoe-een-weduwe-de-nederlandse-staat-deed-buigen-6426428-a1543254.
30   See Katharine McGregor, 'From National Sacrifice to Compensation Claims: Changing Indonesian Representations of the Westerling Massacres in South Sulawesi, 1946–47', in *Colonial Counterinsurgency and Mass Violence: The Dutch Empire in Indonesia*, eds Bart Luttikhuis and A. Dirk Moses (London: Routledge, 2014), 282–307, doi.org/10.4324/9781315767345-14.
31   Stef Scagliola, 'The Silences and Myths of a "Dirty War": Coming to Terms with the Dutch–Indonesian Decolonisation War (1945–1949)', *European Review of History* 14, no. 2 (2007): 235–62, doi.org/10.1080/13507480701433901, at 252.

investigation. In the years that followed, a powerful veterans' lobby was largely able to divert attention from the violence committed by the Dutch military (including at Rawagede).[32]

Despite a culture of silence surrounding the Indonesian revolution in the Netherlands, occasionally veterans spoke out, sometimes triggering responses from the Dutch Government. In the 1960s, Joop Hueting, a former military officer, spoke about atrocities committed in Rawagede in a national television broadcast. This resulted in an extensive public discussion and the Dutch Government initiated an official investigation that resulted in the 1969 *Memorandum of Excesses* (*Excessennota*). The memorandum would set the tone for Dutch Government policy towards violence during the revolution for decades and was based on limited research conducted over a few months by Dutch Government officials, using governmental archives only, summarising archival findings but providing no further analysis.[33] No-one was interviewed—not even well-known Dutch veterans or Indonesian witnesses, although most were alive at the time.[34] The main conclusion of the memorandum was that atrocities were incidences of extreme violence and not of a systemic or structural nature. The term 'war crimes' was purposefully left out of the memorandum and instead 110 'excesses' were identified, including the Rawagede Massacre. In choosing the term 'excesses', the memorandum implied that these were exceptions and presented the violence as responses to the 'guerilla attacks' of revolutionary fighters. While the Dutch Government said it deplored these 'excesses', it determined that 'on the whole the military had behaved correctly in Indonesia'[35] and unilaterally decided that there would be no civil or criminal accountability.[36] This position would be entrenched in Dutch law two years later, when the legislature passed the 1971 Law on the Statute of Limitations ('*Verjaringswet*'). According to this law, and in line with newly formulated international norms,[37] the statute of limitations could not be upheld for war

---

32 Stef Scagliola, 'Cleo's "Unfinished Business": Coming to Terms with Dutch War Crimes in Indonesia's War of Independence', *Journal of Genocide Research* 14, nos 3–4 (2012): 419–39, doi.org/10.1080/14623 528.2012.719374.
33 Vincent J.H. Houben, 'A Torn Soul: The Dutch Public Discussion on the Colonial Past in 1995', *Indonesia* 63 (April 1997): 47–66, doi.org/10.2307/3351510, at 57.
34 Lorenz, 'Can a Criminal Event in the Past Disappear', 225.
35 Houben, 'A Torn Soul', 58.
36 de Volder and de Brouwer, *The Impacts of Litigation*, 11–12.
37 In 1968, the United Nations adopted the Convention on the Non-Applicability of Statutory Limitations to War Crimes and Crimes Against Humanity, which entered into force in 1970. Before the development of this convention, there was a sense that all crimes (including war crimes) were subject to a statute of limitations. The Netherlands is yet to sign or ratify this convention.

crimes. However, the Dutch Government, referring to the *Memorandum of Excesses*, made it clear that the statute of limitations would continue to be upheld for any crimes committed during the revolution.[38]

After the publication of the memorandum, there was from time to time some public attention to colonial violence, although it had little impact on accountability. In the mid-1990s, the Rawagede Massacre gained renewed attention after a traumatised veteran distributed a pamphlet about his involvement and a television documentary was made about the event. Nonetheless, the prosecutor of military legal affairs stated that the documentary had not produced new evidence and, as such, there were no grounds for reopening the case. In line with the memorandum, the state held that legal processes were 'unfeasible'.[39] At the time, there was some criticism of this position and, in an op-ed in the Dutch daily *Trouw*, pastors Jan Eijken and Henk Koetsier rejected the Dutch Government's claims, openly calling the Rawagede Massacre a 'war crime'. Eijken and Koetsier argued that:

> it would be a credit to Parliament and Cabinet if they agree to the earlier requested investigation into the scale of the mass murder … [I]t should be recognised openly that this is a war crime to which the statute of limitations does not apply.[40]

They thus were challenging Dutch legal norms. Eijken and Koetsier wrote extensively to Members of Parliament and ministerial representatives, while a small number of critical veterans also took the initiative to offer apologies to the Indonesian Ambassador in the Netherlands for the violence committed.[41]

Despite these efforts, a broader push towards accountability did not emerge until after the turn of the millennium. This is directly connected with global trends in human rights, apologies and compensation cases, as well as a changed political climate in Indonesia.[42] Indonesian activists started to become more interested in colonial violence and organisations that

---

38 Maurice Swirc, *De Indische Doofpot. Waarom Nederlandse Oorlogsmisdaden in Indonesië Nooit Zijn Vervolgd* [*The Indisch Cover Up: Why Dutch War Crimes in Indonesia Were Never Prosecuted*] (Amsterdam: De Arbeiderspers, 2022), 14.
39 de Volder and de Brouwer, *The Impacts of Litigation*, 11–12.
40 Jan Eijken and Henk Koetsier, 'Mogelijke Oorlogsmisdaad Nog Steeds in Doofpot [Possible War Crime Still Covered Up]', *Trouw*, [Amsterdam], 6 December 1997.
41 Immler and Scagliola, 'Seeking Justice for the Mass Execution in *Rawagede*', 11.
42 McGregor, 'From National Sacrifice to Compensation Claims'.

advocated for its acknowledgement were established. Most prominent was the creation in 2005 of the Dutch–Indonesian Committee of Dutch Debts of Honour (Komite Utang Kehormatan Belanda, KUKB), followed by a Dutch branch two years later. Established by Batara Hutagalung, the son of an Indonesian veteran living in Jakarta, and Jeffry Pondaag, an Indonesian living in the Netherlands, the KUKB would spearhead a string of claims against the Dutch State.

A last avenue

In 2006, Pondaag approached Dutch human rights lawyer Liesbeth Zegveld with the Rawagede dossier. Zegveld, who had no personal or professional ties to Indonesia, was fascinated by the case for it represented a tension between the Netherlands' role as a staunch supporter of international human rights and its unwillingness to face its own human rights transgressions. However, initially, she regarded the Rawagede dossier as a 'great case, but utterly hopeless'[43] and did not focus on bringing it to court.

In 2007, the KUKB visited Balongsari (the present name for Rawagede), after which 10 survivors of the massacre decided to join the organisation to demand accountability and compensation. Initially, the primary strategy to achieve this was attempting to negotiate an out-of-court settlement with the Dutch Government. The government, however, refused the claims and argued that they were time-limited. Nonetheless, because of political pressure on the Dutch Government, in December 2008, the Dutch Ambassador to Indonesia attended the commemoration of the Rawagede Massacre at which he expressed the state's regret.[44] Despite the Dutch State holding onto its argument about the statute of limitations, it was also about this time that embassy representatives met with villagers. As a result, in early 2009, the Dutch Government allocated the village €850,000 in development aid, although it insisted it was not a reparation payment. Then Minister of Foreign Affairs, Maxime Verhagen, added that the government had no intention to respond to the compensation claims and that the Dutch and Indonesian governments had mutually agreed to 'draw a line under the

---

43   Linawati Sidarto, 'Liesbeth Zegveld: The Lawyer Behind the Dutch Apologies', *Jakarta Post*, 13 September 2013, www.thejakartapost.com/news/2013/09/13/liesbeth-zegveld-the-lawyer-behind-dutch-apologies.html.
44   'Nederland Betuigt Spijt in Rawagede [Netherlands Expresses Regret in Rawagede]', *Reformatorisch Dagblad*, [Apeldoorn], 9 December 2008.

past'.⁴⁵ This was echoed by Suparta, the chairperson of the organisation of Rawagede victims, who said: '[W]e belong to a younger generation that are not as personally connected to the tragedy. We want to close this chapter, together with the Netherlands.'⁴⁶

However, in 2009, the persistent refusal of the Dutch Government to address the claims of the families affected led the KUKB to initiate civil proceedings. The claimants were the KUKB, eight widows, one daughter of a victim and the only male survivor of the massacre. They asked the court to hold the Dutch State liable for the damages suffered and the costs of the legal proceedings. This move towards litigation was, in the words of Pondaag, a 'last avenue', as all other efforts had been unsuccessful. Zegveld similarly felt that, given the circumstances, there was no option but to go to court.⁴⁷

While the Dutch State did not deny the events or its responsibility, it held that the claims were time-barred and therefore inadmissible. On 14 September 2011, the court decided against the state and concluded that, based on the seriousness of the event and because the state at the time was aware of what had happened, the statute of limitations could not be upheld. The court found the state responsible for the damages of claimants directly affected by the executions (that is, the eight women whose husbands had been executed and the widow of the surviving man, who passed away during the proceedings). In so doing, the court rejected the claims of the daughter, stating that 'the next generation' was affected to a lesser extent, as well as the KUKB, as the organisation did not exist at the time of the massacre and as such had not suffered damages. A settlement was reached, whereby the state agreed to pay €20,000 to the nine widows.⁴⁸ It also paid the costs of the legal proceedings and extended formal apologies.

---

45 'Rawagede Wil de Bloedige Tragedie uit 1947 Nu Afsluiten [Rawagede Now Wants to Close the Bloody Tragedy of 1947]', *Dagblad van het Noorden*, [Groningen], 21 February 2009; 'Minister Koenders Belooft Rawagede Ontwikkelingshulp [Minister Koenders Promises Rawagede Development Aid]', *Trouw*, [Amsterdam], 21 February 2009.
46 'Rawagede Now Wants to Close the Bloody Tragedy of 1947', *Dagblad van het Noorden*.
47 de Volder and de Brouwer, *The Impacts of Litigation*, 16.
48 The compensation payments were contested in the village: the widows who were awarded compensation were forced to share some of the money with the descendants of other victims. See Immler, 'How to Acknowledge Colonial Injustices?'.

In hearing the case, the court determined that 'Indonesia, until 1949 under the name of the Netherlands East Indies, was part of the Kingdom of the Netherlands'[49] and the victims were 'unarmed subjects'[50] of the realm. As such, the state had 'the obligation to protect the bodily integrity and the life of its subjects and had, in no circumstances, the right to kill or harm people without any kind of process'.[51] Referring to the report of the UN Committee of Good Offices on the Indonesian Question and communication between Spoor and the Attorney-General, the court held that the massacre was unacceptable at the time and the state should have anticipated that it would be held to account.[52]

Even so, the court determined that 'prosecutions of the crimes concerned is no longer possible',[53] referring to both the *Memorandum of Excesses* and the 1971 Law on the Statute of Limitations. The court also reiterated that when in 1971 Dutch legislators determined that the statute of limitations would not be upheld for war crimes, this did not include crimes committed by Dutch soldiers in Indonesia. This position had two implications. First, in general, the statute of limitations was upheld—even if the court decided that, in the case of Rawagede, it did not apply. Second, the crimes committed in Rawagede were not 'war crimes'. It was through this position that the court limited the liability of the Dutch State, resonating with Moreton-Robinson's conceptualisation of patriarchal whiteness, through which the claiming of justice in fact serves to protect the interests of the oppressor.

This manifestation of coloniality is also evident in the two factors that played a decisive role in the court's verdict. First, the court determined that the case was 'a very exceptional situation'[54] because of the gravity of what had happened and because the state, despite knowing what had transpired, failed to address this. In so doing, the court effectively removed the massacre from a broader context 'of a striking amount of injustice and violence'[55] and overlooked the fact that violence was inherent in the colonial system.

---

49   Rechtbank 's-Gravenhage [District Court of The Hague], *Zaaknummer 354119/HA ZA 09-4171* [*Case Number 354119/HA ZA 09-4171, Rawagede Verdict*], 14 September 2011, 2.1.
50   ibid., 4.14.
51   ibid., 4.14.
52   ibid., 4.15.
53   ibid., 2.15.
54   ibid., 4.14.
55   Wouter Veraart, 'Uitzondering of Precedent? De Historische Dubbelzinnigheid van de Rawagede-uitspraak [Exception or Precedent? The Historical Ambiguity of the Rawagede Verdict]', *Ars Aequi* (April 2012): 251–59, at 258.

Second, the court based its decision on the fact the massacre took place in a period that 'has yet to be settled'.[56] Further to this point, the court referred to the fact that the Dutch State, from the late 1990s, has broadened restitutions and compensation payments to Jewish victims of World War II; in these cases, the state had not argued the claims were time-barred. Through this consideration, the court rejected the strict separation the Dutch State has long made between injustices committed in the Netherlands during World War II and colonial violence.[57] However, by limiting the claims of the second generation in the Rawagede case, the court deviated from the Dutch Civil Code, under which liability for deaths can be claimed by children. There was a striking contrast here, for example, with claims from the Dutch Jewish community, for whom the second generation has been explicitly included.[58] By acknowledging only the direct victims of Rawagede, the court limited the scope of the case, further reinforcing its supposedly 'exceptional' nature.

The different treatment of those victimised by colonial violence compared with those impacted by the Holocaust demonstrates how the coloniality of power impacts on which groups have access to political power and thus can apply pressure for recognition. Indeed, the court acknowledged in its verdict that the Rawagede victims had 'until recently, not had a fair chance to put their claims forward to the Dutch State or the Dutch Court'.[59] Moreover, the fact that the Dutch State was willing to broaden restitution and compensation for Holocaust victims suggests there is a high level of awareness of the lack of protection offered to Jews at the time by the Dutch State and society in general.[60] By contrast, there is far less unease with colonial history: according to one survey, half of Dutch people are more proud than ashamed of their country's colonial past.[61] It has been noted that, since the nineteenth century, Dutch colonialism has been projected as a 'different, better type of colonialism than [that of] the larger European

---

56 *Rawagede Verdict*, 4.16.
57 Veraart, 'Exception or Precedent?', 255.
58 ibid., 258.
59 *Rawagede Verdict*, 4.9.
60 In 2020, Dutch prime minister Mark Rutte acknowledged the country's role in the persecution of the Jews and apologised on behalf of the Dutch Government for its failure to protect them—the first Dutch Prime Minister to do so. See 'Holocaust: Dutch PM Apologises Over Failure to Protect Jews', *BBC News*, 26 January 2020, www.bbc.com/news/world-europe-51258081.
61 Matthew Smith, *How Unique are British Attitudes to Empire?*, Report (London: YouGov, 11 March 2020), yougov.co.uk/topics/international/articles-reports/2020/03/11/how-unique-are-british-attitudes-empire.

nations'.[62] This has allowed little space for stories that deviate from this narrative, while self-perceptions as a victim nation in World War II have also made it difficult for the Dutch to consider colonial violence as a war crime.[63] How the past is remembered collectively thus has a direct impact on how and the extent to which claims are responded to.

Rawagede and (de)coloniality

In this section, I examine public discussions of the 2011 Rawagede court case in newspaper reporting by media outlets based in both the Netherlands and Indonesia. As outlined in the introduction, I discuss the extent to which public discussions acknowledged broader contexts of colonialism, foregrounded the voices of the victims and considered the framework that was applied to the case.

Public discussions about Rawagede—whether in the Dutch or the Indonesian media—primarily contextualised the massacre in the 1945–49 period. It is important to note that while the Rawagede case was intensely reported by media outlets in the Netherlands, including frequent opinion pieces, this was not the case in Indonesia, where reports were less numerous and opinion pieces scarce.[64] Instead, news reports in the Indonesian media overwhelmingly focused on a chronology of the killings and the various efforts undertaken to hold accountable those responsible.[65]

By contrast, Dutch media—particularly broadsheet newspapers such as *NRC Handelsblad, de Volkskrant* and *Trouw*—extensively reported on Rawagede, even well before the court handed down its verdict. In 2008, criticism emerged after a delegation of Dutch MPs to Indonesia did not visit Rawagede, with the official reason being that this would interfere with court proceedings, which by then had been initiated. In response to this criticism, delegate Henk Jan Ormel of the Christian Democratic Appeal (Christen-Democratisch Appèl) party stated that Rawagede 'was not the only place

---

62 Paul Bijl, 'Colonial Memory and Forgetting in the Netherlands and Indonesia', *Journal of Genocide Research* 14, nos 3–4 (2012): 441–61, doi.org/10.1080/14623528.2012.719375, at 449.
63 Lorenz, 'Can a Criminal Event in the Past Disappear?', 234.
64 For this chapter, the LexisNexis digital archive was used with 'Rawagede' as a keyword. This search returned well over 800 newspaper articles in Dutch and European media outlets, and only 40 in Indonesian newspapers.
65 Aboeprijadi Santoso, 'Jalan Panjang Memenangkan Gugatan [The Long Road to Winning the Claim]', *Historia*, [Jakarta], 15 September 2011, historia.id/militer/articles/jalan-panjang-memenangkan-gugatan-vQaBv.

where excesses took place ... Why would we go to Rawagede and not to other places?'[66] Ormel further claimed that a visit by parliamentarians, especially in the context of financial compensation, would 'lead to high expectations'. He added that the Dutch State on multiple occasions had expressed its regret, including on this visit to Indonesia during which Ormel offered apologies to vice-president Jusuf Kalla, as well as to representatives of the Indonesian parliament and media. Ormel also suggested that addressing the past was more important to the Dutch than the Indonesian public; 'on all occasions', he argued, 'Indonesian counterparts felt that a line should be drawn under this part of our joint history'. In addition, Ormel said:

> [I]n the Netherlands, people are insufficiently aware of the events in Indonesia after the Second World War. We have pushed this period out of our collective memory. We remember the atrocities of which we became a victim, but apparently, we have difficulty to accept that the Dutch, *after the war*, have also been perpetrators.[67]

Ormel's commentary is interesting for several reasons, including the fact that he acknowledged the violence of the 1945–49 period and Dutch responsibility, and pointed out that the Rawagede killings were by no means exceptional. At the same time, however, Ormel reproduced the discourse of 'excesses' and did not address longer histories of colonialism. While Ormel pointed to a lack of awareness in the Netherlands about its colonial past, by referring to the Dutch as perpetrators of violence only after World War II, his comments suggest that prior to that the Dutch were not involved in such crimes.

A newspaper piece by Cees Fasseur, Emeritus Professor in Indonesian history at Leiden University and secretary of the commission that issued the 1969 *Memorandum of Excesses*, similarly referred to other violent events during the revolution. Fasseur argued that 'Rawagede must not remain an exception', referring to other cases identified in the memorandum. He welcomed the claims brought to the court, stating that 'even 60 years later, the Netherlands must make amends in its former colony ... The Netherlands has a moral responsibility that must be redeemed.'[68] Nonetheless, while Fasseur drew

---

66   Henk Jan Ormel, 'Geen Streep Trekken Onder Executies in Rawagede [No Line Under Rawagede Executies]', *Trouw*, [Amsterdam], 21 October 2008.
67   ibid., [emphasis added].
68   Cees Fasseur, 'Rawagede is Nederlandse Ereschuld, en er Zijn Meer [Rawagede is a Dutch Debt of Honour and There Are More]', *Trouw*, [Amsterdam], 26 November 2008.

attention to other violent events during the revolution, thereby making clear that Rawagede was not an exception, he did not refer to the longer period of colonialism.

This is not to say that there was no acknowledgement of the longer history of colonialism and the inequalities this generated. Historian C.V. Lafeber,[69] for instance, labelled Rawagede a 'war crime' and called for a 'deep expression of regret'. Lafeber drew attention to the violence inherent in colonialism by referring to the 'financial and economic exploitation' of the colonies that 'occurred with contempt for the Indonesian people'. Nonetheless, statements such as Lafeber's were rare and did not represent the general tone of public debates.

Another way through which the Rawagede case had the potential to decolonise public perceptions was by drawing attention to the experiences and voices of those who hitherto had been largely overlooked. Particularly liberal and left-leaning newspapers such as *de Volkskrant* and *NRC Handelsblad* showed much sympathy for the claimants, even if they very rarely foregrounded the women's voices, while the state was criticised as 'lazy' and its reliance on the statute of limitations was largely dismissed. An opinion piece signed by, among others, former pastors Jan Eijken and Henk Koetsier stated that the Dutch Government had to be 'courageous' and admit that Rawagede was 'a debt of honour'.[70] Some commentators also were critical of the inability of the Dutch to give Rawagede 'a fitting position in [their] collective memory', contrasting this with events such as the deportation of Jews from the Netherlands during World War II[71] and, more recently, the Dutch failures in the 1995 mass killings in Srebrenica, in Bosnia and Herzegovina.[72]

---

69   C.V. Lafeber, 'Bloedbad Rawagede was een Oorlogsmisdaad [Rawagede Bloodbath Was a War Crime]', *Trouw*, [Amsterdam], 2 December 2008.
70   Jan Eijken, C.H. Koetsier, Jan Glissenaar, and Henk Baars, 'Regering, Toon Nu Eens Lef. Rawagede is Een Ereschuld [Government, Be Courageous. Rawagede Is a Debt of Honour]', *NRC Handelsblad*, [Amsterdam], 6 December 2008.
71   Sander van Walsum, 'Nederlandse Daders [Dutch Perpetrators]', *de Volkskrant*, [Amsterdam], 22 June 2011.
72   In the Srebrenica massacre, Bosnian Serb forces killed more than 7,000 Bosnian Muslim boys and men. While principal responsibility was placed on senior officers in the Bosnian Serb army, the United Nations was blamed for its failure to protect the Muslim men, women and children of Srebrenica. In 2002, a report from the Netherlands Institute of War Documentation determined that the decision of the Dutch Cabinet to withdraw its troops charged with the protection of the Bosnian Muslims in Srebrenica effectively sealed the fate of the community.

Nonetheless, right-wing popular newspapers *De Telegraaf* and *Algemeen Dagblad* were more critical. In these outlets, commonplace were views that Indonesia should also be held accountable for the violence committed against the Dutch. These newspapers provided an outlet and support for Dutch veterans 'accused for 60 years, while our opponents are never blamed of anything'.[73] In response to the Rawagede verdict, the widow of Simon Spoor commented that the 'verdict is great for those people' and added that, while 'the Dutch have done things wrong, this was also the case the other way around'. A few months later Spoor's widow stated:

> [T]he apologies and money given now are outrageous and insane. Those things happened in the Indies, on both sides. But nothing is ever said about what the Indonesians did. Is Indonesia going to apologise for the Dutch boys they killed?[74]

Similarly, the Association of Indies Veterans (Vereniging Oud Militairen Indiëgangers) stated that all veterans felt affected by the verdict and referred to violence committed by Indonesian troops: 'Of course, something happened there, we should not deny that. Such things happen in a war. But we do not receive apologies for our friends who were tortured and decapitated.'[75] Three years later, and after the Dutch State had provided further compensation in other cases, *De Telegraaf* published an article under a headline that said veterans were 'sick' of the claims and labelled the compensation a 'raid on the state's coffers'[76]—showing a blatant disregard for the financial benefits the Netherlands obtained because of colonialism.

While most liberal and left-leaning media outlets in the Netherlands portrayed the Rawagede widows as 'innocent victims of the decolonisation war',[77] right-wing newspapers suggested that Indonesians were taking advantage of the Netherlands and did not eschew racist commentary. In *De Telegraaf*, an Indo-European couple questioned whether the women existed: '[T]he widows are 84, 86, sometimes even 104 years old. Do they really exist? In Indonesia people do not become very old, especially not if they

---

73 'Veteranen Verontwaardigd; Nederland Betaalt Indische Weduwen Vanwege Oorlogsmisdrijf [Veterans Dismayed; Netherlands Pays Indies Widows Because of War Crime]', *De Telegraaf*, [Amsterdam], 15 September 2011.
74 'Eindelijk Gerechtigheid Voor Volk van Rawagede [Finally Justice for Rawagede People]', *Algemeen Dagblad*, [Rotterdam], 10 December 2011.
75 ibid.
76 Charles Sanders, 'Klopjacht op de Staatskas; Indiëgangers Kotsmisselijk van Indonesische Schadeclaims [Manhunt on the Treasury; Indies Veterans Sick of Indonesian Claims]', *De Telegraaf*, [Amsterdam], 31 December 2014.
77 Immler and Scagliola, 'Seeking Justice for the Mass Execution in *Rawagede*', 5.

come from a *kampong*. Why have there been no DNA tests?'[78] They added that they distrusted the claims as, according to them, most Indonesians 'do not even know the year they were born in! In the lower social classes almost all Indonesians are illiterate.'[79] The article concluded by saying:

> [W]ithout a doubt, some of the collected data on victims of Dutch violence will be found fictitious. Once again, we are the teacher's pet. And there, on the other side of the world, they are dancing in the *kampong*, their bellies shaking with laughter.[80]

These comments are illustrative of the 'undisguised racism'[81] present within segments of the Indo-European community, which has roots in colonial society and has persisted long after this community settled in the Netherlands.

In Indonesia, the widows' success in the Dutch courts was quickly absorbed into the broader narrative of Indonesia's struggle against and eventual victory over its former colonial power. However, this did not necessarily mean that there was more public interest in the stories of the women. Instead, most newspaper reports, as discussed above, strongly featured a chronology of events and in many cases focused on the republican army captain Lukas Kustaryo, for whom the Dutch were looking in Rawagede but did not find, leading to the Dutch troops rounding up and killing the men in the village. This focus on Kustaryo—a male revolutionary figure—reproduces dominant nationalist narratives of this period in Indonesian history. Emphasising masculinity, in these narratives, courage was considered a uniquely male attribute, meaning that women were only rarely considered bold or brave.[82]

This emphasis on the role of men in the story of Rawagede was also raised in the context of the compensation awarded to the widows. For instance, Batara Hutagalung, chairperson of the KUKB in Indonesia, commented that 'the level of compensation needs to consider that this is a rural area.

---

78 Sanders, 'Manhunt on the Treasury'.
79 ibid.
80 ibid.
81 Gert Oostindie, *Postcolonial Netherlands: Sixty-Five Years of Forgetting, Commemorating, Silencing* (Amsterdam: Amsterdam University Press, 2011), 109.
82 Frances Gouda, 'Militant Masculinity and Female Agency in Indonesian Nationalism, 1945–1949', in *Colonialism and the Modern World: Selected Studies*, eds Gregory Blue, Martin Bunton, and Ralph C. Crozier (New York: Routledge, 2002), 200–16, doi.org/10.4324/9781315499338, at 208–9.

The massacre targeted men, and thus the economy was severely affected.'[83] While presenting the widows' claims in nationalist frames that emphasised male heroes of the revolution contributed to significant public interest in the massacre in Indonesia,[84] it also meant that there was limited attention given to how the women experienced the event and how it impacted them.

The Rawagede case was examined in the Dutch Civil Court. Paradoxically, 'justice' was delivered through a system established and administered by the former coloniser, which was being held to account in the same court. What was the response to the verdict and to what extent did these discussions address the colonial structures that enabled this decision? Interestingly, Indonesian media reported on the verdict largely in a matter-of-fact fashion. While reports mentioned that, according to the court, at the time of the massacre Indonesia was part of the Netherlands and the victims were Dutch subjects (*onderdanen*),[85] this was presented as the Netherlands' long refusal to legally acknowledge 17 August 1945 as Indonesia's Independence Day.[86] In fact, it was only in 2023 that the Netherlands recognised this date as Indonesia's official Independence Day, and on the condition that this recognition has no legal consequences.[87]

When in September 2011 the court handed down its verdict, it did not elicit much discussion in Indonesia, and there was no official reaction from the Indonesian Government. Only the National Human Rights Commission (Komisi Nasional Hak Asasi Manusia), an independent state body, expressed its support for the verdict.[88] The Indonesian Government was largely absent from the proceedings, which it considered a civil matter initiated by a private entity (that is, the widows and the KUKB). Unsurprisingly, the government did not openly support the efforts of the KUKB or acknowledge the widows' success. While the Indonesian Embassy in the Netherlands provided the widows with accommodation when they

---

83 'Janda Korban Peristiwa Rawagede Akan Dapat Kompensasi [Rawagede Widows Will Receive Compensation]', *Republika*, [Jakarta], 15 September 2011.
84 Immler and Scagliola, 'Seeking Justice for the Mass Execution in *Rawagede*', 9.
85 *Rawagede Verdict*, 4.14.
86 'Sisi Negatif Kasus Rawagede Bagi Indonesia [Negative Side of the Rawagede Case for Indonesia]', *Viva*, [Jakarta], 22 September 2011; 'Belanda Bertanggung Jawab Atas Pembantaian Rawagede [Netherlands Responsible for Rawagede Massacre]', *BBC*, 8 December 2011; 'Komnas HAM Apresiasi Pengadilan Kasus Rawagede [National Commission on Human Rights Appreciative of Rawagede Court]', *Sindonews*, [Jakarta], 10 December 2011.
87 Yvette Tanamal, 'Dutch PM Recognises 1945 as Indonesia's Independence', *Jakarta Post*, 16 June 2023.
88 'National Commission on Human Rights Appreciative of Rawagede Court', *Sindonews*.

gave testimony in court, embassy representatives were notably absent on the day the verdict was handed down.[89] A few years after the Rawagede verdict, representatives of the Indonesian parliament recognised the apology given as 'a good approach to strengthen the relationship' between the Netherlands and Indonesia,[90] thus emphasising the present and future, rather than addressing the past.

By contrast, the verdict was intensely debated in the Netherlands, although these discussions mainly revolved around the compensation awarded to the widows. The official apology from the Netherlands, issued at the December 2011 commemoration in Rawagede, was received well by the families, as was the compensation issued. Media reports commented that, with this, the Dutch State hoped to 'close the Rawagede chapter'.[91] Liesbeth Zegveld emphasised the apologies, stating that they were 'valuable' and contrasting this with monetary compensation. Regarding the amounts awarded, Zegveld commented that these were 'arbitrary, because crimes like this cannot be expressed in a monetary value. The apologies fill that void and can also be heard by those who have not engaged in litigation.' Zegveld added that, with this outcome, the case could be closed: '[A]t some point, you need to stop.'[92] Thus, for Zegveld, the court process was one to obtain a desirable result for her clients—a common approach for lawyers—not an avenue to address inequalities with roots in colonial times that continue to be applied today.

Following the Rawagede case, Zegveld and the KUKB initiated more claims against the Dutch State, which led to further compensation. In 2021, however, Zegveld announced that she would no longer act as a lawyer for Indonesian victims, citing increased workload. KUKB chairperson Jeffry Pondaag, however, suggested Zegveld's decision was a result of her refusal to address the colonial aspects of the legal process. Pondaag has long lamented both the extensive court processes the victims must endure and the decreasing amounts of compensation being awarded by the courts.[93] He has criticised the persistence of the court's differentiation between

---

89 'Jeffrey Ingin Bongkar Kejahatan Belanda [Jeffrey Wants to Take Apart Dutch Crimes]', *Kompas*, [Jakarta], 22 September 2011.
90 'Pembantaian Rawagede, DPR Terima Permintaan Maaf Belanda [Rawagede Massacre, Parliament Accepts Dutch Apology]', *Merdeka*, [Jakarta], 2 September 2013.
91 'Excuses voor Tragedie Rawagede [Apologies for Rawagede Tragedy]', *Trouw*, [Amsterdam], 10 December 2011.
92 ibid.
93 For instance, Syafiah Paturusi, whose father was executed by Raymond Westerling's troops in 1947, was awarded just over €120 in compensation.

'legitimate' and 'excessive' violence, as well as the fact that victims are able to make their claims only because the legal system continues to consider the Netherlands East Indies as the Netherlands' legitimate property, stating: 'I strongly reject that, because the colony was an illegal occupation which I refuse to accept.'[94] Pondaag added: '[T]his means that the court legitimises colonialism ... What gave the Netherlands the right to consider a country that is thousands of kilometres away as its own?' As such, Pondaag argues that it is important that the colonial aspects of the court process are named, thereby taking aim at Zegveld:

> How can it be that colonialism is legitimised and a lawyer who supports the Indonesian victims does not mention this? Whether you win the case or not, these things must be spoken about within the court. If the court then rejects our criticism on the colonial system, then we can together search for other ways to discuss colonialism.[95]

Pondaag's recent criticism shows that, more than 10 years after the Rawagede verdict, there is some discussion of how coloniality continues to influence the legal process. This exposure of the colonial nature of the legal system and its inherent limitations is important. Nonetheless, it remains unclear what the alternative is.

Conclusion

In this chapter I have drawn on newspaper reports to examine public discussions of the Rawagede case. In asking whether these discourses acknowledged coloniality and, in so doing, contributed to decolonial ways of thinking, I focused on the extent to which there was a contextualisation of the Rawagede massacre in the longer history of colonialism, the centring of subaltern and specifically female voices, as well as a critical appraisal of the legal framework that was applied to the case.

The Rawagede case attracted significant attention and, as such, it certainly generated broader discussions about colonial violence. However, this attention was limited to the 1945–49 period. In confining Rawagede to

---

94   Fitria Jelyta, 'Hoe koloniaal is ons rechtssysteem [How Colonial is Our Legal System]?', *De Kanttekening*, [Rotterdam], 29 September 2021, dekanttekening.nl/samenleving/hoe-koloniaal-is-ons-rechtssysteem/.
95   ibid.

this period, longer histories of colonialism remained untouched, as was any debate about how the violence that was perpetrated during the revolution was a result of colonial structures.

Similarly, the Rawagede case increased attention for ordinary people to their experiences during the revolution. The case also opened discussions on the legitimacy of these claims, with the contrast between left-wing and populist reporting in the Netherlands showing that support for the female claimants was not a given, while racist comments in some reporting are further evidence that the legacies of colonialism have not been undone. Meanwhile, the success of the widows in Indonesia was quickly absorbed within dominant narratives of nationalist struggle, foregrounding and reinforcing the role of men in this process, rather than women's ongoing resilience.

Finally, public discussions, especially at the time of the Rawagede decision, barely addressed the colonial legacies apparent in the legal process. While in some Indonesian news reports comments were made about the court's position that at the time of the massacre the victims were considered Dutch subjects, this was presented as a fact rather than critically discussed.

Without doubt, there are limits to what court processes can achieve in decolonising public discussions. Perhaps this is also a matter of time. Just as the Rawagede case paved the way for more cases to be brought to court and more attention given to colonial histories, so, too, have discussions shifted over time. Recent debates about the nature of the legal process, and the colonial aspects thereof, suggest that the work of naming colonialism for what it was and how it continues to reverberate is an ongoing effort.

References

Primary sources

Algemeen Dagblad. 2011. 'Eindelijk Gerechtigheid voor Volk van Rawagede [Finally Justice for Rawagede People].' *Algemeen Dagblad*, [Rotterdam], 10 December.

BBC. 2011. 'Belanda Bertanggung Jawab Atas Pembantaian Rawagede [Netherlands Responsible for Rawagede Massacre].' *BBC*, 8 December.

BBC News. 2020. 'Holocaust: Dutch PM Apologises Over Failure to Protect Jews.' *BBC News*, 27 January. www.bbc.com/news/world-europe-51258081.

Dagblad van het Noorden. 2009. 'Rawagede Wil de Bloedige Tragedie uit 1947 Nu Afsluiten [Rawagede Now Wants to Close the Bloody Tragedy of 1947].' *Dagblad van het Noorden*, [Groningen], 21 February.

De Telegraaf. 2011. 'Veteranen Verontwaardigd; Nederland Betaalt Indische Weduwen Vanwege Oorlogsmisdrijf [Veterans Dismayed; Netherlands Pays Indies Widows Because of War Crime].' *De Telegraaf*, [Amsterdam], 15 September.

Eijken, Jan, and Henk Koetsier. 1997. 'Mogelijke Oorlogsmisdaad Nog Steeds in Doofpot [Possible War Crime Still Covered Up].' *Trouw*, [Amsterdam], 6 December.

Eijken, Jan, C.H. Koetsier, Jan Glissenaar, and Henk Baars. 2008. 'Regering, Toon Nu Eens Lef. Rawagede is Een Ereschuld [Government, Be Courageous. Rawagede is a Debt of Honour].' *NRC Handelsblad*, [Amsterdam], 6 December.

Fasseur, Cees. 2008. 'Rawagede is Nederlandse Ereschuld, en er Zijn Meer [Rawagede is a Dutch Debt of Honour and There Are More].' *Trouw*, [Amsterdam], 26 November.

Fisher, Max. 2022. 'The Long Road Ahead for Colonial Reparations.' *New York Times*, 27 August. www.nytimes.com/2022/08/27/world/americas/colonial-reparations.html.

Karmini, Niniek. 2011. 'Dutch State Apologizes for 1947 Indonesia Massacre.' *Boston Globe*, 9 December. archive.boston.com/news/world/europe/articles/2011/12/09/dutch_state_apologizes_for_1947_indonesia_massacre/.

Kompas. 2011. 'Jeffrey Ingin Bongkar Kejahatan Belanda [Jeffrey Wants to Take Apart Dutch Crimes].' *Kompas*, [Jakarta], 22 September.

Lafeber, C.V. 2008. 'Bloedbad Rawagede was een Oorlogsmisdaad [Rawagede Bloodbath Was A War Crime].' *Trouw*, [Amsterdam], 2 December.

Merdeka. 2013. 'Pembantaian Rawagede, DPR Terima Permintaan Maaf Belanda [Rawagede Massacre, Parliament Accepts Dutch Apology].' *Merdeka*, [Jakarta], 2 September.

New York Times. 1950. 'Indonesia is Rebuffed; Bid for Westerling's Extradition is Denied in Singapore.' *New York Times*, 4 August.

NRC. 2017. 'Hoe een Weduwe de Nederlandse Staat Deed Buigen [How a Widow Made the Dutch State Bow].' *NRC*, [Amsterdam], 27 January. www.nrc.nl/nieuws/2017/01/27/hoe-een-weduwe-de-nederlandse-staat-deed-buigen-6426428-a1543254.

Ormel, Henk Jan. 2008. 'Geen Streep Trekken Onder Executies in Rawagede [No Line Under Rawagede Executions].' *Trouw*, [Amsterdam], 21 October.

Rechtbank 's-Gravenhage [District Court of The Hague]. 2011. *Zaaknummer 354119/HA ZA 09-4171 [Case Number 354119/HA ZA 09-4171, Rawagede Verdict]*. 14 September.

Reformatorisch Dagblad. 2008. 'Nederland Betuigt Spijt in Rawagede [Netherlands Expresses Regret in Rawagede].' *Reformatorisch Dagblad*, [Apeldoorn], 9 December.

Republika. 2011. 'Janda Korban Peristiwa Rawagede Akan Dapat Kompensasi [Rawagede Widows Will Receive Compensation].' *Republika*, [Jakarta], 15 September.

Sanders, Charles. 2014. 'Klopjacht op de Staatskas; Indiëgangers Kotsmisselijk van Indonesische schadeclaims [Manhunt on the Treasury; Indies Veterans Sick of Indonesian Claims].' *De Telegraaf*, [Amsterdam], 31 December.

Santoso, Aboeprijadi. 2011. 'Jalan Panjang Memenangkan Gugatan [The Long Road to Winning the Claim].' *Historia*, [Jakarta], 15 September. historia.id/militer/articles/jalan-panjang-memenangkan-gugatan-vQaBv.

Sidarto, Linawati. 2013. 'Liesbeth Zegveld: The Lawyer Behind the Dutch Apologies.' *Jakarta Post*, 13 September. www.thejakartapost.com/news/2013/09/13/liesbeth-zegveld-the-lawyer-behind-dutch-apologies.html.

Sindonews. 2011. 'Komnas HAM Apresiasi Pengadilan Kasus Rawagede [National Commission on Human Rights Appreciative of Rawagede Court].' *Sindonews*, [Jakarta], 10 December.

Tanamal, Yvette. 2023. 'Dutch PM Recognises 1945 as Indonesia's Independence.' *Jakarta Post*, 16 June.

Trouw. 2009. 'Minister Koenders Belooft Rawagede Ontwikkelingshulp [Minister Koenders Promises Rawagede Development Aid].' *Trouw*, [Amsterdam], 21 February.

Trouw. 2011. 'Excuses voor Tragedie Rawagede [Apologies for Rawagede Tragedy].' *Trouw*, [Amsterdam], 10 December.

van Walsum, Sander. 2011. 'Nederlandse Daders [Dutch Perpetrators].' *de Volkskrant*, [Amsterdam], 22 June 2011.

Viva. 2011. 'Sisi Negatif Kasus Rawagede bagi Indonesia [Negative Side of the Rawagede Case for Indonesia].' *Viva*, [Jakarta], 22 September.

Secondary sources

Australian Law Reform Commission (ALRC). 2015. *Connection to Country: Review of the* Native Title Act 1993 *(Cth): Final Report*. Sydney: Australian Government. www.alrc.gov.au/wp-content/uploads/2019/08/alrc_126_final_report.pdf.

Bijl, Paul. 2012. 'Colonial Memory and Forgetting in the Netherlands and Indonesia.' *Journal of Genocide Research* 14, nos 3–4: 441–61. doi.org/10.1080/14623528.2012.719375.

Cunneen, Chris. 2005. 'Colonialism and Historical Injustice: Reparations for Indigenous Peoples.' *Social Semiotics* 15, no. 1: 59–80. doi.org/10.1080/1035 0330500059130.

de Volder, Eefje, and Anne-Marie de Brouwer. 2019. *The Impacts of Litigation in Relation to Systematic and Large-Scale Atrocities Committed by the Dutch Military Forces in the 'Dutch East Indies' between 1945–1949*. Amsterdam: Nuhanovic Foundation.

Farid, Hilmar. 2022. 'Dealing with the Legacies of a Violent Past.' In *Beyond the Pale: Dutch Extreme Violence in the Indonesian War of Independence, 1945–1949*, edited by Gert Oostindie, Ben Schoenmaker, and Frank van Vree, 473–86. Amsterdam: Amsterdam University Press.

Gouda, Frances. 2002. 'Militant Masculinity and Female Agency in Indonesian Nationalism, 1945–1949.' In *Colonialism and the Modern World: Selected Studies*, edited by Gregory Blue, Martin Bunton, and Ralph C. Crozier, 200–16. New York: Routledge. doi.org/10.4324/9781315499338.

Houben, Vincent J.H. 1997. 'A Torn Soul: The Dutch Public Discussion on the Colonial Past in 1995.' *Indonesia* 63 (April): 47–66. doi.org/10.2307/3351510.

Immler, Nicole L. 2018. 'Hoe koloniaal onrecht te erkennen? De Rawagede-zaak laat kansen en grenzen van rechtsherstel zien [How to Acknowledge Colonial Injustices? The Rawagede Case Shows Opportunities and Limitations of the Restoration of Rights].' *BMGN–Low Countries Historical Review* 133, no. 4: 57–87. doi.org/10.18352/bmgn-lchr.10613.

Immler, Nicole L., and Stef Scagliola. 2020. 'Seeking Justice for the Mass Execution in Rawagede/Probing the Concept of "Entangled History" in a Postcolonial Setting.' *Rethinking History* 24, no. 1: 1–28. doi.org/10.1080/13642529.2019.1693134.

Jelyta, Fitria. 2021. 'Hoe koloniaal is ons rechtssysteem [How Colonial is Our Legal System]?' *De Kanttekening*, [Rotterdam], 29 September. dekanttekening.nl/samenleving/hoe-koloniaal-is-ons-rechtssysteem/.

Limpach, Rémy. 2016. *De Brandende Kampongs van General Spoor* [*The Burning Kampongs of General Spoor*]. Amsterdam: Boom.

Lorenz, Chris. 2014. 'Can a Criminal Event in the Past Disappear in a Garbage Bin in the Present? Dutch Colonial Memory and Human Rights: The Case of Rawagede.' In *Afterlife of Events: Perspectives of Mnemohistory*, edited by Marek Tamm, 219–42. London: Palgrave Macmillan. doi.org/10.1057/9781137470188_12.

Mara, Darren. 2014. 'The Native Title Act, 20 Years On.' [Transcript]. *SBS World News Radio*, 28 February. www.sbs.com.au/news/article/the-native-title-act-20-years-on/2iqilg3jo.

McGregor, Katharine. 2014. 'From National Sacrifice to Compensation Claims: Changing Indonesian Representations of the Westerling Massacres in South Sulawesi, 1946–47.' In *Colonial Counterinsurgency and Mass Violence: The Dutch Empire in Indonesia*, edited by Bart Luttikhuis and A. Dirk Moses, 282–307. London: Routledge. doi.org/10.4324/9781315767345-14.

Moreton-Robinson, Aileen. 2015. *The White Possessive: Property, Power, and Indigenous Sovereignty*. Minneapolis: University of Minnesota Press. doi.org/10.5749/minnesota/9780816692149.001.0001.

NIOD Institute for War, Holocaust and Genocide Studies. n.d. 'Indonesian War of Independence (In Numbers).' [Online]. Amsterdam: NIOD Institute for War, Holocaust and Genocide Studies. www.niod.nl/en/frequently-asked-questions/indonesian-war-independence-numbers.

Oostindie, Gert. 2011. *Postcolonial Netherlands: Sixty-Five Years of Forgetting, Commemorating, Silencing*. Amsterdam: Amsterdam University Press.

Oostindie, Gert. 2022. 'The Netherlands and Indonesia 1945–1949: The Political-Historical Context.' In *Beyond the Pale: Dutch Extreme Violence in the Indonesian War of Independence, 1945–1949*, edited by Gert Oostindie, Ben Schoenmaker, and Frank van Vree, 35–68. Amsterdam: Amsterdam University Press.

Oostindie, Gert, and Rémy Limpach. 2022. 'The War in Indonesia 1945–1949: The Military-Historical Context.' In *Beyond the Pale: Dutch Extreme Violence in the Indonesian War of Independence, 1945–1949*, edited by Gert Oostindie, Ben Schoenmaker, and Frank van Vree, 69–106. Amsterdam: Amsterdam University Press. doi.org/10.1515/9789048557172-002.

Pearson, Jessica Lynne. 2017. 'Defending Empire at the United Nations: The Politics of International Colonial Oversight in the Era of Decolonisation.' *The Journal of Imperial and Commonwealth History* 45, no. 3: 525–49. doi.org/10.1080/03086534.2017.1332133.

Quijano, Aníbal. 2000. 'Coloniality of Power and Eurocentrism in Latin America.' *International Sociology* 15, no. 2: 215–32. doi.org/10.1177/0268580900015002005.

Rolston, Bill, and Fionnuala Ní Aoláin. 2018. 'Colonialism, Redress and Transitional Justice: Ireland and Beyond.' *State Crime Journal* 7, no. 2: 329–48. doi.org/10.13169/statecrime.7.2.0329.

Scagliola, Stef. 2007. 'The Silences and Myths of a "Dirty War": Coming to Terms with the Dutch–Indonesian Decolonisation War (1945–1949).' *European Review of History* 14, no. 2: 235–62. doi.org/10.1080/13507480701433901.

Scagliola, Stef. 2012. 'Cleo's "Unfinished Business": Coming to Terms with Dutch War Crimes in Indonesia's War of Independence.' *Journal of Genocide Research* 14, nos 3–4: 419–39. doi.org/10.1080/14623528.2012.719374.

Smith, Matthew. 2020. *How Unique are British Attitudes to Empire?* Report, 11 March. London: YouGov. yougov.co.uk/topics/international/articles-reports/2020/03/11/how-unique-are-british-attitudes-empire.

Swirc, Maurice. 2022. *De Indische Doofpot. Waarom Nederlandse Oorlogsmisdaden in Indonesië Nooit Zijn Vervolgd* [*The Indisch Cover Up: Why Dutch War Crimes in Indonesia Were Never Prosecuted*]. Amsterdam: De Arbeiderspers.

van den Herik, Larissa. 2012. 'Addressing Colonial Crimes through Reparations? Adjudicating Dutch Atrocities Committed in Indonesia.' *Journal of International Criminal Justice* 10, no. 3: 693–706. doi.org/10.1093/jicj/mqs033.

Veraart, Wouter. 2012. 'Uitzondering of Precedent? De Historische Dubbelzinnigheid van de Rawagede-uitspraak [Exception or Precedent? The Historical Ambiguity of the Rawagede Verdict].' *Ars Aequi* (April): 251–59.

15

Seeking the Morning Star: Young Papuans and the ongoing struggle against Indonesian colonialism

I Ngurah Suryawan

> Hi Indonesia, the coloniser, you can kill my body, but my soul and spirit are with the eternity. It has been inscribed in the history of the struggle of Papuans forever.[1]

Introduction

The statement above was issued by young Papuan activists from the National Committee for West Papua[2] (Komite Nasional Papua Barat, KNPB) at the memorial service for Martinus Yohame, the chair of the KNPB in Sorong Raya (Greater Sorong). He was found dead on 26 August 2014, his body floating on the shoreline of Nana Island, tightly bound in a sack. He was

---

1   Budi Hernawan, 'Mengapa Indonesia Bunuh Kami Terus? Pembunuhan Politik atas Pegiat KNPB di Papua [Why Does Indonesia Kill Us? Political Assassinations of KNPB Activists in Papua]', *Kyoto Review of Southeast Asia* 21 (March 2017), kyotoreview.org/issue-21/political-assassination-knpb-activists/.
2   West Papua (Papua Barat) refers to the creation of a state, proclaimed on 1 December 1961, prepared by the Dutch with the Papuan elite, through the formation of the Papuan National Committee and state apparatus. The term 'Tanah Papua' ('Land of Papua') emerged after the 1998 reforms in Indonesia and the division of West Irian Jaya Province into Papua, West Papua, Southwest Papua, South Papua, Highland Papua and Central Papua.

killed in secret by the Indonesian military or police. The Indonesian security apparatus uses various forms of violence to suppress young Papuan activists: extrajudicial killings are one such strategy. Two years before Yohame's killing, several armed men who appeared to be police officers shot Mako Tabuni, the first chairperson of the KNPB. Mako was taken to hospital but could not be saved and died soon after.[3] The KNPB statement clearly shows that violence, including the killing of Papuan freedom activists, is a colonial practice of the Indonesian Government and identifies the security apparatus—the police, military and other security organisations—as one of the tools Indonesian colonisers use to suppress the Papuan liberation movement.

Another strategy used by the Indonesian Government to silence Papuan activists is arresting and subjecting them to heavy criminal sanctions. For example, Victor Frederik Yeimo, the international spokesperson for the KNPB and the *Papuan People's Petition* (*Petisi Rakyat Papua*), was arrested by the Nemangkawi Task Force, a joint team of Indonesian military and police, on 9 May 2021 in Jayapura. The authorities justified Yeimo's arrest by arguing that he had incited riots almost two years earlier, on 19 August 2019, while delivering a speech in front of the office of the Governor of Papua.[4] Yeimo was accused of treason (*makar*) based on his speech and participation in a peaceful anti-racism demonstration. As a result, he faced life imprisonment, simply because he expressed his political aspirations. Following his arrest, Yeimo was held in solitary confinement and both his family and his lawyers had trouble meeting with him.[5] While in May 2023 the Jayapura District Court cleared Yeimo of treason charges, he was sentenced to eight months in prison for showing disrespect to the Indonesian Government.[6] He was released from prison in September 2023.[7]

---

3 For a profile of Mako Tabuni, see Benny Mawel, 'Jejak Mako Tabuni; Lahir Besar Bersama Rakyat di Jalanan, Matipun Bersama Rakyat di Jalanan [Mako Tabuni's Footsteps, Born and Raised with the People on the Streets, Died with the People on the Streets]', *Suara Papua* [*Voice of Papua*], 17 September 2016, suarapapua.com/2016/09/17/jejak-mako-tabuni-lahir-besar-bersama-rakyat-di-jalanan-mati-pun-bersama-rakyat-di-jalanan/.
4 Adi Briantika and Riyan Setiawan, 'Mereka yang Menuntut Pembebasan Juru Bicara KNPB Victor Yeimo [Those Demanding the Release of KNPB Spokesperson Victor Yeimo]', *Tirto.id*, [Jakarta], 20 May 2021, tirto.id/mereka-yang-menuntut-pembebasan-juru-bicara-knpb-victor-yeimo-gf7A.
5 'Indonesia: Release Peaceful Anti-Racism Protestor Victor Yeimo', Petition (London: Amnesty International, 3 December 2021).
6 Controversially, Yeimo was convicted based on Article 155(1) of the Criminal Code, which was never cited in the initial charges against him and which was revoked by the Indonesian Constitutional Court in 2007. See Yamin Kogoya, 'Victor Yeimo's Release from Indonesian Prison Unites West Papuans in the Fight Against Racism and Colonialism', *GreenLeft*, [Sydney], 25 September 2023, www.greenleft.org.au/content/victor-yeimos-release-indonesian-prison-unites-west-papuans-fight-against-racism-and.
7 ibid.

At the time of his arrest, Yeimo was charged under Articles 106 and 110 of the Indonesian Criminal Code. Indonesian authorities have used the code, and particularly these articles, to prosecute dozens of peaceful pro-independence Papuan activists who are legally exercising their rights to freedom of expression, association and peaceful assembly. According to Amnesty International Indonesia, in December 2020, at least 77 people were in prison based on Articles 106 and 110 of the Criminal Code, while as of July 2021, at least 13 Papuan political prisoners had been imprisoned for treason based on the same articles.[8] Thus, legal mechanisms are another tool the Indonesian Government uses in the colonisation of Papua and to oppress those who fight for its sovereignty and independence.[9]

Papuan resistance to this colonialism takes the form of an anti-racism movement, which was the reason for the arrest of Victor Yeimo and other young Papuan nationalists, based on the race politics engrained in Papuan political history and its relationship with the Indonesian State. Globally, race politics gained public momentum following the brutal killing in 2020 of African American man George Floyd by the police in Minneapolis. This triggered a global anti-racism movement known as #BlackLivesMatter. Related to this movement was the emergence of global networks of solidarity with Papuan people through digital media known by the hashtag #PapuanLivesMatter, which developed recognition of the oppression of Papuan people and the occupation of their territory by the Indonesian State.[10]

As outlined in Chapter 1 of this volume, the systematic persecution of Papuan activists is an example of how colonialism persists and is practised in, and by, the Indonesian State. This chapter focuses on the hopes and thoughts of a generation of young Papuans about their fight for independence and sovereignty. The chapter traces the continuities between young Papuan activists today and the ideas of young Papuans during the final decades of Dutch colonialism in the 1950s and 1960s. This generation of early Papuan nationalists was sent to the Netherlands to study and

---

8   'Bebaskan Victor Yeimo yang Kondisi Kesehatan Memburuk [Release Victor Yeimo whose Health is Deteriorating]' (Jakarta: Amnesty International Indonesia, 21 August 2021).
9   Development is another tool of colonial oppression. See Cypri Jehan Paju Dale, 'Penjajahan Lewat Pembangunan di Papua [Colonisation Through Development in Papua]', *Rappler*, [Manila], 23 May 2016, www.rappler.com/world/indonesia/133896-penjajahan-lewat-pembangunan-papua/.
10 Timothy P. Daniels, 'Blackness in Indonesia: Articulations of Colonial and Postcolonial Racial Epistemologies', *Ethnos* (2022): 1–22, doi.org/10.1080/00141844.2022.2081239; Veronika Kusumaryati, '#Papuanlivesmatter: Black Consciousness and Political Movements in West Papua', *Critical Asian Studies* 53, no. 4 (2021): 453–75, doi.org/10.1080/14672715.2021.1963794.

developed their nationalist ideas within this context. As this chapter shows, there was division within the movement of young Papuans at the time— namely, between those who aspired for an independent state under Dutch guidance and those who wanted to achieve West Papuan independence without such support. Several young activists pursued their aspirations by establishing Papuan political parties. These early movements departed from the premise that national identity and seeking an acknowledgement of equal human dignity were at the core of the conflict between Indonesia and the Netherlands over independence. Forms of resistance, apart from political access, were also a reaction to the violence that was committed by the Indonesian security apparatus at the time of the transition of power in the 1960s. In this chapter, I reflect on the extent to which the ideas of young Papuan activists today differ from those who opposed Dutch colonialism. How do young Papuans today fight colonialism and coloniality, including racism and widespread discrimination? Why do they consider historical understanding, education and critical awareness of the colonial system important as a basis for West Papua's liberation? To do this, I focus on the KNPB, a leading activist organisation for resistance within West Papua, and the thoughts of one of its prominent leaders, Victor Yeimo.

In its magazine, *KNPB News*,[11] the Central Executive Board of the KNPB says that the state violence it has experienced has made the organisation mature in its resistance to the Indonesian colonial state. The KNPB characteristically uses a peaceful and dignified approach to resistance by focusing on political education and community organising, particularly of youth groups on university campuses in urban areas of Papua, as well as demonstrations. The KNPB's aim is to achieve sovereignty for the people of Papua so they can make their own political decisions, free from intimidation and violence.

Resistance movements led by young Papuans, such as the KNPB, have been born of a cycle of violence and persistent efforts to fight for sovereignty and dignity. The role of young Papuans is vital considering the dissolution of

---

11 *KNPB News* is the official media published by the KNPB. In the June–August 2016 edition, Victor F. Yeimo, then the general chair of the KNPB, wrote: 'KNPB News is a media of information, communication and education for the people of West Papua. We are aware that the people have the right to know correct information about the true reality they are facing, behind the mainstream media coverage which is nothing more than colonialism and capitalism public relations. KNPB hopes that the presence of *KNPB News* can provide credible information and can become the basis for the people of West Papua to make choices about their lives in the present and in the future. We need suggestions, criticism, financial support, and written contributions from the people of West Papua.'

various previous Papuan resistance organisations and the establishment of the KNPB on 19 November 2008. This organisation has since developed into one of the most important, influential and solid social movement organisations to date, with most of its supporters being Papuan students and youth. The KNPB has regional representation in almost all areas of West Papua through local branches, including in the Mnukwar (Manokwari) region, as well as Timika, Jayapura, Sorong and Merauke. Each regional branch coordinates with the organisation's Central Executive Board. All KNPB branches have experienced various acts of intimidation and terror, raids, arrests and even killings that can be considered colonial violence.

This chapter uses the KNPB to reflect on how young Papuans imagine the future. The chapter consists of three parts. The first provides historical context of political emancipation in Tanah Papua ('Land of Papua'), the western half of the island of New Guinea. The second part begins with a background of the founding of the KNPB, its dynamics, ideology and imagination of the future. I pay attention to what is new in their ideas and approaches and am particularly concerned with how sustainability and renewal are carried out by young Papuans within contemporary social movements in West Papua. One characteristic of the movement to which I attend is how young Papuans seek to raise awareness as a basis for their movement and take a stand against the Indonesian Government. Indeed, a defining feature of the Papuan youth movement is its consistency in disseminating discourses of Indonesian colonialism towards the people of West Papua. Their political position has not changed, in that they continue to advocate for a referendum on self-determination for the people of West Papua. In the third part of the chapter, I argue that the goal of the KNPB is to end colonialism and the suffering experienced by the Papuan people. To illustrate this point, I analyse parts of three open letters issued by the KNPB to 'Indonesian colonial slaves'—that is, Papuans who support the Indonesian Government and its colonisation of the Papuan people—the people of West Papua and Indonesian migrants in Papua. Through these letters, I discuss the ideas and attitudes of the KNPB.

Figure 15.1 Victor Yeimo (centre) and, on the left, the late West Papuan independence activist Filep Karma (1959–2022), at Karma's release from Abepura Prison coinciding with the seventh anniversary of the formation of the KNPB, 19 November 2015[12]
Source: Harun Rumbarar.

Antecedents of political emancipation

In 1895, the Netherlands colonised the area that was then known as Netherlands New Guinea (Nederlands Nieuw Guinea) when the island of New Guinea was divided into two parts. The western part (West Papua) came under Dutch control, while the eastern part (Papua New Guinea) was further divided between territory ruled by Germany in the north and the British in the south. British New Guinea was transferred to Australian administrative control in 1906.[13] On the western side of the island in 1898, the Dutch established two centres of government: Manokwari and Fakfak. In 1903, the Dutch started to bring people from Java to the main cities in

---

12 Filep Karma was arrested for taking part in a peaceful ceremony on 1 December 2004, which included the raising of the Morning Star flag. In May 2005, Karma was sentenced to 15 years in prison on charges of treason (*makar*) for having 'betrayed' Indonesia by flying the Papuan flag.

13 The German-controlled colonial territory of the northeastern part of the island came under a League of Nations mandate in 1920. For analysis of the transition to Australian colonial rule in Papua and New Guinea, see Roger C. Thompson, *Australian Imperialism in the Pacific: The Expansionist Era, 1820–1920* (Melbourne: Melbourne University Press, 1980).

West Papua to develop a system of government, agriculture and trade, which benefited the Netherlands. During Dutch rule, Papuans were regarded as colonial subjects who needed to be civilised.

The dispute over the territory that is now known as West Papua began when the Netherlands was defeated in the Indonesian revolution (1945–49). During the Dutch–Indonesian Round Table Conference in The Hague, the fate of Papua, then known as Netherlands New Guinea, was hotly debated. Eventually, it was decided that all areas colonised by the Dutch prior to the Japanese occupation would become part of the Indonesian State, except Papua. Because of this decision, both parties felt that they were entitled to the territory of West Papua. Indonesian claims to this territory were based on nationalist imaginings of the extent of the sovereign Indonesian nation, stretching from the westernmost tip of Aceh in Sumatra to the easternmost extent in Papua—'*from Sabang to Merauke*'.[14] The Dutch wanted Papua to become an independent state under the control of the Kingdom of the Netherlands and therefore started to prepare the territory for independence, leading to the establishment of local Papuan political parties in the 1950s and 1960s. Indeed, Papuan political development peaked in the 1960s when many people from different backgrounds showed interest in politics by forming or joining political parties.[15] This exercising of their freedom to take a political stance of course did not take place in a vacuum: the freedom for political expression in an independent country was still very much subject to the control and power of the Netherlands.

An important period for understanding the development of a Papuan elite is the preparation for West Papua's independence in the 1950s and 1960s. This development was subsequently interrupted by the invasion of West Papua by Indonesia because of the 1962 New York Agreement, which marked the transfer of sovereignty from the Netherlands to Indonesia through the United Nations Temporary Executive Authority (UNTEA). The historical issue that remains today is whether the West Papuan people indeed exercised their right to self-determination, supposedly given to them through the UN-negotiated agreement between the Netherlands and Indonesia. At the

---

14 See, for instance, Sukarno, *From Sabang to Merauke! President Soekarno's Speech on the Fifth Anniversary of Indonesia's Independence—17th August 1950* (Jakarta: Pertjetakan Negara, 1950).

15 See also I Ngurah Suryawan, 'Jalan Berliku Para Elit Papua [The Winding Path of the Papuan Elite]', *IndoPROGRESS*, [Jakarta], 1 November 2018, indoprogress.com/2018/11/jalan-berliku-para-elite-papua/.

heart of the matter is the tension between Dutch efforts to 'prepare' West Papua for independence and Indonesia's manipulation of the transition to seize control over the territory.[16]

The editors of *Majalah Triton* ('*Triton Magazine*'), a Malay-language publication of the Dutch Government's information department, provides insights into the vibrant political developments of 1960–61. The editors of *Majalah Triton*, in a report titled 'Perkembangan Politiek Sudah Mulai [Political Development Has Started]', likened the emergence of political parties to the building of houses, which would come to play an important role in the development of the state of West Papua:

> We must together build our people's homes. Don't let us collect building materials only to bring them to another place, to the point that the house will not be built. Each establishment [of a political party] is the material for building a house, our enthusiasm provides the energy for our work, our goals are the interests of the people, that is what houses are made of.[17]

This period was also the beginning of preparations for the election of Papuan representatives to the New Guinea Council (Nieuw Guinea Raad, NGR), a body that would include representation of educated Papuan groups. The NGR was created on 5 April 1961. Both established and new, young political activists used the NGR as an opportunity to disseminate their political views to the Papuan people. These different activists, however, were united in their desire for the Papuan people to be involved in negotiations to determine the fate of their country.

An important political figure voicing the aspirations of the Papuan people at the time was Johan Ariks, a teacher from Manokwari. Ariks had strongly fought for the representation of Papuan people during the Round Table Conference but was ultimately unsuccessful. Ariks' conversation with P.J. Koet, the director of the cabinet of the representative of the Crown, on 10 February 1949, illustrates clearly that Ariks rejected Papua's inclusion in Indonesia, instead preferring to be part of the Dutch Kingdom:

---

16 Several previous studies have questioned the crucial moments in the 20 years of transition of power in West Papua. See, for instance, John Salford, *The United Nations and the Indonesian Takeover of West Papua, 1962–1969: The Anatomy of Betrayal* (London: Routledge, 2003), doi.org/10.4324/9780203221877.

17 'Perkembangan Politiek Sudah Mulai [Political Development Has Started]', *Majalah Triton* [*Triton Magazine*], [West Papua], no. 1 (January 1961).

> The people of Irian are indeed not yet educated and most of them truly still live in ancient times and conditions, but these people know what they feel in their hearts. For this matter, there are only two questions, namely: Indonesia or the Netherlands, and the answer to this question is, even from a small child: not Indonesia.
>
> This is the opinion of the common people, the uneducated people, people who, according to the Dutch government, cannot express their opinion!
>
> The people of Irian can express their opinion and the Dutch government must follow the decisions and desires of the people. We do not want to be part of the United States of Indonesia, we want to be under the Dutch crown and want to be led by the Dutch nation and take an honourable place within the Dutch empire.[18]

Following a somewhat colonial logic, Ariks suggested Papuans were not yet sufficiently developed and argued firmly that they already knew they would prefer to stay under the governance of the Dutch and did not want to join Indonesia. Continuing into the 1950s, Papuan political movements started to garner support from other countries and disseminated information to people in Papua—for instance, by political figures such as Nicolaas Jouwe. In 1951, Jouwe established the United New Guinea Movement (Gerakan Persatuan New Guinea, GPNG) in Hollandia (now Jayapura). The GPNG would also become influential in regions such as Biak, Manokwari, Sorong and Merauke. The GPNG's goal was to oppose Indonesia, promote the unity of Papuan people and fight for independence.

There were many different political parties in this early period with different geographic sources of support, which contributed to a lack of unity. For example, Barend Mandatjan and Lodewijk Mandatjan, on 20 September 1960, established the United New Guinea Party (Eenheidspartij Nieuw Guinea, or Partai Persatuan Nieuw Guinea). Mandatjan was the party's chairperson and received support from most of the Arfak community in

---

18 Bernarda Materay, *Nasionalisme Ganda Orang Papua* [*The Dual Nationalism of Papuan People*] (Jakarta: Buku Kompas, 2012), 170–71.

Manokwari. Three days later, Johan Ariks established the United People of New Guinea Party (Partai Orang Nieuw Guinea) with O. Manupapami as its deputy chairperson.[19]

The parties that emerged in this early period of political freedom aimed to express the political choices and ideas of the people of West Papua. The basic ideas that emerged from these parties were political access and freedom for West Papuans to express themselves. As part of this, the emancipation of the Papuan people was to include their active involvement in politics, government, the economy, education and other fields that hitherto had been organised by the Dutch Government. Nonetheless, these ideas were expressed in a broader political context that was controlled by the Dutch Government, with the assistance of Papuan elites. These elites—active in politics and government—considered it most important to collaborate with anyone who would give broader political opportunities to the Papuan people.

One example is Eliezer Jan Bonay, who, on 1 December 1961, in collaboration with the Dutch Government, was among a group of Papuan nationalists who declared the independence of West Papua and decided on national symbols such as the anthem and flag, featuring the Morning Star. However, a year later, as sovereignty was transferred from the Netherlands to Indonesia, Bonay joined the Indonesian Government. Bonay— a member of the educated Papuan elite—had by then realised that with the transfer to Indonesia and the establishment of the Province of West Irian, Indonesia would have far more political control. Thus, he placed his hopes in collaborating with the Indonesian Government and that this would lead to autonomy for West Irian, in which there would be more opportunities for political, economic and social development, as well as education. The Indonesian Government, led by president Sukarno, appointed Bonay as the first Governor of Papua (1963–64).[20]

---

19   Other parties, such as the Democratic People's Party (Democratische Volks Partij) and the National Party (Partei Nationaal) were established in Hollandia (Jayapura) and, in Sentani, the Partai Kena U Embay was established on 20 November 1960. In Manokwari, apart from the United New Guinea Party and the United People of New Guinea Party, the Party of the Union of Papuan Youth (Partai Serikat Pemoeda Pemoedi Papoea) was established on 20 October 1960. Meanwhile, in Sorong, the Party of Equal Humans (Partai Sama-Sama Manusia) and the Raja Ampat Christian and Islamic Unity Party (Partai Persatuan Kristen Islam Raja Ampat) was established on 2 December 1960. See Materay, *The Dual Nationalism of Papuan People*, 191–93.
20   The legal basis of the positions of indigenous Papuan leaders under president Sukarno was Presidential Determination No. 1/1962 and was continued by Law No. 12/1969 under the Suharto government.

Bonay was ultimately disappointed. Sukarno was overthrown by Suharto through a 'creeping coup'.[21] In the early years of Suharto's New Order (1966–98), the annexation of West Papua was completed following the so-called 1969 Act of Free Choice, in which Papuan elders were coerced by the Indonesian military to vote for integration into Indonesia.[22] Bonay's dream of organising West Irian's government and preparing Papuans to develop Papua ended, and he began to advocate publicly for Papua's liberation. Bonay took his activism beyond the borders of Indonesia when, in May 1981, he spoke at the Melanesian Solidarity Week in the capital of Papua New Guinea, Port Moresby. The Government of Papua New Guinea then expelled Bonay and he went to Sweden in June. In 1982, he moved to the Netherlands, where he settled in a small town called Wijhe, where he eventually died in 1990. During his exile, he wrote a manuscript entitled 'The History of the Rise of Papuan Nationalism'.[23]

The struggle of these early Papuan leaders in the period of late Dutch colonialism and the Indonesian takeover emphasises the leaders' common belief that the Papuan people knew what they wanted and desired to shape their own future. This period was, however, characterised by a lack of agreement between politicians and the presence of many different parties with local followings, which may have weakened the movement. A clear lesson learned from this period was that, from the beginning of Suharto's rule in 1966, Papuans would not be given a strong role in shaping their future. It was in this context that the military-dominated Suharto regime began to firmly repress political opposition in West Papua. In response, Papuans mounted continuing resistance to the regime through the political activism of, among others, the armed Free Papua Movement (Organisasi Papua Merdeka).

During Suharto's New Order, human rights violations were entrenched in the operations of the security forces, particularly in West Papua. International scrutiny of Indonesia's human rights record was limited in the context of the Cold War because of the country's strong anticommunist stance.[24] However, towards the end of the Suharto regime, there was gradually more

---

21   John Roosa, *Pretext for Mass Murder: The September 30th Movement and Suharto's Coup d'État in Indonesia* (Madison: University of Wisconsin Press, 2006), 4.
22   Ken M.P. Setiawan and Dirk Tomsa, *Politics in Contemporary Indonesia: Institutional Change, Policy Challenges and Democratic Decline* (London: Routledge, 2022), doi.org/10.4324/9780429459511, 160–61.
23   For an analysis of this unpublished manuscript, see Richard Chauvel, *Constructing Papuan Nationalism: History, Ethnicity, and Adaptation*, ed. Muthiah Alagappa (Washington, DC: East–West Center, 2005), www.jstor.com/stable/resrep06503.
24   Setiawan and Tomsa, *Politics in Contemporary Indonesia*, 152.

interest in the human rights situation in West Papua. In 1995, the Irian Jaya Working Group for Justice and Peace was established, which investigated several human rights violations. Papuans also continued to engage in political organisation. One example was the establishment in August 1998, months after the fall of the Suharto regime, of the Irian Jaya People's Forum for Reconciliation (Forum Rekonsiliasi Rakyat Irian Jaya, or FORERI). Established by Papuan intellectuals, church leaders and activists, FORERI sought to explore opportunities for Papuan people to address their own issues through various means, including independence.[25] Indeed, following East Timor's successful referendum for independence in 1999, hopes for self-determination for West Papua were reignited.

The KNPB envisages the liberation of Papua

The National Committee for West Papua (KNPB) was formed on 19 November 2008. Its name refers to Papuans' political engagement over time and, in particular, the establishment of the Papua National Committee (Komite Nasional Papua) and the New Guinea Council at the time sovereignty was transferred from the Netherlands to the United Nations, between 1 December 1961 and 1 May 1963, when the UNTEA's mandate came to an end. The establishment of the KNPB was closely connected to the outrage that followed the 2001 killing by the Indonesian security apparatus of Theys H. Eluay, an elite Papuan leader of the Papua Presidium Council (Presidium Dewan Papua), a liberation organisation formed after the Second Papuan People's Congress (Kongres Rakyat Papua), held in May–June 2000. After Eluay's murder, the Papua Presidium Council was no longer active, and this inspired young activists to establish a new body in the form of the KNPB as a resistance, student and community organisation. At its formation, Buchtar Tabuni and Victor F. Yeimo, who had previously led actions supporting the launch of the International Parliamentarians for West Papua in London (on 15 October 2008), were selected as, respectively, the general chairperson and the first chairperson of the KNPB. The organisation grew out of a longer history of emancipatory

---

25   I Ngurah Suryawan, 'Dari Memoria Passionis ke Foreri: Sejarah Politik Papua 1999–2000 [From Memoria Passionis to Foreri: Political History of Papua 1999–2000]', *Paramita: Historical Studies Journal* 22, no. 2 (2012): 143–56, doi.org/10.15294/paramita.v22i2.2116; Jaap Timmer, 'Erring Decentralization and Elite Politics in Papua', in *Renegotiating Boundaries: Local Politics in Post-Suharto Indonesia*, eds Henk Schulte Nordholt and Gerry van Klinken (Leiden: Brill, 2007), 459–82, doi.org/10.1163/9789004260436_021.

political movements in Tanah Papua. Its formation in 2008 took place in the context of the exodus from Manado, Java and Bali of Papuan students, who returned to the provinces of Papua and West Papua to join student and community activists in Jayapura who occupied a sports field for the funeral of Theys Eluay in Sentani, where they decreed that 'Papua is an Emergency Zone'.

The KNPB held its first congress on 19–22 November 2010. The congress ushered in a focus on the formation of the Regional People's Parliament (Parlemen Rakyat Daerah) and, at its peak, the National Parliament of West Papua (Parlemen Nasional West Papua) as democratic mechanisms to represent the interests of the Papuan political nation. Buchtar Tabuni, who had recently been released from prison, was elected as the head of the National Parliament of West Papua. Other notable peaceful political movements initiated by the KNPB included the mid-2011 demand for a referendum throughout Tanah Papua under the command of Mako Tabuni. Security forces responded by repressing those who supported this idea and Mako Tabuni was shot and killed on 14 July 2012 by the Special Detachment 88 (*Densus 88*) of the Papua Regional Police (*Polda Papua*).

Figure 15.2 KNPB demonstration in support of Papua joining the international Pacific Forum, 7 September 2015
Photo: Harun Rumbarar.

Cohering with the mandate of the First KNPB Congress, activists began to coordinate with various resistance groups and drove the creation of a so-called Reconciliation Team. In reconciliation meetings, the KNPB advocated for unity between various Papuan liberation movements comprising three large factions: the National Parliament of West Papua, the Federal Republic of West Papua (Negara Republik Federal Papua Barat) and the West Papua National Coalition for Liberation. The need for unity between leaders within and outside Papua became increasingly pressing, leading to a meeting in Port Vila in Vanuatu on 6 December 2014. This meeting resulted in the Saralana Declaration, in which the KNPB announced the unification of the three prominent factions to form one coordinating forum, the United Liberation Movement for West Papua. This movement aimed to push for international efforts to realise self-determination for the Papuan nation, while the declaration confirmed the KNPB's ongoing activist role as an organisation for domestic resistance movements. This reflects the KNPB's perspective that the primary basis of resistance must be internal; the West Papuan people must unite in a resistance movement to push the political process towards West Papuan independence.

Reflecting the core principles of the KNPB's struggle, the West Papuan national liberation movement is underpinned by socialist values that are deeply embedded in the cultural life of Papuans. These values include collectivism in democracy, patriotic spirit and a militant mindset, based on truth and humanity as sources of love and thereby equality and egalitarianism. The KNPB's ideology is also shaped by the religious and cultural values of Melanesian Papuans—a differentiating factor of contemporary Papuans, who hold such values close. The contemporary liberation movement also incorporates and shapes activists and the KNPB movement by equipping them with modern socialist thought as a weapon in the struggle of oppressed people against colonialism/neo-colonialism and capitalist imperialism, which have destroyed the nation of Papua.

The KNPB positions the West Papuan people as subjects in the struggle for national liberation, the primary fighters in the revolution to create a socialist Papuan society. In the KNPB's aspiration for a socialist society, the nation is no longer shaped by political and economic classes as sources of the oppression of people by other people. They argue that the expansion of transnational companies which scour the environment and seek to reap the greatest profit possible has marginalised local communities throughout Tanah Papua. These processes of expansion and marginalisation are, in their view, the face of a new colonialism under way in West Papua. The KNPB fights for the life of the nation, advocating for the expulsion of Indonesian colonialism, which is a source of oppression in West Papua today.[26]

The KNPB has never promised independence, but rather focuses on demonstrating what the path to independence might be and prompting ways to advocate for it. Through civic education, the KNPB is currently teaching people that an independent Papua will not arrive from outside the nation, but rather as the result of the efforts of the people of West Papua themselves. This attitude demonstrates a strong desire to strengthen the roots of the Papuan people by building a basis for a movement among members of the younger generation. Such a focus is very different from the first generations of Papuan liberation activists who concentrated on building opportunities for cooperation with external actors, such as the Netherlands and Indonesia. The openness of these previous generations to forge networks and leverage opportunities is intimately linked to the context in which they acted. In that context the Papuan people were forced to decide whether they wanted to become an independent country, a territory under the Netherlands or part of Indonesia.

The silencing of freedom of expression and opinion in West Papua during and beyond the Suharto period reflects the entrenched nature of the authoritarian Indonesian regime. In the Papuan context, this is intensified by ingrained discriminatory attitudes, racism and stigma directed at those considered to be 'separatists' and 'terrorists' in the subconscious of those in power, especially those working in the state apparatus. Intimidation, violence and even the disappearance of members of the Papuan youth movement who voice their aspirations and political stances are like burning coals that will continue to fuel the flames of the Papuan liberation movement. The use of discriminatory violence to contain the Papuan youth movement will further exacerbate the conflict and perpetuate memories of suffering for the Papuan people—of loss of life, loss of their land and therefore loss of their sovereignty.

Among the current younger generation of Papuan activists there is an acute sense of the extent to which Papua is still colonised today and the way in which coloniality functions to legitimise and perpetuate this system of

---

26 'KNPB: Dari Mana Ke Mana [KNPB Where From, Where To]?', *KNPB News*, June–August 2016, [Also published in *Suara Papua* (*Voice of Papua*), 12 August 2019, suarapapua.com/2019/08/12/knpb-dari-mana-ke-mana/, 34–37.

power. One of the Papuan intellectual leaders who has made an important contribution in challenging Papua's colonial status is Benny Giay. In his inspiring book,[27] Giay contends that intellectual projects and activism must respond to the sociopolitical conditions of people who experience a 'culture of silence'. By this he means the silence and the silencing of the Papuan people due to the constant terror of violence and exclusion they experience. Breaking this silence is a challenge for the intellectual work and activism of the Papuan youth movement because solidarity is stifled by a culture of silence and reluctance to speak up. For Giay, the solidarity and ties that already exist between Papuan people—which are built on social relations—can be restored as a source of strength to fight for freedom and justice and work towards a New Papua.

Giay contends that the solidarity of the Papuan people can be strengthened through raising awareness of common experiences under Indonesian rule—for example: first, Papuans being labelled stupid, incapable and drunk; second, being intimidated into making oral and written political statements to release hundreds of hectares of land for development purposes, and statements supporting the political interests of the authorities even though these are often contrary to their own conscience or the interests of the public; third, discrimination in the distribution of jobs, promotions, business opportunities and access to education and health services; and fourth, human rights violations, such as the killing of innocent citizens, indiscriminate detention of community members and terror. Such experiences have resulted in the dissolution of solidarity and created a reluctance to speak out about injustice and violence as well as aspirations. They have given rise to the prioritisation of a pragmatic outlook that is sometimes manipulated by those in power. However, the pragmatism required to ensure one's own safety and sacrifice others to protect oneself has resulted in an erosion of the social solidarity that existed because of the shared experience of occupation.

Giay's focus on how colonialism functions in several domains of society—economic, social and psychological—is similarly conceptualised by Victor F. Yeimo. In his exhilarating essay, 'Looking at the Liberation of Papua', Yeimo[28] emphatically stated that the Papuan people are being colonised and their rich natural resources have been robbed by the state, which cooperates

---

27   Benny Giay, *Menuju Papua Baru: Beberapa Pokok Pikiran Sekitar Emansipasi Orang Papua* [*Towards a New Papua, Several Main Thoughts on the Emancipation of Papuans*] (Jayapura: Deiyai/Elsham Papua, 2000).
28   Victor Yeimo, 'Memandang Pembebasan Papua [Looking at the Liberation of Papua]', *IndoPROGRESS*, [Jakarta], 7 May 2015, indoprogress.com/2015/05/memandang-pembebasan-papua/.

with oligarchic networks of bureaucrats, political and social elites and businesspeople. Tanah Papua has been, and continues to be, used as nothing more than a source of profit. Yeimo has repeatedly argued that awareness of being colonised is vital to challenge the silence of the Papuan people and elites who are controlled by the Indonesian State. On this, Yeimo stated:

> [L]ike it or not, we have to depart from the understanding that the Papuan people are being colonised. The complexity of the problem and the types of misery that befall the Papuan people are a form of modern colonialism which can then be described as imperialism. By understanding it as such, our point of view becomes clear that all the economic, social and political inequalities in West Papua are the biological children of the imperialists whose name is Indonesia.[29]

For Yeimo, the Papuan people's awareness that they are being colonised must be accompanied by wariness of the practice of divide and rule by the state and its security apparatus. This practice is undergirded by a militaristic approach, which ensures that the Papuan people are easily pitted against one another, divided and their spirit of critical awareness and desire for liberation extinguished. The Papuan elite's access to and comfort within spaces granted by the state is ironic considering how other Papuans experience oppression, terror and colonialism in their everyday lives. This cleavage between the elites and the wider population occurred during the early days of the rise of nationalism and the liberation movement in the 1950s and 1960s. The liberation movement at the elite level negotiated with the aim of achieving benefits from the Netherlands and Indonesia; however, they were disappointed, divided and became distanced from the Papuan people.

The question remains one of how to break this cycle. Education is an absolute requirement to give birth to liberation; however, colonialism has also been perpetuated through education, linking education and power, and producing injustice and inequality. Yeimo pointed out that Indonesian schools in Papua teach that demanding Papuan independence is illegal and Indonesia is not a colonial ruler. Papuans thus learn that groups who demand their rights as free humans will be confronted with weapons. In such a context, torture, arbitrary arrests and political executions are thus considered justifiable responses to 'separatist' claims. Education has thus become a tool of colonialism for the Indonesian State. The spread of terror among the Papuan people means they will keep their lips sealed and not

---

29 ibid.

talk about independence. The gagging of the desire for liberation through terror and violence continues to occur in Tanah Papua. The accumulation of violent practices, discrimination and the appropriation of Papua's natural resources is true colonialism. This is what Yeimo calls 'repressive colonialism', which requires the closure of spaces for freedom of expression and the simultaneous and continuous destruction of efforts for independence that emerge as the sociopolitical aspirations of the colonised people.

So, how can this system be opposed? What should be done to raise awareness of colonisation among the Papuan people? According to the KNPB's thinking, historical and cultural education for the Papuan people is important, as an understanding of their history will form the basis of raising awareness and demands for independence as a nation with dignity. Yeimo asserted, following Frantz Fanon's idea, that deeply entrenched colonialism strengthens the spirit of decolonisation—a struggle against colonialism and oppression by the colonised people.[30] This contradiction will then lead to a clash between these two different interests. Accordingly, the only way to resolve ongoing conflicts is to abolish colonialism as the root of the conflict.[31]

Figure 15.3 KNPB street demonstration in Abepura, Jayapura
Source: Harun Rumbarar.

---

30 Frantz Fanon, *The Wretched of the Earth*, trans. Richard Philcox (New York: Grove Press, 2004), 6.
31 Yeimo, 'Looking at the Liberation of Papua'.

Yeimo is very concerned that Papuans should not accept ongoing violence and colonialism as normal, as though there is nothing wrong with these abominations. This would allow the reproduction of violence and colonialism to fully penetrate society and become ingrained to the extent that criticism and voices of resistance are deemed futile. Yeimo emphasises the danger of a false consciousness among people submitting to the structures of power and the hegemony of the state and its security apparatus. The Papuan people have witnessed the oppression, but the political and economic reality has shaped their awareness that submission to Indonesian colonial rule is the only way to live in a safe, peaceful, prosperous and honourable way. To Yeimo, it is unnatural for a colonised nation to remain silent and not fight back. He regards resistance as a series of strategies and tactics that are directed by the people in Tanah Papua. For him, a revolutionary mindset must live in the reality of oppression. Yeimo's article and the work of the KNPB are based on the belief that resistance is part of the awareness-raising process. Peaceful and dignified resistance to Indonesian colonial rule is an effort to awaken the people from their colonial 'mute stupor'. Ongoing resistance not only provides political education to the Papuan people and the public at large, but also generates a new vision of society and a way to leave the culture of silence behind and move towards the formation of a more critical culture.[32] Yeimo represents a new generation of young Papuans who are progressive and critical, but who also offer only limited readings of and reflections on the direction of their movement as they are often preoccupied with theory and do not sufficiently consider or respond to overall dynamics and the lived reality on the ground.

For Yeimo, the creation of a better future for Papua is dependent on the development of a social movement with several elements. The first is a clear sense of belonging to the nation. To this end, Yeimo emphasises the importance of writing the history of the development of the Papuan people as part of the reconstruction of the Papuan nation. The formulation of the reconstruction of the Papuan nation is also part of the spirit of liberation from state narratives and constructions. The second element, which is no less important, is the conceptualisation of ideology. For Yeimo, ideology must be the basis of the struggle of the Papuan people. He formulates a fundamental question for the liberation struggle: what does it offer in terms

---

32 Victor Yeimo, 'Mu Man Minggil, Jalan Menuju Tanah Leluhur Bangsa Papua [Mu Man Minggil, the Road to the Ancestral Land of the Papuan Nation]', in *Suara-Suara yang Dicampakkan: Ontran-Ontran Tak Berkesudahan di Bumi Papua [Abandoned Voices: Endless Upheaval in Papua]*, ed. I Ngurah Suryawan (Yogyakarta: Basa-Basi, 2017), 4–5.

of a better life for the people of Papua? For him, the struggle is for political independence. Furthermore, it is important to define what the substance of Papuan independence would be, as the basis for the Papuan people's struggle. The third element is organisation, which is essential for building awareness and a structured resistance by Papuan people. Yeimo cogently expressed:

> [S]tructures of oppression that continue to be massive over time must be destroyed by the structures of the people's resistance, and this must be done in the awareness of gathering and organising. Thus, there is certainty that the Papuan people have full sovereignty over their ancestors. Should we let the colonial powers have full sovereignty over our destruction? For this reason, the project of containing oppressed classes in various sectors is absolutely necessary.[33]

For Yeimo, organising must involve intellectuals who form a system for the people's resistance as well as the 'oppressed classes' who are made aware of the colonial power system that subjugates them. This shows that one of the fundamental struggles of the young Papuan generation is class awareness, including the major role played by the Papuan elite in manipulating and taking advantage of the colonial process.

The fourth theme that has become a major part of Yeimo's liberation struggle is related to capacity. Yeimo criticises Papuan intellectuals and bureaucrats who claim to be professional but have been educated and sucked into the colonial system. In Yeimo's view, such people fail to recognise the situation of oppression in Papua and choose to act pragmatically. Yeimo links the capacity for struggle with the need for education that can respond to the reality of oppression and resistance experienced by the Papuan people. He believes that Tanah Papua needs a revolution of thought, which could be achieved through education or what he calls the establishment of a new paradigm. Fighting for Papua requires education that is revolutionary. Education in progressive and militant ideology is thus a necessity to equip the Papuan people with the capacity to struggle.[34] In practice, this means that the KNPB and other social movements offer cadre education programs to instil political education in the next generation.

---

33 ibid., 6.
34 ibid., 6–7.

Without awareness-building as a means of struggle, a cycle of division and suspicion among Papuan people continues. For their own interests, loyal community members eventually renounce themselves and cooperate with the authorities to the detriment of their community. Cooperation takes the form of making political statements (both verbal and written) on behalf of the community, handing over land for development and, in some cases, working with the authorities. Rebuilding solidarity and unity is therefore both the task of the Papuan people going forward in fighting for the interests of their fellow Papuans and a pillar of the struggle for a new Papua.[35] Both Yeimo and Giay have articulated new and important strategies to work against Indonesian colonialism. Activism combined with intellectual awareness has created important ways of thinking about the social liberation movement. Of course, the challenge is to collectively transmit this awareness to all members of the youth movement. Both these leaders have tried to disseminate their messages, strategies and perceptions through available means—limited as they are by the environment of continuous repression. The methods they have used include the KNPB's official magazine, *KNPB News*, which—also because of the state of repression—has limited reach.

Ending suffering with dignity

As part of their awareness-raising, in 2016, the KNPB published three open letters in *KNPB News* that explained in detail their vision to end the colonial situation with dignity. The first letter was addressed to those they called 'Indonesian colonial slaves'—namely, Papuans who have completely devoted themselves to the Indonesian colonialists. They criticised indigenous Papuans who have become part of the Indonesian colonial government and whom the KNPB regards as having denied the struggle for Papuan liberation. Touchingly, the last part of this open letter reminds this group that even though they may experience pleasure and enjoy luxury in their positions, eventually, the Indonesian authorities will bring them and their people to the brink of destruction.[36]

---

35 See also I Ngurah Suryawan, 'Victor Yeimo dan Tumbuhnya Generasi Papua Baru [Victor Yeimo and the Growth of a New Papuan Generation]', *Islam Bergerak*, [Jakarta], September 2021, islambergerak.com/2021/09/victor-yeimo-dan-tumbuhnya-generasi-papua-baru/.
36 'Surat Terbuka KNPB bagi Para Budak Kolonial Indonesia [KNPB Open Letter to Indonesian Colonial Slaves]', *KNPB News*, June–August 2016, 28.

Figure 15.4 Women of the KNPB protest on Trikora ('People's Triple Command') Day, Lingkaran Abepura, Jayapura, 19 December 2016
Note: Trikora Day (*Hari Trikora*) marks *Operation Trikora* (1961–62) in which the Indonesian military tried to seize the territory known as Netherlands New Guinea.
Source: Harun Rumbarar.

The second open letter addressed the people of West Papua who are fighters in the struggle for liberation. In this letter, the KNPB considers itself a tool to mediate the struggle of the Papuan people against the oppressors—namely, the colonial rulers, capitalists and all those who are strengthening their self-interests:

> Resistance against colonialism is something that has always existed in the civilisations of nations in this world. Indonesia is a history teacher who has educated us to be … aware of fighting all forms of colonialism in this world. Just as the nations of the archipelago have proven the emergence of a resistance movement against Dutch colonialism, we as a nation have risen here against Indonesian colonialism. The resistance of the colonised people against the colonising people. We are fighting the Indonesian occupation which has taken away the right of political sovereignty for our nation.[37]

---

37 'Surat Terbuka KNPB kepada Rakyat West Papua [KNPB Open Letter to the People of West Papua]', *KNPB News*, June–August 2016, 29–31.

In this letter, the KNPB conveyed their idea that ongoing resistance is not merely a performative script. The ideology underlying the resistance is Papuan socialism, opposing colonialism and capitalism (imperialism) with the aim of reorganising social, economic and political life based on the values of equality, compassion and togetherness (solidarity).

The final open letter, to migrants (*pendatang*) in Papua, conveys the sentiment of the KNPB towards those who are said to have been provoked by the Indonesian authorities to believe that they represent the Unitary State of the Republic of Indonesia (Negara Kesatuan Republik Indonesia) and that all Papuans are indistinguishable from the Free Papua Movement. According to the KNPB, the Indonesian colonists want to create internal conflict (known by the Indonesian acronym SARA, which stands for '*suku, agama, ras dan antar golongan divisi*' or 'ethnicity, religion, race and other social divisions') between the Malay and Melanesian races:

> We have a question for migrant brothers and sisters, do you want to join the ranks of the idiots who are killing the truth that the Papuan people are fighting for [by making this] into a racial issue? You certainly don't want Papuans to see you, migrants, as colonialists, do you? Because for us those connoted as colonists are the rulers of Indonesia who have made us all lose our true national identity by using the jargon 'Bhineka Tunggal Ika [Unity in Diversity]'.
>
> I am sure that there are still many people of the Malay race who genuinely understand the truth about the suffering of the Papuan people. There are still many migrants who view us Papuans as human beings who have the right to determine our own destiny. It is very sad if you see the struggle of the Papuan people from the racial perspective that is being constructed by Indonesia. After all, we admit that there are many migrants who have sincerely contributed to developing the Papuan nation, even though many migrants have been forced to strengthen the cruelty of Indonesian colonial rule in West Papua. The desire of the Papuan people to join the MSG (Melanesian Spearhead Group) sub-regional forum is not driven by racial sentiment. It is also not driven because of religious sentiments either.
>
> Papuans do not hate Malays or any religion. You can see and experience for yourself that the Papuan people have never been hostile or at war with immigrants or people of any religion on Papuan land. We are too kind, you can't even find our kindness anywhere in this world, even though you control all aspects of our life.[38]

---

38 'Surat Terbuka untuk Pendatang di Papua [Open Letter to Migrants in Papua]', *KNPB News*, June–August 2016.

Figure 15.5 KNPB demonstration to protest Trikora Day in Jayapura, 19 December 2016
Source: Harun Rumbarar.

Through this letter, the KNPB thus called on migrants to not be taken in by narratives that suggested Papuan nationalism was stoking hatred against Malays or Muslims, but rather become aware that the nationalist movement seeks to challenge and overthrow the colonial reality.

Reflection

This chapter has described the historical struggles and dynamics of social movements in Tanah Papua. The search for the Morning Star is a long, winding river filled with violence and tears, flowing towards the liberation of Papua and upholding its dignity as a nation. The movement for political emancipation, although criticised for being pragmatic and spontaneous, has deep roots in history as illustrated by the formation of the Papua National Committee and the New Guinea Council during the transition of power from the Netherlands to the United Nations. This river flows into the estuary of imagination as a nation: the raising of the Morning Star on 1 December 1961. This genealogy of political emancipation has been transmitted to the younger generation of Papua, who, despite having received their education from the Indonesian colonial government, continue to imagine Papua's liberation in a social movement that is deeply rooted among the Papuan people.

The KNPB has become a key social movement of the younger generation who believe that the liberation of Papua must be realised. The KNPB's goal is to end colonialism and the suffering experienced by the people of Papua. The writings of the KNPB central governing body, Victor F. Yeimo and its open letters discussed in this chapter illustrate the KNPB's ideas and perspectives, which are almost impossible to discuss openly in Indonesia. In my view, imagination, social movements and the formulation of liberation ideologies will continue to form alongside, and in reaction to, the endless cycle of violence experienced by indigenous Papuans and the denial of their rights to social justice, dignity and worth. Colonisation will always be opposed: the Papuan youth social movement is struggling for the liberation of Papua and will continue to do so.

References

Primary sources

Amnesty International. 2021. 'Indonesia: Release Peaceful Anti-Racism Protestor Victor Yeimo.' Petition, 3 December. London: Amnesty International. action. amnesty.org.au/act-now/indonesia-release-peaceful-anti-racism-protester-victor-yeimo [page discontinued].

Amnesty International Indonesia. 2021. 'Bebaskan Victor Yeimo yang Kondisi Kesehatan Memburuk [Release Victor Yeimo whose Health is Deteriorating].' 21 August. Jakarta: Amnesty International Indonesia. www.amnesty.id/bebaskan-victor-yeimo-yang-kondisi-kesehatannya-memburuk/ [page discontinued].

Briantika, Adi, and Riyan Setiawan. 2021. 'Mereka yang Menuntut Pembebasan Juru Bicara KNPB Victor Yeimo [Those Demanding the Release of KNPB Spokesperson Victor Yeimo].' *Tirto.id*, [Jakarta], 20 May. tirto.id/mereka-yang-menuntut-pembebasan-juru-bicara-knpb-victor-yeimo-gf7A.

Dale, Cypri Jehan Paju. 2016. 'Penjajahan Lewat Pembangunan di Papua [Colonisation Through Development in Papua].' *Rappler*, [Manila], 23 May. www.rappler.com/world/indonesia/133896-penjajahan-lewat-pembangunan-papua/.

KNPB News. 2016. 'KNPB: Dari Mana Ke Mana [KNPB Where From, Where To]?' *KNPB News*, June–August. [Also published in *Suara Papua* (*Voice of Papua*), 12 August 2019. suarapapua.com/2019/08/12/knpb-dari-mana-ke-mana/.

KNPB News. 2016. 'Surat Terbuka KNPB bagi Para Budak Kolonial Indonesia [KNPB Open Letter to Indonesian Colonial Slaves].' *KNPB News*, June–August.

KNPB News. 2016. 'Surat Terbuka KNPB kepada Rakyat West Papua [KNPB Open Letter to the People of West Papua].' *KNPB News*, June–August.

KNPB News. 2016. 'Surat Terbuka untuk Pendatang di Papua [Open Letter to Migrants in Papua].' *KNPB News*, June–August.

Kogoya, Yamin. 2023. 'Victor Yeimo's Release from Indonesian Prison Unites West Papuans in the Fight Against Racism and Colonialism.' *GreenLeft*, [Sydney], 25 September. www.greenleft.org.au/content/victor-yeimos-release-indonesian-prison-unites-west-papuans-fight-against-racism-and.

Majalah Triton. 1961. 'Perkembangan Politiek Sudah Mulai [Political Development Has Started].' *Majalah Triton* [*Triton Magazine*], [West Papua], no. 1 (January).

Mawel, Benny. 2016. 'Jejak Mako Tabuni: Lahir Besar Bersama Rakyat di Jalanan Matipun Bersama Rakyat di Jalanan [Mako Tabuni's Footsteps: Born and Raised with People on the Streets, Died with People on the Streets].' *Suara Papua* [*Voice of Papua*], 17 September. suarapapua.com/2016/09/17/jejak-mako-tabuni-lahir-besar-bersama-rakyat-di-jalanan-mati-pun-rakyat-di-jalanan/.

Sukarno. 1950. *From Sabang to Merauke! President Soekarno's Speech on the Fifth Anniversary of Indonesia's Independence—17th August 1950*. Jakarta: Pertjetakan Negara.

Yeimo, Victor. 2015. 'Memandang Pembebasan Papua [Looking at the Liberation of Papua].' *IndoPROGRESS*, [Jakarta], 7 May. indoprogress.com/2015/05/memandang-pembebasan-papua/.

Secondary sources

Chauvel, Richard. 2005. *Constructing Papuan Nationalism: History, Ethnicity, and Adaptation*. Edited by Muthiah Alagappa. Washington, DC: East–West Center. www.jstor.com/stable/resrep06503.

Daniels, Timothy P. 2022. 'Blackness in Indonesia: Articulations of Colonial and Postcolonial Racial Epistemologies.' *Ethnos*: 1–22. doi.org/10.1080/00141844.2022.2081239.

Fanon, Frantz. 2004. *The Wretched of the Earth*. Translated by Richard Philcox. New York: Grove Press.

Giay, Benny. 2000. *Menuju Papua Baru: Beberapa Pokok Pikiran Sekitar Emansipasi Orang Papua* [*Towards a New Papua: Several Main Thoughts on the Emancipation of Papuans*]. Jayapura: Deiyai/Elsham Papua.

Hernawan, Budi. 2017. 'Mengapa Indonesia Bunuh Kami Terus? Pembunuhan Politik atas Pegiat KNPB di Papua [Why Does Indonesia Kill Us? Political Assassinations of KNPB Activists in Papua].' *Kyoto Review of Southeast Asia* 21 (March). kyotoreview.org/issue-21/political-assassination-knpb-activists/.

Kusumaryati, Veronika. 2021. '#Papuanlivesmatter: Black Consciousness and Political Movements in West Papua.' *Critical Asian Studies* 53, no. 4: 453–75. doi.org/10.1080/14672715.2021.1963794.

Materay, Bernarda. 2012. *Nasionalisme Ganda Orang Papua* [*The Dual Nationalism of Papuan People*]. Jakarta: Buku Kompas.

Roosa, John. 2006. *Pretext for Mass Murder: The September 30th Movement and Suharto's Coup d'État in Indonesia*. Madison: University of Wisconsin Press.

Salford, John. 2003. *The United Nations and the Indonesian Takeover of West Papua, 1962–1969: The Anatomy of Betrayal*. London: Routledge. doi.org/10.4324/9780203221877.

Setiawan, Ken M.P., and Dirk Tomsa. 2022. *Politics in Contemporary Indonesia: Institutional Change, Policy Challenges and Democratic Decline*. London: Routledge. doi.org/10.4324/9780429459511.

Suryawan, I Ngurah. 2012. 'Dari Memoria Passionis ke Foreri: Sejarah Politik Papua 1999-2000 [From Memoria Passionis to Foreri: Political History of Papua 1999–2000].' *Paramita: Historical Studies Journal* 22, no. 2: 143–56. doi.org/10.15294/paramita.v22i2.2116.

Suryawan, I Ngurah. 2018. 'Jalan Berliku Para Elit Papua [The Winding Path of the Papuan Elite].' *IndoPROGRESS*, [Jakarta], 1 November. indoprogress.com/2018/11/jalan-berliku-para-elite-papua/.

Suryawan, I Ngurah. 2021. 'Victor Yeimo dan Tumbuhnya Generasi Papua Baru [Victor Yeimo and the Growth of a New Papuan Generation].' *Islam Bergerak*, [Jakarta], September. islambergerak.com/2021/09/victor-yeimo-dan-tumbuhnya-generasi-papua-baru/.

Thompson, Roger C. 1980. *Australian Imperialism in the Pacific: The Expansionist Era, 1820–1920*. Melbourne: Melbourne University Press.

Timmer, Jaap. 2007. 'Erring Decentralization and Elite Politics in Papua.' In *Renegotiating Boundaries: Local Politics in Post-Suharto Indonesia*, edited by Henk Schulte Nordholt and Gerry van Klinken, 459–82. Leiden: Brill. doi.org/10.1163/9789004260436_021.

Yeimo, Victor. 2017. 'Mu Man Minggil, Jalan Menuju Tanah Leluhur Bangsa Papua [Mu Man Minggil, the Road to the Ancestral Land of the Papuan Nation].' In I Ngurah Suryawan, *Suara-Suara yang Dicampakkan: Ontran-Ontran Tak Berkesudahan di Bumi Papua* [*Abandoned Voices: Endless Upheaval in Papua*]. Yogyakarta: Basa-Basi.

Index

Page numbers in bold text indicate images.

Aceh 17, 99, 109, 327, 409
Aceh Army Museum (Atjehsch Legermuseum) 327
Aceh War 29, 49, 64, 79, 146–71, 327, 380
Acehnese 17
Act of Free Choice (1969) 413
Affif, Ferial 368
Africa 3, 6, 7, 10, 84, 187
    see also *Belanda Hitam*; South Africa; West Africa
Agrarian Law (1870) 126, 133
Alamat Langkapuri 76, 79
Althusser, Louis 51
Ambon 73, 84, 86n25, 158n42, 186, 192, 322, 323
Ambonese 75, 189, 191, 192, 194, 213, 232, 339
    soldiers 147, 158n42, 159, 160–2, 170, 328, 337
America 77, 147, 352
    see also United States of America
Americas 4
    see also Latin America; South America
Anderson, Benedict 76, 103, 246, 298
Angkola-Batak 104
Anker, Marion 11
anthropology 5, 150, 246, 336, 338, 348, 353, 356, 366
    museums 246

anticolonialism 6–10, 93, 95, 112, 180, 301, 351, 357, 359, 365, 366, 367, 371
anticommunism 9, 10, 183, 305n34, 340n78, 413
Antwerp 350, 361–2, 368, **369**
Anwar, Rosihan 180
apologies 23–4, 25, 28, 347, 375–6, 383, 385, 387n60, 389, 391, 394
Arab Indonesians 19, 47, 48, 56, 129, 210, 299, 302, 339
Arabic 71, 76, 79, 106
archaeology 246–7, 326, 327, 328, 330, 334, 335, 366
archival collaboration 276, 280
archival institutions 275–6, 285
    see also individual institutions
archives 18, 26, 78, 247, 273, 278, 285, 362, 363, 366
    colonial 78, 273–4, 276, 289, 367
    coloniality of 21, 26, 31, 78, 162, 246, 273–6, 277, 279, 280, 283, 285, 290–1
    decolonisation of 273–91
    destruction of 275
    invisibility in 78, 92
    repatriation of 18, 31, 243, 261, 273–91, 324
    seizure from Yogyakarta 31, 244, 276, 278, 281, 287
    seizure of 31, 244, 275, 276, 278–83, 285, 287, 288, 289

431

studies 5, 27
see also Djogdja Documenten
Ariks, Johan 410–11, 412
Arsip Nasional Republik Indonesia *see*
   National Archives of the Republic
   of Indonesia
Arung Palakka 322, 336–7, 338
assimilation 14, 56n39, 188, 230, 303,
   304, 309, 352, 377n13
Association of Indies Veterans
   (Vereniging Oud Militairen
   Indiëgangers) 391
Association of Indonesian Museums
   (Asosiasi Museum Indonesia)
   16–17
Atjehsch Legermuseum (Aceh Army
   Museum) 327
atrocities 145–71, 208, 211–13, 214,
   220, 222, 223, 228, 232, 282, 389
   see also massacres; war crimes
Australia 273, 278, 332, 377, 408
authoritarianism 9, 185, 308, 328,
   336, 417

Badan Penyelidikan Usaha Persiapan
   Kemerdekaan Indonesia
   (Investigating Committee
   for Preparatory Work for
   Independence) 302–3
Badulla 79
Badung 147, 151, 151n24, 152, **155**,
   156, 159, **170**
Bagindo Djamaluddin Rasjad 109
Bahasa Indonesia 19, 250, 252, 283,
   284, 285, 302, 339
Bali 147, 151, **155**, 156, 158, 159,
   164, **170**, 171, 415
Bali Museum 332
Balige 107, 363
Balinese 17, 75, 79, 298, 299
Balongsari 375n2, 384
   see also Rawagede
Banda Aceh 327
Banda Islands 186

Bandung 99, 216, 228
Bandung Conference (1955) 3, 6, 7,
   196–7
'Bandung spirit' 6, 7, 196–7
Bangka 54, 221
Banjar 207
Batak 103, 104, 150, 350, 362, 363,
   365, 366, 367, 368
   adat 105, 107, 108
   Angkola-Batak 104
   Tanah Batak 350, 362, 363, 365,
   368
Batak War 350, 361–2, 365, 366, 368,
   369
Batavia 45, 46–7, 52, 53, 75, 84, 98,
   296–8, 328
   Chinese in 48, 50–3, 60, 62,
   209–10, 296–8, 300
   Chinese massacre in (1740)
   209–10, 300
   Old Batavia Museum 328
   Ommelanden ('hinterland') 299
   protests in **46**, 47, 48, 50
   see also Jakarta
Batavia Castle 299
Bataviaasch Nieuwsblad 94, 325
Batavian Society for Art and Sciences
   (Bataviaasch Genootschap voor
   Kunsten en Wetenschappen) 150,
   247, 328
Baubau 187
Baud, Jean Chrétien 262
Belanda Hitam ('Black Dutchmen')
   xiii, 18, 75, 158, 187, 189
Belgium 32, 350, 361, 362, 367
Belitung 54
Beng Seng Sie Wan 301
Bengkulu 323
bersiap ('be ready') xiii, 11–14, 21,
   24–5, 213
Biak 411
binarism 27, 32, 137, 139, 350, 353,
   354, 361, 370
'Black Dutchmen' *see Belanda Hitam*

Blitar 205, **206**, 207
Bonay, Eliezer Jan 412–13
Bone 247–8, 321, 322, 336–8
Borneo 54, 164
Borobudur Temple 247
Boru Lopian 368, **369**
Bosch, F.D.K. 326, 334
Bot, Ben 23
British 72, 79, 190, 283
    and Indonesia 85, 180, 195, 325, 327
    colonialism 29, 79, 85, 125n4, 196
    Empire 18, 29, 74
    in Singapore 380
    Straits Settlements 86
British Ceylon 22, 73, 74, 85, 86, 87
British India 73, 81, 86, 151
British Malaya 22, 85, 189
British New Guinea 408
Bronbeek 157, 246
Brunei 86
Buddhism 81, 82, 247, 261
    Hindu-Buddhist 17, 305, 335, 338
Buginese 75, 329, 321, 326, 334, 336, 338
Bugis Bone 337
Burma 101, 196
Buton 322

Calcutta 81, 180, 196, 197, 198
Candra Naya 305
capitalism 4, 9, 93, 129, 137, 139, 218, 304, 366, 406n11, 416, 424, 425
    and colonialism 4, 62, 93, 110–11, 112, 129, 137, 139, 366, 406n11, 416, 424, 425
    and racialisation 4, 48, 62, 110–11
    anti-capitalist 112
    exploitation 4, 62, 109, 111
categorisation, colonial 5, 6, 13, 18–22, 28, 30, 49, 50, 52, 63–5, 75, 82–3, 92, 101, 103, 187, 189, 194, 298

Celebes 164, 326
    see also Sulawesi
Celebes Museum 326, 330–2, 333, 334, 335, 340
censorship 62, 149, 183, 308
Central Java 127, 208, 220, 223, 224
Ceylon 22, 28–9, 71–87
    see also Sri Lanka
China 19, 52, 53, 54, 56–7, 98, 102, 125n4, 181, 183, 196, 297, 301, 304
Chinatown
    in Batavia/Jakarta 31, 210, 295, 305
    in Makassar 339
    see also Glodok; Pecinan
Chineesche Kamp 300, 301, 316
Chinese 55, 102
    nationalism 46, 56–7, 208n8
Chinese Council 301
Chinese Indonesians 14, 19, 75, 111, 112, 296, 298–300, 311, 339–40
    activism 301, 305
    and agriculture 297, 299, 300
    and Dutch citizenship 56–7, 63
    and Indonesian citizenship 302–5, 340
    and Indonesian history 295–317
    and taxation 21, 28, 45–65, 210, 296, 297
    and war of independence 22, 26n87, 63, 205, 207–8, 209–32
    anti-Chinese sentiment 63, 208, 209, 211, 213, 223, 230, 232, 300, 303, 304–5, 309, 314
    Chineesche Kamp 300, 301, 316
    Chinese Red Cross 218
    classification of 19, 21, 30, 50, 56, 75, 210–11, 295, 298, 299, 304
    colonial exploitation of 28, 45–65
    contributions of 19, 296–8, 304
    cultural objects 327, 332

culture 19, 45, 230, 301, 302, 304, 305, 309, 311, 340
economic influence 50, 52, 53, 55, 56–7, 64, 210, 296–7, 300, 302
economic losses 60–1, 212
economic regulation of 50–1, 52–3, 55, 56, 57–8, 64, 300
elite 53, 55, 57, 130n22
grievances 46, 47, 58, 61–3, 64
identity formation 31–2, 295–317
in social hierarchy 13–14, 50, 52, 57, 63, 64–5, 210–11, 297, 302, 309, 339–40
kapitein ('chiefs') 300, 301
language 211, 230, 304, 305, 309
mass graves 30, 205–9, 224–32
massacres of 30, 52, 53, 205–32, 296, 300
media 30, 47, 50, 59, 61–2, 208n8, 216, 221, 302, 304, 306–15
merchants 129, 207, 212, 298, 299
mobility restrictions 209–10, 300, 302
occupations 52, 53, 54, 55, 296, 297
organisations 19, 45–6, 228, 230, 250, 301, 305
pedagang ('trading class') 295, 298, 302, 306, 309–15, 316
pedagangan ('trading centre') 305
Peranakan xiv, 54, 299, 304, 340
political representation 19, 57, 61, 62–3
politics 50, 295, 306
population size 53–5
portrayal as collaborators with Dutch 191, 208, 209, 213, 217, 218, 302
protests by 28, 45, **46**, 47–8, 58, 61–4, 300
racialisation of 21, 47, 48, 50, 63, 299, 300, 301–17

re-Sinification 211, 308–9
scholarship 19, 21
schools 211, 301, 304
spatial effects of colonialism on 295–317
trade (*dagang*) 31–2, 47, 52, 55, 57, 298, 306, 313–14
violence against 14, 19, 22, 30, 31–2, 63, 191, 205–32, 295, 296, 305–6, 314, 380
see also Chung Hua Tsung Hui
Chinese-Malay 113
Christianity 77, 79, 81, 160–1, 187, 210, 388
Christoffel, Hans 361, 362–3, 368
Chung Hua Tsung Hui (CHTH, Federation of Chinese Organisations in Indonesia) 205, 206, 219, 220, 224, 250
Cirebon 219
Jakarta 219, 220, 224
Magelang 224
Malang 217, 218
Nganjuk 224, 225, **226**
Wonosobo 223, 225
Yogyakarta 223
Cianjur 73
Cilimus 219
Cirebon 219
Citizenship Law 56, 303, 340
Coen, Jan Pieterszoon 328
Cold War 8, 180, 196, 286, 413
Colombo 71, 75, 79, 81, 82, 83, 84
colonial
archives 78, 273–4, 276, 289, 367
categorisation 5, 6, 13, 18–22, 28, 30, 49, 50, 52, 63–5, 75, 82–3, 92, 101, 103, 187, 189, 194, 298
diasporas 22, 29, 71–6, 79, 81, 83, 84, 85, 86, 298
ethnic hierarchies 13–4, 20, 21, 22, 30, 182, 199, 209–10, 295–317, 357

INDEX

exile 72–5, 76, 83–6, 181, 183–4, 198, 199, 221, 326, 356, 413
exploitation xv, 28, 45–65, 84, 112, 114, 133, 135, 390
guilt 28, 49, 349, 362, 363, 371
hierarchies 29–30, 101, 113, 138, 147–8, 161–2, 168, 179, 181, 188–90, 194, 339, 357
ideology 5, 7, 8, 26, 51, 125n4, 181
knowledge production 4, 5, 7, 32, 33, 96, 97, 103, 114, 137, 192, 324, 331, 340, 354
racial hierarchies 5, 13–14, 20, 30, 96, 102, 161, 171, 187, 188, 189, 298–9
structures of power 10, 20–2, 23, 26, 27, 32, 64–5, 84, 97, 110, 182, 309, 378, 381, 393, 396
subjectification 29, 93, 96
war photography 22, 157, 163–71
wars 26, 157, 164, 380
see also decolonisation; postcolonialism
colonialism
and capitalism 4, 62, 93, 110–11, 112, 129, 137, 139, 366, 406n11, 416, 424, 425
and ethnicity 78, 182, 191–9, 208, 210, 211, 302
and modernity 29, 108, 113, 125, 129, 137–9, 246
and racialisation 4, 48, 50–1, 52, 62, 92, 171, 189, 299, 300–1
anticolonialism 6–10, 93, 95, 112, 180, 301, 351, 357, 359, 365, 366, 367, 371
contemporary Indonesian 28, 33, 360, 403–27
cultural legacy of 4, 6, 7, 33, 137, 340
dismantling of 6, 22, 23–8, 30, 137, 199, 276, 291, 323–4, 350, 379
end of 211, 232, 407, 420, 427
enduring nature of 3–4, 5, 28, 30, 33, 65, 147, 405
legacies of 4, 5, 10, 23–8, 30, 31, 32, 33, 65, 78, 85, 87, 185–91, 241, 261–3, 276, 283, 324, 338, 339, 340, 352, 354, 378, 379, 396
neo-colonialism 7, 416
reproduction of 5, 6, 7, 10, 18, 21, 27, 29, 30, 94, 181, 284, 291, 306, 309, 349, 351, 421
resistance to 6–7, 33, 181–2, 184, 195–8, 328–9, 403–27
see also decolonisation
coloniality
and structures of power 4, 5, 347
of archival structures 290–1, 349, 358, 360, 366
of archives 21, 26, 31, 78, 162, 246, 273–6, 277, 279, 280, 283, 285, 290–1
'of power' 4, 50–1, 64, 113, 199, 378, 387
persistence of 12, 23–8, 31
see also decoloniality
colonisation 4, 5, 18, 123, 125n4, 137, 327, 376
cultural 137, 261, 308–9, 330, 331, 334
Dutch attempt at recolonisation 11, 248, 275, 276, 278, 279, 285, 286
limits of 84
of Papua 405, 407, 420, 427
see also decolonisation
Committee for Exhuming Chinese Corpses (Panitia Penggalian Jenazah Tionghoa) 207
Committee for Relocating the Graves of Chinese Victims (Panitia Pemindahan Makam Korban Tionghoa) 224–5

Committee for the Repatriation of Collections from Indonesia in the Netherlands (Tim Repatriasi Koleksi Asal Indonesia di Belanda) 243–4
Committee of Dutch Debts of Honour (Komite Utang Kehormatan Belanda, KUKB) 13, 384, 385, 392, 393, 394
communism 14, 180, 279, 288, 304
   see also anticommunism; Indonesian Communist Party; Pesindo
Consultative Council for Indonesian Citizenship (Badan Permusjawaratan Kewarganegaraan Indonesia) 303
Corpse Excavation Committee (Panitia Penggalian Majat) 225
Crown Prince of Tidore 72
Crown Princess Juliana 97, 98
cultural 84, 97, 98, 101n46, 137, 246, 323, 324, 329
   assimilation 56n39, 188, 230, 352
   collaboration 251–4, 256–8, 261–2, 369
   colonisation 137, 261, 308–9, 330, 331, 334
   connections of Malays 72, 83, 84, 86
   decolonisation 18, 30, 97, 245
   futures 31, 248–53, 263
   heritage 335, 368
   identity 28, 180, 192, 193, 367, 370
   imperialism 261
   impoverishment 334
   institutions, decolonisation of 18, 32, 275, 276, 289, 290, 323–4, 333, 340, 347
   legacy of colonialism 4, 6, 7, 33, 137, 340
   nationalism 97, 99
   ownership/rights 245, 248, 262, 348, 367
   preservation 121n1, 323, 324, 326, 327, 328, 329, 330–1, 337, 338
   repatriation 11–18, 31, 241–63, 273–91, 324, 367, 368, 369
   restoration 276, 325–6, 329
   resurgence 366, 367, 368, 370
   sovereignty 95, 252, 253, 255, 256, 258, 279
   suppression 6, 137, 304, 305–6, 340
   traditions 192, 198
   see also Draft Cultural Agreement
Cultural Committee 245, 250, 251, 252, 253, 256
cultural objects
   acquisition of 246–7, 256
   Chinese Indonesian 327, 332
   defining 17, 255
   looting of 17, 241, 247, 259, 262, 274, 277, 280, 283, 289
   see also archives
culture 85, 94, 137, 182, 259, 262, 289, 378
   Batak 365, 366, 367, 368
   Chinese Indonesian 19, 45, 230, 301, 302, 304, 305, 309, 311, 340
   'Chinese' 301–2, 304, 305, 340
   defining 255
   Dutch 187, 188, 193, 198
   elite 20
   Indonesian 30, 186, 192–3, 245, 248, 250–3, 259, 316, 327, 328, 334, 335, 337, 338
   loss of 334
   Malay 79
   Malay literary 73ns1–2
   Papuan 360, 416, 420
   peranakan subcultures 299, 300
   print 91–114

visual, of war 145–71
Western 334
see also archives; Draft Cultural Agreement

De Cesari, Chiara 356
decoloniality 4, 5, 22, 27, 33, 276
decolonisation 4, 7, 8, 11, 23, 27–8, 30, 33, 86, 191–5, 209, 244, 317, 377, 391, 420
    and Malaysia 86
    and Netherlands 11, 23, 28
    as continuing process 28, 30, 243, 323
    incomplete 4, 5, 184
    limits to 351, 396
    of archives 273–91
    of cultural institutions 18, 32, 275, 276, 290, 323–4, 333, 340, 347
    of knowledge 5, 32, 33, 96–7, 273, 324, 363, 366, 367, 369, 370, 371
    of structures of power 5, 22, 32, 33, 96
    political 5, 245
de Jonge, Bonifacius Cornelis 357
Delft 16, 262
democracy 110, 138, 252, 254–5, 257, 317, 348
    and India 138
    and West Papua 415, 416
    Dutch experiments with 47
    'Guided Democracy' 280
    post New Order 19
democratisation, of knowledge 363, 368
Denpasar 151, 160, **170**, 332
de Zwaan, Tjeerd 375
diasporas 22, 29, 71–6, 79, 81, 83, 84, 85, 86, 298
Dili Massacre 185
Diponegoro, Prince/Pangeran 14, 16, 17, 73, 261–2, 337, 338

Directorate of Museums 334, 335
Djogdja Documenten 18, 31, 244, 261, 273–91
Djumenar, Isye 283
Draft Cultural Agreement (1949) 31, 243, 244, 245, 256, 258, 259–63, 279
Dubois, Eugène 17
Dutch Ceylon *see* Ceylon
Dutch Communist Party 195
Dutch East India Company (Vereenigde Oostindische Compagnie, VOC) 52, 53, 72, 73n2, 158n42, 186, 209, 290, 296, 297, 298, 300, 322, 324–5, 326, 328, 335, 336, 380
Dutch Indies Federation (Federatie Indische Nederlanders) 13
Dutch–Indonesian Round Table Conference (RTC, Konferensi Meja Bundar) (1949) 18, 31, 243, 244–5, 248, 250, 251, 252, 256, 261, 262, 279, 409, 410
Dutch military 5, 49, 64, 132, 147, 148, 247, 278, 288, 325, 326, 327, 328, 362
    atrocities by 145–71, 375, 379, 381–2, 383, 392
    First Dutch Military Aggression 205n2, 214–20, 221, 223, 224, 228
    racialisation in 21, 22, 29–30, 148, 159
    Second Dutch Military Aggression 31, 205n2, 214, 220–4, 244
    subjugation campaigns 145–71, 216
    see also Netherlands East Indies Forces Intelligence Service; Royal Netherlands Army; Royal Netherlands East Indies Army
Dutch Military Aggression
    First 205n2, 214–20, 221, 223, 224, 228

Second 31, 205n2, 214, 220–4, 244
Dutch military police (*marechaussees*) 159, 161, 162, **163**, **169**, 327
Dutch National Museum of Ethnology 17, 246, 262

East Java 198n101, 252, 327
　anti-Chinese violence in 205, 208, 212, 217, 220, 222, 224
　First and Second Dutch Military Aggressions 217, 222
　plantation society 29, 121–40
East Sumatra 54, 197, 252
East Timor 185, 414
　see also Timor-Leste
Eastern Indonesia Cultural Foundation (Yayasan Pusat Kebudayaan Indonesia Timur) 333
Eijken, Jan 383, 390
Eluay, Theys H. 414, 415
'Ethical Policy' 49, 59n47, 64, 94, 109, 148, 210, 356, 358
ethnic
　colonial hierarchies 13–4, 20, 21, 22, 30, 182, 199, 209–10, 295–317, 357
　inter-ethnic conflict 210, 211, 232, 303, 305, 309, 425
　laws 56, 210–11, 230, 303, 304–5, 311
　othering 30, 81–2, 168, 170–1
　populations 45, 54n33, 56, 79, 94, 299, 303, 315, 329, 333, 334, 335, 338
　solidarity 29, 92, 96, 108, 110–11, 113, 371, 408, 423, 425
　stereotypes 30, 81–2, 147, 162, 190, 208, 209, 295, 298, 299, 303, 306, 309
　violence 145–71, 191, 207–8, 209, 211–12, 228, 232, 305
　see also race

ethnicity 30, 209–10, 351, 367
　and citizenship 56–7, 303
　and colonialism 78, 182, 191–9, 208, 210, 211, 302
　and identity 22, 81–2, 102, 108, 113
　and war of independence 199, 207–8, 232
　see also race
ethnographic
　manuscripts 326
　museums 150, 246, 326, 330–1, 333, 334, 335, 347–50, 352–3
　objects 246, 326, 327, 331, 333, 335, 338, 357
　portraits 149, 150
ethnography 363, 368
Eurocentric 8, 108
Europe 8, 59n49, 77, 195, 196, 246, 246, 331, 350

Fanggidaej, Francisca 30, 179–99
Fanggidaej, Gottlieb 180, 185, 186, 187, 188–9, 190, 191
Fanon, Frantz 7, 10, 187–8, 350, 351–2, 353–4, 359, 368, 420
Farid, Hilmar 9, 17, 20–1, 26, 262–3
fascism 193
Fasseur, Cees 389–90
Federal Republic of West Papua (Negara Republik Federal Papua Barat) 416
Firmanto, Agung 'Geger' 362
First Dutch Military Aggression 205n2, 214–20, 221, 223, 224, 228
Flores 164
Fort Kuto Besak 323
Fort Legok Jawa 323
Fort Marlborough 323
Fort Rotterdam 32, 321–40
Fort Ujung Pandang 321–2, 329, 340
Fort Victoria 323
Fort Vredeburg 323

forts 167, 322–3, 325, 371
    Nusantara 322, 330, 340
France 125n4
Free Papua Movement (Organisasi Papua Merdeka) 413, 425
French 125n4, 196, 325
French Indochina 101
Fujian 52, 54n33

Gajah Dompak sword **364**, 365
Galle 81
Gandhi, Mahatma 7
genocide 376n9
    Indonesian 181, 184
    see also Holocaust; NIOD Institute for War, Holocaust and Genocide Studies
Ghana xiii, 187
Giannini, Sara 358
Giay, Benny 418, 423
Glodok (Jakarta's Chinatown) 28, 31, 32, 295–317
Gold Coast (Ghana) xiii, 187
Gonggong, Anhar 14–15
Gowa kingdom 247–8, 321, 322, 336
Gowa, Sultan of 72, 73n1, 321, 322, 336–7, 338
Guangdong 52, 54n33
Gus Dur *see* Wahid, Abdurrahman

Habibie, B.J. 305, 306, 308
Haiti 6, 197
hajj 76, 78
Hasan, Bob 304
Hasanuddin, Sultan 322, 336, 338
Hatta, Mohammad 110, 212, 221, 256, 286, 287
Hegel, Georg Wilhelm Friedrich 350–1, 353
Hindu 79, 82, 100, 101
    Hindu-Buddhist 17, 305, 335, 338
Hollandia (Jayapura) 411, 412n19
Holocaust 353, 387
    see also genocide

Hsia, Ching-lin 220
Huender, W. 49
Hueting, Joop 382
Hutagalung, Batara 384, 392

Ide Anak Agung Gde Agung 252
ideology
    colonial 5, 7, 8, 26, 51, 125n4, 181
    national 328, 407, 416, 421, 422, 425, 427
    racial 63, 181
I Gusti Agung Wesaka Puja 16
I Manriwagau Daeng Bonto Karaeng Lakiung (Tunipalangga Ulaweng) 321
independence, Indonesian *see* Indonesian independence
independence, Papuan *see* Papuan independence
independence war *see* war of independence
India 77, 80–1, 82, 86, 98, 101, 138, 180, 196, 197, 198
    see also British India
Indian 8, 56, 196, 210, 299
Indian Ocean 71
Indo-Eurasian 339
Indo-European 12, 13–14, 20, 182, 209, 213, 232, 391, 392
Indonesian Communist Party (Partai Komunis Indonesia, PKI) 184, 207, 216, 288
Indonesian independence 3, 84, 85, 302–3
    see also Republic of Indonesia; republican movement; war of independence
Indonesian independence, declaration of 8, 180, 194, 196, 212, 250, 323
    diplomatic inequality after 181, 197–8
    Dutch recognition of 23, 279, 393
    Dutch refusal to recognise 11, 214n34, 393

Indonesian–Malay world 72, 76, 85
Indonesian military 283, 286, 287,
    288, 304, 306, 328–9
  and removal of Sukarno 8–9
  funding of 134–5
  in West Papua 404, 413, 424
  interpretation of history 10
  Thirtieth of September Movement
    (1965) xiv, 184, 340n78
  violence 185, 217, 219, 223,
    305n34, 404
  see also militias; republican forces;
    TNI
Indonesian National Armed Forces
  see TNI
Indonesian National Culture 252
Inter-Indonesian Conference 251,
    252–3, 256
International Institute of Social
    History 182, 183
Investigating Committee for
    Preparatory Work for
    Independence (Badan Penyelidikan
    Usaha Persiapan Kemerdekaan
    Indonesia) 302–3
Irian Jaya People's Forum for
    Reconciliation (Forum Rekonsiliasi
    Rakyat Irian Jaya) 414
Irwin, John 335
Iskan, Dahlan 308
Islam 10n28, 74, 76, 78, 80–1, 82, 94,
    106, 219, 335, 338
  and Malays 79–82
  pre-Islamic 83
  see also Muslim; Qur'an
Islamisation 72

Jakarta 213, 245, 247, 280, 284,
    296–9, 305, 315–16, 328, 384
  Chinatown 31, 210, 295, 305
  Chinese in 28, 31, 295, 306, 308,
    314, 315–16

Chung Hua Tsung Hui (Federation
    of Chinese Organisations in
    Indonesia) in 219, 220, 224
  Glodok 28, 31, 32, 295–317
  see also Batavia
Jakarta Fair **307**
Japan 77, 102, 111, 365
Japanese
  capitulation 134, 211, 278
  Empire 12, 134
  living in East Indies 56n38, 210
  military 63, 211, 221
  Navy Administration 328, 332
  occupation (1942–45) 14n42, 63,
    133–4, 180, 191–4, 208n8,
    211–12, 221, 278, 328, 332,
    409
Java 47, 49, 76–7, 85, 86, 94, 126,
    157n39, 179, 180, 188, 212, 247,
    248, 297, 337, 360, 408, 415
  anti-Chinese violence in 14, 205,
    207, 217, 224
  Chinese in 52, 53, **54**, 55, 61, 63
  Dutch military recruits from 73,
    148, 158, 161, 162
  First and Second Dutch Military
    Aggressions **215**, 216, 221
  Japanese occupation of 133, 134,
    332
  placenames 79n13, 83, 86
  taxation of Chinese 55, 61, 296
  see also East Java; Central Java;
    West Java
'Java Man' 17
Java War (1825–30) 73
Javanese 71, 72, 191–2, 287, 299, 339
  antiquities 247, 327
  colonialism 360
  Dutch classification of 75
  elite 75, 186, 261n56, 337, 338
  exiles 72, 83n22
  military police 221
  racial conceptions of 21
  social class 105, 188–9

'Javanisation' 252
Jayapura 404, 407, 411, 412n19, 415, **420**, **424**, **426**
Jewish 81, 276, 387, 390
Jouwe, Nicolaas 411

Kahlon, Rajkamal 349
Kali Tello, NV 127, 128, 131, 132, 136
Kalla, Jusuf 389
Kandy 74n5, 79
Kandy Wars 74–5
Karma, Filep **408**
Kartini, Raden Adjeng 95
Kediri **124**, 207, 231
Kelapa Gading 314, 315–17
Kempees, J.C.J. 150, 151, 156, 160, 161–2
King Amangkurat III 72
King Chulalongkorn 247
King of Kupang 72
King Willem-Alexander 24, 262
Klungkung 17, 262
KNIL *see* Royal Netherlands East Indies Army
KNPB *see* National Committee for West Papua
KNPB News 406, 423
Koet, P.J. 410
Koetsier, Henk 383, 390
Kolopaking, Sunarjo 250
Koninklijk Nederlandsch-Indisch Leger *see* Royal Netherlands East Indies Army
Kunci 350, 354, 355–6, 358, 359, 360
Kupang 72, 186
Kustaryo, Lukas 375, 392

Lafeber, C.V. 390
La Galigo Museum 323, 324, 329, 332–40
Lahore 81
Laskar Hizbullah ('Army of God') 212n24, 217, 219, 222, 223

Laskar Rakjat ('People's Warriors') 212n24, 214, 223
Latin America 366
see also Americas
Law on the Statute of Limitations ('*Verjaringswet*') (1971) 382–3, 386
League of Nations 217, 218, 220, 408n13
Leiden 17, 150, 262
Leiden University 165, 389
Lesser Sunda Islands 186
Liem Bian Sioe 218
Liem Koen Hian 302
Liem Sioe Liong 304
Lifepatch 350, 354, 361–2, 363–4, 365, 366, 367, 368, 369
Linggadjati Agreement 197
Lombok 17, 49, 64, 164, 262
London 81, 414
Lumajang 121, 122, 123, 220
Luwu Kingdom 17

Mabo Case 377, 378
Madiun Affair xiii, 180, 184, 198, 288
Madura 53, **54**, 55, 73, 126, 127, 157n39, 327
'Madurese' 75
Mael, Magda 186, 187, 191, 193
Magassing, Abdul Hamid Daeng 332
Magelang 223, 224, 225
Magfira, Sita 361, 368
Majalah Triton ('*Triton Magazine*') 410
Makassar 32, 72, 73, 84, 85n23, 86, 99, 186, 321–40
'Makassarese' 75
Mako Tabuni 404, 415
Malacca 77, 78
Malang 121–40, 217–18, 231
see also South Malang
Malay 79, 86, 339
  diaspora in Ceylon 22, 29, 71–87
  homelands 72, 76, 78, 81, 84–5, 87
  identity 22, 29, 71, 74, 75, 79, 82–3, 84–7, 101, 102, 105

441

Indonesian–Malay world 72, 76, 85
racial conceptions of 18, 21, 101, 102, 425–6
Malay language 72, 76, 79–80, 81, 83, 105, 106, 188, 194n77, 302
   publications 5, 20–1, 22, 29, 47, 71–87, 91–114, 302, 410
   schools 104, 186
   Sino-Malay 302
Malay Peninsula 73, 76
Malay Regiment 73, 74
Malaya 78, 85, 196
Malaysia 78, 80, 86, 87
Malessy, Sam 194
Malik, Abdul 256
Maluku 147
Manado 73, 415
Mandailing 103, 104, 106, 108
Mandarese 329, 334
Mandatjan, Barend 411
Mandatjan, Lodewijk 411
Mangkunegara VIII 250, 253
Manokwari, 407, 408, 411–12
Manupapami, O. 412
marechaussees (Dutch 'military police') 159, 161, 162, **163**, **169**, 327
Margana, Sri 27, 262, 263n62, 327, 330
'martial Orientalism' 148, 155–63
'martial races' xiii, 18, 21, 22, 30, 74, 147, 161, 171
mass graves 30, 205, 207–8, 218, 224–32
   see also reburial
massacres 32, 52, 53, 145–71, 185, 205–32, 296, 300, 375–96
   see also atrocities; war crimes
Mataram 72
Matthes, Benjamin Frederik 326, 338
Matthes Foundation (Matthes Stichting) 325–6, 332, 333
Mbamban 207
Medan 106, 107, 305

Melanesian 416, 425
Melanesian Solidarity Week 413
Melanesian Spearhead Group 425
Memorandum of Excesses (*Excessennota*) (1969) 24n78, 382, 383, 386, 389
Merauke 407, 409, 411
merdeka ('independence') 182, 195
   see also Indonesian independence
Mignolo, Walter 4, 96, 137, 181, 348
military *see* Dutch military; Indonesian military; Japanese, military
military forts 322, 323, 324–5
militias 165, 190, 221, 232
   attacks on Chinese 205, 207, 212, 214, 216, 217–19, 223
   Laskar Hizbullah ('Army of God') 212n24, 217, 219, 222, 223
   Laskar Rakjat ('People's Warriors') 212n24, 214, 223
Minahasa Peninsula 147
Minahasan 158
Minangkabau 92, 94, 95, 97–108, 110, 111
Minangkabau (periodical) 29, 93, 95, 108, 109–12
Mnukwar (Manokwari) 407
modernisation 9, 102–3, 127, 304, 331, 334
modernity 10, 92, 108, 111, 121–40
   access to 107, 108, 113–14, 130, 140, 361
   and colonialism 29, 108, 113, 125, 129, 137–9, 246
   and conceptions of self 92, 96, 98, 103, 113–14
   and social class 103, 105, 107, 113–14, 130, 139, 140
   criticism of 7, 111
   Eurocentric/Western 108, 137
   participation in 92, 105
Modest, Wayne 358
Mohamad, Goenawan 25, 26, 156
Moluccan 14, 30, 158, 171, 186, 187, 192, 193–4

INDEX

Moluccas 186, 188, 322
Mone, Abdul Rahim Daeng 332
Muntilan 207, 224
Museum aan de Stroom (MAS) 362, 368
Museum Bronbeek 157, 246
Museum Nasional Indonesia 262
Museum Nusantara 16, 262
Museum of Contemporary Art Antwerp (M HKA) 350, 361, 368, **369**
Museum of the Royal Batavian Society of Arts and Science 247–8, 328
Museum of the Tropics *see* Tropenmuseum
museums 17, 246, 262, 274, 321–40, 347–71
  and nationalism 32, 347, 340
  anthropological 246
  colonial 246, 331, 333, 334, 357
  coloniality within 32, 241, 246, 331, 333, 339–40, 352, 354, 357–9
  decolonisation of 28, 32, 241, 324, 333, 340, 347–71
  depictions of Royal Netherlands East Indies Army (KNIL) in 156, 157, 158, 159
  ethnographic 150, 246, 326, 330–1, 333, 334, 335, 347–50, 352–3
  nationalisation of 334–6, 338
  postcolonial 32, 333, 340, 348, 351, 352, 357, 369
  studies 5, 348
  under New Order regime 328, 330, 334, 335–7, 340
  see also individual museums
Museums, Directorate of 334, 335
Muslim 79, 81, 82, 83n20, 94, 106, 108, 161, 299, 390n72, 426
  Muslim-majority societies 77, 80, 81
  see also Islam; Qur'an

Nagaria, Soetjipto 315, 316
Nasoetion-van der Have, Adriana 381
National Archives of the Netherlands (Nationaal Archief, NA) 244, 245, 274, 275, 276, 277, 279–90
National Archives of the Republic of Indonesia (Arsip Nasional Republik Indonesia, ANRI) 245, 274, 275, 277, 280, 282–91
National Archives of Sri Lanka 76
National Committee for West Papua (Komite Nasional Papua Barat, KNPB) 403–4, 406–7, **408**, 414–17, **420**, 421, 422, 423–7
National Human Rights Commission (Komisi Nasional Hak Asasi Manusia) 393
National Museum of Ethnology 246, 262
National Museum of Indonesia 333
National Museum of World Cultures (Nationaal Museum van Wereldculturen) 17, 243n7
National Parliament of West Papua (Parlemen Nasional West Papua) 415, 416
Naturalis Biodiversity Center 17
Nazism 193, 275–6
Neeb, Hendricus Marinus 147, 148, 150, 151, **154**, 155, 156, 158, 159, 161, 166, 170
NEFIS *see* Netherlands East Indies Forces Intelligence Service
Negara Indonesia Timur (State of East Indonesia) 251–2
Negara Jawa Timur (State of East Java) 252
Negara Kesatuan Republik Indonesia (Unitary State of the Republic of Indonesia) 425
Negara Pasundan (State of Pasundan) 252

Negara Republik Federal Papua Barat (Federal Republic of West Papua) 416
Negara Sumatra Timur (State of East Sumatra) 252
Nemangkawi Task Force 404
neo-colonialism 7, 416
Netherlands Citizenship Act 56, 57
Netherlands East Indies Forces Intelligence Service (NEFIS) 244, 261, 277, 278–85, 287–91
Netherlands Institute for Military History 24, 277n10
New Guinea Council (Nieuw Guinea Raad, NGR) 410, 414, 426
New Order regime (1966–98) 9, 10, 182, 304, 305, 308, 316, 328, 334, 335, 336–7, 340, 381, 413
  end of 19, 330, 336–7
  see also Suharto regime
New York Agreement 409
New Zealand 273
Nganjuk 207, 222, 223, 224, 225, **226**
Nieuwenhuis, Christiaan Benjamin 147, 149–50, 151, **153**, 155, 156, **158**, 159–**60**, 162, 164, 166–7, **168**, **169**, 170
NIOD Institute for War, Holocaust and Genocide Studies 24, 243n7
Nkrumah, Kwame 7
North, Frederick 73
North Sumatra 350, 361, 362
Nusantara (Indonesian archipelago) 316
Nusantara forts 322, 330, 340

Old Batavia Museum (Oud Batavia Museum) 328
Ormel, Henk Jan 388–9
'othering', ethnic 30, 81–2, 168, 170–1
Ottoman Empire 77, 80
Oud Batavia Museum (Old Batavia Museum) 328

Outer Islands 53, **54**, 55
Outer Provinces (*Buitengewesten*) 158

pachtstelsel ('tax farming') 51, 53, 57, 58, 210, 302
Pacific 55
Pacific Forum **415**
Padang 74–5, 93, 95, 97, 99, 103–4, 109n85, 164, 214
Pakistan 81, 196
Pakubuwana I 72
Pakubuwana II 83n22
Pakubuwana VI 73
Palembang 74–5, 98, 216, 323
Palopo 339
pan-Asianism 301
Papua *see* West Papua
Papua National Committee (Komite Nasional Papua) 414, 426
Papua New Guinea 360, 408, 413
Papua Presidium Council (Presidium Dewan Papua) 414
Papua Regional Police (Polda Papua) 415
Papuan independence 405–6, **408**, 409–12, 414, 416–17, 419–20, 422, 426
Parakan 221
Pare 207, 223, 231
Pare-Pare 339
Pariaman 74–5, 93, 95, 99, 104, 109, 110, 112–13, 114
'Pecinan' (Chinatown) 210, 295
Pemecutan 151, **155**, 160
Penang 74–5, 77, 78, 86n25, 189
People's Council (*Volksraad*) 48n6, 61, 62, 64, 251
People's Democratic Front (Front Demokrasi Rakyat) 180, 288
Perak 78, 83
Peranakan xiv, 54, 299, 304, 340
Pesindo (Pemuda Sosialis Indonesia; Socialist Youth of Indonesia) 180, 195, 198, 288

Philippines 86, 196
Pita Maha collection 17, 262
Poeze, Harry 195, 282, 283
Pondaag, Jeffry 384, 385, 394–5
Portuguese 73–4, 321
postcolonial
    Chinese identity in Indonesia 31, 295, 302–6, 309
    history 6–10
    India 138
    Indonesia 6–10, 31, 65, 84–7, 156, 295, 302–6, 309, 333, 340, 360, 369
    museums 32, 333, 340, 348, 351, 352, 357, 369
    ordering of space 31
    structures of power 9, 10
    studies 7, 8, 9, 10, 19
postcolonialism 9, 10, 19, 84, 351, 352, 369, 370
Prakoso, Soesilo H. 250, 251, **260**
Prambanan 222
Prambanan Temple 247
Prawiro 217
Prince of Bantam 72
Princessehof Museum 332
Pringgodigdo, Abdul Gaffar 280
propaganda 5, 13, 18, 21, 29, 221, 332
Protestants 188
Provincial and Municipal Historical Museum (Provincial en Stedelijk Historisch Museum) 327
puputan (dynastic 'ending') xiv, 17, 147, 151, 156
Purwokerto 207, 220, 231

Queen Máxima 262
Queen of Tanete 326, 338
Queen Wilhelmina 150
Quijano, Aníbal 4, 378
Qur'an 17, 79, 81

race 7, 13, 18, 20, 21, 30, 92, 94, 187–8, 298, 299, 338
    and Papuans 190, 425
    colonial hierarchies of 5, 13–14, 20, 30, 96, 102, 161, 171, 187, 188, 189, 298–9
    'martial races' xiii, 18, 21, 22, 30, 74, 147, 161, 171
    politics 102, 348, 405
    relations 102, 110–11, 351, 425
    see also ethnicity
racial
    classifications xiii, 19, 21, 50–1, 56, 62, 102, 187, 189, 299
    conceptions of Malays 18, 21, 101, 102, 425–6
    discrimination 14, 63, 110, 182, 209, 210–11, 230, 232, 305, 306, 309–11, 317, 406, 417, 418, 420
    ideology 63, 102, 181
    laws 56, 63, 210–11, 230, 303, 304–5, 311
    logic 48, 50, 52
    regimes 18–21, 29, 171
    segregation 210, 298–9, 300, 301–2
    solidarity 7, 101, 110–11, 405, 413, 418
    vilification 189, 190
    violence against Chinese 14, 19, 22, 30, 31–2, 63, 191, 205–32, 295, 296, 305–6, 314, 380
racialisation 4, 18–19, 21, 29, 30, 48, 50, 110, 171, 300, 301
    and capitalism 4, 48, 62, 110–11
    and colonialism 4, 48, 50–1, 52, 62, 92, 171, 189, 299, 300–1
    in Dutch military 21, 22, 29–30, 147–8, 157–71
    of Chinese Indonesians 21, 47, 48, 50, 63, 295–317

racism 12, 13, 21, 181, 185, 189–90, 303, 305, 331, 377n13, 391, 392, 396, 406, 417
    anti-racism 241, 404, 405
Rais, Amien 312
Rapportage Indonesia 279
Rasad, Fatimah 93, 95, 108, 109, 110, 111, 112–14
Rawagede 32, 375–96
reburial 206n3, 207, 208n7, 218, 224, **226**, **228**, 232
    see also mass graves
recolonisation, Dutch attempt at 11, 248, 275, 276, 278, 279, 285, 286
Reformasi 308, 310
religion 79, 93, 99, 158, 188, 210, 253, 297, 351, 416
    and Malays 72, 74, 75, 80, 81, 83
    see also individual religions
religious
    conflict 217, 218, 219, 425
    exiles 73
    objects 246, 247
    organisations 10n29
    practices 19
Renville Agreement xiv, 157, 197, 286
repatriation, cultural 11–18, 31, 241–63, 273–91, 324, 367, 368, 369
    Dutch committee for 17
    Indonesian committee for 16, 18, 243, 262
Republic of China (Taiwan) 304, 355n27
Republic of Indonesia (1945–49)
    'enemies' of 182
    opposition to 180, 198, 208n8
    political contestation 197–8
    post republic 30, 32, 152, 232, 244, 302, 323, 326, 330, 338
    territory under control of 157n39, 197–8, 207, 213, 214, 216, 221, 248, 251–2
    transfer of sovereignty to 23, 135–6, 232, 243, 244, 248, 254, 255, 258, 380, 409, 412, 414
republican forces 22, 30, 121n1, 207, 212n24, 214, 216, 221, 223, 358, 375, 380, 392
    and Madiun Affair 180, 184, 198n101
    attacks on opponents 180–1, 182, 194, 198
    control of plantations 134, 135, 221
    destruction of infrastructure 121n1, 135–7, 139, 165, 216, 221
    destruction of plantations 135, 140, 216
    militias 205, 207, 212, 214, 216, 217–19, 221, 223, 232
    repression of Pesindo 180, 198
    scorched-earth policy 135–6, 216, 221, 222
    territorial control 157n39, 197–8, 207, 213, 214, 216, 221, 248, 251–2
republican government 31, 63, 197–8, 207, 208n8, 212n24, 213, 224, 232, 244, 379
    and cultural heritage 248, 250, 251–63
    and Dutch invasion 214–24, 278
    and plantations 134, 135
    archives of 274–91
    arrests of members 221
    condemnation of violence 214
    Dutch attempts to discredit 216, 217
    failure to protect citizens 30, 208n8, 212, 232
    independence negotiations 248, 251, 252
    relocation of capital 213, 214, 222
    see also Dutch–Indonesian Round Table Conference; Inter-Indonesian Conference

republican movement 194, 208n8,
  261n56, 278, 283, 392–3, 396
  and decolonisation 3, 22, 30, 244
  and Royal Netherlands East Indies
    Army (KNIL) 148n11, 152
  Chinese support for 208n8,
    213–14, 250, 302
  colonial legacy 31, 181, 197
  ideas about 140, 182, 193, 195
  Investigating Committee for
    Preparatory Work for
    Independence 302–3
  negotiations 197–8, 244, 248,
    254–6, 279
Republik Indonesia Serikat *see* United
  States of Indonesia
Retna Kencana Colliq Pujie Arung
  Pancana Toa Matinroe ri Tucae
  326, 338
'Revolusi! Indonesia Independent'
  (exhibition) 11, 15, 24, 31,
  194n79, 289, 290
revolution *see* war of independence
Ribberink, Ton 280
Rijksmuseum 11, 13, 24, 194n79,
  243n7, 246, 289, 290
Rote 186
Rotenese 186
Round Table Conference *see*
  Dutch–Indonesian Round Table
  Conference
Royal Netherlands Army 146, 150, 170
Royal Netherlands East Indies Army
  (Koninklijk Nederlandsch-Indisch
  Leger, KNIL) 29–30, 146, 147–62,
  164, 167–8, 170–1, 328, 337, 357
Rumphius, Georgius Everhardus 357
Russia 77
  see also Soviet Union
Rutte, Mark 25, 387n60

Saldin, Baba Ounus 74–5, 76
Samalanga 147, 149–50, 151, **153**,
  159, **160**, 164, 167, **168**, **169**

Saralana Declaration 416
Sarekat Ambon 192
Sarekat Minangkabau 110
Sarmadji 356
Sastroamidjojo, Ali 250, 251, 253,
  255–**7**, 261
Secang 221
Second Dutch Military Aggression 31,
  205n2, 214, 220–4, 244
Seram 164
Setiawan, Hersri 183
Sheikh Yusuf 72, 85n23
Si Singamangaraja XII 362, 363, 365,
  366, 367, 368
Siam 76, 77, 101, 102, 247
  see also Thailand
Siaw Giok Tjhan 303
Sidharta, Amir 11
Sigli 147, 149, 150, **153**, 156, 162,
  169
Sim Ki Ay 250, 253
Sin Ming Hui 305
Sin Po 30, **46**, 47, 50, 61–2, 205–32
Sinar Glodok ('*Light of Glodok*') 295,
  306–17
Singapore 61, 76, 77, 86, 380–1
Singosari 218
Singosari Temple 247, 262
Sinhalese 81–3
Sino-Malay 302
Siti Roehana (Ruhana Kuddus) 95n18,
  96
Siwabessy, Gerrit 191n57, 192, 193,
  194
Sjarifuddin, Amir 286
Soemartini, Raden Adjeng 280
Soenting Melajoe ('*Malay Headdress*')
  29, 91–114
Soerabaiasch Handelsblad ('*Surabaya
  Commercial Paper*') 121, 123,
  131–2
Solo 221, 305
Sorong 403, 407, 411, 412n19
South Africa 73n2, 197

South America 3, 77
South Malang 125, 127, 128, 133, 137
South Sulawesi 321–40
   artefacts from 17, 247, 331, 334
   atrocities in 157, 380
   conflict in 164, 325, 336
   exiles from 72, 75
   see also Celebes
Southeast Asia 76, 79, 86, 298, 366
   colonialism in 4, 145, 171n81, 196
Southeast Asian Youth and Students Conference 180, 196, 198
Southeast Sulawesi 324, 332
   see also Celebes
sovereignty
   cultural 95, 252, 253, 255, 256, 258, 279
   Dutch recognition of 224, 279
   Indonesian national 4, 180, 195, 197–8, 251, 252, 253, 255, 256, 279, 310, 333, 409
   Papuan 405, 406, 417, 422, 424
   transfer of 23, 135–6, 232, 243, 244, 248, 254, 255, 258, 380, 409, 412, 414
Soviet Union 8, 180, 198
Special Detachment 88 (Densus 88) 415
Speelman, Cornelis Janszoon 322, 326, 335
Spoor, Simon 381, 386, 391
Sri Lanka 22, 71, 72, 73n2, 74, 75, 76, 79, 81, 82, 83, 84–7
   see also Ceylon
Sri Lanka Malays 71–87
statute of limitations 382–3, 384, 385, 386, 390
   Law on the Statute of Limitations ('*Verjaringswet*') (1971) 382–3, 386
Stevens, Harm 11
Stevens, Mary 348, 352–3
Straits Settlements 86
   see also Singapore

Sudirman 221
Suharto 280, 304, 328, 340, 413
   family 304
Suharto regime 9, 183–4, 185, 230, 304, 305, 316, 328, 334, 340, 381, 412n20, 413–14, 417
   end of 183, 230, 308, 414
   post-regime 10, 295, 306, 308, 315–16, 417
   see also New Order regime
Sukarno 3, 7, 8, 195, 212, 214, 221, 280, 304, 340, 381, 412–13
Sukarnoputri, Megawati 311, 312
Sulawesi 73, 322, 324, 326, 332
   see also Celebes; South Sulawesi
Sultan Abdul Hamid II 80
Sultan Fakhruddin 72
Sultan Hasanuddin 322, 336, 338
Sultan of Gowa 72, 73n1, 321, 322, 336–7, 338
Sumatra 22, 54, 104, 107, 149, 157n39, 164
   Malay-language newspapers in 76, 77, 103, 112
   see also East Sumatra; North Sumatra; West Sumatra
Sungai Ujung 77
Suparta 385
Surabaya 121, **124**, 126, 127, 193, 194, 327
   British attack on 180, 195
   Chinese in 216
   civil unrest 190
Surabaya Commercial Paper (Soerabaiasch Handelsblad) 121, 123, 131–2
Sureq I La Galigo 326, 338
Suripno 195
Susuhunan Pakubuwono XII 250, 253
Sutaarga, Mohammad Amir 334, 335
Swastika, Alia 363

Tabuni, Buchtar 414, 415
Tabuni, Mako 404, 415

Tamil 76, 83n19
Tanah Batak 350, 362, 363, 365, 368
Tanah Jawa 77, 78
Tanah Melayu 78, 79
Tanah Papua 403n2, 407, 415, 416, 419, 420, 421, 422, 426
Tanah Toba 361, 362
Tangerang 212, 214, 216
Tapanuli 29, 93, 103, 106, 107, 113
Tatengkeng, Jan Engelbert 256
taxation
    of Indonesian Chinese 21, 28, 45–65, 210, 296, 297
    'tax farming' (*pachtstelsel*) 51, 53, 57, 58, 210, 302
    war-profit tax 50, 58, 59, 60, 61–2, 64
Ternate 74–5, 86, 322
Teuku Umar 17
Thailand 76, 86, 101, 247
    see also Siam
Thirtieth of September Movement (1965) xiv, 184, 340n78
Tiger Brigade (*Colonnie Matjan*) 362, 363, 365
Timika 407
Timor 164, 180, 186
Timorese 189
Timor-Leste 86, 185
    see also East Timor
Tiong Hoa Hwee Koan (THHK) 45–6, 301
Tiong Hoa Im Gak Hwe 45
TNI (Indonesian National Armed Forces) 165, 315n60, 287
    see also Indonesian military
Tolstoy, Leo 93, 108, 111
Torajans 329, 334, 338
Treaty of Bongaya 322
Triyana, Bonnie 11, 12, 13, 14, **15, 16**, 18
Tropenmuseum (Museum of the Tropics) 246, 350, 355, 356–8
Tuanku Imam Bonjol 73

Tulungagung 207, 223, 231
Türkiye 77, 80, 81
    see also Ottoman Empire

Ujung Pandang *see* Fort Ujung Pandang
Umi Sardjono 184
United Liberation Movement for West Papua 416
United Nations (UN) 220, 245, 248, 279, 379, 382n37, 390n72, 409, 414, 426
    Archives 245
    Security Council 197
United Nations Committee of Good Offices on the Indonesian Question 379, 386
United Nations Educational, Scientific and Cultural Organization (UNESCO) 251, 329
United Nations Temporary Executive Authority (UNTEA) 409, 414
United New Guinea Movement (Gerakan Persatuan New Guinea) 411
United New Guinea Party (Eenheidspartij Nieuw Guinea, or Partai Persatuan Nieuw Guinea) 411–12
United People of New Guinea Party (Partai Orang Nieuw Guinea) 412
United States of America (US) 8, 77, 273, 336, 348
    see also America
United States of Indonesia (Republik Indonesia Serikat, RIS) 197, 243, 248, 252, 279, 411

Valentijn, François 297
van Bommel, Marieke 17
van Daalen, Gotfried Coenraad Ernst 150, 156, 160, 161
van Der Hoop, Dr A.N.J.Th. à Th. 334

van Dijk, Janneke 357
van Dijk, Kees 162
van Griensven, Hans 25
van Heutsz, Joannes Benedictus 149–50, 156, 159, 162
van Rijswijk, Adolphine 362
van Rijswijk, Jan 362
van Tonningen, Marinus Bernardus Rost 151
van Weede, Hendrik Maurits 147, 150–2, **155**, 156, 158, 159–60, 164, 166–8, **170**
Vereenigde Oostindische Compagnie *see* Dutch East India Company
Verhagen, Maxime 384
Vietnam 125n4, 180, 196
VOC *see* Dutch East India Company
Volksraad ('People's Council') 48n6, 61, 62, 64, 251
von Faber, G.H. 327

Wahid, Abdurrahman (Gus Dur) 311–**12**, 313, 340
Wajah Selong 29, 71, 72, 75–87
Walsh, Catherine 4, 96
war crimes 25, 382–3, 386–8, 390
  see also atrocities
war of independence 11, 134, 145–71, 179–99, 278, 279, 288, 328, 337, 376, 406, 409
  alternative views of 6, 158, 179–99, 232
  and class 179–99, 209
  and decoloniality 22
  and ethnicity 30, 199, 207–8, 232
  and modernity 138–40
  and Netherlands East Indies Forces Intelligence Service 278
  and plantation society 133–40, 165
  archives of 31, 274–5, 278, 279, 283, 286
  Chinese Indonesians during 22, 26n87, 63, 205, 207–8, 209–32

class conflict during 182, 209
control over history of 10, 11, 13, 25, 381
Dutch abuses during 23–5, 27, 29–30, 146–71, 376, 379–80, 382–3, 389–90
Dutch areas of control 197, 207n4, 216
Dutch interpretations of 31, 376, 382, 389–90, 288, 391
Dutch recolonisation attempt 11, 248, 275, 276, 278, 279, 285, 286
Indonesian interpretations of 10–11, 26n87, 28
militias 205, 207, 212, 214, 216, 217–19, 221, 223, 232
romanticisation of 22, 27, 135, 209
silences in history of 182, 199, 207–8, 382
targeting of minorities during 13, 30, 209–14, 232
violence against Chinese 14, 19, 22, 30, 31–2, 52, 53, 63, 191, 205–32, 295, 296, 300, 305–6, 314, 380
violence against Indo-Europeans 12, 13–14, 209, 213, 232
  see also *bersiap*; Djogdja Documenten
war-profit tax 50, 58, 59, 60, 61–2, 64
Watampone 339
Wereldmuseum (World Museum) 157, 246
Wertheim, Wim 185
West Africa 158
West Irian Jaya Province 403n2
West Irian Province 412, 413
West Java 218, 219, 228, 323, 375
West Papua 33, 189, 190, 280, 360, 403–27
  independence 405–6, **408**, 409–12, 414, 416–17, 419–20, 422, 426

Tanah Papua 403n2, 407, 415, 416, 419, 420, 421, 422, 426
West Papua National Coalition for Liberation 416
West Sumatra 29, 73, 92, 94, 110
   Malay-language newspapers in 22, 29, 78, 91–114
Westerling, Raymond 157, 380, 394n93
Wijnen, Alphons 381
Wilders, Geert 25
Wilmar, Hugo 147
Wilmers, K.H.M. 256
Wonosobo 207, 221, 223, 225, **227**, 230
World Federation of Democratic Youth 195
World War I 58, 59, 61, 64, 98, 110, 161
World War II 3, 84, 145, 147, 163n58, 196, 278, 322, 332, 387–8, 389, 390

Yamin, Mohammad 9, 250–1, 256
Yeimo, Victor Frederik 33, 404–5, 406, **408**, 414, 418–19, 420–3, 427
Yogyakarta 86n25, 195, 261, 323, 350, 368
   as capital of the republic 213
   Chinese mass graves in 207, 228
   Dutch invasion 221–2, 278, 281, 287
   massacres in 222, 223, **230**
   Second Dutch Military Aggression 31, 244
   seizure of archives from 31, 244, 276, 278, 281, 287
Yohame, Martinus 403, 404
Yudhoyono, Susilo Bambang 336
Yuliastuti, Eni 283

Zegveld, Liesbeth 384, 385, 394–5

www.ingramcontent.com/pod-product-compliance
Lightning Source LLC
Chambersburg PA
CBHW052009290426
44112CB00014B/2177